2024 and 2025 Selected Papers from Algorithms Editorial Board Members

2024 and 2025 Selected Papers from Algorithms Editorial Board Members

Guest Editor

Frank Werner

MDPI

Basel • Beijing • Wuhan • Barcelona • Belgrade • Novi Sad • Cluj • Manchester

Guest Editor
Frank Werner
Faculty of Mathematics
Otto-von-Guericke-University
Magdeburg
Germany

Editorial Office
MDPI AG
Grosspeteranlage 5
4052 Basel, Switzerland

This is a reprint of the Special Issue, published open access by the journal *Algorithms* (ISSN 1999-4893), freely accessible at: https://www.mdpi.com/journal/algorithms/special_issues/86AHBFW0ZR.

For citation purposes, cite each article independently as indicated on the article page online and as indicated below:

Lastname, A.A.; Lastname, B.B. Article Title. *Journal Name* **Year**, *Volume Number*, Page Range.

ISBN 978-3-7258-7260-2 (Hbk)
ISBN 978-3-7258-7261-9 (PDF)
https://doi.org/10.3390/books978-3-7258-7261-9

Contents

About the Editor

Frank Werner

Frank Werner studied mathematics from 1975 to 1980 and graduated from the Technical University of Magdeburg (Germany) with a distinction. He received a Ph.D. degree (with summa cum laude) in Mathematics in 1984 and defended his habilitation thesis in 1989. From this time on, he worked at the Faculty of Mathematics at the Otto-von-Guericke University Magdeburg in Germany, and since 1998, he has worked as an Extraordinary Professor. In 1992, he received a grant from the Alexander von Humboldt Foundation. He has been a manager of several research projects supported by the German Research Society (DFG) and the European Union (INTAS). Since 2019, he has been the Editor-in-Chief of the journal *Algorithms*. He has also been the Associate Editor of *The International Journal of Production Research* since 2012 and *The Journal of Scheduling* since 2014, and a member of the Editorial/Advisory Boards of 19 other international journals. He has been a Guest Editor of Special Issues in ten international journals and has served as a member of the Program Committee of more than 190 international conferences. Frank Werner is an author/editor of 20 books, including the textbooks Mathematics of Economics and Business and A Refresher Course in Mathematics. In addition, he has co-edited four proceedings volumes of the SIMULTECH conferences and published more than 350 journal and conference papers, including in *The International Journal of Production Research, Computers & Operations Research, The Journal of Scheduling, Applied Mathematical Modelling,* and *The European Journal of Operational Research*. He has received Best Paper Awards from *The International Journal of Production Research* (2016) and *IISE Transactions* (2021). His main research subjects are scheduling, discrete optimization, graph theory, and mathematical problems in operations research.

Preface

This is the printed edition of a Special Issue published in the journal *Algorithms*. In addition to the Editorial, this book contains 15 accepted articles of this issue. Among the subjects addressed in this book, we can mention simulation, graph coloring, scheduling, deep learning, data analysis, knapsack, and minimum spanning tree problems, to name a few. Finally, we express our gratitude to all who contributed to the success of this issue: authors from 11 countries, many referees from all over the world, and the staff of the journal *Algorithms*. I hope that the readers of this book will find many stimulating ideas for their own future research in the challenging field of algorithmic aspects.

Frank Werner
Guest Editor

algorithms

rial

ecial Issue "Selected 2024 and 2025 Papers from *Algorithms* itorial Board Members"

k Werner

Faculty of Mathematics, Otto-von-Guericke University Magdeburg, D-39016 Magdeburg, Germany;
frank.werner@ovgu.de; Tel.: +49-391-675-2025

1. Introduction

This is the fourth edition of a Special Issue of *Algorithms* that is of a different nature than the other Special Issues in the journal, which are usually dedicated to a particular subject in the area of algorithms. The Editorial Board of the journal has considerably extended in recent years. Currently, my work as Editor-in-Chief is supported by six Section Editor-in-Chiefs as well as 159 further members of the Editorial Board from many countries. The journal decided to set up a periodical Special Issue because these scientists cover a huge understand the current research conducted by our Editorial Board members.

In 2020, the journal started with the first edition of this Special Issue. This first edition [1] contained 8 papers, and the second edition from 2021 [2] included 12 papers. Then, the journal changed to a 2-year cycle. The third edition including submissions from the years 2023 and 2024 (see [3]) comprised 16 papers, and the next Special Issue with submissions from the years 2024 and 2025 is now available.

2. Special Issue

After a careful refereeing process, 15 papers were selected for this Special Issue. All submissions have been reviewed by two or more experts from the relevant area. Subsequently, the published papers are briefly examined in increasing order of their publication dates in this Special Issue.

In the first accepted study, Piazza et al. considered proportional lumpability, which is an extension of the original lumpability definition, addressing some challenges related to the computation of performance indices for large stochastic models. The authors introduced three distinct characterizations of this novel concept. Their approach suggests that the transition rates of a Markov chain can be modified, leading to a lumpable new Markov chain. An effective polynomial algorithm was introduced.

The second contribution is by Punnen and Dhahan, who investigated the knapsack problem with bipartite conflict graphs. The problem with complete bipartite conflict graphs is shown to be NP-complete but is solvable in pseudo-polynomial time. The authors also present a class of integer programming models for the general problem of this type, which generalizes and unifies existing formulations. A computational comparison of the suggested models is also presented.

Morosanu et al. developed a novel approach for automatic music mixing by deriving a personalized multi-track-leveling method that uses both a customized genetic algorithm and a method based on neural networks. The presented method ensures consistent quality throughout the process and automates the repetitive elements of the mixing process. The authors considered a dataset of 20 songs; 15 were used for training both algorithms, which were then validated on the other 5 songs.

Gussenbauer et al. suggested an approach based on the XGBoost method that transforms the original data into privacy-compliant synthetic copies to ensure the synthetic data can be simulated with the same size of the input data. The parameters are automatically tuned using a modified k-fold cross-validation. If the exact population margins are known, the synthetic data must be calibrated to these margins, which is performed using a simulated annealing algorithm.

The fifth paper, by Mihova and Sotskov, deals with the relationships between scheduling problems with minimizing a bottleneck-function-like makespan or maximum lateness and the optimal colorings of mixed graphs. The authors studied the optimal scheduling of a partially ordered set of multi-processor tasks with allowed interruptions as optimal colorings of the vertices of a corresponding mixed graph. The presented results allow certain generalized scheduling problems to be solved in terms of graph theory.

Caramia and Stecca considered planning problems for collecting, sorting, and recycling in connection with industrial waste management. They propose two interpedendent models, namely, one for waste collection by an operator and the other for the sorting operations in a recycling plant. The models are formulated as mixed-integer linear programs and solved using a new negotiation-based approach. Computational results are presented, and two remaining shortcomings are mentioned, which can stimulate further work in this area.

In the seventh contribution, Gafarov and Werner addressed a subject of high actuality, namely, the development of some models and algorithms for connected and autonomous vehicles. For four types of such problems, which are considered for the first time, mathematical models and solution algorithms are presented. Three algorithms have a polynomial time complexity, and the fourth one is of branch-and-bound type. Finally, two open research questions are formulated for future research in this area.

In the next paper, Carpentieri presents a framework for identifying an optimal choice of compression algorithms, where the objective is maximizing the data compression efficiency under a given time limit. The developed approach was tested on one-dimensional (texts) and two-dimensional (images) data and was found to be effective. In addition, this approach was extended to lossy compression.

Radac et al. examined high-power wind turbines in the Romanian Oravita region. They propose an architecture with two power converters on each of the stator and rotor operating at variable wind speeds in a large interval. Several competitive controllers were designed and tested in the identified operating regions, ensuring the required operation specifications were met for a wide wind speed range.

Kisel at al. developed a deep-learning-based approach with the goal of enhancing the signal/background ratio for Λ particles within the Kalman Filter Particle Finder network. They derived a multi-layer perceptron model that achieved over 98% classification accuracy. Their approach increased the signal/background ratio by a factor of 10.97 and the significance by a factor of 1.14. The results demonstrate the potential of machine learning for increasing particle reconstruction and signal clarity.

Khansari et. al. addressed an important problem in neuroscience and healthcare. They developed a novel seizure prediction method leveraging EEG data by combining a discrete wavelet-transform-based time–frequency analysis, advanced feature extraction, and deep learning using Fourier neural networks. Their experimental results showed that the prediction accuracy of their approach was 98.96 with a zero false positive rate, which outperformed several existing state-of-the-art methods. The study underlines the potential of integrating advanced signal processing and deep learning approaches for reliably predicting șeizures in real time.

Montemanni and Smith considered a generalization of the minimum spanning tree problem, where additional conflict constraints were added to the classical optimization

https://doi.org/10.3390/a190

problem. They developed a mixed-integer linear program and solved the problem with an open-source solver. They solved several benchmark instances for the first time, also improving upon various best-known lower and upper bounds. The developed approach obtained results that were similar to those of more sophisticated existing approaches, but the approach is much easier to implement.

Garagnani and Maniezzo analyzed forecasting univariate time series. They present a detailed breakdown of a minimalist, fundamental, transformer-based architecture for their forecasting. The implemented simplified transformer model was validated a set of standard forecasting benchmarks. This contribution provides a transparent and replicable baseline for both researchers and practitioners to understand the core mechanisms through which the transformers used in connection work with forecasting tasks.

Vakhania et al. studied classical single machine problems and reviewed the existing results at the borderline of polynomial solvability, approximability, and complexity issues. They covered an area that was missing a survey in the existing literature. The authors discuss the basic structural properties of such problems and suggest some subjects requiring further investigation. The discussed polynomially solvable special cases are also of interest with similar problems that do not exactly satisfy the required conditions, where the underlying algorithms can be used as good heuristics.

In the last study, Boccuto et al. investigated the value of remotely tracking motor activity in clinical devices among persons younger than 50 years during early myocardial infarction. This study is valuable due to the rising incidence of this type of infarction. Continuous, noninvasive measurements of the heart rate, oxygen saturation, and physical activity were collected from 62 patients after myocardial infarction over seven days. The results of this study confirmed that the wearable devices provided various benefits in monitoring the motor activity and vital parameters of the patients.

As the current Editor-in-Chief, I thank all the Editorial Board members for their recent support of the journal as well as the complete staff of the Editorial Office for the their cooperation. We will continue with these Special Issues, presenting the recent research results of the Editorial Board members. The call for papers for the issue covering the years 2026 and 2027 is online, and the first paper in this Special Issue has already been published. I cordially invite the members to submit their latest high-quality work to the forthcoming issue.

Conflicts of Interest: The author declares no conflicts of interest.

List of Contributors:

1. Piazza, C.; Rossi, S.; Smuseva, D. Efficient Algorithm for Proportional Lumpability and Its Application to Selfish Mining in Public Blockchains. *Algorithms* **2024**, *17*, 159.
2. Punnen, A.P.; Dhahan, J. The Knapsack Problem with Conflict Pair Constaints on Bipartite Graphs and Extensions. *Algorithms* **2024**, *17*, 219.
3. Morosanu, B.; Negru, M.; Paleologu, C. Automated Personalized Loudness Control for Multi-Track Recordings. *Algorithms* **2024**, *17*, 228.
4. Gussenbauer, J.; Templ, M.; Fritzmann S.; Kowarik, A. Simulation of Calibrated Complex Synthetic Population Data with XGBoost. *Algorithms* **2024**, *17*, 22849
5. Mihova, E.; Sotskov, Y.N. Mixed Graph Colouring as Scheduling a Partially Ordered Set of Interruptible Multi-Processor Tasks with Integer Due Dates. *Algorithms* **2024**, *17*, 299.
6. Caramia, M.; Stecca, G. An Improved Negotiation-Based Approach for Collecting and Sorting Operations in Waste Management and Recycling. *Algorithms* **2024**, *17*, 380.
7. Gafarov, E.R.; Werner, F. Connected and Autonomous Vehicle Scheduling Probems: Some Models and Algorithms. *Algorithms* **2024**, *17*, 421.
8. Carpentieri, B. Data Compression with a Time Limit. *Algorithms* **2025**, *18*, 135.

https://doi.org/10.3390/a19020161

9. Radac, M.-B.; Muller, V.-D.; Ciucurita, S. Control of High-Power Slip Ring Induction Generator Wind Turbines at Variable Wind Speeds in Optimal and Reliable Modes. *Algorithms* **2025**, *18*, 162.
10. Kisel, I.; Lakos, R.; Zischka, G. Deep-Learning-Based Optimization of the Signal/Background Ratio for Λ Particles in the CBM Experiment at FAIR. *Algorithms* **2025**, *18*, 229.
11. Khansari, H.S.; Abbaszadeh, M.; Joonaghany, G.H., Mohagerani, H.; Faraji, F. Epileptic Seizure Prediction Using a Combination of Deep Learning, Time-Frequency Fusion Methods, and Discrete Wavelet Analysis. *Algorithms* **2025**, *18*, 492.
12. Montemanni, R.; Smith, D.H. On Solving the Minimum Spanning Tree Problem with Conflicting Edge Pairs. *Algorithms* **2025**, *18*, 526.
13. Garagnani, F.; Maniezzo, V. Deconstructing a Minimalist Transformer Architecture for Univariate Time Series Forecasting. *Algorithms* **2025**, *18*, 645.
14. Vakhania, N.; Werner, F.; Ramirez-Fuentes, K.J. Single Machine Scheduling Problems: Standard Settings and Properties, Polynomially Solvable Cases, Complexity and Approximability. *Algorithms* **2026**, *19*, 38.
15. Boccuto, F.; Lomoio, U.; Derosa, S.; Torella, D.;Veltri, P.; Guzzi, P.H. Usefulness of Wearable Devices for Monitoring Motor Activity in Patients with Early Myocardial Infarction. **2026**, *19*, 137.

References

1. Werner, F. 2020 Selected Papers from Algorithms' Editorial Board Members. *Algorithms* **2021**, *14*, 32. [CrossRef]
2. Werner, F. 2021 Selected Papers from Algorithms' Editorial Board Members. *Algorithms* **2021**, *14*, 357. [CrossRef]
3. Werner, F. 2022 and 2023 Selected Papers from Algorithms' Editorial Board Members. *Algorithms* **2024**, *17*, 65. [CrossRef]

https://doi.org/10.3390/a190

algorithms

MDPI

le

ficient Algorithm for Proportional Lumpability and Its pplication to Selfish Mining in Public Blockchains

a Piazza [1,*], Sabina Rossi [2] and Daria Smuseva [1]

1 Dipartimento di Scienze Matematiche, Informatiche e Fisiche, Università degli Studi di Udine, Via delle Scienze, 206, 33100 Udine, Italy; daria.smuseva@unive.it

2 Dipartimento di Scienze Ambientali, Informatica e Statistica, Università Ca' Foscari Venezia, Via Torino, 155, 30123 Venezia, Italy; sabina.rossi@unive.it

* Correspondence: carla.piazza@uniud.it

Abstract: This paper explores the concept of *proportional lumpability* as an extension of the original definition of lumpability, addressing the challenges posed by the state space explosion problem in computing performance indices for large stochastic models. Lumpability traditionally relies on state aggregation techniques and is applicable to Markov chains demonstrating structural regularity. Proportional lumpability extends this idea, proposing that the transition rates of a Markov chain can be modified by certain factors, resulting in a lumpable new Markov chain. This concept facilitates the derivation of precise performance indices for the original process. This paper establishes the well-defined nature of the problem of computing the coarsest proportional lumpability that refines a given initial partition, ensuring a unique solution exists. Additionally, a polynomial time algorithm is introduced to solve this problem, offering valuable insights into both the concept of proportional lumpability and the broader realm of partition refinement techniques. The effectiveness of proportional lumpability is demonstrated through a case study that consists of designing a model to investigate selfish mining behaviors on public blockchains. This research contributes to a better understanding of efficient approaches for handling large stochastic models and highlights the practical applicability of proportional lumpability in deriving exact performance indices.

Keywords: Markov chains; lumpability; algorithms; blockchain

1. Introduction

Markov chains serve as the fundamental semantic model for a multitude of modeling formalisms employed in the reliability analysis and performance evaluation of complex systems, including Stochastic Petri nets [1,2], Stochastic Automata Networks [3,4], queuing networks [5,6], and Markovian process algebras [7,8].

Although the utilization of high-level specification formalisms greatly simplifies the creation of compositional and hierarchical quantitative models, even seemingly straightforward models can pose challenges due to a large number of states, making analysis a daunting task. To tackle this problem, exploring models with extensive state spaces without resorting to approximation or simulation techniques involves reducing the state space of the underlying Markov chain by aggregating states that exhibit equivalent behaviors [9,10]. This state-based reduction technique is known as *lumping*. Various notions of lumping, including strong and weak lumping [11], exact lumping [9,12], and strict lumping [13], have been introduced in the literature. The lumpability method enables efficient computation of exact performance indices [14] when the model is lumpable.

It is widely recognized that not all Markov chains are inherently lumpable, particularly those originating from real-world applications. To overcome this limitation, the notion of *quasi-lumpability* was introduced in [15], suggesting that transforming a quasi-lumpable Markov chain into a lumpable one allows for the application of steady state probability bounding methods [15–19] to obtain bounds on the performance indices of the original model.

In [20], the concept of *proportional lumpability* was introduced, expanding upon the original notion of lumpability. Unlike the broader definition of quasi-lumpability, proportional lumpability allows for the derivation of precise performance indices for the original process. Building on this foundation, our research in [21] delves deeper into the topic by juxtaposing proportional lumpability with other lumping definitions, such as weak lumpability [11,22], and the concept of exact lumpability for ordinary differential equations (ODEs) [23,24].

The definition of proportional lumpability entails identifying a function that assigns a positive coefficient to each state of the system. However, given the infinite set of potential functions, devising an efficient algorithmic technique to check or compute proportional lumpability is not immediately evident.

This paper explores the properties of proportional lumpability and elaborates on three alternative characterizations. The first, proven in [21], enables efficient verification of whether a partition of the state space is induced by an equivalence relation representing proportional lumpability. The second, proven in [25], is used to design an algorithm to calculate the coarsest proportional lumpability of a given Markov chain in time $O(|\mathcal{S}|^4)$ with $|\mathcal{S}|$ being the cardinality of the state space of the analyzed model. The third characterization is a novel contribution, and it allows us to improve on the above complexity by obtaining an algorithm for proportional lumpability running in $O(|\mathcal{S}|^2 \log |\mathcal{S}|)$. Similar to partition refinement algorithms used for the traditional concept of strong (or ordinary) lumpability, our approach demonstrates that computing the coarsest proportional lumpability refining a given initial partition is well defined, always yielding a unique solution. Furthermore, we demonstrate that the maximum proportional lumpability over an initial Markov chain, within a specified equivalence relation, can be interpreted as ordinary lumpability over a perturbation of the original chain. Consequently, we can leverage efficient algorithms for calculating the maximum lumpability over a Markov chain.

The effectiveness of proportional lumpability is illustrated through the presentation of a comprehensive case study. This study involves the development and analysis of a proportionally lumpable model specifically tailored for examining selfish mining behaviors within a public blockchain context. Our aim is to provide valuable insights into the concept of proportional lumpability and the broader applications of partition refinement techniques.

This work extends our prior investigations outlined in [25,26]. Expanding upon our earlier research on proportional lumpability [25], we introduce a pivotal, novel, third characterization in this paper. This result allows us to enhance the efficiency of our previously proposed algorithm, resulting in a groundbreaking approach to proportional lumpability. The algorithm now boasts a remarkable time complexity of $O(|\mathcal{S}|^2 \log |\mathcal{S}|)$, where $|\mathcal{S}|$ denotes the cardinality of the state space of the analyzed model, offering the potential to substantially enhance the scalability and applicability of proportional lumpability analyses. Furthermore, we expand on the findings in [25] by offering a thorough case study. This study is inspired by our previous work [26], where a strongly lumpable model for a concrete blockchain problem was presented. The model is carefully designed to investigate selfish mining behaviors within the framework of a public blockchain. In this paper, we present an extended version of the model studied in [26], designed to capture a more realistic configuration of the blockchain state under examination. Our analysis reveals that despite this broadening, the generalized model maintains its computational manageability. This resilience primarily stems from its adherence to a more general definition of lumpability, specifically, proportionally lumpability. Consequently, we can apply the findings presented in this paper to conduct precise analyses of the new model. This comprehensive approach aims to shed light on the dynamics of selfish mining in the real-world context of blockchain technology.

The structure of this paper is as follows: In Section 2, we delve into the theoretical underpinnings of continuous-time Markov chains and revisit the concept of strong (or ordinary) lumpability. Section 3 introduces the notion of proportional lumpability, providing a novel characterization of it along with an efficient algorithm for its verification. We discuss both the accuracy and complexity of the algorithm. In Section 4, we present a case study centered around a proportionally lumpable model for selfish mining in public blockchain. Finally, Section 5 offers concluding remarks and future directions to wrap up the paper.

2. Background

In this section, we provide a brief overview of the basics of continuous-time Markov chains [11,27,28] and introduce the notion of lumpability [22,29,30].

2.1. Stochastic Models

In this paper, we consider Markov chains or Markov processes that are stochastic models describing sequences of possible events in which the probability of each event depends only on the state attained in the previous event. More specifically, we concentrate on Continuous-Time Markov Chains.

A Continuous-Time Markov Chain (CTMC) with finite or countable state space $\mathcal{S}$ is a family $\{X(t) \mid t \in \mathbb{R}^+\}$ of $\mathcal{S}$-valued random variables such that

$$Prob(X(t_{n+1}) = s_{n+1} \mid X(t_1) = s_1, X(t_2) = s_2, \ldots, X(t_n) = s_n) = Prob(X(t_{n+1}) = s_{n+1} \mid X(t_n) = s_n).$$

This condition is the natural continuous-time analogue of the Markov property. It requires that the future behavior of the process is conditionally independent of its past evolution given the present states.

We assume that the Markov properties under consideration satisfy the following properties: a Markov process $X(t)$ is

- *stationary* if its statistical properties do not change by time, i.e., the family of random variables $(X(t_1), X(t_2), \ldots, X(t_n))$ has the same distribution as the collection $(X(t_1+\tau), X(t_2+\tau), \ldots, X(t_n+\tau))$ for all $t_1, t_2, \ldots, t_n, \tau \in \mathbb{R}^+$.
- *time-homogeneous* if the conditional probability $Prob(X(t+\tau) = s \mid X(t) = s')$ remains constant regardless of t, i.e., the behavior of the system does not depend on when it is observed. In particular, the transitions between states are independent of the time at which the transitions occur.
- *irreducible* if all states in its state space $\mathcal{S}$ can be reached from all other states by following the transitions of the process.

Within a Markov process, a state is labeled *persistent* or *recurrent* if the probability of the process eventually returning to that state is one. Otherwise, the state is called *transient*. In terms of a system, the recurrent states correspond to the behavior which is repeatedly exhibited by the system, whereas transient states correspond to a behavior which will be no longer exhibited after a certain time. A recurrent state is termed *positive-recurrent* or *ergodic* if the expected number of steps until the process returns to that state is less than infinity. A Markov process is ergodic if all its states are positive-recurrent. In the context of finite Markov chains, irreducibility alone ensures ergodicity. In this paper, we consider Continuous-Time Markov Chains, which are time-homogeneous, irreducible, and ergodic.

An ergodic Continuous-Time Markov Chain (CTMC) possesses an *equilibrium* (or *steady-state*) *distribution*, defined as the *unique* collection of positive real numbers $\pi(s)$ where $s \in \mathcal{S}$, satisfying the equation:

$$\lim_{t \to \infty} Prob(X(t) = s \mid X(0) = s') = \pi(s)\,.$$

It is worth noting that the above equation for $\pi(s)$ is independent of s'. We denote by $q(s, s')$ the transition rate from state s to state s', where $s \neq s'$. The sum of all transition rates out of state s to any other state in the chain is denoted as $q(s)$. A state s for which

$q(s) = \infty$ is termed an instantaneous state, as it is instantaneously left upon entry. While theoretically possible, we assume throughout that $0 < q(s) < \infty$ for each state s.

The infinitesimal generator matrix $\mathbf{Q}$ of a CTMC $X(t)$ with state space $\mathcal{S}$ is defined as the $|\mathcal{S}| \times |\mathcal{S}|$ matrix. Its off-diagonal elements are the $q(s,s')$'s, and its diagonal elements are the negative sum of the off-diagonal elements of each row, i.e., $q(s,s) = -\sum_{s' \in \mathcal{S},\, s' \neq s} q(s,s')$. For simplicity, we use $q(s,s')$ to denote the components of matrix $\mathbf{Q}$. For $s \in \mathcal{S}$ and $S \subseteq \mathcal{S}$, we write $q(s,S)$ to denote $\sum_{s' \in S} q(s,s')$.

Any non-trivial vector of positive real numbers $\boldsymbol{\mu}$ satisfying the system of global balance equations (GBEs) $\boldsymbol{\mu}\mathbf{Q} = \mathbf{0}$ is referred to as an *invariant measure* of the CTMC.

Given an irreducible CTMC $X(t)$, if $\boldsymbol{\mu}_1$ and $\boldsymbol{\mu}_2$ are two invariant measures of $X(t)$, then there exists a constant $k > 0$ such that $\boldsymbol{\mu}_1 = k\boldsymbol{\mu}_2$. If the CTMC is ergodic, then there exists a unique invariant measure $\boldsymbol{\pi}$ whose components sum to unity, i.e., $\sum_{s \in \mathcal{S}} \pi(s) = 1$. In this case, $\boldsymbol{\pi}$ represents the equilibrium or steady-state distribution of the CTMC.

2.2. Strong (or Ordinary) Lumpability

In the field of performance and reliability analysis, the notion of lumpability introduces a method for aggregating models. This method allows for the development of a reduced Markov chain compared to the original one while maintaining the ability to determine precise results for the original process.

The concept of lumpability is defined by equivalence relations that span the state space of the Markov chain. These relations create a division within the state space of the Markov chain, enabling the grouping of equivalent states into larger macro-states, which ultimately decreases the total state space. When the division fulfills the *strong* (or *ordinary*) lumpability condition [11,31], the equilibrium solution of the condensed process can provide a precise solution for the initial one.

The definition of strong lumpability was originally presented in [11] and has been extensively investigated in subsequent research [13,24,32–34].

Definition 1 (Strong lumpability). *Consider a CTMC $X(t)$ with a state space $\mathcal{S}$, and let $\sim$ denote an equivalence relation over $\mathcal{S}$. We define $X(t)$ to be strongly lumpable with respect to $\sim$ (or, alternatively, $\sim$ is termed a strong lumpability for $X(t)$) if $\sim$ induces a partition on the state space of $X(t)$ such that for any equivalence classes $S_i, S_j \in \mathcal{S}/\sim$ where $S_i \neq S_j$, and for any states $s, s' \in S_i$, the transition rates from s to S_j and from s' to S_j are equal, i.e.,*

$$q(s,S_j) = q(s',S_j)\,.$$

Therefore, an equivalence relation over the state space of a Markov process has a strong lumpability if it divides the space into equivalence classes, ensuring that within each class, the collective transition rates to any other class remain the same. It is important to highlight that every Markov process exhibits strong lumpability with respect to the identity relation, as well as the trivial relation, which comprises only one equivalence class.

In the paper by Kemeny et al. [11], it is demonstrated that for an equivalence relation $\sim$ over the state space of a Markov process $X(t)$, the aggregated process remains a Markov process for any initial distribution if and only if $\sim$ represents a strong lumpability for $X(t)$. Furthermore, the transition rate between two macro-states S_i and S_j in $\mathcal{S}/\sim$ is equal to $q(s,S_j)$ for any s belonging to S_i.

Proposition 1 (Aggregated process for strong lumpability). *Consider a CTMC $X(t)$ with a state space $\mathcal{S}$, infinitesimal generator $\mathbf{Q}$, and equilibrium distribution $\boldsymbol{\pi}$. Let $\sim$ be a strong lumpability for $X(t)$ and $\widetilde{X}(t)$ be the aggregated process with state space $\mathcal{S}/\sim$ and infinitesimal generator $\widetilde{\mathbf{Q}}$ defined by, for any equivalence class $S_i, S_j \in \mathcal{S}/\sim$,*

$$\widetilde{q}(S_i,S_j) = q(s,S_j)$$

for any $s \in S_i$. Then, the equilibrium distribution $\widetilde{\boldsymbol{\pi}}$ of $\widetilde{X}(t)$ is characterized by the property that for any equivalence class $S \in \mathcal{S}/\sim$,

$$\widetilde{\pi}(S) = \sum_{s \in S} \pi(s) .$$

3. Proportional Lumpability

The notion of proportional lumpability made its debut in [20]. Much like the notion of quasi-lumpability [15], which is also known as near-lumpability in [13], proportional lumpability builds upon the initial concept of strong lumpability. Furthermore, in contrast to the broader scope of quasi-lumpability, proportional lumpability allows for the precise derivation of a solution for the original process.

Definition 2 (Proportional lumpability). *Consider a CTMC $X(t)$ with a state space $\mathcal{S}$, and let $\sim$ denote an equivalence relation over $\mathcal{S}$. We define $X(t)$ to be proportionally lumpable with respect to $\sim$ (or, alternatively, $\sim$ is termed a proportional lumpability for $X(t)$) if $\sim$ induces a partition on the state space of $X(t)$ such that for any equivalence classes $S_i, S_j \in \mathcal{S}/\sim$ where $S_i \neq S_j$, and for any states $s, s' \in S_i$,*

$$\frac{q(s, S_j)}{\kappa(s)} = \frac{q(s', S_j)}{\kappa(s')}.$$

*where κ is a function from $\mathcal{S}$ to $\mathbb{R}^+$. We say that $X(t)$ is κ-*proportionally lumpable *with respect to $\sim$ (or, alternatively, $\sim$ is a κ-proportional lumpability for $X(t)$) if $X(t)$ is proportionally lumpable with respect to $\sim$ and function κ.*

The next theorem proven in [20] establishes that proportional lumpability facilitates the calculation of a precise solution for the original model.

Theorem 1 (Aggregated process for proportional lumpability). *Consider a CTMC $X(t)$ with a state space $\mathcal{S}$, infinitesimal generator $\mathbf{Q}$, and equilibrium distribution $\boldsymbol{\pi}$. Let κ denote a function from $\mathcal{S}$ to $\mathbb{R}^+$, $\sim$ be a κ-proportional lumpability for $X(t)$, and $\widetilde{X}(t)$ be the aggregated process over the state space $\mathcal{S}/\sim$ and with infinitesimal generator $\widetilde{\mathbf{Q}}$ defined by, for any equivalence classes $S_i, S_j \in \mathcal{S}/\sim$ where $S_i \neq S_j$, and for any state $s, \in S_i$,*

$$\widetilde{q}(S_i, S_j) = \frac{q(s, S_j)}{\kappa(s)} .$$

Then, $\widetilde{\boldsymbol{\mu}}$ such that for any equivalence class $S \in \mathcal{S}/\sim$,

$$\widetilde{\mu}(S) = \sum_{s \in S} \pi(s)\kappa(s) \tag{1}$$

is an invariant measure of $\widetilde{X}(t)$.

Definition 3 elucidates a technique for perturbing a CTMC that is proportionally lumpable, transforming it into one that is strongly lumpable. Unlike earlier perturbation approaches, Theorem 2 furnishes a method to calculate the stationary probabilities of a proportionally lumpable chain by leveraging those of the perturbed lumpable chain. The proof of Theorem 2 is available in [20].

Definition 3 (Perturbed Markov chains). *Consider a CTMC $X(t)$ with a state space $\mathcal{S}$ and infinitesimal generator $\mathbf{Q}$. Let κ denote a function from $\mathcal{S}$ to $\mathbb{R}^+$. We say that a CTMC $X'(t)$ with infinitesimal generator $\mathbf{Q}'$ is a perturbation of $X(t)$ with respect to κ if $X'(t)$ is obtained from $X(t)$ by perturbing its rates such that for all $s, s' \in \mathcal{S}$ with $s \neq s'$,*

$$q'(s, s') = \frac{q(s, s')}{\kappa(s)}.$$

Theorem 2 (Equilibrium distribution for proportional lumpability). *Let $X(t)$ be a CTMC with state space $\mathcal{S}$, infinitesimal generator $\mathbf{Q}$, and equilibrium distribution $\boldsymbol{\pi}$. Let κ be a function from $\mathcal{S}$ to $\mathbb{R}^+$. For any perturbation $X'(t)$ of the original chain $X(t)$ with respect to κ, as per Definition 3, where $X'(t)$ has an infinitesimal generator $\mathbf{Q}'$ and equilibrium distribution $\boldsymbol{\pi}'$, the equilibrium distribution $\boldsymbol{\pi}$ of $X(t)$ adheres to the following property: let $K = \sum_{s\in\mathcal{S}} \pi'(s)/\kappa(s)$, then for all $s \in \mathcal{S}$,*

$$\pi(s) = \frac{\pi'(s)}{K\,\kappa(s)}.$$

Example 1. *Consider the classic reliability problem concerning a system comprising N components. Each component $i \in 1, \ldots, N$ follows an exponential distribution with rate μ_i for time to failure, independent of the other components. This system type has been extensively researched, as seen in various works such as [35–39]. Following the approach in [38], we posit that upon system failure, it is restored to a new "good" state, and the restoration time follows an exponential distribution with rate λ. At any given time, the system state can be represented as a boolean vector of size N, $\bar{x} = (x_1, \ldots, x_N)$, where $x_i = 1$ signifies the i-th component functioning and $x_i = 0$ denotes failure. Consequently, the set of all feasible states is $\mathcal{S} = \{0,1\}^N$. Under these conditions, the system's state evolution over time can be modeled by a continuous-time Markov chain. The Markov process for a system with 3 components (i.e., $N = 3$) is illustrated in Figure 1. Notably, this system is proportionally lumpable with respect to the given partition: $S_n = \{\bar{x} \in \mathcal{S} : \sum x_i = n\}$ with $n \in \{0,1,2,3\}$, i.e.,*

$$\begin{aligned}
S_0 &= \{(0,0,0)\} \\
S_1 &= \{(1,0,0),(0,1,0),(0,0,1)\} \\
S_2 &= \{(1,1,0),(1,0,1),(0,1,1)\} \\
S_3 &= \{(1,1,1)\}
\end{aligned}$$

and the function κ such that for each state $s \in S_1 \cup S_2$, $\kappa(s) = q(s)$, while for $s \in S_0 \cup S_3$, $\kappa(s) = 1$. Consequently, we can examine the aggregated Markov chain depicted in Figure 2. Utilizing Theorems 1 and 2, we are able to calculate the precise solution for the original model.

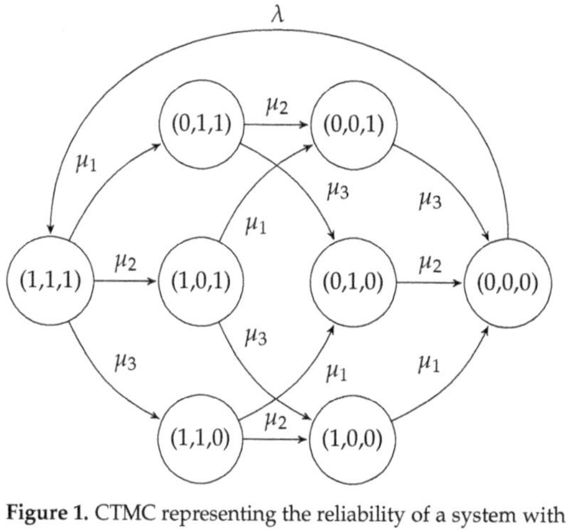

Figure 1. CTMC representing the reliability of a system with 3 components.

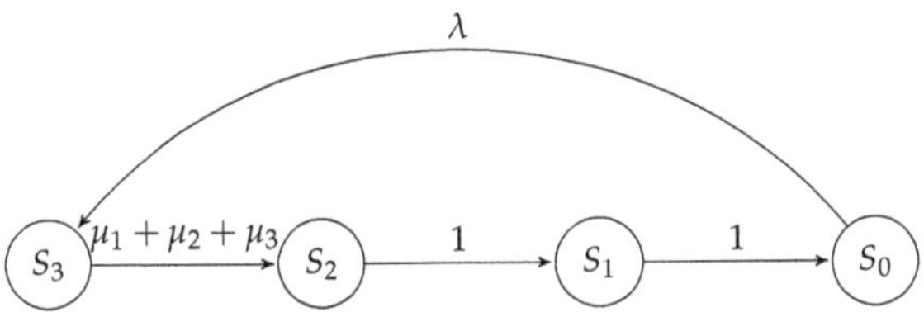

Figure 2. Aggregated CTMC representing the reliability of the system in Figure 1.

3.1. Three Alternative Characterizations of Proportional Lumpability

We introduce three alternative characterizations of proportional lumpability. The first one, proven in [21], provides an efficient method to determine if a partition of a Markov chain's state space is induced by proportional lumpability. The second characterization, outlined in [25], has been utilized to describe an algorithm for computing the coarsest proportional lumpability of a given Markov chain in $O(|\mathcal{S}|^4)$ time. The third characterization is new, and it allows us to improve on the above complexity of obtaining an algorithm running in $O(|\mathcal{S}|^2 \log |\mathcal{S}|)$.

First, for a given equivalence relation $\sim$ over the state space of a CTMC, we denote by $q_\sim(s)$ the sum of all transition rates from the state s to any state t such that $s \not\sim t$, i.e., for all $s \in \mathcal{S}$,

$$q_\sim(s) = \sum_{t \not\sim s} q(s,t).$$

The following theorem shows that proportional lumpability can be characterized in terms of $q_\sim(s)$ by replacing $\kappa(s)$ with $q_\sim(s)$ in the original definition.

Theorem 3 (Characterization 1 of proportional lumpability [21])**.** *Let $X(t)$ be an ergodic CTMC with state space $\mathcal{S}$ and $\sim$ be an equivalence relation over $\mathcal{S}$. The relation $\sim$ is a proportional lumpability for $X(t)$ if and only if for any equivalence classes $S_i, S_j \in \mathcal{S}/\!\sim$ with $S_i \neq S_j$ and $s, s' \in S_i$,*

1. *$q_\sim(s) \neq 0$ if and only if $q_\sim(s') \neq 0$*
2. *if $q_\sim(s) \neq 0$ then*

$$\frac{q(s,S_j)}{q_\sim(s)} = \frac{q(s',S_j)}{q_\sim(s')}.$$

While the aforementioned characterization is useful for efficiently verifying whether a given relation conforms to proportional lumpability, its direct application in an algorithm for computing proportional lumpability refinement from an initial relation is not immediately apparent. As we will demonstrate below, if the relation undergoes changes during computation, $q_\sim$ also changes. Consequently, an equality from item 2 that is false in the current step might become true later. Conversely, the following characterization of proportional lumpability is more straightforward to employ in defining a partition refinement algorithm for proportional lumpability.

Theorem 4 (Characterization 2 of proportional lumpability [25])**.** *Consider a CTMC $X(t)$ with a state space $\mathcal{S}$, and let $\sim$ denote an equivalence relation over $\mathcal{S}$. The relation $\sim$ is a proportional lumpability for $X(t)$ if and only if for any equivalence classes $S_i, S_j, S_k \in \mathcal{S}/\!\sim$ where $S_i \neq S_j$, $S_i \neq S_k$, and $s, s' \in S_i$,*

1. *$q(s,S_k) \neq 0$ if and only if $q(s',S_k) \neq 0$ and*
2. *if $q(s,S_k) \neq 0$, then*

$$\frac{q(s,S_j)}{q(s,S_k)} = \frac{q(s',S_j)}{q(s',S_k)}$$

In order to introduce our new characterization, we need to recall that, as for strong lumpability, also in the case of proportional lumpability the equivalence relation $\mathcal{S} \times \mathcal{S}$ is always a proportional lumpability. However, this is not useful in the applications. On the other hand, the problem of "refining" a given initial equivalence relation in order to obtain a proportional lumpability is a challenging one.

Definition 4 (Maximum Proportional Lumpability Problem). *Let $X(t)$ be a CTMC with state space $\mathcal{S}$ and let $\mathcal{R}$ be an equivalence relation over $\mathcal{S}$. The* maximum proportional lumpability problem *over $X(t)$ and $\mathcal{R}$ consists of finding the largest equivalence relation $\sim$ such that $\sim \subseteq \mathcal{R}$ and $\sim$ is a proportional lumpability for $X(t)$.*

In [25], we proved that the maximum proportional lumpability problem has always a unique solution that can be computed in time $O(|\mathcal{S}|^4)$. The following characterization allows us to improve such time complexity result. We recall that given an equivalence relation $\mathcal{R}$, $q_{\mathcal{R}}(s)$ denotes the sum of all transition rates from s to any state t such that $(s,t) \notin \mathcal{R}$. Notice that in Theorem 3, we referred to a generic equivalence relation $\sim$; hence, since we consider only ergodic CTMCs, the first item is only necessary to cover the case in which the relation $\sim$ is the total relation $\mathcal{S} \times \mathcal{S}$. In the following result, we do not have to explicitly deal with it, since we consider an equivalence relation $\mathcal{R}$ which is not total.

Theorem 5 (Characterization 3 of proportional lumpability). *Let $X(t)$ be an ergodic CTMC with state space $\mathcal{S}$ and $\mathcal{R}$ be an equivalence relation over $\mathcal{S}$ with $\mathcal{R} \neq \mathcal{S} \times \mathcal{S}$. The relation $\sim$ is the maximum proportional lumpability over $X(t)$ and $\mathcal{R}$ if and only if it is the largest equivalence relation included in $\mathcal{R}$ such that for any equivalence classes $S_i, S_j \in \mathcal{S}/\sim$ with $S_i \neq S_j$ and $s, s' \in S_i$,*

$$\frac{q(s,S_j)}{q_{\mathcal{R}}(s)} = \frac{q(s',S_j)}{q_{\mathcal{R}}(s')}$$

Proof. $\Rightarrow$) Suppose that $\sim$ is the maximum proportional lumpability over $X(t)$ and $\mathcal{R}$. This means that $\sim$ is the largest equivalence relation included in $\mathcal{R}$ for which there exists a function κ from $\mathcal{S}$ to $\mathbb{R}^+$ such that $\sim$ is a κ-proportional lumpability. This means that $\sim$ is such that for any equivalence classes $S_i, S_j \in \mathcal{S}/\sim$ with $S_i \neq S_j$ and $s, s' \in S_i$

$$\frac{q(s,S_j)}{\kappa(s)} = \frac{q(s',S_j)}{\kappa(s')}$$

Let B be a union of equivalence classes of $\sim$. It holds that $q(s,B) \neq 0$ if and only if $q(s',B) \neq 0$. Moreover,

$$\frac{q(s,B)}{\kappa(s)} = \frac{q(s',B)}{\kappa(s')}$$

If $q(s,B) \neq 0$, this is equivalent to

$$\frac{\kappa(s)}{q(s,B)} = \frac{\kappa(s')}{q(s',B)}$$

As a consequence,

$$\frac{q(s,S_j)}{q(s,B)} = \frac{q(s,S_j)}{\kappa(s)}\frac{\kappa(s)}{q(s,B)} = \frac{q(s',S_j)}{\kappa(s')}\frac{\kappa(s')}{q(s',B)} = \frac{q(s',S_j)}{q(s',B)}$$

Let B_i be the equivalence class of $\mathcal{R}$ to which s and s' belong. It holds that $S_i \subseteq B_i$. Moreover, $\mathcal{S} \setminus B_i$ is a union of equivalence classes of $\sim$. Since $X(t)$ is ergodic, $\mathcal{R} \neq \mathcal{S} \times \mathcal{S}$, and $s \sim s'$, it has to be $q(s, \mathcal{S} \setminus B_i) = q_{\mathcal{R}}(s) \neq 0$ and $q(s', \mathcal{S} \setminus B_i) = q_{\mathcal{R}}(s) \neq 0$. Hence, $\sim$ satisfies

$$\frac{q(s,S_j)}{q_{\mathcal{R}}(s)} = \frac{q(s',S_j)}{q_{\mathcal{R}}(s')}$$

Finally, $\sim$ has to be the largest equivalence relation included in $\mathcal{R}$ that satisfies such equations, since any equivalence relation included in $\mathcal{R}$ satisfying such equations is a proportional lumpability and $\sim$ is by hypothesis the largest proportional lumpability included in $\mathcal{R}$.

$\Leftarrow$) Suppose that $\sim$ is the largest equivalence relation included in $\mathcal{R}$ that satisfies the equations

$$\frac{q(s,S_j)}{q_{\mathcal{R}}(s)} = \frac{q(s',S_j)}{q_{\mathcal{R}}(s')}$$

Since $\mathcal{R} \neq \mathcal{S} \times \mathcal{S}$ and $X(t)$ is ergodic, it holds that $q_{\mathcal{R}}(s)$ is greater than 0 for each $s \in \mathcal{S}$. Hence, $\sim$ is a proportional lumpability included in $\mathcal{R}$. We still have to prove that it is the largest one. Let us assume by contraddiction that there exists another proportional lumpability $\approx$ included in $\mathcal{R}$ and larger than $\sim$. There exists a function κ from $\mathcal{S}$ to $\mathcal{R}^+$ such that $\approx$ is a κ-proportional lumpability. This means that for any equivalence classes $T_i, T_j \in \mathcal{S}/\approx$ with $T_i \neq T_j$ and $s, s' \in T_i$,

$$\frac{q(s,T_j)}{\kappa(s)} = \frac{q(s',T_j)}{\kappa(s')}$$

As a consequence, if B is a union of equivalence classes of $\approx$, it holds that

$$\frac{q(s,B)}{\kappa(s)} = \frac{q(s',B)}{\kappa(s')}$$

Hence, if $q(s,B) \neq 0$,

$$\frac{\kappa(s)}{q(s,B)} = \frac{\kappa(s')}{q(s',B)}$$

Let B_i be the equivalence class of $\mathcal{R}$ to which s and s' belong. The set $\mathcal{S} \setminus B_i$ is a union of equivalence classes of $\approx$. Therefore $\approx$ also satisfies

$$\frac{q(s,T_j)}{q_{\mathcal{R}}(s)} = \frac{q(s',T_j)}{q_{\mathcal{R}}(s')}$$

which contradicts the fact that $\sim$ was the largest satisfying such equations. □

As a consequence, the maximum proportional lumpability over a CTMC $X(t)$ included in a given equivalence relation $\mathcal{R}$ can be seen as a lumpability over the perturbed chain $X'(t)$ in which the rate $q(s,s')$ is divided by $q_{\mathcal{R}}(s)$.

Corollary 1. *Let $X(t)$ be an ergodic CTMC with state space $\mathcal{S}$ and let $\mathcal{R}$ be an equivalence relation over $\mathcal{S}$ with $\mathcal{R} \neq \mathcal{S} \times \mathcal{S}$. The relation $\sim$ is the maximum proportional lumpability over $X(t)$ and $\mathcal{R}$ if and only if it is the largest lumpability included in $\mathcal{R}$ over the CTMC $X_{\mathcal{R}}(t)$ whose infinitesimal generator $\mathbf{Q}_{\mathcal{R}}$ is defined as*

$$q_{\mathcal{R}}(s,s') = \frac{q(s,s')}{q_{\mathcal{R}}(s)}$$

Hence, we can exploit any efficient algorithm for computing the maximum lumpability included in a given equivalence relation in order to compute the maximum proportional lumpability included in the same equivalence relation, as illustrated in Algorithm 1.

Algorithm 1 Computation of the Maximum Proportional Partition

```
function MAXPROP(S, Q, R)
    if R = S × S then return R
    for s ∈ S do
        q_R(s) = 0
        for s' ∈ S do
            if (s, s') ∉ R then
                q_R(s) = q_R(s) + q(s, s')
    for s ∈ S do
        for s' ∈ S do
            q_R(s, s') = q(s, s') / q_R(s)
    return MAXLUMP(Q_R, R)
```

The correctness of the described algorithm is immediately followed by Corollary 1, while its complexity depends on the complexity of the subroutine used for computing the maximum lumpability.

Corollary 2 (Correctness and Complexity)**.** *Let* MAXLUMP *be an algorithm that, given the infinitesimal generator* $\mathbf{Q}'$ *of a CTMC* $X'(t)$ *and an equivalence relation* $\mathcal{R}$ *over the states of the chain, computes the largest lumpability of* $X'(t)$ *included in* $\mathcal{R}$*. Let* $\mathbf{Q}$ *be the infinitesimal generator of a CTMC* $X(t)$ *over state space* $\mathcal{S}$ *and* $\mathcal{R}$ *be an equivalence relation over* $\mathcal{S}$*. It holds that* MAXPROP$(\mathcal{S}, \mathbf{Q}, \mathcal{R})$ *returns the largest proportional lumpability of* $X(t)$ *included in* $\mathcal{R}$*. Moreover* MAXPROP *has the same time complexity as* MAXLUMP*.*

Currently, the fastest algorithm for computing the largest lumpability runs in time $O(|\mathcal{S}|^2 \log |\mathcal{S}|)$ if the infinitesimal generator of the chain is provided as a matrix [40,41].

3.2. Comparison with Lumpability of the Embedded Markov Chain

We contrast proportional lumpability with the lumpability of the embedded Markov chain, as defined in [21]. Examples 2 and 3 offer fresh insights into this comparison.

One common method for determining the stationary probability distribution of an ergodic continuous-time Markov chain $X(t)$ involves examining its embedded Markov chain $X^E(t)$. Technically, the embedded Markov chain is a regular discrete-time Markov chain (DTMC), sometimes referred to as its jump process. For a given $X(t)$ with state space $\mathcal{S}$, each entry of the one-step transition probability matrix of the corresponding embedded Markov chain is denoted by $p(s, s')$, signifying the conditional probability of transitioning from state s to state s'. This probability is defined as follows:

$$p(s, s') = \frac{q(s, s')}{q(s)} \qquad \text{for } s \neq s'$$

while $p(s, s) = 0$. Let us assume that $X^E(t)$ is aperiodic, and let $\boldsymbol{\pi}^*$ be its steady-state distribution. Therefore, we can compute the equilibrium distribution $\boldsymbol{\pi}$ of $X(t)$ in the following way: let $W = \sum_{s \in \mathcal{S}} \pi^*(s)/q(s)$, then

$$\pi(s) = \frac{\pi^*(s)}{Wq(s)}.$$

It is important to note that our definition of $q_{\sim}(s)$ differs from that of $q(s)$ in general. Therefore, the proportionally lumpable property of $X(t)$ does not necessarily imply that the corresponding embedded Markov chain $X^E(t)$ is lumpable. Conversely, if $X^E(t)$ exhibits lumpability, then $X(t)$ is proportionally lumpable with respect to the function κ from $\mathcal{S}$ to $\mathbb{R}^+$, where $\kappa(s) = q(s)$ for all $s \in \mathcal{S}$. In summary, we can affirm that if $X(t)$ possesses a strongly lumpable embedded process, then it is also proportionally lumpable. However, the reverse is not necessarily true.

Example 2. *Let us reconsider the reliability problem for a system comprising N components. Suppose our focus now shifts to determining the number of operational components at any given time. Thus, the state space* $\mathcal{S} = C_i : 0 \leq i \leq N$, *where* C_i *represents the system state with i functioning components. We posit that in each state* C_i, *the time to failure of a component follows an exponential distribution with rate* μ_i. *Additionally, each component can undergo restoration with a rate of* λ. *In certain scenarios, system failures may occur due to the simultaneous malfunctioning of components resulting from common underlying factors. These common-cause failures could stem from issues like shared power supply failures, environmental conditions (such as earthquakes, floods, humidity, etc.), common maintenance issues, and so forth. Simultaneous failures attributed to common causes may happen at a rate of* μ_c. *The state transition diagram for this system repair model is depicted in Figure 3.*

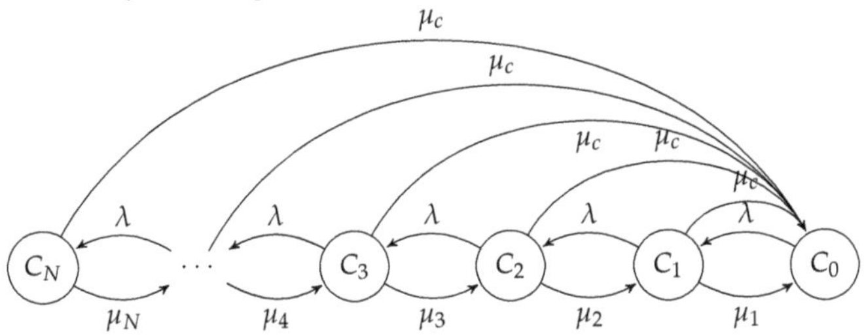

Figure 3. CTMC for system repair model with common-cause failures.

We can prove that this model is proportionally lumpable with respect to the relation $\sim$ *over* $\mathcal{S}$ *given by the reflexive, symmetric, and transitive closure of* $\{(C_i, C_j) : 1 \leq i, j \leq N\}$, *and the function* κ *such that* $\kappa(C_i) = q_\sim(C_i)$ *for* $i \in \{0, \ldots, N\}$. *This relation induces two equivalence classes, named* $S_0 = \{C_0\}$ *and* $S_1 = \{C_1, \ldots, C_N\}$, *and the model in Figure 3 results to be proportionally lumpable, whose aggregated chain is depicted in Figure 4.*

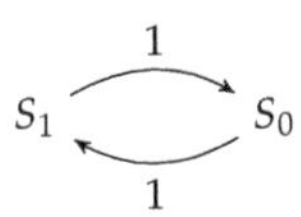

Figure 4. Aggregated CTMC for system repair model with common-cause failures.

In this case, the model in Figure 3 does not have a strongly lumpable embedded process due to the fact that $q(C_i) \neq q_\sim(C_i)$ *for each* $i \in \{0, \ldots, N\}$.

Example 3. *Consider the model described in Example 1. We showed that the CTMC depicted in Figure 1 is proportionally lumpable. It is easy to see that this model has also a strongly lumpable embedded process. Indeed, this is trivially followed by Theorem 3 and the fact that* $q(s) = q_\sim(s)$ *for all* $s \in \mathcal{S}$ *where* $\sim$ *is the relation inducing the partition* $S_n = \{\bar{x} \in \mathcal{S} : \sum x_i = n\}$ *with* $n \in \{0, 1, 2, 3\}$.

4. A Case Study

To articulate our case study, we introduce Performance Evaluation Process Algebra (PEPA) [8] as a high-level formal specification language that is used to study either behavioral or performance properties of complex systems (see, e.g., [42]). This enables us to precisely describe the system slated for analysis.

4.1. The Process Algebra PEPA

In this section, we aim to provide a concise overview of Performance Evaluation Process Algebra (PEPA) and shed light on its notable advantages. One of the primary strengths of PEPA lies in its compositional nature. This inherent compositional quality allows for a modular and scalable approach in modeling complex systems. Further, each PEPA specification corresponds to an underlying stochastic process that, under specific assumptions, takes the form of a continuous-time Markov process.

The practical utility of PEPA is enhanced by the availability of a dedicated tool seamlessly integrated into the Eclipse environment, known as the PEPA Eclipse Plug-in [43]. This tool facilitates the application of PEPA, offering a user-friendly environment for modeling and analysis within the Eclipse framework.

A fundamental aspect of a PEPA system specification is its representation as a collection of active agents or components. These components collaboratively engage in activities to collectively shape the overall system behavior. This cooperative behavior is encapsulated by the interaction of components and their respective activities, forming a structured framework for system analysis.

Importantly, the behavior of each individual component within the PEPA framework is characterized by its activities, providing a nuanced understanding of its role within the larger system context. Moreover, the influence of the environment on each component adds a layer of realism to the model, accounting for external factors that may impact the system dynamics.

To facilitate a clear and standardized representation, the syntax for PEPA terms is rigorously defined by a specific grammar as described below:

$$P ::= P \underset{L}{\bowtie} P \mid P/L \mid S \qquad\qquad S ::= (\alpha, r).S \mid S + S \mid A$$

In this context, the symbols used carry specific meanings within the framework of PEPA. The variable S denotes a sequential component, highlighting a distinct, ordered execution of activities. On the other hand, the variable P represents a model component, which can be obtained as the cooperation of sequential terms, signifying cooperative behavior among them. The operators in PEPA hold distinctive meanings. For instance, $(\alpha, r).S$ denotes an operation where the activity (α, r) is performed, involving an action type α and a corresponding rate r. Subsequently, the system behaves as P. The operator $P + Q$ signifies a system that can exhibit the behavior of either P or Q. The choice combinator $+$ represents competition between components. The term $P + Q$ enables all the current activities of both P and Q. The first activity to complete distinguishes one of the components, P or Q. The other component of the choice is discarded. The component P/L operates by behaving as P but with a modification: any activity of type within the set L undergoes relabeling with the *unknown type* τ.

Introducing constants, denoted by symbols like A, involves defining equations, such as $A \stackrel{def}{=} P$. This equation assigns the behavior of the component P to the constant A, providing a means to encapsulate specific system characteristics within constants.

The cooperation combinator $\underset{L}{\bowtie}$ represents an interaction between two components. The interaction is determined by the set of action types L, referred to as the *cooperation set*. Activities with action types in this set, known as shared activities, require synchronization between the components. It is assumed that components independently proceed with activities whose types do not belong to the cooperation set L. Crucially, the duration of a shared activity is influenced by the rate of the slower participant. If an activity within a component has an unknown rate denoted as $\top$, the rate of the shared activity will align with that of the other component.

4.2. Selfish Mining in Public Blockchains

The problem of selfish mining in public blockchains (see, e.g., [44–48]) arises when a minority mining pool adopts a strategic approach to maximize its rewards at the expense of other miners. This attack strategy involves the mining pool keeping its successfully mined blocks private, creating a fork in the blockchain. Meanwhile, honest miners continue to mine on the public chain, unaware of the pool's private branch. As the selfish miners discover more blocks, they strengthen their lead on the public chain and continue to keep their blocks secret. When the public branch approaches the pool's private branch in length, the selfish miners reveal blocks from their private chain to the public one, causing the public chain to become the shorter branch and their private chain to become the longer one. This results in a waste of resources for honest miners and can lead to a higher number of forks in the blockchain, impacting its performance and security. The selfish mining attack is a significant concern in blockchain systems and requires careful analysis and consideration to develop more robust and efficient solutions.

In the rest of this paragraph, we introduce a PEPA model tailored for the analysis of the selfish mining attack. The model we are about to delineate represents a generalization of the one outlined in [26]. In contrast to the assumptions made in [26], where all miners possess identical computational capabilities for both mining and verification phases, we extend our model to accommodate variations in miners' computational powers. Consequently, the rates at which miners mine or verify blocks may differ. This adjustment mirrors a more realistic configuration of the blockchain state, enabling us to delve into real-world scenarios with greater precision and relevance. It is important to note that the case study presented in this paper is different from the one discussed in [26]. Our focus encompasses an examination of how the verification time influences the effectiveness of the selfish mining strategy. This consideration becomes particularly significant in the context of the evolving landscape of blockchain technology, notably with the advent of smart contracts. As outlined in seminal work [45], the impact of verification time on selfish mining strategies may not be negligible, rendering our model applicable to a broader spectrum of scenarios.

Our investigation specifically centers on the relationship between verification times and the advantages gained by selfish miners. To elaborate further, we present a PEPA model designed for a blockchain network utilizing a Proof-of-Work (PoW) consensus mechanism. This model accounts for a coalition of fair miners alongside a single selfish miner. Each miner, denoted as M_i, operates with an individual computational power represented by γ_i and verifies blocks with a time frame following an exponentially distributed pattern, with a mean duration of β_i^{-1}.

In Table 1, we report the specification of a network composed of $K \geq 3$ fair miners.

Table 1. PEPA model of a network with K fair miners.

M_i	$\stackrel{def}{=}$	$(m_i, \gamma_i).M_i + \sum_{j \neq i} (m_j, \top).V_i$
V_i	$\stackrel{def}{=}$	$\sum_{j \neq i} (v_j, \beta_i).M_i + \sum_{j \neq i} (m_j, \top).V_i$
Network	$\stackrel{def}{=}$	$(..((M_1 \underset{L \cup L_{12}}{\bowtie} M_2) \underset{L \cup L_3}{\bowtie}) \underset{L \cup L_4}{\bowtie} \ldots) \underset{L \cup L_K}{\bowtie} M_K$
where		$i, j \in \{1, \ldots, K\}$ and $L = \{m_1, \ldots, m_K\}, L_{12} = \{v_3, \ldots, v_K\}$, $L_j = \{v_1, \ldots, v_K\} \setminus \{v_j\}$ for $j \geq 3$

Let us inspect the behavior of a single fair (verifying) miner, say M_1.

Miner M_1 initiates block mining with action type m_1 at a rate of γ_1, subsequently returning to its initial state to commence mining another block. Upon receiving a block from the network via an activity $(m_j, \top)$ where $j \in \{2, \ldots, K\}$, M_1 enters the verification process, moving to state V_1. Notice that, when M_1 announces a block, according to the operational semantics of PEPA, m_1 is received by all miners except M_1. Thus, all miners moves to state V_1, while M_1 is still mining. Now, according to the synchronization operation, all miners in V_1 synchronize on $\{v_1\}$, and the block is verified at a rate of $\delta_1 = min(\beta_2, \beta_3, \ldots, \beta_K)$. Once the verification is completed, all the verifying miners simultaneously move to the mining phase. Importantly, M_1 remains capable of receiving new blocks from the network during the verification phase through activities $(m_j, \top)$, where $j \in \{2, \ldots, K\}$.

The derivation graph of the model is depicted in Figure 5, where $\delta_1 = min(\beta_2, \beta_3, \ldots, \beta_K)$, $\delta_2 = min(\beta_1, \beta_3, \ldots, \beta_K), \ldots, \delta_K = min(\beta_1, \beta_2, \ldots, \beta_{K-1})$.

The continuous-time Markov chain underlying the system is depicted in Figure 6a, with states $\{0, 1, \ldots, K\}$ where 0 denotes the state of the network in which all miners are mining and $j \in \{1, \ldots, K\}$ denotes the state in which M_j is mining while all the other miners are verifying. It would be interesting to aggregate fair miners into a fair environment according to a relation $\mathcal{R}$ such that $i\mathcal{R}j$ for all $i, j \in \{1, \ldots, K\}$. By applying Theorem 4, one can easliy find that the maximum proportional lumpability for this system with respect to $\mathcal{R}$ is the one induced by the partition:

$$\begin{aligned} S_1 &= \{0\} \\ S_2 &= \{1, \ldots, K\} \end{aligned}$$

and the function κ such that for each state $s \in S_2$, $\kappa(s) = q(s)$, while for $s \in S_1$, $\kappa(s) = 1$. The resulting aggregated CTMC is represented in Figure 6b. As the number of miners in a blockchain can be significantly high, an aggregated model can prove useful in reducing the state space and efficiently calculating performance indices of interest.

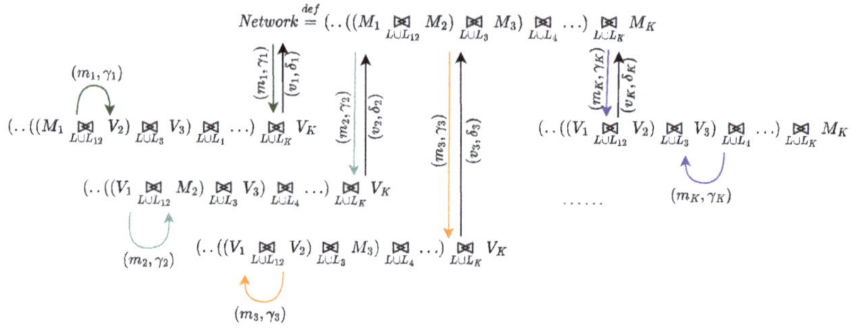

Figure 5. Derivation graph of the model presented in Table 1.

Figure 6. (**a**) Markov chain underlying the model presented in Table 1 and (**b**) its aggregation according to proportional lumpability.

Let us now consider a scenario where a network includes a selfish mining pool exercising control with hash power $w\gamma$, utilizing action types m_{S_1} and m_{S_2} for block mining. The PEPA specification for this network, comprising K honest miners and one selfish miner (M_S representing the mining pool), is detailed in Table 2. The action type m_{S_1} denotes the first block privately mined by the selfish pool, creating a separate branch, while m_{S_2} represents the second successful block. Upon the production of the second block, two blocks are revealed from the private branch to the public, prompting the rest of the network to transition from the shorter public branch to the newly disclosed blocks. This behavior is reflected in the model, where all network nodes align on the action type v_S upon the announcement of the selfish pool's second block.

Note that, for modeling simplicity, the selfish miner discloses two blocks from the private branch to the public. However, it is important to acknowledge that the model can be expanded to accommodate a more extended queue of blocks.

Figure 7 represents the derivation graph of the model presented in Table 2, while the Markov process corresponding to the system with K fair components and one selfish pool is represented in Figure 8a. Also in this case, if we define a relation $\mathcal{R}$ among states such that $i\mathcal{R}j$ for all $i, j \in 1, \ldots, K$, this would enable the aggregation of all fair miners into a fair environment. Indeed, by applying Theorem 4, one can find that the maximum proportional lumpability contained in $\mathcal{R}$ is the one induced by the state partition:

$$
\begin{array}{lcl}
S_0 & = & \{0\} \\
S_K & = & \{1, \ldots, K\} \\
S_{K+1} & = & \{K+1\} \\
S_{K+2} & = & \{K+2\} \\
S_{K+3} & = & \{K+3\}
\end{array}
$$

and the function κ such that for each state $s \in S_K$, $\kappa(s) = q(s)$, while for $s \in S_0 \cup S_{K+1} \cup S_{K+2} \cup S_{K+3}$, $\kappa(s) = 1$. Thus, we can analyze the aggregated Markov chain represented in Figure 8b and, by Theorems 1 and 2, we can compute the exact solution to the original model.

Table 2. PEPA model of a network with K fair miners and one selfish pool M_S.

M_{F_i}	$\stackrel{def}{=}$	$(m_{F_i}, \gamma_i).M_{F_i} + \sum_{j \neq i}(m_{F_j}, \top).V_i + (m_{S_2}, \top).V_{i_S}$
V_i	$\stackrel{def}{=}$	$\sum_{j \neq i}(v_j, \beta_j).M_{F_i} + \sum_{j \neq i}(m_{F_j}, \top).V_i$
V_{i_S}	$\stackrel{def}{=}$	$(v_S, \beta).M_{F_i} + (m_{S_2}, \top).V_{i_S}$
M_S	$\stackrel{def}{=}$	$(m_{S_1}, w\gamma).C + \sum_{i}(m_{F_i}, \top).V_S$
C	$\stackrel{def}{=}$	$(m_{S_2}, w\gamma).M_S + \sum_{i}(m_{F_i}, \top).V_S$
V_S	$\stackrel{def}{=}$	$\sum_{i}(v_i, \beta).M_S + \sum_{j \neq i}(m_{F_j}, \top).V_S$
Network	$\stackrel{def}{=}$	$M_S \underset{L \cup V}{\bowtie} (..((M_{F_1} \underset{L \cup V_{12}}{\bowtie} M_{F_2}) \underset{L \cup V_3}{\bowtie} M_{F_3}) \ldots) \underset{L \cup V_K}{\bowtie} M_{F_K})$
where		$i, j \in \{1, \ldots, K\}$ and $L = \{m_{S_2}, m_1, \ldots, m_K\}, V = \{v_1, \ldots, v_K\}$, $V_{12} = \{v_S, v_3, \ldots, v_K\}, V_j = \{v_S, v_1, \ldots, v_K\} \setminus \{v_j\}$ for $j \geq 3$

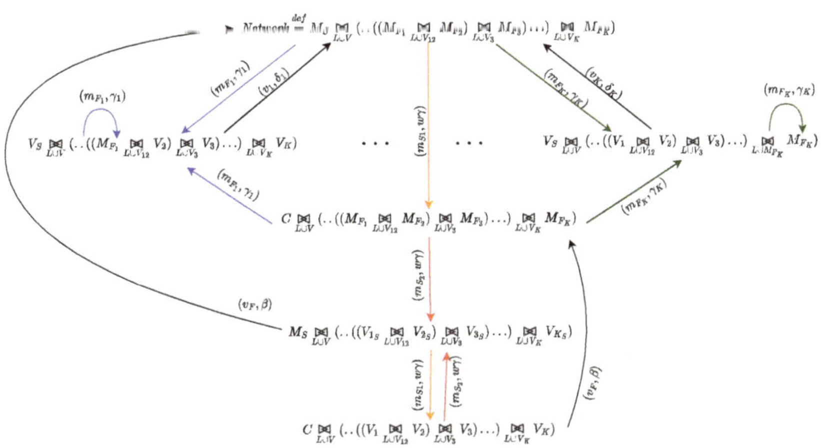

Figure 7. Derivation graph of the model presented in Table 2.

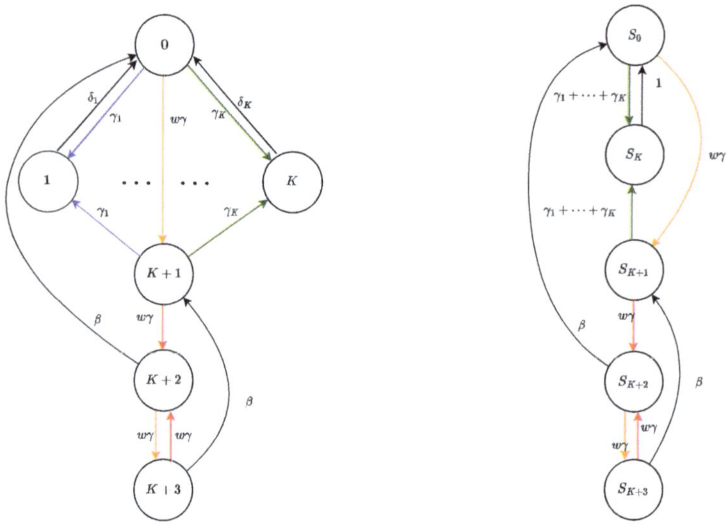

(**a**) (**b**)

Figure 8. (**a**) Markov chain underlying the model presented in Table 2 and (**b**) its aggregation according to proportional lumpability.

The symbolic expression of the steady-state probabilities of the Markov chain underlying the lumped network depicted in Figure 8b are:

$$\pi(S_0) = \frac{\beta^2(\Gamma + w\gamma) + \beta w\gamma(2\Gamma + \gamma))}{G}, \quad \pi(S_k) = \frac{\beta^2\Gamma(\Gamma + 2w\gamma) + \beta\Gamma w\gamma(2\Gamma + 3\gamma))}{G}$$

$$\pi(S_{K+1}) = \frac{w\gamma\beta(\beta + 2w\gamma)}{G}, \qquad \pi(S_{K+2}) = \frac{w\gamma^2(\beta + w\gamma)}{G}, \qquad \pi(S_{K+3}) = \frac{w\gamma^3}{G},$$

where $\Gamma = \gamma_1 + \ldots, \gamma_K$, while G is the normalizing constant

$$G = \beta^2\Gamma(1+\Gamma) + 2\beta(1+\Gamma)(\beta+\Gamma)w\gamma + \beta(4+3\Gamma)w\gamma^2 + 2w\gamma^3.$$

By applying Theorem 1, we derive the steady-state probability of the original system; in particular, referring to Figure 8, we obtain:

$$\pi(0) = \pi(S_0) =, \quad \pi(K+1) = \pi(S_{K+1}), \quad \pi(K+2) = \pi(S_{K+1}), \quad \pi(K+3) = \pi(S_{K+3})$$

$$\pi(i) = \frac{\beta \prod_{j=1, j\neq i}^{K} \delta_j \gamma_i (\beta\Gamma + 2(\beta+\Gamma)w\gamma + 3w\gamma^2)}{G}.$$

5. Conclusions

In this study, we have delved into the concept of proportional lumpability and have introduced three distinct characterizations of this novel notion. These characterizations have laid the groundwork for the development of an efficient algorithm designed to automatically check the property of proportional lumpability for, even complex, CTMCs.

The first characterization, as outlined in [21], provides a streamlined method for verifying whether a given relation aligns with proportional lumpability. Building upon this, a second characterization presented in [25] enables the creation of an algorithm for computing proportional lumpability by iteratively refining an initial relation. In this paper. we introduced a novel characterization that significantly enhances computational efficiency, leading to the development of an algorithm for proportional lumpability with a time complexity of $O(|\mathcal{S}|^2 \log |\mathcal{S}|)$.

To demonstrate the efficacy of proportional lumpability, we conducted an extensive case study akin to the approach outlined in [26]. Specifically, we expanded upon the findings in [26] by analyzing a strongly lumpable model meticulously designed to probe selfish mining behaviors within the context of a public blockchain. The model examined in this paper represents an extended, more general version of the one presented in [26], tailored to capture a more realistic depiction of the blockchain state under investigation. Unlike the assumptions in [26], where all miners are assumed to possess identical computational capabilities for both mining and verification phases, our extended model acknowledges variations in miners' computational powers. This adjustment offers a more authentic portrayal of the blockchain state, enabling a deeper exploration of real-world scenarios with enhanced accuracy and relevance.

It is crucial to emphasize that the case study presented in this paper diverges from the one discussed in [26]. Our primary focus revolves around investigating how verification time influences the efficacy of the selfish mining strategy. This examination assumes particular importance in the context of the dynamic landscape of blockchain technology, especially with the emergence of smart contracts. As highlighted in seminal work such as [45], the impact of verification time on selfish mining strategies cannot be underestimated, thereby rendering our model applicable to a wider array of scenarios.

Our objective is to offer valuable insights into the concept of proportional lumpability and highlight the broader applications of partition refinement techniques.

As part of our future research endeavors, we aim to explore the possibility of further relaxing the definition of proportional lumpability by introducing approximated semantics, aligning with the spirit of the proposed approaches, e.g., in [49–53]. This future direction aims to enhance the flexibility and applicability of proportional lumpability in various modeling scenarios.

Furthermore, we aim to delve into the concept of *component substitution* as outlined in [54], specifically for approximating solutions of stochastic models expressed within the framework of Performance Evaluation Process Algebra (PEPA). This approach is introduced to tackle the computational complexity inherent in analyzing PEPA models. The proposed method involves substituting certain components within the models to simplify the analysis process, potentially leading to more efficient and scalable solutions. This methodology hinges upon the notion of *behavioral independence* [55] to delineate specific restricted classes of models. Essentially, this property affirms that the actions of a specific group of components within a model are unaffected by the actions of other components. This characteristic serves as a valuable means of discerning independent and semi-independent behaviors. The authors suggest substituting a component in a model with a simplified version of itself. This streamlined component maintains the same interactions as the original but usually has fewer states. As a result, the ensuing model generates a significantly smaller Continuous-Time Markov Chain (CTMC), simplifying the solution process. However, determining the transition rates within the simplified component is often challenging. Therefore, an iterative approach, in the spirit of the one proposed in [56], is employed to converge between two or more reduced models. As a future work, we plan to investigate a variant of component substitution grounded in the concept of proportional lumpability. This endeavor will enable us to leverage the findings presented in this paper to efficiently compute an exact solution for the model under consideration. This strategy is in line with the overarching goal of improving the practical usability of PEPA models within real-world systems, thus aiding in the optimization of performance evaluation procedures in computer and digital systems.

Author Contributions: All authors equally contributed to the paper. All authors have read and agreed to the published version of the manuscript.

Funding: This reasearch was partially funded by the Project PRIN 2020 "Nirvana—Noninterference and Reversibility Analysis in Private Blockchains" (20202FCJMH, CUP G23C22000400005), by the project SERICS (PE00000014) under the MUR National Recovery and Resilience Plan funded by the

European Union—NextGenerationEU, and by the GNCS INdAM project 2024 "Strutture di matrici e di funzioni per la sintesi di circuiti quantistici efficienti" (CUP E53C23001670001).

Data Availability Statement: All data in support of the results are available in the paper.

Acknowledgments: We thank the anonymous reviewers.

Conflicts of Interest: The authors declare no conflict of interest.

References

1. Molloy, M.K. Performance Analysis Using Stochastic Petri Nets. *IEEE Trans. Comput.* **1982**, *31*, 913–917. [CrossRef]
2. Valk, R.; Vidal-Naquet, G. Petri nets and regular languages. *J. Comput. Syst. Sci.* **1981**, *23*, 299–325. [CrossRef]
3. Plateau, B. On the stochastic structure of parallelism and synchronization models for distributed algorithms. *Sigmetrics Perf. Rev.* **1985**, *13*, 147–154. [CrossRef]
4. Fourneau, J.M.; Plateau, B.; Stewart, W.J. Product form for stochastic automata networks. In Proceedings of the ValueTools Conference, ICST, Brussels, Belgium, 22–27 October 2007; pp. 1–10.
5. Balsamo, S.; Marin, A. Queueing Networks in Formal methods for performance evaluation. In *LNCS*; Springer: Berlin/Heidel Germany, 2007; Chapter 2, pp. 34–82. [CrossRef]
6. Lazowska, E.D.; Zahorjan, J.L.; Graham, G.S.; Sevcick, K.C. *Quantitative System Performance: Computer System Analysis U Queueing Network Models*; Prentice Hall: Englewood Cliffs, NJ, USA, 1984.
7. Hermanns, H. *Interactive Markov Chains*; Springer: Berlin/Heidelberg, Germany, 2002. [CrossRef]
8. Hillston, J. *A Compositional Approach to Performance Modelling*; Cambridge University Press: Cambridge, UK, 1996. [CrossR
9. Schweitzer, P. Aggregation Methods for Large Markov Chains. In Proceedings of the International Workshop on Comp Performance and Reliability, Pisa, Italy, 26–30 September 1983; pp. 275–286.
10. Stewart, G. Computable error bounds for aggregated Markov chains. *J. ACM* **1983**, *30*, 271–285. [CrossRef]
11. Kemeny, J.G.; Snell, J.L. *Finite Markov Chains*; Springer: Berlin/Heidelberg, Germany, 1976. [CrossRef]
12. Baarir, S.; Dutheillet, C.; Haddad, S.; Iliè, J.M. On the use of exact lumping in partially symmetrical Well-formed Petri Net Proceedings of the International Conference on the Quantitative Evaluaiton of Systems (QEST'05), Torino, Italy, 19–22 Septe 2005; pp. 23–32. [CrossRef]
13. Buchholz, P. Exact and Ordinary lumpability in finite Markov chains. *J. Appl. Probab.* **1994**, *31*, 59–75. [CrossRef]
14. Kant, K. *Introduction to Computer System Performance Evaluation*; McGraw-Hill: New York, NY, USA , 1992.
15. Franceschinis, G.; Muntz, R. Bounds for quasi-lumpable Markov chains. *Perform. Eval.* **1994**, *20*, 223–243. [CrossRef]
16. Courtois, P.J.; Semal, P. Computable Bounds for Conditional Steady-State Probabilities in Large Markov Chains and Queu Models. *IEEE J. Sel. Areas Commun.* **1986**, *4*, 926–937. [CrossRef]
17. Franceschinis, G.; Muntz, R. Computing Bounds for the Performance Indices of Quasi-Lumpable Stochastic Well-Formed *IEEE Trans. Softw. Eng.* **1994**, *20*, 516–525. [CrossRef]
18. Baarir, S.; Beccuti, M.; Dutheillet, C.; Franceschinis, G. From partially to fully lumped Markov chains in stochastic well for Petri nets. In Proceedings of the Valuetools 2009 Conference, Pisa, Italy, 20–22 October 2009; ACM: New York, NY, USA, p. 44. [CrossRef]
19. Milios, D.; Gilmore, S. Component aggregation for PEPA models: An approach based on approximate strong equival *Perform. Eval.* **2015**, *94*, 43–71. [CrossRef]
20. Marin, A.; Piazza, C.; Rossi, S. Proportional Lumpability. In Proceedings of the International Conference on Formal Mod and Analysis of Timed Systems, FORMATS, Amsterdam, The Netherlands, 27–29 August 2019; Springer: Berlin/Heidel Germany, 2019; pp. 265–281. [CrossRef]
21. Marin, A.; Piazza, C.; Rossi, S. Proportional Lumpability and Proportional Bisimilarity. *Acta Inform.* **2021**, *59*, 211–244. [Cros
22. Ledoux, J. A necessary condition for weak lumpability in finite Markov processes. *Oper. Res. Lett.* **1993**, *13*, 165–168. [Cros
23. Kuo, J.; Wei, J. Lumping analysis in monomolecular reaction systems. analysis of approximately lumpable system. *Ind. Chem. Fundam.* **1969**, *8*, 124–133. [CrossRef]
24. Li, G.; Rabitz, H. A general analysis of exact lumping in chemical kinetics. *Chem. Eng. Sci.* **1989**, *44*, 1413–1430. [CrossRef]
25. Piazza, C.; Rossi, S. Reasoning about Proportional Lumpability. In Proceedings of the Quantitative Evaluation of Systems, France, 23–27 August 2021; Springer: Berlin/Heidelberg, Germany, 2021; Volume 12846, pp. 372–390. [CrossRef]
26. Smuseva, D.; Marin, A.; Rossi, S. Selfish Mining in Public Blockchains: A Quantitative Analysis. In Proceedings of the International Conference on Performance Evaluation Methodologies and Tools, Crete, Greece, 6–7 September 2023; Spri Berlin/Heidelberg, Germany, 2023; pp. 18–32. [CrossRef]
27. Ross, S.M. *Stochastic Processes*, 2nd ed.; John Wiley & Sons: Hoboken, NJ, USA, 1996.
28. Taylor, H.M.; Karlin, S. *An Introduction to Stochastic Modeling*; Academic Press: Cambridge, MA, USA, 1998; Chapter IX.
29. Jacobi, M.N. A robust spectral method for finding lumpings and meta stable states of non-reversible Markov chains. *Elect. Numer. Anal.* **2010**, *37*, 296–306.
30. Derisavi, S.; Hermanns, H.; Sanders, W.H. Optimal state-space lumping in Markov chains. *Elsevier Inf. Process. Lett.* *87*, 309–315. [CrossRef]

Baarir, S.; Beccuti, M.; Dutheillet, C.; Franceschinis, G.; Haddad, S. Lumping partially symmetrical stochastic models. *Perform. Eval.* **2011**, *68*, 21–44. [CrossRef]

Sumita, U.; Rieders, M. Lumpability and time-reversibility in the aggregation-disaggregation method for large Markov chains. *Commun. Stat. Stoch. Models* **1989**, *5*, 63–81. [CrossRef]

Wei, J.; Kuo, J.C. Lumping analysis in monomolecular reaction systems. Analysis of the exactly lumpable system. *Ind. Eng. Chem. Fundam.* **1969**, *8*, 114–123. [CrossRef]

Tomlin, A.S.; Li, G.; Rabitz, H.; Tóth, J. The effect of lumping and expanding on kinetic differential equations. *SIAM J. Appl. Math.* **1997**, *57*, 1531–1556. [CrossRef]

Frostig, E. Jointly optimal allocation of a repairman and optimal control of service rate for machine repairman problem. *Eur. J. Oper. Res.* **1999**, *116*, 274–280. [CrossRef]

Hooghiemstra, G.; Koole, G. On the convergence of the power series algorithm. *Perform. Eval.* **2000**, *42*, 21–39. [CrossRef]

Katehakis, M.; Derman, C. Optimal Repair Allocation in a Series System. *Math. Oper. Res.* **1984**, *9*, 615–623. [CrossRef]

Katehakis, M.; Smit, L. A successive lumping procedure for a class of markov chains. *Probab. Eng. Informational Sci.* **2012**, *26*, 483–508. [CrossRef]

Ungureanu, V.; Melamed, B.; Katehakis, M.; Bradford, P. Deferred Assignment Scheduling in Cluster-Based Servers. *Clust. Comput.* **2006**, *9*, 57–65. [CrossRef]

Valmari, A.; Franceschinis, G. Simple O(m logn) Time Markov Chain Lumping. In Proceedings of the International Conference on TACAS, Edinburgh UK, 15–19 July 2010; Springer Verlag: Berlin/Heidelberg, Germany, 2010; Volume 6015, pp. 38–52. [CrossRef]

Groote, J.F.; Rivera Verduzco, J.; De Vink, E.P. An Efficient Algorithm to Determine Probabilistic Bisimulation. *Algorithms* **2018**, *11*, 131. [CrossRef]

Hillston, J.; Marin, A.; Piazza, C.; Rossi, S. Persistent stochastic non-interference. *Fundam. Informaticae* **2021**, *181*, 1–35. [CrossRef]

Tribastone, M.; Duguid, A.; Gilmore, S. The PEPA Eclipse Plug-in. *Perf. Eval. Rev.* **2009**, *36*, 28–33. [CrossRef]

Carlsten, M.; Kalodner, H.; Weinberg, S.M.; Narayanan, A. On the instability of bitcoin without the block reward. In Proceedings of the ACM SIGSAC Conference on Computer and Communications Security, Vienna, Austria, 24–28 October 2016; pp. 154–167. [CrossRef]

Eyal, I.; Sirer, E.G. Majority is not enough: Bitcoin mining is vulnerable. *Commun. ACM* **2018**, *61*, 95–102. [CrossRef]

Göbel, J.; Keeler, H.P.; Krzesinski, A.E.; Taylor, P.G. Bitcoin blockchain dynamics: The selfish-mine strategy in the presence of propagation delay. *Perform. Eval.* **2016**, *104*, 23–41. [CrossRef]

Wright, C.S. The Fallacy of the Selfish Miner in Bitcoin: An Economic Critique. *Soc. Sci. Res. Netw.* **2018**. [CrossRef]

Motlagh, S.G.; Mišić, J.; Mišić, V.B. The Impact of Selfish Mining on Bitcoin Network Performance. *IEEE Trans. Netw. Sci. Eng.* **2021**, *8*, 724–735. [CrossRef]

Pattipati, K.R.; Kostreva, M.M.; Teele, J.L. Approximate mean value analysis algorithms for queuing networks: Existence, uniqueness, and convergence results. *J. ACM* **1990**, *37*, 643–673. [CrossRef]

Chandy, K.M.; Hergox, U.; Woo, L. Approximate Analysis of General Queueing Networks. *IBM J. Res. Dev.* **1975**, *19*, 43–49. [CrossRef]

Miner, A.S.; Ciardo, G.; Donatelli, S. Using the exact state space of a Markov model to compute approximate stationary measures. In Proceedings of the 2000 ACM SIGMETRICS International Conference on Measurement and Modeling of Computer Systems, New York, NY, USA, 18–21 June 2000; pp. 207–216. [CrossRef]

Gilmore, S.; Hillston, J.; Ribaudo, M. An Efficient Algorithm for Aggregating PEPA Models. *IEEE Trans. Softw. Eng.* **2001**, *27*, 449–464. [CrossRef]

Casagrande, A.; Dreossi, T.; Piazza, C. Hybrid Automata and ϵ-Analysis on a Neural Oscillator. In Proceedings of the Proceedings First International Workshop on Hybrid Systems and Biology, HSB, Newcastle Upon Tyne, UK, 3 September 2012 ; Volume 92, pp. 58–72. [CrossRef]

Thomas, N.; Bradley, J.T.; Thornley, D.J. Approximate solution of PEPA models using component substitution. In *Proceedings of the IEE Proceedings—Computers and Digital Technique*; IET Digital Library: Stevenage, UK, 2023; Volume 150, pp. 67–74. [CrossRef]

Thomas, N. Behavioural independence and control in PEPA. In *Proceedings of the First Workshop on Process Algebra with Stochastic Timed Activities (PASTA'02), Edinburgh, UK, 2002*; Newcastle University Library: Newcastle Upon Tyne, UK, 2002.

Gribaudo, M.; Sereno, M. Approximation Technique of Finite Capacity Queuing Networks Exploiting Petri Net Analysis. In Proceedings of the Fourth International Workshop on Queuing Networks with Finite Capacity (QNETs 2000), lkley, UK, 20–21 July 2000.

algorithms

Article

The Knapsack Problem with Conflict Pair Constraints on Bipartite Graphs and Extensions

Abraham P. Punnen and Jasdeep Dhahan *

Department of Mathematics, Simon Fraser University, Surrey, BC V5A 1S6, Canada; apunnen@sfu.ca
* Correspondence: jasdeep_dhahan@sfu.ca

Abstract: In this paper, we study the knapsack problem with conflict pair constraints. After a thorough literature survey on the topic, our study focuses on the special case of bipartite conflict graphs. For complete bipartite (multipartite) conflict graphs, the problem is shown to be NP-hard but solvable in pseudo-polynomial time, and it admits an FPTAS. Extensions of these results to more general classes of graphs are also presented. Further, a class of integer programming models for the general knapsack problem with conflict pair constraints is presented, which generalizes and unifies the existing formulations. The strength of the LP relaxations of these formulations is analyzed, and we discuss different ways to tighten them. Experimental comparisons of these models are also presented to assess their relative strengths. This analysis disclosed various strong and weak points of different formulations of the problem and their relationships to different types of problem data. This information can be used in designing special purpose algorithms for KPCC involving a learning component.

Keywords: knapsack problem; stable sets; conflict pair constraints; combinatorial optimization; algorithms

1. Introduction

Let $G = (V, E)$ be an undirected graph, and for each $i \in V = \{1, 2, \ldots, n\}$ an ordered pair (c_i, a_i) is prescribed such that $a_i, c_i \geq 0$ for all i. This non-negativity assumption can be relaxed in some of the results discussed in this paper. We refer to c_i as the *cost* of i and a_i as the *weight* of i. Let $b \in \mathbb{R}^{=} \cup \{0\}$ be a given budget. For any $S \subseteq V$, let $c(S) = \sum_{i \in S} c_i$ be its cost and $a(S) = \sum_{i \in S} a_i$ be its weight. Then, the *knapsack problem with conflict pair constraints* (KPCC) is to find a stable set S in G satisfying $a(S) \leq b$ such that $c(S)$ is as large as possible. The KPCC can be formulated as a 0-1 programming problem as follows:

$$\begin{aligned} \text{Maximize} \quad & \mathbf{cx} \\ \text{Subject to:} \quad & \mathbf{ax} \leq b \\ & x_i + x_j \leq 1 \text{ for all } (i,j) \in E \\ & \mathbf{x} \in \{0,1\}^n \end{aligned}$$

where $\mathbf{c} = (c_1, c_2, \ldots, c_n)$, $\mathbf{a} = (a_1, a_2, \ldots, a_n)$ and $\mathbf{x}^T = (x_1, x_2, \ldots, x_n)$.

The KPCC has been investigated by many researchers, and it is known under different names. Some authors call it the *maximum independent set problem with a budget constraint* [1–3], while some others call it the *disjunctively constrained knapsack problem* [4–10]. We use the name knapsack problem with conflict pair constraints since it belongs to the broader class of combinatorial optimization problems with conflict pair constraints [11–20].

Bandyapadhyay [1] notes that the maximum weight stable set problem (MWSS) has many applications in various fields, including scheduling, wireless networks, computer graphics, map labeling, and molecular biology. The budget restriction has a relevant interpretation in most of these applications, and it provides motivation to study KPCC. Moreover, specific applications of KPCC include job scheduling in computers and selecting a non-interfering set of transmitters [1]. Other applications of KPCC also have been discussed in the literature. Further, KPCC is used in the Dantzig–Wolfe decomposition formulation of the two-dimensional bin packing problem [21].

2. Literature Review

Combinatorial optimization problems with conflict pair constraints have recently received considerable attention from the research community. These include conflict pair versions of the minimum spanning tree problem [11–14,19,20], shortest path problem [14], minimum cost matching problem [14,17], minimum cost bin packing [22,23], and maximum flow problem [18]. KPCC is yet another member in this class of optimization problems. Conflict pair constraints can easily be absorbed into a quadratic objective function. Thus, these types of problems can be formulated as quadratic combinatorial optimization problems. However, the special structure of the conflict pair constraints makes the problem interesting to study independently.

The multiple choice knapsack problem studied by Chandra et al. [24] and Nauss [25] in 1975 is essentially a KPCC, where the underlying graph is a collection of disjoint cliques. The continuous version of this problem was investigated by Ibaraki et al. [26]. Another special case of KPCC, where $c_j = 1$ for all j, was mentioned by Bar-Noy et al. [27] in the context of resource allocation. The general problem KPCC was introduced by Yamada, Kataoka, and Watanab [10], and they proposed exact and heuristic algorithms to solve the problem. Hifi and Michrafy [6] presented different exact algorithms based on MIP formulations. Bettinelli, Cacchiani, and Malaguti [28] proposed yet another class of the branch and bound algorithm, along with extensive experimental analysis. Moreover, they presented comparisons of MIP formulations using general purpose solvers. Salem et al. [29] investigated the convex hull of feasible solutions of KPCC, i.e., the KPCC polytope. The authors obtained necessary and sufficient conditions for odd cycle inequalities associated with the stable set problem to be facet-defining for the KPCC polytope. Similar conditions were developed for the cover inequalities of the knapsack polytope in connection with the KPCC polytope. They also analyzed different lifting procedures to obtain additional valid inequalities. Exploiting these inequalities, the authors proposed an effective branch and bound algorithm to solve KPCC and reported the results of extensive computational experiments.

Heuristic algorithms for KPCC have been investigated by many researchers, and the results of extensive experimental analysis with these algorithms are available. Hifi and Michrafy [5] developed a reactive-local-search-based algorithm and also generated a class of test instances based on the ideas from [10]. Akeb et al. [4] proposed local-branching-based heuristics and provided an experimental analysis based on instances generated by [5]. Hifi and Otmani [7] proposed a scatter-search-based metaheuristic algorithm along with results of an experimental analysis using test instances from [5]. Recently, Hifi [9] proposed an iterative-rounding-search-based algorithm. Their experimental results using test instances from [5] were promising and were able to obtain the best known solutions for many benchmark instances. Salem et al. [30] developed a probabilistic tabu search algorithm to solve KPCC and reported extensive computational results.

Pferschy and Schauer [31] investigated KPCC for several special cases of the graph G. They showed that KPCC can be solved in pseudo-polynomial time when G is a tree and more generally when G is a graph with bounded treewidth or chordal. Fully polynomial-time approximation schemes (FPTASs) are also derived for these classes of graphs. Further, they proved that KPCC remains strongly NP-hard on perfect graphs. It may be noted that the stable set problem is polynomial-time-solvable on perfect graphs. Bandyapadhyay [1] also considered KPCC on trees, but the algorithm discussed in [31] is faster for this case. Moreover, [1] presents pseudopolynomial algorithms for cycles, forests, k-outerplanar graphs, and interval graphs. In another paper, Pferschy and Schauer [32] investigated approximation algorithms for KPCC under various restrictions on G. They showed that KPCC admits FPTASs on weakly chordal graphs and is solvable by PTAS (not FPTASs) on planar graphs.

Kalra et al. [2] studied another special case of KPCC, where $a_j = 1$ for all $j = 1, 2, \ldots, n$ and G is a multipartite graph. They proposed a $\frac{1}{k}$-approximation algorithm, where k is the number of partite sets, and proved that the performance bound established is tight. If $a_j = 1$ and c_j equal to the degree of j, for $j = 1, 2, \ldots, n$, KPCC reduces to the maximum independent vertex coverage problem (MIVC). The authors proved approximation hardness results for MIVC and showed that MIVC is NP-hard on bipartite graphs. Further, they established bounds on the integrality for the LP relaxation of a clique-based formulation of MVIP. Bandyapadhyay [1] investigated another special case of KPCC, where $c_j = 1$ for all j. This problem is called the maximum budget independent set problem (MBIS), and the author presented a factor d polynomial time approximation algorithm for the problem on $(d+1)$-claw free graphs.

In KPCC, if we restrict the budget constraint to be satisfied as an equality, we obtain an instance of the *exact knapsack problem with conflict pair constraints* (KPCC-exact). The feasibility version of this problem was investigated by Milanic and Monnot [3,33], where it was shown that the problem is strongly NP-complete on bipartite graphs with maximum vertex degree of three. The authors also presented a pseudo-polynomial algorithm for the problem in cographs, chordal graphs, and interval graphs.

A generalization of KPCC involving more than one knapsack constraint was studied by Gabriel [34], where a Dantzig–Wolfe decomposition scheme was proposed. Atamtürk et al. [35] used conflict graphs in developing algorithms for 0-1integer programs.

The *quadratic knapsack problem* (QKP) [36] can be stated as

$$\begin{aligned} \text{Maximize} \quad & \mathbf{x}^t Q\mathbf{x} + \mathbf{c}\mathbf{x} \\ \text{Subject to:} \quad & \mathbf{a}\mathbf{x} \leq b \\ & \mathbf{x} \in \{0,1\}^n \end{aligned}$$

where $Q = (q_{ij})$ is an $n \times n$ matrix.

Although the QKP appears to be more general than KPCC, we now observe that QKP and KPCC are essentially equivalent, in the sense that one is a special case of the other.

Theorem 1. *QKP and KPCC are equivalent.*

Proof. Define the matrix $Q = (q_{ij})$ such that $q_{ij} = -M$, where M is a large positive number if $(i, j) \in E$ and $q_{ij} = 0$ otherwise. With this choice of Q, the problem KPCC reduces to QKP. Thus, KPCC is a special case of QKP.

Let us now prove the converse. That is, QKP is a special case of KPCC. This is, however, achieved by appropriate modifications in the well-known reduction of a quadratic unconstrained binary optimization problem (QUBO) to the maximum weight stable set problem [37,38] to handle the budget constraint. Thus, KPCC can be viewed as a generalization of QKP. □

For further details on QUBO, refer to [39]. The major contributions of the paper can be summarized as follows.

- We present new complexity results on KPCC along with a thorough state-of-the-art review of the literature. Also, we show that KPCC and QKP are equivalent.
- When the conflict graph is a complete bipartite graph, it is shown that KPCC decomposes into two knapsack problems. As a consequence, we have new polynomially solvable (and pseudo-polynomially solvable) special cases of KPCC and have special cases of KPCC that admit FPTASs. These results are extended to more general classes of graphs that accept a blakbox oracle with special properties. On a star (which is a special bipartite graph), the problem is shown to be NP-hard.
- A new integer programming formulation that unifies and generalizes existing formulations of KPCC on general graphs is given. The strengths of the LP relaxation of this formulation and of special cases are analyzed theoretically.

- Different methods are proposed to tighten our general integer programming formulation, and these methods are compared using the general purpose solver Gurobi.

3. KPCC on Bipartite Graphs

Let $G = (V_1 \cup V_2, E)$ be a bipartite graph with the generic bipartition of its vertex set as $V_1 \cup V_2$, where $V_1 = \{1, 2, \ldots, m\}$ and $V_2 = \{m+1, m+2, \ldots, m+n\}$. Note that KPCC is trivial to solve when G is a complete graph and is the same as the knapsack problem when G is a collection of isolated nodes. When G is a tree, Pferschy and Schauer [31] showed that KPCC is NP-hard but solvable in $O(nb^2)$ time and $O(nb)$ space. Further, they showed that the algorithm can be modified to obtain a fully polynomial approximation scheme (FPTASs) for KPCC. Trees, in some sense, can be viewed as an extreme case of sparse connected bipartite graphs. Let us now look at KPCC on the complete bipartite graph $K_{m,n} = (V_1 \cup V_2, E)$. Although KPCC is trivial on a complete graph, this simplicity does not extend to $K_{m,n}$.

Theorem 2. *KPCC is NP-hard even if the conflict graph is a star (i.e., $K_{1,n}$). Further, on a complete bipartite graph, KPCC can be solved in pseudopolynomial time and it admits FPTASs.*

Proof. It is not difficult to reduce the knapsack problem to a KPCC on $K_{1,n}$ and this establishes the first part of the theorem. To prove the second part, note that for any solution $\mathbf{x}$ of a KPCC on $K_{m,n}$, if $x_i = 1$ for any $i \in V_1$ then by the conflict pair constraints, $x_i = 0$ for all $i \in V_2$ and vice versa. Thus, KPCC on $K_{m,n}$ reduces to two knapsack problems

$$\begin{aligned} \text{KP1: Maximize } & \sum_{j \in V_1} c_j x_j \\ \text{Subject to: } & \sum_{j \in V_1} a_j x_j \le b \\ & x_j \in \{0,1\} \text{ for all } j \in V_1 \end{aligned}$$

and

$$\begin{aligned} \text{KP2: Maximize } & \sum_{j \in V_2} c_j x_j \\ \text{Subject to: } & \sum_{j \in V_2} a_j x_j \le b \\ & x_j \in \{0,1\} \text{ for all } j \in V_2 \end{aligned}$$

The best solution amongst the solutions of KP1 and KP2 solves KPCC on $K_{m,n}$. Since the knapsack problem can be solved in pseudopolynomial time and it admits FPTASs, the second part of the theorem follows. □

From the above theorem, if KP1 and KP2 are solvable in polynomial time, then the corresponding KPCC on $K_{m,n}$ is also solvable in polynomial time. If $a_j = 1$ for all $j \in V_1 \cup V_2$, then obviously KP1 and KP2 are solvable in polynomial time; hence, the corresponding KPCC on $K_{m,n}$ is also solvable in polynomial time. This is interesting since KPCC on a general bipartite graph is NP-hard even if $a_j = 1$ for all j [31]. Deineko and Woeginger [40] showed that the cross-ratio-ordered bounded knapsack problem on n variables can be solved in $O(n)$ time. This, together with Theorem 2, leads to the following theorem.

Theorem 3. *If the costs c_i and weight a_i for $i \in V_1 \cup V_2$ satisfy $\frac{a_{i+1}}{a_i} \le \left\lfloor \frac{c_{i+1}}{c_i} \right\rfloor$ for $i = 1, 2, \ldots m-1$ and $\frac{a_{i+1}}{a_i} \le \left\lfloor \frac{c_{i+1}}{c_i} \right\rfloor$ for $i = m+1, m+2, \ldots m+n-1$, then KPCC on $K_{m,n}$ can be solved in polynomial time.*

We can also mix conditions for different solvable cases for KP1 and KP2 to obtain solvable instances of KPCC on $K_{m,n}$. For example, if $a_i = \alpha$ for all $i \in V_1$ and $\frac{a_{i+1}}{a_i} \leq \left\lfloor \frac{c_{i+1}}{c_i} \right\rfloor$ for $i = m+1, m+2, \ldots m+n-1$, then KPCC on $K_{m,n}$ can also be solved in polynomial time. Later, we present additional conditions for polynomially solvable special cases of the knapsack problem that can be used in different combinations for KP1 and KP2 to produce polynomially solvable cases of KPCC on $K_{m,n}$.

Let $G = (V_1 \cup V_2, E)$ be an undirected graph such that the subgraphs induced by V_1 and V_2 belong to a family $\mathcal{F}$ of graphs with specific properties. We call such graphs $\mathcal{F}$-bipartite (see Figure 1 for an example). If an $\mathcal{F}$-bipartite graph contain all edges (i, j) for $i \in V_1, j \in V_2$, then it is called a complete $\mathcal{F}$-bipartite graph. Bonamy et al. [41] studied $\mathcal{F}$-bipartite graphs, where the induced subgraph of V_1 is a collection of isolated nodes and the induced subgraph of V_2 is a k-degenerate graph. Depending on the properties imposed on the family $\mathcal{F}$, the $\mathcal{F}$-bipartite structure can have algorithmic advantages in solving some optimization problems. For example, $\mathcal{F}$ could contain all classes of graphs on which the KPCC can be solved in pseudo-polynomial time. In this case, $\mathcal{F}$ includes graphs that are isolated vertices, trees, complete bipartite graphs, complete graphs, chordal graphs, interval graphs, cographs, and circular arc graphs.

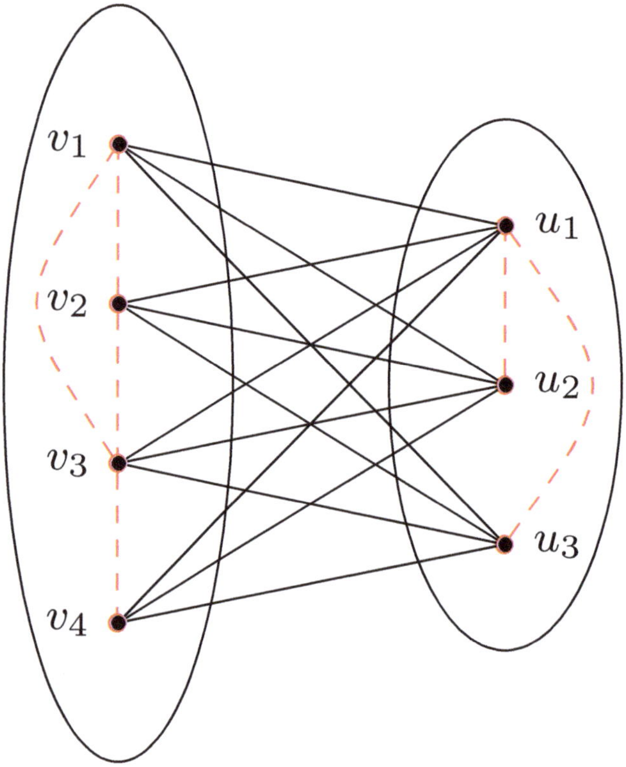

Figure 1. A complete $\mathcal{F}$-bipartite graph with $V_1 = \{v_1, v_2, v_3, v_4\}$ and $V_2 = \{u_1, u_2, u_3\}$. The subgraph induced by V_1 is a cycle and a pendant vertex, and the subgraph induced by V_2 is tree (path).

Assume that for a $\mathcal{F}$-bipartite graph, the bipartition V_1 and V_2 along with the structure of the subgraphs induced by V_1 and V_2 are given. Then, the results obtained in the previous sections on the solvability of KPCC can be extended to $\mathcal{F}$-bipartite graphs.

Theorem 4. *KPCC can be solved in pseudo-polynomial time on a complete $\mathcal{F}$-bipartite graph $G = (V_1 \cup V_2, E)$ if KPCC can be solved in pseudo-polynomial time on graphs in $\mathcal{F}$. Further, KPCC admits FPTASs on G whenever KPCC admits FPTASs on graphs in $\mathcal{F}$.*

Proof. The proof of the above theorem is similar to that of Theorem 2, except that instead of KP1 and KP2 we will have problems of the type KPCC but with reduced sizes. However, we present the complete proof of the theorem here to facilitate further related discussions. Let $G_1 = (V_1, E_1)$ be the subgraph of G induced by V_1 and $G_2 = (V_2, E_2)$ be the subgraph of G induced by V_2. Since every vertex in V_1 is connected to every vertex in V_2, for any solution $\mathbf{x}$ of the KPCC, if $x_i = 1$ for any $i \in V_1$ then $x_i = 0$ for all $i \in V_2$ and vice versa. Thus, KPCC reduces to the following reduced KPCCs.

$$\begin{aligned} \text{KPCC1: Maximize } & \sum_{j \in V_1} c_j x_j \\ \text{Subject to: } & \sum_{j \in V_1} a_j x_j \leq b \\ & x_i + x_j \leq 1 \text{ for } (i,j) \in E_1 \\ & x_j \in \{0,1\} \text{ for all } j \in V_1 \end{aligned}$$

and

$$\begin{aligned} \text{KPCC2: Maximize } & \sum_{j \in V_2} c_j x_j \\ \text{Subject to: } & \sum_{j \in V_2} a_j x_j \leq b \\ & x_i + x_j \leq 1 \text{ for } (i,j) \in E_2 \\ & x_j \in \{0,1\} \text{ for all } j \in V_2 \end{aligned}$$

The best solution amongst the solutions of KPCC1 and KPCC2 provides an optimal solution to KPCC. By assuming the properties of $\mathcal{F}$, KPCC1 and KPCC2 can be solved in pseudo-polynomial time. The proof of the second part of the theorem also follows in an analogous way. □

Theorem 4 is a proper generalization of Theorem 2.

The results discussed above extend in a natural way to complete multi-partite graphs. However, to take any computational advantage we need to know the partite sets a priori or need to compute them. Bipartite graphs can be recognized in polynomial time but recognizing p-partite graphs for $p > 2$ is NP-complete [42]. If there are p partite sets, then we will be solving p knapsack problems.

General Bipartite Graphs

We now consider KPCC on a general bipartite graph $G = (V_1 \cup V_2, E)$, where $V_1 = \{1, 2, \ldots, m\}$ and $V_2 = \{m+1, m+2, \ldots, m+n\}$. Note that we are considering a maximization problem. Consider the maximization version of a combinatorial optimization problem such that the objective function value of its feasible solutions are positive. Let $\mathbf{x}^*$ be any feasible solution to such a problem and $\mathbf{x}^0$ be a corresponding optimal solution. Then, $\mathbf{x}^*$ is said to be ϵ-optimal if $\frac{OBJ(\mathbf{x}^0)}{OBJ(\mathbf{x}^*)} \leq \epsilon$, where $OBJ(\mathbf{x})$ is the objective function value of the solution $\mathbf{x}$. When $\epsilon = 1$, then $\mathbf{x}^*$ is an optimal solution. Consider KP1 and KP2, as indicated in Theorem 2. Let $\bar{x_1}$ and $\bar{x_2}$ be ϵ-optimal solutions to KP1 and KP2, respectively. Define the solutions $\hat{\mathbf{x}}^1$ and $\hat{\mathbf{x}}^2$, where

$$\hat{x}^1_j = \begin{cases} \bar{x}^1_j & \text{if æ} \in V_1 \\ 0 & \text{otherwise} \end{cases} \text{ and } \hat{x}^2_j = \begin{cases} \bar{x}^2_j & \text{if æ} \in V_2 \\ 0 & \text{otherwise} \end{cases}$$

Theorem 5. *The best solution amongst* $\hat{\mathbf{x}}^1$ *and* $\hat{\mathbf{x}}^2$ *is a* 2ϵ*-optimal solution to KPCC on* $G = (V_1 \cup V_2, E)$.

Proof. Let $\mathbf{x}^0$ be an optimal solution to KPCC on $G = (V_1 \cup V_2, E)$. Define the solutions $\mathbf{x}^*$ and $\mathbf{x}^{**}$ such that

$$x_j^* = \begin{cases} x_j^0 & \text{if æ} \in V_1 \\ 0 & \text{otherwise} \end{cases} \text{ and } x_j^{**} = \begin{cases} x_j^0 & \text{if æ} \in V_2 \\ 0 & \text{otherwise} \end{cases}$$

Let $\mathbf{x}^{1*}$ be the restriction of $\mathbf{x}^*$ to V_1 and $\mathbf{x}^{2**}$ be the restriction of $\mathbf{x}^{**}$ to V_2. Then, $\mathbf{x}^{1*}$ and $\mathbf{x}^{2**}$ are feasible solutions of KP1 and KP2, respectively. Then, by the ϵ-optimality of $\hat{\mathbf{x}}_1$ and $\hat{\mathbf{x}}_2$ to KP1 and KP2, we have

$$\sum_{j \in V_1} c_j \hat{x}_j^1 \leq \epsilon \left(\sum_{j \in V_1} c_j x_j^{1*} \right) = \epsilon \mathbf{c}\mathbf{x}^* \tag{1}$$

and

$$\sum_{j \in V_2} c_j \hat{x}_j^2 \leq \epsilon \left(\sum_{j \in V_2} c_j x_j^{2**} \right) = \epsilon \mathbf{c}\mathbf{x}^{**} \tag{2}$$

Without a loss of generality, assume $\mathbf{c}\hat{\mathbf{x}}^1 \geq \mathbf{c}\hat{\mathbf{x}}^2$. Then,

$$\mathbf{c}\mathbf{x}^0 = \mathbf{c}\mathbf{x}^* + \mathbf{c}\mathbf{x}^{**} \leq \epsilon \mathbf{c}\hat{\mathbf{x}}^1 + \epsilon \mathbf{c}\hat{\mathbf{x}}^2 \leq 2\epsilon \mathbf{c}\hat{\mathbf{x}}^1.$$

□

An approximation algorithm $\mathcal{A}$ for a combinatorial optimization problem (in maximization form) is said to be a *δ-fully polynomial time approximation scheme* (δ-FPTASs) if it guarantees a solution $\mathbf{x}^*$ such that $OBJ(X^0) \leq \delta(1+\epsilon)OBJ(\mathbf{x}^*)$, where $\mathbf{x}^0$ is an optimal solution and $\mathcal{A}$ runs in polynomial time in the input size and $\frac{1}{\epsilon}$ for any $\epsilon > 0$. Thus, a $1 - FPTASs$ is precisely an $FPTASs$. Since KP1 and KP2 admits FPTASs, from Theorem 5, KPCC admits $2 - FPTASs$. This result is interesting because the problem is strongly NP-complete on bipartite graphs with maximum vertex degree of three [3,33]. Further, when KP1 and KP2 are solvable in polynomial time, KPCC on a general bipartite graph can be solved by a polynomial time 2-approximation algorithm. When $a_j = 1$ for all j, Theorem 5 reduces to a corresponding result obtained by Kalra et al. [2], and for the special case, they showed that the performance bound is asymptotically tight. We summarize these observations in the following corollary.

Corollary 1. *KPCC on a bipartite graph admits* 2*-FPTASs. Further, when KP1 and KP2 are solvable in polynomial time, then a* 2*-optimal solution to KPCC on a bipartite graph can be obtained in polynomial time, and in this case the bound* 2 *is asymptotically tight.*

The concept of $\mathcal{F}$-bipartite graphs can be extended to the more general case of $\mathcal{F}$-multipartite graphs. Let $G = \left(\cup_{k=1}^{p} V_k, E\right)$ be an undirected graph such that the subgraphs induced by V_k for any $k = 1, 2, \ldots, p$ belong to the family $\mathcal{F}$. We call G a $\mathcal{F}$-multipartite graph. If $(i,j) \in E$ for any $i \in V_r, j \in V_s$ for $r \neq s, r, s = 1, 2, \ldots p$, then G is called a complete $\mathcal{F}$-multipartite graph. Theorem 4 and the discussions that follow extend in a natural way to complete $\mathcal{F}$-multipartite graphs.

4. Integer Programming Formulations

Let us now discuss some integer programming formulations of the KPCC. For each vertex $i \in V$, let $A(i) = \{j \in V : (i,j) \in E\}$ and the sets $N_i(1), N_i(2), \ldots, N_i(p_i)$ be a given partition of $A(i)$, where $N_i(k) \neq \emptyset$ for any $k = 1,2,\dots p_i$, $N_i(r) \cap N_i(s) = \emptyset$ whenever $r \neq s$, and $A(i) = \cup_{k=1}^{p_i} N_i(k)$. Then, KPCC can be formulated as the 0-1 programming problem

$$\begin{aligned}
\text{StarIP: Maximize} \quad & \sum_{j\in V} c_j x_j \\
\text{Subject to:} \quad & \sum_{j\in V} a_j x_j \leq b \\
& \sum_{j\in N_i(k)} x_j \leq |N_i(k)|(1-x_i) \text{ for } k = 1,2,\dots p_i, i = 1,2,\dots n \\
& x_j \in \{0,1\} \text{ for all } j \in V
\end{aligned} \tag{3}$$

The above formulation reduces to the standard integer programming formulation of the KPCC when each $N_i(k)$ is singleton, i.e., $p_i = |A(i)|$ for all i. When $p_i = 1$ for all i then $N_i(1) = A(i)$, and the above integer program reduces to

$$\begin{aligned}
\text{MaxStarIP: Maximize} \quad & \sum_{j\in V} c_j x_j \\
\text{Subject to:} \quad & \sum_{j\in V} a_j x_j \leq b \\
& \sum_{j\in A(i)} x_j \leq |A(i)|(1-x_i) \text{ for } i = 1,2,\dots n \\
& x_j \in \{0,1\} \text{ for all } j \in V
\end{aligned} \tag{4}$$

Thus, our general integer programming framework StarIP provides a class of integer programming formulations of KPCC that subsumes two well-studied formulations.

Theorem 6. *Among all of the choices of the partition $N_i(1), N_i(2), \dots, N_i(p_i)$ for StarIP, the standard formulation is the strongest and MaxStarIP is the weakest in terms of their LP relaxation values.*

Proof. Let $\mathbf{x}^* = (x_1^*, x_2^*, \dots, x_n^*)$ be any feasible solution to the LP relaxation of the standard formulation. Then,

$$x_i^* + x_j^* \leq 1 \text{ for all } (i,j) \in E \tag{5}$$

We successfully show that $\mathbf{x}^*$ is a feasible solution to the LP relaxation of StarIP for any partition $N_i(1), N_i(2), \dots, N_i(p_i)$. Choose a set $N_i(k)$ for the vertex i. Now, by adding the edge inequalities from (5) for all $(i,j) \in E$ such that $j \in N_i(k)$, we obtain

$$\sum_{j\in N_i(k)} (x_i^* + x_j^* \leq 1) = \sum_{j\in N_i(k)} x_j^* \leq |N_i(k)|(1-x_i^*).$$

Thus, any feasible solution to the standard integer programming formulation of the KPCC is also a solution to the StarIP. Thus, the LP relaxation of the standard formulation is the strongest among the LP relaxation of any formulation within the class of StarIP. The second part of the theorem can be proved in an analogous way. □

Note that, for the LP relaxation of StarIP (for any choice of the partition of $A(i)$), $x_i = \frac{1}{2}$ for all i as a feasible solution, provided that $\frac{1}{2}\sum_{j\in V} a_j \leq b$. One way to strengthen or tighten StarIP is by computing upper bounds on the stability number of the subgraph $G(i,k)$ induced by $N_i(k)$. For example, if this subgraph is perfect, we can calculate the stability number exactly. If α is the largest cardinality of a matching in this graph, then $|N_i(k)|$ can be replaced by $|N_i(k)| - \alpha$. Another way to tighten the formulation StarIP is as follows: let $\gamma(i,k)$ be the objective function value of the LP relaxation of the standard formulation of KPCC restricted to $G(i,k)$, where $c_i = 1$ for all i. Then, $|N_i(k)|$ can be replaced by $\lfloor \gamma(i,k) \rfloor$. This number can be viewed as a fractional budgeted stability number. We can use other similar upper bounds to strengthen StarIP. For a review of different upper bounds that can be easily calculated, we refer to [43]. By tightening StarIP this way, we can obtain a better formulation for KPCC.

Let $A'(i) = \{j \in V : (i,j) \in E, j < i\}$ and $N_i'(1), N_i'(2), \ldots, N_i'(p_i)$ be a given partition of $A'(i)$. We can replace $N_i(k)$ by $N_i'(k)$ in StarIP to obtain a valid formulation, say StarIP$'$, of KPCC. Likewise, we can replace $A(i)$ by $A'(i)$ in MaxStarIP to obtain a valid formulation, say MaxStarIP$'$, for KPCC. The formulation MaxStarIP$'$ has been studied by Hifi et al. [6]. The coefficient matrices of these modified formulations are sparser. However, tightening the resulting formulations by using upper bounds as discussed above are likely to yield weaker LP relaxations, in general, compared to tightening the corresponding formulation of StarIP and MaxStarIP. Moreover, any possible computational advantage achieved by sparsity over the suspected weaker LP relaxation needs to be analyzed experimentally.

Based on the ideas used in Theorem 2, we now present a single integer programming formulation of KPCC on $K_{m,n}$.

$$\text{KPCC}_{m,n}\text{: Maximize} \quad \sum_{j \in V_1 \cup V_2} c_j x_j$$

$$\text{Subject to: } \sum_{j \in V_1} a_j x_j \leq b$$

$$\sum_{j \in V_2} a_j x_j \leq b$$

$$\sum_{j \in V_1} x_j \leq m(1 - x_i) \text{ for } i \in V_2 \tag{6}$$

$$\sum_{j \in V_2} x_j \leq n(1 - x_i) \text{ for } i \in V_1 \tag{7}$$

$$x_j \in \{0,1\} \text{ for all } j \in V_1 \cup V_2$$

Note that constraint (6) guarantees that if any $x_i = 1$ for $i \in V_2$ then $x_i = 0$ for all $i \in V_1$. Likewise, constraint (7) guarantees that if any $x_i = 1$ for $i \in V_1$ then $x_i = 0$ for all $i \in V_2$.

4.1. Experimental Analysis

The formulation MaxStarIP$'$ has been studied and used in algorithms to solve KPCC [6]. There are also effective branch-and-bound algorithms to solve KPCC for general graphs [6,28,44]. However, to the best of our knowledge, there is no computational study available that compares the different formulations of KPCC. Note that the complexity of KPCC can vary significantly depending on the structure of the underlying graph and the level of tightness of the budget constraint. Also, tight efficiently computable upper bound estimates on the stability number of a graph can affect the efficacy of our formulations StarIP and MaxStarIP. The following Table 1 provides some easily computable upper bounds on the stability number of the graph $G = (V, E)$.

In the table above, Δ denotes the maximum degree and δ denotes the minimum degree of vertices in the graph $G = (V, E)$.

Recall that the integer programming formulation MaxStarIP belongs to the class StarIP. Therefore, it can be strengthened by replacing $|A(i)|$ with an upper bound on the stability number of the subgraph $G(i)$ of G induced by $A(i)$. When MaxStarIP is strengthened using the bound UBk obtained from $G(i)$ to replace $|A(i)|$, $k = 1,2,3,4,5,6$, we denote the resulting MaxStarIP formulation by MaxStarIPk. Thus, in addition to MaxStarIP, we have the strengthened formulations MaxStarIP1, MaxStarIP2, MaxStarIP3, MaxStarIP4, MaxStarIP5, and MaxStarIP6. The major goals of the experimental analysis were to:

1. Compare the relative performance of the standard KPCC formulation given in the introduction, MaxStarIP, and its variations MaxStarIPk, $k = 1,2,3,4,5,6$ using the general purpose solver GUROBI.
2. Study the impact of the tightness of the budget constraints on the formulations that we compare.
3. Study the impact of sparsity of G on the formulations that we compare.

4. Explore the heuristic value of the formulations.

It may be noted that UB1 will be at least as tight as UB2 and that UB4 applies to a connected graph. For these reasons, we will not use UB2 and UB4 in our experiments.

Table 1. Easily computable stability number bounds.

	Bound	Name
UB1	$\lfloor \gamma(G) \rfloor$	fractional budgeted stability number
UB2	$\lfloor \alpha_f(G) \rfloor$	fractional stability number [43]
UB3	$\lfloor \frac{1}{2} + \sqrt{\frac{1}{4} + \lvert V\rvert^2 - \lvert V\rvert - 2\lvert E\rvert} \rfloor$	Hansen [45]
UB4	$\lfloor \frac{(\Delta-1)n+1}{\Delta} \rfloor$	Borg [46]
UB5	$\lfloor \lvert V\rvert - \frac{\lvert E\rvert}{\Delta} \rfloor$	Kwok [47]
UB6	$\lvert V\rvert - \delta$	Minimum degree [43]

All of the computational experiments were carried out on a PC with the Windows 10 Enterprise 64-bit operating system, Intel(R) Core(TM) i7-3770 CPU @ 3.40GHz, and 16.0 GB of memory. The calling program was written in Python (Python 3.6.1) and called GUROBI 9.0 using the interface gurobipy. The time limit for GUROBI was set to 3600 s. Most of the test problems were solved to optimality within this time limit, except some large or structured instances.

4.2. Benchmark Instances

Our experiments used benchmark instances selected from Bettinelli et al. [28] and instances generated using the DIMACS clique graph library [48]. The instances of Bettinelli et al. [28] have three data sets: R1, R2, and R10. Each data set consists of eight classes, and each class has many instances. For the data set R1, in the first four classes, the items have a uniformly distributed weight from the range [20, 100], and the knapsack capacity is set to $b = 150$. The number n of items is 120, 250, 500, and 1000, respectively. The last four classes have uniformly distributed weights from [250, 500], and the knapsack capacity is set to $b = 1000$. The conflict graphs were generated randomly. For the data set R1, classes 1 to 4 have a total of 360 instances and classes 5 to 8 have a total of 360 instances. Thus, the data set R1 has a total of 720 instances. The data set R3 is similar to R1 except that the budget b is set to $3 \times 150 = 450$. Likewise, the data set R10 is almost identical to R1 except that the budget b is set to $10 \times 150 = 1500$. For details on these instances, we refer to the paper [28].

For our computational experiments, we selected instances from the first four classes of each of the data sets R1, R3, and R10. We categorized these instances further into small, medium, and large. The small instances consist of conflict graphs with 120 to 250 vertices, the medium instances consist of conflict graphs with 500 vertices, and the large instances consist of conflict graphs with 1000 vertices. From each category, we selected 120 instances using a prescribed selection rule. We refer to the aforementioned class of instances as random data instances.

The DIMACS clique graph library consists of unweighted graphs. We generated two sets of KPCC benchmarks out of these instances, called positively correlated problems and negatively correlated problems. For positively correlated problems, the costs and weights have the same ordering, whereas for the negatively correlated problems, the costs and weights have opposite ordering. We used graphs that consist of 171 to 1024 vertices. These instances are further classified into small, medium, and large sizes. The small instances consist of graphs with 171 to 378 vertices, the medium instances consist of graphs with 400 to 500 vertices, and the large instances consist of 700 to 1024 vertices. There are 23 small instances, 24 medium instances, and 13 large instances. The DIMACS graphs were originally generated as clique benchmarks. To obtain stable set instances, we took the complement of these graphs. Let $G = (V, E)$ be such a complement graph. For each $i \in V$, we generated the cost c_i and the weight a_i as uniformly distributed random integers in the range $[1, |V|]$. To obtain positively correlated data, we first sort the vectors **c** and **a** in non-decreasing order and then apply the same random index permutation to both vectors. Negatively correlated instances are constructed in a similar manner but with opposite ordering. The budgets for the correlated instances are set as follows. First, we generate a random subset S of the vertices of G such that the cardinality of S is the known size of the maximum cardinality stable set on G and set $b = \sum_{i \in S} a_i$. Then, instances are generated by setting the budget equal to the value b scaled by the factors 0.25, 0.50, and 0.75. The instances we used in our experiments are available at https://github.com/jasdeepdhahan/kpcc_instances.git.

4.3. Experimental Results

Let us now discuss the experimental outcomes of our analysis. First, we compared the standard KPCC formulation given in the introduction to MaxStarIP and its variations MaxStarIP1, MaxStarIP3, MaxStarIP5, and MaxStarIP6 using all of the test instances. Table 2 provides some insight into the relative strength of our formulations based on average running times (in seconds). The numbers marked in bold letters correspond to the lowest computational time taken. The experimental results disclose that there is no consistently superior formulation of KPCC among the ones we tested.

Table 2. Average running times (in seconds).

Data Set	Standard	MaxStarIP	MaxStarIP1	MaxStarIP3	MaxStarIP5	MaxStarIP6
Random Small	**3.9525**	4.1754	4.3713	9.2690	8.9970	9.2855
Random Medium	547.0358	546.1085	**532.7913**	542.4379	562.4661	540.5295
Random Large	1165.9380	1232.1670	**1116.0310**	1267.2090	1235.8030	1284.1800
Positive Small	0.4756	0.4833	0.4683	0.4874	0.4883	**0.4606**
Positive Medium	117.7284	108.5378	112.0652	**105.2428**	105.8007	109.7333
Positive Large	499.7824	506.0453	417.1473	418.3175	446.0069	**407.9784**
Negative Smal	**1.3642**	1.9495	1.7018	1.9759	1.7312	1.6509
Negative Medium	427.9115	499.4719	443.6538	431.8717	432.7311	**422.1719**
Negative Large	1866.9380	1937.1970	1780.2640	1723.5700	**1698.0620**	1742.0950

The efficacy of various formulations could also be dependent on how tight the budget constraint is and what special structure the underlying graph has. Table 3 presents the experimental results after classifying the budget constraint in the test instances as tight, very tight, and moderately tight. Table 4 presents the experimental results after classifying the random test instances based on tightness of the budget constraints as well as the density of the underlying graph. We sometimes refer to a KPCC instance as sparse or dense. A *sparse (dense)* KPCC instance has a sparse (dense) underlying graph. The results on the correlated test instances are classified only with respect to budget tightness since the density of the underlying graphs was uniform and generally sparse. These results are presented in Table 5.

After this categorized analysis, the standard formulation appears as the preferred formulation overall, if one is constrained to recommend only one formulation. However, it may be noted that MaxStarIP appears to be more suited for sparse small instances with the tightest and loosest budgets. In addition, MaxStarIP outperforms the standard formulation on sparse medium and large instances with the tightest budgets. For our medium and large instances, as the underlying graph density increased the standard formulation became more robust than MaxStarIP. It is also important to point out that 8 out of 120 medium-sized instances were not solved to optimality within the time limit provided, either by the standard formulation or by the MaxStarIP type formulations. In addition, 30 of the 120 large instances with the loosest budget were not solved to optimality within the time limit specified by either of the aforementioned formulations.

Now, let us compare the standard formulation and MaxStarIP type formulations over the correlated data. We found that the positively correlated instances were easier to solve than the negatively correlated instances. Increasing the budget within limits generally increased the running time of our formulations. Large negatively correlated instances often hit the time limit set for the experiments. The standard formulation generally outperformed MaxStarIP over our negatively correlated data set. We further observed that MaxStarIP is slightly better than the standard formulation for negatively correlated large instances with the loosest budget. For positively correlated data, MaxStarIP is best suited for medium instances and the standard formulation is the strongest for our small and large instances.

It may also be noted that the standard formulation is the most robust in terms of running times, followed by MaxStarIP1, and there is no clear formulation that wins third place. MaxStarIP1 outperformed our other KPCC formulations over denser and larger random instances, while the standard formulation showed superiority on sparser large random instances. Each of the formulations MaxStartIP, MaxStarIP3, MaxStarIP5, and MaxStarIP6 were found to be the preferred formulation for at least one of the random data set classifications in Table 4. Based on this, we conclude that there is no one formulation that is best suited for our positively correlated data set. The standard formulation is best suited for our medium and small negatively correlated data. In addition, MaxStarIP3 outperformed the other formulations over our larger negatively correlated instances with the tightest budgets, and MaxStarIP5 outperformed the other formulations in Table 5 for the remaining large negatively correlated KPCC instances.

Table 3. Average running times (in seconds) by budget.

ata Set	Budget	Standard	MaxStarIP	MaxStarIP1	MaxStarIP3	MaxStarIP5	MaxStarIP6
ndom Small	very tight	0.17025	0.2180	**0.1535**	14.48525	14.46275	14.4683
ndom Small	tight	**0.8165**	1.4390	0.98075	0.93225	0.95875	1.0078
ndom Small	moderate tight	10.871	**10.86925**	11.97975	12.3895	11.56975	12.3805
ndom Medium	very tight	**1.2145**	1.78725	1.602	1.89275	1.769	1.87975
ndom Medium	tight	24.9155	47.09275	**21.021**	51.623	63.196	37.62275
ndom Medium	moderate tight	1614.97725	1589.4455	1575.751	1573.798	1622.43325	**1582.0860**
ndom Large	very tight	**5.5705**	10.0915	12.59575	10.38025	10.95975	11.4418
ndom Large	tight	491.50875	593.444	484.346	806.51925	**796.03675**	837.51325
ndom Large	moderate tight	3000.7355	3092.9655	**2851.1515**	2984.729	2900.411	3003.5857
sitive Small	very tight	0.2232	**0.1991**	0.2173	0.2155	0.2045	0.2245
sitive Small	tight	0.4123	**0.3786**	0.4532	0.4936	0.4955	0.4745
sitive Small	moderate tight	0.7914	0.8723	0.7345	0.7532	0.7650	**0.6827**
sitive Medium	very tight	5.4561	4.7843	3.5357	3.6765	3.6857	3.7887
sitive Medium	tight	47.9278	33.6848	35.3148	32.3804	**29.4691**	32.3991
stive Medium	moderate tight	299.8013	287.1443	297.34522	**279.6713**	284.2474	293.0122
sitive Large	very tight	**29.4941**	35.5012	41.20824	45.17471	47.0088	41.72882
sitive Large	moderate tight	1093.12647	1082.2853	918.3300	919.5976	959.8629	**908.9182**
sitive Large	tight	376.7265	400.34941	291.9035	290.1800	331.1488	**273.2882**
egative Small	very tight	**0.3973**	0.4814	0.52410	0.5064	0.4745	0.4614
egative Small	tight	**0.9173**	1.2236	1.17409	1.2859	1.13911	1.3295
egative Small	moderate tight	**2.7782**	4.1436	3.4073	4.1354	3.5800	3.1618
egative Medium	very tight	**6.5067**	10.5179	7.8883	9.2575	9.2071	8.8704
egative Medium	tight	**266.1083**	292.6083	276.6429	274.4096	299.2258	270.0600
egative Medium	moderate tight	1011.11958	1195.2896	1046.4300	1011.9479	989.7604	**987.5854**
egative Large	very tight	721.0029	857.0400	667.3035	**649.35523**	666.8012	658.71412
egative Large	tight	2095.2776	2210.1188	2010.5912	1965.06882	**1879.2935**	1955.7835
egative Large	moderate tight	2784.5333	2744.4318	2662.8976	2556.2859	**2548.0912**	2611.7882

Table 4. Average running times (in seconds) by budget and density.

Data Set	Budget	Density	Standard	MaxStarIP	MaxStarIP1	MaxStarIP3	MaxStarIP5	MaxStarIP
Random Small	very tight	0.10–0.30	0.0657	0.04500	**0.0421**	40.7564	40.75	40.7564
Random Small	tight	0.10–0.30	**0.1957**	0.2893	0.2364	0.2621	0.2986	0.2707
Random Small	moderate tight	0.10–0.30	12.5571	**12.3421**	20.2229	17.135	17.52	18.2271
Random Small	very tight	0.40–0.60	0.1557	0.1700	**0.1486**	0.1614	0.155	0.1586
Random Small	tight	0.40–0.60	**0.7914**	1.6179	0.8986	1.0443	0.9907	1.0564
Random Small	moderate tight	0.40–0.60	15.6157	15.7507	**11.5864**	12.2021	11.8821	12.4986
Random Small	very tight	0.70–0.90	0.3092	0.4758	**0.2892**	0.5467	0.4867	0.4933
Random Small	tight	0.70–0.90	**1.5700**	2.5717	1.945	1.5833	1.6917	1.8108
Random Small	moderate tight	0.70–0.90	3.0409	3.1609	**2.5527**	5.5382	2.9364	5.3027
Random Medium	very tight	0.10–0.30	0.3307	0.2493	0.2779	0.2471	**0.2386**	0.2421
Random Medium	tight	0.10–0.30	**1.2657**	1.8571	1.6014	2.3179	1.7207	1.7429
Random Medium	moderate tight	0.10–0.30	1807.6836	1792.2193	1933.2079	1802.3836	1830.6364	**1778.0714**
Random Medium	very tight	0.40–0.60	0.91	0.8462	0.8869	0.8215	0.8654	**0.8023**
Random Medium	tight	0.40–0.60	**16.8238**	29.1508	18.8531	21.9731	23.0215	21.1769
Random Medium	moderate tight	0.40–0.60	2456.7877	2391.1946	**2309.3023**	2380.9877	2421.0185	2427.7085
Random Medium	very tight	0.70–0.90	**2.4708**	4.3846	3.7431	4.7362	4.3208	4.7208
Random Medium	tight	0.70–0.90	58.4762	113.75	**44.1023**	134.3708	169.5746	92.7085
Random Medium	moderate tight	0.70–0.90	565.6369	569.3246	**457.2462**	520.4392	599.6292	525.4023
Random Large	very tight	0.10–0.30	1.3021	1.2186	1.2957	1.1879	1.1857	**1.1764**
Random Large	tight	0.10–0.30	**7.3279**	12.9400	8.505	13.2321	8.8986	9.1857
Random Large	moderate tight	0.10–0.30	**2475.0386**	2547.7179	2487.0064	2504.4529	2519.53	2556.8364
Random Large	very tight	0.40–0.60	**4.3062**	4.6062	5.6438	4.4131	4.5692	4.4046
Random Large	tight	0.40–0.60	**211.7485**	328.7346	303.8569	476.9715	466.3538	451.49
Random Large	moderate tight	0.40–0.60	3600.2546	3601.3262	3600.0577	3600.0585	3600.0546	3600.0592
Random Large	very tight	0.70–0.90	**11.4315**	25.1323	31.7169	26.2469	27.8762	29.5338
Random Large	tight	0.70–0.90	1292.6946	1483.3115	**1177.2792**	1990.3762	1973.4069	2115.5815
Random Large	moderate tight	0.70–0.90	2967.3515	3171.7946	**2494.4015**	2886.62	2610.9469	2888.2269

Table 5. Average running times (in seconds) by budget and density.

Data Set	Budget	Density	Standard	MaxStarIP	MaxStarIP1	MaxStarIP3	MaxStarIP5	MaxStarI
Positive Small	very tight	Sparse	0.2232	**0.1991**	0.2173	0.2155	0.2045	0.2245
Positive Small	tight	Sparse	0.4123	**0.3786**	0.4532	0.4936	0.4955	0.4745
Positive Small	moderate tight	Sparse	0.7914	0.8723	0.7345	0.7532	0.7650	**0.6827**
Positive Medium	very tight	Sparse	5.4561	4.7843	3.5357	3.6765	3.6857	3.7887
Positive Medium	tight	Sparse	47.9278	33.6848	35.3148	32.3804	**29.4691**	32.3991
Positive Medium	moderate tight	Sparse	299.8013	287.1443	297.34522	**279.6713**	284.2474	293.0122
Positive Large	very tight	Sparse	**29.4941**	35.5012	41.20824	45.17471	47.0088	41.72882
Positive Large	moderate tight	Sparse	1093.12647	1082.2853	918.3300	919.5976	959.8629	**908.9182**
Positive Large	tight	Sparse	376.7265	400.34941	291.9035	290.1800	331.1488	**273.2882**
Negative Small	very tight	Sparse	**0.3973**	0.4814	0.52410	0.5064	0.4745	0.4614
Negative Small	tight	Sparse	**0.9173**	1.2236	1.17409	1.2859	1.13911	1.3295
Negative Small	moderate tight	Sparse	**2.7782**	4.1436	3.4073	4.1354	3.5800	3.1618
Negative Medium	very tight	Sparse	**6.5067**	10.5179	7.8883	9.2575	9.2071	8.8704
Negative Medium	tight	Sparse	**266.1083**	292.6083	276.6429	274.4096	299.2258	270.0600
Negative Medium	moderate tight	Sparse	1011.11958	1195.2896	1046.4300	1011.9479	989.7604	**987.5854**
Negative Large	very tight	Sparse	721.0029	857.0400	667.3035	**649.35523**	666.8012	658.71412
Negative Large	tight	Sparse	2095.2776	2210.1188	2010.5912	1965.06882	**1879.2935**	1955.7835
Negative Large	moderate tight	Sparse	2784.5333	2744.4318	2662.8976	2556.2859	**2548.0912**	2611.7882

The frequency distribution of the fastest running times can provide further insight into the complexity of KPCC that averaging out the running times could not provide. For this analysis, we consider only the test instances that were solved to optimality within the time limit specified. In the event of a tie, any formulations in a tie for the fastest running time were considered to be equally good. From Table 6, we observe that the standard formulation is the preferred formulation followed by MaxStarIP1, and there is no clear winner for third place, based on frequency analysis.

Table 6. Frequency distribution of fastest running times.

a Set	Standard	MaxStarIP	MaxStarIP1	MaxStarIP3	MaxStarIP5	MaxStarIP6
dom Small	**62**	12	38	17	25	14
dom Medium	**41**	14	29	9	17	17
dom Large	**41**	6	21	6	15	11
tive Small	**22**	2	9	2	3	4
itive Medium	**16**	15	9	8	12	12
itive Large	**20**	5	5	6	2	11
gative Small	**35**	5	10	3	8	9
gative Medium	**23**	4	16	6	9	10
gative Large	**15**	1	3	4	8	3

5. Conclusions

In this paper, we studied the KPCC from various points of views. After a thorough literature survey on the topic, we focussed our attention on bipartite conflict graphs. For a complete bipartite (multipartite) graphs, the problem is shown to be NP-hard but solvable in pseudo-polynomial time and admits FPTASs. Extensions of these results to more general classes of graphs are also presented. We then introduced an integer programming model for KPCC with general conflict graphs, which generalizes and unifies existing formulations. The strength of the LP relaxations of these formulations are analyzed and also discussed in different ways to tighten them. An experimental comparison of our models is also presented to assess their relative strengths. This analysis disclosed various strong and weak points of our formulations and their linkages to the structure of the problem data. The analysis shows some preference towards the standard formulation; none of the formulations uniformly dominated others in all categories of the test data. In any case, the insights generated could be used effectively in the design of special purpose algorithms for KPCC involving some learning components. Such approaches proved useful in the case of other combinatorial optimization problems (e.g., [49]). This study can be followed on with future work.

Author Contributions: Conceptualization, A.P.P.; methodology, A.P.P. and J.D.; software, J.D.; validation, J.D.; formal analysis, A.P.P. and J.D.; investigation, A.P.P. and J.D.; resources, A.P.P.; data curation, J.D.; writing – original draft preparation, J.D.; writing—review and editing, A.P.P.; visualization, J.D.; supervision, A.P.P.; project administration, A.P.P.; funding acquisition, A.P.P. All authors have read and agreed to the published version of the manuscript.

Funding: This work was supported by an NSERC discovery grant awarded to Abraham P. Punnen.

Data Availability Statement: Our data is available to the public from " https://github.com/jasdeep dhahan/kpcc_instances.git".

Conflicts of Interest: The authors declare no conflict of interest.

erences

Bandyapadhyay, S. A variant of the maximum weight independent set problem. *arXiv* **2014**, arXiv:1409.0173.
Kalra, T.; Mathew, R.; Pal, S.P.; Pandey, V. Maximum weighted independent with a budget. In Proceedings of the Algorithms and Discrete Applied Mathematics: Third International Conference, CALDAM 2017, Sancoale, Goa, India, 16–18 February 2017; Gaur, D., Narayanaswamy, N., Eds.; Proceedings 3; Springer: Cham, Switzerland, 2017; Volume 10156, pp. 254–266.
Milanic, M.; Monnot, J. The exact weighted independent set problem in perfect graphs and related classes. *Electron. Notes Discret. Math.* **2009**, *35*, 317–322. [CrossRef]
Akeb, H.; Hifi, M.; Mounir, M. Local branching-based algorithms for the disjunctively constrained knapsack problem. *Comput. Ind. Eng.* **2011**, *60*, 811–820. [CrossRef]
Hifi, M.; Michrafy, M. A reactive local search algorithm for the disjunctively constrained knapsack problem. *J. Oper. Res. Soc.* **2006**, *57*, 718–726. [CrossRef]
Hifi, M.; Michrafy, M. Reduction strategies and exact algorithms for the disjunctively constrained knapsack problem. *Comput. Oper. Res.* **2007**, *34*, 2657–2673. [CrossRef]
Hifi, M.; Otmani, N. An algorithm for the disjunctively constrained knapsack problem. *Int. J. Oper. Res.* **2012**, 13, 22–43. [CrossRef]
Hifi, M.; Saleh, S.; Wu, L.; Chen, J. A hybrid guided neighborhood search for the disjunctively constrained knapsack problem. *Cogent Eng.* **2015**, *2*, 1068969. [CrossRef]

9. Hifi, M. An iterative rounding search-based algorithm for the disjunctively constrained knapsack problem. *Eng. Optim.* **201** 1109–1122. [CrossRef]
10. Yamada, T.; Kataoka, S.; Watanabe, K. Heuristic and exact algorithms for the disjunctively constrained knapsack problem *Process Soc. Jpn. J.* **2002**, *43*, 2864–2870.
11. Carrabs, F.; Cerrone, C.; Pentangelo, R. A multiethnic genetic approach for the minimum conflict weighted spanning tree prob *Networks* **2019**, *74*, 134–147. [CrossRef]
12. Carrabs, F.; Cerulli, R.; Pentangelo, R.; Raiconi, A. Minimum spanning tree with conflicting edge pairs: A branch-and approach. *Ann. Oper. Res.* **2021**, *298*, 65–78. [CrossRef]
13. Darmann, A.; Pferschy, U.; Schauer, J. Determining a minimum spanning tree with disjunctive constraints. In *Lecture N in Computer Science*; including subseries Lecture Notes in Artificial Intelligence and Lecture Notes in Bioinformatics; Spri Berlin/Heidelberg, Germany, 2009; pp. 414–423.
14. Darmann, A.; Pferschy, U.; Schauer, J.; Woeginger, G.J. Paths, trees and matchings under disjunctive constraints. *Discret. Math.* **2011**, *159*, 1726–1735. [CrossRef]
15. Elhedhli, S.; Li, L.; Gzara, M.; Naoum-Sawaya, J. A branch-and-price algorithm for the bin packing problem with conf *INFORMS J. Comput.* **2011**, *23*, 404–415. [CrossRef]
16. Gendreau, M.; Laport, G.; Semet, F. Heuristics and lower bounds for the bin packing problem with conflicts. *Comput. Oper.* **2004**, *31*, 347–358. [CrossRef]
17. Oncan, T.; Zhang, R.; Punnen, A.P. The minimum cost perfect matching problem with conflict pair constraints. *Comput. Oper.* **2013**, *40*, 920–930 [CrossRef]
18. Pferschy, U.; Schauer, J. The maximum flow problem with disjunctive constraints. *J. Comb. Optim.* **2013**, *26*, 109–119. [Cross
19. Zhang, R.; Kabadi, S.N.; Punnen, A.P. The minimum spanning tree problem with conflict constraints and its variations. *Di Optim.* **2011**, *8*, 191–206. [CrossRef]
20. Samer, P.; Urrutia, S. A branch and cut algorithm for minimum spanning trees under conflict constraints. *Optim. Lett.* **201** 41–55. [CrossRef]
21. Pisinger, D.; Sigurd, M. Using decomposition techniques and constraint programming for solving the two-dimensional packing problem. *INFORMS J. Comput.* **2007**, *19*, 36–51. [CrossRef]
22. Sadykov, R.; Vanderbeck, F. Bin packing with conflicts: A generic branch-and-price algorithm. *INFORMS J. Comput.* **2013** 244–255. [CrossRef]
23. Fernandes-Muritiba, A.E.; Iori, M.; Malaguti, E.; Toth, P. Algorithms for the bin packing problem with conflicts. *INFORM Comput.* **2010**, *22*, 401–415. [CrossRef]
24. Chandra, A.K.; Hirschberg, D.S.; Wong, C.K. Approximate algorithms for the knapsack problem and its generalizations. In *Research Report*; RC5616; IBM T. J. Watson Research Center: New York, NY, USA, 1975.
25. Nauss, R.M. *The 0-1 Knapsack Problem with Multiple Choice Constraints*; University of Missouri-St. Louis: St. Louis, MO, USA, (Revised in 1976).
26. Ibaraki, T.; Hasegawa, T.; Teranaka, K.; Iwase, J. The multiple choice knapsack problem. *J. Oper. Res. Soc. Jpn.* **1978**, *21*, 59–9
27. Bar-Noy, A.; Bar-Yehuda, R.; Freund, A.; Naor, J.; Schieber, B. A unified approach to approximating resource allocation scheduling. *J. ACM* **2001**, *48*, 1069–1090. [CrossRef]
28. Bettinelli, A.; Cacchiani, V.; Malaguti, E. A branch-and-bound algorithm for the knapsack problem with conflict graph. *INFO J. Comput.* **2017**, *29*, 457–473. [CrossRef]
29. Salem, M.B.; Taktak, R.; Mahjoub, A.R.; Ben-Abdallah, H. Optimization algorithms for the disjunctively constrained knap problem. *Soft Comput.* **2018**, *22*, 2025–2043. [CrossRef]
30. Salem, M.B.; Hanafi, S.; Taktak, R.; Ben-Abdallah, H. Probabilistic Tabu search with multiple neighborhoods for the Disjuncti Constrained Knapsack Problem. *RAIRO-Oper. Res.* **2017**, *51*, 627–637. [CrossRef]
31. Pferschy, U.; Schauer, J. The knapsack problem with conflict graphs. *J. Graph Algorithms Appl.* **2009**, *13*, 233–249. [CrossRef]
32. Pferschy, U.; Schauer, J. Approximation of knapsack problems with conflict and forcing graphs. *J. Comb. Optim.* **2017** 1300–1323. [CrossRef]
33. Milanic, M.; Monnot, J. The complexity of the exact weighted independent set problem. In *Combinatorial Optimization-Theore Computer Science: Interfaces and Perspectives*; Wiley-ISTE: NewYork, NY, USA, 2008; pp. 393–432.
34. Gabrel, V. Dantzig-Wolfe Decomposition for Linearly Constrained Stable Set Problem; hal-00116732; France 2006. Avail online: https://hal.science/hal-00116732/ (accessed on 23 February 2024)
35. Atamtürk, A.; Nemhauser, G.L.; Savelsbergh, M.W.P. Conflict graphs in solving integer programming problems. *Eur. J. Oper.* **2000**, *121*, 40–55. [CrossRef]
36. Gallo, G.; Hammer, P.; Simeone, B. Quadratic knapsack problems. In Combinatorial Optimization; Mathematical Programm Studies; Padberg, M., Ed.; Springer: Berlin, Germany, 1980; Volume 12, pp. 132–149.
37. Hammer, P.L.; Hansen, P.; Simone, B. Roof duality, complementations, and persistency in quadratic 0–1 optimization. *M Program.* **1984**, *28*, 121–155. [CrossRef]
38. Punnen, A.P. (Ed.) Introduction to QUBO. In *The Quadratic Unconstrained Binary Optimization Problem: Theory, Algorithms, Applications*; Springer: Cham, Switzerland, 2022.

Punnen, A.P. (Ed.) *The Quadratic Unconstrained Binary Optimization Problem: Theory, Algorithms, and Applications*; Springer: Cham, Switzerland, 2022.
Deineko, V.G.; Woeginger, G.J. A well-solvable special case of the bounded knapsack problem. *Oper. Res. Lett.* **2011**, *39*, 118–120. [CrossRef]
Bonamy, M.; Dabrowski, K.K.; Feghali, C.; Johnson, M.; Paulusma, D. Recognizing Graphs Close to Bipartite Graphs. In *42nd International Symposium on Mathematical Foundations of Computer Science (MFCS 2017)*; Leibniz International Proceedings in Informatics; Larsen, K.G., Bodlaender, H.L., Raskin, J.-F., Eds.; Schloss Dagstuhl-Leibniz-Zentrum für Informatik GmbH: Wadern, Germany, 2017; pp. 70:1–70:14.
Garey, M.R.; Johnson, D.S. *Computers and Intractability: A Guide to the Theory of NP-Completeness*; W.H. Freeman Co.: New York, NY, USA, 1979.
Willis, W. Bounds for the Independence Number of a Graph. Master's Thesis, College of Humanities and Sciences, Virginia Commonwealth University, Richmond, VA, USA, 2011.
Li, J.; Lan, Y.; Chen, F.; Han, X.; Blazewicz, J. A Fast Algorithm for Knapsack Problem with Conflict Graph. *Asia-Pac. J. Oper. Res.* **2021**, *38*, 2150010. [CrossRef]
Hansen, P. Degrés et nombre de stabilité d'un graphe. *Cah. Centre Études Rech. Opér.* **1975**, *17*, 213–220.
Borg, P. A sharp upper bound for the independence number. *arXiv* **2010**, arXiv:1007.5426.
West, D. *Introduction to Graph Theory*, 2nd ed.; Prentice Hall Inc.: Upper Saddle River, NJ, USA, 2001.
Rossi, R.; Ahmed, N. The Network Data Repository with Interactive Graph Analytics and Visualization. *Proc. AAAI* **2015**, *29*, 4292–4293. [CrossRef]
Karapetyan, D.; Punnen, A.P.; Parkes, A.J. Markov chain methods for the bipartite Boolean quadratic programming problem. *Eur. J. Oper. Res.* **2017**, *260*, 494–506. [CrossRef]

algorithms

Article

Automated Personalized Loudness Control for Multi-Track Recordings

Bogdan Moroșanu †, Marian Negru † and Constantin Paleologu *

Faculty of Electronics, Telecommunications, and Information Technology, National University of Science and Technology Politehnica Bucharest, 060042 Bucharest, Romania; bogdan.morosanu@upb.ro (B.M.); marian.negru@upb.ro (M.N.)
* Correspondence: pale@comm.pub.ro
† These authors contributed equally to this work.

Abstract: This paper presents a novel approach to automated music mixing, focusing on the optimization of loudness control in multi-track recordings. By taking into consideration the complexity and artistic nature of traditional mixing processes, we introduce a personalized multi-track leveling method using two types of approaches: a customized genetic algorithm and a neural network-based method. Our method tackles common challenges encountered by audio professionals during prolonged mixing sessions, where consistency can decrease as a result of fatigue. Our algorithm serves as a 'virtual assistant' to consistently uphold the initial mixing objectives, hence assuring consistent quality throughout the process. In addition, our system automates the repetitive elements of the mixing process, resulting in a substantial reduction in production time. This enables engineers to dedicate their attention to more innovative and intricate jobs. Our experimental framework involves 20 diverse songs and 10 sound engineers possessing a wide range of expertise, offering a useful perspective on the adaptability and effectiveness of our method in real-world scenarios. The results demonstrate the capacity of the algorithms to mimic decision-making, achieving an optimal balance in the mix that resonates with the emotional and technical aspects of music production.

Keywords: automatic mixing; loudness control; genetic algorithms; multi-track level optimization; sound engineering; music production; neural networks

1. Introduction

Music mixing is an intricate process that transforms multi-track material—recorded, sampled or synthesized—into a cohesive multi-channel format [1]. This process is not merely technical; it significantly influences the emotional connection between the music and its audience. A well-executed mix can profoundly affect the experience of the listener, emphasizing the artistry in sound engineering.

The field of music mixing is experiencing significant changes due to the introduction of automated solutions. The goal of incorporating automation in music mixing is to mimic or assist the complex and artistic process that has traditionally relied on the skill of a professional. This particular expertise is essential for modifying the dynamics, spatial characteristics, timbre and pitch in multi-track recordings. The alteration of these components involves a sequence of procedural stages that employ both linear and nonlinear processes to achieve the desired auditory outcome [2]. The following steps can be outlined:

- Gain Adjustment—this initial stage in mixing involves setting the overall volume levels of different tracks to obtain a well-balanced mix, preventing any single element from dominating the others;
- Equalization (EQ)—this is the deliberate adjustment of specific frequency ranges to improve the clarity and balance of the mix. This technique ensures that each instrument or voice has its own distinct sonic presence;

- Panning—this involves manipulating the stereo position of each track to create a sense of spatial depth in the mix. This technique enhances the listening experience by replicating the placement of sounds in a three-dimensional space, resulting in a more immersive effect;
- Dynamic Range Compression (DRC)—this is a technique that reduces the difference between the softest and loudest sounds in audio signals. It accomplishes this by amplifying soft sounds and attenuating loud sounds, resulting in a more uniform volume level across the mix. This technique is essential for preserving energy and guaranteeing the audible presence of all components;
- Artificial reverberation—this is the process of incorporating reverb effects to imitate different acoustic settings, ranging from compact chambers to large venues. This technique enhances the sonic dimension and ambiance of the audio mix.

Loudness, in the realm of audio engineering, refers to the subjective perception of the power or magnitude of a sound. Unlike objective measures of sound pressure like decibels (dB), loudness is a subjective sense that is affected by frequency and impacted by the unique characteristics of the human auditory system [3]. The intricacy of perceiving loudness has resulted in the creation of multiple standards and models to accurately and meaningfully measure it, such as the International Telecommunication Union's ITU-R BS.1770 [4] and the European Broadcasting Union's EBU R128 recommendation [5]. Loudness is not solely determined by amplitude, but rather it is a psycho-acoustic characteristic that reflects how humans perceive the intensity of sound.

The perception of sound is influenced by various elements, including the frequency content, duration and the surrounding context in which it is heard [6]. The challenge of audio mixing is to achieve a harmonic and enjoyable listening experience by balancing the perceptions of diverse audio tracks. Gain adjustment in the mixing process is indeed grounded on loudness measurements, tailored to the auditory perception of the engineer. This phase is crucial in the mixing process, if this step is not executed correctly, it can adversely impact all subsequent stages in the mixing workflow. Loudness management guarantees that the ultimate blend achieves a perceived volume that aligns with industry norms and listener expectations, while preserving the dynamic range and sound quality. The volume of each track in a mix is a crucial factor that can greatly impact the overall sound and clarity of the finished result. Engineers could use diverse strategies to manage track loudness, which might be influenced by their distinct views, target audience and the specific music genre they are working on.

In the domain of automatic music mixing, significant strides have been made towards developing algorithms that can emulate the nuanced decisions of human engineers. The inception of 'Automatic Mixing' can be traced back to 1975 with Dugan's speech application focusing on microphone gain control [7]. Significant contributions to the field include the work of González et al. [8], who introduced an automatic maximum gain normalization technique that forms the basis for many subsequent developments in audio mixing automation. Their methodology, detailed in the Journal of the Audio Engineering Society, provided a cornerstone for gain and fader control algorithms in live and recorded music scenarios. Scott et al. [9] focused on the analysis of acoustic features for automated multi-track mixing, offering insights into how different elements of a mix can be automatically balanced to achieve a desired sonic quality. Their work underscores the importance of understanding the acoustic characteristics of individual tracks for effective automation. Ward et al. [10] contributed to the field with their research on multi-track mixing using models of loudness and partial loudness. Their approach, aiming to improve the clarity and balance of mixes by addressing energetic masking, demonstrates the complexity of achieving a well-balanced mix through automated processes. Fentom et al.'s [11] research on automatic mixing using modified loudness models presents a method for level balancing that considers the psycho-acoustic phenomenon of loudness perception. This work is pivotal in understanding how listeners perceive the loudness of different sources within a mix and how this perception can be modeled and applied in automatic mixing systems. Moffat et al.'s [12] exploration of automatic mixing level balancing, enhanced through source interference identification, adds a layer of sophistication to automated mixing by addressing the issue of source interference. Their work proposes solutions for identifying and mitigating interference between sources, thereby enhancing the clarity and quality of the mix. Wilson et al.'s [13] research addresses the challenge of achieving desired audio outcomes by leveraging the flexibility and efficiency of genetic algorithms, which can evolve solutions based on user preferences and feedback. This method stands out by facilitating a more intuitive interaction between the user and the mixing process, enabling the user to influence the evolution of the mix in real time.

Further emphasizing the role of technological advancements in audio processing, recent studies in uncertainty estimation provide a crucial foundation for enhancing automated mixing systems. Adiloglu et al. [14] discuss the integration of probabilistic source separation with feature extraction to robustly estimate audio features despite errors in separation, particularly useful in under-determined scenarios such as polyphonic music recordings. Extending to multimodal contexts, Fang et al. [15] introduce an uncertainty-driven hybrid fusion model for audio-visual phoneme recognition, which adaptively manages unreliable visual inputs to enhance accuracy. Additionally, Sefidgar et al. [16] tackle the challenge of source feature extraction in multi-source recordings by employing deep learning to handle uncertainty, aiming to improve both the accuracy and robustness of separations. Xu et al. [17] provide a novel approach to the challenge of compressive blind mixing matrix estimation of audio signals, focusing on directly estimating the mixing matrix from compressive measurements without the need for reconstructing the mixtures to enhance the speed and accuracy of audio signal processing. These contributions highlight the increasing reliance on sophisticated algorithms to address complex challenges in audio engineering, aligning well with the ongoing developments in automated mixing technologies.

The significance of our work lies in its personalized approach to automated music mixing, distinguishing it from existing methodologies that generally aim for a one-size-fits-all solution. Unlike the broad strategies employed in previous studies, our research focuses on emulating the unique preferences and styles of individual engineers. This distinction is crucial because artists often seek out specific engineers for their distinctive sound and approach to mixing. The ability of our algorithm to learn and adapt to the preferences of different engineers represents a paradigm shift in automated mixing technology. It not only automates the technical aspects of mixing but also captures the creative signature essence of the engineer, thus offering a more tailored and artistically sensitive solution. Our methodology incorporates the `pyloudnorm` Python system, which adheres to the ITU-R BS.1770-4 standard and EBU R128 recommendation for measuring loudness [18]. By using the Loudness Units Full Scale (LUFS) meter, we can measure the volume in a manner that is consistent with both human perception and industry norms. Through the process of measuring and standardizing the loudness of each track, we provide a uniform starting point for our algorithm. This guarantees that the final mix attains the intended aural equilibrium and quality.

In this paper, we further investigate the implementation of automation in music mixing by proposing an experimental configuration that evaluates an individualized multi-track leveling method across a total of 20 songs and 10 engineers. This approach, which is based on our prior research [19], aims to improve the automation of the mixing process by focusing on crucial components such as loudness control and reproduction of creative decision-making similar to that of skilled audio engineers. The current experiment aims to evaluate the capacity of the algorithm to adjust to different musical genres and multiple engineering preferences, thus tackling the difficulty of automating music mixing with a sophisticated approach that considers the nuances of creative intention and technological implementation. Through the analysis of the algorithm's performance on a wide range of songs and mixing styles, our goal is to confirm its effectiveness and adaptability, which is a crucial milestone in addressing the challenges of automating music mixing. In this article we seek to enhance our previous discoveries from [19] and make a substantial contribution to the area by showcasing an advanced technique for obtaining customized loudness control and innovative decision-making in automated music mixing.

This paper is organized as follows. In Section 2, details about the used dataset, signal-processing operations and our applied methods for loudness control are presented. The results of our work are highlighted in Section 3. An analysis of the experiments is carried out as a discussion in Section 4. Finally, Section 5 concludes this work.

2. Materials and Methods

In this section, we provide a comprehensive explanation of the approaches and tools utilized to successfully accomplish our goals in creating a customized automated loudness control system for multi-track recordings. First, we provide a summary of the composition of dataset and the standards used for selecting songs, which guarantee a diverse representation of many musical genres. Subsequently, we explain the standardization procedure used on the audio files to ensure uniformity across all experimental inputs. Next, we analyze the development of the problem by creating a mathematical model that incorporates different variables. This section is essential for establishing a basic understanding of our methodologies and tactics prior to exploring specific algorithms, such as the genetic algorithm and neural network approach, which are explained in later subsections.

2.1. Dataset

For this paper, a dataset of 20 songs was meticulously curated, combining tracks from the Cambridge Music Technology database [20] and recordings from local Romanian bands sourced by the participating engineers. These selections encompass a wide range of genres and styles, providing a robust foundation for examining the nuances of audio mixing. The multi-track collection spans a deliberately broad spectrum of musical genres and styles, including Soul, Indie Pop, Alternative Rock, Country, Hip-Hop, Latin Pop, Funk, Rock 'n' Roll, Blues Rock, Indie-Psych Rock, R&B, Soft Rock, Pop Rock, Funk/Soul, Art Rock, Power Pop, Metal and more. This eclectic selection is critical for a comprehensive analysis of the diverse mixing techniques preferred by different sound engineers. The decision to include such a varied range of genres serves multiple purposes. Firstly, it mirrors the wide-ranging musical landscape that sound engineers encounter in professional settings, ensuring our findings have broad applicability. Secondly, it allows us to examine how different musical styles influence the mixing process, particularly in terms of dynamic range, tonal balance and spatialization, which can vary significantly from genre to genre. This diversity not only enriches our dataset but also strengthens our investigation into the adaptability and effectiveness of the personalized multi track leveling algorithm in mimicking the nuanced approach that engineers bring to projects across the musical spectrum.

The effectiveness of our tailored multi-track leveling process relies heavily on the expertise and subjective assessments of sound engineers. In order to assess the efficacy and versatility of our algorithm, we enlisted the participation of 10 sound engineers with diverse levels of expertise, ranging from beginners to professionals in the music industry. The selection process aimed to include individuals with a range of mixing techniques and preferences, in order to thoroughly evaluate the performance of the algorithm across various artistic approaches. Before starting the experiment, the sound engineers undertook a training session to become acquainted with the details of the algorithm. This encompassed a comprehensive examination of its design concepts and operational mechanics.

2.2. Data Preparation

As a pre-processing step, all audio files in the dataset were uniformly converted to a standard sampling rate in music of 44.1 kHz [21]. This conversion ensures consistency across all tracks, facilitating a more accurate and controlled analysis of the mixing processes employed by the engineers. The standardization of the sampling rate is a crucial step in maintaining the integrity and comparability of the data, as recommended in the Audio

Engineering Society's standard [22]. To avoid unwanted artifacts caused by quantization, we maintained the bit depth at its original value. In order to improve the organization of our dataset, we created a custom Python script to methodically rename audio files, using precise keywords extracted from a comprehensive multi-track database [20]. The process of renaming is not solely administrative; it fulfills a crucial analytical purpose by guaranteeing that tracks of similar categories throughout multiple songs are consistently labeled, hence greatly streamlining data administration and analysis. As an example, the recordings are consistently renamed according to a convention like 'Index_KickIn', 'Index_BassDi', 'Index_Piano', 'Index_LeadVocals_2', 'Index_LeadVocals_3', enabling quick identification and comparison of related parts throughout the collection. Our track list template consists of 66 general tracks conform to the industry standard and is generated through the analysis of several multi-track recordings. It enables a more focused and nuanced examination of the individual contributions of each group to the overall mix, as well as how engineers approach the process of mixing different instrument kinds in different genres:

- 00–17—Drums and related instruments (e.g., KickIn, SnareUp, HiHat);
- 18–24—Synthesized and electronic percussion (e.g., KickSynth, PercSynthLow);
- 25–30—Bass tracks (e.g., BassDi, BassSynth);
- 31–36—Guitars (e.g., AccGuitarDi, ElGuitarClean);
- 37–45—Keyboards, Piano and synthesized instruments (e.g., ElectricPiano, KeySynthLow);
- 46–58—Orchestral, world instruments and other cinematic instruments (e.g., Woodwinds, Vio1, WorldInstrLow);
- 59–65—Vocals and other (e.g., LeadVox, BackingMed, Other).

This methodical approach addresses the lack of a common naming convention among artists and recording engineers, an issue in the profession that we sought to overcome. By using a systematic naming convention, we enhance the organization and accessibility of the dataset. This ensures that tracks are not only uniformly titled, but also classified and arranged in a manner that reflects industry standards.

As a post-mixing step, for each sound engineer, the loudness parameters for each track of each song were meticulously extracted and documented, in order to properly represent the preferences of each individual. We created a Python script specifically designed to apply ITU loudness standards [4] for quantifying important loudness measures in every engineer's mix. This script additionally validates the accurate naming of tracks and detects any additional tampering apart from gain adjustment, that might have taken place. The main purpose of this method for loudness extraction was to examine perceptive audio level parameters, offering a quantitative perspective to evaluate the mixing decisions of each engineer. The advantage of this method is represented by its capacity to process a wide range of audio data inputs, guaranteeing consistency in parameter extraction regardless of the file format and duration. Nevertheless, the process was not devoid of obstacles. Novice engineers exhibited inconsistent compliance to protocols, resulting in a deviation from established mixing procedures and causing unanticipated changes in loudness parameters. The extraction algorithm faced considerable obstacles due to inconsistencies in naming standards and unanticipated changes in bit depth, and required human intervention.

One very important step in automatic learning using any type of data is to ensure that all the examples are in the same distribution and within a similar range of values. Because the loudness control is a problem of human perception, we needed to make sure that each song has the same loudness volume. This operation was carried out in order to ensure that the mix created by each engineer is always at the same loudness level, and only the coefficients between tracks are different. Additionally, each original song has its own multi-tracks at different loudness levels, therefore, it is important to normalize all the initial tracks to a fixed loudness. To ensure consistency and optimal listening conditions, we normalized each input track to −45 LUFS and set the loudness of every original mix to −23 LUFS. The decision to use −45 LUFS for individual tracks stems from a widely adopted practice among sound engineers, who prefer to start with lower volumes to have greater control during the mixing process. This initial low volume also surpasses the loudness threshold gate, below which measurements by loudness meters may not be reliable, ensuring accuracy in our loudness assessments. The selection of −23 LUFS for the mixed audio volume is rooted in its recognition as a level that aligns closely with human auditory perception, offering a balance that preserves both clarity and dynamic range, without inducing listener fatigue over extended periods. This choice mirrors the standards set forth by international broadcasting guidelines, such as the EBU R128 standard [18], which recommends a target loudness of $-23(\pm 2)$ LUFS to ensure a consistent and comfortable listening experience across various platforms and media types. However, obtaining an accurate loudness reading for audio tracks with only small brief moments of useful signal, such as a single clap or a snare strike, can be quite difficult. It is well known that the length of the useful signal should be at least 3 s for a proper loudness measurement. In the case of such exceptional cases with very brief useful signal and small amplitude levels, the Root Mean Square (RMS) value was used instead of LUFS implementation in order to scale the track. For this paper, we consider the reference mix level at −23 LUFS, and the input track level at −45 LUFS.

For audio processing, it is usually quite challenging to work with the entire signal, therefore, splitting the audio into multiple overlapped windows is commonly practiced. However, for the problem of a fixed loudness level for the entire track, we discovered that there is no need to look at all the signal windows, but instead, use only one of them, because the scale factor will be the same over the entire track. In other words, instead of processing entire tracks, we focus on key segments, thereby reducing processing time without compromising on the accuracy of loudness estimation. Additionally, based on the human auditory sensitivity differences across frequencies, we also recognized that the maximum loudness perception is between 250 Hz and 4000 Hz [23]. For this reason, as an optimization step, we realized that we could downsample the audio at a lower frequency rate, maintaining quality while reducing computational load. The following multi-step procedure was applied for each track in every song:

1. Downsample the entire track to 16 kHz, in alignment with human auditory sensitivity and the equal-loudness contours, which emphasize the 2–5 kHz range where clarity and loudness perception are most significant [3];
2. Divide the audio signal into windows of 3 s, with a hop size of 1 s (66% overlap);
3. Find the best window within the audio. We consider the best window the one with the highest RMS value, which can approximate the loudness level with some degree (it is a representantion of the power of the signal, without the human perception factor), but is much faster to compute;
4. Repeat steps (2) and (3), but with a window size of 1024 samples and hop size of 512 (50% overlap), representing a window of 64 ms in time. This was done in order to further shrink the input data size for a faster training loop.

2.3. Problem Formulation

Music mixing, inherently a blend of art and science, necessitates a nuanced understanding of audio signal interplay. A musical piece, essentially a combination of various frequencies and timbres, can be deconstructed into its constituent tracks. This separation is key to our approach, as it allows for the manipulation of individual elements before reassembling them into a harmonious mixture. At the heart of our method, Equation (1) presents a mathematical model [24] representing a mixed song as a sum of its constituent tracks, each modulated by a specific coefficient:

$$m(t) = \sum_{i=1}^{N} \lambda_i x_i(t), \tag{1}$$

where $m(t)$ denotes the mixed audio at time sample t, $x_i(t)$ symbolizes an individual track and λ_i is the corresponding mixing coefficient. N represents the maximum number of possible tracks, and is equal to 66 in our case. This model encapsulates the essence of mixing—blending various elements (tracks) into a cohesive auditory experience.

When analyzing the mixing process from an optimization perspective, we view it as a search for the best combination of λ_i values that result in a balanced blend. The difficulty lies in automating this process of optimization, which has traditionally been carried out by human professionals. In our situation, the coefficient λ_i represents the level or loudness of each recording as perceived in the mix.

2.4. Genetic Algorithm for Loudness Optimization

We propose the utilization of genetic algorithms [25,26] to effectively handle this complex and multi-solution problem. Our approach leverages a genetic algorithm to iteratively refine the mixing coefficients, driving towards an optimal mix. The algorithm mimics natural selection, evolving solutions over generations to arrive at a superior mix.

The genetic algorithm begins with a population of randomly generated solutions (mixing coefficient sets). Through processes akin to biological evolution—selection, crossover and mutation—this population evolves over generations. A generic pseudo-code for genetic algorithms is represented in Algorithm 1.

Algorithm 1 Genetic Algorithm

```
Set: Population size, chromosome length
Init: Create population using random bounded values
while stop criterion not met do
    Evaluation: Calculate the fitness of each individual in the population
    Parents selection: Choose individuals for reproduction based on their fitness
    for i = 0 to length list of parents do
        Choose pair of parents
        if random probability crossover ≤ crossover probability then
            Crossover: Perform crossover between parents to create a new offspring
        else
            Select a parent as the new offspring
        end if
    end for
    for each offspring do
        for each gene in offspring do
            if random probability mutation ≤ mutation probability then
                Mutation: Apply random mutation to introduce changes in the offspring
            end if
        end for
    end for
    Update: Create a new population based on the generated offsprings
end while
```

Our customized genetic algorithm ensures that only the fittest solutions (those producing the most harmonious mixes) survive and propagate their traits. Given the unique demands of music mixing, we customize the standard genetic algorithm to suit our specific needs:

- Population and Solution Representation—the population consists of vectors of mixing coefficients (chromosomes). Each vector represents a potential solution for the problem, where one element (gene) corresponds to a coefficient for a track. For our problem, each solution will always be represented by a vector of 66 elements. Instead of creating a high population, we chose to use a highly competitive small population of only 5 chromosomes, in order to extract the optimal solution from this group of best candidates. Using the model described in Equation (1), we define a chromosome based on the vector representation specified in Equation (2):

$$c = [\lambda_0, \lambda_1, \ldots, \lambda_{65}]. \tag{2}$$

- Fitness Function—our fitness function evaluates the quality of a mix based on the Mean Absolute Error (MAE) between the desired and produced audio samples across tracks. The main difference is that instead of computing the loss function for each song and average all the errors, we instead compute the error for each track in all songs (Equations (3) and (4)), in order to better approximate the track coefficients.

$$e_i^k = \frac{1}{T^k} \sum_{t=0}^{T^k-1} |y_i^k(t) - \lambda_i x_i^k(t)| = \text{MAE}\left(y_i^k, \hat{y}_i^k\right), \tag{3}$$

$$e_i = \sum_{k=1}^{M} e_i^k, \tag{4}$$

where $k \in [1, M]$ represents the index of a song out of M possible examples, and T^k is the length of the signal k. At each track i for a song k, the error e_i^k (MAE function) is calculated between the original track y_i^k and the product of coefficient λ_i and input track x_i^k at -45 LUFS, which represents the predicted track $\hat{y}_i^k$.

The MAE function, defined in both Equations (3) and (5), measures the differences between the ground truth track samples y_i^k and predicted samples $\hat{y}_i^k$. Summing these errors on a track level helps us better minimize a loss function as the average of the track errors over all songs M. In other words, we are trying to reduce the differences between the loudness of the predicted track and the original one, for all available musical pieces.

$$\mathcal{L} = -\frac{1}{N} \sum_{i=0}^{N-1} e_i = -\frac{1}{N} \sum_{i=0}^{N-1} \sum_{k=1}^{M} \text{MAE}\left(y_i^k, \hat{y}_i^k\right). \tag{5}$$

- Selection Process—we employ a 3-Way Tournament selection, ensuring diversity while favoring higher-fitness solutions. This means that a parent is extracted as the best solution from 3 random candidates. The best solution is always saved to the next generation using the Elitism method, and there are 4 mating parents for the crossover and mutation operations.
- Crossover and Mutation—a tailored crossover strategy ensures optimal trait inheritance, while a controlled mutation process introduces necessary variability, preventing stagnation. Instead of a probability approach, we always apply a custom crossover operation between 2 parents. Each gene is selected from the 2 parents as the best one by comparing the gene error e_i at each track i, using Equations (3) and (4). For the mutation operation, we use an adaptive mutation [27,28] probability of 10% for the parent-crossing solutions and 1% for the elite chromosome.

The customized genetic algorithm can represent a good solution for the loudness control problem because it finds a fixed set of coefficients as the best approximation for multiple songs. However, one of the problem with this approach is that there will always be the same values for the coefficients (unless retraining is demanded). Because of this, if the training songs are very different between each other, the genetic algorithm will try to find the best solution that can obtain the minimal fitness function, but this may not always be the best auditory experience when mixing the tracks with the corresponding coefficients.

2.5. Neural Network for Loudness Optimization

In order to test the eligibility of our proposed method, in addition to the customized genetic algorithm, we also implemented a neural network that can solve the automatic loudness control problem in an adaptive way instead of a fixed solution. We chose a Convolutional Neural Network (CNN) architecture because it has the ability to extract useful information from correlated data, in our case, the successive audio samples. Because stereo channels usually have correlated information with many similarities, we simplified the problem by stacking both channels into a single one using a Fortran-like index order (the left sample is followed by its corresponding right sample). This enables us to use 1D convolution instead of the 2D operation, ensuring a better representation for the extracted time features.

A big advantage when using a neural network is its ability to generalize by learning on a batch of data, instead of one single example. In our case, since the number of audio mixes in the dataset is limited, we chose our batch size as the entire train data size (15 songs), allowing the model to extract information from all musical pieces available for training. The output of our architecture will be represented by a vector of 66 coefficients, ensuring that all the tracks have a corresponding scaling factor (the same as the genetic algorithm output). Usually, augmenting operations for extending the training dataset are applied, e.g., overlapping windows for audio are treated as different examples in the input of the model. However, because we decided to use only the best segment of 1024 stereo samples in the genetic algorithm, we kept the same input for our neural network as well, therefore, only one segment was used from each track. The only difference is that the input for the genetic algorithm is stereo, while the neural network receives the stacked mono signal. The architecture of the model is represented in Figure 1.

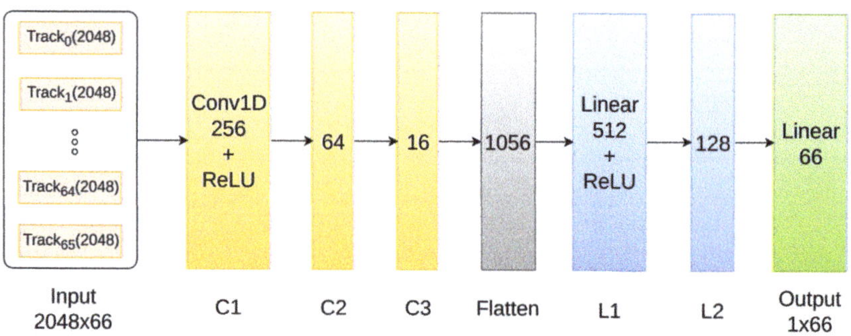

Figure 1. Overview of the neural network architecture. The **C** blocks consists in an 1D-convolutional layer and an ReLU activation function. The **L** blocks are represented by a fully connected layer, followed by ReLU function. For each layer the value in the block represents the number of filters (for Conv1D) or the number of neurons (for Linear). The last layer consists the output of the model, which is a vector of 66 coefficients.

Note that we used a simple model in order to learn the track coefficients, because this problem does not require very complex architectures, since this is only a scaling task. However, we mention that any type of architecture can be used here, and more large models might be required for bigger datasets. The loss function used is the same one presented in Equation (5). This means that we did not apply the MAE function between real and predicted coefficients, but rather on the input samples multiplied with the predicted coefficients and compared with the ground truth samples. An explication for this will be the fact that the MAE function between audio signals can give better results than an error between only 66 values. This neural network was implemented only to test its functionality for this problem and can be considered as a baseline for all the next tasks in automatic mixing, e.g., EQ, panning, DRC or even artificial reverberation.

3. Results

Both our methods (genetic algorithm and neural network) were applied for each of the 10 sound engineers, in order to capture the preferences of each individual. For this reason, 10 solutions from the customized genetic algorithm were obtained, as well as 10 trained machine learning models. In order to correctly conduct a comparison of the two methods, we divided the dataset composed of 20 songs in 15 songs used for train and 5 musical pieces for validation purposes, for both algorithms. The 5 mixtures for validation were selected based on their uniqueness and their differences between other songs. Those validation songs were considered outliers, or in other words, musical pieces too difficult to extract the correct coefficients when combined with other songs.

For the training process, it is important to mention that usually songs have multiple versions of the same track (e.g., guitar1, guitar2, violin1, violin2, etc.). When recording or mixing both symphonic and modern music, it is typical to combine similar instrument tracks to make the best use of technical resources and improve artistic expression. For instance, when there are several violinists in an orchestra section or multiple guitar parts in a song, they are frequently combined into a single track during the mixing process. This method saves the channels of the mixing console, decreases the amount of processing required and reduces the size of files, making it easier to handle and save them. From an artistic standpoint, when tracks that perform the same part, such as double tracking guitar riffs or a violin section, are combined, it results in a cohesive and more dense sound. To address this issue, we consider a single track x^k (e.g., guitar) which represents the mean of all the possible versions x_j^k of the corresponding track, as presented in Equation (6):

$$x_i^k = \frac{1}{V} \sum_{j=0}^{V-1} x_{i,j}^k, \tag{6}$$

where j represents the index of the current variant from all possible V versions for track k of song i.

By doing this, we are always able to keep the same number of 66 tracks, no matter the song. However, one constraint is that for both methods, the algorithm will optimize one single coefficient value for the corresponding track, instead of a multitude of them. While all sound engineers had the possibility to change all available tracks (including their variants), the automatic approaches can only approximate the track composed from grouping all available variants. This means that all track versions will have the same mean coefficient at prediction, therefore, it will always be at least a small difference between the predicted mix and its reference. Nevertheless, having the same coefficient value for a group of the same tracks can give a smooth audio sensation and might actually be better perceived by the listener.

For the subjective listening test, each engineer participating in the project received four distinct forms of a mix: the RAW, unedited tracks summed after recording; the artist's MIX, which is the engineer's personal mix used as a reference for the algorithms; and the versions generated by the GA and NN algorithms. The engineers were given the songs in a random order and labeled in a manner that prevented them from knowing what version they were reviewing. In order to preserve consistency and assure reliable assessment, each engineer examined the songs in their private studio using their familiar setup that they are used to for mixing. This method helped in reducing any variations in the listening environment that could potentially impact their evaluations of the audio quality. For the subjective listening test described, the engineers used the same digital audio workstation (DAW) software that they are most accustomed to for mixing to conduct the evaluations. This choice is significant as it ensures that the engineers are working within a familiar audio processing environment, reducing the learning curve and potential biases that might arise from unfamiliarity with new software tools. This ensured an impartial evaluation. The engineers were instructed to listen to each version 3 times in order to acquaint themselves with the subtleties of each mix. After participating in these listening sessions, participants were given the task of evaluating each version using the ITU standard grading scale, which ranges from 1 to 5. A rating of 1 indicates the lowest quality, while a rating of 5 indicates the highest quality. The average of these three scores was then calculated to generate a final score for each mix version for every engineer. The results for the training dataset are presented in Tables 1 and 2 for validation.

Table 1. Mean listening scores over the training dataset of 15 songs. The last column represents the average over all 10 subjects for each of the 4 versions.

Version	S1	S2	S3	S4	S5	S6	S7	S8	S9	S10	All
original (RAW)	3.5	3.9	3.5	3.1	3.5	2.9	3.7	1.2	3.5	1.5	3.0
artist's mix (MIX)	4.3	4.1	4.0	3.7	3.3	3.3	4.3	2.2	4.0	4.0	3.7
genetic algorithm (GA)	4.6	3.9	4.2	3.6	3.1	3.4	3.9	2.9	4.2	4.5	3.9
neural network (CNN)	4.5	4.2	4.5	3.7	3.1	3.7	4.1	3.3	4.5	3.7	3.9

Table 2. Mean listening scores over the validation dataset of 5 songs. The last column represents the average over all 10 subjects for each of the 4 versions.

Version	S1	S2	S3	S4	S5	S6	S7	S8	S9	S10	All
original (RAW)	3.4	3.7	3.6	3.2	2.2	1.6	3.5	1.4	3.6	1.6	2.8
artist's mix (MIX)	4.7	4.0	4.3	3.8	2.9	3.2	4.6	2.8	4.3	4.0	3.9
genetic algorithm (GA)	4.3	3.2	3.8	2.8	3.2	2.6	3.8	2.2	3.8	2.2	3.2
neural network (CNN)	4.3	3.5	4.0	3.8	2.0	3.0	3.7	2.2	4.0	2.2	3.3

Upon reviewing the listening test results for the 15 songs used to train the algorithms, we observe that the genetic algorithm achieved a score that was equal to or greater than the human-engineered mix in half of the cases, specifically for 5 out of the 10 engineers. The CNN also performed notably, matching or surpassing the MIX in 4 out of the 10 instances. In the scenarios where the GA and CNN did not outscore the MIX, their performance remained close to the reference, indicating a marginal difference. This tight competition between the algorithms and the human MIX scores underscores the sophistication and potential of these automated mixing tools to closely approximate, if not enhance, the nuanced craft of human audio engineering.

In the validation phase of our study, we assessed the performance of the algorithms on a set of 5 complex songs, selected for their challenging nature in terms of mixing. The results for these songs are revealing in terms of the capability of both GA and CNN to handle complicated audio tasks. The RAW tracks, which had no processing, received scores that highlight the inherent difficulties present in the unaltered recordings, with mean scores ranging from 1.4 to 3.7 across the engineers. In contrast, the human-engineered MIX versions, which represent the benchmark of professional quality, scored significantly higher, with means spanning from 2.8 to 4.7, reflecting the engineers' ability to enhance and refine the tracks. Notably, the GA and CNN both showed strong performances in this challenging scenario. The scores from GA were consistently competitive, ranging from 2.2 to 4.3, closely trailing the MIX scores and, in some cases, matching them. The CNN mirrored this robust performance with scores from 2.0 to 4.3, demonstrating that the advanced modeling and learning capabilities of CNNs are effective even with the most complex mixes.

These results suggest that both automated methods are adept at navigating the intricacies of sophisticated song structures and mixing requirements. Their performance in this validation set reinforces the potential of these algorithms to act as valuable tools in the mixing process, providing high-quality results even when confronted with demanding audio material. In the realm of audio engineering, professionals are often distinguished by varying levels of proficiency, each characterized by distinct skill sets, experiences and contributions to the music-production process. Our participant engineers might be categorized based on their competence level as follows:

- S1 and S6: Professional Engineers (Pro);
- S8, S9 and S10: Semi-Professional Engineers (Semi-Pro);
- S5 and S7: Aspiring Engineers (Aspiring);
- S2, S3 and S4: Amateur Engineers (Amateur).

In reinterpreting the data based on the level of proficiency, we observe distinct trends in how the different engineer categories perceive the quality of mixes produced by the algorithms compared to the raw and human-engineered mix. The Pro engineers rated their mix highest, which is expected as it aligns with their high standards and experience in creating polished mixes. However, it is noteworthy that both the GA and CNN also received high ratings from these engineers, often very close to their MIX scores. This suggests that the algorithms are producing results that approach professional quality, even in the eyes of seasoned engineers. Semi-Pro engineers provided a diverse range of scores. Interestingly, the algorithms, especially CNN, received scores that were competitive with the MIX, occasionally surpassing them. This indicates that the Semi-Pro engineers found the automatic mixed tracks to be of a high standard, suggesting that these tools could be particularly beneficial for those in this category looking to enhance their output. Aspiring engineers demonstrated a wide range of responses, possibly reflecting their developing ears and mixing preferences. The algorithms' scores were generally favorable, sometimes matching the MIX, which could indicate that these tools might serve as educational aids, helping aspiring engineers understand and achieve better mixing standards. For the Amateur engineers, the MIX and the algorithmic outputs were also rated better than the RAW version, with the algorithms often scoring on par with the human mixes. This reflects the potential for the GA and CNN to serve as effective tools for amateurs, helping them achieve a more professional sound that might otherwise be beyond their current skill level.

In Figure 2, we chose to illustrate a comparison between the mean preferences of one Pro artist over the 20 songs, and the two automatic proposed methods (GA and NN). The loudness variance of the original artist mixes for all 20 songs is delimited in the rectangle blue boxes, showing significant variations between songs.

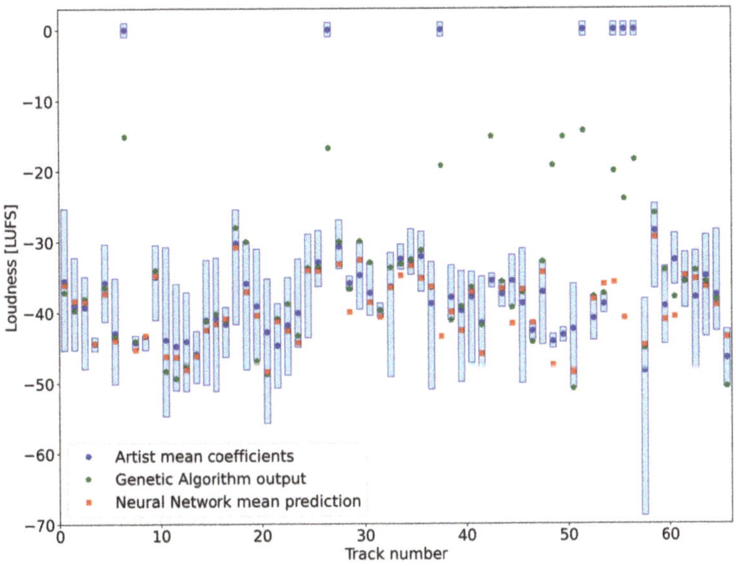

Figure 2. Comparison between the mean preferences of 1 Pro sound engineer and GA and NN.

The blue dots represent the mean computed over the 20 songs for the artist's coefficient for each track. The green pentagons are illustrated by the output of the genetic algorithm, and the red squares are the mean predicted coefficients from the neural network. As you can notice, both automatic methods are close to the user's mean preferences. The genetic algorithm will always output the same constant coefficients, which makes it a consistent method. On the other hand, the neural network always tries to adjust to the received input, therefore, the prediction will be different based on audio, which makes it an interesting adaptive algorithm. The advantage of GA is that the prediction is very fast because it only loads the best solution, but it has the disadvantage that it is not adaptable. On the other hand, the neural network is very flexible, but requires more time to predict because it needs to receive the audio input, which has to go through all the pre-processing operations previously mentioned. Our findings showed that Pros spent about 5 min on simpler songs and up to 30 min on more complex tracks to achieve their mix. In contrast, amateur engineers sometimes required up to an hour to reach satisfactory results, illustrating the steep learning curve and time investment needed without the aid of automation. Once trained, our methods significantly reduced this time expenditure, showing the potential of these algorithms not only to assist engineers by automating the initial, labor-intensive steps of mixing but also to expedite the overall mixing process.

The training and inference processes were conducted on a laptop with Nvidia GeForce RTX 2060 as GPU, which proves that both our methods can be used on common computers, representing a big advantage for artists because they can use this program on their personal laptops. The custom genetic algorithm was trained for 30,000 iterations, while the neural network was trained for 200 epochs. For training the NN, we used the Adam [29] optimizer with a learning rate of 1×10^{-4} and a batch size of 20. We minimized a MAE loss function between the ground truth audio samples and the input samples multiplied by the predicted coefficients, as depicted in Equation (5).

4. Discussion

Our comprehensive analysis yielded compelling results: both GA and CNN displayed a remarkable ability to not only improve upon the raw, unprocessed tracks, but also to meet—and occasionally exceed—the quality of mixes engineered by humans. This was evidenced across a training set of 15 songs and a validation set of 5 complex songs, where the automated algorithms consistently achieved scores close to or surpassing those of the human-engineered mix. The findings from our study are not an indicator that the role of the audio engineer is being replaced by algorithms, but rather that these technologies are emerging as sophisticated assistants in the mixing process. The GA and CNN demonstrate an ability to lay the groundwork according to an engineer's preferences, effectively setting the stage for them to concentrate on the more creative and subjective aspects of mixing. This symbiosis could see engineers leveraging AI (Artificial Inteligence) to handle initial and time-consuming tasks, such as balancing levels and applying basic EQ settings, thereby freeing up more time for them to delve into the artistic nuances that truly define a mix. Despite the promising outcomes, our results are not without limitations. The current algorithms, while proficient in technical execution, may not yet fully replicate the creative and intuitive aspects of human mixing—the 'art' that goes beyond the 'science'. Moreover, the listening tests were confined to specific genres and mixing styles, which may not represent the full spectrum of music production. Future research should explore the incorporation of creative and stylistic decision-making into the algorithms to capture the artistry of human engineers more faithfully. Additionally, expanding the dataset to include a wider variety of musical genres and engineering styles could provide a more comprehensive understanding of the capabilities of the algorithms. Investigating user-friendly interfaces for these technologies could also facilitate their adoption by professionals in the field, enhancing the collaborative potential between humans and AI in audio engineering. As we look to the future, our research will not rest at the threshold of leveling algorithms. We plan to expand this personalized approach to encompass other critical aspects of mixing, including equalization, compression and saturation. By extending the scope of our algorithm to these domains, we aim to offer an even more comprehensive and intuitive mixing tool, one that further blurs the lines between professional studio quality and accessible home recording setups.

5. Conclusions

In this paper, we present a novel approach that centers around a highly personalized multi-track leveling algorithm for automatic mixing. This implementation is designed to reflect the individual preferences of any user by learning their specific style and applying these preferences to the mixing process. We provide two algorithms for resolving the automatic loudness control: a customized genetic algorithm and a convolutional neural network, where both are adept at adjusting to the unique requirements of the user and executing precision-based loudness control across a multitude of tracks. We created a dataset of 20 songs, ranging from diverse genres and complexity. Both the genetic algorithm and neural network were trained on 15 songs and validated on 5 other songs, where the validation set was chosen as the most different musical pieces compared to the others from the dataset. This creative approach presents a novel multi-track leveling technique specifically designed to greatly simplify the mixing process for music producers and sound engineers. Upon receiving a new set of multi-tracks for a song, our approach not only efficiently organizes and arranges the tracks based on a specific order, but also does preliminary processing on each individual track, a process that is normally carried out manually. This preprocessing aligns each track with the precise mixing preferences of the engineer, guaranteeing that they are optimally prepared for import into the desired DAW. This tailored design enables producers to concentrate more effectively on enhancing and finalizing the remaining activities in the production process. This virtual assistant technology promotes creative freedom and makes high-quality mixing available to a greater variety of music enthusiasts and professionals by responding to the particular styles and requirements of each producer, thereby democratizing access.

Author Contributions: Conceptualization, B.M. and M.N.; methodology, B.M. and M.N.; software, M.N.; validation, B.M.; data curation, B.M.; writing—original draft preparation, B.M. and M.N.; writing—review and editing, C.P.; funding acquisition, C.P.; formal analysis, C.P. All authors have read and agreed to the published version of the manuscript.

Funding: This work was supported by a grant of the Ministry of Research, Innovation and Digitization, CNCS-UEFISCDI, project number PN-III-P4-PCE-2021-0780, within PNCDI III.

Data Availability Statement: Samples are available online on onedrive (https://shorturl.at/kwFTX (accessed on 15 May 2024)).

Conflicts of Interest: The authors declare no conflict of interest.

Abbreviations

The following abbreviations are used in this manuscript:

AI	Artificial Inteligence
CNN	Convolutional Neural Network
DAW	Digital Audio Workstation
DRC	Dynamic Range Compression
EBU	European Broadcasting Union
EQ	Equalization
GA	Genetic Algorithm
GPU	Graphics Processing Unit
ITU	The International Telecommunication Union
LUFS	Loudness Units relative to Full Scale
MAE	Mean Absolute Error
NN	Neural Network
RMS	Root Mean Square

erences

De Man, B. Towards a Better Understanding of Mix Engineering. Ph.D. Thesis, Queen Mary University of London, London, UK, 2017.
Izhaki, R.B. The Process of Mixing. In *From Demo to Delivery*; Routledge: New York, NY, USA, 2013; pp. 107–123.
Fletcher, H.; Munson, W.A. Loudness, its Definition, Measurement and Calculation. *Bell Syst. Tech. J.* **1933**, *12*, 377–430. [CrossRef]

4. Series, B.S. Algorithms to Measure Audio Programme Loudness and True-Peak Audio Level. *Int. Telecommun. Union Radiocom Assem.* 2011. Available online: https://lokaaldigitaal.vlaanderen/Documenten/R-REC-BS.1770-4-201510-I%21%21PDF-E (accessed on 15 May 2024).
5. European Broadcasting Union. EBU Tech 3341: Loudness Normalisation and Permitted Maximum Level of Audio nals. *Ebu Recomm. R128.* 2014. Available online: https://www.rosseladvertising.be/sites/default/files/techspecs/TV/ recommendation.pdf (accessed on 15 May 2024).
6. Bech, S.; Zacharov, N. *Perceptual Audio Evaluation-Theory, Method and Application*; John Wiley & Sons: Hoboken, NJ, USA, 20
7. Dugan, D. Automatic Microphone Mixing. In Proceedings of the Audio Engineering Society Convention 51, Audio Enginee Society, Los Angeles, CA, USA, 13–16 May 1975.
8. Reiss, J.D.; Perez Gonzalez, E. An Automatic Maximum Gain Normalization Technique with Applications to Audio Mixin Proceedings of the Audio Engineering Society Convention 124, Audio Engineering Society, Amsterdam, The Netherlands, 1 May 2008.
9. Scott, J.J.; Kim, Y.E. Analysis of Acoustic Features for Automated Multi-Track Mixing. In Proceedings of the 12th Internati Society for Music Information Retrieval Conference (ISMIR 2011), Miami, FL, USA, 24–28 October 2011; pp. 621–626.
10. Ward, D.; Reiss, J.D.; Athwal, C. Multitrack Mixing Using a Model of Loudness and Partial Loudness. In Proceedings o Audio Engineering Society Convention 133, Audio Engineering Society, San Francisco, CA, USA, 26–29 October 2012.
11. Fenton, S. Automatic Mixing of Multitrack Material Using Modified Loudness Models. In Proceedings of the Audio Enginee Society Convention 145, Audio Engineering Society, New York, NY, USA, 17–20 October 2018.
12. Moffat, D.; Sandler, M. Automatic Mixing Level Balancing Enhanced Through Source Interference Identification. In Proceed of the Audio Engineering Society Convention 146, Audio Engineering Society, Dublin, Ireland, 20–23 March 2019.
13. Wilson, A.; Fazenda, B.M. User-Guided Rendering of Audio Objects Using an Interactive Genetic Algorithm. *J. Audio Eng.* **2019**, *67*, 522–530. [CrossRef]
14. Adiloglu, K.; Vincent, E. An Uncertainty Estimation Approach for the Extraction of Source Features in Multisource Recordin *Sound Music. Audio Eng.* **2011**, *5*, 123–145.
15. Fang, B.; Frintrop, S.; Gerkmann, T. Uncertainty-Driven Hybrid Fusion for Audio-Visual Phoneme Recognition. *J. Audiov. Process.* **2023**, *1*, 99–118. [CrossRef]
16. Sefidgar, S.A.; Liu, J.; Wang, Y. Modern Approach for Estimating Uncertainty of a Precision Optoelectronic Phase N Measurement. *Int. J. Electron. Meas.* **2023**, *11*, 77–92. [CrossRef]
17. Xu, H.; Fu, N.; Qiao, L.; Yu, W.; Peng, X. Compressive Blind Mixing Matrix Estimation of Audio Signals. *IEEE Trans. Inst Meas.* **2014**, *63*, 1253–1261. [CrossRef]
18. De Man, B. Evaluation of Implementations of the EBU R128 Loudness Measurement. In Proceedings of the Audio Enginee Society Convention 145, Audio Engineering Society, New York, NY, USA, 17–20 October 2018.
19. Moroşanu, B.; Negru, M.; Neacşu, A.; Negrescu, C.; Paleologu, C. Personalized Multi-Track Leveling Algorithm. In Proceed of the 2023 International Conference on Speech Technology and Human-Computer Dialogue (SpeD), Bucharest, Romania, 2 October 2023; pp. 24–29. [CrossRef]
20. Senior, M. *Mixing Secrets for the Small Studio*; Routledge: London, UK, 2018.
21. Schouhamer Immink, K.A. The Compact Disc Story. *J. Audio Eng. Soc.* **1998**, *46*, 458–465.
22. Audio Engineering Society. AES TD1002.2.15-02: Recommendation for Delivery of Recorded Music Projects. *Audio Eng. Soc.* Available online: https://www.aes.org/technical/documents/AESTD1002.2.15-02_1.pdf (accessed on 15 May 2024).
23. Wilson, A.D.; Fazenda, B.M. Perception & Evaluation of Audio Quality in Music Production. In Proceedings of the 16th Inte tional Conference on Digital Audio Effects (DAFx-13), Digital Audio Effects (DAFx), Maynooth, Ireland, 2–4 September 20
24. Terrell, M. The Mathematics of Mixing. *J. Audio Eng. Soc.* **2013**, *61*, 904–913. [CrossRef]
25. Mirjalili, S. Genetic Algorithm. In *Evolutionary Algorithms and Neural Networks: Theory and Applications*; Sprir Berlin/Heidelberg, Germany, 2019; pp. 43–55.
26. Katoch, S.; Chauhan, S.S.; Kumar, V. A Review on Genetic Algorithm: Past, Present, and Future. *Multimed. Tools Appl.* **202** 8091–8126. [CrossRef] [PubMed]
27. Marsili Libelli, S.; Alba, P. Adaptive Mutation in Genetic Algorithms. *Soft Comput.* **2000**, *4*, 76–80. [CrossRef]
28. Rajakumar, B. Impact of Static and Adaptive Mutation Techniques on the Performance of Genetic Algorithm. *Int. J. Hybrid I Syst.* **2013**, *10*, 11–22. [CrossRef]
29. Kingma, D.P.; Ba, J. Adam: A method for stochastic optimization. *arXiv* **2014**, arXiv:1412.6980.

algorithms

MDPI

icle

mulation of Calibrated Complex Synthetic Population Data ith XGBoost

annes Gussenbauer [1], Matthias Templ [2,*], Siro Fritzmann [3] and Alexander Kowarik [1]

[1] Statistics Austria, 1110 Vienna, Austria; johannes.gussenbauer@statistik.gv.at (J.G.); alexander.kowarik@statistik.gv.at (A.K.)
[2] School of Business, University of Applied Sciences and Arts Northwestern, 4600 Olten, Switzerland
[3] Medgate, 4052 Basel, Switzerland; siro.fritzmann@medgate.ch
* Correspondence: matthias.templ@fhnw.ch

Abstract: Syntheticdata generation methods are used to transform the original data into privacy-compliant synthetic copies (twin data). With our proposed approach, synthetic data can be simulated in the same size as the input data or in any size, and in the case of finite populations, even the entire population can be simulated. The proposed XGBoost-based method is compared with known model-based approaches to generate synthetic data using a complex survey data set. The XGBoost method shows strong performance, especially with synthetic categorical variables, and outperforms other tested methods. Furthermore, the structure and relationship between variables are well preserved. The tuning of the parameters is performed automatically by a modified k-fold cross-validation. If exact population margins are known, e.g., cross-tabulated population counts on age class, gender and region, the synthetic data must be calibrated to those known population margins. For this purpose, we have implemented a simulated annealing algorithm that is able to use multiple population margins simultaneously to post-calibrate a synthetic population. The algorithm is, thus, able to calibrate simulated population data containing cluster and individual information, e.g., about persons in households, at both person and household level. Furthermore, the algorithm is efficiently implemented so that the adjustment of populations with many millions or more persons is possible.

Keywords: privacy; complex survey data; synthetic populations; XGBoost; calibration of populations

1. Introduction

The generation of synthetic data is one way to comply with general data protection laws [1]. However, this is not the only way to solve the problem of confidentiality. Data can be shared in different forms. In traditional anonymization, data are anonymized under the paradigm of high data utility to create scientific or public use files. In this process, the data are altered so that the risk of disclosure to individuals falls below a certain threshold, under the condition that the data are as useful as possible. Remote execution, secure labs and remote access are other data-sharing options (with synthetic data required for remote execution). Query servers deal with perturbed aggregated results using differential privacy [2], secondary cell suppression [3], or the cellKey method [4] or target record swapping (see, e.g., [5]). Black-box methods for obtaining predictions on test data are a way to share not data but predictions on single sensitive variables without having access to training data. Typically, this is used in a federated learning environment where data sources are not centralized but distributed across multiple peers [6].

Synthetic data avoid the costly remote access and federated learning approaches and are an attractive and well-established alternative to the aforementioned approaches.

1.1. Synthetic Data

Synthetic data are used as training data in machine learning, for augmented data or in the form of population data, and as *twin* data for the public or for sharing within an organization to speed things up so that data can already be used before administrative issues regarding data access are solved. Instead of introducing changes in the original data, central structures of the data and relationships between variables are used to generate new data. The methods for creating synthetic data stem from the machine learning (ML), AI and statistical modeling domains. They learn the parameters of the models on the original data and use them to generate artificial data. Synthetic data are associated with low disclosure risk [7–9] and advantages in the simplicity of the process—once synthetic data are generated.

Synthetic data have surged in popularity and are now utilized across a myriad of scenarios where real-world data were traditionally employed. They offer a cost-effective and hassle-free testing environment that can subsequently be verified with real-world data. This shift underscores the significant role that synthetic data play in modern data analytics. This applies to various research areas. For instance, a commonly used synthetic data set in the literature are the synthetic data of the European Statistics on Income and Living Conditions (EU-SILC), created by [10], or the synthetic version of the Structure of Earnings Survey [11], both conducted in all member states of the European Union (as well as some other countries, such as Switzerland).

The basic motivation to create synthetic data is either to compare methods in simulation studies or to find a way to share confidential data. For both, the quality of synthetic data is crucial, and the synthetic data need to reflect the properties of real data.
But what is meant by close-to-reality/realistic data? (see, similarly, also [12])

- Socio-demographic-economic structure of persons and strata need to be reflected.
- Marginal distributions and interactions between variables should be represented correctly.
- Hierarchical and cluster structures have to be preserved.
- Certain marginal distributions must exactly match known values.
- Data confidentiality must be ensured; thus, replication of units (e.g., using a bootstrap approach) should be avoided.

1.2. Synthetic Populations

Simulating not only a sample survey but the entire population has some advantages. For example, in agent-based and/or micro-simulation approaches, information about individuals in the whole population is needed. For example, to simulate the epidemic spread of COVID-19 under certain conditions in a micro-simulation environment, socioeconomic and health information is needed on all individuals at a given time.

Note that if only a synthetic sample survey is required, it can be drawn from the synthetic population using a realistic sampling plan. In this way, the creation of the whole population is richer in application and more general.

Software for synthetic data simulation in `R` is, for example, provided by `synthpop` [13] for data without any of the mentioned complicated structures (e.g., persons in households) and surveys obtained with simple random sampling. `simPop` [14] is the only software that considers complex data sets to allow hierarchical and cluster structures and samples from complex survey designs, including sampling weights from complex sampling procedures. Realistic cluster structures are important, e.g., not to create households with only children or an 80-year-old mother with a young son, to give some simplified illustrative examples. `simPop` additionally allows for population simulation.

1.3. Non-Linear Synthesizers

Recently, non-linear methods from artificial neural networks have also been used to synthesize data, for example, using generative additive networks (GAN) [15] as a joint modeling approach. Clearly, using deep learning methods to learn all relationships, e.g., that a household cannot consist only of children or more complicated logical conditions, is often not possible and parameter tuning must be performed with great care. Also joint modeling of all variables in a data set is naturally only visible for a small number of variables, and it is quite obvious that, e.g., when applying a joint modeling approach (e.g., with GAN), it becomes too noisy with a high number of variables, e.g., when simulating a complex data set with 25 variables or more. This is also naturally true for LLMs used for synthetic data generation as, e.g., in [16].

Therefore, fully conditional modeling approaches come into play, where variables are simulated sequentially. A type of non-linear method that uses a fully conditional modeling approach and which is well implemented in software (e.g., in the `R` packages `synthpop` [13] and `simPop`) is random forest adapted to synthesize variables in a data set.

1.4. Calibration

One should not stop at having synthetic twin data sets simulated with a synthesizer, but additionally modify the synthetic data so that certain marginal sums match the original data set and/or known characteristics of the population. To give an illustrative example. Imagine a user calculating the total number of 45–50-year-old men and women for each region. He would be confused if the results from the synthetic data differed (even slightly) from the official figures from the national agency. Therefore, some marginal totals have to be estimated accurately with synthetic data, and synthetic data have to be calibrated to known population characteristics.

Calibration should always be used when auxiliary information is available [17], not only for the consistency named before, but also for the reason of using all available information that improves the synthetic data. In general, it can be said that there is no calibration approach if no auxiliary information is available, since there is nothing to calibrate against. In the case of synthetic data, either population characteristics are known from administrative data, or/and characteristics such as marginal totals are known from the original data. Calibration can, therefore, be used to adjust the synthetic population to the known external population totals.

In `R`, there is a lot of software for calculating calibration weights, e.g., the packages `survey` and `surveysd` are two of them. These weights are calibrated using auxiliary information from administrative registers, other accurate sources, or even original data sets. However, with these tools and methods, it is not possible to calibrate synthetic populations.

1.5. Calibration of Populations

The previously weight-based approaches cannot be used for synthetic populations because the selection probability of each individual in the population is 1 and, therefore, the weights should be 1. The recalibration step presented in this paper is a combinatorial optimization problem with the aim of drawing clusters (such as households) from the synthetic population (of individuals) in such a way that the difference between the margins from selection and a given set of population margins is minimized and substantially extends existing methods. In this way, the cluster information is preserved while the margins are respected.

In practice, it is a typical situation that auxiliary information is available not only for persons but also for households or enterprises (employers) and also for employees, etc. In this case, several different types of multiple margins are known, and these margins are defined for different types of units in a data set.

1.6. Outline

The framework and workflow are illustrated in Figure 1. Essentially, the framework comprises three steps, with the second and third steps introducing new contributions to literature and software. The three items below match the numbers in Figure 1.

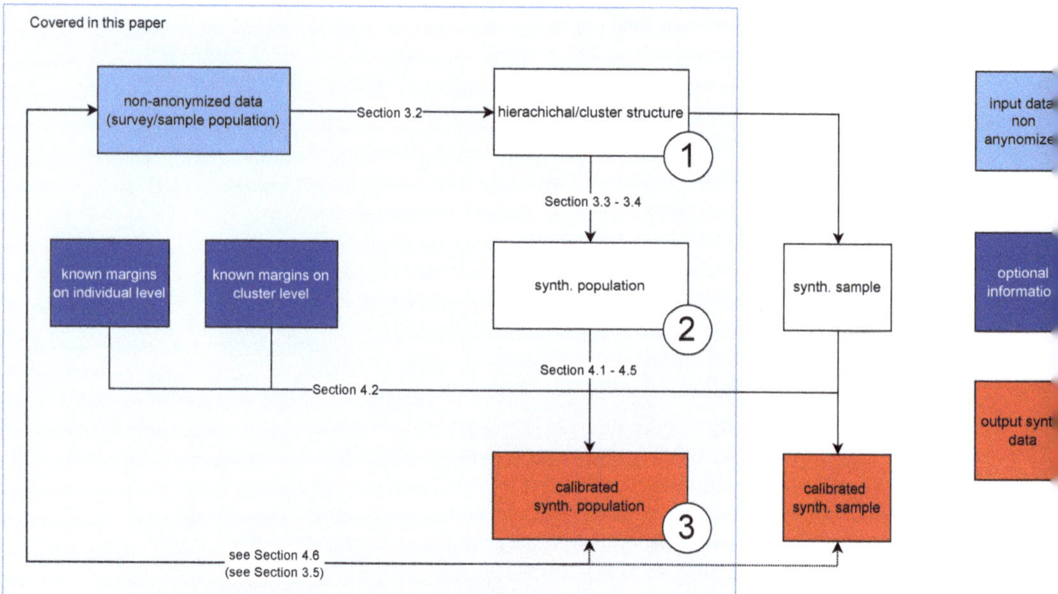

Figure 1. The workflow to produce a synthetic population and to calibrate it. The contribution covers the large light blue area together with the synthesis step 2 using XGBoost. The corresponding text passages are linked to section numbers in the Figure.

1. The synthetic hierarchical structure is simulated, e.g., age and gender of persons in households.
2. Synthetic data simulation with XGBoost to simulate synthetic population data with (possible) complex structures (like persons in households) from complex samples with (possible) complex sampling plans.
3. Calibration of the simulated population to known margins with a new calibration technique that allows multiple margins for different information (e.g., household information and personal information simultaneously).

All these steps might be needed to simulate realistic synthetic populations, and we show the benefits of these new developments.
The remainder of the essential parts of the article is structured as follows.

- In Section 2.3, the well-known XGBoost method is introduced in a general manner. After this short introduction, the simulation of the synthetic population is shown.
- The first aim is to create a synthetic structural file (Section 2.2, cf. Figure 1, first point) that includes the cluster information.
- Using the information of the non-anonymized data and the synthetic hierarchical/cluster structure, the remaining variables can now be simulated using XGBoost (cf. Figure 1, second point). While random forests build their regression trees independently (for each variable to be simulated), XGBoost improves the selection of trees at each step. XGBoost thus generally combines two important aspects: non-linear adjustments and improvements (due to a loss function) in each selected tree. The adaption of XGBoost to be used to simulate synthetic variables is described in Section 2.3.3 and the information used is visible in Figure 1. The cross-validation procedure to determine the hyperparameters in XGBoost is also reported in Section 2.3.4. After simulation of the synthetic population (see Figure 1, third step), the quality of the simulated data is discussed in Section 2.4.
- Section 3 then shows how the simulated population can be calibrated to known multiple population margins (e.g., margins on households and information on persons

in Section 3.2) considering the cluster structure in the data. Several subsections (Sections 3.3–3.5) are dedicated to this problem. Note that the draft version of this calibration method was already implemented in the R package `simPop` but has never been published in a scientific journal, and we have considerably extended the methods within this contribution.

- Section 3.6 shows the impact of calibration on several statistics.
- Section 4 discusses the implications of these methods for applications and science.
- Since we have also implemented the methods in software, we outline the use of this software using complex data sets in the Appendices A–C. The corresponding data set is described in Section 2.1. The illustration with code in an application allows the reader to see the connection from theory to application in software and to obtain an impression of how the methods can be used in practice.

2. Synthetic Data Generation

2.1. Data Set Used in the Method Application

This study uses the 2013 Austrian EU-SILC public use data set, consisting of 13,513 observations and 62 variables, to demonstrate developed methods. The EU-SILC survey collects cross-sectional and longitudinal data on income, poverty, social exclusion and living conditions from households and individuals across Europe, supporting the EU's social policy objectives. Data include detailed income components, social exclusion, housing conditions, labor, education and health information. The data are weighted for design and non-response, with stratification and calibration based on Austrian Census characteristics. For more details on data selection and variables, see Appendix A and sources given therein.

2.2. Simulation of Cluster Structures

As seen in Figure 1 (point 1), the first objective is to generate realistic cluster structures (such as households of persons). In this way (see also Figure 2), some basic variables, such as age and sex, are directly sampled from the survey. An example of an unrealistic household would be a household solely with children or a 95-year-old woman with a young child. As bootstrapping from the sample poses a risk of re-identification, as few variables as possible should be chosen in this step.

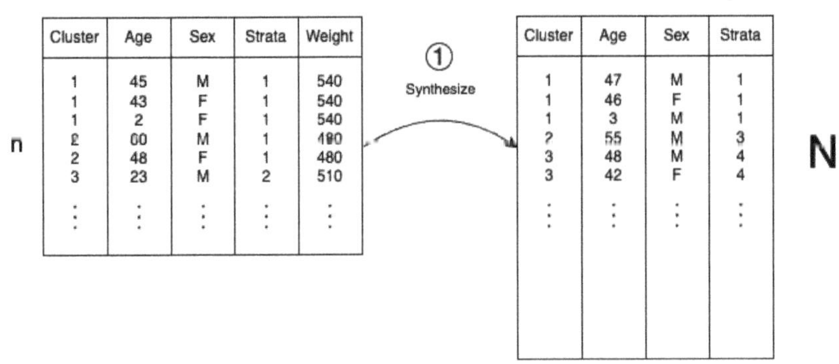

Figure 2. Step 1: To simulate a basic structure of the data, for example, here, the household structure by age and sex in each stratum and by considering the sampling weights. n determines the size of the data to be synthesized and N the size of the synthetic population. Unrealistic clusters (here, household compositions) are avoided.

The structure of the household of the synthetic population U' is generated separately for each combination of strata k and the size of the household l. The number of households by combination M_{kl} is estimated with the Horwitz–Thompson estimator from [18] by

$$\hat{M}_{kl} := \sum_{h \in H_{kl}^S} w_h \tag{1}$$

where H_{kl}^S is the set of all households in stratum k and w_h the household weights. To create realistic household structures, basic variables such as age or sex are sampled with the alias sampling method proposed by [19]. Each population household $h \in H_{kl}^U$ has a selection probability of

$$p_h = \frac{w_h}{\hat{M}_{kl}}. \tag{2}$$

To generate, for example, a household structure, input the cluster structure, stratification variable(s), and sampling weights of the data to be synthesized (see Algorithm 1).

Algorithm 1 Simulate cluster structure using `simPop`

1: Let `X` be the data to be synthesized.
2: **set** `inp` ▷ input data structure from the data set to be synthesized
  choose `clusterID` ▷ optional variable of `X` with cluster information
  choose `strata` ▷ optional variable(s) of `X` with stratification information
  choose `weight` ▷ optional variable of `X` with sampling weights
3: **set** `basicVariables` ▷ basic variables (such as age and gender)
4: Estimate the number of households $\hat{M}_{kl}$ in the population using Equation (1)
5: Calculate selection probabilities p_h for clusters from Equation (2)
6: **create** `simPop` ← simulate structure (`X`, `inp`, `basicVariables`, $\hat{M}_{kl}$, p_h)

The code snipped in Appendix C.1 shows the detailed application in software using `simPop`.

2.3. *Synthetic Data Generation with XGBoost*

2.3.1. General Comments on XGBoost

Extreme Gradient Boosting (XGBoost) is a highly sophisticated distributed gradient boosting algorithm. XGBoost builds many consecutive decision trees to correct errors in previous trees. There are two main types of decision trees: classification and regression trees. XGBoost works for both regression and classification, and both types are implemented in various software products, such as the R package `XGBoost` (see [20]).

Boosting is an ensemble method with its origin in computer science, which is opposite to the statistical approach of bagging (bootstrap aggregating) used in random forests. The general idea is to boost the performance of weak learners, which are slightly better than random chance, by weighting and combining them. Gradient boosting is the formulation of the boosting approach as gradient descent optimization with an arbitrary differentiable loss function. It then minimizes the loss by iteratively adding regression (or classification) trees, also known as CART (Classification and Regression Tree). Since overfitting is a massive problem in regression trees, ref. [20] proposed adding a regularization term. This regularization is similar to the regularized greedy forest (RGF) of [21] and favors smaller and more predictive trees. In addition to the first regularization method, ref. [20] included two other regularization techniques: shrinkage developed by [22] and feature (column) subsampling used in random forest. The latter improves the computation time and prevents overfitting. Shrinkage scales newly added weights, and thus decreases the dependency on individual trees. Furthermore, ref. [20] introduced an evaluation function to measure the quality of a tree structure, which is similar to the tree impurity function used in decision trees and random forest. Ref. [20] added more improvements to standard tree boosting.

2.3.2. Advantages of XGBoost for Synthetic Data Generation

- Ensemble methods such as XGBoost are widely used in the data science community due to their solid out-of-the-box performance [23] allowing, e.g., also non-linear relationships. This solid out-of-the-box performance makes the XGBoost algorithm an optimal candidate for synthetic data generation, as the underlying distributions are often unknown.
- The key improvements to previous ensemble methods are subsampling the data set with replacement and choosing a random feature set. These improvements lead to highly independent base classifiers, and thus the XGBoost algorithm is robust to overfitting.
- The XGBoost algorithm is scalable and generally faster than the classical gradient boost machine (GBM), which makes it an excellent choice for generating large synthetic data sets.
- Another important advance that makes this algorithm convenient in practice is its sparsity awareness. With the sparsity-aware split finding, it works with missing values by default. The split-finding algorithm learns the default direction at each branch directly from the non-missing data.
- Cache awareness and out-of-core computing are improvements that allow XGBoost for parallel computing.
- For both regression and classification, both types are implemented in various software products, such as the R package `XGBoost` (see [20]).

However, if existing XGBoost implementations are used without adaptations to simulate synthetic data, complex structures, such as people in households and complex sample designs, cannot be taken into account. In this contribution and the software provided `simPop`, the application of XGBoost is adapted in such a way (see Section 2.3.3) to allow synthesizing complex data and procedures made available for hyperparameter tuning. In this contribution, we have adapted the application of XGBoost (and provided the new tools in the software `simPop`) to synthesize complex data. We have also made available procedures for hyperparameter tuning. See Section 2.3.3 for more details.

2.3.3. Sequentional Approach to Simulate Variables of a Data Set Using XGBoost

After the simulation of the household structure of the population, other variables can be generated (cf. Figure 1, point 2). An additional variable is simulated using the (simplified) scheme below. In the XGBoost training step, one response variable of the original survey $\mathbf{S}$ is predicted using variables $\mathbf{x}^S_{\cdot,1}, \ldots, \mathbf{x}^S_{\cdot,j}$ as a predictor matrix with n observations and j dimension. The predictors must already be simulated in the synthetic data set.

$$\mathbf{S} = \begin{pmatrix} \overbrace{\begin{matrix} x^S_{1,1} & x^S_{1,2} & \cdots & x^S_{1,j} \\ x^S_{2,1} & x^S_{2,2} & \cdots & x^S_{2,j} \\ \vdots & \vdots & \ddots & \vdots \\ x^S_{n,1} & x^S_{n,2} & \cdots & x^S_{n,j} \end{matrix}}^{\text{predictors}} & \overbrace{\begin{matrix} x^S_{1,j+1} \\ x^S_{2,j+1} \\ \vdots \\ x^S_{n,j+1} \end{matrix}}^{\text{response}} & \overbrace{\begin{matrix} x^S_{1,j+2} \\ x^S_{2,j+2} \\ \vdots \\ x^S_{n,j+2} \end{matrix}}^{\text{additional}} & \begin{matrix} \cdots \\ \cdots \\ \cdots \\ \cdots \end{matrix} \end{pmatrix} \tag{3}$$

In the synthesis step, the new variable in position $j+1$ is generated for the synthesized population U with observations N using a prediction with the XGboost parameters formerly trained.

$$\mathbf{U}' = \begin{pmatrix} \overbrace{x^{U'}_{1,1} & x^{U'}_{1,2} & \cdots & x^{U'}_{1,j}}^{\text{input}} & \overbrace{x^{U'}_{1,j+1}}^{\text{predicted}} & \overbrace{x^{U'}_{1,j+2}}^{\text{next}} & \cdots \\ x^{U'}_{2,1} & x^{U'}_{2,2} & \cdots & x^{U'}_{2,j} & x^{U'}_{2,j+1} & x^{U'}_{2,j+2} & \cdots \\ \vdots & \vdots & \ddots & \vdots & \vdots & \vdots & \cdots \\ x^{U'}_{N,1} & x^{U'}_{n,2} & \cdots & x^{U'}_{N,j} & x^{U'}_{N,j+1} & x^{U'}_{N,j+2} & \cdots \end{pmatrix} \tag{4}$$

After simulating the $j+1$ variable, the training of the parameters for the next $(j+2)$ variable can be performed again based on the original data set, and the $j+1$ variable can be generated for the population using the trained parameters for the already simulated input variables. Please note that the "predictors" in Equations (3) and (4) may not represent directly the predictor variables but a design matrix that also reflects interactions of predictor variables, transformations of predictors, quadratic terms of predictors, etc.

In our case, the generation of additional categorical values is performed by sampling from conditional distributions estimated by an XGBoost classifier. For each stratum, the XGBoost model is fitted to the sample data $\mathbf{x}^S_{j+1}$ with the variables $x^S_{1j+1}, \ldots, x^S_{nj+1}$, where n is the number of individuals in the sample S. Each record is weighted by the respective sampling weights $\mathbf{w} = (w_1, \ldots, w_n)'$. For each stratum k and the synthetic population variable $\mathbf{x}^{U'}_j = (x^{U'}_{1j}, \ldots, x^{U'}_{Nj})'$, the conditional probabilities $p^{U'}_{ir} := P(x^{U'}_{ij} = r | x^{U'}_{i,1}, \ldots, x^{U'}_{i,j})$ of the new variable $\mathbf{x}^{U'}_{j+1}$ are estimated from the already generated variables $\mathbf{x}^{U'}_1 \ldots \mathbf{x}^{U'}_j$ by the XGBoost algorithm with the softmax objective functions (see Equation (5)).

$$\hat{p}^{U'}_{i,r} = \frac{e^{z_{i,r}}}{\sum_{j=1}^{R} e^{z_{j,r}}}, \tag{5}$$

where $r \in \{1, \ldots, R\}$ is the set of R categories and $z_{i,r}$ is the XGBoost prediction score for the respective category r. The category of $x_{n,j+1}$ is then chosen with a weighted sampling, where the weights are the estimated conditional probabilities $\hat{p}^{U'}_{i,r}$.

The proposed method has the advantage that predicted variables can contain random zeros, which are combinations that do not occur in the sample but are present in the population. Algorithm 2 describes how to generate additional categorical variables. XGBoost has many hyperparameters, such as the learning rate (η), minimum loss reduction to make further partitions (γ), and the maximum depth of the tree.

In Appendix C.2, it is shown how to simulate in an exemplary way two new variables (economic status and citizenship of a person) in software.

In addition to categorical variables, an XGBoost implementation is also available for continuous variables. The `simPop` function `simContinuous` has a similar structure to that of its categorical counterpart but is not further explained in this paper.

2.3.4. Modified k-Fold Cross-Validation

To tune the XGBoost hyperparameters accordingly, a slightly modified k-fold cross-validation procedure is proposed. For every additional variable $\mathbf{x}^{U'}_j$, the hyperparameter grid is k-fold cross-validated on the resulting new synthetic variable compared to the sample variable $\mathbf{x}^S_j$.

The basis of comparing the sample and the synthetic population variable is computing a weighted contingency table. Each $t^{S,U'}_i$ of the one-dimensional contingency tables $\mathbf{t}^S$ and $\mathbf{t}^{U'}$ with R categories is estimated by the Horwitz–-Thompson estimator. Then, the residuals (e) are calculated by

$$e_i = t^{U'}_i - t^S_i \tag{6}$$

and the MSE is used to compare the discrepancies between the expected t_i^S and the realized $t_i^{U'}$ frequencies.

$$\text{MSE} = \frac{1}{n}\sum_{i=1}^{n}(e_i)^2 \tag{7}$$

The hyperparameters with the lowest average MSE are then used to generate the variable for the synthetic population U'.

A grid/combination of various hyperparameters can be set for which the optimal combination is then selected. Such hyperparameters are, for example, the maximum depth of a tree, the learning rate and the evaluation metric. A complete list is provided here https://xgboost.readthedocs.io/en/latest/parameter.html (accessed on 6 May 2024).

Algorithm 2 Simulate an Additional Variable using `XGBoost`

Use `X` the data to be synthesized
choose one of the following:
  Option 1: **set** `simPop` ← result from Algorithm 1
  Option 2: **set** `simPop` ← result from Algorithm 1 plus already simulated additional variables with Algorithm 2.
set `availablevars` ← variables of `simPop`
set `newvar` ← variable to be simulated in the synthetic population
Define model parameters for the XGBoost algorithm

- **set** `max.depth` $\in [0, \infty]$ ▷ maximum depth of a tree. 0: no limit on depth.
- **set** `eta` $\in [0, 1]$ ▷ learning rate. The higher the more conservative boosting.
- **set** `gamma` $\in [0, \infty]$ ▷ minimum loss reduction required
- **set** . . . ▷ additional hyperparameters

set `objective` ← "multi:softprob" for categorical response und squared error für continuous response as default (can be overwritten)
Initialize `xgboost_params` with `max.depth`, `eta`, `gamma`, `...`, `objective`
`fitted_params` ← train XGBoost (`X`, `availablevars`, `newvar`, `model_params`) . Fit on the data to be synthetized using the same variables as contained in `simPop` and `newvar` as shown in Equation (3). ▷ Hyperparameter training with cross validation
update `simPop` ← simulate variable (`simPop`, `availablevars`, `newvar`, `xgboost_params`, `fitted_params`) ▷ Demonstrated in Equation (4)

Appendix C.3 shows a selection of hyperparameters and the corresponding cross-validation procedure with the help of the R package `simPop`.

2.4. Synthetic Data Validation

Evaluating the quality of simulated synthetic data is a crucial step to ensure that the generated data are useful, reliable and fit for their intended purpose. The primary dimensions and methods used to assess synthetic data quality from an "absolute" perspective are the following:

- **Statistical similarity** measures how well the synthetic data replicate the statistical properties of the real data. Key aspects include descriptive statistics, distributional properties and correlation structures.
- **Data utility** measures how well synthetic data can be used in place of real data for specific tasks. This includes the predictive performance by training the machine learning models on the synthetic data and evaluating their performance on real data. Moreover, models trained on synthetic data should generalize well to real data, indicating that the synthetic data capture the essential patterns and relationships.
- **Integrity and consistency checks** ensure that the synthetic data maintain logical and business rules inherent in the real data:
- While synthetic data should closely resemble real data, they should also introduce some **variability**, e.g., ensure the synthetic data contain new combinations of features

that are plausible within the context of the real data but were not present in the original data set.

In the following, we concentrate on statistical similarity and utility, indicating that variability is guaranteed by the simPop framework and consistency is mainly modeled by design (see Section 2.2).

The newly proposed XGBoost synthetic generation method was compared to the multinomial approach developed by [14]. Both methods generated 100 synthetic versions of the Austrian European Union Statistics on Income and Living Conditions (EU-SILC) survey from 2019. First, a single generated synthetic population is examined, and second, all 100 synthetic populations together are compared. The mosaic plots in Figure 3 show the comparison for a single synthetic population for the two categorical variables, marital status (P114000) and chronic disease (P103000). The red areas show a lower than expected group frequency, so under-representation of the respective group, whereas the blue areas indicate an over-representation. The XGBoost approach shows promising results, as the overall deviation from the sample is smaller than that of the multinomial approach. As this is only an excerpt of one combination of one generated population, Figure 4 shows a comparison across all 100 synthetic populations. The color scale ranges from white (small mean chi-square test statistic) to red (large mean chi-square test statistic) for the variable combinations. As seen for the single population comparison, the multi-run comparison confirmed the good performance of the XGBoost approach.

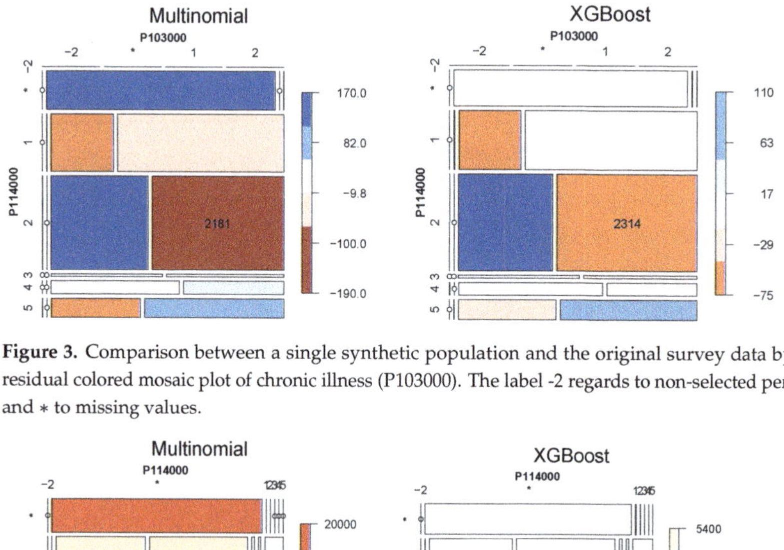

Figure 3. Comparison between a single synthetic population and the original survey data by the residual colored mosaic plot of chronic illness (P103000). The label -2 regards to non-selected persons and ∗ to missing values.

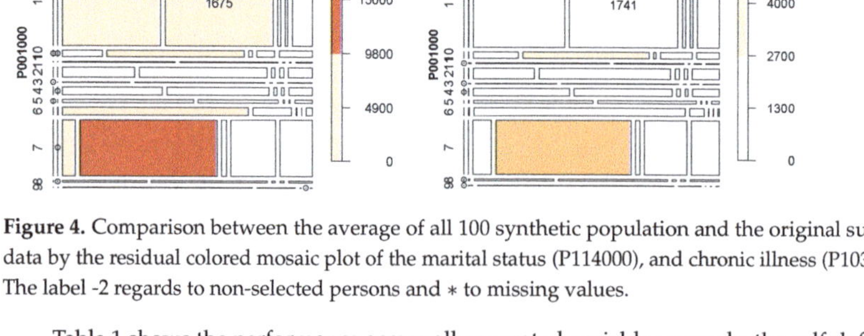

Figure 4. Comparison between the average of all 100 synthetic population and the original survey data by the residual colored mosaic plot of the marital status (P114000), and chronic illness (P103000). The label -2 regards to non-selected persons and ∗ to missing values.

Table 1 shows the performance across all generated variables, namely, the self-defined current economic status (P001000), citizenship (P111010nu), marital status (P114000) and highest level of education achieved (P137000) in all synthetic populations, and chronic illness (P103000). The XGBoost approach outperforms the multinomial for all three performance metrics: mean squared error (MSE), mean absolute error (MAE) and the χ^2 test statistics.

Table 1. Overview of the categorical performance metrics for both XGBoost and multinomial approach across all generated 100 synthetic populations.

	MSE	MAE	χ^2 Test Statistics
Multinomial	42	0.42	117.381
XGBoost	5	0.21	121.291

3. Calibration of a Population

3.1. Post-Calibration with Combinatorial Optimization

The post-calibration step can be described as a combinatorial optimization problem that aims to select households from the synthetic population in such a way that the difference between the margins from the selection and a given set of population margins is minimized. To be more precise, let $\mathbf{U}'$ be a synthetic population generated from a sample $\mathbf{S}$, let $f(\mathbf{t}, \hat{\mathbf{t}})$ be an objective function that measures the difference between two sets of margins $\mathbf{t}$ and $\hat{\mathbf{t}}$, then the optimization problem can be defined as follows:

$$\min_{\hat{\mathbf{t}}} f(\mathbf{t}, \hat{\mathbf{t}}) \tag{8}$$

$$\hat{\mathbf{t}} = \begin{pmatrix} \hat{t}_1 \\ \vdots \\ \hat{t}_M \end{pmatrix} \tag{9}$$

$$\hat{t}_m = \sum_{i=1}^{N} \delta_i \mathbf{1}_{[\text{individual } i \text{ part of margin cell } m]} \quad m = 1, \ldots, M \tag{10}$$

$$\delta_i \in \{0,1\},\ i = 1, \ldots, N \tag{11}$$

$$\delta_i = \delta_j \ \forall \text{ individuals } j \text{ in same household as individual } i, \tag{12}$$

with N as the number of people in the synthetic population and $\mathbf{1}_{[.]}$ representing the indicator functions that equal 1 if the expression in [.] is true. The vectors $\mathbf{t}$ and $\hat{\mathbf{t}}$ represent the target population margins and the population margins of the selected synthetic population, respectively. Each t_m, $m = 1, \ldots, M$ contains the number of people for a set of variables, e.g., number of people by age, sex and geographic region. Setting $\delta_i = 1$ implies that the individual i is selected from the synthetic population $\mathbf{U}'$, and to preserve the household structure, so are all individuals j belonging to the same household as the individual i.

The use of combinatorial optimization to create synthetic populations was presented in [24,25]. Since such problems are difficult to solve, they are often split into several smaller problems by dividing the synthetic population into non-overlapping groups, typically representing small geographical areas for which the margins $\mathbf{t}$ are available. Many smaller problems are easier to solve than one large problem. When solving combinatorial optimization problems, so-called metaheuristics are usually used. These algorithms try to comb the search space of possible solutions in an efficient way to find at least a local minima of $f()$ in a reasonable amount of time. The meta-heuristic used in this contribution is the so-called simulated annealing algorithm (SA; [26,27]). SA is inspired by a physical process in which the material is cooled in a controlled manner. The pseudo-code of the SA as implemented in `simPop` for the post-calibration problem is presented in Algorithm 3.

A more detailed description of the SA algorithm is given in the Appendix B.1.

An important aspect of SA is that worse solutions can be accepted, especially at the beginning of the algorithm when the temperature T is high. This can prevent SA from getting trapped in local optima. Ref. [28] compared the SA algorithm with deterministic re-weighting and conditional probabilities to create a synthetic population at different spatial scales and concluded that the SA algorithm consistently outperformed the other two methods.

Algorithm 3 has the following disadvantages:

- It is only possible to supply one target distribution $\mathbf{t}$ as constraint. This can be a major limitation if only the marginal and not the joint distribution of variables for re-calibration are not available or accessible.
- Convergence of the SA is very slow because households are replaced using simple random sampling. Applying this algorithm to real-world applications, a population of tens of millions of people will yield costly run times and possibly fail to converge.
- Parameters T, c and n can strongly influence the convergence of the SA and adopting the choice of these parameters when the problem is split into multiple smaller subgroups is not supported.

Algorithm 3 Calibration of the Synthetic Population using Simulated Annealing

1: Set starting values regarding:
  - Maximum number of iterations
  - Starting temperature T, cooldown rate and maximum number of cooldowns c
  - Initial swap rate n
  - Allowed relative error $\epsilon > 0$

2: Initialize a first selection $\Delta = (\delta_1, \ldots, \delta_{N'})$, calculate initial synthetic margins $\mathbf{m}$, and the value of the objective function:

$$Obj = f(\mathbf{t}, \hat{\mathbf{t}}) = \sum_{m=1}^{M} |t_m - \hat{t}_m|$$

3: Randomly add and remove n persons, including all household members, resulting in a new selection Δ_{new}.
4: Calculate the new value of the objective function Obj_{new} using Δ_{new}.
5: **if** $\frac{Obj_{new}}{N} \leq \epsilon$ **then**
6:     Convergence reached, terminate the algorithm and return Δ_{new}.
7: **end if**
8: **if** $Obj_{new} < Obj$ **then**
9:     Update $\Delta \leftarrow \Delta_{new}$.
10: **else**
11:     Update current selection Δ with new selection Δ_{new} if $u < \exp\left(-\frac{Obj_{new} - Obj}{T}\right)$ where u is drawn from $U(0,1)$; otherwise, keep Δ.
12: **end if**
13: Increment counters and reduce temperature, if needed.
14: **if** Maximum number of iteration or minimum temperature reached **then**
15:     Terminate the algorithm and return current selection Δ.
16: **else**
17:     Go to step 3.
18: **end if**

In [29], applying the SA algorithm to a synthetic population of the Bangladesh Coastal Zone revealed various challenges. The population, which consists of 37.2 million individuals, was generated using a micro data set from the 2011 Bangladesh National Census through IPUMS (see [30]). The improvements to the SA algorithm discussed here are largely influenced by its application to this real-life data set. Subsequently, we will present the SA improvements in detail.

3.2. Including Multiple Different Target Margins

The SA has been adopted to support the use of multiple target margins that can refer to margins of persons and households, e.g., number of persons by age and geographic region and number of households by tenancy and geographic region.

Let $\mathbf{t}_1, \ldots, \mathbf{t}_M$ be the different set of target population margins, where each $\mathbf{t}_i$ contains the population totals on either number of households or number of people, for a set of variables, e.g., number of households by household size and geographic region.

$$\mathbf{t}_m = \begin{pmatrix} t_{m,1} \\ \vdots \\ t_{m,R_m} \end{pmatrix} \quad m = 1, \ldots, M \tag{13}$$

In addition, let $\hat{\mathbf{t}}_1, \ldots, \hat{\mathbf{t}}_M$ be the corresponding number of households or people in the current synthetic population. We propose the following objective function when dealing with multiple sets of margins:

$$f(\mathbf{t}, \hat{\mathbf{t}}) = \sqrt{\frac{1}{M} \sum_{m=1}^{M} \left(\sum_{r=1}^{R_m} |t_{m,r} - \hat{t}_{m,r}| \right)^2} \ . \tag{14}$$

For the case $p = 1$, where only one contingency table is used, this objective function reduces to the sum of the absolute differences between the target and synthetic margins. Although not explicitly needed to apply the SA algorithm, it is strongly recommended that the sum over each of the margins $\mathbf{t}_1, \ldots, \mathbf{t}_M$ yields either the same number of households or the same number of people.

$$\sum_{r=1}^{R_m} t_{m,r} = \begin{cases} N_H & \text{if } \mathbf{t_m} \text{ corresponds to household margins} \\ N_P & \text{if } \mathbf{t_m} \text{ corresponds to person margins} \end{cases} \tag{15}$$

$$m = 1, \ldots, M \tag{16}$$

With changing the objective function $f(\mathbf{t}, \hat{\mathbf{t}})$, we also slightly adopted the termination criterion, which means that the SA algorithm will terminate if

$$\begin{aligned} N_H \epsilon_H &\geq \sum_{r=1}^{R_m} |t_{m,r} - \hat{t}_{m,r}| \quad \text{if } \mathbf{t_m} \text{ corresponds to household margins} \\ N_P \epsilon_P &\geq \sum_{r=1}^{R_m} |t_{m,r} - \hat{t}_{m,r}| \quad \text{if } \mathbf{t_m} \text{ corresponds to person margins} \end{aligned} \tag{17}$$

for all $m = 1, \ldots, M$, where ϵ_H and $\epsilon_P \in (0, 1)$ and N_H and N_P refer to the number of households and people in the target margins, respectively. ϵ_H and ϵ_P can be loosely interpreted as the maximum allowed average rate of the absolute difference between the target margins $\mathbf{t}_1, \ldots, \mathbf{t}_M$ and the margins of the current selection Δ. Equation (17) allows the SA algorithm to terminate even if for not all cells of the target margins the absolute difference is lower than $\frac{N_H}{R_m}\epsilon_H$ or $\frac{N_P}{R_m}\epsilon_P$, making the use of very detailed target margins more feasible.

3.3. Efficient Re-Sampling of Households

The slow convergence rate of the SA can be improved by selecting and deselecting individuals in a more targeted way. Instead of a purely random sample of individuals, the improved version of the SA selects individuals with a certain probability. For individuals belonging to margins where the current person or household count is higher (lower) than specified by the target margins, they should be deselected (selected) with a higher probability. Thus, the improved sampling aims to calculate sampling probabilities for each person based on their impact on the objective function. Let us denote $e_{m,r}$ as the differences between the target population counts, $t_{m,r}$, and the synthetic counts $\hat{t}_{m,r}$

$$e_{m,r} = t_{m,r} - \hat{t}_{m,r} \quad r = 1, \ldots, R; \; t = 1, \ldots, M_r. \tag{18}$$

For each individual i, we calculate the values $e_{1,r(1,i)}, \ldots, e_{M,r(M,i)}$, which correspond to all the differences between the target and the synthetic counts for the categories the individual i is part of. When adding persons and subsequently households, e.g., changing δ_i from 0 to 1, we propose a sampling probability p_i for individual i with

$$p_i = \begin{cases} \frac{v_i}{N_i} & \text{if } v_i > 0 \\ \exp(-\sum\limits_{u: v_u \leq 0} \frac{v_u}{N_u}) & \text{otherwise} \end{cases} \tag{19}$$

with

$$v_i = \frac{1}{M} \sum_{m=1}^{M} \left| e_{m,r(m,i)} \right| \cdot \operatorname{sgn}\left(\sum_{m=1}^{M} e_{m,r(m,i)} \right) \tag{20}$$

and N_i as the number of people in the synthetic population that belong to the same set of margins $t_{1,r(1,i)}, \ldots, t_{M,r(M,i)}$ as individual i. If $v_i < 0$, individuals belonging to the same set of margins as individual i are over-represented in the synthetic data, e.g., individual i should not be additionally included to the synthetic population. In this case, i has a diminishing small sampling probability $\exp(-\sum\limits_{u: v_u \leq 0} \frac{v_u}{N_u})$. In the case $p = 1$, the sampling probability reduces to

$$\frac{e_{1,r(i)}}{N_i} = \frac{t_{1,r(i)} - \hat{t}_{1,r(i)}}{N_i}, \tag{21}$$

with the objective function $\sum\limits_{i=r}^{R_1} |t_{1,r} - \hat{t}_{1,r}|$. That is, the sampling probability for the individual i is proportional to $t_{1,r(i)} - \hat{t}_{1,r(i)}$, in other words, its contribution to the objective function. The sampling probability for removing individuals from the synthetic population, e.g., changing δ_i from 1 to 0, is calculated in the same way as described before with the only difference that $e_{m,r}$ is calculated by

$$e_{m,r} = \hat{t}_{m,r} - t_{m,r}, \quad m = 1, \ldots, M, \; r = 1, \ldots, R_m. \tag{22}$$

Since sampling with probability can be very computationally intensive if the set to be drawn from is very large, e.g., exceeds the order of 10^4, we use the efficient implementation for weighted sampling from the R package `wrswoR` (see [31]).

3.4. Initialise and Adjust Number of Swaps N

The initial number of swaps (n) significantly affects the convergence of the Simulated Annealing (SA) algorithm. A high n increases the acceptance rate of worse solutions, while a low n limits improvement of the objective function. The initial swap rate n should depend on the objective function and population size, with a practical starting value given by specific equations. The swap rate can be adjusted during the SA process to maintain population stability and ensure convergence. Appendix B.2 reports the details of selecting the number of swaps.

3.5. Automatically Choosing T and Forcing Cooldowns

The starting temperature T also influences SA convergence; too high a T causes aimless searching, while too low a T risks premature convergence to a local optimum. The temperature T_{adj} can be adjusted automatically based on the objective function. Additionally, a procedure to force cooldowns helps avoid stagnation by reducing iterations if the objective function remains unchanged over several iterations. Details on the automatic choice of T are given in Appendix B.3.

3.6. Application of the SA Algorithm

The SA algorithm including the improvements is fully implemented in the function `calibPop()` in the R package `simPop`. Some parameters have been added that reflect various hyperparameters described above (see Appendix B.4).

For demonstration purposes, we post-calibrate the synthetic population from the previous section and use the data set `eusilcP` as the target population. We choose the following two post-calibration scenarios to highlight the improvements to the algorithm:

- Post-calibrate the synthetic population on a single target margin using the number of individuals by region, gender and citizenship
- Post-calibrate the synthetic population on two target margins using the number of individuals by region, gender and citizenship and number of households by region and household size.

In both scenarios, a value of $\epsilon = 0.1$ was set as default. The R code to apply the post-calibration scenarios to the synthetic data can be found in the Appendix C under Appendices C.4 and C.5. We performed this calculation on a server running Ubuntu 18.04 Intel(R) Xeon(R) CPU E5-2690 v4 @ 2.60 GHz with 8 cores and 125 GB memory. With the improved version of SA using only the single target margin, the algorithm converges in a few seconds instead of almost 50 min when using the older version implemented in `simPop 1.2.1`. When running the improved version with $\epsilon = 0.01$, it converges in almost 10 s.

The results of the first scenario are shown in Figure 5, where the distribution of the variables used for post-calibration is displayed. The colors indicate the distribution before calibration, after calibration using the old implementation `SA 1.2.1`, the improved implementation `SA 2.1.2` and the improved implementation using $\epsilon = 0.01$ `SA eps = 0.01`. The black lines represent the target distribution. Citizenship `pb220a` is shown in the horizontal panels and gender `rb090` in the vertical panels. The distributions using the improved method seem to be more similar to the target margins, especially for large populations, e.g., the box on the left for people with the nationality "AT". Table 2 shows the mean absolute error (MAE), the mean absolute percentage error (MAPE), as well as the average Aitchison distance (see [32,33]), compared to the target distribution. Using the improved implementation instead of the old, the MAE and MAPE are drastically reduced, especially for $\epsilon = 0.01$. For the average Aitchison distance, we observe similar values for the old and new improvements, but again a drastic improvement for $\epsilon = 0.01$.

Figure 6 shows the results of the second scenario using two target distributions—one for the number of individuals and one for the number of households As a comparison the distribution before calibration and the distribution using only one set of target margins are displayed. The upper part of the Figure 6 shows that the margins for the number of people are reproduced slightly worse when multiple margins are used. The distribution on the number of households is, however, represented better when also considered during calibration, as can be seen in the bottom part of Figure 6.

Table 3 shows the MAE, the MAPE and the average Aitchison distance compared to the target distribution for the second scenario. Using multiple margins yields slighter higher error measures for the person margins but much lower ones for the household margins. The household margins before the calibration yield a low average Aitchison distance because the relative distribution is already quite similar to the relative target distribution.

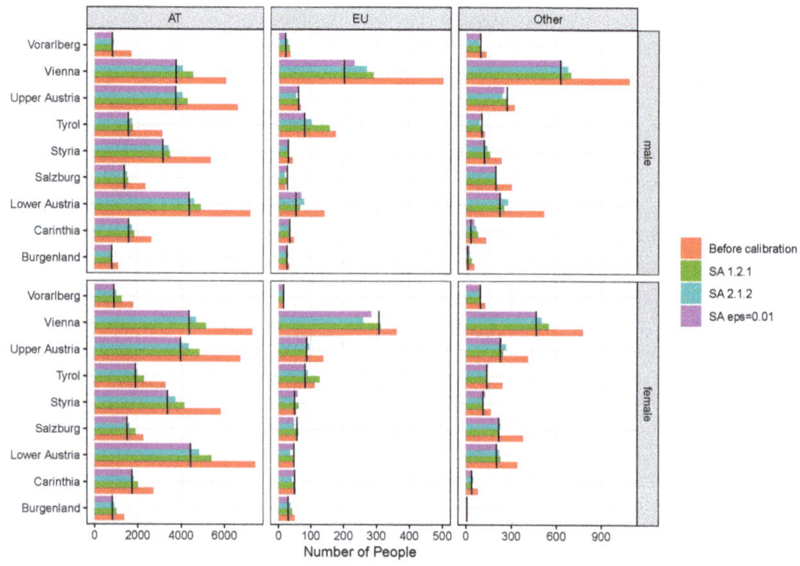

Figure 5. Distribution of people after post-calibration by variables "db040", citizenship (horizontal panels) and gender (vertical panels). Colored bars show the distribution after applying the old version of calibPop (SA 1.2.1), the improved version of calibPop (SA 2.1.2) and the improved version of calibPop with $\epsilon = 0.01$. The black lines represent the target distribution, the red bars the distribution before calibration.

Table 2. Mean absolute error, mean absolute percentage error and average Aitchison distance between target totals and population totals before and after calibration from the first scenario.

	MAE	MAPE	Avg. Aitchison
Before calibration	618.31	71.31	2.52
SA 1.2.1	158.47	22.13	1.68
SA 2.1.2	75.26	17.36	1.73
SA $\epsilon = 0.01$	8.02	7.41	1.27

Table 3. Mean absolute error, mean absolute percentage error and average Aitchison distance between target totals and population totals before and after calibration from calibration from the first scenario.

		MAE	MAPE	Avg. Aitchison
Person margins	Before calibration	618.20	71.31	2.52
	Single margins	75.26	17.36	1.73
	Multiple margins	80.44	29.72	2.33
Household margins	Before calibration	280.22	40.03	0.31
	Single margins	113.19	16.83	1.24
	Multiple margins	54.72	9.75	0.48

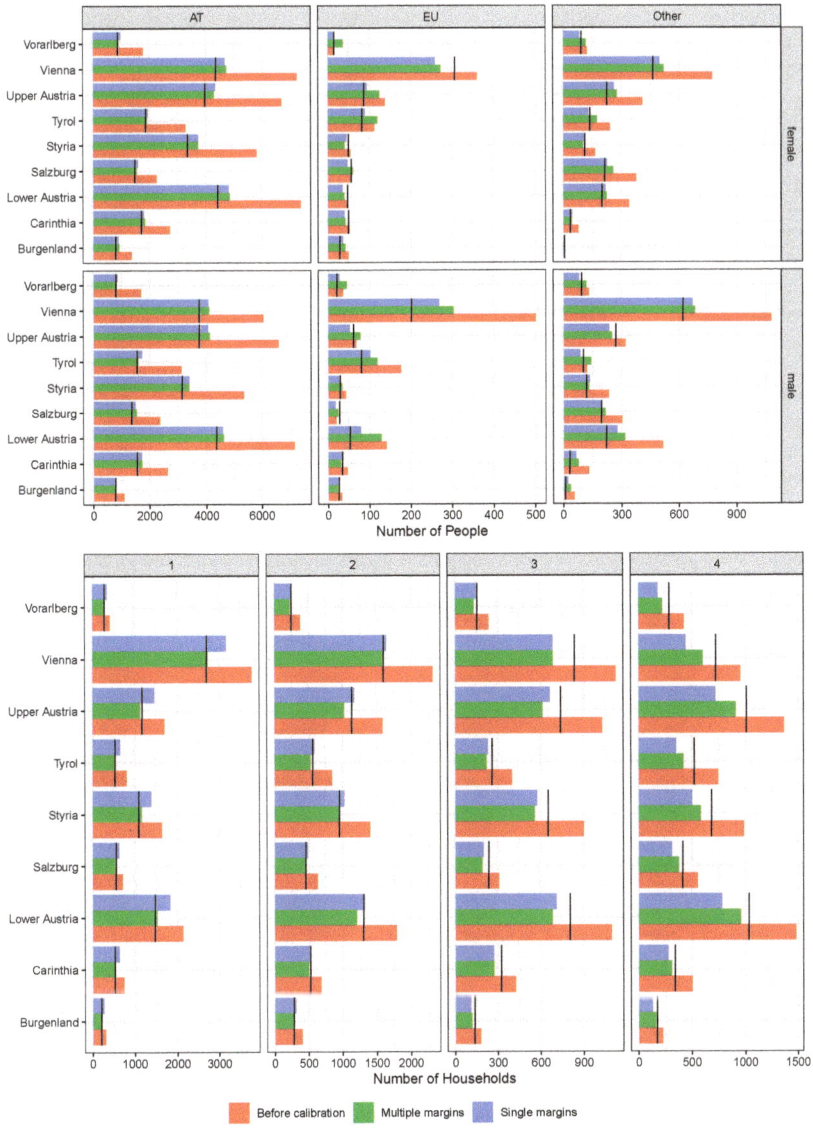

Figure 6. Distribution of people (left side) and households after post-calibration. The colors indicate using only one set of target margins (single margins) on people and target margins on people and households simultaneously (multiple margins). The black lines represent the target distribution, the red bars the distribution before calibration.

4. Conclusions

Important improvements for the synthesis of complex data sets using the R package simPop were presented. Although the methods work to simulate synthetic data from simple structured data sets, they are also able to deal with more complex situations that are not addressed in the literature or other software. The methods can also be used for complex samples conducted with complex survey designs and calibrated samples that additionally contain information on multiple margins of different types of unit (e.g., persons and households). Thus, values on specified margins of the synthesized data correspond to the values of margins of the original data and/or the additional information on known population characteristics.

With the presented methods and tools, one can even create a whole population from a complex sample. This is especially important for micro-simulation and agent-based simulations. Hereby, in a first step, a population is generated with the help of our presented methods. For micro-simulation tasks, this population is then stochastically extrapolated up to a defined time horizon, taking into account various relevant scenarios, e.g., for policy measures, demographic development, migration, etc. The base population is then used as a proxy for the real and unknown population.

Another important feature not detailed in this paper is that the synthetic data set can be generated from multiple inputs. These inputs can be census or sample data.

The integration of XGBoost as a fully conditional simulation method into the R package simPop has been carried out in such a way that it fully matches the S4 class structure of the package to allow its application to data including the challenges mentioned. In addition, hyperparameter tuning is built-in—an important point in achieving better results than with fixed default settings. XGBoost has been shown to be a competitive method for synthesizing data. Realistic cluster structures and logical conditions are naturally considered by construction, and multiple relationships are considered by sequentially synthesizing variables.

After synthesizing the data, we developed a post-calibration to calibrate for multiple margins. It is now possible to calibrate against multiple margins even if they are defined for different types of units (e.g., persons and households) at the same time.

All of these improvements raise the simulation of synthetic data to a higher level and account for many practical and complex real-world problems.

Author Contributions: Conceptualization, M.T.; methodology, J.G. and S.F.; software, J.G. and S.F.; validation, M.T. and A.K.; formal analysis, J.G. and S.F.; investigation, J.G. and S.F. and M.T.; data curation, S.F.; writing—original draft preparation, J.G. and M.T.; writing—review and editing, J.G. and M.T.; visualization, S.F. and J.G.; supervision, M.T. and A.K.; project administration, M.T.; funding acquisition, M.T. All authors have read and agreed to the published version of the manuscript.

Funding: This research was partly funded by the Swiss National Science Foundation (SNSF) under the project titled "Harnessing event and longitudinal data in industry and health sector through privacy preserving technologies", Grant number 211751, Funding scheme Bridge Discovery.

Data Availability Statement: All data sets underlying the results of this study are freely available on the Comprehensive R Archive Network (CRAN) in the R package simPop [14].

Conflicts of Interest: The authors do not report any potential conflicts of interest.

Appendix A. Details on Selected Variables of the EU-SILC Data

A representative real-world data set from the European Union Statistics of Income and Living Conditions (EU-SILC) survey was selected for this study to demonstrate the application of the developed methods. These data sets primarily serve to measure Europe's risk of poverty and social cohesion, playing an instrumental role in monitoring progress towards the Lisbon 2010 strategy and Europe 2020 objectives outlined by the European Union. The core objective of EU-SILC is the timely and comparable acquisition of cross-sectional and longitudinal data, focusing on income, poverty, social exclusion and living conditions. The survey includes data collected from households and individuals, with around 90% of its output comprising annual variables. The remaining data are either modules collated every three or six years or ad hoc modules designed to address specific policy needs. Participating countries send data on individuals and households to Eurostat in accordance with legally determined deadlines and agreed guidelines and procedures.

In particular, this study uses the Austrian EU-SILC public use data set from 2013 with 13,513 observations and 62 variables. These cross-sectional data include variables on income, poverty, social exclusion and other living conditions. Information on social exclusion and housing conditions is collected primarily at the household level, while labor, education and health information is sourced from individuals aged 16 years and older. Income variables at the detailed component level are also collected predominantly from individuals. The equivalized household income variable and household sizes are shown in the Appendix A in Table A1. Other relevant variables are shown in the Appendix A in Table A2, where the official names of the variables according to Eurostat are also displayed.

Design and non-response weights are calculated differently for the primary sampling units (PSU) and the higher-order sampling units (second to fourth order). For PSUs, the Austrian Central Statistical Office calculates the design weights according to the stratified simple random sample with 70 strata. The stratification is based on several criteria, including the province, the number of households in the survey area and the characteristics of the target group. For the latter, households with foreigners and a higher risk of poverty were oversampled. A logistic regression model estimates the response probabilities for the calculation of the non-response weights. The non-response weights for higher-order sampling units are calculated in a similar way as for the primary sampling units. A logistic regression model estimates the response probabilities. Since more information is available from the previous survey, the regression model contains more variables than the PSU model. The model contains 43 predictors ranging from survey attributes, e.g., contact attempt, to characteristics of income and living conditions, e.g., net income. Finally, the weights of the data are calibrated to match the known population characteristics from the Austrian Census.

Table A1. Overview and description of the Austrian EU-SILC variables used to generate synthetic data including the distribution of income and household size. (Part I)

Name	Description	Type	Distribution
Equivalized household income	Yearly income according to OECD equivalence scale	continuous (median = 26.5)	
HID	Longitudinal section household ID	multinomial 5983 levels	
D004010	Household size	continuous (median = 2)	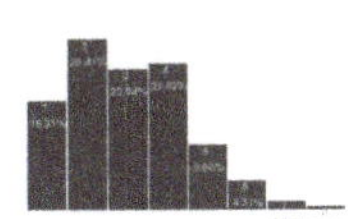

Table A2. Overview and description of the Austrian EU-SILC variables used to generate synthetic data. (Part II).

Name	Desc	Type	Distribution
sex	Sex	multinomial 2 levels	
age	Age	continuous median 46	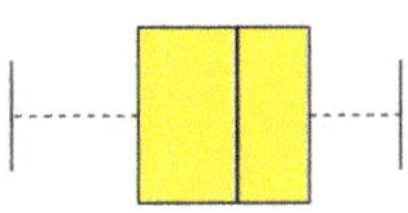

Table A2. *Cont.*

Name	Desc	Type	Distribution
bundesld	Region	multinomial 9 levels	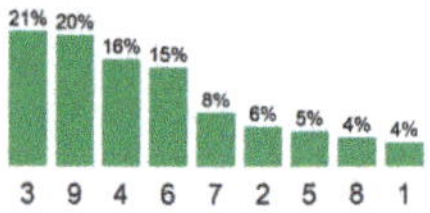
P001000	Economic status	multinomial 12 levels	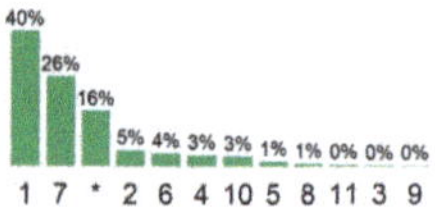
P111010nu	Citizenship 1	multinomial 7 levels	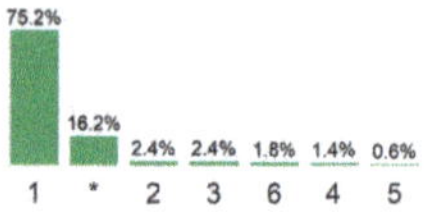
P114000	Marital status	multinomial 7 levels	
P137000	Highest education level	multinomial 7 levels	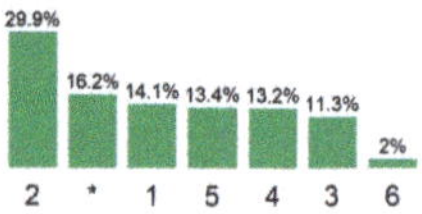
P103000	chronic illness	multinomial 4 levels	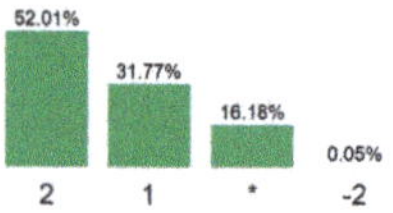

For a comprehensive description of the variables used and more information on this data set, the package manual of `R` package `laeken` [34,35] provides a detailed guide.

Appendix B. Details on the Simulated Annealing Algorithm for the Calibration of Populations

Appendix B.1. Detailed Calibration Algorithm

Algorithm A1 presents the Simulated Annealing algorithm in more detail.

Algorithm A1 Detailed calibration algorithm

1: Duplicate the synthetic population K times to include $N' = N \cdot K$ individuals, increasing the likelihood of finding a composition $(\delta_1, \ldots, \delta_N)$.

2: Set the initial conditions:

- Start temperature $T > 0$
- Cooling rate $r_T \in (0, 1)$
- Minimum temperature T_{min}
- Maximum number of cooldowns $C > 100$
- Counter for number of cooldowns $N_C = 1$
- Initial number of selections/deselections $n = Obj \cdot \frac{med_{hsize}}{5}$
- Reduction rate for number of swaps $r_n \in (0, 1)$
- Allowed relative error $\epsilon > 0$
- Number of iterations until cooling c
- Counter for iterations until next cooldown $n_c = 1$

3: Initialize a first selection $\Delta = (\delta_1, \ldots, \delta_{N'})$, calculate initial synthetic margins $\mathbf{m}$, and the value of the objective function:

$$Obj = f(\mathbf{t}, \hat{\mathbf{t}}) = \sum_{m=1}^{M} |t_m - \hat{t}_m|$$

4: Randomly add and remove n persons, including all household members, from the selection Δ by setting $\delta_i = 0$ or $\delta_i = 1$ for each member of the drawn household, resulting in a new selection Δ_{new}.

5: Calculate the new value of the objective function Obj_{new} using Δ_{new}.

6: **if** $\frac{Obj_{new}}{N} \leq \epsilon$ **then**

7: Convergence reached, terminate the algorithm and return Δ_{new}.

8: **end if**

9: **if** $Obj_{new} < Obj$ **then**

10: Update $\Delta \leftarrow \Delta_{new}$.

11: **else**

12: Update current selection Δ with new selection Δ_{new} if $u < \exp\left(-\frac{Obj_{new} - Obj}{T}\right)$ where u is drawn from $U(0, 1)$; otherwise, keep Δ.

13: **end if**

14: Increment n_c; if $n_c > c$, start the next cooldown, otherwise, repeat from step 4:

- $n \leftarrow \max(1, \lfloor n \cdot r_n \rfloor)$
- $T \leftarrow T \cdot r_T$
- $N_C \leftarrow N_C + 1$
- $n_c \leftarrow 1$

15: **if** $N_C > C$ or $T < T_{min}$ **then**

16: Terminate the algorithm and return current selection Δ.

17: **else**

18: Go to step 4.

19: **end if**

Appendix B.2. Initialise and Adjust Number of Swaps N

The convergence of the SA algorithm is greatly influenced by the initial number of swaps (n). Choosing a very high n can lead to frequent changes in Δ due to a high acceptance rate for a worse solution. In contrast, selecting a very low n can limit the potential to improve the objective function. Naturally, n should depend on the initial value of $f(\mathbf{t}, \hat{\mathbf{t}})$ and the size of the synthetic population. An initial choice of the swap rate n is as follows:

$$n = \min(\max_{m,r}(|t_{m,r} - \hat{t}_{m,r}|) \cdot \frac{2}{3}, 0.05 \cdot \frac{N_P}{med_{hsize}}). \tag{A1}$$

The first part is related to the objective function, and the second to the size of the target population. This suggested starting value proved practical during the work in [29].

The swap rate n can also be controlled during the SA algorithm for faster convergence. When selecting or deselecting individuals, the whole household is chosen; thus, the number of individuals in the synthetic population can change, affecting the algorithm's convergence. To address this, a scaling factor is introduced to maintain the total number of individuals or households at the same level as the target margins. Before the sampling step, the number of draws for the selection of persons and households to be included and excluded is adjusted by

$$n_{in} = \max(\lceil n - gap \rceil, 1) \tag{A2}$$

$$n_{out} = \max(\lceil n + gap \rceil, 1) \quad , \tag{A3}$$

where

$$gap = r_{re} \cdot \frac{1}{\sum_{r=1}^{R} M_r} \left(\sum_{m=1}^{M} \sum_{r=1}^{R_m} t_{m,r} - \hat{t}_{m,r} \right) \tag{A4}$$

$$r_{re} \in (0,1). \tag{A5}$$

For $\sum_{r,t} t_{m,r} - \hat{t}_{m,r} > 0$, the number of individuals or households selected is overall smaller than the target population margins. Multiplying with the factor $\frac{1}{\sum_{r=1}^{R} M_r}$ yields an estimate of the average number of individuals or households missing in each of the margin cells of the synthetic population. On the other hand $\sum_{r,t} t_{m,r} - \hat{t}_{m,r} < 0$ implies that too many individuals or households have been selected. The value gap is, thus, an estimated difference to the desired total population in terms of individuals N_P or households N_H. Considering Equations (A2) and (A3), it is clear to see that choosing $r_{re} = 1$ would imply that n_{in} and n_{out} can overcompensate for this difference calculated in Equation (A4) and the solutions would likely begin to jump above and below the desired total $\sum_{t=1}^{M_r} t_{m,r}$. With a value of $r_{re} = 0.5$, half of the estimated difference is addressed when adding and removing individuals from the current selection. Thus, the value of $r_{re} = 0.5$ is recommended to stabilize the solutions.

Appendix B.3. Automatically Choosing T and Forcing Cooldowns

The starting temperature T can strongly influence the convergence of the SA. If T is chosen too high, the algorithm jumps aimlessly through the search space and, depending on the cooling rate r_T, it takes some time for the SA to narrow down to a solution. If T, on the other hand, is chosen too small, the SA may become stuck in a local optimum too early and have no possibility to improve further. The starting temperature T_{adj} can optionally be adjusted automatically in the initialization phase of the SA by

$$T_{adj} = \max(T, r_a \frac{1}{\sum_{r=1}^{R} M_r} \sum_{m=1}^{M} \sum_{r=1}^{R_m} t_{m,r} \epsilon_m) \tag{A6}$$

$$\epsilon_m = \begin{cases} \epsilon_H & \text{if } \mathbf{t_m} \text{ corresponds to household margins} \\ \epsilon_P & \text{if } \mathbf{t_m} \text{ corresponds to person margins} \end{cases} \tag{A7}$$

$$m = 1, \ldots, M, \tag{A8}$$

where $r_a \in (0,1)$. Besides the individual adjustment of T, the SA algorithm can become stuck between cooldowns and further improvements of the current solution can only be achieved after successive cooldowns with decreasing T as well as n. Since c usually sets the number of iterations between cooldowns to several hundreds, we implemented a procedure that forces a cooldown if the value of the objective function has not changed since h iterations and the previous h values of the objective function, $Obj_1, \ldots, Obj_h$, satisfy

$$\frac{\sigma_{Obj}}{\overline{Obj}} < r_h, \tag{A9}$$

with σ_{Obj} as the standard deviation and $\overline{Obj}$ as the arithmetic mean of $Obj_1, \ldots, Obj_h$. This addition has the sole purpose of decreasing the number of iterations if the solution starts to become stuck for a given n and T. For the work in [29], we chose $r_a = 0.2$ and $r_h = 0.05$.

Appendix B.4. Hyperparameters in Package simPop for Population Calibration

Table A3 shows the connection of parameters in the equations above to function arguments in the software implementation.

Table A3. Some of the new function arguments of function `calibPop()`.

Function Argument	Parameter
`choose.temp.factor`	r_a
`scale.redraw`	r_{re}
`observe.times`	h
`observe.break`	r_h
`hhTables, persTables`	$\mathbf{t}_1, \ldots, \mathbf{t}_M$

We refer to other newly added parameters, such as `splitUpper`, `redist.var` and `redist.var.factor`, to the help page `?calibPop`. They can be useful for calibrating synthetic data with a high geographic resolution, such as local administrative units level 2 (LAU2) or more granular.

Appendix C. R-Code Examples

The proposed synthetic data generation and calibration tools have been implemented in the R package `simPop` and the extensive source code is available in the functions `simCategorical`, `simContinuous`, `crossValidation`, `addKnownMargins` and `calibPop`. A demonstration of an application of these functions on the EU-SILC data set is illustrated below.

Appendix C.1. Simulation of Synthetic Data with XGBoost

The following code snipped shows how to simulate a cluster structure in software R. To generate the household structure, first, the data input is specified naming the data set, the (optional) cluster structure, the (optional) stratification variable(s) (in each strata, the simulation is taken independently), and the (optional) vector of sampling weights. Secondly, the function `simStructure` is used, with the basic household variables specified in the function argument `basicHHvars`. Note that there are different methods available, such as "direct" with estimation of the population totals for each combination of stratum and household size using the Horvitz–Thompson estimator, "multinom" with the estimation of the conditional probabilities within the strata using a multinomial log-linear model and random draws from the resulting distributions, or "distribution" with random draws from the observed conditional distributions within the strata.

```
R> library(simPop)
R> ## load the demo data set
R> data(eusilcS)
R>
```

```
R> ## create the structure
R> inp <- specifyInput(data = eusilcS,
R>                    hhid = "db030",   # variable with cluster information
R>                    strata = "db040", # optional stratification
R>                    weight = "db090") # variable with sampling weights
R>
R>
R> simPop <- simStructure(data = inp,    # data structure
R>                        method = "direct",
R>                        basicHHvars = c("age", "rb090"))
```

In doing so, `simStructure` requires all information about the structure of a data set. For surveys with complex sampling designs, more information has to be provided (e.g., function argument `weight`) than for the simulation of survey samples obtained with simple random sampling or by simulating census data. In our case, the data set is collected on the basis of a complex sample design, and in addition, there is a household structure, e.g., all persons within a household are surveyed (function argument `hhid`). To reflect heterogeneity in the population, samples are often drawn within strata, e.g., regions (functional argument `strata`). Note that `specifyInput` generates a S4-class object [36] including all necessary information.

```
R> class(simPop)

[1] "simPopObj"
attr(,"package")
```

The implemented print method already shows some basic information.

```
R> simPop

--------------
synthetic population  of size
81838 x 7

build from a sample of size
11725 x 20
--------------

variables in the population:
db030,hhsize,db040,age,rb090,pid,weight
```

Appendix C.2. Synthesizing Additional Variables

In the example below, two new variables, "pl030" (person's economic status) and "pb220a" (citizenship)), are simulated for the population. All function arguments and parameters for the xgboost algorithm can be passed through `model_params`. The complete list of the hyperparameters is listed in [37].

```
R> model_params <- list(max.depth = 10, # maximum depth of a tree
R>                      eta = 0.5,      # learning rate
R>                      nrounds = 5,    # max number of boosting iterations
R>                      objective = "multi:softprob") # softmax objective
R>
R> simPop <- simCategorical(simPop,
R>                          additional = c("pl030", "pb220a"),
R>                          method = "xgboost",
R>                          model_params = model_params)
```

The print method shows the successful simulation of these two new variables.

```
R> simPop

--------------
synthetic population  of size
81838 x 9

build from a sample of size
11725 x 20
--------------

variables in the population:
db030,hhsize,db040,age,rb090,pid,weight,pl030,pb220a
```

The population now consists of the basic variables, the structure variables and the newly generated categorical variables ("pl030" (person's economic status) and "pb220a" (citizenship)). Table A4 displays a snippet of the initial five observations from the already simulated data.

Table A4. An excerpt of the synthetic population generated by the proposed XGBoost approach.

	db030	hhsize	db040	Age	rb090	Pid	Weight	pl030	pb220a
1	4570	1	Lower Austria	68	male	4570.1	1.00	5	AT
2	1735	1	Carinthia	65	male	1735.1	1.00	5	AT
3	655	2	Burgenland	55	female	655.1	1.00	5	AT
4	836	3	Burgenland	64	female	836.1	1.00	7	AT
5	2984	4	Carinthia	13	female	2984.4	1.00	4	AT

Appendix C.3. Hyperparameter Tuning for XGBoost

```
R> grid <- expand.grid(nrounds = c(5, 10),
R>                     max_depth = 10,
R>                     eta = c(0.2, 0.3, 0.5),
R>                     eval_metric = "mlogloss",
R>                     stringsAsFactors = F)

R> additionals <- c("pl030", "pb220a")
R>
R> # Remove variables and regenerate with crossValidation
R> simPop@pop@data[, (additionals) := NULL]
R>
R> simPop <- crossValidation(simPop,
R>                           additionals = additionals,
R>                           fold = 3, #
R>                           hyper_param_grid = grid)
R>
R> simPop

--------------
synthetic population  of size
81838 x 9

build from a sample of size
11725 x 20
--------------
```

```
variables in the population:
db030,hhsize,db040,age,rb090,pid,weight,pl030,pb220a
```

Appendix C.4. Post-Calibration First Scenario

```
R> data(eusilcP) # use to derive target margins
R>
R> # build target margins
R> margins <- xtabs( ~ region + gender + citizenship,
R>                   data = eusilcP)
R> margins <- as.data.frame(margins)
R> # rename to match column names in synthetic data
R> colnames(margins) <- c("db040", "rb090", "pb220a", "freq")
R>
R> # add target margins to simPop-object
R> simPop <- addKnownMargins(simPop, margins)

R> # apply simulated annealing for each "db040"
R> simPop_adj <- calibPop(simPop,
R>                        split = "db040",
R>                        epsP.factor = 0.1,
R>                        choose.temp = TRUE,
R>                        choose.temp.factor = 0.2,
R>                        nr_cpus = 1,
R>                        verbose = FALSE)
```

Appendix C.5. Post-Calibration Second Scenario

```
R> # target margins for persons
R> persTables <- xtabs(~ region + gender + citizenship,
R>                     data = eusilcP)
R> persTables <- as.data.frame(persTables)
R> colnames(persTables) <- c("db040", "rb090", "pb220a", "Freq")
R>
R> # target margins for households
R> filter_hid <- !duplicated(eusilcP$hid)
R> # re-code household size
R> eusilcP$hsize4 <- pmin(4, as.numeric(eusilcP$hsize))
R> simPop@pop@data$hhsize4 <- pmin(4, as.numeric(simPop@pop@data$hhsize))
R>
R> hhTables <- xtabs(~ region + hsize4,
R>                   data = eusilcP[filter_hid, ])
R> hhTables <- as.data.frame(hhTables)
R> colnames(hhTables) <- c("db040", "hhsize4", "Freq")
R>
R> # run simulated annealing
R> simPop_adj_2tables <- calibPop(simPop, split = "db040",
R>                                temp=1, epsP.factor = 0.1,
R>                                epsH.factor = 0.1,
R>                                persTables = persTables,
R>                                hhTables = hhTables,
R>                                nr_cpus = 1, verbose = TRUE)
```

erences

United Nations Economic Commission for Europe. *Synthetic Data for Official Statistics: A Starter Guide*; Technical Report, Report No. ECE/CES/STAT/2022/6; United Nations: Rome, Italy, 2022.

Dwork, C. Differential Privacy. In *International Colloquium on Automata, Languages, and Programming*; Springer: Berlin/Heidelberg, Germany, 2006; pp. 1–12. [CrossRef]

Fischetti, M.; Salazar-González, J. Complementary Cell Suppression for Statistical Disclosure Control in Tabular Data with Linear Constraints. *J. Am. Stat. Assoc.* **2000**, *95*, 916–928. [CrossRef]

Enderle, T.; Giessing, S.; Tent, R. Calculation of Risk Probabilities for the Cell Key Method. In *Privacy in Statistical Databases: UNESCO Chair in Data Privacy, Proceedings of the International Conference PSD 2020, Tarragona, Spain, 23–25 September 2020*; Springer: Berlin/Heidelberg, Germany, 2020; pp. 151–165. [CrossRef]

Novák, J.; Sixta, J. Visualization of Record Swapping. *Austrian J. Stat.* **2024**, *53*, 1–16. [CrossRef]

Yin, X.; Zhu, Y.; Hu, J. A Comprehensive Survey of Privacy-Preserving Federated Learning: A Taxonomy, Review, and Future Directions. *ACM Comput. Surv.* **2021**, *54*, 1–36. [CrossRef]

Templ, M.; Alfons, A. Disclosure Risk of Synthetic Population Data with Application in the Case of EU-SILC. In *Privacy in Statistical Databases*; Lecture Notes in Computer Science; Springer: Berlin/Heidelberg, Germany, 2010; pp. 174–186. [CrossRef]

Templ, M. Providing Data with High Utility and No Disclosure Risk for the Public and Researchers: An Evaluation by Advanced Statistical Disclosure Risk Methods. *Austrian J. Stat.* **2014**, *43*, 247–254. [CrossRef]

McClure, D.; Reiter, J. Assessing Disclosure Risks for Synthetic Data with Arbitrary Intruder Knowledge. *Stat. J. IAOS* **2016**, *32*, 109–126. [CrossRef]

Alfons, A.; Kraft, S.; Templ, M.; Filzmoser, P. Simulation of Close-to-Reality Population Data for Household Surveys with Application to EU-SILC. *Stat. Methods Appl.* **2011**, *20*, 383–407. [CrossRef]

Templ, M.; Filzmoser, P. Simulation and Quality of a Synthetic Close-to-Reality Employer–Employee Population. *J. Appl. Stat.* **2014**, *41*, 1053–1072. [CrossRef]

Münnich, R.; Schürle, J. *On the Simulation of Complex Universes in the Case of Applying the German Microcensus*; DACSEIS Research Paper Series No. 4; University of Tübingen: Tubingen, Germany, 2003.

Nowok, B.; Raab, G.; Dibben, C. synthpop: Bespoke Creation of Synthetic Data in R. *J. Stat. Softw.* **2016**, *74*, 1–26. [CrossRef]

Templ, M.; Meindl, B.; Kowarik, A.; Dupriez, O. Simulation of Synthetic Complex Data: The R Package simPop. *J. Stat. Softw.* **2017**, *79*, 1–38. [CrossRef]

Mendelevitch, O.; Lesh, M. Beyond Differential Privacy: Synthetic Micro-Data Generation with Deep Generative Neural Networks. In *Security and Privacy from a Legal, Ethical, and Technical Perspective*; IntechOpen: London, UK, 2020; pp. 1–14. [CrossRef]

Solatorio, A.V.; Dupriez, O. REaLTabFormer: Generating Realistic Relational and Tabular Data using Transformers. *arXiv* **2023**, arXiv:2302.02041. https://doi.org/10.48550/arXiv.2302.02041.

Särndal, E. The Calibration Approach in Survey Theory and Practice. *Surv. Methodol.* **2007**, *33*, 99–119.

Horvitz, D.G.; Thompson, D.J. A Generalization of Sampling Without Replacement from a Finite Universe. *J. Am. Stat. Assoc.* **1952**, *47*, 663–685. [CrossRef]

Walker, A.J. An Efficient Method for Generating Discrete Random Variables with General Distributions. *ACM Trans. Math. Softw. (TOMS)* **1977**, *3*, 253–256. [CrossRef]

Chen, T.; Guestrin, C. XGBoost: A Scalable Tree Boosting System. In Proceedings of the 22nd ACM SIGKDD International Conference on Knowledge Discovery and Data Mining, KDD '16, New York, NY, USA, 13–17 August 2016; pp. 785–794. [CrossRef]

Johnson, R.; Zhang, T. Learning Nonlinear Functions Using Regularized Greedy Forest. *IEEE Trans. Pattern Anal. Mach. Intell.* **2013**, *36*, 942–954. [CrossRef] [PubMed]

Brandt, S. Statistical and Computational Methods in Data Analysis. *Am. J. Phys.* **1971**, *39*, 1109–1110. [CrossRef]

Vorhies, W. Want to Win Competitions? Pay Attention to Your Ensembles. 2016. Available online: https://www.datasciencecentral.com/profiles/blogs/want-to-win-at-kaggle-pay-attention-to-your-ensembles (accessed on 25 February 2021).

Huang, Z.; Williamson, P. *A Comparison of Synthetic Reconstruction and Combinatorial Optimization Approaches to the Creation of Small-Area Micro Data*; Working Paper 2001/02; Department of Geography, University of Liverpool: Liverpool, UK, 2001.

Voas, D.; Williamson, P. An Evaluation of the Combinatorial Optimisation Approach to the Creation of Synthetic Microdata. *Int. J. Popul. Geogr.* **2000**, *6*, 349–366. [CrossRef] [PubMed]

Kirkpatrick, S.; Gelatt, C.; Vecchi, M. Optimization by Simulated Annealing. *Science* **1983**, *220*, 671–680. [CrossRef] [PubMed]

Cerný, V. Thermodynamical Approach to the Traveling Salesman Problem: An Efficient Simulation Algorithm. *J. Optim. Theory Appl.* **1985**, *45*, 41–51. [CrossRef]

Harland, K.; Heppenstall, A.; Smith, D.; Birkin, M. Creating Realistic Synthetic Populations at Varying Spatial Scales: A Comparative Critique of Population Synthesis Techniques. *J. Artif. Soc. Soc. Simul.* **2012**, *15*, 1. [CrossRef]

Rubinyi, S.; Verschuur, J.; Goldblatt, R.; Gussenbauer, J.; Kowarik, A.; Mannix, J.; Bottoms, B.; Hall, J. High-Resolution Synthetic Population Mapping for Quantifying Disparities in Disaster Impacts: An Application in the Bangladesh Coastal Zone. *Front. Environ. Sci.* **2022**, *10*, 1033579. [CrossRef]

Minnesota Population Center. *Integrated Public Use Microdata Series, International: Version 7.3 [Dataset]*; IPUMS: Minneapolis, MN, USA, 2020. [CrossRef]

Müller, K. *wrswoR: Weighted Random Sampling without Replacement*; R package Version 1.1.1. 2020. Available online:

https://CRAN.R-project.org/package=wrswoR (accessed on 1 May 2024).
32. Fačevicová, K.; Hron, K.; Todorov, V.; Templ, M. Compositional Tables Analysis in Coordinates. *Scand. J. Stat.* **2016**, *43*, 962-
[CrossRef]
33. Fačevicová, K.; Hron, K.; Todorov, V.; Templ, M. General approach to coordinate representation of compositional tables. *Scan Stat.* **2018**, *45*, 879–899. [CrossRef]
34. Alfons, A.; Templ, M. Estimation of Social Exclusion Indicators from Complex Surveys: The R Package laeken. *J. Stat. S* **2013**, *54*, 1–25. [CrossRef]
35. Templ, M. *Imputation and Visualization of Missing Values*; Springer International Publishing: Cham, Switzerland, 2023; p. *in print*.
36. Chambers, J. *Extending R*; Chapman & Hall/CRC the R Series; CRC Press, Taylor & Francis Group: Boca Raton, FL, USA, 2
37. XGBoost Developers. XGBoost Parameters. 2020. Available online: https://xgboost.readthedocs.io/en/latest/parameter.h (accessed on 15 December 2020).

algorithms

MDPI

cle

ixed Graph Colouring as Scheduling a Partially Ordered Set Interruptible Multi-Processor Tasks with Integer Due Dates

ngelina I. Mihova [1] and Yuri N. Sotskov [2,*]

1 Mathematical Institute, Faculty of Mathematics, Computer Science and Statistics, Ludwig-Maximilians-Universitat Munich, Geschwister-Scholl-Platz, 1, 80539 Munich, Germany; evangelinamihova@gmail.com

2 United Institute of Informatics Problems, National Academy of Sciences, 6 Surganov Street, 220012 Minsk, Belarus

* Correspondence: sotskov48@mail.ru; Tel.: +375-17-249-61-20

Abstract: We investigate relationships between scheduling problems with the bottleneck objective functions (minimising makespan or maximal lateness) and problems of optimal colourings of the mixed graphs. The investigated scheduling problems have integer durations of the multi-processor tasks (operations), integer release dates and integer due dates of the given jobs. In the studied scheduling problems, it is required to find an optimal schedule for processing the partially ordered operations, given that operation interruptions are allowed and indicated subsets of the unit-time operations must be processed simultaneously. First, we show that the input data for any considered scheduling problem can be completely determined by the corresponding mixed graph. Second, we prove that solvable scheduling problems can be reduced to problems of finding optimal colourings of corresponding mixed graphs. Third, finding an optimal colouring of the mixed graph is equivalent to the considered scheduling problem determined by the same mixed graph. Finally, due to the proven equivalence of the considered optimisation problems, most of the results that were proven for the optimal colourings of mixed graphs generate similar results for considered scheduling problems, and vice versa.

Keywords: scheduling; maximal lateness; makespan; multi-processor task; mixed graph colouring

1. Introduction

For optimal production planning and scheduling, it is required to construct an optimal schedule for processing a set of tasks (jobs) using existing equipment (processors). Optimisation of a schedule is a key factor in improving efficiency, as it allows a scheduler to reduce production costs, the time of the execution of incoming customer orders and the timely supply of production processes with raw materials and other components that are required for the manufacture of final products. Practical production scheduling (planning) problems are diverse in terms of conditions, restrictions and the objectives to be achieved by optimal schedules. To solve a large number of scheduling problems, special models and algorithms have been developed that take into account the specific conditions and objectives of concrete production planning. An extension of the application areas of scheduling algorithms can be based on a generalisation of scheduling models for complicated multistage systems in order to present different problem sets and to develop universal methods for constructing optimal schedules on the basis of the generalised scheduling models.

It is well known that the construction of the makespan-optimal schedule for fulfilling operations of equal duration reduces the construction of the optimal colouring of vertices of the graph. If it is required to consider precedence constraints specified on the operation set and the impossibility of processing two or more tasks simultaneously on the same processor, then, to determine the makespan-optimal schedule for fulfilling the unit-time operations, one can use the optimal colouring of the mixed graph [1,2].

In this paper, we focus on scheduling problems with integer operation durations and job release dates to minimize the makespan C_{max} or maximal lateness L_{max} of the given jobs with integer due dates.

Let $G = (V, A, E)$ be a mixed graph with the set $V = \left\{v_1, v_2, \dots, v_{|V|}\right\} \neq \varnothing$ of vertices, the set A of arcs and the set E of edges. Each arc determines an ordered pair of vertices from the set V. Each edge determines an unordered pair of vertices. The mixed graph G considered in this paper does not contain loops, multiple arcs and multiple edges. For the empty set of arcs, we obtain the graph $G = (V, \varnothing, E)$. For the empty set of edges, we obtain the directed graph $G = (V, A, \varnothing)$ (the digraph for short).

In [3], a colouring of the mixed graph was defined.

Definition 1 ([3]). *A function $c : V \to \{1, 2, \dots, t\}$ is called a colouring $c(G)$ of a mixed graph $G = (V, A, E)$ if the inequalities $c(v_i) \leq c(v_j)$ hold for all arcs $(v_i, v_j) \in A$ and the relations $c(v_p) \neq c(v_q)$ hold for all edges $[v_p, v_q] \in E$. A colouring $c(G)$ is optimal if this colouring uses a minimal number $\chi(G)$ of colours $c(v_i) \in \{1, 2, \dots, t\}$. The minimal number $\chi(G)$ is called a chromatic number of the mixed graph G.*

If the equality $A = \varnothing$ holds, then the colouring $c(G)$ is an ordinary colouring of the graph $G = (V, \varnothing, E)$. The mixed graph (V, A, E) with the non-empty set of arcs and the non-empty set of edges may not be colourable [3].

Theorem 1 ([3]). *A colouring $c(G)$ of vertices of mixed graph $G = (V, A, E)$ exists if and only if the directed graph $(V, A, \varnothing)$ has no circuit containing the adjacent vertices in the graph $(V, \varnothing, E)$.*

Finding an optimal colouring of the vertices of the mixed graph $G = (V, A, E)$ is an NP-hard problem, even if $A = \varnothing$; see [4]. The NP-hardness of the optimisation problem means that it is unlikely that there exists a polynomial algorithm for solving this problem, since there is a polynomial reduction to this problem from a huge number of NP-hard problems, while there is no polynomial algorithm for each of them yet.

In [1,2], it is proven that a job-shop problem with equal (unit) durations of operations with the objective of minimising a schedule length (i.e., makespan) reduces to a problem of finding the optimal colouring of the mixed graph $G = (V, A, E)$.

In this paper, we show that finding the optimal colouring $c(G)$ reduces to the problem of constructing a schedule that minimizes a maximal lateness for processing multi-processor tasks with integer durations, integer due dates and allowed operation interruptions. The converse is also proven. Processing a multi-processor task requires several dedicated processors; see Chapter 10 of the monograph [5]. Moreover, two types of precedence constraints can be specified for the multi-processor tasks, and the unit-time operations of the indicated subset must be processed simultaneously.

The remaining part of this paper is organised as follows. The settings of considered scheduling problems, preliminary results and notation are given in Section 2. Related papers are cited, where it has been shown that the problem of finding an optimal colouring of the mixed graph reduces to finding a makespan-optimal schedule for partially ordered operations with unit processing times. Scheduling problems are discussed in increasing order of their complexity. Section 3 demonstrates that the problem of optimal colouring of the mixed graph reduces to finding a makespan-optimal schedule of the multi-processor tasks with equal durations. In Section 4, we discuss scheduling problems of minimising maximal lateness of completing jobs with respect to integer due dates. New results are proven, demonstrated, and discussed in Sections 4–8. The possibility of interruptions processing integer-time tasks is studied in Section 5. A theorem is proven on the reduction of the optimal colouring $c(G)$ to the scheduling problems with a minimisation of the makespan for the interrupted integer–time tasks with integer release dates of the jobs. An illustrative example of the studied scheduling problem is solved in Section 6. Section 7 includes a theorem on the equivalence of scheduling problems with a maximal lateness objective and the problem of finding optimal colourings of the mixed graphs. Due to the proven equivalence of the problems of constructing optimal schedules and mixed graph colouring problems, many claims that have been proven for scheduling problems can be applied to the problems of optimal mixed graph colourings, and vice versa. In Section 8, we discuss new findings and their potential implications. Section 9 contains concluding remarks and promising future research directions. The new theorems and most of the theorems presented in the survey section are demonstrated in the numerical examples in the main text and in Sections A and B.

2. Related Works, Definitions, and Preliminaries

In the following, terminology from [5] is used for scheduling problems and terminology from [6,7] is used for graph theory. To classify scheduling problems, a three-field notation $\alpha|\beta|\gamma$ [5] is used, where α determines the processing system, field β determines the characteristics of the jobs, and field γ an objective function.

2.1. Minimum Length Unit-Time Job-Shop Problems

We begin by examining the unit-time scheduling problem $J|t_{ij}=1|C_{\max}$ of constructing a makespan-optimal schedule for fulfilling the set $J=\left\{J_1,J_2,\ldots,J_{|J|}\right\}$ of the given jobs by the dedicated processors $M=\left\{M_1,M_2,\ldots,M_{|M|}\right\}$. The execution of the job $J_i\in J$ entails the execution of the ordered set $Q^{(i)}=\left\{Q_{i1},Q_{i2},\ldots,Q_{i,|Q^{(i)}|}\right\}$ of operations with unit (equal) durations $t_{ij}=1$ in the strict linear order $(Q_{i1},Q_{i2},\ldots,Q_{i,|Q^{(i)}|})$ on the corresponding processors from the set M. The operation $Q_{ij}\in Q^{(i)}$ is performed by the processor $M_{\mu(ij)}\in M$.

This processing system is called a job-shop, denoted $\alpha=J$ in the three-field notation $J|t_{ij}=1|C_{\max}$ used for this problem. The notation $C_{\max}$ is used to specify the optimality criterion of minimising the makespan $C_{\max}=\max\{C_i:J_i\in J\}$ (the schedule length) in the desired optimal schedule, where C_i denotes the completion time of the job $J_i\in J$. All jobs in the set $J=\left\{J_1,J_2,\ldots,J_{|J|}\right\}$ are ready for processing from the same release date $r=0$. Interruptions are not allowed during the execution of an operation $Q_{ij}\in Q^{(i)}$ with $J_i\in J$. A schedule S for processing the job set $J=\left\{J_1,J_2,\ldots,J_{|J|}\right\}$ is determined either by the start times $S(Q_{ij})\geq 0=t$ or by the completion times $C(Q_{ij})=S(Q_{ij})+t_{ij}$ of the operations $Q_{ij}\in Q:=\cup_{i=1}^{|J|}Q^{(i)}$. The length (makespan) of the schedule S is equal to $C_{\max}(S)=\max\{C(Q_{ij}):Q_{ij}\in Q\}$.

Let the subset Q_k of the set Q consist of operations to be fulfilled by the processor $M_k\in M$. Given that every pair of operations within the set Q_k must not be executed simultaneously, any schedule that exists for a job-shop problem $J|t_{ij}=1|C_{\max}$ determines $|M|$ strict linear orders of the operations Q_k fulfilled by the processors $M_k\in M$. An optimal schedule for the problem $J|t_{ij}=1|C_{\max}$.

$$S=(C(Q_{1,1}),C(Q_{1,2}),\ldots,C(Q_{1,|Q^{(1)}|}),C(Q_{2,1}),C(Q_{2,2}),\ldots,C(Q_{2,|Q^{(2)}|}),\ldots, \tag{1}$$

$$C(Q_{|J|,1}),C(Q_{|J|,2}),\ldots,C(Q_{|J|,|Q^{(|J|)}|}))$$

has the minimum length $C_{\max}(S)$ among all schedules that exist for this problem.

The objective function for each regular criterion is a non-decreasing function of the arguments $C_i:=C(Q_{i,|Q^{(i)}|})$, where $J_i\in J$. When solving the scheduling problem $\alpha|\beta|\gamma$ with a regular criterion γ, the optimal schedule can be found within the set of semiactive schedules [5].

Definition 2 ([5]). *The schedule S for the problem $\alpha|\beta|\gamma$ is semiactive, if the execution of every operation cannot be processed earlier without violating the operation order in schedule S or another operation is processed later than in this schedule.*

2.2. Optimal Strict Colourings of Mixed Graphs and Equivalent Unit-Time Job-Shop Problems

The paper [3] introducing Definition 1 was published in Russian. In 1997, another colouring of mixed graph $c_<(G)$ was introduced in the paper [8], published in English.

Definition 3 ([8]). *The function $c_< : V \to \{1,2,\ldots,t\}$ is a strict colouring $c_<(G)$ of the mixed graph $G = (V,A,E)$, if the inequalities $c_<(v_i) < c_<(v_j)$ hold for all arcs $(v_i,v_j) \in A$ and the relations $c_<(v_p) \neq c_<(v_q)$ hold for all edges $[v_p,v_q] \in E$. The strict colouring $c_<(G)$ is optimal, if this colouring uses a minimum number of colours $c_<(v_i) \in \{1,2,\ldots,t\}$.*

We can use colouring $c(G)$ instead of strict colouring $c_<(G)$ of vertices of the mixed graph $G = (V,A,E)$ provided that the following implication holds for every arc $(v_i,v_j) \in A$:

$$(v_i,v_j) \in A \Rightarrow [v_i,v_j] \in E \tag{2}$$

If the mixed graph $G = (V,A,E)$ includes the arc $(v_i,v_j) \in A$ and the implication (2) does not hold, one can add an edge $[v_i,v_j]$ to the mixed graph G for each such arc $(v_i,v_j) \in A$. A strict colouring $c_<(G)$ of the mixed graph G can be represented as a colouring $c(G)$ of the mixed graph obtained by including all such edges to the mixed graph G. Thus, the following lemma is obtained.

Lemma 1. *A strict colouring $c_<(G)$ of the mixed graph $G = (V,A,E)$ can be interpreted as a special case of the colouring $c(G)$, if the inclusion $(v_i,v_j) \in A$ implies the inclusion $[v_i,v_j] \in E$.*

A criterion for the existence of a strict colouring of vertices of the mixed graph $G = (V,A,E)$ is determined by Corollary 1 of Theorem 1.

Corollary 1 ([1]). *A strict colouring $c_<(G)$ exists if and only if the digraph $(V,A,\varnothing)$ does not contain a circuit.*

Theorem 2 was proven in [1].

Theorem 2 ([1]). *The unit-time scheduling problem $J|t_{ij} = 1|C_{\max}$ is equivalent to the problem of finding the optimal strict colouring of vertices of the mixed graph $G = (V,A,E)$ with $V = Q$, provided that two conditions hold as follows:*

(a) $(Q,A,\varnothing) = \cup_{i=1}^{|J|}(Q_i,A_i,\varnothing)$, *where each subgraph $(Q_i,A_i,\varnothing)$ is a path passing through the vertices Q_i and equality $Q_i \cap Q_j = \varnothing$ holds for indexes $i \neq j$;*

(b) $(Q,\varnothing,E) = \cup_{k=1}^{|M|}(Q^{(k)},\varnothing,E^{(k)})$, *where each subgraph $(Q^{(k)},\varnothing,E^{(k)})$ is a complete graph on the set Q_i and equality $Q^{(k)} \cap Q^{(l)} = \varnothing$ holds for indexes $k \neq l$.*

Due to Lemma 1 and Theorem 2, one can obtain the following corollary.

Corollary 2 ([1]). *The unit-time scheduling problem $J|t_{ij} = 1|C_{\max}$ is equivalent to the problem of determining the optimal colouring of the mixed graph $G = (V,A,E)$, where the relations*

$$\{v_1,v_2,\ldots,v_{|V|}\} = V = Q = \{Q_{1,1},Q_{1,2},\ldots,Q_{1,|Q_1|},Q_{2,1},Q_{2,2},\ldots,Q_{2,|Q_2|},\ldots,Q_{|J|,1},Q_{|J|,2},\ldots,Q_{|J|,|Q_{|J|}|}\}$$

hold along with the above conditions (2), (a) and (b).

To illustrate Corollary 2, we consider Example 1 of the problem $J|t_{ij} = 1|C_{\max}$, whose input data are determined by the corresponding mixed graph G.

Remark 1. *Since all operations $Q_{ij} \in Q_i$ in the unit-time scheduling problem $J|t_{ij} = 1|C_{\max}$ have unit processing times, we represent each operation as a vertex in the mixed graph $G = (V,A,E)$ with indexing the vertices in the set V in the lexicographic order of the pairs $\{i,j\}$ of* *the indexes of the corresponding operations* $Q_{ij} \in Q_i$, $J_i \in J$. *Thus, we obtain the following set* $V = \left\{v_1, v_2, \ldots, v_{|V|}\right\}$ *of vertices, where the equality* $\left|V\right| = \sum_{i=1}^{|J|} \left|Q^{(i)}\right|$ *holds.*

Example 1. *The dedicated processors* $M = \{M_1, M_2, M_3, M_4\}$ *must process jobs* $J = \{J_1, J_2, J_3, J_4, J_5\}$, *where processing the job* $J_1 \in J$ *consists of the singleton* $V^{(1)} = \{v_1\}$. *The job* $J_2 \in J$ *is represented as a union of the path* (v_2, v_3) *in the digraph* $(V, A, \varnothing)$ *and the chain* (v_2, v_3) *in the graph* $(V, \varnothing, E)$. *The job* $J_3 \in J$ *contains the set* $V^{(3)} = \{v_4, v_5, v_6, v_7\}$ *of the ordered operations* (v_4, v_5, v_6, v_7). *The job* $J_3 \in J$ *is represented as a union of the path* (v_4, v_5, v_6, v_7) *in the digraph* $(V, A, \varnothing)$ *and the chain* (v_4, v_5, v_6, v_7) *in the graph* $(V, \varnothing, E)$. *The job* $J_4 \in J$ *contains the set* $V^{(4)} = \{v_8, v_9, v_{10}\}$ *of the linearly ordered operations* (v_8, v_9, v_{10}). *The job* $J_4 \in J$ *is represented as a union of the path* (v_8, v_9, v_{10}) *in the directed graph* $(V, A, \varnothing)$ *and the* (v_8, v_9, v_{10}) *in graph* $(V, \varnothing, E)$. *The job* $J_5 \in J$ *contains the set* $V^{(5)} = \{v_{11}, v_{12}\}$ *of the ordered operations* (v_{11}, v_{12}). *The job* $J_5 \in J$ *is represented as a union of the path* (v_{11}, v_{12}) *in directed graph* $(V, A, \varnothing)$ *and the chain* (v_{11}, v_{12}) *in graph* $(V, \varnothing, E)$.

Let the set $V_1 = \{v_1, v_5, v_7\}$ be defined as a set of operations processed on the processor M_1. The forbiddance to process the operations of the set V_1 simultaneously is determined by the clique $\{v_1, v_5, v_7\}$ in the graph $(V, \varnothing, E)$; see Figure 1. Let the processor M_2 have to process the operations $V_2 = \{v_2, v_4\}$. The forbiddance to process operations of the set V_2 simultaneously is determined by the edge $[v_2, v_4]$. Let the processor M_3 have to process the operations $V_3 = \{v_3, v_9, v_{11}\}$. The forbiddance to process operations of the set V_3 simultaneously is determined by the clique $\{v_3, v_9, v_{11}\}$. Let the processor M_4 have to process the operations $V_3 = \{v_9, v_{11}, v_{15}\}$. The forbiddance to process any pair of operations of the set V_3 simultaneously is determined by the clique $\{v_9, v_{11}, v_{15}\}$. Let the processor M_4 have to process the operations $V_4 = \{v_6, v_8, v_{10}, v_{12}\}$. The forbiddance to process any pair of operations of the set V_4 simultaneously is determined by the clique $\{v_6, v_8, v_{10}, v_{12}\}$.

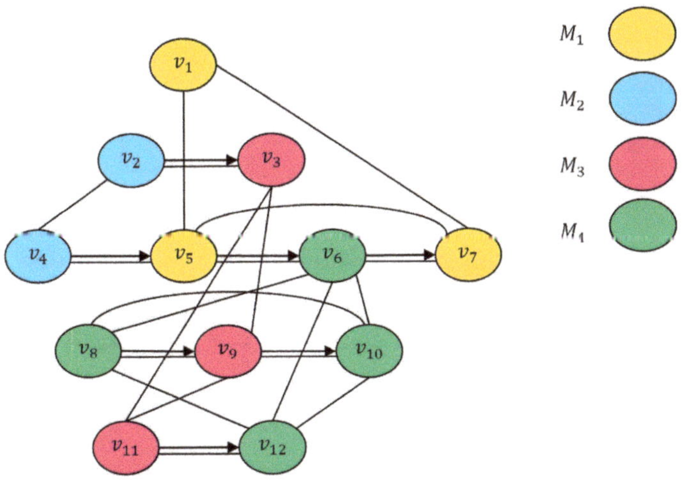

Figure 1. Mixed graph G that determines input data for Example 1.

A specific colour is used for indicating the operations $V_i = \left\{v_{i_1}, v_{i_2}, \ldots, v_{i_{|V_i|}}\right\} \subseteq V$ that are processed on the processor $M_i \in M$; see Figure 1. It is clear that the mixed graph depicted in Figure 1 possesses properties (1), (a) and (b), and the indexing of all vertices of the set V satisfies Remark 1. The optimal colouring of the mixed graph G is defined as follows: $c(v_1) = 1$, $c(v_2) = 2$, $c(v_3) = 3$, $c(v_4) = 1$, $c(v_5) = 2$, $c(v_6) = 3$, $c(v_7) = 4$, $c(v_8) = 1$, $c(v_9) = 2$, $c(v_{10}) = 4$, $c(v_{11}) = 1$ and $c(v_{12}) = 2$. The optimality of the colouring $c(G)$ follows from the fact that the graph $(V, \varnothing, E)$ contains the chain (v_4, v_5, v_6, v_7) with four vertices and the digraph $(V, A, \varnothing)$ contains the path (v_4, v_5, v_6, v_7). So, the chromatic number $\chi(G)$ is not less than four. The optimality of the colouring c(G) follows also from the clique $\{v_6, v_8, v_{10}, v_{12}\}$.

Due to Corollary 2, an optimal colouring $c(G)$ defines the following optimal semiactive schedule S for Example 1 with the input data shown in Figure 1:

$$S = (C(Q_{1,1}) = 1, C(Q_{2,1}) = 2, (Q_{2,2}) = 3, C(Q_{3,1}) = 1, C(Q_{3,2}) = 2, C(Q_{3,3}) = 3, C(Q_{3,4}) = 4, \\ C(Q_{4,1}) = 1, C(Q_{4,2}) = 2, C(Q_{4,3}) = 4, C(Q_{5,1}) = 1, C(Q_{5,2}) = 2$$

Due to Corollary 2, we obtain the chromatic number $\chi(G) = 4 = C_{max}(S)$.

2.3. General Shop Minimum-Length Unit-Time Scheduling Problems

The general shop scheduling problem $G_c|t_{ij} = 1|C_{\max}$ is a generalisation of the job-shop scheduling problem $J|t_{ij} = 1|C_{\max}$. In the former problem $G_c|t_{ij} = 1|C_{\max}$, in addition to the strict order that is determined on the set of operations $Q^{(i)}$ of the same job $J_i \in J$, precedence constraints can be defined between operations of different jobs. Moreover, indicated unit-time operations must be processed simultaneously. In [9], completion-start precedence constraints and start-start precedence constraints between operations of different jobs were also considered.

The processing job $J_k \in J$ consists of the set $V^{(k)}$ of linearly ordered operations. The duration t_i of every operation v_i of the set $V = \cup_{k=1}^{|J|} V^{(k)}$ equals one; $t_i = 1$. We represent the job $J_k \in J$ as a union of the path $(v_{k_1}, v_{k_2}, \ldots, v_{k_{r_k}})$ in the directed graph $(V, A, \varnothing)$ and the chain $(v_{k_1}, v_{k_2}, \ldots, v_{k_{r_k}})$ in the graph $(V, \varnothing, E)$, which are subgraphs of the mixed graph $G = (V, A, E)$ determining input data of the problem $G_c|t_{ij} = 1|C_{\max}$. Thus, we obtain the vertex set $V = \cup_{k=1}^{|J|} V^{(k)}$ of the desired mixed graph $G = (V, A, E)$, the subset $E^* = \cup_{k=1}^{|J|} \left\{ [v_{k_1}, v_{k_2}], [v_{k_2}, v_{k_3}], \ldots, [v_{k_{r_k}-1}, v_{k_{r_k}}] \right\}$ of edges $E \supseteq E^*$ and the subset A^* of arcs A such that the implication (3) holds:

$$[v_i, v_j] \in E^* \Rightarrow (v_i, v_j) \in A^* \tag{3}$$

In the general shop unit-time scheduling problem $G_c|t_{ij} = 1|C_{\max}$, along with a linear strict order given on the set $V^{(k)}$ of all operations of the job $J_k \in J$, there are given precedence constraints between operations belonging to different jobs in the set J Let $A \backslash A^*$ denote a subset of the set A such that the implication (2) does not hold for each arc $(v_i, v_j) \in A \backslash A^*$. In the unit-time scheduling problem $G_c|t_{ij} = 1|C_{\max}$, one processor of the set M is needed to process an operation $v_i \in V = \cup_{k=1}^{|J|} V^{(k)}$. Let the set $V_i = \left\{ v_{i_1}, v_{i_2}, \ldots, v_{i_{|V_i|}} \right\} \subseteq V$ be a set of operations, which must be processed on the processor $M_i \in M$. A pair of operations processed on the processor $M_i \in M$ cannot be processed simultaneously. Such a capacity constraint for processing operations $V_i \subseteq V$ on the processor $M_i \in M$ is represented by the clique $\left\{ v_{i_1}, v_{i_2}, \ldots, v_{i_{|V_i|}} \right\}$ in the subgraph $(V, \varnothing, E \backslash E^*)$ of the desired mixed graph $G = (V, A, E)$.

The general shop unit-time scheduling problem $G_c|t_{ij} = 1|C_{\max}$ is to find a schedule S for processing the set $V = \cup_{i=1}^{|M|} V_i = \cup_{k=1}^{|J|} V^{(k)}$ of partially ordered operations, whose length $C_{\max}(S)$ is minimal among the lengths of all semiactive schedules existing for the general shop scheduling problem $G_c|t_{ij} = 1|C_{\max}$. The input data for the general shop unit-time scheduling problem $G_c|t_{ij} = 1|C_{\max}$ are determined by the mixed graph $G = (V, A, E)$, where the vertex set V is a set of operations, the arc set A determines precedence constraints and the edge set E determines capacity constraints.

The union $A^* \cup E^*$ of the arc set A^* and the edge set E^* determines $|J|$ subsets $V^{(k)}$ of the linearly ordered operations of the jobs $J_k \in J$. The subset $E \backslash E^*$ of the edges determines $|M|$ cliques $\left\{ v_{i_1}, v_{i_2}, \ldots, v_{i_{|V_i|}} \right\}$ in the subgraph $(V, \varnothing, E \backslash E^*)$, where all operations $\left\{ v_{i_1}, v_{i_2}, \ldots, v_{i_{|V_i|}} \right\}$ must be processed on the same processor $M_i \in M$. The precedence constraints between operations belonging to different jobs are determined by the directed subgraph $(V, A \backslash A^*, \varnothing)$ of the mixed graph $G = (V, A, E)$.

If the completion time c_{k_p} of the operation v_{k_p}, $J_k \in J$, must precede the start time s_{l_q} of the operation v_{l_q} belonging the job $J_l \in J$ with $k \neq l$, then the mixed graph $G = (V, A, E)$ must contain both arc $(v_{k_p}, v_{l_q}) \in A$ and edge $[v_{k_p}, v_{l_q}] \in E$; see Definition 1. We denote this completion-start constraint as $v_{k_p} \Rightarrow v_{l_q}$. If the constraint $v_p \Rightarrow v_q$ holds for the unit-time scheduling problem $G_c|t_{ij} = 1|C_{\max}$, then the implication (1) holds for the arc $(v_p, v_q) \in A$ (the implication $(v_p, v_q) \in A \Rightarrow [v_p, v_q] \in E^*$ holds for the edges $E^* \subseteq E$). If the start time s_{k_p} of the operation v_{k_p} of the job $J_k \in J$ must precede the start time s_{l_q} of the operation v_{l_q}, $J_l \in J$, where $k \neq l$, then the desired mixed graph $G = (V, A, E)$ contains arc $(v_{k_p}, v_{l_q}) \in A$. We denote this weak precedence constraint as follows: $v_{k_p} \rightarrow v_{l_q}$. If the precedence constraint $v_p \rightarrow v_q$ holds for the problem $G_c|t_{ij} = 1|C_{\max}$, then the implication (1) does not hold for the arc $(v_p, v_q) \in A$.

Due to the use of weak precedence constraints, it is possible to require that a subset $V(k) \subset V$ of the unit-time operations must be processed simultaneously. To represent such a requirement, it is necessary to construct a circuit containing all vertices of the set $V(k)$. As shown in [9], the constructed mixed graph $G = (V, A, E)$ completely determines the input data for a general shop unit-time problem $G_c|t_{ij} = 1|C_{\max}$.

Definition 4. *If a mixed graph $G = (V, A, E)$ completely determines the input data for the scheduling problem $\alpha|\beta|\gamma$, then this individual problem $\alpha|\beta|\gamma$ is called a scheduling problem $\alpha|\beta|\gamma$ on the mixed graph G.*

Theorem 3 was proved in [9].

Theorem 3 ([9]). *A general shop unit-time problem $G_c|t_{ij} = 1|C_{\max}$ on the mixed graph $G = (V, A, E)$ reduces to the problem of determining the optimal colouring $c(G)$.*

It should be noted that there are problems in finding optimal colourings of the mixed graph that cannot be represented as a general shop unit-time scheduling problem $G_c|t_{ij} = 1|C_{\max}$. In Appendix A, we solve Example A1 of the unit-time scheduling problem $G_c|t_{ij} = 1|C_{\max}$ to illustrate Theorem 3.

3. Colouring Vertices of Mixed Graphs and Unit-Time Scheduling Problems

In contrast to shop scheduling problems $J|t_{ij} = 1|C_{\max}$, $G_c|t_{ij} = 1|C_{\max}$ and other scheduling problems [5], where one machine performs each operation (task), in the multi-stage system, with multi-processor tasks [5,10,11], the task may require one processor or several dedicated processors during the entire time of processing this task. The tasks that require a common processor cannot be processed simultaneously.

Chapter 10 of the monograph [5] is devoted to unit-time scheduling problems $GMPT|t_{ij} = 1|C_{\max}$ with multi-processor tasks. In [9], the more general unit-time scheduling problem $G_cMPT|t_{ij} = 1|C_{\max}$ was introduced including the unit-time scheduling problem $GMPT|t_{ij} = 1|C_{\max}$. In the unit-time scheduling problem $G_cMPT|t_{ij} = 1|C_{\max}$, two types of the precedence relations $v_{k_p} \rightarrow v_{l_q}$ and $v_{k_h} \Rightarrow v_{l_g}$ can be given in the input data. It may also be required that a set $V(k) = \{v_{k_1}, v_{k_2}, \ldots, v_{k_{|V(k)|}}\} \subseteq V$ of multi-processor tasks has to be performed simultaneously in each schedule. To present this condition, the circuit $(v_{k_1}, v_{k_2}, \ldots, v_{k_{|V(k)|}}, v_{k_1})$ must be included in the digraph $(V, A, \varnothing)$ such that the following is true:

$$A'_c = \{(v_{k_1}, v_{k_2}), (v_{k_2}, v_{k_3}), \ldots, (v_{k_{|V(k)|-1}}, v_{k_{|V(k)|}}), (v_{k_{|V(k)|}}, v_{k_1})\} \subseteq A.$$

We assume that the input data of the considered unit-time scheduling problem $G_cMPT|t_{ij} = 1|C_{\max}$ includes w subsets $V(1), V(2), \ldots, V(w)$ of the given set

$V = \{v_1, v_2, \ldots, v_n\}$ such that all tasks of the subset $V(k)$ must be performed simultaneously; $k \in \{1, 2, \ldots, w\}$. Since all unit-time tasks of the set $V(k) = \left\{v_{k_1}, v_{k_2}, \ldots, v_{k_{|V(k)|}}\right\}$ must be fulfilled simultaneously, we obtain the following set of arcs:

$$A_c = \bigcup_{k=1}^{w} \left\{(v_{k_1}, v_{k_2}), (v_{k_2}, v_{k_3}), \ldots, (v_{k_{|V(k)|-1}}, v_{k_{|V(k)|}}), (v_{k_{|V(k)|}}, v_{k_1})\right\} \subseteq A \tag{4}$$

The example of the unit-time problem $G_cMPT|t_{ij} = 1|C_{\max}$ defines the mixed graph $G = (V, A, E)$ with arc set $A \supseteq A_c$. Theorems 4 and 5 are proven in [9].

Theorem 4 ([9]). *The unit-time problem $G_cMPT|t_{ij} = 1|C_{\max}$ on the mixed graph $G = (V, A, E)$ is solvable if and only if the directed subgraph $(V, A, \varnothing)$ has no circuit containing adjacent vertices in the subgraph $(V, \varnothing, E)$.*

Theorem 5 ([9]). *Every solvable unit-time problem $G_cMPT|t_{ij} = 1|C_{\max}$ on the mixed graph $G = (V, A, E)$ is equivalent to the problem of finding an optimal colouring $c(G)$ of the mixed graph G. For every colourable mixed graph $G = (V, A, E)$ there exists a unit-time problem $G_cMPT|t_{ij} = 1|C_{\max}$ determined by the same mixed graph G, which is equivalent to finding an optimal colouring $c(G)$ of the mixed graph G.*

Theorems 4 and 5 are illustrated by solving Example A2 of the problem $G_cMPT|t_{ij} = 1|C_{\max}$ on the mixed graph G depicted in Figure A2; see Appendix B.

4. Minimising Maximal Lateness and Equivalent Minimising Makespan for Jobs with Integer Release Dates

The unit-time problem $G_cMPT|[r_i], t_{ij} = 1|C_{\max}$ with integer release dates $r_i \geq 0$ of the jobs $J_i \in J$ has been studied in [12]. Since release dates r_i are non-negative integers and operations have unit durations, the input data of the problem $G_cMPT|[r_i], t_{ij} = 1|C_{\max}$ can be determined by the mixed graph G; see Sections 2 and 3.

4.1. Minimising Makespan for Unit-Time Tasks as Optimal Mixed Graph Colouring

In the problem $G_cMPT|[r_i], t_{ij} = 1|C_{\max}$, the multi-processor task $v_i \in V$ is considered as a job J_i. A job consisting of a single operation is referred to as a simple job in Theorem 6 which follows. Note that the first part of this theorem has been proven in [12] by generating a mixed graph $G\prime$, which determines the problem $G_cMPT|t_{ij} = 1|C_{\max}$ to the mixed graph $G = (V, A, E)$ determining the input data for the problem $G_cMPT|[r_i], t_{ij} = 1|C_{\max}$. Due to the demonstrated correspondence of the terms used in optimal coloring $c(G)$ and those used in solving a unit-time problem $G_cMPT|[r_i], t_{ij} = 1|C_{\max}$, the following first part of Theorem 6 was proven in [12]: *Any solvable unit-time problem $G_cMPT|[r_i], t_{ij} = 1|C_{\max}$ on the mixed graph $G = (V, A, E)$ is equivalent to the problem of finding an optimal colouring of the mixed graph $G = (V, A, E)$.*

Theorem 6. *Any solvable unit-time problem $G_cMPT|[r_i], t_{ij} = 1|C_{\max}$ on the mixed graph G is equivalent to the problem of finding an optimal colouring of the mixed graph G. Conversely, for any colourable mixed graph G, there exists a unit-time problem $G_cMPT|[r_i], t_{ij} = 1|C_{\max}$ on the mixed graph G, which is equivalent to the problem of finding optimal colouring $c(G)$.*

Proof of the second part of Theorem 6. We next prove the claim as follows: *for any colorable mixed graph $G = (V, A, E)$, there exists a unit-time problem $G_cMPT|[r_i], t_{ij} = 1|C_{\max}$ on the mixed graph G, which is equivalent to the problem of finding optimal colouring $c(G)$.* Let set Ω denote a set of all circuits existing in the digraph $(V, A, \varnothing)$.

We will treat two possible cases, I and II.

Case I. Let set Ω be empty; $\Omega = \varnothing$.

The unit-time scheduling problem $G_cMPT||[r_i], t_{ij} = 1|C_{\max}$ on the mixed graph $G = (V, A, E)$ may be constructed based on Algorithm 1, which follows.

Case II. Let set Ω be not empty; $\Omega \neq \varnothing$.

The mixed graph $G = (V, A, E)$ is colourable. So, due to Theorem 1, each circuit $(v_{k_1}, v_{k_2}, \ldots, v_{k_{|V(k)|}}, v_{k_1})$ in set Ω has no vertices that are adjacent in the graph $(V, \varnothing, E)$. Therefore, all tasks of the set $\left\{v_{k_1}, v_{k_2}, \ldots, v_{k_{|V(k)|}}\right\} = V(k)$ must be processed simultaneously in the unit-time problem $G_cMPT||[r_i], t_{ij} = 1|C_{\max}$ on the mixed graph $G = (V, A, E)$ with the circuit $(v_{k_1}, v_{k_2}, \ldots, v_{k_{|V(k)|}}, v_{k_1})$ existing in the directed subgraph $(V, A, \varnothing)$. Assume that $\Omega = \bigcup_{k=1}^{w} V(k) = \bigcup_{k=1}^{w}\left\{(v_{k_1}, v_{k_2}, v_{k_3}, \ldots, v_{k_{|V(k)|-1}}, v_{k_{|V(k)|}}, v_{k_1})\right\}$. We delete arcs A_c determined in (4) from the mixed graph $G = (V, A, E)$ and apply Algorithm 1 to the constructed mixed graph $G^0 = (V, A \backslash A_c, E)$. Thus, we construct the unit-time problem $G_cMPT||[r_i], t_{ij} = 1|C_{\max}$ on the mixed graph $G^0 = (V, A \backslash A_c, E)$, which is equivalent to the problem of finding the optimal coloring $c(G^0)$. This unit-time problem $G_cMPT||[r_i], t_{ij} = 1|C_{\max}$ on the mixed graph $G = (V, A, E)$ is equivalent to the problem of finding the optimal colouring $c(G)$ of the mixed graph G. □

Algorithm 1: Determining the unit-time problem $G_cMPT\Big|[r_i], t_{ij} = 1\Big|C_{\max}$, which is equivalent to the problem of finding an optimal colouring $c(G)$.

Input: A mixed graph $G = (V, A, E)$ with a circuit-free digraph $(V, A, \varnothing)$.

Output: The unit-time problem $G_cMPT\Big|[r_i], t_{ij} = 1\Big|C_{\max}$ on the mixed graph $G = (V, A, E)$ that is equivalent to the problem of finding the optimal colouring $c(G)$.

Step 1: Partition graph $(V, \varnothing, E)$ into maximal number of the connected components: $(V, \varnothing, E) = (V_1, \varnothing, E_1) \cup \ldots \cup V_m, \varnothing, E_m) \cup (V_{m+1}, \varnothing, \varnothing) \ldots \cup (V_{m+r}, \varnothing, \varnothing)$, where subgraphs $(V_k, \varnothing, E_k)$ are connected components of the graph $(V, \varnothing, E)$ for $k \in \{1, 2, \ldots, m\}$, $|V_k| \geq 2$, and each subgraph $(V_j, \varnothing, \varnothing)$ determines an isolated vertex for index $j \in \{m+1, m+2, \ldots, m+r\}$. Denote isolated vertices as follows: $\left\{v_{j_1}\right\} = V_j$. Set $M = \varnothing$, $k = 1, i = 0$, and $l_0 = 0$.

Step 2: **IF** $k = m + 1$ **GOTO** step 5 **ELSE** find all maximum complete vertex-induced subgraphs $(V_k^1, \varnothing, E_k^1), \ldots, (V_k^{l_k}, \varnothing, E_k^{l_k})$ of the graph $(V_k, \varnothing, E_k)$. Set $r = 1, i := i + l_{k-1} + 1$.

Step 3: **FOR** every index i, add the new processor M_i to the already constructed set; $M := M \cup \{M_i\}$. State that all tasks of the clique V_k^r of the graph $(V_k, \varnothing, E_k)$ will be processed on the processor M_i; $V_k^r = V_i = \left\{v_{i_1}, v_{i_2}, \ldots, v_{i_{|V_i|}}\right\}$, where all tasks $\left\{v_{i_1}, v_{i_2}, \ldots, v_{i_{|V_i|}}\right\}$ will be processed on the processor M_i. Set $i := i + 1$.

Step 4: **IF** $i = \sum_{h=0}^{k} l_h$ **THEN** $k := k + 1$ **GOTO** step 2 **ELSE** $r := r + 1$ **GOTO** step 3.

Step 5: **FOR** every index $j \in \{m+1, \ldots, m+r\}$, add the new processor M_{i+j-m} to the already constructed set M; $M := M \cup \left\{M_{i+j-m}\right\}$. State that task v_{j_1}, $V_j = \left\{v_{j_1}\right\}$, which is isolated in the graph $(V, \varnothing, E)$, will be processed on processor M_{i+j-m}. Processor M_{i+j} will process only task v_{j_1}. Set $M := M \cup \{M_{i+1}, \ldots, M_{i+r}\}$.

Step 6: **FOR** every arc $(v_p, v_q) \in A$, for which the implication (2) does not hold, determine the weak precedence constraint $v_p \rightarrow v_q$.

Step 7: **FOR** every arc $(v_p, v_q) \in A$, for which the implication (2) holds, determine the precedence constraint $v_p \Rightarrow v_q$.

Step 8: The unit-time problem $G_cMPT\Big|[r_i], t_{ij} = 1\Big|C_{\max}$ on the mixed graph $G = (V, A, E)$ is constructed, where the precedence constraints on the set V are defined at steps 6 and 7. The set M of the processors is defined at steps 3 and 5. **STOP.**

The above Algorithm 1 shows us how to construct the unit-time problem $G_cMPT||[r_i], t_{ij} = 1|C_{\max}$ on the mixed graph $G = (V, A, E)$, which is equivalent to the problem of finding an optimal coloring $c(G)$ of the mixed graph $G = (V, A, E)$, all jobs in the set J being simple.

To illustrate Theorem 6, we solve Example 2 of the unit-time problem $G_cMPT||[r_i], t_{ij} = 1|C_{\max}$ on the mixed graph $G = (V, A, E)$ depicted in Figure 2.

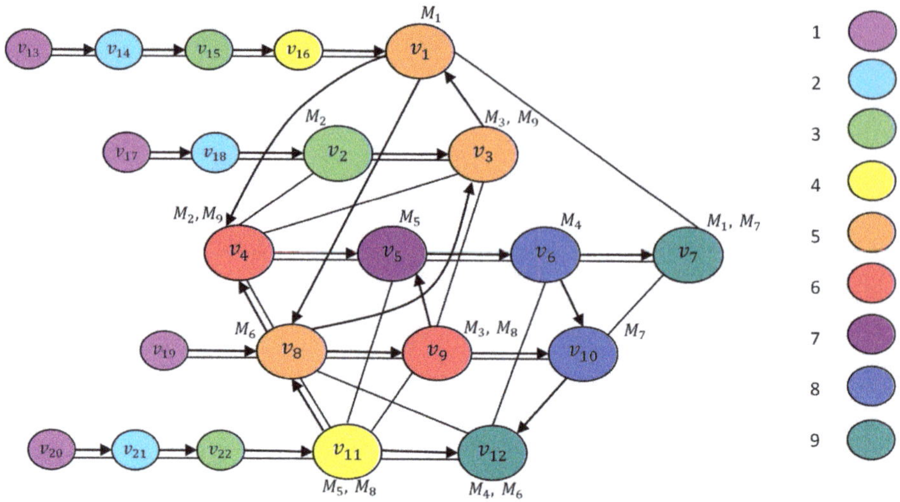

Figure 2. Mixed graph $G^{**} = (V^{**}, A^{**}, E^{**})$ determining input data for Example 2.

Example 2. *This example is similar to Example A2 with the input data shown in Figure A2; see Appendix B. The only difference is that the input data for Example 2 include the following release dates for the jobs* $\{J_1, J_2, \ldots, J_5\} = J$: $r_1 = 4$, $r_2 = 2$, $r_3 = 0$, $r_4 = 1$, $r_5 = 3$. *We determine the input data for Example 2 based on a mixed graph* $G^{**} = (V^{**}, A^{**}, E^{**})$ *that includes the subgraph* $G = (V, A, E)$ *presented in Figure 2. The release date* $r_1 = 4$ *of the job* $J_1 \in J$ *is represented by the union of path* $(v_{13}, v_{14}, v_{15}, v_{16}, v_1)$ *in the directed graph* $(V^{**}, A^{**}, \varnothing)$ *and chain* $(v_{13}, v_{14}, v_{15}, v_{16}, v_1)$ *in the graph* $(V^{**}, \varnothing, E^{**})$. *The release date* $r_2 = 2$ *of the job* $J_2 \in J$ *is represented by the union of path* (v_{17}, v_{18}, v_2) *in the directed graph* $(V^{**}, A^{**}, \varnothing)$ *and chain* (v_{17}, v_{18}, v_2) *in the graph* $(V^{**}, \varnothing, E^{**})$. *The release date* $r_4 = 1$ *of the job* $J_4 \in J$ *is represented by the union of arc* (v_{19}, v_8) *in the directed graph* $(V^{**}, A^{**}, \varnothing)$ *and edge* $[v_{19}, v_8]$ *in the graph* $(V^{**}, \varnothing, E^{**})$. *The release date* $r_5 = 3$ *of the job* $J_5 \in J$ *is represented by the union of path* $(v_{20}, v_{21}, v_{22}, v_{11})$ *in the directed graph* $(V^{**}, A^{**}, \varnothing)$ *and chain* $(v_{20}, v_{21}, v_{22}, v_{11})$ *in the graph* $(V^{**}, \varnothing, E^{**})$.

The directed subgraph $(V^{**}, A^{**}, \varnothing)$ of the mixed graph $G^{**} = (V^{**}, A^{**}, E^{**})$ contains the single circuit (v_1, v_8, v_3, v_1). Since this circuit has no vertices that are adjacent in the subgraph $(V^{**}, \varnothing, E^{**})$ of the mixed graph $G^{**} = (V^{**}, A^{**}, E^{**})$, there exists a semiactive schedule for Example 2 of the unit-time problem $G_cMPT||[r_i], t_{ij} = 1|C_{\max}$ on the mixed graph $G^{**} = (V^{**}, A^{**}, E^{**})$; see Theorem 4. One can construct the following optimal colouring of the mixed graph $G^{**} = (V^{**}, A^{**}, E^{**})$ depicted in Figure 2: $c(v_1) = 5$ $c(v_2) = 3$, $c(v_3) = 5$, $c(v_4) = 6$, $c(v_5) = 7$, $c(v_6) = 8$, $c(v_7) = 9$, $c(v_8) = 5$, $c(v_9) = 6$, $c(v_{10}) = 8$, $c(v_{11}) = 4$, $c(v_{12}) = 9$, $c(v_{13}) = 1$, $c(v_{14}) = 2$, $c(v_{15}) = 3$, $c(v_{16}) = 4$, $c(v_{17}) = 1$, $c(v_{18}) = 2$, $c(v_{19}) = 1$, $c(v_{20}) = 1$, $c(v_{21}) = 2$, $c(v_{22}) = 3$.

The colouring $c(G)$ with $\chi(G) = 9$ is optimal for Example 2 since digraph $(V^{**}, A^{**}, \varnothing)$ contains a path $(v_{20}, v_{21}, v_{22}, v_{11}, v_8, v_4, v_5, v_6, v_7)$ and the graph $(V^{**}, \varnothing, E^{**})$ contains a chain $(v_{20}, v_{21}, v_{22}, v_{11}, v_8, v_4, v_5, v_6, v_7)$ whose lengths are equal to 9. Because of this path and chain, the inequality $\chi(G^{**}) \geq 9$ holds. Based on Theorem 6, the colouring $c(G^{**})$ defines the following optimal semiactive schedule for Example 2:

$$S = (C(Q_{1,1}) = 5, C(Q_{2,1}) = 3, C(Q_{2,2}) = 5, C(Q_{3,1}) = 6, C(Q_{3,2}) = 7, C(Q_{3,3}) = 8, C(Q_{3,4}) = 9,$$

$$C(Q_{4,1}) = 5, C(Q_{4,2}) = 6, C(Q_{4,3}) = 8, C(Q_{5,1}) = 4, C(Q_{5,2}) = 9)$$

The correspondence between operations Q and vertices V is based on Remark 1. Due to Theorem 6, the following equalities hold: $\chi(G^{**}) = 9 = C_{\max}$.

4.2. Equivalent Scheduling Problems for Minimising either Makespan or Miximal Lateness

In [12], it was proven that the scheduling problem $G_cMPT\big|[r_i], t_{ij} = 1\big|C_{\max}$ reduces to the scheduling problem $G_cMPT\big|t_{ij} = 1, [D_i]\big|L_{\max}$ with the objective of minimising the maximal lateness $L_{\max} = \max\{C_i - D_i : J_i \in J\}$, where the given due dates $D_i \geq 0$ are integers.

Theorem 7 ([12]). *Every solvable unit-time problem $G_cMPT\big|[r_i], t_{ij} = 1\big|C_{\max}$ on the mixed graph G with integer release dates $r_i \geq 0$ reduces to unit-time problem $G_cMPT\big|t_{ij} = 1, [D_i]\big|L_{\max}$ with non-negative integer due dates, and vice versa.*

For illustrating Theorem 7, we solve Example 2 of the unit-time problem $G_cMPT\big|[r_i], t_{ij} = 1\big|C_{\max}$ on the mixed graph $G^{**} = (V^{**}, A^{**}, E^{**})$ shown in Figure 2 and the following Example 3 of the unit-time problem $G_cMPT\big|t_{ij} = 1, [D_i]\big|L_{\max}$.

Example 3. *In Example 3 of the problem $G_cMPT\big|t_{ij} = 1, [D_i]\big|L_{\max}$ on the mixed graph $G = (V, A, E)$ depicted in Figure 3, the set of jobs J_1, J_2, J_3, J_4 and J_5 are ready for processing on the processors $M = \{M_1, M_2, \ldots, M_9\}$ from a release date of zero. Each processor $M_k \in M$ must process the same subset of jobs as in Example 2. However, the orders for processing the same operations are opposite to the linear orders determined in Example 2. If the precedence constraints $v_i \to v_j$ and $v_p \Rightarrow v_q$ are given between operations belonging to different jobs in Example 2, the inverse precedence constraints $v_j \to v_i$ and $v_q \Rightarrow v_p$ must be given in Example 3 of the general shop scheduling problem $G_cMPT\big|t_{ij} = 1, [D_i]\big|L_{\max}$. For Example 3, the due dates of the given jobs J_1, J_2, J_3, J_4, J_5 are defined as follows: $D_1 = \max\{r_j : J_j \in J\} - r_1 = 4 - 4 = 0$, $D_2 = 4 - r_2 = 4 - 2 = 2$, $D_3 = 4 - r_3 = 4 - 0 = 4$, $D_4 = 4 - r_4 = 4 - 1 = 3$, $D_5 = 4 - r_5 = 4 - 3 = 1$.*

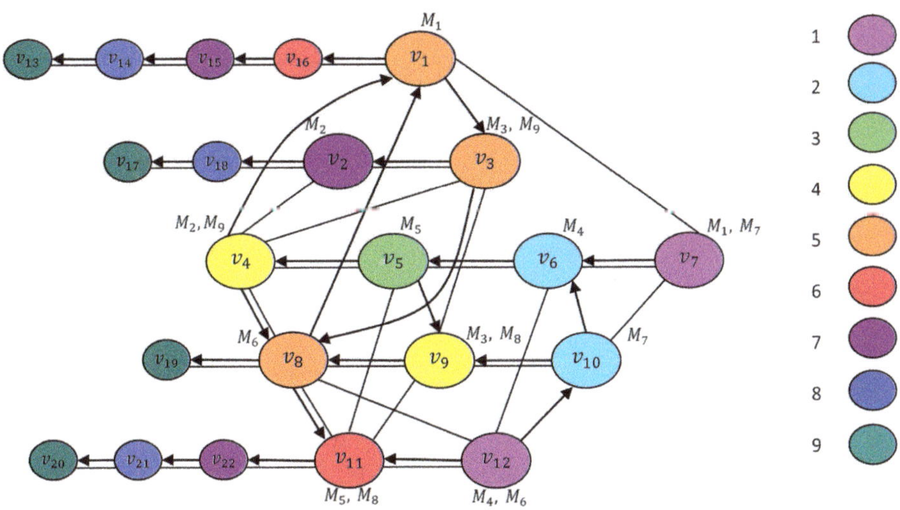

Figure 3. The colouring $c(G^{\leftarrow})$ determining the optimal semiactive schedule for the unit-time problem $G_cMPT\big|t_{ij} = 1, [D_i]\big|L_{\max}$.

The input data for Example 3 are given by the mixed graph $G^{\leftarrow} = (V^{**}, A^{\leftarrow}, E^{**})$ presented in Figure 3. The set V^{**} of vertices and the set E^{**} of edges in the mixed graph $G^{\leftarrow}$ are the same as those depicted in Figure 3 for the mixed graph G.

Compare the mixed graph depicted in Figure 3 for the problem $G_cMPT|t_{ij} = 1, [D_i]|L_{\max}$ and the mixed graph $G^{**} = (V^{**}, A^{**}, E^{**})$ depicted in Figure 2 for the problem $G_cMPT||r_i], t_{ij} = 1|C_{\max}$. By Theorems 6 and 7, for Example 3 of the general shop unit-time scheduling problem $GcMPT|t_i = 1, [D_i]|L_{\max}$ on the mixed graph $G^{\leftarrow} = (V^{**}, A^{\leftarrow}, E^{**})$, the optimal semiactive schedule S is determined by the optimal colouring of mixed graph $G^{\leftarrow} = (V^{**}, A^{\leftarrow}, E^{**})$ shown in Figure 3: $c(v_1) = 5$ $c(v_2) = 7$, $c(v_3) = 5$, $c(v_4) = 4$ $c(v_5) = 3$, $c(v_6) = 2$, $c(v_7) = 1$, $c(v_8) = 5$, $c(v_9) = 4$, $c(v_{10}) = 2$, $c(v_{11}) = 6$, $c(v_{12}) = 1$, $c(v_{13}) = 9$, $c(v_{14}) = 8$, $c(v_{15}) = 7$, $c(v_{16}) = 6$, $c(v_{17}) = 9$, $c(v_{18}) = 8$, $c(v_{19}) = 6$, $c(v_{20}) = 9$, $c(v_{21}) = 8$, $c(v_{22}) = 7$.

The colouring $c(G^{\leftarrow})$ defines the following optimal schedule for Example 3:

$$S = (C(Q_{1,1}) = 5, C(Q_{2,1}) = 7, C(Q_{2,2}) = 5, C(Q_{3,1}) = 4, C(Q_{3,2}) = 3, C(Q_{3,3}) = 2, C(Q_{3,4}) = 1,$$
$$C(Q_{4,1}) = 5, C(Q_{4,2}) = 4, C(Q_{4,3}) = 2, C(Q_{5,1}) = 6, C(Q_{5,2}) = 1)$$

The optimal maximum lateness is equal to $\chi(G^{\leftarrow}) - \max\{r_i : J_i \in J\} = 9 - 4 = 5$.

5. An Optimal Schedule of Interruptible Operations with Integer Processing Times

We investigate the scheduling problem $G_cMPT||r_i], [t_{ij}], pmtn|C_{\max}$ with integer release dates, positive integer operation durations, and allowed operation interruptions. In the three-field notation, *pmtn* indicates allowed preemptions of the operations and $[t_{ij}]$ ($[r_i]$, respectively) means that the operation durations (release dates of the jobs) are positive (non-negative) integers.

5.1. Partitions of the Interruptible Operations with Integer Duration into Unit-Time Operations

If interruptions of the operation are allowed, then a set of schedules is usually larger than a set of schedules of non-interruptible operations of the set Q. The larger set of schedules may complicate optimal scheduling [11]. Obviously, allowing interruptions of the operations from the set Q may decrease an optimal value of the objective function. Thus, for most scheduling problems, it is desirable to reduce the number of allowed interruptions of the operations Q without losing an optimal semiactive schedule.

Lemma 2. *If the release dates r_i of the jobs $J_i \in J$ are non-negative integers and the operations $Q_{ij} \in Q$ have positive integer durations $t_{ij} > 0$, then there exists an optimal semiactive schedule such that interruptions in processing operations occur only at the integer times.*

Proof. The interruption of the operation $Q_{ij} \in Q$ can reduce the value of a regular objective function in the semiactive schedule without interruptions only if the interruption is at a completion time of at least one operation $Q_{ij} \in Q$. In fact, due to such interruption of the operation $Q_{ij} \in Q$ processed on the processor $M_{\mu(i.j)} \in M$, another operation $Q_{uv} \in Q$ with $u \neq i$ can start its processing on the same processor $M_{\mu(i.j)} = M_{\mu(u,v)}$, since this processor becomes free.

Since the release dates r_i of the given jobs $J_i \in \left\{J_1, J_2, \ldots, J_{|J|}\right\}$ are non-negative integers and operations have positive integer durations, in any semiactive schedule without operation interruptions, the realisation of each operation can be completed only at integer times. Lemma is proven. □

Due to Lemma 2, operations $Q_{1,1} \in Q^{(1)}$ with positive integer durations can be partitioned into $t_{1,1}$ unit-time operations. We denote these unit-time operations as follows: $\left\{v_1, v_2, \ldots, v_{t_{1,1}}\right\}$. Let $\left\{v_{t_{1,1}+1}, v_{t_{1,1}+2}, \ldots, v_{t_{1,1}+t_{1,2}}\right\}$ be a set of all unit-time operations generated by similar partitioning the operation $Q_{1,2} \in Q^{(1)}$. Similarly, we partition operations $Q^{(1)} \setminus \{Q_{1,1}, Q_{1,2}\}$ into unit-time operations and assign sequential indexes to the generated unit-time operations.

Continuing the above partitioning procedure of operations from set $Q^{(1)}$ with integer durations, we generate the following set of unit-time operations:

$$W_1 = \left\{v_1, v_2, \ldots, v_{|W_1|}\right\}, \text{ where } |W_1| = \sum_{j=1}^{|Q^{(1)}|} t_{1,j}. \tag{5}$$

The generated unit-time operations will be ordered as follows: $(v_1, v_2, \ldots, v_{|W_1|})$ within any feasible schedule; see Lemma 2.

Remark 2. *We represent all unit-time operations generated by the above partition of operations Q as vertices in the mixed graph $G = (V, A, E)$. Here and elsewhere, the generated unit-time operations are linearly ordered in the ascending order of their indexes. For each job $J_i \in J$, the unit-time operations generated by the above partitioning procedure of the integer-time operations $Q^{(i)}$ will be fulfilled in the ascending order of their indexes in any semiactive schedule.*

We continue with the generated unit-time operation $v_{|W_1|+1}$ by sequentially indexing the generated unit-time operations into which integer-time operations from set $Q^{(2)} = \left\{Q_{2,1}, Q_{2,2}, \ldots, Q_{2,|Q^{(2)}|}\right\}$ contained in the job $J_2 \in J$ are partitioned. Thus, we obtain the following set of the unit-time operations:

$$W_2 = \left\{v_{|W_1|+1}, v_{|W_1|+2}, \ldots, v_{|W_2|}\right\}, \text{where } |W_2| = |W_1| + \sum_{j=1}^{|Q^{(2)}|} t_{2,j}, \tag{6}$$

of the linearly ordered unit-time operations generated from integer-time operations of job J_2; see Remark 2. Using the above partitioning technique, we index the unit-time operations of the jobs in set $J \setminus \{J_1, J_2\}$ in the increasing order of job indexes and indexes of all generated unit-time operations. At the end of this partitioning process, for operations with integer job durations $J_{|J|} \in J$, the following set is obtained:

$$W_{|J|} = \left\{v_{|W_{|J|-1}+1}, v_{|W_{|J|-1}+2}, \ldots, v_{|W_{|J|}|}\right\}, \text{ where } |W_{|J|}| = |W_{|J|-1}| + \sum_{j=1}^{|Q^{(|J|)}|} t_{|J|,j}, \tag{7}$$

of the ordered unit-time operations generated by the integer-time operations belonging to the job $J_{|J|}$. All jobs from the set J will be processed based on Remark 2 applied to the set $W := \cup_{i=1}^{|J|} W_i$ of all generated unit-time operations. Furthermore, for each job $J_i \in J$, the unit-time operations of the set W_i generated by the above partitioning procedure applied to the integer-time operations of the set $Q^{(i)}$ are fulfilled in increasing order of their indexes during the realisation of each semiactive schedule.

5.2. Relationships between Scheduling Problems and Optimal Mixed Graph Colourings

We next prove Theorem 8, which generalizes Theorem 5 to the problem $G_cMPT|[r_i], [t_{ij}], pmtn|C_{\max}$ of constructing an optimal schedule for fulfilling jobs $J_i \in J$ with integer release dates $r_i \geq 0$ and positive durations $t_{ij} > 0$ of the operations $Q_{ij} \in Q^{(i)} \subseteq Q$ with allowed interruptions.

Theorem 8. *Every solvable scheduling problem $G_cMPT|[r_i], [t_{ij}], pmtn|C_{\max}$ pseudo-polynomially reduces to a problem of constructing an optimal colouring of vertices of the mixed graph $G = (V, A, E)$. For every colourable mixed graph G, there exists a scheduling problem $G_cMPT|[r_i], [t_{ij}], pmtn|C_{\max}$ on the mixed graph G, which is equivalent to the problem of finding the optimal colouring $c(G)$ of vertices of the same mixed graph G.*

Proof. We consider arbitrary solvable scheduling problem $G_cMPT\big|[r_i],[t_{ij}],pmtn\big|C_{\max}$ of constructing a makespan-optimal schedule for fulfilling jobs $J=\left\{J_1,J_2,\ldots,J_{|J|}\right\}$ by the available dedicated processors $M=\left\{J_1,J_2,\ldots,J_{|M}\right\}$. We show how to construct the mixed graph $G=(V,A,E)$ such that optimal colouring $c(G)$ defines a solution to the problem $G_cMPT\big|[r_i],[t_{ij}],pmtn\big|C_{\max}$.

Due to Lemma 2, there exists an optimal semiactive schedule such that interruptions in the operations (if any) occur only at the integer time moments. Thus, to construct the mixed graph $G=(V,A,E)$, we will determine a set of unit-time operations

$$W=\left\{v_1,v_2,\ldots,v_{|W|}\right\}=\cup_{i=1}^{|J|}W_i$$

generated by the above partitioning of the integer-time operations belonging to jobs $J_i\in J=\left\{J_1,J_2,\ldots,J_{|J|}\right\}$ into the unit-time tasks sequentially, as shown in Section 5.1. The Formula (5) determines the set W_1 of the unit-time tasks generated by integer-time tasks $Q^{(1)}$ belonging to a job J_1.

The Formula (6) determines the set W_2 of the unit-time tasks generated by the integer-time tasks $Q^{(2)}$ belonging to the job J_2.

Similar formulas for sets $Q^{(3)},Q^{(4)},\ldots,Q^{(|J|-1)}$ of the integer-time tasks sequentially determine sets $W_3,W_4,\ldots,W_{|J|-1}$, respectively, of the generated unit-time tasks.

Finally, the Formula (7) determines the set $W_{|J|}$ of the unit-time tasks generated by the integer-time tasks $Q^{(|J|)}$ belonging to the last job $J_{|J|}\in J$.

The above partitioning(see Section 5.1) of the integer-time tasks $Q=\bigcup_{i=1}^{|J|}Q^{(i)}$ into the unit-time tasks determines a subgraph $(W,\varnothing,\varnothing)$ with an empty set of arcs and an empty set of edges in the indicated mixed graph $G=(V,A,E)$, where $W\subset V$. Based on Remark 2, every job $J_i\in J$ consisting of the ordered set of the integer-time tasks $Q^{(i)}$ is partitioned into the linearly ordered set of the unit-time tasks of the following form: $W_i=\left\{v_{|W_{i-1}|+1},v_{|W_{i-1}|+2},\ldots,v_{|W_i|}\right\}$.

In any semiactive schedule, the unit-time tasks W_i have to be executed in ascending order of indexes of the unit-time tasks $v_k\in W_i$; see Remark 2. By Definition 1, the desired mixed graph $G=(V,A,E)$ must contain the set of arcs $A_i=\{(v_{|W_{i-1}|+1},v_{|W_{i-1}|+2}),(v_{|W_{i-1}|+2},v_{|W_{i-1}|+3}),\ldots,(v_{|W_i|-1},v_{|W_i|})\}$ and the following set of edges: $E_i=\left\{[v_{|W_{i-1}|+1},v_{|W_{i-1}|+2}],[v_{|W_{i-1}|+2},v_{|W_{i-1}|+3}],\ldots,[v_{|W_i|-1},v_{|W_i|}]\right\}$.

The sets of arcs A_i and edges E_i will determine the linear order for the execution of the unit-time tasks from set W_i when implementing any semiactive schedule for the problem $G_cMPT\big|[r_i],[t_{ij}],pmtn\big|C_{\max}$; see Remark 2.

Thus, we constructed a subgraph $(W,\cup_{i=1}^{|J|}A_i,\cup_{i=1}^{|J|}E_i)$ of the desired mixed graph $G=(V,A,E)$ where inclusion $W\subset V$ holds. For every processor $M_k\in M$, set Q_k of all integer-time tasks fulfilled by the processor M_k defines set V_k of unit-time tasks fulfilled by the processor M_k. The cardinality of set V_k is equal to the total processing time of the integer-time tasks for fulfilling all jobs in the set $J^{(k)}=:\left\{J_{k_1},J_{k_2},\ldots,J_{|J^{(k)}|}\right\}$. So, the following equality holds:

$$\left|V_k\right|=\sum\nolimits_{J_i\in J^{(k)}}t_{ik} \tag{8}$$

Set V_k is partitioned into $\left|J^{(k)}\right|$ subsets V_k^j of the tasks with unit durations for fulfilling jobs $J_{k_j}\in J^{(k)}$, i.e., the equality $V_k=V_k^1\cup V_k^2\cup\ldots\cup V_k^{|J^{(k)}|}$ holds, where $V_k^j\neq\varnothing$ and $V_k^j\cap V_k^h=\varnothing$ for each indices $j\neq h$. As can be easily verified, the forbiddance to simultaneously execute every pair of the unit-time tasks of the set V_k in a semiactive schedule is determined by the complete $\left|J^{(k)}\right|$-partite subgraph $(V_k,\varnothing,E_k)$ of the mixed graph $G=(V,A,E)$ with the following set $\left\{V_k^1, V_k^2, \ldots, V_k^{|J^{(k)}|}\right\}$ of vertices and the following edge set E_k with the cardinality determined as follows:

$$|E_k| = \sum_{i=1}^{|J^{(k)}|-1} \sum_{j=i+1}^{|J^{(k)}|} \left\{\left|V_k^i\right| \times \left|V_k^j\right|\right\} \tag{9}$$

Together with the precedence constraints determined above between tasks belonging to the same job $J_i \in J$, the input data for the problem $G_cMPT\big|[r_i], [t_{ij}], pmtn\big|C_{\max}$ may include the precedence constraints defined on the set of tasks, which belong to different jobs of the set J. Let these precedence constraints be determined as follows:

$$R_{\Rightarrow} = \left\{v_{k_1} \Rightarrow v_{k_2},\ v_{k_3} \Rightarrow v_{k_4}, \ldots, v_{k_{|k|}-1} \Rightarrow v_{k_{|k|}}\right\} \tag{10}$$

Moreover, the following weak precedence constraints on the set of tasks, which belong to different jobs of the set J, may also be determined:

$$R_{\rightarrow} = \left\{v_{h_1} \rightarrow v_{h_2},\ v_{h_3} \rightarrow v_{h_4}, \ldots, v_{h_{|h|}-1} \rightarrow v_{h_{|h|}}\right\} \tag{11}$$

According to Definition 1, we introduce the precedence constraints (10) by adding the set $A_{|J|+1} = \left\{(v_{k_1}, v_{k_2}), (v_{k_2}, v_{k_3}), \ldots, (v_{k_{|k|}-1}, v_{k_{|k|}})\right\}$ of the arcs and the set $E_{|J|+1} = \left\{[v_{k_1}, v_{k_2}], [v_{k_2}, v_{k_3}], \ldots, [v_{k_{|k|}-1}, v_{k_{|k|}}]\right\}$ of the edges in the mixed graph $G = (V, A, E)$.

To determine the weak precedence constraints (11), it is sufficient to add the following set $A_{|J|+2} = \left\{(v_{h_1}, v_{h_2}), (v_{h_2}, v_{h_3}), \ldots, (v_{h_{|h|}-1}, v_{h_{|h|}})\right\}$ of the arcs in the desired mixed graph $G = (V, A, E)$. Let the input data for the scheduling problem $G_cMPT\big|[r_i], [t_{ij}], pmtn\big|C_{\max}$ include the subsets $V(1), V(2), \ldots, V(l)$ of the unit-time operations from the set Q such that operations of the subset $V(g) = \left\{v_{g_1}, v_{g_2}, \ldots, v_{g_{|V(g)|}}\right\} \subset Q$ must be executed simultaneously in any schedule, where $g \in \{1, 2, \ldots, l\}$. Therefore, the set of weak precedence constraints $R_{\rightarrow}$ determined in (11) must contain the following subset:

$$\cup_{g=1}^{l}\left\{v_{g_1} \rightarrow v_{g_2}, v_{g_2} \rightarrow v_{g_3}, \ldots, v_{g_{|g|}-1} \rightarrow v_{g_{|g|}}, v_{g_{|g|}} \rightarrow v_{g_1}\right\}$$

It is clear that the above constructed set $A_{|J|+2}$ of the arcs must contain the following set of the arcs: $A_{|J|+3} = \cup_{g=1}^{l}\left\{(v_{g_1}, v_{g_2}), (v_{g_2}, v_{g_3}), \ldots, (v_{g_{|g|}-1}, v_{g_{|g|}}), (v_{g_{|g|}}, v_{g_1})\right\}$; see Definition 1. We have constructed the arc set $A^o = \left\{\cup_{i=1}^{|J|} A_i\right\} \cup A_{|J|+1} \cup A_{|J|+2} \cup A_{|J|+3}\}$, the edge set $E^o = \left\{\cup_{i=1}^{|J|} E_i\right\} \cup E_{|J|+1}$ and the vertex set $W = \left\{v_1, v_2, \ldots, v_{|W|}\right\} = \cup_{i=1}^{|J|} W_i$, where each vertex determines the unit-time operation (task) generated by the operation from the set Q with integer durations. Thus, we have constructed the mixed graph (W, A^o, E^o), which is a subgraph of the desired mixed graph G.

The input data for the considered solvable problem $G_cMPT\big|[r_i], [t_{ij}], pmtn\big|C_{\max}$ include also the non-negative integer release dates $r_1, r_2, \ldots, r_{|J|}$ of the jobs $J_1, J_2, \ldots, J_{|J|}$, respectively. Therefore, for every job $J_i \in J$, the set $W(r_i) = \left\{v_{i_1^0}, v_{i_2^0}, \ldots, v_{i_{r_{i-1}}^0}\right\}$ of the vertices and the path $(v_{i_1^0}, v_{i_2^0}, \ldots, v_{i_{r_{i-1}}^0})$, whose length is equal to $r_i \geq 0$, are determined. We add all these vertices and arcs of the following paths: $(v_{i_1^0}, v_{i_2^0}, \ldots, v_{i_{r_{i-1}}^0})$ to subgraph $(W, A^o, \varnothing)$ of mixed graph (W, A^o, E^o).

We also add the edges of the following chains $(v_{i_1^0}, v_{i_2^0}, \ldots, v_{i_{r_{i-1}}^0})$ to subgraph $(W, \varnothing, E^o)$ of mixed graph (W, A^o, E^o). Let $G = \{V, A, E)$ be a mixed graph generated by the mixed graph (W, A^o, E^o) after adding all the vertices $\bigcup_{i=1}^{|J|} W(r_i)$, all the arcs of paths $(v_{i_1^0}, v_{i_2^0}, \ldots, v_{i_{r_i-1}^0})$ and all the edges of chains $(v_{i_1^0}, v_{i_2^0}, \ldots, v_{i_{r_i-1}^0})$.

Thus, we have constructed the desired mixed graph $G = (V, A, E)$. For the constructed mixed graph, the following equality $V = W + \bigcup_{i=1}^{|J|} W(r_i)$ holds. Due to the above construction of the mixed graph, the precedence constraints defined on the set of tasks for the problem $G_cMPT\|[r_i], [t_{ij}], pmtn|C_{\max}$ are determined by graph (W, A^o, E^o). The prohibition of simultaneously fulfilling every pair of unit-time tasks of the set $V^{(k)}$ in any semiactive schedule is determined by the complete $|J^{(k)}|$-partite graph $(V^{(k)}, \varnothing, E^{(k)})$ with the vertex set $\left\{V_k^1, V_k^2, \ldots, V_k^{|J^{(k)}|}\right\}$. The given release dates $r_1, r_2, \ldots, r_{|J|}$ of the given jobs $J_1, J_2, \ldots, J_{|J|}$ are defined by a subgraph $(\bigcup_{i=1}^{|J|} W(r_i), A \setminus A^o, E \setminus E^o)$ of the constructed mixed graph $G = (V, A, E)$.

As can be easily verified, the constructed mixed graph $G = (V, A, E)$ completely defines the input data of the considered scheduling problem $G_cMPT\|[r_i], [t_{ij}], pmtn|C_{\max}$. Hence, for the solvable general scheduling problem $G_cMPT\|[r_i], [t_{ij}], pmtn|C_{\max}$ determined on mixed graph $G = (V, A, E)$, there exists a semiactive schedule

$$S = (C(v_1), C(v_2), \ldots, C(Q_{|W|})) \tag{12}$$

which defines the colouring $c(G)$ of the constructed mixed graph $G = (V, A, E)$ as follows: the equality $c(v_i) = C(v_i)$ holds for every vertex $v_i \in V$. It is clear that the optimal semiactive schedule S that exists for the solvable scheduling problem $G_cMPT\|[r_i], [t_{ij}], pmtn|C_{\max}$ on the mixed graph $G = (V, A, E)$ defines the optimal colouring $c(G)$ of the constructed mixed graph $G = (V, A, E)$.

Compare the form (1) of semiactive schedules existing for unit-time problems and the form (12) of semiactive schedules existing for problem $G_cMPT\|[r_i], [t_{ij}], pmtn|C_{\max}$ with the aim to construct a makespan-optimal schedule for fulfilling jobs $J_i \in J$ with the positive integer processing times $t_{ij} > 0$ of the operations $Q_{ij} \in Q$, provided that operation interruptions are allowed. Along with the completion times of the given operations $Q_{ij} \in Q^{(i)} \subseteq Q$, with integer processing times, the latter semiactive schedule must define the completion times of the unit-time operations generated by the above partitioning procedure of the operations $Q_{ij} \in Q^{(i)}$ with integer processing times. Due to the equalities (8) and (9), the described reduction of the general scheduling problem $G_cMPT\|[r_i], [t_{ij}], pmtn|C_{\max}$ to the problem of finding the optimal colouring $c(G)$ of the constructed mixed graph $G = (V, A, E)$ is pseudo-polynomial.

The proof of the first part of Theorem 8 is completed.

It should be noted that an optimal semiactive schedule existing for the problem $G_cMPT\|[r_i], [t_{ij}], pmtn|C_{\max}$ with positive integer durations of all given operations, integer non-negative release dates of the given jobs, and allowed operation interruptions can be obtained from the optimal semiactive schedule existing for the unit-time scheduling problem $G_cMPT\|[r_i], t_{ij} = 1|C_{\max}$, and vice versa. Indeed, if the integer-time operations $Q_{ij} \in Q$ are partitioned into the unit-time operations W based on the above partitioning procedure described in Section 5.1 (see Lemma 2 and Remark 2), the operation interruptions of the set W cannot reduce the value $C_{\max}$ for the optimal semiactive schedule. Thus, the possibilities of interrupting the operations in the scheduling problem $G_cMPT\|[r_i], [t_{ij}], pmtn|C_{\max}$ can be ignored when constructing a makespan-optimal semiactive schedule that exists for the considered scheduling problem.

Hence, the problem $G_cMPT\|[r_i], [t_{ij}], pmtn|C_{\max}$ can be solved as a special case of the unit-time scheduling problem $G_cMPT\|[r_i], t_{ij} = 1|C_{\max}$; see Section 4.1. Therefore, the proof of the second part of Theorem 8 follows directly from the second part of Theorem 6. Theorem 8 is proved. □

6. Example 4 of General Scheduling Problem with Interruptible Operations

To illustrate Theorem 8, we describe Example 4 of solvable scheduling problem $G_cMPT||[r_i],[t_{ij}],pmtn|C_{\max}$ with a set of jobs $J=\{J_1,J_2,J_3,J_4\}$, seven dedicated processors $M=\{M_1,M_2,\ldots,M_7\}$, integer release dates $r_i\geq 0$, integer processing times $t_{ij}>0$ of the multi-processor tasks, two types of the precedence constraints between operations, and allowed interruptions of the integer-time operations.

Example 4. *The main part of the input data for Example 4 is presented in* Table 1. *Other input data for Example 4 will be determined after constructing a mixed graph with a set W of the vertices corresponding to unit-time operations generated by partitioning the integer-time operations $Q_{ij}\in Q$ based on Remark 2.*

Table 1. A main part of the input data for Example 4.

Operations $Q_{1,j}$ of the job J_1	$Q_{1,1}$	$Q_{1,2}$	-	-
Processors $M_{\mu(1,j)}$	M_1,M_2	M_7	-	-
Duration $t_{1,j}$ of operation $Q_{1,j}$	2	1	-	-
Operations $Q_{2,j}$ of the job J_2	$Q_{2,1}$	$Q_{2,2}$	$Q_{2,3}$	-
Processors $M_{\mu(2,j)}$	M_3,M_7	M_1	M_2,M_6	-
Duration $t_{2,j}$ of operation $Q_{2,j}$	2	1	3	-
Operations $Q_{3,j}$ of the job J_3	$Q_{3,1}$	$Q_{3,2}$	$Q_{3,3}$	$Q_{3,4}$
Processors $M_{\mu(2,j)}$	M_3	M_1	M_4	M_5,M_6
Duration $t_{3,j}$ of operation $Q_{3,j}$	1	1	2	2
Operations $Q_{4,j}$ of the job J_4	$Q_{4,1}$	$Q_{4,2}$	-	-
Processors $M_{\mu(4,j)}$	M_1,M_3	M_4,M_5	-	-
Duration $t_{4,j}$ of operation $Q_{4,j}$	1	3	-	-

Using the constructive proof of the first part of Theorem 8, we next show how to construct the mixed graph determining the input data of Example 4. Based on Lemma 2, we first partition the integer-time operations $Q_{1,j}\in Q^{(1)}$ into operations $W_1=\{v_1,v_2,v_3\}$ with unit durations. Similarly, we partition the integer-time operations $Q_{2,j}\in Q^{(2)}$ into operations $W_2=\{v_4,v_5,v_6,v_7,v_8,v_9\}$ with unit durations. Then, we partition the integer-time operations $Q_{3,j}\in Q^{(3)}$ into operations $W_3=\{v_{10},v_{11},v_{12},v_{13},v_{14},v_{15}\}$ with unit durations. Finally, we partition the operations $Q_{4,j}\in Q^{(4)}$ of the last job into the operations $W_4=\{v_{16},v_{17},v_{18},v_{19}\}$ with unit durations. As a result, we construct the following set of operations: $W=\{v_1,v_2,\ldots,v_{19}\}=\cup_{i=1}^{4}W_i$ with unit durations generated from the integer-time operations of four given jobs $J=\{J_1,J_2,J_3,J_4\}$.

Due to Remark 2 and Definition 1, the mixed graph $G=(V,A,E)$ contains a set of arcs A_i and a set of edges E_i that determine the linear order of the operations of the set W_i in the semiactive schedule that exists for Example 4. The set of arcs A_i and the set of edges E_i must be constructed for each job $J_i\in\{J_1,J_2,J_3,J_4\}$. Thus, we have constructed a subgraph $(W,\cup_{i=1}^{|J|}A_i,\cup_{i=1}^{|J|}E_i)$ of mixed graph $G=(V,A,E)$ with inclusion $W\subset V$; see Figure 4, where the desired mixed graph G is depicted.

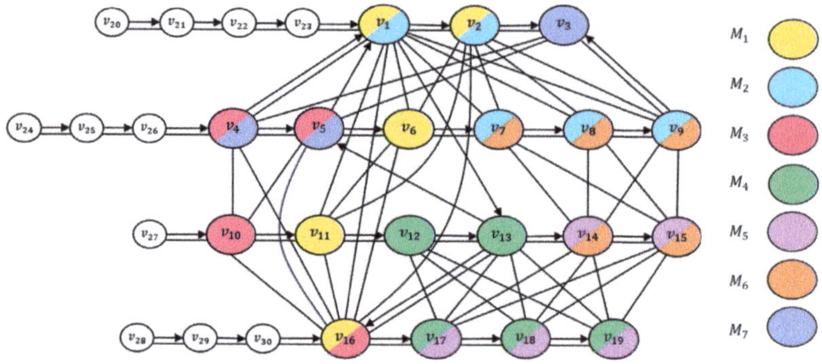

Figure 4. The mixed graph defining input data for Example 4 of the problem $G_cMPT\left|[r_i], [t_{ij}], pmtn\right|C_{\max}$.

For each processor $M_k \in M$, the operation set Q_k defines the set V_k of operations with unit durations to be executed on that processor M_k. The cardinality $|V_k|$ of set V_k is equal to the total processing time of the integer-time operations for fulfilling a set of the jobs $J^{(k)} = \left\{J_{k_1}, J_{k_2}, \ldots, J_{|J^{(k)}|}\right\}, k \in \{1,2,\ldots,7\}$. Based on the Formula (8), we calculate these cardinalities as follows:

$$|V_1| = \sum_{J_i \in J^{(1)}} t_{i,1} = 2+1+1+1 = 5, |V_2| = \sum_{J_i \in J^{(2)}} t_{i,2} = 2+3 = 5,$$
$$|V_3| = \sum_{J_i \in J^{(3)}} t_{i,3} = 2+1+1 = 4, |V_4| = \sum_{J_i \in J^{(4)}} t_{i,4} = 2+3 = 5,$$
$$|V_5| = \sum_{J_i \in J^{(5)}} t_{i,5} = 2+3 = 5, |V_6| = \sum_{J_i \in J^{(6)}} t_{i,6} = 3+2 = 5,$$
$$|V_7| = \sum_{J_i \in J^{(7)}} t_{i,7} = 1+2 = 3.$$

The prohibition of simultaneously executing each pair of unit-time operations of set V_k on the processor M_k in any semiactive schedule is determined by the complete $\left|J^{(k)}\right|$-partite subgraph $(V_k, \varnothing, E_k)$ with vertex set $\left\{V_k^1, V_k^2, \ldots, V_k^{|J^{(k)}|}\right\}$ as $\left|J^{(k)}\right|$ parts in the $\left|J^{(k)}\right|$-partite subgraph $(V_k, \varnothing, E_k)$ and edge set $E_k, k \in \{1,2,\ldots,7\}$.

Based on the Formula (9), we calculate the cardinalities $|E_k|, k \in \{1,2,3,4\}$, as follows:

$$|E_1| = \sum_{i=1}^{|J^{(1)}|-1} \{\sum_{j=i+1}^{|J^{(1)}|}\left\{\left|V_1^i\right| \times \left|V_1^j\right|\right\}\} = \{\{2\times1\}+\{2\times1\}+\{2\times1\}\}+\{\{1\times1\}+\{1\times1\}\}+\{\{1\times1\}\} = 9,$$
$$|E_2| = \sum_{i=1}^{|J^{(2)}|-1} \{\sum_{j=i+1}^{|J^{(2)}|}\left\{\left|V_1^i\right| \times \left|V_1^j\right|\right\}\} = 2\times3 = 6, |E_3| = \sum_{i=1}^{|J^{(3)}|-1} \{\sum_{j=i+1}^{|J^{(3)}|}\left\{\left|V_1^i\right| \times \left|V_1^j\right|\right\}\} = \{\{2\times1\}+\{2\times1\}\}+\{1\times1\} = 5,$$
$$|E_4| = |E_5| = |E_6| = |E_2| = 2\times3 = 6, |E_7| = 1\times2 = 2.$$

It is clear that, due to the 4-partite graph $(V_1, \varnothing, E_1)$, it is forbidden to simultaneously fulfill a pair of the operations of set V_1 on the processor M_1. Due to the tripartite graph $(V_3, \varnothing, E_3)$, it is forbidden to simultaneously fulfill a pair of operations from the V_3 on the processor M_3. Due to the bipartite graph $(V_2, \varnothing, E_2)$, it is forbidden to simultaneously fulfill a pair of the operations of set V_2 on the processor M_2. Due to the bipartite graph $(V_4, \varnothing, E_4)$, it is forbidden to simultaneously fulfill a pair of the operations of set V_4 on the processor M_4. Due to the bipartite graph $(V_5, \varnothing, E_5)$, it is forbidden to simultaneously fulfill a pair of the operations of set V_5 on the processor M_5. Due to the bipartite graph $(V_6, \varnothing, E_6)$, it is forbidden to simultaneously fulfill a pair of the operations of set V_6 on the processor M_6. Due to the bipartite graph $(V_7, \varnothing, E_7)$, it is forbidden to simultaneously fulfill a pair of the operations of set V_7 on the processor M_7.

Let precedence constraints determined on a set of operations belonging to different jobs in Example 4 be given as follows: $R_{\Rightarrow} = \{v_4 \Rightarrow v_1,\ v_9 \Rightarrow v_3, v_{13} \Rightarrow v_{16},\}$. *Let the weak precedence constraints in Example 4 be given as follows:* $R_{\rightarrow} = \{v_1 \rightarrow v_{13},\ v_{13} \rightarrow v_5, v_5 \rightarrow v_1\}$.

To include the precedence constraints $R_{\Rightarrow}$ in the input data of Example 4, we add the set of arcs $A_{|J|+1} = \{(v_4, v_1), (v_9, v_3), (v_{13}, v_{16})\}$ and the edge set $E_{|J|+1} = \{[v_1, v_4), \{v_3, v_9], [v_{13}, v_{16}]\}$ to the mixed graph $G = (V, A, E)$. To include weak precedence constraints $R_{\rightarrow}$ in the input data of Example 4, we add the arc set $A_{|J|+2} = \{(v_1, v_{13}), (v_{13}, v_5), (v_5, v_1)\}$ to the mixed graph $G = (V, A, E)$. We see that set of arcs $A_{|J|+2}$ determines circuit (v_1, v_{13}, v_5, v_1) in the directed graph $(V, A, \varnothing)$. Therefore, unit-time operations of set $\{v_1, v_{13}, v_5\}$ have to be simultaneously fulfilled.

Let the following release dates of the jobs $J = \{J_1, J_2, J_3, J_4\}$ be given as a part of the input data of Example 4: $r_1 = 4$,$r_2 = 3$, $r_3 = 1$, $r_4 = 3$.

Release date $r_1 = 4$ of the job $J_1 \in J$ is determined by the union of path $(v_{20}, v_{21}, v_{22}, v_{23}, v_1)$ in the directed graph $(V, A, \varnothing)$ and chain $(v_{20}, v_{21}, v_{22}, v_{23}, v_1)$ in the subgraph $(V, \varnothing, E)$ of the mixed graph $G = (V, A, E)$. Release date $r_2 = 3$ is presented by the union of path $(v_{24}, v_{25}, v_{26}, v_4)$ in the directed graph $(V, A, \varnothing)$ and chain $(v_{24}, v_{25}, v_{26}, v_4)$ in the subgraph $(V, \varnothing, E)$ of the desired mixed graph $G = (V, A, E)$. Release date $r_3 = 1$ of the job $J_3 \in J$ is presented by the union of arc (v_{27}, v_{10}) in the directed graph $(V, A, \varnothing)$ and edge $[v_{27}, v_{10}]$ in the subgraph $(V, \varnothing, E)$ of the desired mixed graph $G = (V, A, E)$. Release date $r_4 = 3$ of the job $J_4 \in J$ is presented by the union of path $(v_{28}, v_{29}, v_{30}, v_{16})$ in the directed graph $(V, A, \varnothing)$ and chain $(v_{28}, v_{29}, v_{30}, v_{16})$ in the subgraph $(V, \varnothing, E)$ of the desired mixed graph $G = (V, A, E)$. Now, the desired mixed graph G is constructed. Figure 4 presents the constructed mixed graph G determining the whole input data for Example 4 of the problem $G_cMPT|[r_i], [t_{ij}], pmtn|C_{\max}$ with four jobs $J = \{J_1, J_2, J_3, J_4\}$ and seven dedicated processors $M = \{M_1, M_2, \ldots, M_7\}$.

Due to Theorem 8, a solvable problem $G_cMPT|[r_i], [t_{ij}], pmtn|C_{\max}$ (like Example 4) reduces to determining optimal colouring $c(G)$. An existing semiactive schedule for the scheduling problem with possible interruptions of the operations is determined by set (12) of completion times of the unit-time operations of set W. The semiactive schedule is determined by the colouring $c(G)$ of the mixed graph G, in which the equality $c(v_i) = C(v_i)$ holds for the vertices $v_i \in W$. The makespan-optimal semiactive schedule that exists for Example 4 is determined by the optimal colouring $c(G)$, where $c(v_1) = 5$, $c(v_2) = 10$, $c(v_3) = 11$, $c(v_4) = 4$, $c(v_5) = 5$, $c(v_6) = 6$, $c(v_7) = 7$, $c(v_8) = 8$, $c(v_9) = 9$, $c(v_{10}) = 2$, $c(v_{11}) = 3, c(v_{12}) = 4, c(v_{13}) = 5, c(v_{14}) = 6, c(v_{15}) = 7, c(v_{16}) = 7, c(v_{17}) = 8, c(v_{18}) = 9$, $c(v_{19}) = 10$. To show that the colouring $c(G)$ is optimal, we next prove the inequality $\chi(G) \geq 11$.

In the mixed graph G depicted in Figure 4, there is a path $(v_{24}, v_{25}, v_{26}, v_4, v_5, v_6, v_7, v_8, v_9, v_3)$ in the directed subgraph $(V, A, \varnothing)$ and a chain $(v_{24}, v_{25}, v_{26}, v_4, v_5, v_6, v_7, v_8, v_9, v_3)$ in the subgraph $(V, \varnothing, E)$. Therefore, a minimal colour of the vertex v_9 is not less than 9, $c(v_9) \geq 9$ and the minimal colour of the vertex v_3 is not less than 10; $c(v_3) \geq 10$. In mixed graph $G = (V, A, E)$, there is a path $(v_{20}, v_{21}, v_{22}, v_{23}, v_1, v_2, v_3)$ in the directed subgraph $(V, A, \varnothing)$ and a chain $(v_{20}, v_{21}, v_{22}, v_{23}, v_1, v_2, v_3)$ in the subgraph $(V, \varnothing, E)$. Therefore, a minimal colour of the vertex v_2 is not less than 6; $c(v_2) \geq 6$. However, we see that the minimal colour of the vertex v_2 cannot be equal to 6, 7, 8 and 9, because the following four inclusions hold: $[v_2, v_6] \in E$, $[v_2, v_7] \in E$, $[v_2, v_8] \in E$, $[v_2, v_9] \in E$. There is a path $(v_{24}, v_{25}, v_{26}, v_4, v_5, v_6, v_7, v_8, v_9, v_3)$ in the directed subgraph $(V, A, \varnothing)$ and a chain $(v_{24}, v_{25}, v_{26}, v_4, v_5, v_6, v_7, v_8, v_9, v_3)$ in the subgraph $(V, \varnothing, E)$. Thus, a minimal possible colour of the vertex v_2 is not less than 10, i.e., the inequality $c(v_2) \geq 10$ holds. Hence, the minimal possible colour of the vertex v_3 is not less than 11 because of the inclusions $[v_2, v_3] \in E$ and $(v_2, v_3) \in A$. The inequality $\chi(G) \geq 11$ holds, so the constructed colouring $c(G)$ is optimal. We obtain the optimal semiactive schedule $S = (C(v_1, C(v_2, \ldots, C(v_{|W|})$ such that equality $c(v_i) = C(v_i)$ holds for each vertex $v_i \in W$.

7. Minimising the Schedule Length for Interruptible Integer-Time Operations with Integer Release Dates and Equivalent Minimisation of the Maximal Lateness

We next show that finding a makespan-optimal schedule for the general scheduling problem $G_cMPT|[r_i], [t_{ij}], pmtn|C_{\max}$ with integer release dates and interruptible integer-time operations Q_{ij} is similar to finding the optimal schedule for the problem $G_cMPT\big|[t_{ij}], pmtn, [D_i]\big|L_{\max}$ with integer due dates $D_i \geq 0$, $J_i \in J$, and interruptible integer-time operations Q_{ij}.

Theorem 9. *Every solvable scheduling problem $G_cMPT\big|[r_i], [t_{ij}], pmtn\big|C_{\max}$ with integer release dates $r_i \geq 0$, $J_i \in J$, and interruptible integer-time operations Q_{ij}, $J_i \in J$, is equivalent to the solvable scheduling problem $G_cMPT\big|[t_{ij}], pmtn, [D_i]\big|L_{\max}$ with integer due dates $D_i \geq 0$, $J_i \in J$, and interruptible integer-time operations Q_{ij}, $J_i \in J$.*

Proof. The problem $G_cMPT\big|[r_i], [t_{ij}], pmtn\big|C_{\max}$ was considered in Theorem 8. The proof of Theorem 8 showed how to construct a mixed graph G that completely determines the input data for a solvable scheduling problem $G_cMPT\big|[r_i], [t_{ij}], pmtn\big|C_{\max}$. Since the considered scheduling problem $G_cMPT\big|[r_i], [t_{ij}], pmtn\big|C_{\max}$ is solvable, this mixed graph G must be colourable according to Theorem 4 and Theorem 8. From Theorem 1 it follows that the directed graph $(V, A, \varnothing)$ does not have a circuit containing adjacent vertices in the graph $(V, \varnothing, E)$.

For the given scheduling problem $G_cMPT\big|[r_i], [t_{ij}], pmtn\big|C_{\max}$ on the above mixed graph $G = (V, A, E)$, we will show how to construct the corresponding problem $G_cMPT\big|[t_{ij}], pmtn, [D_i]\big|L_{\max}$, where due dates $D_i \geq 0$ are integer for all jobs $J_i \in J$, operations Q_{ij} have integer durations for all jobs $J_i \in J$, and interruptions are allowed for all operations.

In the corresponding problem $G_cMPT\big|[t_{ij}], pmtn, [D_i]\big|L_{\max}$, jobs $J = \left\{J_1, J_2, \ldots, J_{|J|}\right\}$ have a release date of zero $r_i = 0$, $J_i \in J$. Jobs $J = \left\{J_1, J_2, \ldots, J_{|J|}\right\}$ have to be processed by the same set $M = \left\{M_1, M_2, \ldots, M_{|M|}\right\}$ of the dedicated processors. We assume that in the general scheduling problem $G_cMPT\big|[t_{ij}], pmtn, [D_i]\big|L_{\max}$, each processor $M_i \in M$ must process the same set $V_i = \left\{v_{i_1}, v_{i_2}, \ldots, v_{i_{|V_i|}}\right\} \subseteq V$ of the jobs as in the general problem $G_cMPT\big|[r_i], [t_{ij}], pmtn\big|C_{\max}$ considered in Sections 5 and 6.

In the corresponding problem $G_cMPT\big|[t_{ij}], pmtn, [D_i]\big|L_{\max}$, integer due date $D_i \geq 0$ is given for every job $J_i \in J$ as follows: $D_i = \max\{r_j : J_j \in J\} - r_i$.

Let us define a strict order $(v_{k_{|V^{(k)}|}}, v_{k_{|V^{(k)}|-1}}, \ldots, v_{k_2}, v_{k_1})$ for processing the operations $V^{(k)} = \left\{v_{k_1}, v_{k_2}, \ldots, v_{k_{|V^{(k)}|}}\right\}$. It is clear that this strict order $(v_{k_{|V^{(k)}|}}, v_{k_{|V^{(k)}|-1}}, \ldots, v_{k_2}, v_{k_1})$ is opposite to the strict order $(v_{k_1}, v_{k_2}, \ldots, v_{k_{|V^{(k)}|}})$ determined for the corresponding problem $G_cMPT\big|[r_i], [t_{ij}], pmtn\big|C_{\max}$ for processing integer-time operations $V^{(k)}$.

If the precedence constraints $v_i \Rightarrow v_j$ and the weak precedence constraints $v_p \rightarrow v_q$ are defined on the set of operations belonging to different jobs in the corresponding problem $G_cMPT\big|[r_i], [t_{ij}], pmtn\big|C_{\max}$, then the inverse precedence constraint $v_j \Rightarrow v_i$ and the inverse weak precedence constraints $v_q \rightarrow v_p$ have to be given for the problem $G_cMPT\big|[t_{ij}], pmtn, [D_i]\big|L_{\max}$.

It follows from Theorem 8 that the optimal semiactive schedule for the roblem $G_cMPT\big|[r_i], [t_{ij}], pmtn\big|C_{\max}$ determined by the mixed graph $G = (V, A, E)$ can be defined by the optimal colouring $c(G)$. This colouring $c(G)$ also defines an optimal semiactive schedule for the problem $G_cMPT\big|[t_{ij}], pmtn, [D_i]\big|L_{\max}$. It is clear that the optimal maximal lateness may be determined as follows: $L_{\max} = \chi(G) - \max\{r_i : J_i \in J\}$. Thus, we proved the following claim.

Every solvable scheduling problem $G_cMPT\big|[r_i], [t_{ij}], pmtn\big|C_{\max}$ with given integer release dates $r_i \geq 0$, $J_i \in J$, and integer durations of interruptible operations Q_{ij} is equivalent to the scheduling problem $G_cMPT\big|[t_{ij}], pmtn, [D_i]\big|L_{\max}$ with integer due dates $D_i = \max\{r_j : J_j \in J\} - r_i$, $J_i \in J$, and integer durations of the interruptible operations Q_{ij}, $J_i \in J$.

Obviously, the above arguments are reversible. This allows us to prove the following claim in a similar way.

Every solvable scheduling problem $G_cMPT\big|[t_{ij}], pmtn, [D_i]\big|L_{\max}$ with given integer due dates $D_i \geq 0$, $J_i \in J$, and integer durations of the interruptible operations Q_{ij}, is equivalent to the scheduling problem $G_cMPT\big|[r_i], [t_{ij}], pmtn\big|C_{\max}$ with given integer release dates $r_i = \max\{D_j : J_j \in J\} - D_i$ and integer durations of the interruptible operations Q_{ij}, $J_i \in J$.

Theorem 9 is proved. □

The following corollary follows directly from Theorem 8 and Theorem 9.

Corollary 3. *If the job due dates and durations of operations Q_{ij}, $J_i \in J$, are integers for the solvable scheduling problem $G_cMPT\big|[t_{ij}], pmtn, [D_i]\big|L_{\max}$, then an semiactive optimal schedule for this problem is presentable as an optimal colouring of vertices of the mixed graph G that determines the input data of this scheduling problem.*

To illustrate Theorem 9 and Corollary 3, we solve Example 5 of the problem $G_cMPT\big|[t_{ij}], pmtn, [D_i]\big|L_{\max}$ with four jobs $J = \{J_1, J_2, J_3, J_4\}$, seven dedicated processors $M = \{M_1, M_2, \ldots, M_7\}$, integer due dates $D_i \geq 0$, integer processing times $t_{ij} > 0$ of the multi-processor operations, precedence constraints between operations of different and the same jobs, and allowed interruptions of the integer-time operations.

Example 5. *In Example 5 of the scheduling problem $G_cMPT\big|[t_{ij}], pmtn, [D_i]\big|L_{\max}$ on the mixed graph $G = (V, A, E)$ depicted in Figure 5, the set of jobs J_1, J_2, J_3 and J_4 are ready for processing on set $M = \{M_1, M_2, \ldots, M_9\}$ of the dedicated processors from time zero $t = 0$. Each processor $M_k \in M$ must process the same subset of the jobs as in Example 4. However, the orders for fulfilling the same set of operations are opposite to the linear orders determined in Example 4.*

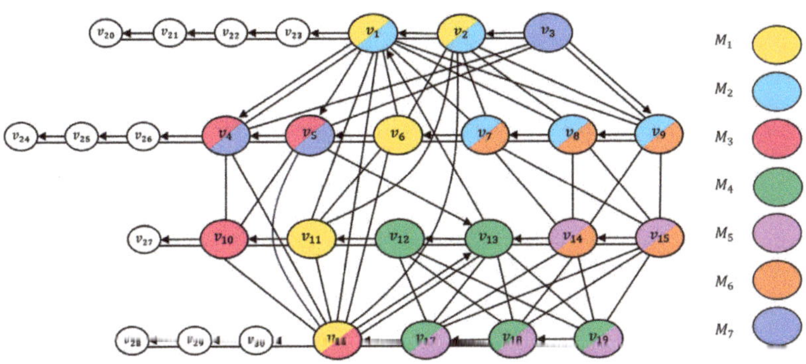

Figure 5. Mixed graph $G^{\leftarrow} = (V, A^{\leftarrow}, E)$ determining Example 5 of the problem $G_cMPT\big|[t_{ij}], pmtn, [D_i]\big|L_{\max}$.

While the precedence constraints $v_i \rightarrow v_j$ and $v_p \Rightarrow v_q$ are determined between operations different jobs in Example 4, the inverse precedence constraints $v_j \rightarrow v_i$ and $v_q \Rightarrow v_p$ are determined in Example 5 of the scheduling problem $G_cMPT\big|[t_{ij}], pmtn, [D_i]\big|L_{\max}$. Thus, in Example 5, the due dates of the given set of jobs $J_i \in J = \{J_1, J_2, J_3, J_4\}$ are defined as follows: $D_1 = \max\{r_j : J_i \in J\} - r_1 = 4 - 4 = 0$, $D_2 = 4 - r_2 = 4 - 3 = 1$, $D_3 = 4 - r_3 = 4 - 1 = 3$, $D_4 = 4 - r_4 = 4 - 3 = 1$.

The input data for Example 5 are determined by the mixed graph $G^{\leftarrow} = (V, A^{\leftarrow}, E)$ depicted in Figure 5. Set V of the vertices and set E of the edges in the mixed graph $G^{\leftarrow}$ are the same as those in the mixed graph G presented in Figure 4.

Compare mixed graph $G^{\leftarrow}$ depicted in Figure 5 for scheduling problem $G_cMPT\big|[t_{ij}], pmtn, [D_i]\big|L_{\max}$ with mixed graph G for scheduling problem $G_cMPT\big|[r_i], [t_{ij}], pmtn\big|C_{\max}$ depicted in Figure 4. According to Theorem 9 and Corollary 3, for Example 5 of the scheduling problem $G_cMPT\big|[t_{ij}], pmtn, [D_i]\big|L_{\max}$ on the mixed graph $G^{\leftarrow} = (V, A^{\leftarrow}, E)$, the optimal semiactive schedule S is determined by the following optimal colouring $c(G^{\leftarrow})$: $c(v_1) = 7, c(v_2) = 2, c(v_3) = 1, c(v_4) = 8, c(v_5) = 7, c(v_6) = 6,$ $c(v_7) = 5, c(v_8) = 4, c(v_9) = 3, c(v_{10}) = 10, c(v_{11}) = 9, c(v_{12}) = 8, c(v_{13}) = 7, c(v_{14}) = 6,$ $c(v_{15}) = 5, c(v_{16}) = 5, c(v_{17}) = 4, c(v_{18}) = 3, c(v_{19}) = 2.$

The colouring $c(G^{\leftarrow})$ determines the optimal semiactive schedule:

$$C(Q_{1,1}) = c(v_3) = 1,\ C(Q_{1,2}) = c(v_1) = 7,\ C(Q_{2,1}) = c(v_7) = 5,\ C(Q_{2,2}) = c(v_6) = 6,$$
$$C(Q_{2,3}) = c(v_4) = 8, C(Q_{3,1}) = c(v_{14}) = 6, C(Q_{3,2}) = c(v_{12}) = 8, C(Q_{3,3}) = c(v_{11}) = 9,$$
$$C(Q_{4,1}) = c(v_{17}) = 4, C(Q_{4,2}) = c(v_{16}) = 5.$$

We compute the optimal objective value as follows:

$$L_{\max} = \chi(G^{\leftarrow}) - \max\{r_i : J_i \in J\} = 11 - 4 = 7.$$

8. Discussion

This research is a continuation of the works [1,2,10–22], where graph colouring models and algorithms were developed for solving various scheduling problems. The developed method is based on graph-theoretic models for scheduling problems. We have studied relationships between optimal colourings of the mixed graphs and general scheduling problems $G_cMPT|[t_{ij}], pmtn, [D_i]|L_{\max}$ and $G_cMPT|[r_i], [t_{ij}], pmtn|C_{\max}$. In both investigated scheduling problems, it is necessary to construct optimal schedules for fulfilling partially ordered sets of integer-time multi-processor tasks with allowed operation interruptions. Precedence constraints of the two types of completion–start and start–start can be given on the set of integer-time operations. Furthermore, specified subsets of the operations with unit durations must be executed simultaneously.

The propositions proved in Sections 4–7 can be used to construct mixed graphs for representing the entire input data of the numerous scheduling problems with interruptible integer-time operations. It is proven that to construct an optimal semiactive schedule for any studied scheduling problem, it is sufficient to determine the optimal colouring of the vertices of the mixed graph representing all input data of the considered scheduling problem.

It is also shown that notions of graph theory are quite sufficient for the formulation of the problems $G_cMPT|[t_{ij}], pmtn, [D_i]|L_{\max}$ and $G_cMPT|[r_i], [t_{ij}], pmtn|C_{\max}$, and a huge number of their special cases. To illustrate the obvious benefits of using graph theory terminology instead of terminology of scheduling theory, we list the scheduling terms used in Sections 1–7: *processing system (multi-stage); production planning (scheduling); job-shop, general shop; equipment, machine, processor; schedule (semiactive, feasible, optimal); schedule optimality criterion (makespan, maximal lateness,; production cost); manufacture; raw material; final product; job (simple, first, second, last) task; release date (equal, integer); input data; planning horizon; schedule length; operation (multi-processor, interruptible); (allowed) interruption, preemption; machine route, (first, last) operation; operation duration (unit, integer), operation order (linear, strict); operation assignment to machine; simultaneous execution of operations; fulfill; process; ready for processing; (operation, job, task) start; (operation, job, task) completion; (operation, task) interruption, schedule (makespan, length); three-field notation; capacity constraint; (week) precedence constraints (completion-start, start-start), unit-time operation (task), integer-time (operation, job, task) operation (task) processing time (duration), production conditions (efficiency), due date (integer).*

To obtain and present the same results in notions of mixed graphs, only fewer terms were used, namely: *vertex (incidental, adjacent); arc, edge (multiple); graph (finite, directed, mixed, k-partite, bipartite, tripartite, complete, colourable); digraph; (vertex-induced) subgraph, clique, connected component (graph); colouring (strict, optimal); vertex colour, chromatic number; loop; path, passing; chain (length); circuit.*

In Sections 5 and 7, we proved that every solvable problem of constructing an optimal colouring of the mixed graph reduces to problems $G_cMPT|[r_i], [t_{ij}], pmtn|C_{\max}$ and $G_cMPT|[t_{ij}], pmtn, [D_i]|L_{\max}$. Thus, for many of the statements proved so far for these scheduling problems and their various special cases, there are similar statements for the problems of defining optimal colourings of the vertices of the mixed graphs.

It is shown that each solvable problem $G_cMPT|[r_i],[t_{ij}],pmtn|C_{\max}$ (as well as the solvable problem $G_cMPT|[t_{ij}],pmtn,[D_i]|L_{\max}$) pseudo-polynomially reduces to finding the optimal colouring of a mixed graph. It is worth noting that the pseudo-polynomiality of this reduction is based on the fact that all input data for both scheduling problems are determined by mixed graphs to be coloured for solving these scheduling problems. Therefore, it is unclear and probably impossible to find a polynomial reduction of these scheduling problems to mixed graph colouring problems.

The statements proved for finding optimal colourings of the mixed graphs [6,7,15,17,23–32] could be used for finding a solution of the NP-hard scheduling problems $G_cMPT|[r_i],[t_{ij}],pmtn|C_{\max}$ and $G_cMPT|[t_{ij}],pmtn,[D_i]|L_{\max}$. To apply the developed mixed graph colouring models, methods, and algorithms, solvable scheduling problems must have positive integer processing times of the multi-processor tasks, non-negative integer release dates of all jobs for the schedule length minimisation (and non-negative integer due dates for the minimisation of the maximal lateness). It should be noted that there is no restriction on the mixed graphs for using the scheduling algorithms for constructing optimal colourings of vertices of the mixed graph.

The results presented and proved in this article can be considered as a substantiation of graph-theoretic methods for solving scheduling problems by reducing them to finding optimal colouring of mixed graphs, which determine the input data of scheduling problems. Conditions and limitations of an individual scheduling problem are determined by the corresponding mixed graph. For the individual scheduling problem, such a mixed graph is defined uniquely.

It should be noted that different scheduling problems $G_cMPT|[r_i],[t_{ij}],pmtn|C_{\max}$ and $G_cMPT|[t_{ij}],pmtn,[D_i]|L_{\max}$ can be defined by the same mixed graph. Thus, the results proven for colourings of the particular mixed graph $G=(V,A,E)$ are applicable, as a rule, for a whole set of the scheduling problems $G_cMPT|[r_i],[t_{ij}],pmtn|C_{\max}$ or problems $G_cMPT|[t_{ij}],pmtn,[D_i]|L_{\max}$. In particular, most results presented and proven in this paper can be used for studying colourings of the specified classes of mixed graphs, which are generated by the scheduling problems $G_cMPT|[r_i],[t_{ij}],pmtn|C_{\max}$ and $G_cMPT|[t_{ij}],pmtn,[D_i]|L_{\max}$. This can help attract graph theorists to solve the multistage scheduling problems and their numerous special cases.

9. Conclusions

This paper presents efficient reformulations of a huge number of scheduling problems into mixed graph colouring ones. Sections 1–3 provide an overview of the preliminary results used in the proofs of the new results presented in Sections 4–8. We studied the optimal scheduling of a partially ordered set of multi-processor tasks with allowed interruptions as optimal colourings of the vertices of the corresponding mixed graphs. We proved that the problem of optimal colouring of vertices of an arbitrary mixed graph reduces to the problem of constructing schedules that minimise a maximal lateness for processing partially ordered sets of multi-processor tasks with integer durations, integer due dates and allowed interruptions. We also proved the inverse statements that problems of constructing schedules minimising a maximal lateness for fulfilling partially ordered sets of multi-processor tasks pseudo-polynomially reduce to problems of optimally coloring the vertices of the mixed graphs, which determines all input data of the considered scheduling problems.

The established relationship between the generalisations of scheduling problems and problems of finding an optimal colouring of the vertices of mixed graphs presented in the article makes it possible to solve any solvable problems $G_cMPT|[r_i],[t_{ij}],pmtn|C_{\max}$ and $G_cMPT|[t_{ij}],pmtn,[D_i]|L_{\max}$, as well as numerous special cases of these problems in terms of graph theory, and not to use the special terms of schedule theory, which are related to the practical production planning problems. It turned out that the terms of graph theory are quite enough to formulate any problem $G_cMPT|[r_i],[t_{ij}],pmtn|C_{\max}$ or $G_cMPT|[t_{ij}],pmtn,[D_i]|L_{\max}$, and for the development of algorithms for solving problems of schedule theory as a result of the search for optimal coloring of the mixed graphs that determine the input data of scheduling problems.

The presented and generalised theorems and results (Sections 1–3) and new results proved in Sections 4–7 allow making scheduling theory more abstract due to the possibility to use abstract models, effective methods and algorithms for optimal colouring the vertices of the mixed graphs for solving most scheduling problems with bottleneck objectives. Such investigations of the relationships between optimisation problems of scheduling theory and those of graph theory may be continued further.

Future research directions may be oriented towards developing mixed graph colouring models and algorithms suitable for solving scheduling problems with other regular optimality criteria. In particular, non-bottleneck criteria are widely used in scheduling theory [5,6,9,22–26]. It should be noted that both criteria considered in this paper are bottleneck criteria. We plan to study other scheduling problems that are reducible or equivalent to colouring the vertices of the corresponding mixed graphs. A promising research may be aimed to usage of the mixed graph models for developing efficient algorithms for scheduling the cloud computations. One could assume that durations of all tasks are integer and operation preemptions are allowed. Both studied objectives (schedule length and maximal lateness) may be considered for cloud computations.

We plan to study other classes of the multistage scheduling problems that are equivalent to problems of optimal colorings of vertices of the mixed graphs. We plan also to consider polynomially solvable multistage scheduling problems, which will allow us to discover polynomially solvable cases of the problem of finding optimal colourings $c(G)$ of the specific mixed graphs $G = (V, A, E)$.

Author Contributions: Conceptualisation, Y.N.S.; methodology, Y.N.S.; validation, E.I.M.; formal analysis, E.I.M.; investigation, E.I.M. and Y.N.S.; data curation, E.I.M.; writing—original draft, Y.N.S.; writing—review and editing, Y.N.S.; visualisation, E.I.M. All authors have read and agreed to the published version of the manuscript.

Funding: The research of Y.S. was funded by Belarusian Republican Foundation for Fundamental Research, grant number Ф23РНФ-017.

Data Availability Statement: The original contributions presented in the study are included in the article, further inquiries can be directed to the corresponding author.

Conflicts of Interest: The authors declare no conflicts of interest.

Appendix A

Example A1. *The individual problem* $G_c|t_{ij} = 1|C_{\max}$ *determined by mixed graph* $G^* = (V, A^*, E^*)$ *is analogous to Example 1 of a job-shop unit-time problem* $J|t_{ij} = 1|C_{\max}$*, with the exception that there are given start-start constraints and completion-start constraints on the set of operations of different jobs of set* J*. All the additional constraints are determined as follows:* $v_1 \Rightarrow v_4$*;* $v_4 \Rightarrow v_3$*;* $v_3 \rightarrow v_1$*;* $v_8 \rightarrow v_4$ *and* $v_{12} \rightarrow v_9$*. Thus, the appropriate mixed graph* $G^* = (V, A^*, E^*)$ *has to contain an additional subset of arcs and subset set of edges defined as follows:*

$$A^* = A \cup \{(v_1, v_4), (v_4, v_3), (v_3, v_1), (v_8, v_4), (v_{12}, v_9)\};\ E^* = E \cup \{[v_8, v_4], [v_{12}, v_9]\}.$$

Note that the operations v_1, v_3 and v_4 have to be fulfilled simultaneously in ever schedule since circuit (v_1, v_4, v_3, v_1) exists in digraph $(V, \varnothing, E^*)$, which is a subgraph of the mixed graph $G^* = (V, A^*, E^*)$ dipicted in Figure A1. At the right side of Figure A1, the colors of coloring $c(G^*)$ are presented instead of the natural numbers: $c(v_1) = 2$, $c(v_2) = 1$, $c(v_3) = 2$, $c(v_4) = 2$, $c(v_5) = 3$, $c(v_6) = 4$, $c(v_7) = 5$, $c(v_8) = 1$, $c(v_9) = 3$, $c(v_{10}) = 5$, $c(v_{11}) = 1$, $c(v_{12}) = 2$. The colouring $c(G^*)$ is optimal, $\chi(G^*) = 5$, since directed graph $(V, A^*, \varnothing)$ contains path $(v_8, v_4, v_5, v_6, v_7)$ and graph $(V, \varnothing, E^*)$ contains chain $(v_8, v_4, v_5, v_6, v_7)$, whose lengths are equal to 5.

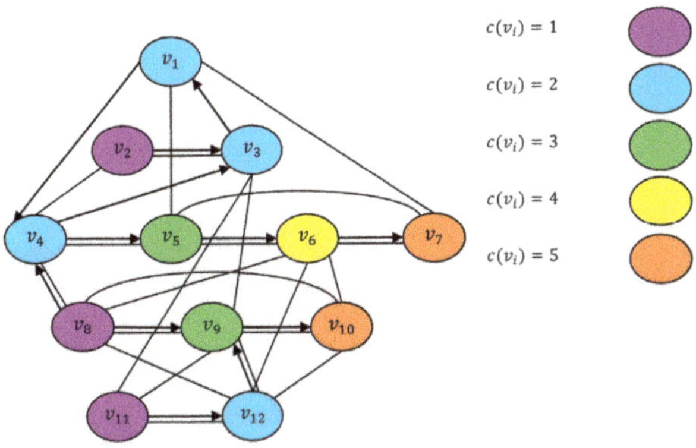

Figure A1. Mixed graph $G^* = (V, A^*, E^*)$ that determines Example A1 of the scheduling problem $G_c|t_{ij} = 1|C_{\max}$.

Due to these path and chain, the following inequality holds: $\chi(G^*) \geq 5$. From Theorem 3, it follows that the optimal colouring $c(G^*)$ defines the following schedule S that is optimal for Example A1 of the unit-time problem $G_c|t_{ij} = 1|C_{\max}$, where the input data are determined by mixed graph G^* depicted in Figure A1.

$$S = (C(Q_{1,1}) = 2, C(Q_{2,1}) = 1, (Q_{2,2}) = 2, C(Q_{3,1}) = 2, C(Q_{3,2}) = 3, C(Q_{3,3}) = 4, C(Q_{3,4}) = 5,$$
$$C(Q_{4,1}) = 1, C(Q_{4,2}) = 3, C(Q_{4,3}) = 5, C(Q_{5,1}) = 1, C(Q_{5,2}) = 2)$$

The correspondence of the operations $Q_{ij} \in Q$ and the vertices $v_k \in V$ is determined based on Remark 1. The equalities $\chi(G^*) = 5 = C_{\max}$ hold due to Theorem 3.

Appendix B

Example A2. *In Example A2, the set $J = \{J_1, J_2, J_3, J_4, J_5\}$ of jobs is the same as in Example 1 and Example A1. The set of processors is increased from four processors in Examples 1 and Example A1 to nine processors in Example A2: $M = \{M_1, M_2, \ldots, M_9\}$.*

The processor M_1 processes the operations $V_1 = \{v_1, v_7\}$. In Figure A2, the forbiddance to process the operations from the set V_1 simultaneously on the processor M_1 is determined by the edge $[v_1, v_7]$ in the graph $(V, \varnothing, E)$. The processor M_2 processes the operations $V_2 = \{v_2, v_4\}$. The forbiddance to process the operations from the set V_2 simultaneously on the processor M_2 is determined by the edge $[v_2, v_4]$.

Similarly, the forbiddance to process operations from the set $V_3 = \{v_3, v_9\}$ simultaneously on the processor M_3 is determined by the edge $[v_3, v_9]$. The forbiddance to process this pair of operations from the set $V_4 = \{v_6, v_{12}\}$ simultaneously on the processor M_4 is determined by the edge $[v_6, v_{12}]$ in the graph $(V, \varnothing, E)$. The forbiddance to process operations from the set $V_5 = \{v_5, v_{11}\}$ simultaneously on the processor M_5 is determined by the edge $[v_5, v_{11}]$. The forbiddance to process the operations from the set $V_6 = \{v_8, v_{12}\}$ simultaneously on the processor M_6 is determined by the edge $[v_8, v_{12}]$. The forbiddance to process the operations from the set $V_7 = \{v_7, v_{10}\}$ simultaneously on the processor M_7 is determined by the edge $[v_7, v_{10}]$. The forbiddance to process the operations from the set $V_8 = \{v_9, v_{11}\}$ simultaneously is determined by the edge $[v_9, v_{11}]$. The forbiddance to process the operations from the set $V_9 = \{v_3, v_4\}$ simultaneously on processor M_9 is determined by the edge $[v_3, v_4]$. The processors, which are used to process the operation $v_i \in V$, are presented near the vertex v_i in Figure A2. The precedence constraints established between operations of different jobs are given as follows: $v_1 \Rightarrow v_4$; $v_1 \Rightarrow v_8$; $v_3 \Rightarrow v_1$; $v_8 \Rightarrow v_3$; $v_6 \Rightarrow v_{10}$; $v_{10} \Rightarrow v_{12}$; $v_8 \rightarrow v_4$; $v_{11} \rightarrow v_8$. These precedence constraints are represented by seven arcs $\{(v_1, v_4), (v_1, v_8), (v_3, v_1), (v_8, v_3), (v_6, v_{10}), (v_{10}, v_{12}), (v_8, v_4)\} \subset A$ and two edges $\{[v_4, v_8], [v_8, v_{11}]\} \subset E$.

The digraph $(V, A, \varnothing)$ has one circuit (v_1, v_8, v_3, v_1) and this circuit has no adjacent vertices in the graph $(V, \varnothing, E)$. Since the digraph $(V, A, \varnothing)$ has no circuit with adjacent vertices in the graph $(V, \varnothing, E)$, there exists a schedule for Example A2 of the general unit-time problem $G_c MPT|t_i = 1|C_{\max}$ that is completely determined by the mixed graph G; see Theorem 4. We construct the following colouring $c(G)$ of the mixed graph $G = (V, A, E)$: $c(v_1) = 2$, $c(v_2) = 1$, $c(v_3) = 2$, $c(v_4) = 3$, $c(v_5) = 4$, $c(v_6) = 5$, $c(v_7) = 6$, $c(v_8) = 2$, $c(v_9) = 3$, $c(v_{10}) = 5$, $c(v_{11}) = 1$, $c(v_{12}) = 6$. The colouring $c(G)$ is optimal, $\chi(G) = 6$, since the directed graph $(V, A, \varnothing)$ contains the path $(v_{11}, v_8, v_4, v_5, v_6, v_7)$ and the subgraph $(V, \varnothing, E)$ of the mixed graph G contains the chain $(v_{11}, v_8, v_4, v_5, v_6, v_7)$, whose lengths are equal to 6. Because of this path and chain, the inequality $\chi(G) \geq 6$ holds. By Theorem 5, the optimal colouring $c(G)$ defines the optimal semiactive schedule (1) for Example A2 of the unit-time problem $G_c|t_{ij} = 1|C_{\max}$, whose input data is determined by the mixed graph G depicted in Figure A2. Based on Remark 1 about the correspondence of operations $Q_{ij} \in Q$ and vertices $v_k \in V$, we obtain the following makespan-optimal semiactive schedule:

$$S = (C(Q_{1,1}) = 2, C(Q_{2,1}) = 1, (Q_{2,2}) = 2, C(Q_{3,1}) = 3, C(Q_{3,2}) = 4, C(Q_{3,3}) = 5, C(Q_{3,4}) = 6,$$
$$C(Q_{4,1}) = 2, C(Q_{4,2}) = 3, C(Q_{4,3}) = 5, C(Q_{5,1}) = 1, C(Q_{5,2}) = 6)$$

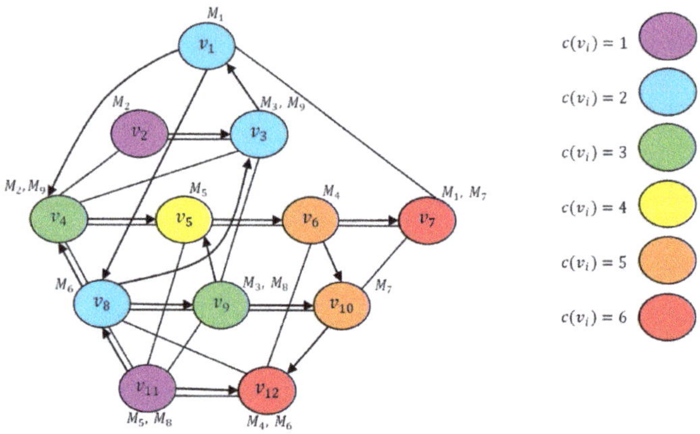

Figure A2. Mixed graph $G = (V, A, E)$ that defines the input data for Example A2.

By Theorem 5, the equality $\chi(G) = 6 = C_{\max}(S)$ must hold.

Note that Theorem 5 is only valid for colourable mixed graphs. For example, if the precedence constraint $v_{12} \Rightarrow v_9$ is added to the input data of Example A2, we obtain the following mixed graph: $G^+ = (V, A \cup \{(v_{12}, v_9)\}, E)$. The obtained mixed graph becomes un-colourable due to the existence of a circuit $(v_{12}, v_9, v_{10}, v_{12})$ such that the vertices v_9 and v_{10} are adjacent in the graph $(V, \varnothing, E)$, which is a subgraph of the mixed graph $G^+ = (V, A \cup \{(v_{12}, v_9)\}, E)$; see Theorem 1. Therefore, the modified Example A2 (with the additional precedence constraint $v_{12} \Rightarrow v_9$) has no feasible schedule due to Theorem 4.

References

1. Sotskov, Y.N.; Dolgui, A.; Werner, F. Mixed graph coloring for unit-time job-shop scheduling. *Int. J. Math. Algorithms* **200** 289–323.
2. Sotskov, Y.N.; Tanaev, V.S.; Werner, F. Scheduling problems and mixed graph colorings. *Optimization* **2002**, *51*, 597–624.
3. Sotskov, Y.N.; Tanaev, V.S. A chromatic polynomial of a mixed graph. *Vestsi Akad. Navuk BSSR Ser. Fiz. Mat. Navuk* **1976**, *6*, 20 (In Russian)
4. Karp, R.M. Reducibility among combinatorial problems. In *Complexity of Computer Computations*; Miller, R.E., Thatcher, J.W., E Plenum Press: New York, NY, USA, 1972; pp. 85–103.
5. Brucker, P. *Scheduling Algorithms*; Springer: Berlin, Germany, 1995.
6. Harary, F. *Graph Theory*; Reading; Addison-Wesley: Boston, MA, USA, 1969.
7. Thulasiraman, K.; Swamy, M.N.S. *Graphs: Theory and Algorithms*; John Wiley & Sons, Inc.: Toronto, ON, Canada, 1992.

Hansen, P.; Kuplinsky, J.; de Werra, D. Mixed graph colorings. *Math. Methods Oper. Res.* **1997**, *45*, 145–160. [CrossRef]
Sotskov, Y.N. Mixed graph colouring as scheduling multi-processor tasks with equal processing times. *J. Belarusian State Univ. Math. Inform.* **2021**, *2*, 67–81. [CrossRef]
Giaro, K.; Kubale, M.; Obszarski, P. A graph coloring approach to scheduling of multiprocessor tasks on dedicated machines with availability constraints. *Discret. Appl. Math.* **2009**, *157*, 3625–3630. [CrossRef]
Hoogeveen, J.A.; Lenstra, J.K.; Veltman, B. Preemptive scheduling in a two-stage multiprocessor flow shop is NP-hard. *Eur. J. Oper. Res.* **1996**, *89*, 172–175. [CrossRef]
Sotskov, Y.N.; Mihova, E.I. Scheduling multiprocessor tasks with equal processing times as a mixed graph coloring problem. *Algorithms* **2021**, *14*, 246. [CrossRef]
De Werra, D. Restricted coloring models for timetabling. *Discret. Math.* **1997**, *165/166*, 161–170. [CrossRef]
De Werra, D. On a multiconstrained model for chromatic scheduling. *Discret. Appl. Math.* **1999**, *94*, 171–180. [CrossRef]
Damaschke, P. Parameterized mixed graph coloring. *J. Comb. Optim.* **2019**, *38*, 326–374. [CrossRef]
Kouider, A.; Ait Haddadne, H.; Ourari, S.; Oulamara, A. Mixed graph coloring for unit-time scheduling. *Int. J. Prod. Res.* **2017**, *55*, 1720–1729. [CrossRef]
Kouider, A.; Ait Haddadene, H.; Oulamara, A. On minimization of memory usage in branch-and-bound algorithm for the mixed graph coloring: Application to the unit-time job shop scheduling. *Comput. Oper. Res.* **2019**, *4967*, 1001–1008.
Kouider, A.; Ait Haddadne, H. A bi-objective branch-and-bound algorithm for the unit-time job shop scheduling: A mixed graph coloring approach. *Comput. Oper. Res.* **2021**, *132*, 105319. [CrossRef]
Baaziz, A.; Haddadene, H.A.; Oulamara, A.; Kouider, A. Scheduling preemptive jobs on parallel machines with a conflict graph: A graph multi-colouring approach. *Int. J. Math. Oper. Res.* **2023**, *25*, 47–67. [CrossRef]
Beck, M.; Blado, D.; Crawford, J.; Jean-Louis, T.; Young, M. On weak chromatic polynomials of mixed graphs. *Graphs Comb.* **2015**, *31*, 91–98. [CrossRef]
Niu, D.; Liu, B.; Zhang, H.; Yin, M. Improving local search for the weighted sum coloring problem using the branch-and-bound algorithm. *Knowl. Based Syst.* **2022**, *246*, 108703. [CrossRef]
Jacqueline, O.; Alden, M.; Golshan, M.; Seyedamirabbas, M. Graph-based modeling in shop scheduling problems: Review and extensions. *Appl. Sci.* **2021**, *11*, 4741. [CrossRef]
Liang, P.; Fu, Y.; Gao, K. Multi-product disassembly line balancing optimization method for high disassembly profit and low energy consumption with noise pollution constraints. *Eng. Appl. Artif. Intell.* **2024**, *130*, 107721. [CrossRef]
Fu, Y.; Zhou, M.; Guo, X.; Qi, L.; Gao, K.; Albeshri, A. A multiobjective scheduling of energy-efficient stochastic hybrid open shop with brain storm optimization and simulation evaluation. *IEEE Trans. Syst. Man Cybern. Syst.* **2024**, *54*, 4260–4272. [CrossRef]
Fu, Y.; Ma, X.; Gao, K.; Li, Z.; Dong, Y. Multi-objective home health care routing and scheduling with sharing service via a problem-specific knowledge-based artificial bee colony algorithm. *IEEE Trans. Intell. Transp. Syst.* **2024**, *25*, 1706–1719. [CrossRef]
Ma, X.; Fu, Y.; Gao, K.; Zhu, L.; Sadollah, A. A multi-objective scheduling and routing problem for home health care services via brain storm optimization. *Complex Syst. Model. Simul.* **2023**, *3*, 32–46. [CrossRef]
Andrade, E.; Bonifácio, A.E.; Robbiano, M.; Rodríguez, J.; Tapia, K. Some families of integral mixed graphs. *Linear Algebra Appl.* **2022**, *641*, 48–66. [CrossRef]
Mostafaie, T.; Modarres Khiyabani, F.; Navimipour, N.J. A systematic study on meta-heuristic approaches for solving the graph coloring problem. *Comput. Oper. Res.* **2020**, *120*, 104850. [CrossRef]
Balakrishnan, S.; Suresh, T.; Marappan, R.; Venkatesan, R.; Sabri, A. New hybrid decentralized evolutionary approach for DIMACS challenge graph coloring & wireless network instances. *Int. J. Cogn. Comput. Eng.* **2023**, *4*, 259–265.
Astuti, W.; Adiwijaya. Graph coloring based on evolutionary algorithms to support data hiding scheme on medical images. *Procedia Comput. Sci.* **2015**, *74*, 173–177. [CrossRef]
Agrawal, J.; Agrawal, S. Acceleration based particle swarm optimization for graph coloring problem. *Procedia Comput. Sci.* **2015**, *60*, 714–721. [CrossRef]
Assi, M.; Halawi, B.; Haraty, R.A. Genetic algorithm analysis using the graph coloring method for solving the university timetable problem. *Procedia Comput. Sci.* **2018**, *126*, 899–906. [CrossRef]

algorithms

MDPI

Article

An Improved Negotiation-Based Approach for Collecting and Sorting Operations in Waste Management and Recycling

Massimiliano Caramia [1,*,†] and Giuseppe Stecca [2,†]

[1] Department of Enterprise Engineering, University of Rome "Tor Vergata", 00133 Rome, Italy
[2] Institute of Systems Analysis and Computer Science "Antonio Ruberti", National Research Council, 00185 Rome, Italy; giuseppe.stecca@iasi.cnr.it
* Correspondence: caramia@dii.uniroma2.it
† These authors contributed equally to this work.

Abstract: This paper addresses the problem of optimal planning for collection, sorting, and recycling operations. The problem arises in industrial waste management, where distinct actors manage the collection and the sorting operations. In a weekly or monthly plan horizon, they usually interact to find a suitable schedule for servicing customers but with a not well-defined scheme. We proposal an improved negotiation-based approach using an auction mechanism for optimizing these operations. Two interdependent models are presented: one for waste collection by a logistics operator and the other for sorting operations at a recycling plant. These models are formulated as mixed-integer linear programs where costs associated with sorting and collection are to be minimized, respectively. We describe the negotiation-based approach involving an auction where the logistics operator bids for collection time slots, and the recycling plant selects the optimal bid based on the integration of sorting and collection costs. This approach aims to achieve an optimization of the entire waste management process. Computational experiments are presented.

Keywords: waste management; optimization; auctions; negotiation approaches

1. Introduction and Literature Review

The purpose of this study is to provide a model based on negotiation in the field of waste management and recycling. The paper is inspired by previous work [1] in which a similar approach was proposed for a waste collection problem. Several efforts are reported in countries and/or local administrations to incentivize waste collection and material circularity through incentives and negotiation mechanisms. In this area, particular attention has been devoted to the collection and sorting processes. Collection refers to the process of gathering and collecting waste from various sources, such as households, businesses, and public areas. It involves the use of waste collection vehicles and containers to transport waste to designated collection points or facilities. Sorting, on the other hand, involves the separation and categorization of different types of waste materials. This process is necessary to ensure that different recyclable materials (i.e., fractions of recyclable materials) are properly identified and separated from non-recyclable waste. Sorting can be performed manually or with the help of automated systems and technologies.

The main research gap covered in this work is the proposal of an improved combinatorial auction system that takes into account the specific characteristics of industrial waste recycling, leveraging the interactions among logistics and sorting operators. In particular, the main innovation of the proposal lies in the different and improved design of the bidding phase. Thanks to the improved auction system, the bidders can generate more different bids, covering a larger solution space. In particular, bids are generated not only by looking at the objective of the logistics operator but also at the objective of the sorting decision maker to obtain more robust solutions. This led to solving the winner determination problem more effectively compared to standard methods, as we will show in the following.

The interaction between collection and sorting is crucial for waste management. Here is how they work together.

- Waste collection systems need to be well planned and organized to ensure that waste is collected regularly and efficiently. Proper collection routes and schedules are established based on the type of waste, the volume of waste generated, and the specific needs of the area. By implementing effective collection practices, waste can be gathered and transported to sorting facilities in a timely and cost-effective manner.
- Sorting plays a vital role in separating recyclable materials from non-recyclable waste. Once waste reaches the sorting facility, trained personnel or automated systems sort through the waste to identify and separate materials such as paper, plastic, glass, metal, and organic waste. This segregation allows for the recycling of valuable materials and prevents them from being disposed of in landfills or incinerators.
- By effectively sorting waste, recyclable materials can be diverted from landfills and sent to recycling facilities. Sorting also enables the recovery of valuable resources from waste, promoting a circular economy and reducing the need for raw material extraction.
- Not all waste materials can be recycled. Sorting ensures that non-recyclable waste is properly identified and disposed of in appropriate ways, such as landfilling or waste-to-energy facilities. By separating non-recyclable waste, the focus can be placed on maximizing the recycling potential of the remaining materials.

In summary, collection and sorting are interconnected steps in waste management. The efficient collection ensures that waste is gathered and transported to sorting facilities, while sorting allows for the separation of recyclables from non-recyclable waste. This collaboration is essential for effective waste management practices that promote recycling, resource conservation, and proper disposal.

Negotiation plays an important role in waste management, especially when it comes to addressing the interests of various stakeholders and finding mutually beneficial solutions. Here is how negotiation works in waste management.

- The first step in the negotiation process is identifying the relevant stakeholders involved in waste management. This may include government agencies, waste management companies, environmental organizations, local communities, and residents.
- Each stakeholder will have different interests, objectives, and concerns when it comes to waste management. It is crucial to understand these interests and objectives to facilitate effective negotiations. For example, waste management companies may prioritize cost-efficiency and profitability, while environmental organizations may focus on sustainability and minimizing environmental impact.
- Successful negotiations require building relationships and establishing trust among the stakeholders. This involves open communication, active listening, and acknowledging the perspectives of all parties involved. Building trust creates a collaborative environment where stakeholders are more willing to work together to find common ground.
- Transparency and sharing of relevant information are essential in waste management negotiations. This includes data on waste generation, recycling rates, waste treatment technologies, and regulatory requirements. Sharing information helps stakeholders make informed decisions and facilitates the development of effective waste management strategies.
- Negotiations in waste management aim to find win–win solutions that address the interests and concerns of all stakeholders involved. For example, waste management companies may agree to invest in more environmentally friendly technologies in exchange for regulatory incentives or public support.
- In complex negotiations, mediators or facilitators may be involved to assist in the negotiation process. They help manage conflicts, guide discussions, and ensure that all

parties have an equal opportunity to express their views. Mediators can help bridge the gap between different stakeholders and facilitate productive negotiations.

- Once an agreement is reached, it needs to be implemented and monitored to ensure compliance. This may involve developing waste management plans, implementing new policies or regulations, and monitoring progress toward waste reduction and recycling targets. Regular review and evaluation of the agreement can help identify areas for improvement and ensure its effectiveness over time.

The literature addressed solid waste management in different ways, and several authors analyzed the topic from the strategic, tactical, and operational side. Cerqueira-Streit et al. [2] detail in their survey how waste management is a critical factor in turning the circular economy into a profitable business. To address the complexity of waste management processes, Cardoso et al. [3] propose a method based on a literature review and apply evidence-based decision making to resolve conflicts in electronic waste management. However, profitability can only be reached if the underlying waste management processes are optimized. For a comprehensive review of the literature on strategic and tactical issues in the management of solid waste, the readers are referred to the following surveys [4–6].

Combinatorial auctions (CAs) are a well-consolidated method to mathematically formalize and solve shared resource allocation problems between different actors. In particular, they are useful when the bidder is interested in bidding not only on a single item but also on a combination of them [7]. In recent years, we assisted a renewed interest in CAs as methods to solve multi-actor problems in shared economy or for eco-sustainable service systems. Triki [8] uses CAs to formalize and optimize the interactions among actors in crowd shipping, where occasional drivers are considered and the winner determination problem is used to solve the vehicle routing problem. The problem of allocating energy storage to optimize social welfare and prices is addressed by Zhong et al. [9] using CAs. In [10], the design of online CAs is considered when supply chain costs are considered. Another recent application of CAs is in the renewal energy industry and market. As illustrated by the survey of Ehrhart et al. [11], the characteristics of complementary and substitute relationships between renewal energy projects can be exploited by CAs. CAs show good perspectives in circular economy, reverse logistics, and green supply chains. Ma et al. [12] use CAs to improve the performances of an online used-car platform with the aim of social welfare maximization and considering incentive compatibility conditions. The authors use both price and non-price attributes in bid generation, such as environmental compliance, service level, and car rating. CAs in the circular economy are also used in [13] to optimally compute, through the winner determination problem, the reselling prices in secondary markets. The remanufacturing of end-of-life products is the application case for an automated demand–supply matching negotiation algorithm proposed by Fernández et al. [14]. Reverse CAs are studied by Triki et al. [15] for real applications in food industries. Incentives for recycling in the international supply chain is the topic addressed in the work by Bimonte et al. [16], where the strategic decision is addressed with a Stackelberg game. In [17], auctions are used to regulate the relations between a carrier and several shippers in the waste collection process. Auction allocation and routing problems are solved by metaheuristics. The paper proposes the auction framework as a carrier-centric pattern in addition to solving synchronization issues. Differently, our proposal focuses on the relations between the logistics operators and the sorting/recycling plant. The work in [18] studies auctions for the battery recycling industry. The authors propose a multi-unit trade reduction mechanism that is demonstrated to be efficient for resource allocation in the electric vehicle battery recycling market. The work is aimed at supporting the decision-maker in evaluating policies for developing the EVBR market. In [19], a multi-objective approach for the circular economy is proposed. The importance of using a similar approach to the one presented in the previous paper is underlined in [20] where the literature on zero defect manufacturing has been classified. The investigation on how to combine optimization and negotiation to minimize recycling costs, taking into account the collection process and material sorting cost, has also been studied in [21] where the authors proposed a mixed-integer linear formulation for the multiperiod planning problem.

We are interested in solution approaches that use market-based mechanisms, as described in [22], negotiations, cooperation, and auctions. Auctions and CAs make it possible to formally describe the problem of assigning shared and limited resources among customers and suppliers, as shown in [7]. Some applications can be found in flexible manufacturing [23], healthcare [24] and value creation in manufacturing [25]. Simulation is used in [26] to study negotiation protocols in a closed supply chain and to assess reusing policies. Ref. [27] consider the importance of multiple criteria analysis in waste collection. Another study is presented in [17] in which waste collection is solved using an auction-based system. The authors assume that the carrier plays the auctioneer role to decide on who wins the bids and the corresponding payments, while the shippers are the bidders.

Notwithstanding the renewed interest in combinatorial auctions in applications such as the shared economy and eco-sustainability, there are a few applications in waste recycling and in particular bidding auction systems specifically designed to improve waste management operations. In contrast, in our manuscript, we propose a model based on combinatorial auctions able to efficiently allocate resources in the joint process of industrial solid waste collection and sorting.

The remainder of the paper is as follows. Section 2 presents the mathematical models of the two problems. Section 3 formalizes the negotiation-based approach to integrate these models. Section 4 details the experiments and results; Section 5 provides the conclusions.

2. Models for Sorting and Logistics Operators

In this section, we model collection and sorting planning in an industrial solid waste management system. The processes of the case studied are sketched in Figure 1 for transport and in Figure 2 for sorting. Transport is carried out by a specialized logistics operator that serves customers by transporting empty containers to their location and picking full containers to be delivered to the sorting plant. Several industries produce mixed waste that must be sorted. In particular, warehouses and transport operators are a source of recyclable waste where different types of plastic and paper are grouped. In the analyzed sorting plant, waste goes through a sorting cabin where it is visually inspected and separated into its components. After several other sequential operations, the separated waste is transformed into secondary raw material and can be sent to other processing plants.

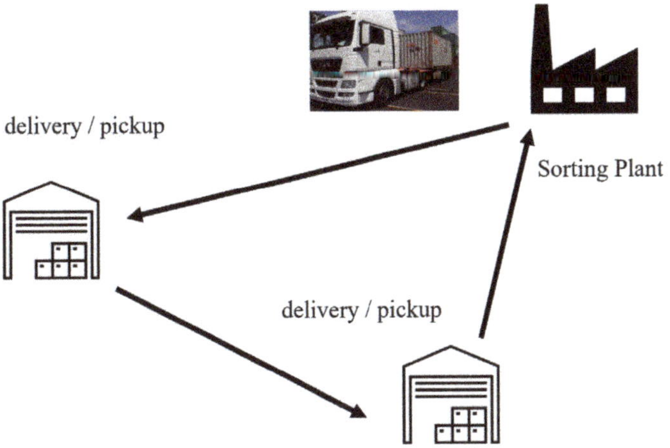

Figure 1. Diagram of the process operated by the carriers.

Different technologies can be used to improve the automation and digitization phases of the collection and sorting processes both at the operational and planning levels. Arebey et al. [28] surveyed how tracking technologies, such as RFID and GPS, could support waste management. In particular, RFID and image recognition applied to bins are used to track waste production and improve planning processes. Recently, Abdallah et al. [29] surveyed the research literature considering artificial intelligence applications to municipal waste management. Artificial intelligence and computer vision can be applied to sorting to automatically separate waste [30]. In this context, our case study is related to an industrial waste recycling network, where RFID is used to track the position of containers located in customer locations or in a sorting plant.

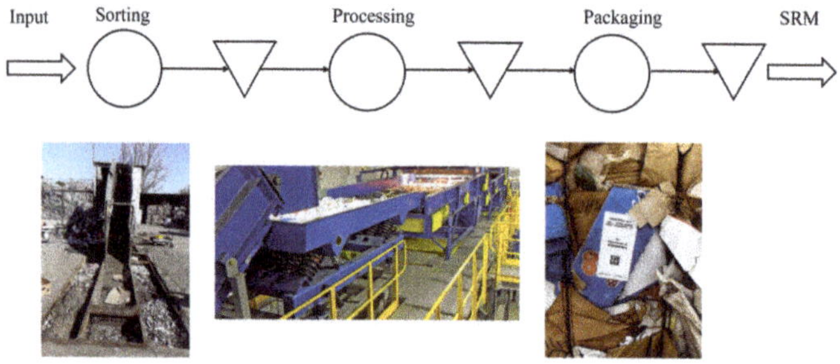

Figure 2. Diagram of sorting plant with the main waste treatment phases from the input of solid waste to secondary raw materials (SRM).

The sorting process is still not automated, and visual inspection coupled with manual sorting at the cabin is performed. Customers, the logistics operator, and the sorting operator are connected through email and the Enterprise Resource Planning (ERP) system. The planning of the two processes is scheduled every week/month independently by the sorting and the logistics operators. This leads to peaks in daily sorting operations because the customers interact directly only with the logistics operator. In the studied case, only a not formally specified interaction between logistics and sorting operator occurs, mostly by phone call, to synchronize transports with sorting operations.

Starting with these premises, we decided to focus on negotiation as a way to manage our waste management problem. In particular, the decision process that needs optimization and is studied in this paper is as follows. Business customers establish contracts with recycling operators. They generate waste during their business processes, which is stored in local buffers (e.g., containers). Once the buffers are full, a recycling request is generated to the logistics operator in charge to define a transportation plan. Once the transportation schedule is established and communicated to the sorting operator, the latter can plan the sorting operations at the plant. The plant operates sequential sorting stations that require setup and staffing. Additionally, waste buffers have limited capacity and incur occupancy costs. After the sorting/recycling operations, the recycled material can be directed to secondary raw material markets. Although the planning of these two subproblems (collection and sorting) is usually completed sequentially and separately, this study proposes an effective method to optimize and integrate both planning phases. We use an improved auction-based scheme to solve the sorting and collection problems in an integrated way and obtain an optimal multiperiod schedule for the two sub-processes. In particular, concerning the approach described in [1], the bid generation scheme is designed to produce a more robust transport plan and thus greater opportunities for the sorting operators to optimize the sorting plan.

The sorting operator aims to minimize the cost function of the sorting operations in the plant formed of variable and fixed components. The variable component considers both sorting and inventory costs based on the amount of commodity processed, while the fixed component considers the setup cost of the working stations involved. In fact, the model is a variant of lot sizing applied to a reverse logistics problem.

The commodity to be sorted in the sorting plant must be moved from waste generation points, where customer demands are assumed to be generated; to this end, a logistics operator aims to minimize such collection cost by optimally routing a fleet of vehicles. To model its decision problem, the logistics operator has to estimate some core parameters such as the planning time horizon and its discretization in time slots, where customers are located, their demands, the unit collection cost (time and customer dependent), the fleet of vehicles, and their capacities.

The connection between the two problems (collection and sorting) is that the optimal quantity a_t to be sorted in each time slot t should be equal to the total amount of commodity collected by the logistics operator from customers in the same time slot. In the following, we first define the formulation of the two problems, and next, we show how to tunnel information between the latter.

2.1. Formulation of the Sorting Problem

The sorting problem aims to define the optimal amount of waste to be sorted within a planning horizon, discretized into $|T_s|$ time slots, for every sorting facility. To this end, we introduce a nonnegative variable x_{jt} defining the quantity of material to be sorted in time slot $t \in T_s$, and a binary decision variable y_{jt} that is equal to 1 if the sorting station (facility) $j \in J$ is opened in $t \in T_s$ and 0 otherwise. Opening a sorting facility in $t \in T_s$ implies a setup time, as detailed in the following; therefore, it is important to correctly evaluate which facilities must operate and which must be closed. I_{jt} is the level of inventory of the upstream buffer of station $j \in J$ in time slot $t \in T_s$ with the condition $I_{j0} = 0$, $\forall j \in J$. Here are the parameters:

- c_t^s, f_j, h_j are the variable sorting costs in time slot $t \in T_s$, the fixed setup time for station $j \in J$, and the inventory holding cost for station $j \in J$, respectively;
- a_t is the quantity of material arriving at the sorting plant at time slot $t \in T_s$;
- E_j, M_j are the minimum and maximum allowed sorting quantity for station $j \in J$, respectively, in case it is activated;
- α is the loss factor considering the mean percentage of material that is discarded after selection at each sorting stage;
- LC_j is the inventory capacity for station $j \in J$.

The P1 sorting model is the following:

$$\min\ Z_s = \sum_{j\in J}\sum_{t\in T_s} c_t^s \cdot x_{jt} + \sum_{j\in J}\sum_{t\in T_s} f_j \cdot \max(0, y_{jt} - y_{j,t-1}) + \sum_{j\in J}\sum_{t\in T_s} h_j \cdot I_{jt} \tag{1}$$

s.t.

$$E_j y_{jt} \le x_{jt} \le M_j y_{jt}, \quad \forall j \in J, \forall t \in T_s, \tag{2}$$

$$I_{1,t} = I_{1,t-1} + a_{t-1} - x_{1,t-1}, \quad \forall t \in T_s \setminus \{0\}, \tag{3}$$

$$I_{j,t} = I_{j,t-1} + \alpha x_{j-1,t-1} - x_{j,t-1}, \forall t \in T_s \setminus \{0\}, j \in J \setminus \{1\}, \tag{4}$$

$$I_{jt} \le LC_j, \quad \forall j \in J, t \in T_s, \tag{5}$$

$$x_{jt} \ge 0,\ y_{jt} \in \{0,1\}, \forall t \in T_s, \forall j \in J. \tag{6}$$

Equation (1) is the objective function of the problem aiming at minimizing the sorting cost, the setup time cost, and the inventory holding cost. Constraint (2) limits x_{jt} values. Constraints (3) and (4) define the inventories. We note that (3) embeds the quantities to be collected from the customers. Constraints (5) limit the inventory level to a maximum capacity, while (6) defines the variable domains.

Model P1 has a nonlinearity in the objective function that can be easily linearized as follows:

$$\min Z_s = \sum_{j \in J} \sum_{t \in T_s} c_t^s \cdot x_{jt} + \sum_{j \in J} \sum_{t \in T_s} f_j \cdot \bar{y}_{jt} + \sum_{j \in J} \sum_{t \in T_s} h_j \cdot I_{jt} \tag{7}$$

s.t.

$$E_j y_{jt} \leq x_{jt} \leq M_j y_{jt}, \quad \forall j \in J, \forall t \in T_s, \tag{2'}$$

$$I_{1,t} = I_{1,t-1} + a_{t-1} - x_{1,t-1}, \quad \forall t \in T_s \setminus \{0\}, \tag{3'}$$

$$I_{j,t} = I_{j,t-1} + \alpha x_{j-1,t-1} - x_{j,t-1}, \forall t \in T_s \setminus \{0\}, j \in J \setminus \{1\}, \tag{4'}$$

$$I_{jt} \leq LC_j, \quad \forall j \in J, t \in T_s, \tag{5'}$$

$$x_{jt} \geq 0, \ y_{jt} \in \{0,1\}, \forall t \in T_s, \forall j \in J. \tag{6'}$$

$$\bar{y}_{jt} \geq y_{jt} - y_{j,t-1}, \quad \forall j \in J, t \in T_s, \tag{8}$$

$$\bar{y}_{jt} \geq 0, \quad \forall j \in J, t \in T_s. \tag{9}$$

2.2. Formulation of the Collection Problem

In the collection problem, we have a set I of customers who require the collection of quantities $q_i, \forall i \in I$, of waste material to be sorted/recycled during the time horizon T_c with $T_c \leq T_s$. The logistics operator uses a fleet H of vehicles, which each have a limited capacity C. The cost c_{it}^c measures the expenses for the logistics operator to collect the waste commodity from customer $i \in I$ in time slot $t \in T_c$. The binary decision variable $z_{iht} \in \{0,1\}$ is equal to 1 if customer $i \in I$ is serviced by vehicle $h \in H$ in time slot $t \in T_c$, and it is zero otherwise. The resulting collection model P2 is the following:

$$\min Z_c = \sum_{i \in I} \sum_{h \in H} \sum_{t \in T_c} c_{it}^c \cdot z_{iht} \tag{10}$$

s.t.

$$\sum_{h \in H} \sum_{t \in T^c} z_{iht} = 1, \forall i \in I, \tag{11}$$

$$\sum_{i \in I} q_i \cdot z_{iht} \leq C, \forall h \in H, \forall t \in T_c, \tag{12}$$

$$z_{iht} \in \{0,1\}, \forall i \in I, h \in H, t \in T_c. \tag{13}$$

Equation (22) is the objective cost function. Constraint (11) imposes that each customer has to be serviced only once, while (12) defines capacity restrictions for each vehicle in each timeslot. Constraint (13) defines the domain of variables z_{iht}. While model P1 is a variant of the lot sizing model and a variant of the model presented in [21], model P2 defines a multiperiod allocation problem which can be considered a variant of the knapsack problem.

3. The Negotiation-Based Approach

As mentioned previously, the two models are interdependent because the quantity to be sorted in each time slot is determined based on the decision on when to collect materials from customers. In particular, the binding between the two models is defined by the following equation:

$$a_t = \sum_{i \in I} \sum_{h \in H} q_i \cdot z_{iht}. \tag{14}$$

Since the two problems are addressed, in general, by two different decision-makers, a negotiation-based approach can support the selection of a solution, taking into account the distinct objectives of the two actors of the system. Negotiation-based approaches have been applied in several forms in the literature (see, e.g. [7]) to address different applications. In this paper, we solve the problem by proposing a negotiation scheme with an auction model depicted in Figure 3 and described in the following. The interactions among the actors start from the customers and the sorting operator sides simultaneously; indeed, the first send requests q_i and the latter send the available capacities over time. Once all the data are received, the logistics operator defines the bids and sends them to the sorting operator. Then, the plant operator, based on the bids received, chooses the best bid solving a winner determination problem. Once the best bid is made, the sorting operator sends this information to the logistics operator who prepares the collection plan and informs the customers of the collection schedule. In the following, we detail how bids are generated and how the winner determination problem is defined.

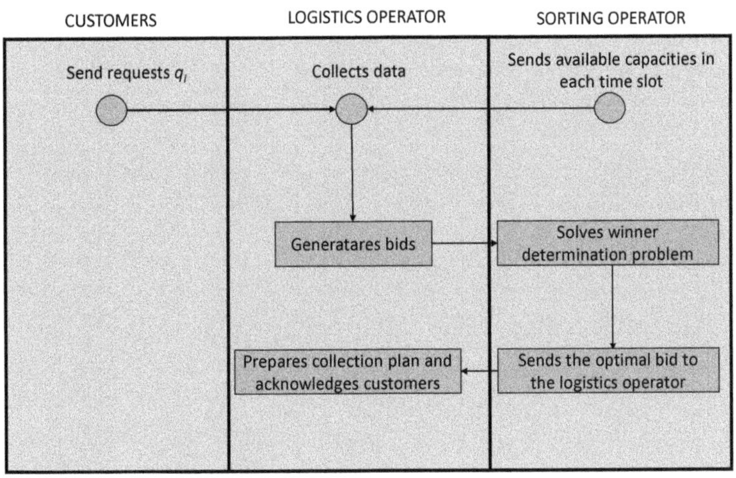

Figure 3. Scheme of the auction-based negotiation.

3.1. The Bid Generation Problem

The bid is the vector (γ, τ) where γ is a row vector of dimensions $|I|$ that corresponds to the quantities to be processed from each customer and τ is a vector of dimensions $|I|$ of the time slots chosen in the bid to serve each customer. A set of K bids is generated by iteratively solving the problem P2. In particular, at each iteration k, the solution obtained in iteration $(k-1)$ is totally or partially prohibited in problem P2 by adding a specific constraint in the k-th bid generation problem. The proposed bid generation scheme guarantees different bids that are feasible for the logistics operator and near-optimal. At each iteration k, let $N^{k-1} = \{(i,h,t) : z^*_{iht} = 1\}$ in bid $k-1$ (clearly $N^0 = \emptyset$). To generate a bid at iteration $k \geq 1$, we introduce a tabu list L^k_{iht} such that

$$L^k_{iht} = \begin{cases} 0, & \text{if } k = 1, \\ L^{k-1}_{iht} - 1, & \text{if } k > 1 \text{ and } (i,h,t) \in N^{k-1} \text{ and } L^{k-1}_{iht} > 1, \\ r, & \text{if } k > 1 \text{ and } L^{k-1}_{iht} = 0. \end{cases}$$

List L acts as a tabu list; in fact, the idea is to prevent client i from being serviced by vehicle h at time t in iteration k if it has been serviced by the same vehicle at the same time in the previous iteration. This allows for diversifying the solutions associated with the bids to be given in input to the collection problem in the next winner-determination problem. However, in order not to possibly prohibit all the assignments of the previous iteration, guaranteeing both diversification and intensification, we define an aspiration criterion such that

$$z_{iht} \leq \rho^k_{iht} + \zeta^k_{iht} \tag{15}$$

where

$$\rho_{iht}^k = \begin{cases} 0, & \text{if } L_{iht}^k > 0, \\ 1, & \text{if } L_{iht}^k = 0. \end{cases}$$

and

$$\zeta_{iht}^k = \begin{cases} 1, & \text{if } Uniform(0,1) > 1 - \frac{Z_c^{(k-1)} - Z_c^{(k-2)}}{Z_c^{(k-2)}}, \\ 0, & \text{otherwise.} \end{cases}$$

Parameter ζ_{iht}^k has the following effect: assume that the algorithm is processing iteration k in the bid generation problem. Let $Z_c^{(k-1)}$ and $Z_c^{(k-1)}$ be the optimal solution value of the bid generation problem in iterations $(k-1)$ and $(k-2)$, respectively. The ratio $\frac{Z_c^{(k-1)} - Z_c^{(k-2)}}{Z_c^{(k-2)}}$ is the percentage of variation of the optimal objective of the bids associated with the iterations mentioned. If the variation is positive and large, that is, the cost is increased by a sufficiently large amount, the algorithm is not prone to intensify this solution; therefore, if an assignment that may restore a previous more profitable solution is prohibited, the algorithm tries to activate an aspiration criterion to override the tabu list status. As can be seen, if ρ_{iht}^k is zero and the ratio $\frac{Z_c^{(k-1)} - Z_c^{(k-2)}}{Z_c^{(k-2)}}$ is large, $1 - \frac{Z_c^{(k-1)} - Z_c^{(k-2)}}{Z_c^{(k-2)}}$ is small, say close to zero, and there is a greater chance that ζ_{iht}^k becomes 1 by its definition.

The overall problem to solve to find the k-th bid is the following.

$$\min \sum_{i \in I} \sum_{h \in H} \sum_{t \in T_c} c_{it}^c \cdot z_{iht} + \sum_{t \in T_c} \max\{0, [a_t - \sum_{j \in J}(LC_j - I_{jt})]\} \tag{16}$$

s.t.

$$\sum_{h \in H, t \in T_c} z_{iht} = 1, \forall i \in I, \tag{17}$$

$$\sum_{i \in I} q_i \cdot z_{iht} = a_t, \forall h \in H, \forall t \in T_c, \tag{18}$$

$$a_t \le C, \forall t \in T_c, \tag{19}$$

$$z_{iht} \le \rho_{iht}^k + \zeta_{iht}^k, \forall i \in I, \forall h \in H, \forall t \in T_c, \tag{20}$$

$$z_{iht} \in \{0,1\}, \forall i \in I, \forall h \in H, \forall t \in T_c. \tag{21}$$

Note that the objective function takes into account two components. The first component is exactly the collection cost; the second part of the objective tries to infer the state of occupancy of the resources that the sorting operator will use. In fact, the term $[a_t - \sum_{j \in J}(LC_j - I_{jt})]$ penalizes scenarios in which there is no residual capacity in the sorting facilities at time t. Instead, if a_t is smaller than the residual capacity at time t, then the second term of the objective is zero. Note that even though this second term is nonlinear, it can be easily linearized as follows:

$$\min \sum_{i \in I} \sum_{h \in H} \sum_{t \in T_c} c_{it}^c \cdot z_{iht} + \sum_{t \in T_c} R_t \tag{22}$$

s.t.

$$\sum_{h \in H, t \in T_c} z_{iht} = 1, \forall i \in I, \tag{23}$$

$$\sum_{i \in I} q_i \cdot z_{iht} = a_t, \forall h \in H, \forall t \in T_c, \tag{24}$$

(25)

$$a_t \leq C, \forall t \in T_c, \tag{26}$$

$$z_{iht} \leq \rho^k_{iht} + \zeta^k_{iht}, \forall i \in I, \forall h \in H, \forall t \in T_c, \tag{27}$$

$$R_t \geq [a_t - \sum_{j \in J}(LC_j - I_{jt})], \forall t \in T_c, \tag{28}$$

$$R_t \geq 0, \forall t \in T_c, \tag{29}$$

$$z_{iht} \in \{0,1\}, \forall i \in I, \forall h \in H, \forall t \in T_c. \tag{30}$$

3.2. The Winner Determination Problem

The winner determination problem starts from problem P1 and considers Equation (14). To embed the bids into the model, we consider the following reformulation. The k-th bid $(\gamma, \tau)^k$ can be rewritten by introducing parameter q^k_{it}, $\forall i \in I, \forall t \in T_c, \forall k \in K$, such that

$$q^k_{it} = \begin{cases} q_i, & \text{if customer } i \text{ is serviced in timeslot } t \in T_c \text{ in bid } k, \\ 0, & \text{otherwise.} \end{cases}$$

Note that $q^k_{it} = 0, \forall t \in T_s \setminus T_c$. Moreover, a bid selection binary variable $u^k \in \{0,1\}, \forall k \in K$, is needed such that

$$u^k = \begin{cases} 1 & \text{if bid } k \text{ is selected,} \\ 0 & \text{otherwise.} \end{cases}$$

Thus, Equation (3) can be rewritten as

$$I_{1,t} = I_{1,t-1} + \sum_{i \in I, k \in K} q^k_{i,t-1} \cdot u^k - x_{1,t-1} \quad \forall t \in T_s \setminus \{0\} \tag{31}$$

To ensure only one bid is the winner, the following constraint is added

$$\sum_{k \in K} u^k = 1 \tag{32}$$

The winner determination problem is then:

$$\min Z_c \tag{33}$$

s.t.
Equations (2), (4), (5), (6), (31) and (32),
$u^k \in \{0,1\}, \forall k \in K$.

4. Experimental Results

The algorithm and the models have been implemented in Python 3.12.0 and solved with Gurobi^{TM} on a Windows machine equipped with an Intel Core^{TM} i7-12700K @ 3.60 GHz, 12 core and 32 GB RAM. The instance used for experimentation is adapted from a real recycling plant composed of two stations. The number of customers is 30. The collection time horizon is 25 days; the sorting problem time horizon is 30 days. The cost of collection is set to a uniform distribution such that $c^c_i \in [5, 15]$, while quantities are chosen uniformly at random in the interval $[3, 5]$, and the maximum capacity for trucks is fixed and equal to 10. The variable selection cost c^s_i is set to 3, while the setup cost is 5 and the inventory storage cost per unit of quantity and time is set to 1. The inventory capacity is 50, while the minimum and maximum production capacity for stations for a unit of time are 0 and 10, respectively. No loss is considered, i.e., $\alpha = 1$.

Figure 4 reports the results when the algorithm is run with the number of bids generated ranging from 1 to 20. If we have only one bid, the logistics operator proposes its optimal solution to the recycling plant that is used to solve the plant planning problem. In that case, we have the minimum cost for the collection process and the maximum cost for the sorting process. In the other cases, the winner determination problem defines the bid to be selected. Figure 4a shows the number of the selected bids. The objective values of the collection and sorting problems are reported in Figures 4b and 4c, respectively. The total cost, that is, the sum of the two objectives, is reported in Figure 4d.

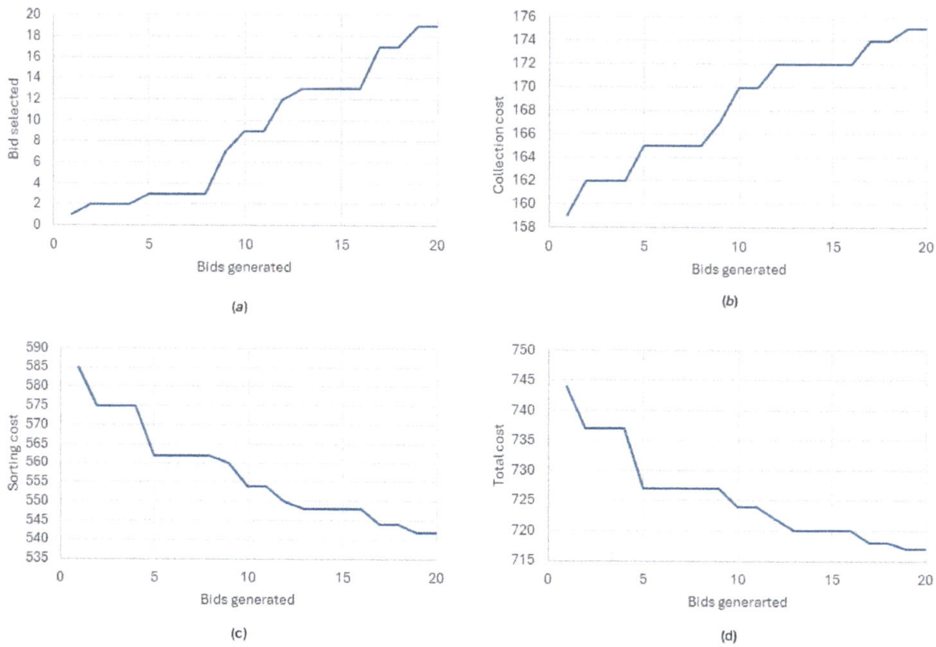

Figure 4. Results obtained by the proposed approach. (**a**) shows the number of bids generated and the number of selected bids; (**b**) shows the number of bids generated and the collection cost; (**c**) shows the number of bids generated and the sorting cost; (**d**) shows the number of bids generated and the total cost.

As can be seen by analyzing the results, as the number of bids generated by the algorithm increases, the collection cost tends to increase as well (see Figure 4b), while the sorting cost shows a nonincreasing behavior (see Figure 4c). However, in general, they produce a decreasing total cost. In fact, even though the percentage of increase and the percentage of reduction of the two cost functions are substantially the same, that is, about 10%, the total cost exhibits a 5% overall reduction (see Figure 4d).

For comparison, in Figure 5, we report the results obtained by implementing a competing approach [1] on the same testbed. As can be seen, while the sorting cost decreased with the increasing number of bids and the collection cost was reduced instead, similarly to what happened with our approach, the overall total cost increased by about 2%. This shows the effectiveness of the ingredients used in the proposed algorithm and the models to improve the overall efficiency of the system.

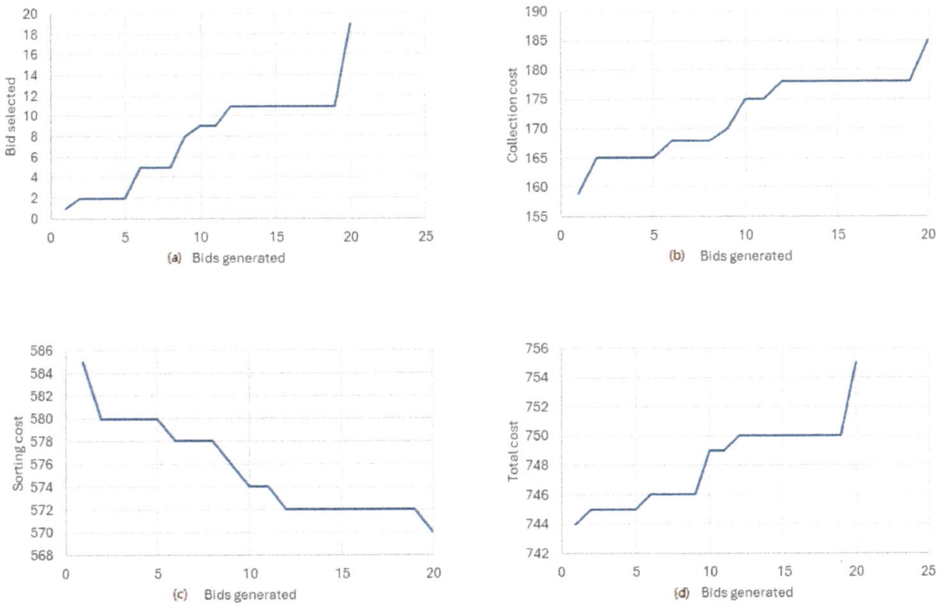

Figure 5. Results obtained by a competing approach. (**a**) shows the number of bids generated and the number of selected bids; (**b**) shows the number of bids generated and the collection cost; (**c**) shows the number of bids generated and the sorting cost; (**d**) shows the number of bids generated and the total cost.

Further Comparison with an Integrated Model and Increasing Instance Size

In this section, we compare the proposed model with a reference integrated model defined in a single decision-maker environment where the decision-maker optimizes simultaneously the two (i.e., collection and sorting) problems, minimizing the objective of the sorting problem. The model (denoted P3) is formed by the constraints of both model P1 and model P2 and is detailed in the following.

$$\min Z_c = \sum_{i \in I} \sum_{h \in H} \sum_{t \in T_c} c^c_{it} \cdot z_{iht}$$

s.t.

$$E_j y_{jt} \leq x_{jt} \leq M_j y_{jt}, \forall j \in J, \forall t \in T_s,$$

$$I_{1,t} = I_{1,t-1} + \sum_{i \in I} \sum_{h \in H} q_i \cdot z_{ih,t-1} - x_{1,t-1}, \forall t \in T_s \setminus \{0\},$$

$$I_{j,t} = I_{j,t-1} + \alpha x_{j-1,t-1} - x_{j,t-1}, \forall t \in T_s \setminus \{0\}, j \in J \setminus \{1\},$$

$$I_{jt} \leq LC_j, \forall j \in J, t \in T_s,$$

$$\sum_{h \in H} \sum_{t \in T^c} z_{iht} = 1, \forall i \in I,$$

$$\sum_{i \in I} q_i \cdot z_{iht} \leq C, \forall h \in H, \forall t \in T_c,$$

$$x_{jt} \geq 0,\ y_{jt} \in \{0,1\}, \forall t \in T_s, \forall j \in J,$$

$$z_{iht} \in \{0,1\}, \forall i \in I, h \in H, t \in T_c.$$

We tested P3 in the same test scenario used before and found that P3 produces an optimal solution value of 542, which is the same solution value as that found by our approach when 20 bids are generated.

Repeating the same test considering the variant of P3 where the objective function is replaced by the objective of the collection problem P1 leads to the same results as the one obtained when only one bid is allowed.

To complete our experimental campaign, we tested our approach by increasing the instance size considering 30 and 70 customers. The number of bids is 20. The results of these tests are reported in Table 1. As can be seen in the last column, the gain in terms of the total cost (the sum of collection and sorting costs) of our approach compared to the competing approach [1] increases with an increasing number of customers, passing from 4.9% (30 customers) to 9.4% (70 customers), indicating the effectiveness of our approach.

Table 1. Test for an increasing number of customers.

Customers	Collection Time Horizon (Days)	Sorting Time Horizon (Days)	Collection Cost	Sorting Cost	Gain in the Total Cost
30	25	30	175	542	4.9%
40	25	30	222	721	5.4%
50	30	35	278	812	7.5%
60	30	35	329	1025	8.9%
70	35	40	389	1144	9.4%

5. Conclusions

This paper addressed a problem that arises in waste management when recycling operations must be optimized while coordinating a logistics operator that must minimize the collection cost of the commodity to be disposed of and a recycling plant to minimize sorting operations. We formulated two multiperiod planning problems and proposed a new negotiation scheme based on auctions. The results show that the approach is promising, as the total cost can be lowered when the number of bids generated by the logistics operator increases. As a follow-up of this approach, further large-scale tests are planned, and additional details in the formulations of the two problems will be considered.

This research has two main shortcomings. The first is that the proposed methodology needs the actors to be integrated with an information system (a virtual marketplace) where the bids can be exchanged automatically. A second flaw is that we did not consider the possibility of having the participation of spot actors, such as occasional logistics operators. Future development of the paper could consider these kinds of extensions to our proposal as well as the opportunity to measure the robustness of the approach to varying the input to the problem.

Author Contributions: Conceptualization, M.C. and G.S.; methodology, M.C. and G.S.; software, M.C. and G.S.; validation, M.C. and G.S.; formal analysis, M.C.; investigation, M.C. and G.S.; data curation, M.C. and G.S.; writing—original draft preparation, M.C. and G.S.; writing—review and editing, M.C. and G.S. All authors have read and agreed to the published version of the manuscript.

Funding: This research received no external funding.

Institutional Review Board Statement: Not applicable.

Data Availability Statement: Data available upon request to authors.

Conflicts of Interest: The authors declare no conflicts of interest.

References

1. Stecca, G.; Kaihara, T. Negotiation based approach for collecting and recycling operations in circular economy. *Procedia C* **2021**, *104*, 200–205. [CrossRef]

Cerqueira-Streit, J.A.; Guarnieri, P.; de Oliveira, L.H.; Demajorovic, J. From Trash to Profit: How Packaging Waste Management Has Driven the Circular Economy—An Integrative Literature Review. *Logistics* **2023**, *7*, 66. [CrossRef]
Cardoso, L.N.P.; Miranda, K.D.d.O.; da Silva, E.F.V.; Guarnieri, P.; Leão e Silva Filho, J.; e Silva, L.C. E-Waste Management: An Analysis under the Perspective of Conflicts and Shared Responsibility. *Logistics* **2023**, *7*, 74. [CrossRef]
Ghiani, G.; Laganà, D.; Manni, E.; Musmanno, R.; Vigo, D. Operations research in solid waste management: A survey of strategic and tactical issues. *Comput. Oper. Res.* **2014**, *44*, 22–32. [CrossRef]
Das, S.; Lee, S.H.; Kumar, P.; Kim, K.H.; Lee, S.S.; Bhattacharya, S.S. Solid waste management: Scope and the challenge of sustainability. *J. Clean. Prod.* **2019**, *228*, 658–678. [CrossRef]
Sandoval-Reyes, M.; He, R.; Semeano, R.; Ferrão, P. Mathematical optimization of waste management systems: Methodological review and perspectives for application. *Waste Manag.* **2024**, *174*, 630–645. [CrossRef]
De Vries, S.; Vohra, R.V. Combinatorial auctions: A survey. *INFORMS J. Comput.* **2003**, *15*, 284–309. [CrossRef]
Triki, C. Using combinatorial auctions for the procurement of occasional drivers in the freight transportation: A case-study. *J. Clean. Prod.* **2021**, *304*, 127057. [CrossRef]
Zhong, W.; Xie, K.; Liu, Y.; Yang, C.; Xie, S. Multi-resource allocation of shared energy storage: A distributed combinatorial auction approach. *IEEE Trans. Smart Grid* **2020**, *11*, 4105–4115. [CrossRef]
Tan, X.; Leon-Garcia, A.; Wu, Y.; Tsang, D.H. Online combinatorial auctions for resource allocation with supply costs and capacity limits. *IEEE J. Sel. Areas Commun.* **2020**, *38*, 655–668. [CrossRef]
Ehrhart, K.M.; Ott, M.; Seifert, S.; Wang, R. Combinatorial auctions for renewable energy—Potentials and challenges. *Energy Policy* **2024**, *186*, 113988. [CrossRef]
Ma, G.; Zhou, Z.; Wang, S.; Zhou, K.; Zheng, J.; Wang, C. Combinatorial Auction of Used Cars Considering Pro-Environment Attribute: A Social Welfare Perspective. *Sustainability* **2023**, *15*, 12512. [CrossRef]
Özer, A.H. A fair, preference-based posted price resale e-market model and clearing heuristics for circular economy. *Appl. Soft Comput.* **2021**, *106*, 107308. [CrossRef]
Fernández, S.; Bodin, U.; Synnes, K. An automated demand-supply matching (DSM) ranking model for the circular economy. In Proceedings of the IECON 2022–48th Annual Conference of the IEEE Industrial Electronics Society, Brussels, Belgium, 17–20 October 2022; pp. 1–6.
Triki, C.; Akil, J.; Al-Asmakh, H. Optimisation models for the procurement through reverse combinatorial auctions in the logistics and food industries. *Int. J. Procure. Manag.* **2023**, *16*, 530–548. [CrossRef]
Bimonte, G.; Ioppolo, G.; Senatore, L.; Trincone, B. Government eco-innovation incentives in a recycling system: A Stackelberg-type model. *Bus. Strategy Environ.* **2023**, *32*, 3792–3800. [CrossRef]
Shao, S.; Xu, S.X.; Huang, G.Q. Variable neighborhood search and tabu search for auction-based waste collection synchronization. *Transp. Res. Part B Methodol.* **2020**, *133*, 1–20. [CrossRef]
Xu, S.X.; Feng, J.; Huang, G.Q.; Zhai, Y.; Cheng, M. Toward efficient waste electric vehicle battery recycling via auction-based market trading mechanisms. *Int. J. Prod. Res.* **2023**, *61*, 8598–8617. [CrossRef]
Mourtzis, D.; Vlachou, E.; Boli, N.; Gravias, L.; Giannoulis, C. Manufacturing networks design through smart decision making towards frugal innovation. *Procedia CIRP* **2016**, *50*, 354–359. [CrossRef]
Psarommatis, F.; May, G.; Dreyfus, P.A.; Kiritsis, D. Zero defect manufacturing: State-of-the-art review, shortcomings and future directions in research. *Int. J. Prod. Res.* **2020**, *58*, 1–17. [CrossRef]
Pinto, D.M.; Stecca, G. Optimal Planning of Waste Sorting Operations Through Mixed Integer Linear Programming. In *Graphs and Combinatorial Optimization: From Theory to Applications; CTW2020 Proceedings*; Springer: Cham, Switzerland, 2021; pp. 307–320.
Kaihara, T. Multi-agent based supply chain modelling with dynamic environment. *Int. J. Prod. Econ.* **2003**, *85*, 263–269. [CrossRef]
Baffo, I.; Confessore, G.; Stecca, G. A decentralized model for flow shop production with flexible transportation system. *J. Manuf. Syst.* **2013**, *32*, 68–77. [CrossRef]
Baffo, I.; Confessore, G.; Liotta, G.; Stecca, G. A cooperative model to improve hospital equipments and drugs management. In Proceedings of the Working Conference on Virtual Enterprises, Thessaloniki, Greece, 7–9 October 2009; Springer: Berlin/Heidelberg, Germany, 2009; pp. 43–50.
Suginouchi, S.; Kokuryo, D.; Kaihara, T. Value co-creative manufacturing system for mass customization: Concept of smart factory and operation method using autonomous negotiation mechanism. *Procedia CIRP* **2017**, *63*, 727–732. [CrossRef]
Tanimizu, Y.; Matsui, K.; Shimizu, Y.; Iwamura, K.; Sugimura, N. Negotiation strategy for economical reuse in closed-loop supply chains. In *Proceedings of the Advances in Production Management Systems. Innovative and Knowledge-Based Production Management in a Global-Local World: IFIP WG 5.7 International Conference, APMS 2014, Ajaccio, France, 20–24 September 2014*; Proceedings, Part II; Springer: Berlin/Heidelberg, Germany, 2014; pp. 382–389.
Nowakowski, P.; Król, A.; Mrówczyńska, B. Supporting mobile WEEE collection on demand: A method for multi-criteria vehicle routing, loading and cost optimisation. *Waste Manag.* **2017**, *69*, 377–392. [CrossRef]
Arebey, M.; Hannan, M.; Basri, H.; Begum, R.; Abdullah, H. Integrated technologies for solid waste bin monitoring system. *Environ. Monit. Assess.* **2011**, *177*, 399–408. [CrossRef]

29. Abdallah, M.; Talib, M.A.; Feroz, S.; Nasir, Q.; Abdalla, H.; Mahfood, B. Artificial intelligence applications in solid wa management: A systematic research review. *Waste Manag.* **2020**, *109*, 231–246. [CrossRef] [PubMed]
30. Alawi, A.E.B.; Saeed, A.Y.; Almashhor, F.; Al-Shathely, R.; Hassan, A.N. Solid waste classification using deep learning techniq In Proceedings of the 2021 International Congress of Advanced Technology and Engineering (ICOTEN), Taiz, Yemen, 4–5 2021; pp. 1–5.

algorithms

MDPI

cle

onnected and Autonomous Vehicle Scheduling Problems: ome Models and Algorithms

eny R. Gafarov [1,†] and Frank Werner [2,*,†]

1 V.A. Trapeznikov Institute of Control Sciences, Russian Academy of Sciences, Profsoyuznaya St. 65, Moscow 117997, Russia; axel73@mail.ru
2 Faculty of Mathematics, Otto-von-Guericke-Universität Magdeburg, PSF 4120, 39016 Magdeburg, Germany
* Correspondence: frank.werner@ovgu.de
† These authors contributed equally to this work.

Abstract: In this paper, we consider some problems that arise in connected and autonomous vehicle (CAV) systems. Their simplified variants can be formulated as scheduling problems. Therefore, scheduling solution algorithms can be used as a part of solution algorithms for real-world problems. For four variants of such problems, mathematical models and solution algorithms are presented. In particular, three polynomial algorithms and a branch and bound algorithm are developed. These CAV scheduling problems are considered in the literature for the first time. More complicated NP-hard scheduling problems related to CAVs can be considered in the future.

Keywords: scheduling; optimization; dynamic programming; connected and autonomous vehicle; precedence relations

MSC: 90 B 35; 90 C 27; 68 Q 25; 68 W 40

JEL Classification: D8; H51

1. Introduction

Connected and autonomous vehicle systems contain a set of vehicles that can automatically coordinate their routing, owing to vehicle-to-vehicle communications and a centralized scheduler (computer). The vehicles are controlled by the centralized scheduler residing in the network (e.g., a base station in the case of cellular systems) or a distributed scheduler, where the scheduler is autonomously selected by the vehicles. Such vehicle systems can coordinate the vehicles in order to speed up the traffic, minimize traffic jams, and they also take into account environment aspects by reducing emissions.

Vehicle routing and scheduling problems have been intensively investigated over the last decades. There exist a huge number of papers dealing with particular aspects or also covering relationships with related research fields, see, for instance, refs. [1–5] to name only a few papers. A complete special issue with 16 papers on different aspects of vehicle routing and scheduling has been edited by Repoussis and Gounaris [6]. For surveys in this field, the reader is referred to the papers [7–9]. During the last years, new challenges arose in connection with autonomous driving of vehicles.

Vehicle-to-vehicle (V2V) communications can be used as a potential solution to many problems arising in the area of traffic control. Several approaches have been developed including the modeling of a complete autonomous driving system as a multi-agent system, where the vehicles interact to ensure an autonomous functionality such that emergency braking and traffic jam are avoided as much as possible. Nowadays, vehicle systems are developed towards fully connected and fully autonomous systems. Vehicular communication technologies have been considered, for instance, in the papers [10,11].

In [12], the authors dealt with the optimization of the departure times, travel routes, and the longitudinal trajectories of connected and autonomous vehicles and also the control of the signal timings at the intersections to obtain a stable traffic flow in such a way that the vehicles do not need to stop before they enter an intersection. In addition, the vehicle queues before the intersections should not become too large. In this paper, all the data (i.e., the departure times, travel routes, and signal timings) are determined by a central controller, but the trajectories of the vehicles are fixed by distributed roadside processors, which constitute a hierarchical traffic management scheme together.

In [13], the authors considered the control of the required lane changes of a system of autonomous vehicles on a road segment with two lanes before the vehicles arrive at a given critical position. This paper presents an algorithm that realizes the lane change of an individual vehicle in the shortest possible time. Then, this algorithm is iteratively used to manage all the lane changes which are necessary on the road segment under consideration in such a way that traffic safety is maintained.

In the paper by [14], the problem of scheduling a CAV, which crosses an intersection, was considered with the goal to optimize the traffic flow at the intersection. In addition, a solution algorithm was presented.

In [15], the problem of scheduling the time phases of a traffic light was considered with the objective to improve the traffic flow by reducing the waiting time of the traveling vehicles at the indicated road intersections.

To the best of our knowledge, in this paper, simplified CAV problems are formulated as classical scheduling problems for the first time. Scheduling solution algorithms can be used as a part of solution algorithms for real-world CAV problems. In the future, more sophisticated NP-hard scheduling models can be considered.

The aim of the paper is to encourage the researchers to consider CAV problems as scheduling problems and to use classical methods of scheduling theory to investigate the complexity and to solve them.

Although the solution algorithms presented have a large running time and are somehow still useless in practice, we have shown that some CAV problems are polynomially solvable. Solution algorithms can be advanced in future research.

In this paper, we consider four scheduling problems that arise in connection with CAVs. The remainder of this paper is as follows. In each of the Sections 2–5, we consider one of these problems. The problem with a road of two lanes and one lane closure is considered in Section 2. Section 3 deals with the case of a turn to a main road. Section 4 considers the case of a road with three lanes and a lane closure on the middle lane. Section 5 deals with a crossroad having dividing lanes. For each of these cases, an appropriate scheduling problem is formulated and a solution algorithm is given. Finally, Section 6 gives a few concluding remarks.

2. A Road with Two Lanes and One Lane Closure

In this section, we consider a road with two lanes, where two sets of CAVs, N_1 and N_2, are given. The CAVs from the set N_1 go on lane 1, and the CAVs from the set N_2 go on lane 2. Both lanes have the same direction. On lane 2, there is a lane closure and the CAVs from the set N_2 have to move to lane 1, see Figure 1.

We have to find a sequence of passing the lane closure by the CAVs from the sets N_1 and N_2 in order to minimize a given objective function, e.g., the total passing time.

We assume that

- a maximal feasible speed of the CAVs is given. The CAVs either go with the maximal feasible speed or brake in order to let another CAV change the lane.
- an acceleration is not taken into account.
- the time needed to change the lane is not taken into account, i.e., it is equal to zero.
- the CAVs have the same length.
- the safe distance between two CAVs is the same for all vehicles.

Since the problems investigated in this paper have not been considered in the literature so far, these assumptions are made for the first time to obtain simplified models. In real-world problems, these assumptions can be false, although solution algorithms for simplified models can be used to solve sub-problems or to obtain lower or upper bounds.

Figure 1. A road with two lanes and one lane closure.

The same problem arises, e.g., on railway sections and in automated warehouses of logistics companies with autonomous robot transporters. This simplified problem can be formulated as a single machine scheduling problem as follows.

Given a set $N = N_1 \bigcup N_2$ of n jobs that have to be processed on a single machine from time 0 on. For each job j, a processing time $p_j = p > 0$, a release date $r_j \geq 0$, a due date $d_j \geq 0$, and a weight $w_j > 0$ are given. The machine can process no more than one job at a time. The processing time p can be computed from the maximal feasible speed and the length of a CAV. The value r_j corresponds to the earliest time when the processing of the vehicle can start, resulting from the position of the CAV j on the road.

For example, let the speed of each car be 60 km per hour and the length of the closed road section be 100 m. Thus, a car needs 6 s to pass the road closure. Therefore, we assume $p = 6$ (in seconds). Let a car j be 0 m from the beginning of the road closure and a car i be 200 m behind. So, we assume $r_j = 0$ and $r_i = 12$ according to their speed and the distances. Moreover, let the starting time of any schedule computed be 05:00:00 a.m. which we consider as time 0. Let the due date for car i be 05:00:15, then we assume $d_i = 15$. It is obvious that the tardiness of car i is no less that $6 + 12 - 15 = 3$ seconds in any feasible schedule.

We call a feasible schedule active if one cannot reduce the objective function value by shifting a single job to an earlier time without violating the constraints. Without loss of generality, we consider only active schedules in this paper.

A schedule is uniquely determined by a permutation π of the CAVs of the set N. Let $S_j(\pi)$ be the starting time of job j in the schedule π. Then, $C_j(\pi) = S_j(\pi) + p$ is the completion time of job j in the schedule π. A precedence relation can be defined as follows. For the jobs from the set $N_1 = \{j_1, j_2, \ldots, j_{n_1}\}$, we have $j_1 \to j_2 \to \cdots \to j_{n_1}$, where $n_1 = |N_1|$ and $j \to i$ means that the processing of job j precedes the processing of job i. Thus, there is a chain of jobs on lane 1. Analogously, a chain of jobs is defined for the set $N_2 = \{i_1, i_2, \ldots, i_{n_2}\}$.

For the single machine scheduling problem of minimizing total completion time, the goal is to find an optimal schedule π^* that minimizes

$$\sum C_j = \sum_{j \in N} C_j(\pi). \tag{1}$$

Here, the completion time of a job is equal to the time when the vehicle passes the closed lane segment. We denote this problem by $1|2\ chains, p_j = p, r_j|\sum C_j$ according to the traditional three-field notation $\alpha|\beta|\gamma$ for scheduling problems proposed by [16], where α describes the machine environment, β gives the job characteristics and further constraints, and γ describes the optimization criterion.

Let

$$T_j(\pi) = \max\{0, C_j(\pi) - d_j\}$$

be the tardiness of job j in the schedule π. If $C_j(\pi) > d_j$, then job j is tardy and we have $U_j = 1$; otherwise, $U_j = 0$.

Subsequently, we consider also the following objective functions:

$$\begin{aligned}\sum w_jC_j &= \sum w_jC_j(\pi) \text{ — total weighted completion time,}\\ \sum T_j &= \sum T_j(\pi) \text{ — total tardiness,}\\ \sum w_jT_j &= \sum w_jT_j(\pi) \text{ — total weighted tardiness;}\\ \sum w_jU_j &= \sum w_jU_j(\pi) \text{ — weighted number of tardy jobs,}\\ C_{max} &= \max\{C_j(\pi)\} \text{ — makespan}\end{aligned}$$

It is known that the problems $1|chains, p_j = p, r_j|\sum w_jC_j$ and $1|chains, p_j = p, r_j|\sum w_jT_j$ with an arbitrary number of chains are NP-hard, see [17]. This has been proven by a reduction from the 3-partition problem.

In [18], polynomial time dynamic programming algorithms have been presented to solve the problems $1|p_j = p, r_j|\sum T_j$ and $1|p_j = p, r_j|\sum w_jU_j$.

In an optimal schedule for the problem $1|2\ chains, p_j = p, r_j|\sum C_j$, the jobs are processed in non-decreasing order of the values r_j. This can be easily proven by contradiction. Assume that we have an optimal schedule $\pi = (\dots, j_2, j_1, \dots)$, where $r_{j_1} < r_{j_2}$. Then, for the schedule $\pi' = (\dots, j_1, j_2, \dots)$, we have $\sum C_j(\pi) \geq \sum C_j(\pi')$. For an illustration of the concepts introduced above, we consider the following small Example 1.

Example 1. *Let* $N_1 = \{1, 2\}$, $N_2 = \{3, 4\}$. *Moreover, the values* $p = 2$, $r_1 = 0$, $r_2 = 3$, $r_3 = 1$, $r_4 = 4$, *and* $d_1 = d_2 = 10$, $d_3 = 3$, $d_4 = 6$ *are given. For the chosen job sequence* $\pi = (1, 3, 2, 4)$, *we obtain*

$$S_1(\pi) = 0,\ S_3(\pi) = 2,\ S_2(\pi) = 4,\ S_4(\pi) = 6$$

and

$$C_1(\pi) = 2,\ C_3(\pi) = 4,\ C_2(\pi) = 6,\ C_4(\pi) = 8.$$

Thus, we obtain

$$\sum_{j=1}^{4} C_j(\pi) = 20 \qquad and \qquad \sum_{j=1}^{4} T_j(\pi) = 1 + 2 = 3.$$

For the job sequence $\pi' = (3, 4, 1, 2)$, *we obtain*

$$\sum_{j=1}^{4} T_j(\pi') = 0.$$

We note that there exists a set Θ of possible completion times of all jobs with $|\Theta| \leq n^2$ since:

- without loss of generality, we consider only active schedules, where no job can be processed earlier without loss of feasibility;
- there are no more than n different values r_j;
- all processing times are equal to p and thus, for any job $j \in N$, its completion time is equal to $r_i + lp,\ i \in N, l \leq n$.

The problems $1|2\ chains, p_j = p, r_j|f,\ f \in \{\sum w_jC_j, \sum w_jT_j, \sum w_jU_j\}$ can be solved by a dynamic program (DP). In the DP, we consider the jobs $i_1, i_2, \dots, i_{n_2} \in N_2$ one by one, where $i_1 \to i_2 \to \dots \to i_{n_2}$. Thus, at each stage k of the dynamic program, we consider a single job i_k, $k = 1, 2, \dots, n_2$. Moreover, at each stage $k > 1$ we consider all states $(f^{k-1}, C^{k-1}_{max}, pos^{k-1})$ and the corresponding best partial solutions (sequences of jobs) stored at the previous stage. The meaning of the above triplet is as follows. Here, f^{k-1} is the value of the considered objective function for the partial solution. $C^{k-1}_{max} = C_{i_{k-1}} \in \Theta$ denotes the completion time of job i_{k-1} in the corresponding partial solution. Finally, $pos^{k-1} \in \{0, 1, 2, \dots, n_1\}$ describes the position of a job, and this means that job i_{k-1} is processed between the jobs $j_{pos} \in N_1$ and $j_{pos+1} \in N_1$, $0 < pos < n_1$. For each job i_k and a state $(f^{k-1}, C^{k-1}_{max}, pos^{k-1})$, we compute new states (f', C'_{max}, pos'), where $pos' \geq pos$, and C'_{max} is the completion time of job i_k in a new partial solution, where job i_k is scheduled after job $j_{pos'} \in N_1$. If, at any stage, there are two states (f', C'_{max}, pos') and $(f'', C''_{max} pos')$ with $f' \leq f''$ and $C'_{max} \leq C''_{max}$, we only keep the state (f', C'_{max}, pos'). After the last stage, we have to select the best found complete solution among all states generated.

Let us explain a state (f^1, C^1_{max}, pos^1) by means of Example 1. In Algorithm 1, at stage $k = 1$, we have $i_k = 3$. Thus, we consider the partial schedule $\pi = (1,3)$ and the corresponding state (f^1, C^1_{max}, pos^1). For the objective function $\sum C_j$, we have

$$(f^1, C^1_{max}, pos^1) = (C_1(\pi) + C_3(\pi), C_3(\pi), 1) = (6, 4, 1).$$

For the objective function $\sum T_j$, we have

$$(f^1, C^1_{max}, pos^1) = (T_1(\pi) + T_3(\pi), C_3(\pi), 1) = (1, 4, 1).$$

Algorithm 1: A pseudo-code of Algorithm 1 is presented below.

1. $StatesSet = \{(0,0,0)\}$;
2. FOR EACH $i_k \in N_2$ DO
   - 2.1 $NewStatesSet = \{\}$;
   - 2.2 FOR EACH $(f^{k-1}, C^{k-1}_{max}, pos^{k-1}) \in StatesSet$ DO
     - 2.2.1 Let $PositionsList = \{pos^{k-1}, pos^{k-1} + 1, \ldots, n_1\}$;
     - 2.2.2 FOR EACH $pos' \in PositionsList$ DO
       - 2.2.2.1 Calculate f' for the resulting partial solution, if job i_k is processed after $j_{pos'}$, according to the partial solution corresponding to state $(f^{k-1}, C^{k-1}_{max}, pos^{k-1})$;
       - 2.2.2.2 Add (f', C'_{max}, pos') to $NewStatesSet$. If in $NewStatesSet$, there is a state (f'', C''_{max}, pos') with $f' \leq f''$ and $C'_{max} \leq C''_{max}$, then exclude the state (f'', C''_{max}, pos') from $NewStatesSet$;
       - 2.2.2.3 If i_k is the last job in the set N_2, then schedule all unscheduled jobs from the set N_1 at the earliest possible time.
   - 2.3 $StatesSet := NewStatesSet$;
3. Select the best found complete solution among all states generated.

Theorem 1. *The problems $1|2\ chains, p_j = p, r_j|f$, $f \in \{\sum w_j C_j, \sum w_j T_j, \sum w_j U_j\}$ can be solved in $O(n^5)$ time by a dynamic program.*

Proof. Dynamic programming is a mathematical optimization method, where a complicated problem is split into simpler sub-problems in a recursive manner.

In Algorithm 1, each state (f, C_{max}, pos) (here we skip the upper index for simplicity of the notations), calculated at stage $k-1$, divides the problem into two sub-problems. In the first sub-problem, all jobs $j \in \{j_1, j_2, \ldots, j_{pos}\}$ and all jobs $i \in \{i_1, \ldots, i_{k-2}\}$ are considered. In the second sub-problem, all jobs $j \in \{j_{pos+1}, \ldots, j_{n_1}\}$ and all jobs $i \in \{i_k, \ldots, i_{n_2}\}$ are considered. Let π' be an optimal solution for the first sub-problem and π'' be an optimal solution for the second one. Then $\pi = (\pi', i_{k-1}, \pi'')$ is an optimal solution corresponding to state (f, C_{max}, pos).

The proof of optimality of Algorithm 1 can be performed by induction. Let, for an instance of a problem, $\pi^* = (\pi_1, i_k, \pi_2)$ be an optimal solution and f^* be the optimal value of the considered objective function. Moreover, let $pos_k \in \{0, 1, \dots, n_1, n_1 + 1\}$, $k = 1, \dots, n$, be the position of job $i_k \in N_2$ in the job sequence. This means that job j_{pos_k} is processed before job i_k and job j_{pos_k+1} is processed after it, where j_0 means that job i_k is processed before job j_1 and j_{n_1+1} means hat job i_k is processed after job j_{n_1}. Let f' be the objective function value for the job sub-sequence (π_1, i_k).

Next, we prove the following Property (*).

Property (*): At each stage k of Algorithm 1, for each job i_k the state (f_k, C_{i_k}, pos_k) and the corresponding partial job sequence (π^k, i_k) will be considered, where $C_{i_k}(\pi^*) = C_{i_k}$ and $f' = f_k$.

For stage 1, Property (*) holds since we consider and save in the set of states all $n_1 + 1$ possible positions for job i_1. Let Property (*) hold for stage $k - 1$, i.e., the state $(f_{k-1}, C_{i_{k-1}}, pos_{k-1})$ is contained in the set of states.

Then, according to step [2.2.2] of Algorithm 1, the state (f_k, C_{i_k}, pos_k) will be considered and stored in the set of states.

So, according to step [3.] of Algorithm 1, the job sequence π will be constructed with the objective function value $f = f^*$ and the problems $1|2\ chains, p_j = p, r_j|f,\ f \in \{\sum w_j C_j, \sum w_j T_j, \sum w_j U_j\}$ can be solved by a dynamic program.

There are $O(n)$ stages and $O(n^3)$ states (f, C_{max}, pos) at each stage, since $C_{max} \in \Theta$ with $|\Theta| \leq n^2$, and $pos \in \{0, 1, \dots, n_1\}$. At the next stage, for each state generated at the previous stage in step [2.2.2], we need to consider $O(n)$ new states.

To perform all steps [2.2.2.1] in [2.2.2], we need $O(n)$ operations. In step [2.2.2.1], to construct a partial solution, we need to schedule the jobs $j_{pos^{k-1}+1}, j_{pos^{k-1}+2}, \dots, j_{pos'}$ into the partial solution, i.e., to calculate their starting times according to C^{k-1}_{max}, the release dates, and the processing time. We need $O(1)$ operations to calculate the starting time of each job, and we calculate the starting time for a job only once in step [2.2.2], e.g., the starting time of job $j_{pos^{k-1}+1}$ is calculated only once in [2.2.2]. So, to perform all steps [2.2.2.1] in the cycle [2.2.2], we need $O(n)$ operations, and to perform all steps [2.2.2.1] in Algorithm 1, we need $O(n^5)$ operations.

To perform step [2.2.2.2] in $O(1)$ time, we additionally keep *PositionsList* in a 2-dimensional array with $O(n^2)$ rows corresponding to all possible values C_{max} and $O(n)$ columns corresponding to all possible values *pos*. We initiate the array in step [2.1]. So, to check a dominated value, we need $O(1)$ time. Thus, we need $O(n^5)$ operations to perform all steps [2.2.2.1] in Algorithm DP.

To perform all steps [2.2.2.3] in Algorithm 1, we need $O(n^5)$ time, since it is performed only for the last job in the set N_2.

So, the running time of Algorithm 1 is $O(n^5)$.

The theorem has been proven. □

We conjecture that there are other solution algorithms with a running time less than $O(n^5)$. Here, our motivation is only to show that the problems are polynomially solvable. For real-world problems, there are more parameters and constraints that have to be taken into consideration, and they can be possibly solved by other methods than dynamic programming.

3. Turn to a Main Road

There is a set N_1 of CAVs going along a main road and a set N_2 of CAVs turning into the main road from a side road (see Figure 2). In contrast to the problems $1|2\ chains, p_j = p|f,\ f \in \{C_{max}, \sum w_j C_j, \sum w_j T_j, \sum w_j U_j\}$, we have now $p_j = p^1$, $j \in N_1$ and $p_j = p^2$, $j \in N_2$. We denote these problems by $1|2\ chains, p_j \in \{p^1, p^2\}, r_j|f,\ f \in \{C_{max}, \sum w_j C_j, \sum w_j T_j, \sum w_j U_j\}$.

These problems can be solved by the same Algorithm 1. In Algorithm 1, we describe the states in the same way: (f, C_{max}, pos). For any job $j \in N$ in an active schedule for these problems, its completion time is equal to $r_i + lp^1 + vp^2$, $i \in N, l \leq n, v \leq n$. Thus, we have $|\Theta| \leq n^3$, and the running time of Algorithm 1 is $O(n^6)$.

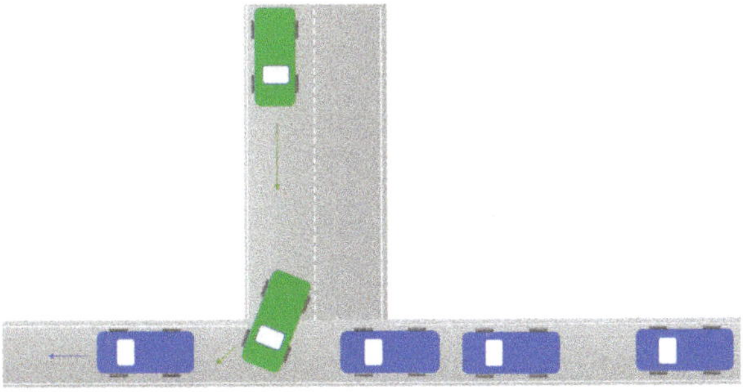

Figure 2. Turn to a main road.

4. A Road with Three Lanes and a Road Closure on the Middle Lane

In addition to the problems $1|2\ chains, p_j = p, r_j|f,\ f \in \{C_{max}, \sum w_jC_j, \sum w_jT_j, \sum w_jU_j\}$, there are an additional lane 3 and a subset N_3 of jobs (see Figure 3). The jobs of the set N_1 should be processed on machine M_1, and the jobs of the set N_3 should be processed on machine M_3. The jobs of the set N_2 can be processed on any of these two machines. Precedence relations among the jobs of the set N_3 can be defined as a chain of jobs.

Figure 3. A road with three lanes and a closure on the middle lane.

We denote these problems by $P2|dedicated, 3\ chains, p_j = p, r_j|f, f \in \{C_{max}, \sum w_jC_j, \sum w_jT_j, \sum w_jU_j\}$. These problems can be solved by a modified Algorithm 1, where we consider the positions *pos* between the jobs of the set N_1 and between the jobs of the set N_3.

We illustrate the dynamic programming algorithm for this problem by the following Example 2.

Example 2. *Let* $N_1 = \{1,2\}$, $N_2 = \{3,4\}$, $N_3 = \{5,6\}$. *Moreover, the values* $p = 2$, $r_1 = 0$, $r_2 = 3$, $r_3 = 1$, $r_4 = 4$, $r_5 = 1$, $r_6 = 4$, *and* $d_1 = 2$, $d_2 = 5$, $d_3 = 3$, $d_4 = 6$, $d_5 = 3$, $d_6 = 8$ *are given. We consider the minimization of total tardiness, i.e.,* $f = \sum T_j$. *Denote by* M_1 *the machine, where the jobs from the set* N_1 *have to be processed and by* M_3 *the machine, where the jobs from the set* N_3 *have to be processed. The initial positions of the jobs and an optimal schedule are presented in Figure 4.*

In Algorithm 1, at each stage we consider all states

$$(pos^1, C^1_{max}, pos^3, C^3_{max}, f)$$

stored at the previous stage. Here, pos^1 *is the first possible position for the current job on machine* M_1, C^1_{max} *denotes the completion time of the last job scheduled on machine* M_1, pos^3 *gives the first possible position for the current job on machine* M_3, *and* C^3_{max} *denotes the completion time of the last job scheduled on machine* M_3.

In the following Table 1, all states computed in the two stages for the jobs $j = 3$ *and* $j = 4$ *are presented. In the first column S1, the index numbers of the states are given. In the second column S2, we present the original state from which the current state is computed.* P^1 *represents* pos^1, C^1 *denotes* C^1_{max}, P^3 *represents* pos^3, *and* C^3 *denotes* C^3_{max}. π^1 *gives the corresponding job sequence on machine* M_1 *and* π^3 *describes the corresponding job sequence on machine* M_3. *In the columns* C_j, $j = 1, \ldots, 6$, *the corresponding completion times are given. In the columns* T_j, $j = 1, \ldots, 6$, *the corresponding tardiness values are given. In the last column, the resulting total tardiness values* $f = \sum T_j$ *are presented.*

Table 1. Calculations of Algorithm 1 for Example 2.

								r_1 0	r_2 3	r_3 1	r_4 4	r_5 1	r_6 5	d_1 2	d_2 5	d_3 3	d_4 6	d_5 3	d_6 8	
*S*1	*S*2	P^1	C^1	P^3	C^3	π_1	π_3	C_1	C_2	C_3	C_4	C_5	C_6	T_1	T_2	T_3	T_4	T_5	T_6	f
Stage $j = 3$																				
1		0	3			3				3				0	0	0	0	0	0	0
2		1	4			1, 3		2		4				0	0	1	0	0	0	1
3		2	7			1, 2, 3		2	5	7				0	0	4	0	0	0	4
4				0	3		3			3				0	0	0	0	0	0	0
5				5	7		5, 3			5		3		0	0	2	0	0	0	2
6				6	9		5, 6, 3			9		3	7	0	0	6	0	0	0	6
Stage $j = 4$																				
7	1	0	6			3, 4, 1, 2	5, 6	8	10	3	6	3	7	6	5	0	0	0	0	1
8	1	1	7			3, 1, 4, 2	5, 6	5	9	3	7	3	7	3	4	0	1	0	0	8
9	1	2	9			3, 1, 2, 4	5, 6	5	7	3	9	3	7	3	2	0	3	0	0	8
10	1	0		0	5	3, 1, 2	4, 5, 6	5	7	3	6	8	10	3	2	0	0	5	2	1
11	1	0		5	6	3, 1, 2	5, 4, 6	5	7	3	6	3	8	3	2	0	0	0	0	5
12	1	0		6	9	3, 1, 2	5, 6, 4	5	7	3	9	3	7	3	2	0	3	0	0	8
13	2	1				1, 3, 4, 2	5, 6	2	8	4	6	3	7	0	3	1	0	0	0	4
14	2	2				1, 3, 2, 4	5, 6	2	6	4	8	3	7	0	1	1	2	0	0	4
15	2	1		0	6	1, 3, 2	4, 5, 6	2	6	4	6	8	10	0	1	1	0	5	2	9
16	2	1		5	6	1, 3, 2	5, 4, 6	2	6	4	6	3	8	0	1	1	0	0	0	2
17	2	1		6	9	1, 3, 2	5, 6, 4	2	6	4	9	3	7	0	1	1	3	0	0	5
18	3	2		2	9	1, 2, 3, 4	5, 6	2	5	7	9	3	7	0	0	4	3	0	0	7
19	3	2		0	5	1, 2, 3	4, 5, 6	2	5	7	9	11	13	0	0	4	3	8	5	2
20	3	2		5	6	1, 2, 3	5, 4, 6	2	5	7	9	3	11	0	0	4	3	0	3	1
21	3	2		6	9	1, 2, 3	5, 6, 4	2	5	7	9	3	7	0	0	4	3	0	0	7
22	4	0	6			4, 1, 2	3, 5, 6	8	10	3	6	5	7	6	5	0	0	2	0	1
23	4	1	6			1, 4, 2	3, 5, 6	2	8	3	6	5	7	0	3	0	0	2	0	5
24	4	2	7			1, 2, 4	3, 5, 6	2	5	3	7	5	7	0	0	0	1	2	0	3
25	4			0	6	1, 2	3, 4, 5, 6	2	5	3	6	8	10	0	0	0	0	5	2	7
26	4			5	7	1, 2	3, 5, 4, 6	2	5	3	7	5	9	0	0	0	1	2	1	4
27	4			6	9	1, 2	3, 5, 6, 4	2	5	3	9	5	7	0	0	0	3	2	0	5
28	5	0	6	5		4, 1, 2	5, 3, 6	9	11	5	7	3	7	7	6	2	1	0	0	1
29	5	1	7	5		1, 4, 2	5, 3, 6	2	9	5	7	3	7	0	4	2	1	0	0	7
30	5	2	7	5		1, 2, 4	5, 3, 6	2	5	5	7	3	7	0	0	2	1	0	0	3
31	5			5		1, 2	5, 3, 4, 6	2	5	5	7	3	9	0	0	2	1	0	1	4
32	5			6		1, 2	5, 3, 6, 4	2	5	5	9	3	7	0	0	2	3	0	0	5
33	6	0	11	6		4, 1, 2	5, 6, 3	13	15	9	11	3	7	11	10	6	5	0	0	3
34	6	1	6	6		1, 4, 2	5, 6, 3	2	13	9	11	3	7	0	8	6	5	0	0	1
35	6	2	11	6		1, 2, 4	5, 6, 3	2	5	9	11	3	7	0	0	6	5	0	0	1
36	6			6	11	1, 2	5, 6, 3, 4	2	5	9	11	3	7	0	0	6	5	0	0	1

An optimal solution is found in state 16. Let us consider an extended instance with an additional job 7 in the set N_2, where $3 \to 4 \to 7$. Then, in Algorithm DP, we will have 3 stages. At the state 15, we will have $(pos^1, C^1_{max}, pos^3, C^3_{max}, f) = (1,4,0,6,2)$, $\pi^1 = (1,3)$ and $\pi^2 = (4)$. At the state 16, we will have $(pos^1, C^1_{max}, pos^3, C^3_{max}, f) = (1,4,1,6,2)$, $\pi^1 = (1,3)$ and $\pi^2 = (5,4)$. So, we only keep the state 16, since pos^3 is larger for state 16 and the other parameters of the states are the same.

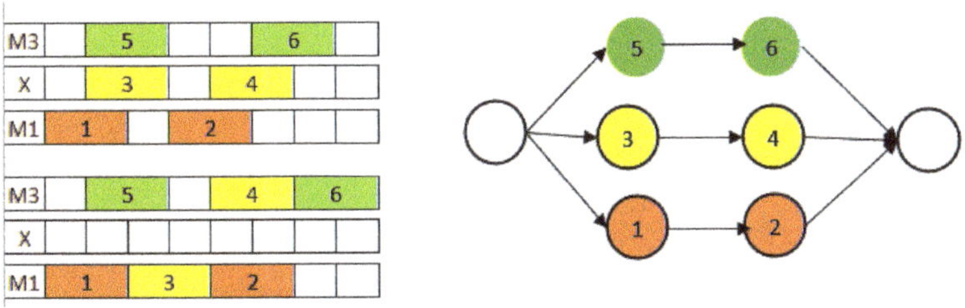

Figure 4. The initial positions of the jobs and an optimal schedule for Example 2.

5. A Crossroad with Dividing Lines

In this section, we consider a crossroad with dividing lines and four sets, N_1, N_2, N_3, N_4, of CAVs. They share four sectors of a crossroad denoted by M_1, M_2, M_3, M_4 (see Figure 5). We have to find an optimal sequence of passing these sectors.

We can formulate the following job shop scheduling problem with four machines. There are four sets, N_1, N_2, N_3, N_4, of jobs and four machines corresponding to the sectors M_1, M_2, M_3, M_4. Each job j consists of two operations. For each job $j \in N_1$, its first operation has to be processed on machine M_1 and its second one has to be processed on machine M_2. For each job $j \in N_2$, its first operation has to be processed on machine M_2 and its second one has to processed on machine M_4. For each job $j \in N_3$, its first operation has to be processed on machine M_3 and its second one has to be processed on machine M_1. For each job $j \in N_4$, its first operation has to be processed on machine M_4 and its second one has to be processed on machine M_3. The processing times of the operations are equal to p. Precedence relations can be given as chains of jobs.

If the lengths of the dividing lines are equal to 0, then the second operation of a job j should be processed immediately after the first one. Otherwise, for each of the sets N_1, N_2, N_3, N_4, there are four buffers of limited capacities, namely b_1, b_2, b_3, b_4 jobs for the corresponding set of jobs. At any moment, for the set N_1, there can be up to b_1 jobs for which the first operation is completed and the second one is not yet started. We denote these problems by $J4|4\ chains, p_j = p, r_j|f,\ f \in \{C_{max}, \sum w_jC_j, \sum w_jT_j, \sum w_jU_j\}$.

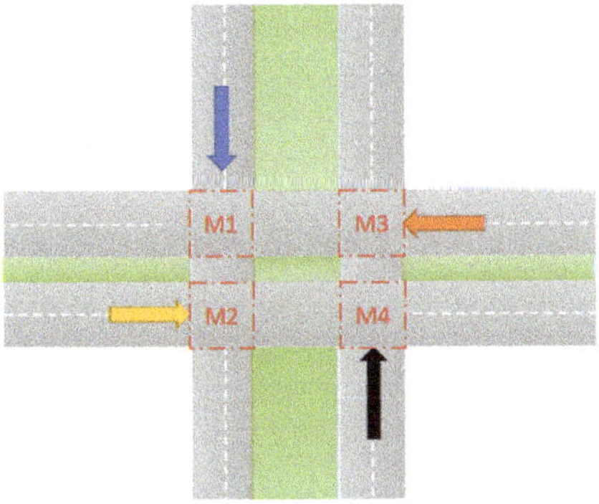

Figure 5. A crossroad with dividing lines.

The problems $J4|4\ chains, p_j = p, r_j|f,\ f \in \{C_{max}, \sum w_jC_j, \sum w_jT_j, \sum w_jU_j\}$ can be solved by a branch-and-bound (B&B) algorithm. The search (rooted) tree is constructed by the following branching rule. For any node of the tree, we consider the following 8 possible branches:

- Schedule the first unscheduled possible operation for a job $j \in N_1$ on machine M_1 at the earliest possible starting time. If there is no such an operation, skip this branch.
- Schedule the first unscheduled possible operation for a job $j \in N_3$ on machine M_1 at the earliest possible starting time.

- Schedule the first unscheduled possible operation for a job $j \in N_1$ on machine M_2 at the earliest possible starting time.
- Schedule the first unscheduled possible operation for a job $j \in N_2$ on machine M_2 at the earliest possible starting time.
- Schedule the first unscheduled possible operation for a job $j \in N_3$ on machine M_3 at the earliest possible starting time.
- Schedule the first unscheduled possible operation for a job $j \in N_4$ on machine M_3 at the earliest possible starting time.
- Schedule the first unscheduled possible operation for a job $j \in N_2$ on machine M_4 at the earliest possible starting time.
- Schedule the first unscheduled possible operation for a job $j \in N_4$ on machine M_4 at the earliest possible starting time.

Thus, there are up to $2^3 = 8$ branches for each node to be considered. Since there are $2n$ operations, where $n = |N_1 \cup N_2 \cup N_3 \cup N_4|$, there are no more than $2n$ levels in the search tree. Thus, we have no more than $(2^3)^{2n} = 2^{6n}$ nodes to be considered. If some of the values b_1, b_2, b_3, b_4 are equal to 0, we have fewer nodes. As an example, if each of them is equal to 0, then we have only 2^{3n} nodes.

Moreover, we can use the following trivial upper and lower bounds for the problem $J4|4\ chains, p_j = p, r_j|C_{max}$.

Upper bound. To construct a feasible solution, we use a list scheduling algorithm. In this algorithm, we consider the unscheduled operations one-by-one according to a non-decreasing order of the release dates of the corresponding jobs. We schedule the next unscheduled operation at the earliest possible starting time according to the current partial schedule. To order the set of jobs, we need $O(n \log n)$ operations. In addition, we need $O(n)$ operations to construct a feasible solution.

Lower bound. Consider a set of unscheduled operations N'. For each of them, we calculate the earliest possible starting time according to the current partial schedule without taking into account the other unscheduled operations. In such a way, we obtain a schedule π that can be infeasible. Let $C_{M_1}(\pi)$ be the makespan (i.e., the maximal completion time of an operation assigned to the machine) for machine M_1, $IT_{M_1}(\pi)$ be the idle time on machine M_1 between the operations of the set N', and $OT_{M_1}(\pi)$ be the total overlap time, where more than one operation is processed at the same time. Moreover, let

$$C'_{M_1}(\pi) = C_{M_1}(\pi) + \max\{0, OT_{M_1}(\pi) - IT_{M_1}(\pi)\}.$$

Similarly, we can define $C'_{M_j}(\pi)$ for $j = 2, 3, 4$. Then,

$$LB1 = \max\{C'_{M_1}(\pi), C'_{M_2}(\pi), C'_{M_3}(\pi), C'_{M_4}(\pi)\}$$

is a lower bound. It is easy to check that we need $O(n)$ operations to calculate this bound.

If we use an upper bound and lower bound, then the B&B algorithm requires $O(n2^{6n})$ operations.

6. Concluding Remarks

In this note, four models of scheduling problems for CAVs have been given. Three of them can be solved by a dynamic programming algorithm in polynomial time. For the fourth problem, a B&B algorithm has been presented. The investigations in this paper are only a first step in the development of scheduling algorithms for CAV problems. The presented algorithms can handle only very special problems. However, they can be potentially used as a part of more complex algorithms for more general CAV problems (e.g., considering more lanes, different speeds of the cars, or a closure of more lanes). For real-world problems related to the scheduling of CAVs, fast metaheuristics and online algorithms can be developed in the future. Finally we give two specific research questions that are worth considering:

- Are the problems $J4|4\,chains, p_j = p, r_j|f, f \in \{C_{max}, \sum w_jC_j, \sum w_jT_j, \sum w_jU_j\}$ NP-hard or can they be solved in polynomial time?
- Are there problems with CAVs having equal processing times and a fixed number of chains of jobs, which is an NP-hard problem?

Author Contributions: Conceptualization, E.R.G. and F.W., investigation, E.R.G. and F.W., visualization, E.R.G.; writing—original draft preparation, F.W. All authors have read and agreed to the published version of the manuscript.

Funding: This research received no external funding.

Informed Consent Statement: Informed consent was obtained from all subjects involved in the study.

Data Availability Statement: The data are available from the authors on request.

Conflicts of Interest: The authors declare no conflicts of interest.

erences

Ullrich, C. Integrated Machine Scheduling and Vehicle Routing with Time Windows. *Eur. J. Oper. Res.* **2012**, *1*, 152–165.
Afifi, S.; Dang, D.-C.; Moukrim, A. Heuristic Solutions for the Vehicle Routing Problem with Time Windows and Synchronized Visits. *Optim. Lett.* **2016**, *10*, 511–525. [CrossRef]
Norouzi, N.; Sadegh-Amalnick, M.; Tavakkoli-Moghaddam, R. Modified Particle Swarm Optimization in a Time-Dependent Vehicle Routing Problem: Minimizing Fuel Consumption. *Optim. Lett.* **2017**, *11*, 121–134. [CrossRef]
Nasiri, M.M.; Rahbari, A.; Werner, F.; Karimi, R. Incorporating Supplier Selection and Order Allocation into the Vehicle Routing and Multi-Cross-Dock Scheduling Problem. *Intern. J. Prod. Res.* **2018**, *56*, 6527–6552. [CrossRef]
Rahbari, A.; Nasiri, M.M.; Werner, F.; Musavi, M.; Jolai, F. The Vehicle Routing and Scheduling Problem with Cross-Docking for Perishable Products under Uncertainty: Two Robust Bi-objective Models. *Appl. Math. Modell.* **2018**, *70*, 605–625. [CrossRef]
Repoussis, P.P.; Gounaris, C.E. Special Issue on Vehicle Routing and Scheduling: Recent Trends and Advances. *Optim. Lett.* **2013**, *7*, 1399–1403. [CrossRef]
Bunte, S.; Kliewer, N. An Overview on Vehicle Scheduling Models. *Public Transport.* **2009**, *1*, 299–317. [CrossRef]
Han, M.; Wang, Y. A Survey for Vehicle Routing Problems and its Derivatives. *IOP Conf. Ser. Mater. Sci. Eng.* **2018**, *452*, 042024. [CrossRef]
Mor, A.; Speranza, M.G.: Vehicle Routing Problems over Time: A Survey. *4OR* **2020**, *18*, 129–149. [CrossRef]
Bazzal, M.; Krawczyk, L.; Govindarajan, R.P.; Wolff, C. Timing Analysis of Car-to-Car Communication Systems Using Real-Time Calculus: A Case Study. In Proceedings of the 2020 IEEE 5th International Symposium on Smart and Wireless Systems within the Conferences on Intelligent Data Acquisition and Advanced Computing Systems (IDAACS-SWS), Dortmund, Germany, 17–18 September 2020; pp. 1–8.
Şahin, T.; Khalili, R.; Boban, M.; Wolisz, A. Reinforcement Learning Scheduler for Vehicle-to-Vehicle Communications Outside Coverage. In Proceedings of the 2018 IEEE Vehicular Networking Conference (VNC), Taipei, Taiwan, 5–7 December 2018; pp. 1–8.
Qian, G.; Guo, M.; Zhang, L.; Wang, Y.; Hu, S.; Wang, D. Traffic scheduling and control in fully connected and automated networks. *Transp. Res. Part C Emerg. Technol.* **2021**, *126*, 103011. [CrossRef]
Atagoziev, M.; Schmidt, E.G.; Schmidt, K.W. Lane change scheduling for connected and autonomous vehicles.*Transp. Res. Part C Emerg. Technol.* **2023**, *147*, 103985. [CrossRef]
Ma, M. Optimal Scheduling of Connected and Autonomous Vehicles at a Reservation-Based Intersection. Ph.D. Thesis, University of Louisville, Louisville, KY, USA, 2022.
Bani Younes, M.; Boukerche, A. An Intelligent Traffic Light scheduling algorithm through VANETs. In Proceedings of the 39th Annual IEEE Conference on Local Computer Networks Workshops, Edmonton, AB, Canada, 8–11 September 2014; pp. 637–642.
Graham, R.L.; Lawler, E.L.; Lenstra, J.K.; Rinnooy Kan, A.H.G. Optimization and Approximation in Deterministic Machine Scheduling: A Survey. *Ann. Discr. Math.* **1979**, *5*, 287–326.
Lenstra, J.K.; Rinnooy Kan, A.H.G. Complexity results for scheduling chains on a single machine. *Eur. J. Oper. Res.* **1980**, *4*, 270–275. [CrossRef]
Baptiste, P. Scheduling equal-length jobs on identical parallel machines. *Discret. Appl. Math.* **2000**, *103*, 21–32. [CrossRef]

algorithms

MDPI

Article

Data Compression with a Time Limit

Bruno Carpentieri

Dipartmento di Informatica, Università di Salerno, 84084 Fisciano, SA, Italy; bcarpentieri@unisa.it

Abstract: In this paper, we explore a framework to identify an optimal choice of compression algorithms that enables the best allocation of computing resources in a large-scale data storage environment: our goal is to maximize the efficiency of data compression given a time limit that must be observed by the compression process. We tested this approach with lossless compression of one-dimensional data (text) and two-dimensional data (images) and the experimental results demonstrate its effectiveness. We also extended this technique to lossy compression and successfully applied it to the lossy compression of two-dimensional data.

Keywords: data compression; digital transmission; convex hull

1. Introduction

Digital technologies have revolutionized our daily lives in a short period. Thanks to mobile devices, modern personal computers, and high-speed mobile networks, we are always connected and can share photos or videos with a click.

These important changes, along with the new applications emerging from recent innovations, have been readily accepted by end-users. However, these users remain largely unaware of the underlying mechanisms and functions: for example, how the process of playing a video or sending an image over the internet works.

Whether you surf the internet, listen to a piece of music, watch a video or scroll through images, few people know how fundamental the data compression process is for these activities.

Communication today is largely based on the exchange of digital information on data networks, such as the internet. In fact, one might say that these infrastructures are now fundamentally based on data compression, which enables easier and faster exchange of digital data and information. Moreover, compression is often combined with encryption to guarantee the privacy of communication.

Typically, the choice of compression algorithms to use and the technical details to rely on depend on the application that will use the digital file and/or the destination of the message sent.

The goal of data compression algorithms is to maximize the level of compression given the limitations of processing resources.

Deciding how to allocate processing resources for compression tasks is not a trivial problem. In this paper, we focus on a framework that begins with multimedia data compression and studies the optimal allocation of compression resources. Our goal is to maximize the efficiency of data compression given limited computational resources, particularly with respect to a time limit (see [1,2]).

The paper is structured as follows: Section 2 discusses past related work and the optimization algorithm. Section 3 presents our experimental results for the lossless compression of one-dimensional and two-dimensional data. Section 4 refines the technique used for lossless compression to perform efficient lossy compression of images and presents experimental results on lossy compression. Finally, Section 5 provides conclusions and outlines possible new research directions.

2. Data Compression with a Time Limit

The compression process, especially in the case of large databases, is characterized by a trade-off between time and space that the user must be aware of and on which they must make a decision. There are various compression algorithms that allow you to optimize the degree of compression, or the time needed for this process.

Individual compression algorithms often also allow a more fine-grained choice by specifying a compression level, where a low level represents the desire for a minimum required time, while a high level represents the need for maximum compressibility of the supplied document.

With the advent of cloud computing and the service-based and pay-per-use model widely used nowadays, one can easily imagine the need to be able to set a specific time budget for a certain activity such as data compression. As specific activities, one can imagine the creation of hourly or event-related dumps. A concrete case specific to cloud computing can be imagined by considering the *FaaS* ("Function as a Service") model.

The cost of this model is directly proportional to the number of calls performed and, in particular, to the duration of each.

2.1. Past Related Work

Data compression is nowadays a very active field of research: every reduction in the size of digital data allows us to transmit them faster, and therefore has a significant economic impact.

In lossless compression algorithms, the decoded output of the compression system is identical, bit for bit, to the original data. In contrast, lossy compression algorithms produce an "acceptable" approximation (depending on the application) of the original input.

Textual data, including text and HTML pages, are typically not stored in compressed form since they need to be searchable. In contrast, raster data such as audio, images, and video are generally stored in compressed formats and are often created in compressed form by the devices that generate them. Lossy compression is used exclusively for raster data.

Zohar and Cassuto in [1] studied for the first time the problem of optimizing the lossless compression of one-dimensional data when there is a time limit within which the compression process must be completed. They experimentally demonstrated that the optimization is possible.

Carpentieri in [2] resumed the work of Zohar and Cassuto and extended it to the lossless compression of two-dimensional data (images).

In the paper of Liao, Moffat, Petri, and Wirth [3], a comprehensive model for the total retention cost (TRC) of a data archiving system is established, integrating cloud computing provider charging rates to quantify costs across various compression strategies. This analysis serves as a foundation for developing innovative, cost-efficient alternatives that surpass the effectiveness of existing methods.

Wiseman and Schwan [4] investigate the application of compression techniques to enhance middleware-based information exchange in interactive and collaborative distributed systems. In these environments, achieving high compression ratios must be balanced with compression speeds that align with sustainable network transfer rates. Their approach dynamically monitors network and processor resources, evaluates compression efficiency, and autonomously selects the most suitable compression methods to optimize performance.

In this paper, we study data compression with a time limit in both the one-dimensional and the two-dimensional case and in the case of both lossless and lossy compression.

Lossless compression algorithms are often based on the text substitution model introduced by Lempel, Ziv, and Storer in the 1970s. and later used for text and image compression (see for example [5–7]), or using Huffman or arithmetic coding (see for example [8,9]).

The approach we have presented for the optimization of compression given a time limit is totally independent of the algorithms used in the experiments. For simplicity, we have chosen to use in the experiments some of the most popular compression tools. Obviously, this choice has no impact on the optimization process other than providing data different from others.

In this paper, regarding the lossless compression of one-dimensional data, we have used in our experiments *gzip* (see [10]), *xz* (based on LZMA: deriving from the seminal work of Lempel and Ziv [4,5]), and *bzip2* (based on the Burrows Wheeler transform, see [11]), *arithmetic coding* (see [9]).

Lossless and lossy image compression algorithms often use the "modeling + coding" approach in which a prediction of the current pixel is built consistently by encoder and decoder depending on a chosen context of already coded samples, and then a prediction error, i.e., the difference between the real value of the current pixel and the prediction made, is sent from the encoder to the decoder.

As for lossless image compression, we used *PNG* (see [12]), *TIFF* (based on the LZW algoritym, see [13]), *JPEG-LS* (see [14]), *JPEG200* (see [15]), *BMP* (see [16]), and *FELICS* (see [17]) in the testing phase.

Saha in [18] presents a review of lossy image compression algorithms. For lossy compression of images, in our tests we used *JPEG* (see [19]) and *WEBP* (see [20]).

When lossy image coding is used, it is important to balance the compression obtained and the quality of the decompressed image. Here, to evaluate the quality of the decompressed image we used the *SSIM* metric (see [21]).

2.2. A Data Compression Algorithm with a Time Limit

Generally speaking, the framework proposed in [1] is a specialization of the more general approach with respect to the basic mechanism of compression algorithms related to the configuration of effort levels.

It is not necessary to specify the compression algorithms to be used, since the approach is agnostic with respect to them. The simplified idea is to use a set of configurations of a specific algorithm, each on a partition of the data to be compressed. The percentage of data to be compressed with each algorithm is chosen to maximize the use of the available time, provided as input budget, in order to maximize the degree of compressibility obtained.

In the case of single documents, this set of configurations can specify the use of a single algorithm or a pair of algorithms.

For multiple documents, instead, combinations of algorithms will be used where each will be executed on a specific document. Each element of these combinations can be a single algorithm or a pair of algorithms, but it can be experimentally shown that in all cases it is sufficient to use a pair of algorithms, at most only for one document, using a single algorithm for the remaining documents. Therefore, in this paper we are not considering the possibility of compressing a single document in parts, with more than one data compression algorithm, because doing so would only bring a low gain that does not justify the increase in complexity due to the decoding.

Assuming a function that compresses a given set of data, a time optimization activity would allow us to reduce the economic costs of our system without sacrificing more than necessary the reductions in data size.

When we normally apply data compression, all the data we want to compress are input into a single compression tool which will try to reduce the size of the input data (while keeping the same information content) in a certain time t, and the tool will return as its output the compressed data.

The focus is frequently placed on the algorithm's compression efficiency, while the time required for compression is often overlooked, provided it remains within a reasonable limit.

This way of doing may not be convenient in situations where you want to specify a time t' that could also be less than t, within which you want to complete the compression process: that is, when you are trying to optimize compression performance while respecting specified time limits.

Recall that a convex surface, or convex hull, of a set of points S is the intersection of all convex sets that contain S and that the lower polygon chain contains all points that minimize the second coordinate (y, which in our case will be the size of the compressed document) for each x (in our case, time) of the convex surface.

If we consider the optimization of the compression of a single document, with the notions of a convex surface and lower polygon chain it is possible to obtain the set of optimal mixes of algorithms for any time budget.

The basic idea is to obtain the lower polygon chain of the best algorithms for each time budget, representing them on a two-dimensional plane by choosing as coordinates the time required (x) and the resulting dimension from the execution of the algorithm (y).

By best algorithms, we mean the input algorithms sorted by the time required, filtered by taking only those that lead to an improvement in terms of compression compared to the previous algorithm.

This filtering activity removes two classes of algorithms.

The algorithms that would cause a worse resulting dimension for the same time budget compared to another mix are excluded. In case two algorithms require the same amount of time, the one with the smaller resulting dimension is preferred.

By building the convex surface of the remaining algorithms, we can obtain the lower polygon chain composed of the algorithms involved in each possible optimal mix. This step is necessary because there may still be algorithms that are better than the previous one but that involve a non-optimal mix.

By definition of a convex surface, there cannot be points below it, while points above the lower polygonal chain will not correspond to optimal algorithms due to a larger resulting dimension. For each possible time budget, we will then have two possible options. It will be possible to use a specific algorithm, or the document can be partitioned into two parts, where each will be compressed by one of the two members of the optimal algorithm pair for that time budget.

If we consider the optimization of the compression of multiple documents, an important feature of the resulting polygon chain is the slope of the segments connecting two algorithms. This slope captures the concept of benefit obtained by switching from one algorithm to another. A more significant slope will result in a greater benefit.

The optimization of the compression of multiple documents starts from the lower polygon chains built through the process seen previously for each document. The idea is to join these chains to obtain an overall chain representing the entire set of documents.

The resulting lower polygon chain will be made up of points representing combinations of algorithms to be used, one for each document involved in the process. Each point of this lower polygon chain will be chosen in order to maximize the benefit for that specific time budget. This maximization is obtained by changing, with respect to the previous combination, only one algorithm. Once the overall lower polygon chain is obtained, the mixing process will be similar to the one seen previously. The optimal algorithms will correspond to the extremes of the segment where the time budget falls.

Following the work of Zohar and Cassuto in [1], let us suppose we find ourselves in a situation where we want to compress a single file f or a large data set D by using a compressor. In real life, we will have many compressors and setups to choose from, but here, for simplicity let us consider the situation in which we have two possible compressors available, or two possible configurations of a single compressor called, respectively, *setup1* and *setup2*: it could be easy then to generalize the following discussion to multiple compressors and multiple setups.

Suppose setup1 takes less time to compress than setup2, but that setup2 compresses more than setup1. Now, suppose that the execution must finish within a certain time t' (let us call this value *time-budget*).

We define t_1 as the time taken by setup1, t_2 the time taken by setup2.

1. $t' < t_1$: it is not possible to compress with either setup, since the time budget is less than the time taken by the fastest compressor (setup1).
2. $t' > t_2$: it is possible to compress with both setup1 and setup2. We choose to compress with setup2, since compression is more effective in terms of output size.
3. $t_1 < t' < t_2$: it is not possible to compress with setup2 because the time budget is not sufficient. We therefore decide to use setup1.

If we find ourselves in situation 3, the system manages to compress f (or D) through setup1; however, the time value $\Delta(t) = t' - t_1$ in which the system remains unused is not negligible since the chosen setup finished its execution before the set time t'. Compression optimization tries to reduce, if not to eliminate, the $\Delta(t)$ value, considering not one, but a mix of setups.

In our previous example, if we found ourselves in a situation in which the time-budget is $t_1 < t' < t_2$, we could think of adopting a "mixing" strategy in which a part of the file f (or of the data set D) to be compressed goes as input to setup1, while the remaining part to setup2.

This strategy, compared to the classic application of a single compression tool, could lead to the use of the entire time budget initially chosen and to a reduction in the output size. The proposed algorithm searches for an *optimal-mix*, i.e., an optimal setup configuration (among many considered) that can be used to compress a file f, given a time budget. As we will see, the search is not a trivial process, as it adopts a technique that builds a function that will consider potential setups that could be part of the mixing, and subsequently, among all the candidates, two or more are chosen.

The algorithm that is described next allows you to obtain all the *useful-setups* for a certain file f to be compressed. Subsequently, it will be possible to obtain the optimal mix once the time budget t' has been set. The inputs of the algorithm are pairs (b_i, t_i), where each pair represents a setup: t_i represents the time taken by the setup to compress the file f, while b_i is the resulting size, as in [1].

The algorithm for finding the optimal mix consists of four main steps, listed below:

1. Determination of the pairs (b_i, t_i) for each setup; these pairs are obtained by running each compression tool individually on the file f or by simply estimating its performance.
2. Sorting the setups in an ascending manner by t_i, with b_i used as the second index in descending order.
3. Removal of the worst setups and construction of the convex hull of the remaining points:

  i. Between two setups that take the same time to execute, the one that gives the largest output size is discarded.
  ii. All setups that give an output size that is too large compared to others that take less time are discarded.

4. Acquisition of the *optimal-mix* given a time budget t'.

Phase 3 will build what in computational geometry is called the convex hull, that is, given a set of points, the determination of the smallest convex set that can contain them all. As proved in [1], the setups located at the vertices of the lower part of the convex hull are the only *useful-setups*.

Useful-mixes will always be two setups connected by an arc on the bottom edge of the polygon. Given m useful setups arranged in ascending order of running time and a time budget t', the goal is to identify the optimal combination of setups, a and b, along with the fractions of files, r_a and r_b, that each setup will handle.

In the non-trivial case where $t_1 < t' < t_2$, the chosen combination consists of the two adjacent setups, a and b, such that $t_b < t' < t_a$. After finding the optimal mix, the percentage of data D that must be compressed with the chosen compression tools is calculated as in [1]. Assuming we have two setups s_a and s_b with times t_a and t_b, respectively, choosing t' as the time budget such that $t_b < t' < t_a$, the fraction of the file f to compress with s_a will be:

$$r_a = (t' - t_b)/(t_a - t_b)$$

The fraction of D compressed by the s_b setup will be:

$$r_b = 1 - r_a.$$

In a multi-document context, each document typically possesses its own unique convex hull. Consequently, optimizing compression requires addressing multiple convex hulls simultaneously. Since the effectiveness of a particular tool or configuration depends on the document's specific information characteristics, the set of optimal configurations will vary across documents.

A critical part of the solution involves an algorithm that consolidates the individual convex hulls into a unified convex hull. This unified structure allows the system to determine the best configuration for a given computational time constraint with ease, as explained in [1].

To illustrate how the merged sequence facilitates finding the optimal configuration for any compute-time limit, as outlined in [1], the process begins by calculating the compute time required when the least resource-intensive configurations are applied across all documents. The algorithm then iterates through successive configuration vectors in the merged sequence, recalculating the compute time at each step. This progression continues until the system encounters the last configuration within the allowed compute-time limit. As the system approaches the budget, the time constraint will eventually lie between two adjacent configurations in the sequence.

At this point, much like the single-document scenario, the solution involves blending two adjacent configurations. Since only one document transitions between setups in adjacent configurations, the final allocation will result in most documents sticking to a single configuration, with at most one document employing a mix of two configurations across its instances.

3. Lossless Compression

We experimented this approach by using lossless compressors on one-dimensional data (text) and on two-dimensional data (images); the obtained results follow.

3.1. Lossless Compression of One-Dimensional Data with a Time Limit

We began testing on a set of 1000 html pages that have similar contents and that were downloaded through the web crawler Wibbi by Stanford University, obtaining a resulting document of size 34 Mb.

We tested the following compression tools: *gzip, xz, bzip2, arithmetic coding* all in the default configuration.

For this experiment, we used a Mac Book Air with 8 Gb of RAM and a 1.7 Ghz Intel Core i7 processor. These, in Table 1, are the results of running the compression tools on this test data set:

Table 1. Compression of 1000 html pages.

Algorithm	Compressed Size (Bytes)	Time to Compress (milliseconds)
Gzip	7,700,660	1784
XZ	6,793,836	25,974
Bzip2	7,216,597	16,514
Arithmetic Coding	13,906,174	7928

Gzip is the fastest of all the tools, probably because it is implemented in the java.util.zip library and this makes it optimized. Arithmetic Coding, although faster than all the other setups except Gzip, returns a significantly larger output size than the other compressors: about 100% more. The best setup in terms of output size is XZ, even though it takes on this platform the longest time: about 26 s. In this experiment, we decided to limit our optimal mix to only two algorithms and to compress each file with a single compressor. We tested two different time budgets: 22,000 milliseconds and 10,000 milliseconds.

For the time budget of 22,000 milliseconds, the optimal mix turns out to be composed of Bzip2 and XZ. A total of 632 html pages were compressed by using XZ and the remaining 368 by using Bzip2. The compressed file size for this test was 6,935,454 bytes long and the total time to compress was 22,566 milliseconds, i.e., slightly more that the assigned time budget: an error of about 0.0257%. This depends on the fact that we had chosen to compress each file with a single compressor. By removing this constraint, we can likely adhere precisely to the assigned time budget.

For the time budget of 10,000 milliseconds, the optimal mix turns out to be composed of Bzip2 and Gzip. A total of 557 html pages were compressed by using Gzip and the remaining 443 by using Bzip2. The compressed file size for this test was 7,401,784 bytes long and the total time to compress was 9703 milliseconds, i.e., slightly less that the assigned time budget.

3.2. Lossless Compression of Two-Dimensional Data with a Time Limit

We evaluated the performance of the algorithm by conducting experiments on different types of inputs. The following four cases were initially analyzed:

- Compression of a set of animated images with similar scenes.
- Compression of a set of animated images with different scenes.
- Compression of a set of non-animated images with similar scenes.
- Compression of a set of non-animated images with different scenes.

The time budgets used are different for each experiment.

The tests on the lossless compression of images with a time limit were conducted on a personal computer with the following specifications:

- CPU: Intel Core i7-2630QM CPU 2.00 GHz;
- RAM: 8.00 GB;
- Operating system: Windows 10 Pro;
- Mass storage: 128 GB Samsung Pro SSD.

The following Table 2 lists all the compression tools used, their configuration adopted, and the download link for the compression libraries (accessed last time on 19 November 2024):

Table 2. Compression tools.

Tool	Download	Configuration
PNG	https://www.idrsolutions.com/jdeli	Lossless
TIFF	https://www.idrsolutions.com/jdeli	Deflate
JPEG-LS	http://www.labs.hp.com/research/info_theory/loco/locodownold.html	Lossless 8 bits
JPEG2000	http://www.dclunie.com/jj2000/JPEG%202000%20implementation%20in%20Java.html	Lossless
BMP	https://github.com/jai-imageio/jai-imageio-core	Compression with uncompressed pixel map (BI RGB)
FELICS	Java implementation	Lossless 8 bits

The images were extracted from videos currently available at the following links (accessed last time on 19 November 2024):

- https://www.youtube.com/watch?v=FmiRX9Oh_0g;
- https://www.youtube.com/watch?v=5FNFBgubeqI;
- https://www.youtube.com/watch?v=u5CZs4y53UE;
- https://www.youtube.com/watch?v=CkEowmI7a3w.

Each video was downloaded by connecting to the portal http://it.savefrom.net/ and then specifying the link and format (MP4 360p).

To perform the subdivision into frames, we used a GOM Player tool (available at the link https://www.gomlab.com/). The input images are in uncompressed TIFF format.

3.2.1. Compression of a Set of Animated Images with Similar Scenes

The dataset D to be compressed consisted of 1000 images, for a total size of 659 MB (691,744,000 bytes). Single runs of the compression tools yielded the following pairs (b_i, t_i).

Table 3 shows us that the fastest compressor was BMP while the slowest was JPEG2000. From the point of view of the compression obtained, the best compressor was JPEG-LS, while the worst was BMP.

Table 3. Animated images with similar scenes.

Tool	Size of Output in Bytes	Compression Time in ms.
PNG	183,362,330	70,806
TIFF	169,626,226	91,082
JPEG-LS	129,232,679	116,263
JPEG2000	145,893,942	564,370
BMP	691,254,004	37,975
FELICS	201,865,197	42,952

The *useful-setup* is therefore composed of the compressors BMP, FELICS, PNG, TIFF, and JPEG-LS. With an assigned time budget t_1 = 39,000 ms then the optimal mix is given by the mix of the BMP and FELICS setups, and it is closer to the BMP setup. All this is shown in Figure 1:

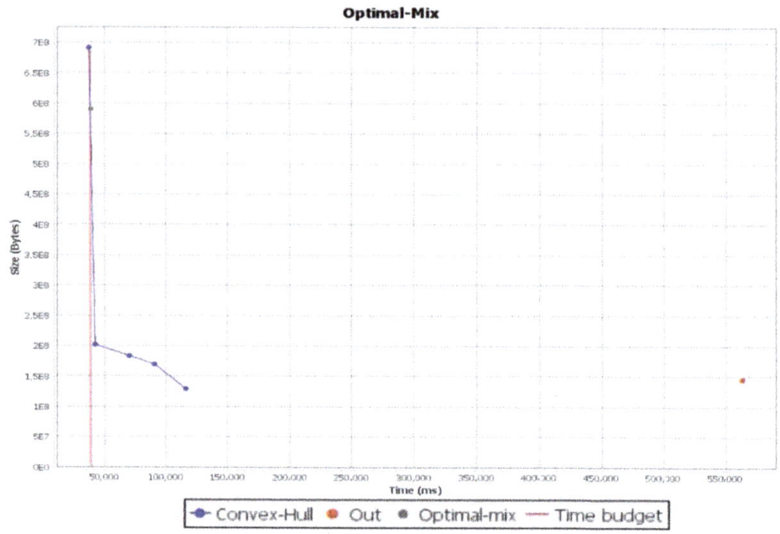

Figure 1. Optimal mix, t = 39,000 ms.

In this case, the optimum is perfectly intersected with the convex hull. A total of 794 images will be compressed using BMP, the other 206 with FELICS. We therefore compressed D as suggested by the algorithm: the compression time was 39,141 ms and the output size 563 MB (590,397,633 bytes).

For t_2 = 89,000 ms, instead, the optimal mix is given by the mix between the TIFF and PNG configurations, and it is very close to the TIFF configuration. Figure 2 shows it:

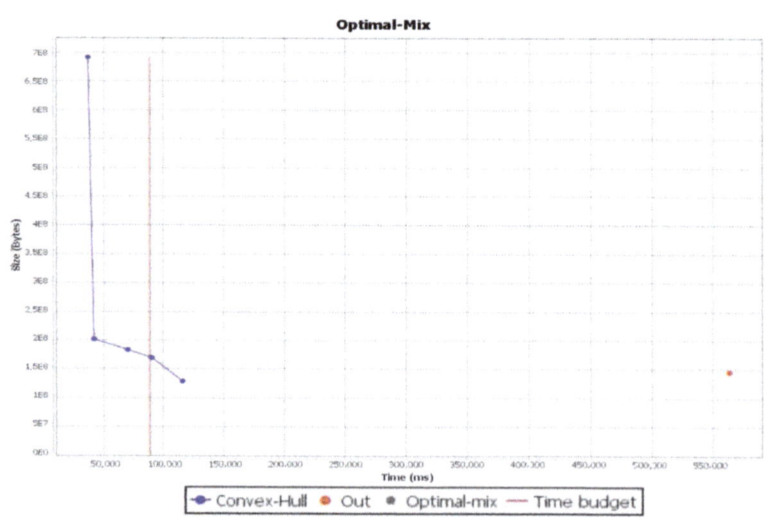

Figure 2. Optimal mix, t = 89,000 ms.

Here too, the optimum intersects the convex hull. The number of images to compress with TIFF was 897, while for PNG it was 103.

The compression time was 89,546 ms., while the output size was 163 MB (170,978,001 bytes).

3.2.2. Compression of a Set of Animated Images with Different Scenes

The dataset D to be compressed consisted again of 1000 images, for a total size of 659 MB (691,744,000 bytes). Single runs of the compression tools yielded the following pairs (b_i, t_i):

Table 4 shows us that the fastest compressor was BMP while the slowest was JPEG2000. From the point of view of the compression obtained, the best compressor was JPEG2000, while the worst was BMP.

Table 4. Animated images with different scenes.

Tool	Size of Output in Bytes	Compression Time in ms.
PNG	278,923,712	83,538
TIFF	263,128,720	93,542
JPEG-LS	188,777,508	127,575
JPEG2000	174,971,373	578,176
BMP	691,254,300	36,992
FELICS	252,695,812	58,873

The *useful-setup* is therefore composed of the compressors BMP, FELICS, JPEG-LS, and JPEG2000. Two time budgets were set to experiment the algorithm. With an assigned time budget, t_1 = 571,000 ms then the optimal mix is given by the mix of the JPEG-LS and JPEG2000 setups, and it is very close to the JPEG2000 setup. All this is shown in Figure 3:

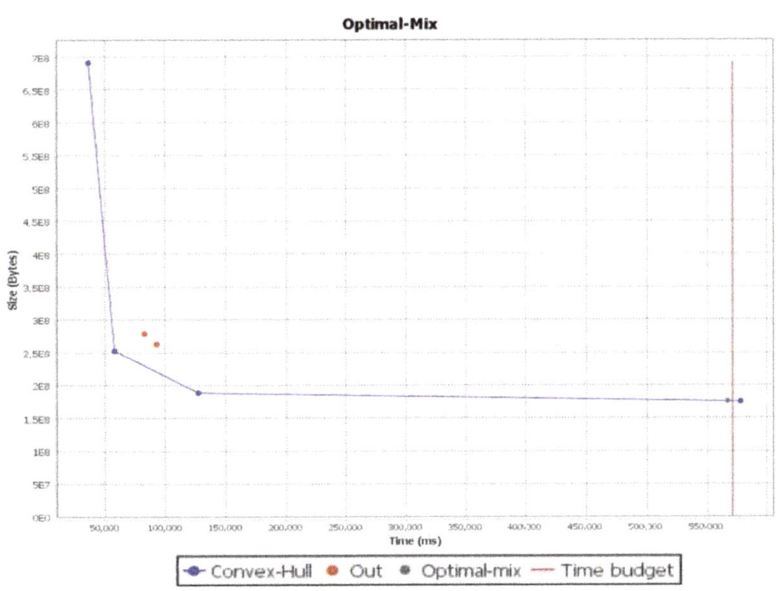

Figure 3. Optimal mix, t = 571,000 ms.

Here, the optimal mix is at the intersection point.

A total of 16 images must be compressed using JPEG-LS, the other 984 with JPEG2000.

The compression time was 566,798 ms, while the output size was 167 MB (175,356,694 bytes).

In this case, the time budget is not used completely: the compression ends about 5 s earlier: this difference is to be considered acceptable considering that a very large time budget has been used, and that the compression is performed one file at a time.

For t_2 = 69,000 ms, instead, the optimal mix is given by the mix between the JPEG-LS and FELICS configurations, and it is in their center. Figure 4 shows it:

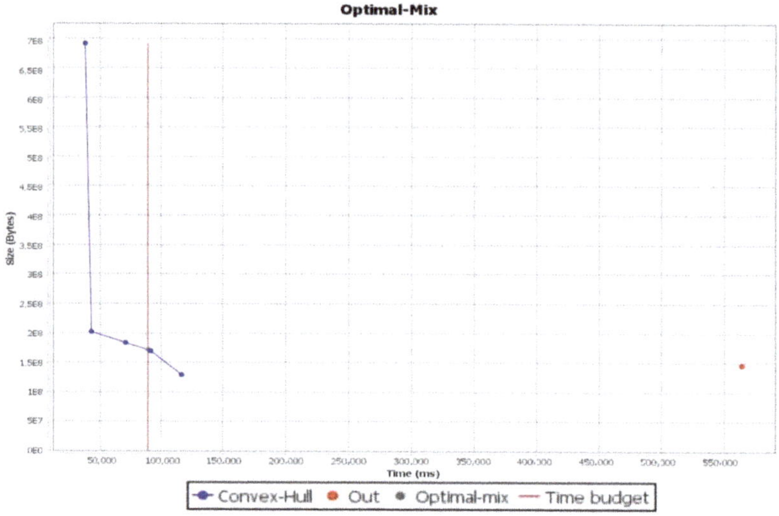

Figure 4. Optimal mix, t = 69,000 ms.

The results are consistent with all the previous tests and the optimal mix is at the intersection point.

The number of images we compress with JPEG-LS is 147, while for FELICS it is 853.

The compression time was 68,541 ms., while the output size was 232 MB (243,538,616 bytes).

3.2.3. Compression of a Set of Non-Animated Images with Similar Scenes

The data set D to be compressed was composed of 1000 images, for a total size of 659 MB (691,744,000 bytes).

Single runs of the compression tools yielded the following pairs (b_i, t_i).

Table 5 shows that the fastest tool was BMP, while the slowest was JPEG2000. The best tool for output size was JPEG2000, while the worst was BMP. The calculated useful-setup was made up of the tools BMP, FELICS, JPEG-LS, and JPEG2000.

Table 5. Non-animated images with similar scenes.

Tool	Size of Output in Bytes	Compression Time in ms.
PNG	367,459,743	89,924
TIFF	356,243,190	89,626
JPEG-LS	237,640,546	132,333
JPEG2000	206,645,155	595,192
BMP	691,254,001	36,900
FELICS	316,963,000	75,920

With an assigned time budget, t_1 = 58,000 ms then the optimal mix is given by the mix of the BMP and FELICS setups, and it is found in the center between them.

All this is shown in Figure 5:

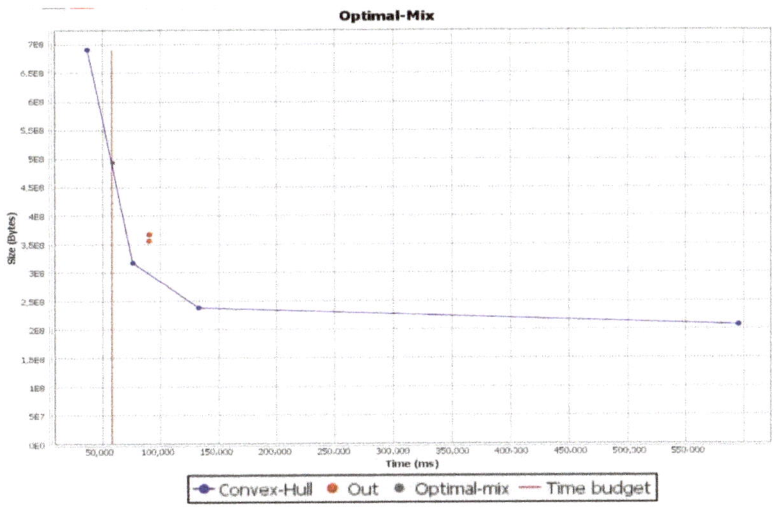

Figure 5. Optimal mix, t = 58,000 ms.

Here too, the optimum intersects the convex hull. The number of images to compress with BMP was 459, while for FELICS it was 541.

The compression time was 58,600 ms, while the output size was 471 MB (493,429,735 bytes).

If we increase the time budget to t_2 = 130,000 ms, the optimal mix is given by the mix between the JPEG-LS and FELICS configurations, and it is very close to the JPEG-LS configuration.

Figure 6 shows it:

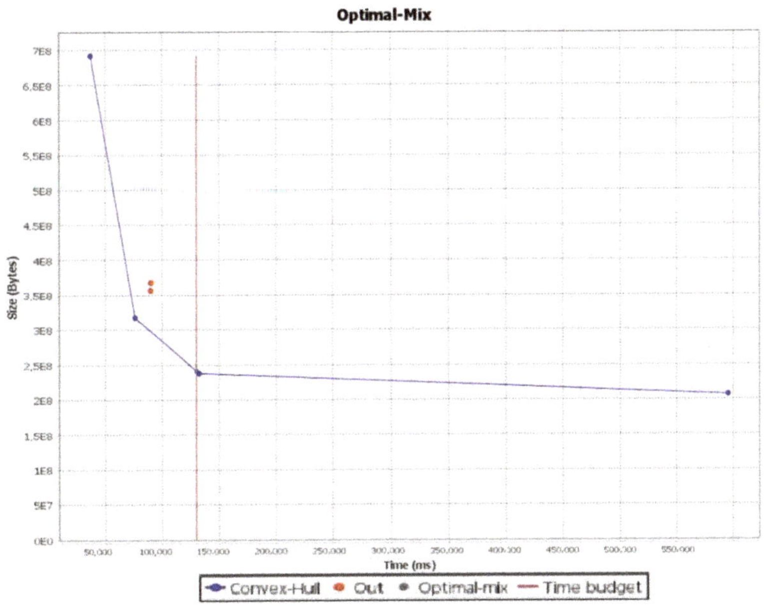

Figure 6. Optimal mix, t = 130,000 ms.

A total of 959 images will be compressed using JPEG-LS, the other 41 with FELICS.

The compression time was 130,292 ms and the output size 245 MB (240,675,273 bytes). We had to use slightly more than the expected budget: about 292 ms more.

3.2.4. Compression of a Set of Non-Animated Images with Different Scenes

The dataset D to be compressed consisted again of 1000 images, for a total size of 306 MB (320,864,256 bytes). Single runs of the compression tools yielded the following pairs (b_i, t_i).

Table 6 shows us that the fastest compressor was BMP, while the slowest was JPEG2000.

Table 6. Non-Animated images with different scenes.

Tool	Size of Output in Bytes	Compression Time in ms.
PNG	326,568,532	97,109
TIFF	311,831,649	100,836
JPEG-LS	226,142,667	130,656
JPEG2000	182,808,175	569,792
BMP	691,254,002	36,708
FELICS	289,826,020	67,992

From the point of view of the compression obtained, the best compressor was JPEG2000, while the worst was BMP. The *useful-setup* is therefore composed of the compressors BMP, FELICS, JPEG-LS, and JPEG2000.

Again, two time budgets were set to experiment the algorithm.

With an assigned time budget, t_1 = 61,000 ms then the optimal mix is given by the mix of the BMP and FELICS setups, and it is very close to the FELICS setup. All this is shown in Figure 7:

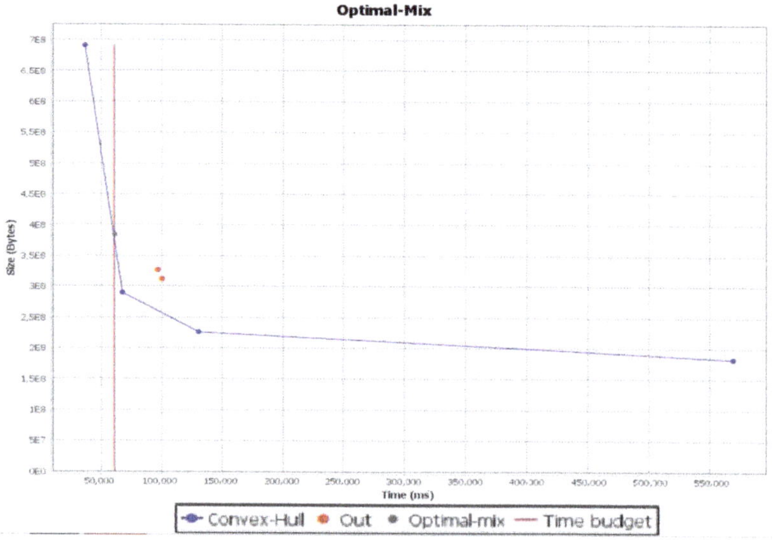

Figure 7. Optimal mix, t = 61,000 ms.

The optimum is on the convex hull. The number of images to compress with BMP was 224, while for FELICS it was 776. The compression time was 61,215 ms., while the output size was 366 MB (383,557,600 bytes).

If we increase the time budget to t_2 = 132,000 ms then the optimal mix is given by the mix between the JPEG-LS and FELICS configurations, and it is very close to the JPEG-LS configuration. Figure 8 shows it:

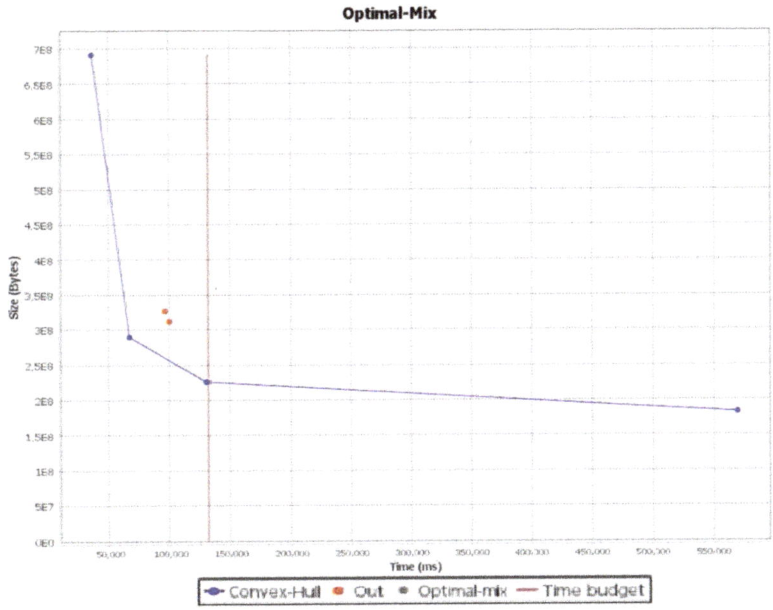

Figure 8. Optimal mix, t = 132,000 ms.

The optimum is on the convex hull. The number of images to compress with JPEG-LS was 997, while for JPEG2000 it was 3.

The compression time was 132,764 ms, while the output size was 216 MB (226,036,083 bytes).

4. Lossy Compression

As seen so far, the optimization algorithm allows us to obtain all the useful setups when we use lossless compressors. From these useful setups, it is then possible to obtain the so-called optimal mix once the time within which the compression must be completed has been set.

If instead of using lossless compressors we consider lossy compressors, we will have to consider a third parameter: *quality*. This is because lossy compression leads to a trade-off between loss of information and compression obtained and it is necessary to evaluate the result of the compression not only in terms of compression but also in terms of quality of the decompressed image. The amount of data loss is determined by the level of compression achievable, as explained by rate-distortion theory.

Lossy compression optimization becomes important, for example, in situations where compression must be performed every time data are to be transmitted because the quality is individually chosen by the remote user.

In general, for many lossy compression tools, such as JPEG and WebP, when we perform the compression, it is possible to set the quality, often in a range of 0–100, where low values mean lower quality (and greater compression). Therefore, the greater the reduction in the size of the digital image is, the greater the loss of information relating to the image will be (and, consequently, the quality will be reduced).

We have therefore chosen to add a third parameter to the optimization algorithm: the *SSIM index*.

The SSIM (Structural Similarity Index) is used to measure the similarity between two images. It is a perceptual metric that qualifies the degradation of image quality caused by processing, such as compression or loss of information in data transmission.

This metric evaluates the similarity between two images of the same acquisition: in our case, an original reference image and an image first compressed and then decompressed. The SSIM was designed to improve traditional evaluation methods such as *PSNR* and mean square error (*MSE*).

The idea was to ask the user to set a limit on the SSIM parameter at the beginning of the optimization. Subsequently, we generate the pairs (b_i, t_i), obtained by sequentially executing the compression algorithms on a data set D (in our case, the images) and then used as input for the useful setup search algorithm, but we select only those pairs whose compression returns us an SSIM value greater than or equal to of the SSIM limit value set.

In detail, the optimization algorithm for lossy image compression (which we called *SSIM_Adaptive*) receives as input the SSIM parameter that we obtain by compressing with the maximum settable quality. Starting from this SSIM, the algorithm at each iteration compresses with a different, lower, quality that is calculated to obtain an SSIM value that is close to the SSIM limit and inserts each setup it tries into an array.

At the end, we obtain q that indicates the minimum quality (0–100) to use during compression to obtain a SSIM that is closest and higher than the quality limit that was set.

It is important to clarify that the SSIM value calculated during the execution of the *SSIM_Adaptive* algorithm is a weighted average on the SSIM values of all the images given as input.

Therefore, in addition to the set-up with the q received as output, we also take all the set-ups that have a quality greater than q. By carrying out this pre-processing, we are sure that among the algorithms that will be chosen from the optimal mix only those with a quality that respects that entered by the user or even higher will appear.

In this way, we can compress D, respecting the time budget and using only the algorithms with a quality greater than or equal to the fixed one.

We experimentally tested our approach on images that were acquired as we did in Section 3.2. The images were extracted from videos that were currently available at the following links (accessed last time on 19 November 2024):

- https://www.youtube.com/watch?v=FmiRX9Oh_0g;
- https://www.youtube.com/watch?v=5FNFBgubeqI;
- https://www.youtube.com/watch?v=u5CZs4y53UE;
- https://www.youtube.com/watch?v=CkEowmI7a3w.

Each video was downloaded by connecting to the portal http://it.savefrom.net/ and then specifying the link and format (MP4 360p).

To perform the subdivision into frames, we used the GOM Player tool (available at the link https://www.gomlab.com/). The input images are in PPM format.

The tests on the lossy compression of images with a time limit were conducted on a personal computer with the following specifications:

- CPU: 8 Core Intel Core i9 CPU 2.3 GHz;
- RAM: 16.00 GB;
- Operating system: Mac OS;

The following Table 7 lists all the compression tools used, the tool to compute the SSIM, and the download link for the compression libraries:

Table 7. Compression tools.

Tool	Download	Configuration
JPG	https://github.com/LuaDist/libjpeg	JPEG lossy optimized
WEBP	https://github.com/webmproject/libwebp	WebP lossy
JPEG NO OPTIMIZE	https://github.com/LuaDist/libjpeg	JPEG lossy not optimized
SSIM	https://imagemagick.org/index.php	SSIM

We tested this lossy approach by using various configurations of time limits and quality limit. Here, we report a few.

4.1. Test 1

The dataset D to be compressed consisted of 1000 images, for a total size of 138.2 MB (138,243,000 bytes). Single runs of the compression tools with the indicated quality setups yielded the following results shown in Table 8:

Table 8. Test 1.

Tool	Size of Output in Bytes	Time in ms.	Quality Parameter	SSIM
JPG1	60,837,185	3652	95	0.987475
WEBP2	43,938,844	4894	95	0.988174
JPEG-NO OPTIMIZE3	63,865,873	5745	95	0.987482
JPEG4	16,576,161	5636	40	0.942975
JPEG5	15,107,663	5632	34	0.940295
JPEG6	14,934,171	5754	33	0.939170
JPEG7	14,607,030	5693	32	0.937845
WEBP8	12,025,946	3791	40	0.949340
WEBP9	9,976,364	3560	27	0.937786
WEBP10	9,481,598	3524	24	0.934067
WEBP11	9,313,614	3548	23	0.932677
JPEG-NO OPTIMIZE12	17,732,502	5888	40	0.942941
JPEG-NO OPTIMIZE13	16,365,984	6046	34	0.940250
JPEG-NO OPTIMIZE14	16,206,014	6030	33	0.939123
JPEG-NO OPTIMIZE15	15,901,162	6172	32	0.937797

From Figure 9, it is possible to observe that the fastest tool was WEBP10 while the slowest was JPEG_NO_OPTIMIZE15.

The best tool for output size was WEBP11, while the worst was JPEG_NO_OPTIMIZE3.

Figure 10 shows the useful setups.

Figure 11 shows the optimal mix. If the time limit is 3530 ms and the SSIM quality limit is set to 0.933483, the optimal mix is given by the mix of the WEBP10 and WEBP11 setups.

It is possible to observe how the optimum is perfectly intersected with the convex hull.

The number of images to be compressed with WEBP10 is equal to 750 with quality 24, while for WEBP11 it is 250 with quality 23.

Compressing D as suggested by the algorithm resulted in a compression time of 3683 ms, while the output size in bytes is equal to 9,433,432 bytes with a quality indicated by an SSIM index of 0.931679.

The time budget was used entirely. The very small margin of error, about 153 ms, is certainly negligible and can depend on many factors strictly related to the system (CPU usage, RAM, file reading/writing, etc.).

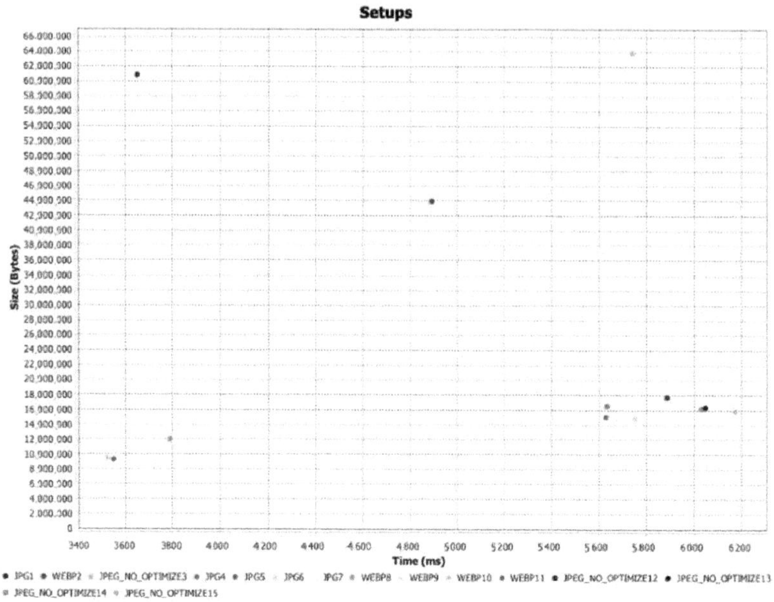

Figure 9. Setups.

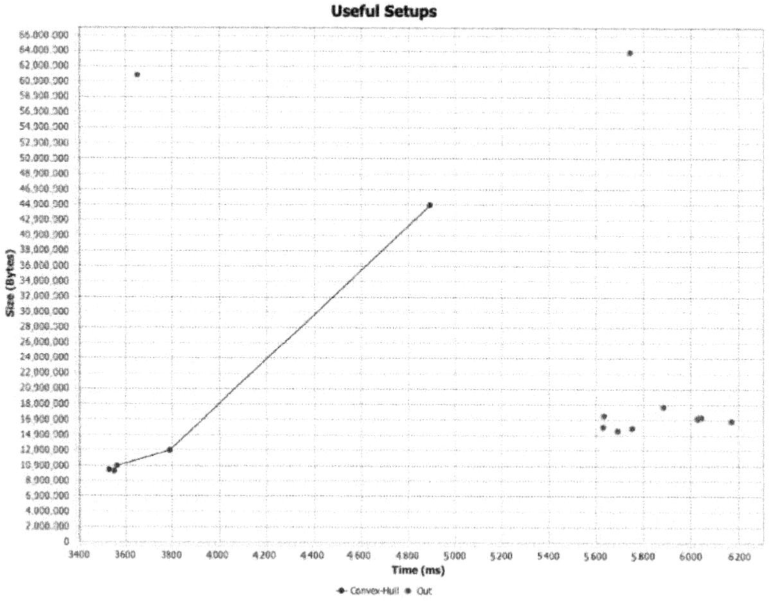

Figure 10. Useful setups.

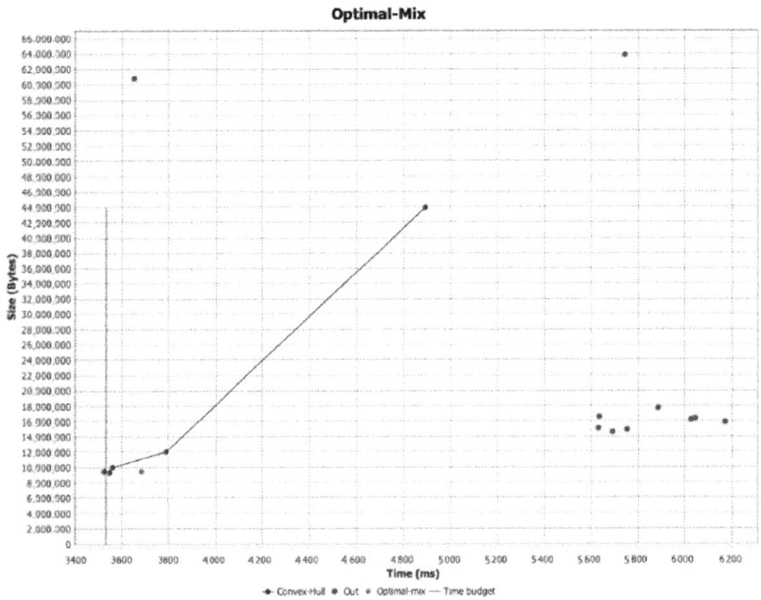

Figure 11. Optimal mix.

4.2. Test 2

The dataset D to be compressed consisted of 1000 images, for a total size of 692.2 MB (691,215,000 bytes). Single runs of the compression tools with the indicated quality setups yielded the following results shown in Table 9:

Table 9. Test 2.

Tool	Size of Output in Bytes	Time in ms.	Quality Parameter	SSIM
JPG1	66,567,945	3140	95	0.984874
WEBP2	45,131,526	4321	95	0.985433
PEG-NO OPTIMIZE3	70,390,195	5305	95	0.984874
JPEG4	21,543,285	5680	48	0.944169
JPEG5	15,001,444	5613	25	0.907689
JPEG6	13,186,571	5683	20	0.889513
JPEG7	12,510,155	5667	18	0.882732
WEBP8	13,685,922	3482	48	0.95248
WEBP9	10,041,668	3283	25	0.93276
WEBP10	8,200,328	3384	14	0.91429
WEBP11	5,839,634	4032	3	0.874497
PEG-NO OPTIMIZE12	22,619,623	5732	48	0.944170
PEG-NO OPTIMIZE13	16,340,793	5938	25	0.907669
PEG-NO OPTIMIZE14	14,648,964	6368	20	0.889482
PEG-NO OPTIMIZE15	14,017,389	5984	18	0.882703

From Figure 12 it is possible to observe that the fastest tool was JPG1 with a quality setup of 95, while the slowest was JPEG_NO_OPTIMIZE14 with a quality setup of 20. The best tool for output size was WEBP11 with a quality setup of 3, while the worst was JPEG_NO_OPTIMIZE3 with a quality setup of 95.

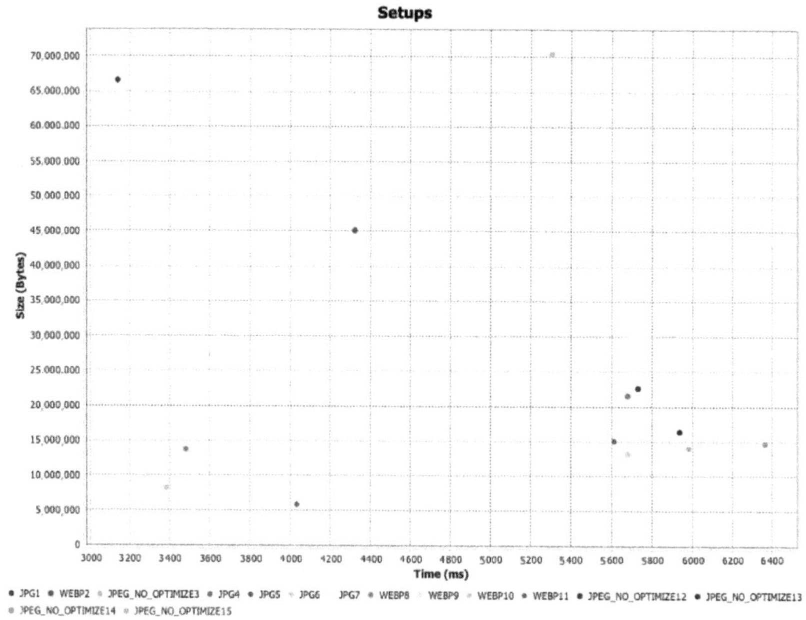

Figure 12. Setups.

Figure 13 shows the useful setups.

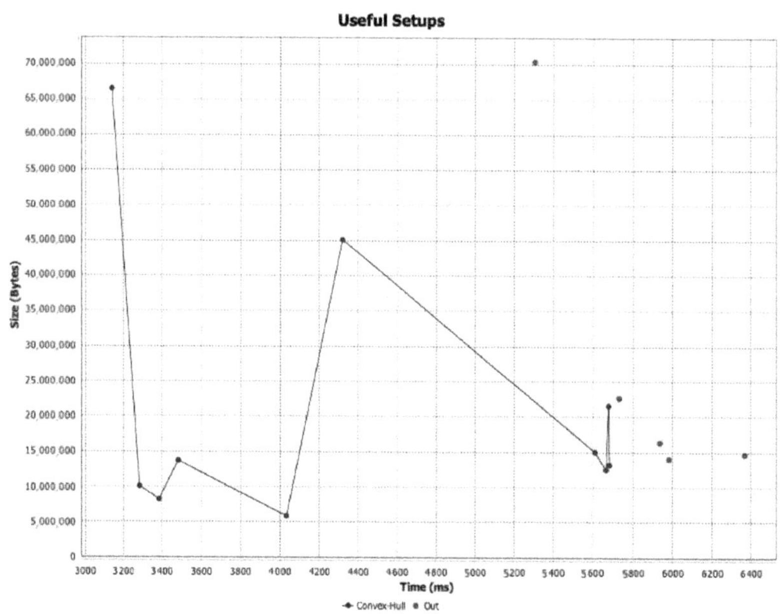

Figure 13. Useful setups.

Figure 14 shows the optimal mix.

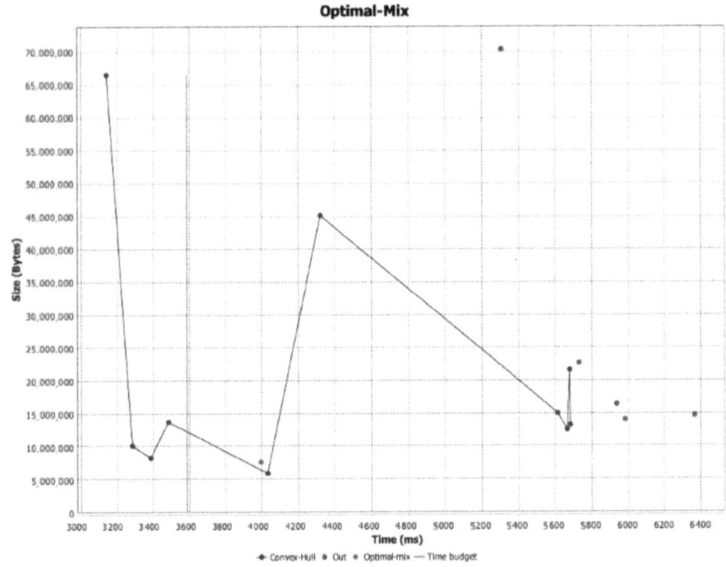

Figure 14. Optimal mix.

In the case where the time limit is 3300 ms. and the SSIM quality limit is set to 0.874144, ms., the optimal mix is given by the mix of the WEBP9 and WEBP10 setups.

The number of images to compress with WEBP9 was found to be 832 with a quality of 25, while for WEBP11 it was 168 with a quality of 14.

Compressing *D* as suggested by the algorithm resulted in a compression time of 3768 ms.

The output size was 9,751,208 bytes with an SSIM quality index of 0.927159.

The time budget was practically used entirely.

Also, in this case there was a small margin of error of about 468 ms.

4.3. Test 3

The dataset *D* to be compressed consisted of 1000 images, for a total size of 692.2 MB (691,215,000 bytes). Single runs of the compression tools with the indicated quality setups yielded the following results shown in Table 10:

Table 10. Test 3.

Tool	Size of Output in Bytes	Time in ms.	Quality Parameter	SSIM
JPG1	43,432,750	5672	95	0.972077
WEBP2	25,647,408	4728	95	0.980147
JPEG-NO OPTIMIZE3	45,836,232	5911	95	0.972077
JPEG4	13,738,395	5795	48	0.912076
JPEG5	9,696,851	5493	25	0.8863093
JPEG6	8,613,749	5974	20	0.8786752
JPEG7	8,198,962	5741	18	0.8743648
WEBP8	3,603,432	4914	1	0.8735347
JPEG-NO OPTIMIZE9	14,969,285	6431	48	0.912082
JPEG-NO OPTIMIZE10	11,228,397	6629	25	0.886300
JPEG-NO OPTIMIZE11	10,266,529	6980	20	0.878630
JPEG-NO OPTIMIZE12	99,131,536	6999	18	0.874339

From Figure 15 it is possible to observe that the fastest tool was WEBP2 with a quality setup of 95, while the slowest was JPEG_NO_OPTIMIZE12 with a quality setup of 18.

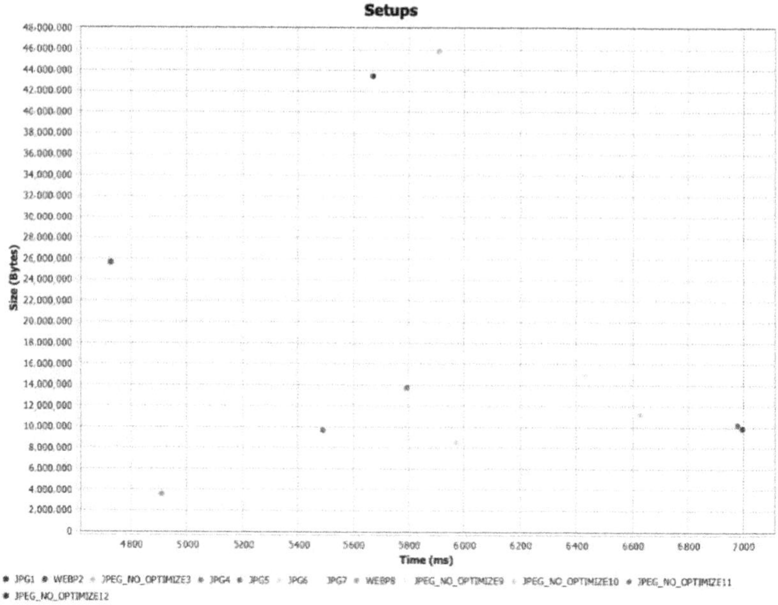

Figure 15. Setups.

The best tool for output size was WEBP8 with a quality setup of 1, while the worst was JPEG_NO_OPTIMIZE3 with a quality setup of 95.

Figure 16 shows the useful setups.

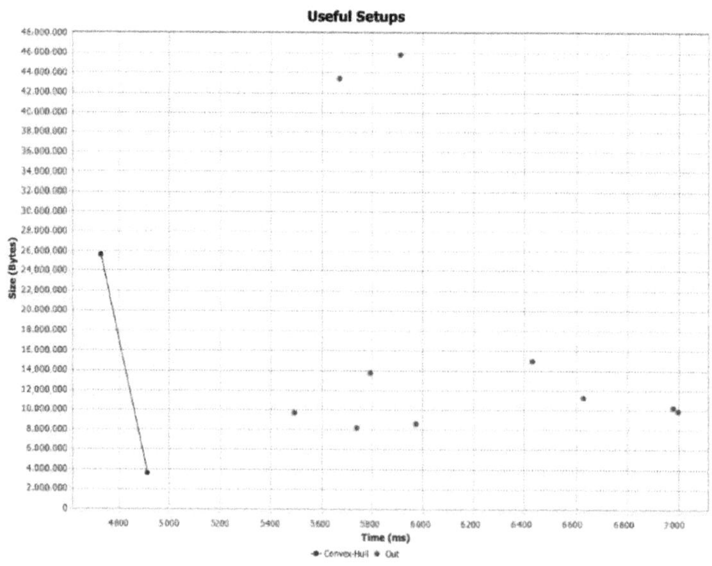

Figure 16. Useful setups.

Figure 17 shows the optimal mix.

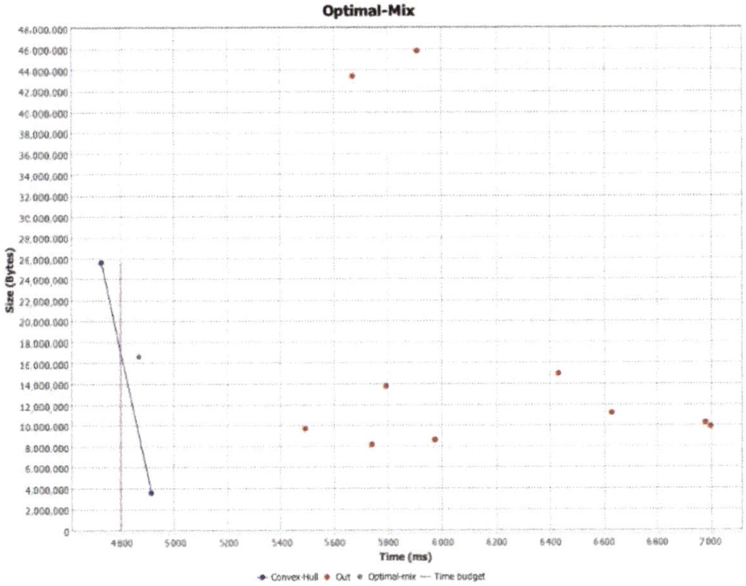

Figure 17. Optimal mix.

In the case where the time budget is t′ = 4800 and the SSIM quality limit is 0.873483 ms, the optimal mix is given by the mix of the WEBP2 and WEBP8 setups.

The number of images to be compressed with WEBP2 is equal to 613 with a quality of 95, while for WEBP8 the images are 387 with a quality of 1.

Compressing D as suggested by the algorithm resulted in a compression time of 4868 ms, while the output size was 16,623,908 bytes and an SSIM of 0.927159.

The time budget was used practically entirely.

In this case, there was a very small margin of error of about 68 ms.

4.4. Test 4

The dataset *D* to be compressed consisted of 1000 images, for a total size of 692.2 MB (691,215,000 bytes). Single runs of the compression tools with the indicated quality setups yielded the following results shown in Table 11:

Table 11. Test 4.

Tool	Size of Output in Bytes	Time in ms.	Quality Parameter	SSIM
JPG1	55,165,877	5096	95	0.983708
WEBP2	34,071,556	4251	95	0.98584
JPEG-NO OPTIMIZE3	57,648,359	5201	95	0.983713
JPEG4	17,071,808	5658	51	0.9462306
JPEG5	12,384,938	5702	29	0.9226299
JPEG6	11,053,309	5536	24	0.9121278
JPEG7	10,516,324	5875	22	0.9027293
JPEG8	9,873,987	5781	20	0.90005430
WEBP9	4,908,124	3260	4	0.90047801
WEBP10	4,688,350	3158	3	0.8955097
JPEG-NO OPTIMIZE11	18,071,969	5913	51	0.946195
JPEG-NO OPTIMIZE12	13,702,370	5926	29	0.922539
JPEG-NO OPTIMIZE13	12,492,529	6028	24	0.912026
JPEG-NO OPTIMIZE14	12,018,149	6018	22	0.902617
JPEG-NO OPTIMIZE15	11,446,486	6135	20	0.899925

In this test, assuming that the quality desired is lower or equal than SSIM 0.8955097, a single setup will be chosen to compress: the WEBP10 setup with a quality of 3.

This is because it is the best setup among all both in terms of compression and output size. The final output size will be 4,688,350 bytes, and it will take 3158 ms. Therefore, there will not be a mix of two setups that will be able to do better.

5. Conclusions

In this paper, we first explore a framework (closely aligned with the one proposed in [1]) for determining the optimal selection of compression algorithms in order to achieve the best allocation of computing resources in large-scale data storage environments. This approach is experimentally validated through the lossless compression of one-dimensional and two-dimensional data. We then extended this technique for lossy compression, and we successfully tested it on the lossy compression of bidimensional data.

The results of our experiments demonstrate that the proposed framework is highly efficient for compressing large quantities of images within a specified time budget. Across all input scenarios, it was observed that, compared to a traditional strategy, the optimized compression approach, that is based on identifying an optimal combination of algorithms, effectively eliminated idle periods in the system. By doing so, it maximized the use of the allocated time budget, leading to more efficient processing.

The algorithm performed reliably with all types of images (both animated and non-animated), regardless of whether the scenes were similar or varied. Additionally, the algorithm was evaluated in scenarios where the time budget was set very close to the runtime of one of the two optimal compression algorithms. Even in these cases, the algorithm performed correctly, distributing files among the compressors to ensure that the entire time budget was utilized effectively.

However, a key challenge remains in calculating the metrics of individual algorithms. If we assume that this activity can be performed once for a document and then the metrics can be reused for all future similar documents, then the proposed framework remains highly effective. On the other hand, if metrics have to be recalculated for each new document, it will be necessary to develop a method to estimate them as quickly as possible, which warrants further investigation.

Future research will focus on extending the algorithm's experimentation to other types of digital data, such as medical or hyperspectral images (see [22,23]), or even to hybrid situations in which different types of digital data must be compressed together: sometimes using lossless compression, and at other times using lossy compression. The ability to handle a broad range of data types in an efficient and adaptive manner will be a valuable addition to this framework. In addition, as in [4], it could be interesting to study a mechanism that involves frequent sampling of the data stream to detect changes in its characteristics.

Funding: This work was partially supported by project SERICS (PE00000014) under the NRRP MUR program funded by the EU—NGEU.

Data Availability Statement: No new data were created or analyzed in this study. Data sharing is not applicable to this article.

Acknowledgments: The author wishes to thank his students Giuseppe Cantisani, Vincenzo Ceci, Francesco Foglia, Alfonso Guarino, Christian Iodice, Pasquale Priscio, Andrea Sessa, and Antonio Sfera who developed, at different times, preliminary versions of the software that was used for the experimental tests in this paper.

Conflicts of Interest: The author declares no conflict of interest.

ferences

Zohar, E.; Cassuto, Y. Data Compression Cost Optimization. In Proceedings of the Data Compression Conference (DCC 2015), Snowbird, UT, USA, 7–9 April 2015; pp. 393–402. [CrossRef]

Carpentieri, B. Data Compression in Massive Data Storage Systems. In Proceedings of the International Conference on Artificial Intelligence, Computer, Data Sciences and Applications (ACDSA 2024), Victoria, Seychelles, 1–2 February 2024; pp. 343–348.

Liao, K.; Moffat, A.; Petri, M.; Wirth, A. A Cost Model for Long-Term Compressed Data Retention. In Proceedings of the Tenth ACM International Conference on Web Search and Data Mining (WSDM '17), Hannover, Germany, 10–14 March 2017; pp. 241–249. [CrossRef]

Wiseman, Y.; Schwan, K.; Widener, P. Efficient End to End Data Exchange Using Configurable Compression. In Proceedings of the 24th IEEE Conference on Distributed Computing Systems (ICDCS 2004), Tokyo, Japan, 24–26 March 2004; pp. 228–235.

Ziv, J.; Lempel, A. A universal algorithm for sequential data compression. *IEEE Trans. Inf. Theory* **1977**, *23*, 337–343. [CrossRef]

Ziv, J.; Lempel, A. Compression of individual sequences via variable-rate coding. *IEEE Trans. Inf. Theory* **1978**, *24*, 530–536. [CrossRef]

Rizzo, F.; Storer, J.A.; Carpentieri, B. LZ-based image compression. *Inf. Sci.* **2001**, *135*, 107–122. [CrossRef]

Moffat, A. Huffman encoding. *ACM Comput. Surv.* **2019**, *52*, 85.

Witten, I.H.; Neal, R.M.; Cleary, J.G. Arithmetic coding for data compression. *Commun. ACM* **1987**, *30*, 520–540. [CrossRef]

Deutsch, P. *Rfc 1952: GZIP File Format Specification Version 4.3*; RFC Editor: Marina del Rey, CA, USA, 1996. [CrossRef]

Burrows, M.; Wheeler, D.J. *A Block–Sorting Lossless Data Compression Algorithm*; Research Report; Digital Systems Research Center: North Syracuse, NY, USA, 1994.

Roelofs, G.; Koman, R. *PNG: The Definitive Guide*; O'Reilly Media: Sebastopol, CA, USA, 1999.

Welch, T.A. A Technique for High-Performance Data Compression. *Computer* **1984**, *17*, 8–19. [CrossRef]

Weinberger, M.J.; Seroussi, G.; Sapiro, G. The LOCO-I lossless image compression algorithm: Principles and standardization into JPEG-LS. *IEEE Trans. Image Process.* **2000**, *9*, 1309–1324. [CrossRef] [PubMed]

Skodras, A.; Christopoulos, C.; Ebrahimi, T. The JPEG 2000 still image compression standard. *IEEE Signal Process. Mag.* **2001**, *18*, 36–58. [CrossRef]

Sharma, K.; Gupta, K. Lossless data compression techniques and their performance. In Proceedings of the 2017 International Conference on Computing, Communication and Automation (ICCCA), Greater Noida, India, 5–6 May 2017; pp. 256–261. [CrossRef]

Howard, P.G.; Vitter, J.S. Fast and efficient lossless image compression. In Proceedings of the DCC '93: Data Compression Conference, Snowbird, UT, USA, 30 March–1 April 1993; pp. 351–360. [CrossRef]

Saha, S. Image compression—From DCT to wavelets: A review. *XRDS Crossroads ACM Mag. Stud.* **2000**, *6*, 12–24. [CrossRef]

Wallace, G. The JPEG still picture compression standard. *IEEE Trans. Consum. Electron.* **1992**, *38*, 18–34. [CrossRef]

Ginesu, G.; Pintus, M.; Giusto, D.D. Objective assessment of the WebP image coding algorithm. *Signal Process. Image Commun.* **2012**, *27*, 867–874. [CrossRef]

Wang, Z.; Bovik, A.C.; Sheikh, H.R.; Simoncelli, E.P. Image Quality Assessment: From Error Visibility to Structural Similarity. *IEEE Trans. Image Process.* **2004**, *13*, 600–612. [CrossRef] [PubMed]

Pizzolante, R.; Carpentieri, B. Multiband and Lossless Compression of Hyperspectral Images. *Algorithms* **2016**, *9*, 16. [CrossRef]

Pizzolante, R.; Carpentieri, B. Lossless, low-complexity, compression of three-dimensional volumetric medical images via linear prediction. In Proceedings of the 18th International Conference on Digital Signal Processing (DSP 2013), Fira, Greece, 1–3 July 2013; pp. 1–6. [CrossRef]

algorithms

MDPI

Article

Control of High-Power Slip Ring Induction Generator Wind Turbines at Variable Wind Speeds in Optimal and Reliable Modes

Mircea-Bogdan Radac [1,*], Valentin-Dan Muller [2] and Samuel Ciucurită [3]

[1] Department of Automation and Applied Informatics, Politehnica University of Timisoara, 300223 Timisoara, Romania
[2] Department of Automation, Industrial Engineering, Textiles and Transport, "Aurel Vlaicu" University of Arad, 310330 Arad, Romania; valentin.muller@uav.ro
[3] Department of Electrical Engineering, Politehnica University of Timisoara, 300223 Timisoara, Romania; samuel.ciucurita@student.upt.ro
* Correspondence: mircea.radac@upt.ro

Abstract: This work analyzes high-power wind turbines (WTs) from the Oravita region, Romania. These WTs are based on slip ring induction generator with wound rotor and we propose a modified architecture with two power converters on both the stator and on the rotor, functioning at variable wind speeds spanning a large interval. Investigations developed around a realistic WT model with doubly fed induction generator show how WT control enables variable wind speed operations at optimal mechanical angular speed (MAS), guaranteeing maximal power point (MPP), but only up to a critical wind speed value, after which the electrical power must saturate for reliable operation. In this reliable operating region, blade pitch angle control must be enforced. Variable wind speed acts as a time-varying parameter disturbance but also imposes the MPP operation setpoint in one of the two analyzed regions. To achieve null tracking errors, a double integrator must appear within the MAS controller when the wind speed disturbance is realistically modeled as a ramp-like input; however, inspecting the linearized model reveals several difficulties as described in the paper, together with the proposed solution tradeoff. The study developed around the Fuhrlander-FL-MD-70 1.5[MW] WT model shows that several competitive controllers are designed and tested in the identified operating regions of interest, as they validate the reliable and performant functioning specifications.

Keywords: wind turbine; energy system; variable wind speed; control algorithm; mathematical model; slip ring induction generator; wound rotor; maximum power point; power converters; reliability

1. Introduction

This work analyzes functioning regimes for high-power wind turbines (WTs) with wound rotor induction generators, at large wind speed variations under the requirement of optimal operation at maximum power point (MPP). The wind speed value $V(t)$ is fundamental in this context, as it imposes the optimal mechanical angular speed (MAS), n_{OPTIM}, that ensures MPP operation for the WT.

To this day, WTs have developed a variety of types and sizes, some reaching up to 6 [MW] installed capacity and with blades diameters up to 150 [m]. Repurposed for either small area operations (even for personal locations used within islanded micro-grids) or for mass energy production in wind farms covering large areas (sometimes offshore), the

WTs capture and convert the wind energy to electric energy that is meant to be delivered to some electrical grid to which the WTs are connected. To this end, the main research topics revolve around modeling [1–5], control [6–9] and operation analysis [10–13].

On the power transformation pipeline, a series of energy transformations occur which must be optimized from an efficiency point of view by the designers/manufacturers [10–15]. In this respect, there are WTs with or without a reducer. In reducer-based ones with ratios beyond 1:100 with the generator having nominal MAS of about 3000 [rpm], power losses occur; however, the generator mass is small [16–20]. In those without a reducer mechanism, there are no additional power losses, but the generator mass must be carefully designed in order to work at such small MAS, while the materials needed for producing such a device have significantly higher costs (supermagnet alloys from neodymium, iron, boron—Nd2Fe14B) [21–23].

Modern WTs are equipped with blade pitch angle control systems; therefore, when the wind speeds are too high, the angle of attack of the blade is adapted to keep the MAS within safe bounds. The blade angle typically varies from 0 to 90 angular degrees, with the higher-end value being applied to stop the WT's rotor during violent windstorms. A blade pitch angle control system bases its feedback on anemometer measurements for wind speed and on the MAS (or the generated electrical power).

Remark 1. *Automatic blade pitch angle control also keeps the energy conversion in reliable condition by avoiding mechanical stress in the WT's tower structure, within bearing and within the transmission elements. Hence, it increases the WT lifespan and decreases the maintenance costs. It is due to this that the blades pitch angle β is based on three independent actuation systems powered by alternative energy sources.*

In the specialized literature, only induction generators with wound rotors having a single power converter in the rotor are generally analyzed (see works [10–13,17–20]). In this work, we analyze the induction generator with two power converters in both the stator and in the rotor. In the Oravita (Romania) region, there are six Fuhrlander FL-MD-70 WTs of 1.5 [MW] capacity, each equipped with an induction generator with a wound rotor [24]. In this case, by imposing the rotor voltage U_R, the optimal MAS can be tracked. The value U_R is intended to control the additional rotor resistance R_{ad}. The group of six WTs from Oravita work at wind speeds ranging from 3 up to 25 [m/s], then the MAS, depending linearly on the wind speed, should adapt within its own range at a ratio of about 3/25 = 1/8.3333 set by the wind speed variation. At this high wind speed variation, two power convertors are needed: one in the stator circuit controllable by the stator frequency f, which delivers the stator power P_{stator}, and a second converter for the rotor, which is responsible for the rotor delivered power P_{rotor} [25–27].

Remark 2. *The power converter from the rotor circuit changes the rotor resistance through the rotor voltage in a way that, apparently, an additional R_{ad} resistance is introduced.*

The wind speed variation is divided into two regions. The first one ranges within [3; 11] [m/s] and corresponds to small to medium wind speeds. The second one is [m/s] and corresponds to high wind speeds. In the first interval, the WT operates in MPP, with optimal MAS at the value n_{OPTIM}, with optimal stator frequency value f_{OPTIM} and with optimal rotor additional resistance $R_{ad-OPTIM}$. These values are realized by the stator power converter for f_{OPTIM} and by the rotor power converter for $R_{ad-OPTIM}$. In the second range, for limiting the electrical and mechanical stress within admissible bounds, under high wind speeds, both the WT power and MAS are saturated; the WT power is regulated through the blade pitch angle β, while the generator power is characterized by the stator working at constant frequency f and the rotor working at constant R_{ad} actuated by the rotor converter. In this regime, the generator power changes only subject to the MAS value n but it is the WT power characteristic selected as the controller quantity.

Remark 3. *In the first interval corresponding to small up to medium wind speeds, the blade pitch angle $\beta = 0$ is constant, while in the second interval, it is changed as it enters the active control role.*

Recent results on blade pitch angle control are analyzed from the literature. Improved WT operation under individual pitch control was proposed by the authors of [28]. A linear quadratic pitch angle controller was designed for a variable speed WT of 850 [kW] in [29]. Intelligent genetic algorithms were used to optimize the parameters of a PID for WT blade pitch controller in [30], while for WT load mitigation, individual pitch controllers were proposed by Han et al. in [31]. Comparisons of different metaheuristic optimizers were provided by the authors of [32] for the same blade pitch control problem. A similar optimal-based control approach is followed by [33] but for a doubly fed induction generator in WT, based on evolutionary algorithm. Machine learning is a novel approach dedicated to pitch angle control in WTs and was among the first reported in the work of [34,35]. Actuator faults were considered for improving the load mitigation in WTs through fault-tolerant pitch control by the authors of [36]. Yet another machine learning control, this time a reinforcement learning approach, was proposed for the same control problem in the work [37]. A wider and theoretically oriented work towards stability analysis under several controllers is proposed in [38]. Under large wind speed variation, which is also the topic of concern in this work, the pitch control was considered by Chen et al. in [39]. Adaptive control for improved tracking performance of WTs through blade pitch angle control is proposed by Zhou et al. in [40]. For offshore WTs, the control robustness issue under high wind and waves was considered and proven feasible by the authors of the work [41].

For variable speed wind turbine operation, the wind speed is the most important factor, as it is simultaneously a time-varying parameter in the dynamical model and also imposes the optimal MAS reference input value to ensure MPP tracking. On short time intervals lasting from several seconds to several tens of seconds, the wind speed can be accepted to follow a ramp-like temporal variation schedule. In effect, this also drives a ramp-like MAS reference input variation. The internal model principle in control requires a double integrator to ensure null steady state tracking error; however, the WT model analyzed in this work shows that this is not possible in the operating region where MAS control is required, so a tradeoff must be made. On the other hand, at higher wind speeds, corresponding to the operating region where the blade pitch angle is used to control the WT power, the linearized dynamics show that a double integrator is feasible and therefore implemented.

Different from the analyzed literature, this paper works out several distinct contributions. First, a real-world case study analysis is proposed, based on WT models operating in the Oravita region, Romania. Secondly, the high wind speed variation in continental locations forces the WTs to operate in different regions, aimed at either maximum operation efficiency (maximum power point) or at maximally reliable operation through saturation of the powers and MAS. This aspect is clearly analyzed in our work. Thirdly, with two identified operating regions corresponding to small wind speeds and large wind speeds, feasible control is proposed dedicated to improved tracking performance under disturbance rejection. For this, realistic ramp-like linear wind speed variation disturbances are considered and the possibility of reducing the steady-state errors in the controller variables of interest is investigated. Using a linearized model, we show that in the MPPT operation mode of the first analyzed region corresponding to smaller wind speeds, we cannot use a stabilizing double integrator within the MAS controller, as required by the internal model principle from control theory. The discussion and validation of control approaches in such a wide operating range of wind speed variation has not been tackled properly in the analyzed literature. Fourthly, we propose the original application of modern control algorithms and compare their performances. These algorithms are VRFT control, sliding-mode control and model predictive adaptive control (MPAC). Comparing the performances of such controllers requires careful design and preparation, which are discussed in detail herein. Last but not least, the use of an architecture with two power converters in the proposed combination of WT and doubly fed induction generator is a first proposal in the literature, aimed at maximizing energy capture over the entire wind speed operation range.

This paper discusses the mathematical model of the analyzed WT in Section 2, both in the blade power characteristic identification and in the complete characterization of the electric doubly fed induction generator and its associated stator and rotor converters. Section 3 is dedicated to the WT control in the operating region corresponding to low wind speeds and it is aimed at ensuring MPP operation. Section 4 aims for reliable WT control in the second operating region of interest corresponding to high wind speeds, where the MAS and the generator value must be saturated. Section 5 concludes the results and points out future research directions.

2. Mathematical Models of the WT and of the Doubly Fed Induction Generator

2.1. WT Mathematical Model and Parameters

The wind system control is focused on the main variables that define its functioning at the WT's MPP: the angular speed $n[\text{ rps}]$, which must track the optimal value n_{OPTIM}, and the stator current I_S, which must be constrained at the nominal value $I_N = 724.64$ [A] for the analyzed WT model. In the deep continental Oravita area, the wind speeds typically reach 25 [m/s] during summer windstorms. Here, the Fuhrlander FL-MD-70 WTs of 1.5 [MW] capacity is three-bladed with 70 [m] diameter and with an equivalent inertial moment of $J = 136\ [\text{kgm}^2]$. These WTs automatically start whenever the wind speed increases beyond 3 [m/s]. The WT is meant to function in dynamic regime at variable wind speeds [2–7]. Given the dynamical process [2–7], the kinetic moment equation is

$$J\frac{d\omega}{dt} = M_{TV} - M_{GE}, \tag{1}$$

where ω is the mechanical angular speed (MAS) at the electric generator's shaft, J is the equivalent moment of inertia, M_{TV} is the torque of the WT at the generator's shaft and M_{GE} is the electromagnetic torque of the generator's shaft. In terms of powers, the equivalence of the previous equation becomes

$$J\frac{d\omega}{dt}\omega = P_{TV} - P_{GE}, \tag{2}$$

with P_{TV} being the WT power and P_{GE} being the generator electromagnetic power. Expressing $\omega = 2\pi n = 6.28n$ and considering the inertial moment $J = 136\ [\text{kgm}^2]$, Equation (2) is particularized at $\overline{J} = 5369.1\ [\text{kgm}^2]$ as

$$\overline{J}\frac{dn}{dt}n = P_{TV} - P_{GE}. \tag{3}$$

The term P_{TV} in the previous equation generally depends on the wind speed and the MAS, while P_{GE} depends on the MAS, on the voltage and on the frequency of the generator's stator and rotor, respectively. When the WT is started, it is required to bring it to the maximum power point as soon as possible. After coupling the generator to the power grid by WT MAS control, the MPP should be tracked at all times. Up to a maximal wind speed value of $V_{MAX} = 10.788$ [m/s], P_{TV} can be absorbed by the generator functioning at nominal flux and current values on the stator. Beyond the mentioned wind speed value, the power captured by the generator will saturate from above.

The WT mathematical model (MM) is completely defined by the characteristic $P_{TV}(n, V, \beta)$ [1–5]. Based on data collected in the Oravita location, the $P_{TV}(n, V, \beta)$ characteristic was fitted to a widely used literature model, $P_{TV}(n, V, \beta, \theta) = aV^3 e^{-c\frac{V}{n}}(\frac{1}{2\pi}\frac{V}{n}e^{-d\beta} - b)$ with parameters $\theta = [a, b, c, d]$:

$$P_{TV}(n, V, \beta, \theta) = 5.692 \times 10^5 V^3 e^{-\frac{6.6041V}{n}} \left(0.15915\frac{V}{n}e^{-3.0303\times10^{-2}\times\beta} - 1.7488 \times 10^{-2}\right). \quad (4)$$

Generally, the parameters of the model P_{TV} can be identified in two steps. First, for $\beta = 0$, the main parameters a, b, c can be identified through nonlinear regression on (4) about the values n, V measured at the time points when $\frac{dn}{dt} = 0$ and using measured P_{GE}, for which it holds that $P_{TV} = P_{GE}$. This approach avoids knowing dn/dt, which is difficult to obtain in practice, as the sampling period is not sufficiently high. However, if dn/dt is available, then P_{TV} can be computed at any point in time, accepting a known measured P_{GE}.

Then, there are several solutions for finding parameter d. For example, when the WT works under no load, the stationary condition $P_{TV}(n, V, \beta) = 0$ leads to $\beta = d\ln\left(\frac{9.1005V}{n_{MAX}}\right)$, meaning that, by measuring the blade's pitch angle, the maximum MAS value n_{MAX}, at some wind speed value V, the coefficient d can be determined. This operation is not safe enough, as it lets the WT accelerate to high MAS values, which may damage the structure.

Another possibility is to increase wind speed until reaching the stationary condition $P_{TV} = P_{GE}$ for a constant and known value P_{GE}, again for a prior set value $\beta \neq 0$, from which, based on the above relationship (4), we find d. This approach is mostly impractical and should be performed in a wind tunnel with controllable wind speed.

Finally, if dn/dt is measured at any point in time, then from (4) and with the WT operating at $\beta \neq 0$, we could obtain all parameters from θ simultaneously, via nonlinear regression. A closeup of the P_{TV} curve for $V = 11$ [m/s] is revealed in Figure 1 where the MPP corresponds to an optimal MAS value. Although the power curve P_{TV} in Figure 1 is a classical one from the literature, its shape is instrumental in analyzing the dynamic optimal operation behavior. Unstable dynamics observed by linearization at the MPP will challenge how the MPP tracking performance will manifest in response to variable wind speed.

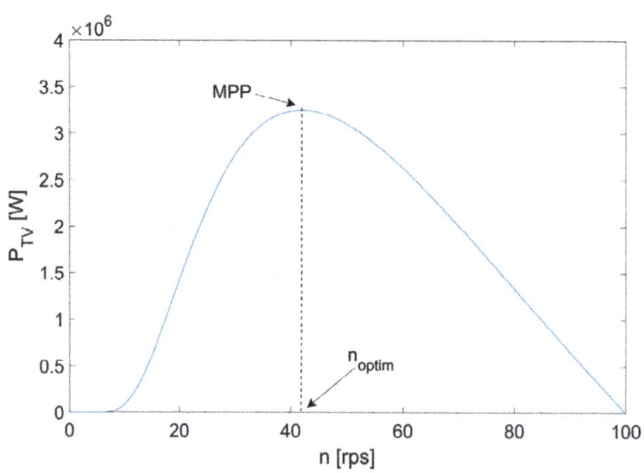

Figure 1. WT power characteristic $P_{TV}(n,\ V,\ \beta)$ plotted at $V = 11$ [m/s] for $\beta = 0$ [deg].

The above MM is critical for deducing optimal operation at various wind speeds [3–6]. For the WT to operate at MPP, the optimal MAS control is ensured by changing the load at the electric generator, based on wind speed variation [9–12]. We note another issue with adapting to quick wind speed variation due to the high mechanical inertia of the WT [18–22,42].

2.2. Mathematical Model of the Slip Ring Induction Generator

The Fuhrlander FL-MD-70 models have the following nominal data: equivalent moment of inertia $J = 136\ \left[\mathrm{kgm}^2\right]$, nominal power $P_N = P_{GE} = 1.5$ [MW], nominal voltage $U_N = 690$ [V], nominal current $I_N = 724.64$ [A], pole number equal to four ($2p_1 = 4$), nominal MAS $n_N = 1518.3$ [rpm], nominal slip $s_N = -1.2231 \times 10^{-2}$ [24].

The doubly fed slip ring induction wound rotor generator parameters are as follows [43]. The short circuit impedance $Z_{sc} = 0.1058$ [Ω], and the short circuit resistance is $R_{sc} = R_s + R_R = 4.7610 \times 10^{-2}$ [Ω], where $R_S = R_R = 2.3805 \times 10^{-2}$ [Ω] are the stator and rotor resistances, respectively. The short circuit nominal reactance is $X^n_{sc} = 0.10309$ [Ω] at 50 [Hz], which at different frequencies f becomes $X_{sc} = X^n_{sc} \cdot \frac{f}{50}[\Omega]$. At the stator voltage $\underline{U}_S$ ($\underline{o}$ means phasor notation for "o") and frequency f, the generator stator and rotor currents $\underline{I}_s, \underline{I}_R$ are (at negligible magnetization current)

$$\underline{I}_S = \frac{\underline{U}_S}{R_S + \frac{R_R}{s} + jX_{Sc}} = \frac{\underline{U}_S}{2.3805 \times 10^{-2} + \frac{2.3805 \times 10^{-2}}{s} + j\frac{0.10309f}{50}},$$
$$\underline{I}_R = -\frac{\underline{U}_S}{2.3805 \times 10^{-2} + \frac{2.3805 \times 10^{-2}}{s} + j\frac{0.10309f}{50}}. \quad (5)$$

where s is the slip at non-nominal operation. Note that the slip depends on the frequency f and MAS value n according to

$$s = \frac{n_1 - n}{n1} = \frac{\frac{f}{p_1} - n}{\frac{f}{p_1}} = \frac{\frac{f}{2} - n}{f/2} = \frac{f - 2n}{f} = 1 - \frac{2n}{f}, \quad (6)$$

The generator's nominal power at the shaft is equivalently expressed as

$$P_{GE} = 3\frac{p_1 U_S^2 (R_R/s)}{\left(R_S + \frac{R_R}{s}\right)^2 + (2.0618 \times 10^{-3})^2 f^2}, \quad (7)$$

where $2p_1$ is the number of poles.

With a single stator converter in the generator, wind energy can only be captured within a reduced wind speed domain. Thus, we propose an additional rotor converter within the architecture, which maximizes the wind energy capture over the full interval of wind speeds under which the WT operates. With a wound rotor, the rotor voltage $\underline{U}_R$ can be used to control the desired MAS as follows. Through a rotor converter, it is $\underline{U}_R$ that can change the rotor parameters R_R through an additional additive resistance defined as

$$R_{ad} = \underline{U}_R / \underline{I}_R. \quad (8)$$

Therefore, by proper adaptation of the rotor additional resistance R_{ad}, we can change $R_R + R_{ad}$, in turn modifying the equivalent generator's characteristic to make it depend on the wind speed value V. As a consequence, since R_{ad} will be more significant than R_R, the rotor electric power P_{rotor} injected into the grid will be approximated with

$$P_{rotor} = 3R_{ad}I_R^2. \quad (9)$$

Ultimately, it is the rotor converter that changes R_{ad} through $\underline{U}_R$, to result in P_{rotor}. At variable frequency, the asynchronous generator works at the constant stator flux value

$$\Psi = \frac{U_N}{\omega} = \frac{U_N}{2\pi f} = \frac{690}{2\pi 50} = 2.1963\ [\text{Wb}], \quad (10)$$

at which the "U/f" ratio in the stator becomes $\frac{U_s}{f} = \Psi \times 2\pi = 13.8$ [Vs], leading to the final generator power influenced by R_{ad} to be obtained as

$$P_{GE} = \frac{3 \times 13.8^2 \times (2.3805 \times 10^{-2} + R_{ad})/(1 - 2n/f)}{\left(\frac{2.3805\times10^{-2}+(2.3805\times10^{-2}+R_{ad})/(1-2n/f)}{f}\right)^2 + (2.0618 \times 10^{-3})^2}, \quad (11)$$

Remark 4. *With the generator operating at variable frequency, two limitations are imposed:*

(1) *The controlled stator flux has maximal value of* $\Psi = 2.1963$ [*Wb*].
(2) *The stator current* I_s *is saturated at nominal value* $I_N = 724.64$ [*A*].

The wind speed value used to discriminate between the two operating regions being analyzed is $V_{MAX} = 10.788$ [m/s] and was obtained by the nonlinear equation system formed with the conditions $P_{TV-MAX} = 2442.3V^3 = P_{GE}$, plus $I_S = I_N = 724.64$ [A], plus the nominal slip condition $1 - 2n/f = -1.2231 \times 10^{-2}$. Solving the above nonlinear equation leads to $f = 101.55$ [Hz], $n = 51.394$ [rps] and $V_{MAX} = 10.788$ [m/s]. The value V_{MAX} is a threshold between the two operating regions in our work.

Notice that the power converters and the generator have their own internal transient dynamics; however, the time scale is much faster than that of the WT control, so static relationships in terms of current, voltage and power are acceptable.

We briefly underline some critical analysis between induction generators and permanent magnet synchronous ones. Induction generators (with slip rings) have the following advantages. (1) They do not have permanent magnets (PMs), so there will not be failures when the PM demagnetizes. (2) They are generally cheaper compared to synchronous generators with PM. (3) They can very easily switch to motor mode when a quick start of the turbine is desired. Several disadvantages of the induction generators: (1) They cannot provide reactive power. (2) They absorb reactive power from the grid in order to operate.

Synchronous generators with PM have the following advantages. (1) They can provide reactive power. (2) They can operate without voltage from the grid. Some disadvantages include the following. (1) When the PM demagnetizes, they can no longer operate. (2) They require more complex power electronics converters, which may increase the cost and complexity of the system.

3. Wind System Control at Variable Wind Speeds from 3 [m/s] up to V_{MAX} [m/s]

With the determined mathematical model of the WT, there are two operation ranges (ORs) under consideration that depend on the wind speed value. The first OR—named OR1—is for $3 \leq V(t) \leq V_{MAX} = 10.788$ [m/s], where the wind power from the WT can still be captured at the generator that works at nominal stator flux and stator current values. Here, the control objective is to regulate the MAS n to the value n_{OPTIM}, where the latter depends linearly on the wind speed value $V(t)$. This control is achievable through the generator frequency f. The second OR—called OR2—is for $V_{MAX} \leq V(t) \leq 21$ [m/s], where the operation forces the generator power to saturate and the objective is to regulate P_{TV} through the blade pitch angle β, which will be analyzed later.

For wind speeds up to the value V_{MAX}, the MPP must ensure **optimal operation** for the wind system based on the following equations that define the mechanical Equation (3), considered for the case $\beta = 0$ specific to OR1:

$$
\begin{aligned}
P_{TVMAX}(V) &= 2442.3V^3, \\
P_{GE} &= -\frac{571.32 \times \frac{\left(2.3805 \cdot 10^{-2} + R_{ad}\right)}{1-\frac{2n}{f}}}{\left(\frac{2.3805 \cdot 10^{-2} + \frac{\left(2.3805 \cdot 10^{-2} + R_{ad}\right)}{1-\frac{2n}{f}}}{f}\right)^2 + \left(2.0618 \cdot 10^{-3}\right)^2}, \\
I_N &= 724.64 \\
&= \frac{13.8}{\sqrt{\left(\frac{2.3805 \cdot 10^{-2} + \frac{\left(2.3805 \cdot 10^{-2} + R_{ad}\right)}{1-\frac{2n}{f}}}{f}\right)^2 + \left(2.0618 \cdot 10^{-3}\right)^2}}, \\
P_{TV}(n, V) &= 5.692 \times 10^5 V^3 e^{-\frac{6.6041V}{n}} \left(0.15915\frac{V}{n} - 1.7488 \times 10^{-2}\right)
\end{aligned}
\quad (12)
$$

where $P_{TVMAX}(V)$ is obtained from the MPP on the $P_{TV}(n, V)$ characteristic, at which point the optimal MAS setpoint is $n = n_{OPTIM} = 3.8269 \times V$.

Using the converter block displaced between the generator and the electrical grid, the optimal values of the stator frequency and of the additional rotor resistance f_{OPTIM} and $R_{ad-OPTIM}$ are realized, respectively. From the prescribed ratio "U/f", the stator voltage U_S follows immediately, with a value that makes the flux constant. The generator's electrical power P_{GE} injected to the grid is the summed effect of the stator and rotor powers, that is, $P_{GE} = Pstator + Protor$ (see Figure 2).

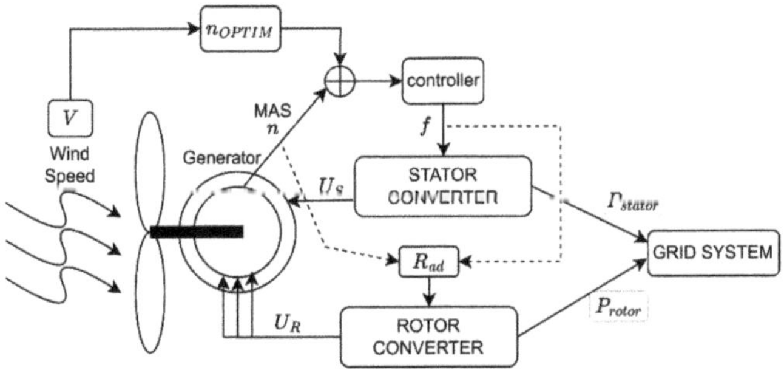

Figure 2. The wind system control architecture at WT's maximum power point. The doubly fed induction generator has the stator and rotor voltages controlled by converters.

From a control analysis perspective, the stator current needs to flow at the nominal value $I_N = 724.64$ [A] and the MAS n must track the optimal value n_{OPTIM}. To smartly decouple the control problem, we extract the solution for R_{ad} that ensures $I_S = I_N$ from the previous equation, which results in R_{ad} as a function of n and V:

$$
\begin{aligned}
R_{ad}(n, V) &= R_{ad-OPTIM}(n, V) \\
&= \left(\tfrac{2}{f}n - 1\right)\left(1.8932 \times 10^{-2} f - \frac{2.3805 \times 10^{-2}}{\frac{2}{f}n - 1}\right) \\
&\quad + 2.3805 \times 10^{-2},
\end{aligned}
\quad (13)
$$

Then, the remaining control objective concerns the control of the MAS value n seen as the controlled output, through the stator frequency f seen as the control input. With the resulting values f, n, the $R_{ad-OPTIM}$ above ensures nominal stator current value.

3.1. Linearized System Analysis and Control

Equation (3) is transformed to a more common shape under the assumption $\beta = 0$, as in

$$\frac{dn}{dt} = \frac{1}{Jn}(P_{TV}(n, V) - P_{GE}(n, f)). \tag{14}$$

Define n to be a state variable and further rewrite the state space model

$$\begin{aligned} \tfrac{dn(t)}{dt} &= g(n(t), f(t), V(t)), \\ y(t) &= h(n(t), f(t), V(t)) = n(t), \end{aligned} \tag{15}$$

where $g(.)$ is the state equation and $h(.)$ is the output equation. A small signal analysis around a constant operating point is next performed. Let this point be $\mathcal{P}(V_0, n_0, f_0)$. Using the first order linearization around $\mathcal{P}$, we can write

$$\begin{aligned} \tfrac{d\Delta n(t)}{dt} &= \nabla_n g|_{V_0,n_0,f_0}\Delta n + \nabla_f g\Big|_{V_0,n_0,f_0}\Delta f + \nabla_V g|_{V_0,n_0,f_0}\Delta V, \\ \Delta y(t) &= \nabla_n h|_{V_0,n_0,f_0}\Delta n + \nabla_f h\Big|_{V_0,n_0,f_0}\Delta f + \nabla_V h|_{V_0,n_0,f_0}\Delta V = \Delta n(t), \end{aligned} \tag{16}$$

where we denote with ∇ the Jacobian of the functions g, h with respect to their arguments at the operating point $\mathcal{P}(V_0, n_0, f_0)$ and Δ means the small variation of the argument about the linearization value. Subsequently, the variation notation with Δ will be discarded and we use only absolute notation f, V, n. The variables' roles are as follows. f is the control input, V is the disturbance input, n is the control output. In the Laplace transform domain of the variable "s", the following transfer functions result: $H_{f\to n}(s) = K_f/(1 + sT)$ and $H_{V\to n}(s) = K_v/(1 + sT)$.

Remark 5. *Linearization around several points $\mathcal{P}(V_0,\ n_0,\ f_0)$ reveals crucial observations that have critical impact upon the control design. We classify two main cases:*

Case 1. When linearization is performed at the MPP by imposing the operating point constraint $n_0 = 3.8269f_0$, we obtain that $K_f > 0, K_v < 0$ and $T < 0$.

Case 2. When the linearization is performed at arbitrary point $\mathcal{P}(V_0, n_0, f_0)$, we observe the following. (a) When $n_0 > 3.8269f_0$ (operation to the right of the MPPT on the P_{TV} curve), we have $K_f < 0, K_v > 0$ and $T > 0$, making for an open-loop stable transfer function; (b) when $n_0 < 3.8269f_0$ (operation to the left of the MPPT on the P_{TV} curve), we have $K_f > 0, K_v < 0$ and $T < 0$, making for an open-loop unstable transfer function.

With the nonlinear process as the one in (12), there are several tradeoffs to be accounted for, when linear control is to be used: robustness under the time varying process nature, stability and performance. When operating at variable wind speeds, the design choices become more stringent. For a reasonable ramp-like variation of the wind speed value $V(t)$, a double integrator should be included in the controller (according to the internal model principle); however, this reduces the stability margin. Two options are considered:

Option (1) The feedback controller is a proportional–integral (PI) controller with the transfer function $C(s) = (p_1s + p_0)/s$. With the closed-loop transfer function from MAS setpoint, the controlled MAS is $(K_fp_1s + K_fp_0)/(Ts^2 + (1 + K_fp_1)s + K_f\,p_0)$ with the characteristic polynomial of the closed loop being $Ts^2 + (1 + K_fp_1)s + K_f\,p_0$, which allows for flexible and robust design. However, there will be nonzero steady state tracking error with respect to ramp-like disturbance $V(t)$ as well as for ramp-like MAS reference input imposed by $V(t)$ via linear dependence, based on the MPP principle. For both Case 1 and Case 2b in Remark 5, there exist negative values of $p_1 < 0, p_0 < 0$ that will make the closed loop stable. For Case 2a in Remark 5, again, a suitable combination of p_1, p_0 can be found to stabilize the closed loop.

Option (2) The feedback controller is a double integrator with transfer function $C(s) = (p_1 s + p_0)/s^2$. The closed-loop characteristic polynomial will be $Ts^3 + s^2 + K_f p_1 s + K_f p_0$ which may still offer stability for proper choice of p_1, p_0, but stability margin is significantly smaller. In this case, since the coefficient of s^2 is 1, then for $T < 0$ (Cases 1 and 2b from Remark 5), it will be impossible to make a stable closed loop by any selection of p_1, p_0. We conclude that a double integrator is not feasible to be designed at the MPP; however, it may be designed at a suboptimal operating point such as in Case 2a in Remark 5.

We consider a reasonable ramp-like variation for the wind speed as in $V(t) = 2.0071 \times 10^{-3}t + 3$, starting from $V(0) = 3\ [\frac{\text{m}}{\text{s}}]$ and up to the value V_{MAX}. After extensive testing with selected pair values (p_1, p_0) that make the closed loop stable around the linearization point, when testing in dynamic regime for the ramp-like $V(t)$, only marginally stable control is achieved. This motivates the selection of the plain PI control algorithm revealed under Option 1, which will drive the control to be stable, fast and with acceptable steady state tracking error. For the operating point characterized by $\mathcal{P}(V_0 = 4\ [\text{m/s}], n_0 = 15.30\ [\text{rps}], f_0 = 0.953\ [\text{Hz}])$, we select $p_1 = -10,\ p_0 = -30$ as the PI controller gain parameters leading to $C_{PI}(s) = -(10s + 30)/s$.

3.2. A Competitive Linear VRFT Controller for Nonlinear Control

For comparison, we design a competitive PI controller algorithm based on the VRFT principle [44–49] which was proposed for automated tuning based on (but not limited to) reference model specification. For data collection, we fix the wind speed value $V = 5$ [m/s] and use a pre-stabilizing feedback controller with transfer function $-20 - 0.2/s$ applied to the closed-loop error $e(t) = n_{ref}(t) - n(t)$. Here, $11 \leq n_{ref} \leq 20$ [rps] is generated as piece-wise constant uniform random samples with periodic switching at 3 [s] additionally filtered with a lowpass second-order filter with function $1/(s^2 + 2s + 1)$. The control input f is saturated below at zero and it is further excited with a wide power spectrum uniform random noise with amplitude in $[-4; 4]$ with period 0.1 [s]. The collected input f and controlled output n are recorded at a sampling period of $T_s = 0.05$ [s] and are shown in Figure 3. The tuned PI controller is to be implemented in discrete time; thus, it is parameterized as $C_{PI}^{VRFT}(q) = (p_0 + p_1 q^{-1})/(1 - q^{-1})$. Here, q is the discrete-time single step forward operator, analogous to the z operator.

The reference model for setting up the desired behavior from n_{ref} to n in closed loop is picked as $M(s) = 10^2/(s^2 + 2 \cdot 0.9 \cdot 10 \cdot s + 10^2)$ and discretized accordingly at $T_s = 0.05$ [s], to reach $M(q)$ discrete-time representation. Let the dataset of input–output samples be $DS = \{f_k, n_k\}$ with sample index $1 \leq k \leq N$, where in our case study, we measured $N = 4000$ sample points. A discrete-time VRFT prefilter is a common option for filtering the virtual feedback error defined as $e_k^v = M^{-1}(q)n_k - n_k$ and also for filtering f_k. This prefilter used in our case is set to $0.8/(1 - 0.2q^{-1})$ with sampled period T_s. The loss function to be minimized is $L_{VRFT} = 1/N\sum_{k=1}^{N}(f_k - C_{PI}^{VRFT}(q)e_k^v)^2$. The resulting identified controller is $C_{PI}^{VRFT}(q) = (-4.0534 + 0.6495q^{-1})/(1 - q^{-1})$.

Comparative control results obtained with $C_{PI}(s)$ and $C_{PI}^{VRFT}(s)$ (the latter being implemented in discrete time) are offered in Figure 4. Note that in the testing phase, $V(t) = 3 + 2.0071 \times 10^{-3}t$, and it acts, as a parametric disturbance on the model P_{TV} but also imposes the setpoint as $n_{ref} = n_{OPTIM} = 3.8269 \times V$. Initial conditions for the test scenario are set as $f_0 = 0.953$ [Hz], $n_0 = 11.481$ [rps].

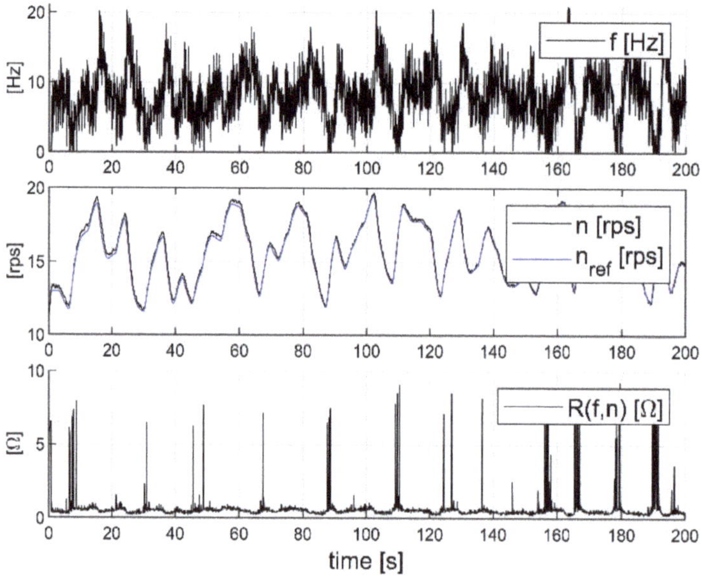

Figure 3. The closed-loop collected data for VRFT PI controller design in the exploration phase. In the bottom subplot, the value of the additional resistance $R_{ad}(n, f)$ from (13) affects both P_{GE} and I_N and it is plotted for informative purposes.

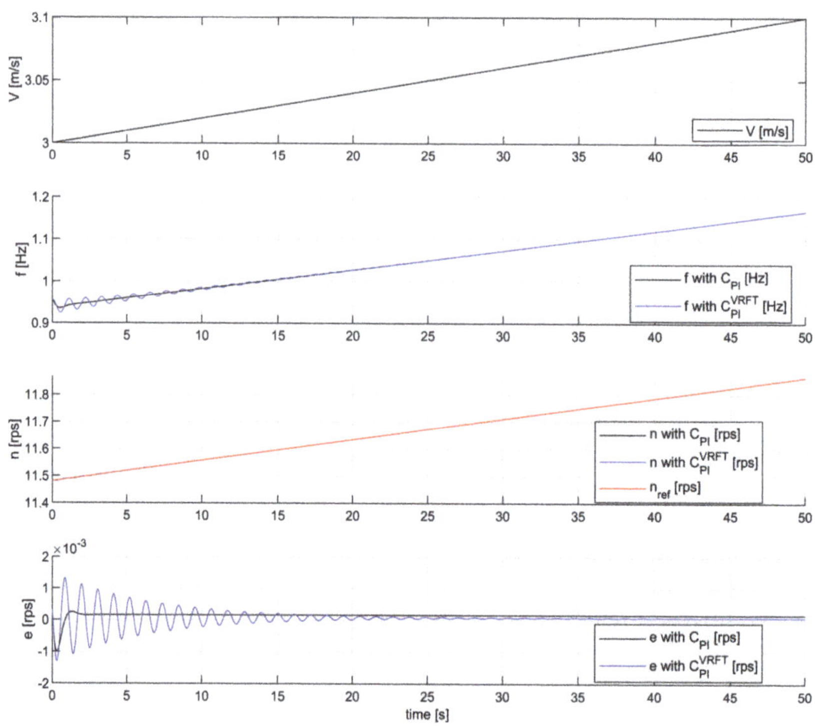

Figure 4. The closed-loop testing with $C_{PI}(s)$ and $C_{PI}^{VRFT}(q)$ in the operating region OR1.

We observe the following. Acceptable tracking control is obtained with respect to n_{ref} and relatively small steady-state errors are visible with respect to the ramp-like $V(t)$. We stress that the underlying process is nonlinear time-varying due to the parameter $V(t)$ acting as disturbance but also imposing the MPP operation via n_{OPTIM}. Surprisingly, given the oscillatory nature of the transient response obtained with the VRFT-trained PI controller, it shows a reduced steady-state tracking error under time-varying $V(t)$, when compared with the simple PI controller.

Regarding the sensitivity of the design with respect to the parameter's choice, the VRFT controller seemed very sensitive to the choice of the reference model bandwidth. There may be several reasons for it, namely the linear VRFT formulation needing to cope with the nonlinear system, although the collected data span quite a wide range near the operating point, thus not perfectly fitting a linear process model description. We underline that the data collection is performed on the nonlinear model, although the linearity assumptions about the method were enforced. Secondly, the time-varying nature of the process due to the wind speed value is another important factor affecting the hypothesis.

On the other hand, the linear PI controller has fewer design parameters, namely the proportional and integrator gains, and we could observe larger domain of values under which the closed loop was stable. We aimed for two criteria, in this order: (1) fast transient response, and (2) as small as possible steady-state error with respect to the ramp-like wind speed variation. The PI controller served as a baseline for performance, while the VRFT one was tuned (via the method hyperparameters) to outperform this behavior. The achieved compromise for a stable design was met by smaller steady-state tracking errors, with larger oscillations in the initial transients.

4. Wind System Control at Variable Wind Speeds from V_{MAX} [m/s] up to 21 [m/s]

In the region OR2 where $V_{MAX} \leq V(t) \leq 21$ [m/s], the **reliable** WT operation requires the generator power to saturate, and the objective is to regulate P_{TV} via the blade pitch angle β. The control process unfolds as follows. Firstly, the values of f and R_{ad} are calculated at V_{MAX}, assuming constant steady state optimal MPP operation. In this case, the optimal MAS will be $n_{OPTIM} = 3.8269 \times V_{MAX} = 3.8269 \times 10.788 = 41.285$ [rps]. Two conditions are used to saturate the generator power, namely $P_{GE} = 1.5 \times 10^6$ [W] and $I_S = I_N = 724.64$ [A]. The following nonlinear system of equations:

$$\begin{aligned} P_{GE} &= -\frac{571.32 \times \frac{\left(2.3805 \cdot 10^{-2} + R\right)}{1 - \frac{2n}{f}}}{\left(\frac{2.3805 \cdot 10^{-2} + \frac{\left(2.3805 \cdot 10^{-2} + R\right)}{1 - \frac{2n}{f}}}{f}\right)^2 + \left(2.0618 \cdot 10^{-3}\right)^2}, \\ I_N = 724.64 &= \frac{13.8}{\sqrt{\left(\frac{2.3805 \cdot 10^{-2} + \frac{\left(2.3805 \cdot 10^{-2} + R\right)}{1 - \frac{2n}{f}}}{f}\right)^2 + \left(2.0618 \cdot 10^{-3}\right)^2}}, \end{aligned} \tag{17}$$

is used for the value $n = n_{OPTIM} = 41.285$ [rps] to solve for stator frequency $f^* = 49.038$ [Hz] and for the additional rotor resistance $R_{ad-OPTIM} = 0.6273$ [Ω] that saturate P_{GE} to the maximal value of 1.5 [MW]. Under this consideration, with fixed values for $f = f^*$ and $R_{ad} =$

$R_{ad-OPTIM}$, we are left with $P_{GE} = \frac{371.99}{\left[\left(\frac{1.3278 \cdot 10^{-2}}{4.0785 \times 10^{-2} n - 1} - 4.8544 \times 10^{-4}\right)^2 + 4.251 \times 10^{-6}\right](4.0785 \times 10^{-2} n - 1)}$, which only depends on the MAS value n. The dynamical system is now

$$\begin{aligned} \frac{dn}{dt} &= \frac{1}{Jn}(P_{TV}(n, V, \beta) - P_{GE}(n)), \\ P_{TV}(n, V, \beta) &= 5.692 \times 10^5 V^3 e^{-\frac{6.6041V}{n}} \left(0.15915 \frac{V}{n} e^{-3.0303 \times 10^{-2} \times \beta} - 1.7488 \times 10^{-2}\right), \\ P_{GE} &= \frac{371.99}{\left[\left(\frac{1.3278 \cdot 10^{-2}}{4.0785 \times 10^{-2} n - 1} - 4.8544 \times 10^{-4}\right)^2 + 4.251 \times 10^{-6}\right](4.0785 \times 10^{-2} n - 1)}, \end{aligned} \tag{18}$$

which is ready to be used for control purposes. Next, the control analysis and design are attempted within region OR2.

4.1. Linearized System Analysis and Control

We bring the dynamical system (18) again to a controllable object form where

$$\begin{aligned} \frac{dn(t)}{dt} &= g(n(t), V(t), \beta(t)), \\ y(t) &= h(n(t), V(t), \beta(t)) = P_{TV}(n, V, \beta), \end{aligned} \tag{19}$$

and now the control objective is to regulate P_{TV} at the setpoint $P^*_{TV} = 1.5$ [MW] using the blade pitch angle $\beta(t)$ as the control input variable. Let us consider again a linearization point $\mathcal{P}(V_0 = V_{MAX}, n_0 = 3.8269 \times V_0, \beta_0 = 0)$ to reflect operation near the MPP. Using the first-order linearization around $\mathcal{P}$, we can write

$$\begin{aligned} \frac{d\Delta n(t)}{dt} &= \left.\frac{dg}{dn}\right|_{V_0, n_0, \beta_0} \Delta n + \left.\frac{dg}{df}\right|_{V_0, n_0, \beta_0} \Delta\beta + \left.\frac{dg}{dV}\right|_{V_0, n_0, \beta_0} \Delta V, \\ \Delta y(t) &= \left.\frac{dh}{dn}\right|_{V_0, n_0, \beta_0} \Delta n + \left.\frac{dh}{df}\right|_{V_0, n_0, \beta_0} \Delta\beta + \left.\frac{dh}{dV}\right|_{V_0, n_0, \beta_0} \Delta V = \Delta n(t), \end{aligned} \tag{20}$$

where we obtain the Jacobian of the functions g, h with respect to their arguments at the operating point $\mathcal{P}(V_0, n_0, \beta_0)$ and Δ means the small variation of the argument about the linearization value. The transfer functions that result are $H_{\beta \to P_{TV}}(s) = -1.603 \times 10^5$ $(1.70716s + 1)/(1.70719s + 1)$ and $H_{V \to P_{TV}}(s) = 8.527 \times 10^5 (1.70716s + 1)/(1.70719s + 1)$. Notice that the numerator and denominator time constants are only slightly different in both cases; therefore, pole-zero cancellation is safely employed, which means that in the linearized model, we write $P_{TV}(s) = k_\beta \beta(s) + k_V V(s)$, which renders the process a static one. Of course, the underlying system is nonlinear time-varying and the values k_β, k_V will change with the operating point.

The role of $V(t)$ will be important, since it will be modeled as a ramp-like disturbance. This time, different from OR1, the control goal will not be MPP tracking (which adapts n_{OPTIM} based on V) but the WT operation imposed by regulating P_{TV} at the setpoint of $P^*_{TV}(t) = 1.5$ [MW]. In this context, the control must be designed so as to deliver both reference tracking and disturbance rejection. With the underlying analyzed process transfer function, a straightforward option is to use a double integrator feedback controller on the feedback error $e(t) = P^*_{TV}(t) - P_{TV}(t)$, namely $C(s) = (p_1 s + p_0)/s^2$.

4.2. A Nonlinear Sliding Mode Controller

For a sliding mode control algorithm design [50–52], the dynamical system (18), (19) is transformed to input affine form. First, let

$$\dot{y}(t) = \nabla_n h \cdot \dot{n} + \nabla_V h \cdot \dot{V} + \nabla_\beta \dot{\beta}, \tag{21}$$

with $\nabla_n h = \frac{dh(n,V,\beta)}{dn}$, $\nabla_V h = \frac{dh(n,V,\beta)}{dV}$, $\nabla_\beta h = \frac{dh(n,V,\beta)}{d\beta}$ and let us augment the dynamical system with the integrator $\dot{\beta} = u$. Then, use the MAS equation $\dot{n} = \frac{1}{Jn}(y - P_{GE}(n))$ to further arrive at

$$\begin{aligned}\dot{y} &= \tfrac{\nabla_n h}{Jn} y + \nabla_\beta h \cdot u + \nabla_V h \cdot V - \tfrac{\nabla_n h}{Jn} P_{GE} \\ &:= \varphi(n, V, \beta) \cdot y + B(n, V, \beta) \cdot u + \sigma(n, V, \beta),\end{aligned} \tag{22}$$

where $\varphi(n, V, \beta) := \frac{\nabla_n h}{Jn}$ is the output multiplicative factor in the output differential equation, $B(n, V, \beta) := \nabla_\beta h$ is the input multiplicative factor and $\sigma(n, V, \beta) := \nabla_V h \cdot V - \frac{\nabla_n h}{Jn} \cdot P_{GE}(n)$ is the uncertainty factor.

Assumption 1. *The input multiplicative factor $B(n, V, \beta)$ and its reciprocal $1/B(n, V, \beta)$ are well defined within the entire operating region OR2.*

Assumption 2. *The uncertainty factor $\sigma(n, V, \beta)$ is bounded within the operating region OR2. Let this bound $\overline{\sigma}$ satisfy $|\sigma| < \overline{\sigma}$.*

Remark 6. *Normally, the uncertainty term σ is partially measurable since its expression is well defined and all arguments n, V, β are measurable. However, original model uncertainty, parameter aging and unmodeled dynamics will be lumped inside this term altogether. Take, e.g., $\varphi + \hat{\varphi}$ and $B + \hat{B}$ as additive uncertainties about nominal values φ, B, then $\hat{\varphi} y + \hat{B} u$ could easily be lumped inside σ. Both Assumption 1 and Assumption 2 are very reasonable and hold for quite wide operating conditions.*

Let the following controller be used:

$$u = B^{-1}\left(\dot{y}^* - \varphi y\right) - B^{-1} K sgn(g), \tag{23}$$

where $g := e$ is the switching variable, which is also the control error $e = y - y^*$ for $y^* = P^*_{TV}$, a reference input. In the proposed control law, $K > 0$ is a design gain. The factor $B^{-1}\left(\dot{y}^* - \varphi y\right)$ is the equivalent control component and $B^{-1} K sgn(g)$ is called the switching component. The most direct stability analysis can be formalized with the next theorem.

Theorem 1. *The control system obtained by the output Equation (22) coupled with controller (23) is stable for $K > \overline{\sigma}$.*

Proof of Theorem 1. Substitute u from (23) in (22) and we obtain $\dot{y} = \dot{y}^* - K sgn(g) + \sigma$, which is equivalent to $\dot{g} = -K sgn(g) + \sigma$.
Define the Lyapunov function $V(g) = 0.5 g^2$ and calculate $\dot{V} = g\dot{g}$.
Case (1) When $g > 0$, $sgn(g) = 1$ and $\dot{g} = -K + \sigma \leq -K + \overline{\sigma} < 0$, which makes $\dot{V} = g\dot{g} < 0$.
Case (2) When $g < 0$, $sgn(g) = -1$ and $\dot{g} = K + \sigma \geq K - \overline{\sigma} > 0$, which makes $\dot{V} = g\dot{g} < 0$.
Based on the two cases above, from the fact that $g := e$ and $e = y - y^*$ depends on bounded y^* and on y, the control system is Lyapunov-stable with bounded y. □

Remark 7. *The upper bound $\overline{\sigma}$ may be estimated more or less accurately in practice. It is customary to choose a large enough $K > \overline{\sigma}$ to allow for a safe robustness margin. The advantage with respect to the linear double integral controller is the stability certification.*

Remark 8. *Although the proposed control draws inspiration from the sliding mode method, it is seen as a particular type of sliding mode, as explained next. For one, the equivalent control component $B^{-1}(\dot{y}^* - \varphi y)$ found within the control law, does not compensate for some nominal value σ of the uncertainty. In other words, the equivalent control $B^{-1}(\dot{y}^* - \varphi y)$ is constructed for an equivalent null uncertainty. As a consequence, it will make the control forever chatter in a limited bandwidth around $g = 0$, to be analyzed next. Secondarily, the sliding motion is missing, i.e., the proposed controller consists only of the reaching phase, as it follows from the definition of $g := e$. This way, the control may be seen as a discontinuous switching one, where the factor $-B^{-1}Ksgn(g)$ is introduced exactly to compensate for the uncertainty. The control is thus formulated directly as a tracking objective. We can gain deeper insight into the control behavior as follows.*

First, notice that $\dot{V} = g\dot{g} = g(-Ksgn(g) + \sigma) = -K|g| + g\sigma$. Since $|g\sigma| \le |g|\,\overline{\sigma}$, we find that $\dot{V} \le -K|g| + \overline{\sigma}|g| = (-K + \overline{\sigma})\,|g|$, which makes $\dot{V} < 0$ bounded away from zero for all $g \neq 0$ and $K > \overline{\sigma}$. When $g = 0$, we notice that $\dot{g} = \sigma \neq 0$, which means that the surface $g = 0$ is not invariant and the trajectory will bounce back to a vicinity of $g = 0$ from where the switching component will again push it towards $g = 0$. This will make the system permanently chatter around $g = e = 0$, and therefore, y will oscillate around y^* within an acceptable boundary layer. Also, a finite reaching time of $g = 0$, starting from an initial condition $g(t_0)$, is measured (by integration) to be less than $\frac{|g(t_0)|}{K-\overline{\sigma}}$.

When the control implementation is digitalized, the sampling delay introduces chattering irrespective of how is K selected about $\overline{\sigma}$. With existing smooth implementations of the switching function $sgn(.)$, chattering is reduced but not completely removed. Generally, a good practical compromise can be achieved for proper selection of K , and we note that there exists a major advantage, since σ is considered completely unknown; hence, it does not require recalculation for it to be compensated. Should a reliable estimate of σ be plugged in (23), a smaller K will reduce the chattering further.

4.3. A Model Predictive Adaptive Controller

A model predictive adaptive controller (MPAC) is next designed [53–59], starting from the linearized model $P_{TV}(s) = k_\beta \beta(s) + k_V V(s)$. The design is carried out with respect to the input channel β, thus ignoring the effect of V directly; however, for model uncertainty and disturbance rejections, we augment the control input channel with an integrator. Hence, the augmented model for MPAC design becomes $P_{TV}(s) = \frac{k_\beta}{s}\,\beta'(s)$, with β' the control input derivative. We discretize the model using the zero-order hold method and arrive at

$$P_{TV,k} = P_{TV,k-1} + k_\beta T_s \beta'{}_k = P_{TV,k-1} + k_d \beta'_k, \tag{24}$$

which incorporates the sampling period T_s. Let the output predictors $\hat{P}_{TV,k+i}, i = 1, \ldots, N$ be unfolded over time as

$$\begin{pmatrix} \hat{P}_{TV,k+1} \\ \hat{P}_{TV,k+2} \\ \vdots \\ \hat{P}_{TV,k+N} \end{pmatrix} = \begin{pmatrix} P_{TV,k} \\ P_{TV,k} \\ \vdots \\ P_{TV,k} \end{pmatrix} + \begin{pmatrix} k_d & 0 & \ldots & 0 \\ k_d & k_d & \ldots & 0 \\ \vdots & \vdots & \ddots & \vdots \\ k_d & k_d & \ldots & k_d \end{pmatrix} \begin{pmatrix} \beta'_k \\ \beta'_{k+1} \\ \vdots \\ \beta'_{k+N-1} \end{pmatrix} \leftrightarrow \hat{\mathrm{P}}_{\mathrm{TV}} = \Psi + PB, \tag{25}$$

where the $\hat{P}_{TV}$ vector stacks the future outputs, the Ψ vector is the current state context and $B = \left[\beta'_k, \ldots, \beta_{k+N-1'}\right]^T$ stacks the present and future control input derivatives, P is the input predictor matrix. Define the receding horizon cost

$$J(k) = \sum_{i=1}^{N} \left(r_{k+i} - \hat{P}_{TV,k+i}\right)^2 + \lambda\left(\beta'_{k+i-1}\right)^2 = \left(R - \hat{P}_{TV}\right)^T \left(R - \hat{P}_{TV}\right) + \lambda B^T B, \tag{26}$$

where $R = [r_{k+1}, \ldots, r_{k+N}]^T$ stacks the future reference inputs and λ is a control energy/effort penalty. The cost is written as $J(k) = B^T(P^TP + \lambda I)B - 2M^TPB + M^TM$ with $M = R - \Psi$ and I the identity matrix of appropriate size. Define the inequality type constraints $\beta_{min} \leq \beta'_{k+i} < \beta_{max}, i = 1, \ldots N-1$ and rewrite in matrix form as

$$\begin{pmatrix} I \\ -I \end{pmatrix} B \leq \begin{pmatrix} B_{max} \\ -B_{min} \end{pmatrix}, \tag{27}$$

where $B_{max} = [\beta_{max}, \ldots, \beta_{max}]^T \in \mathbb{R}^N, B_{min} = [\beta_{min}, \ldots, \beta_{min}]^T \in \mathbb{R}^N$ capture the upper and lower bound constraints on the control input derivative, in linear form. A more compact form of the linear constraints in the input is $AB \leq N,\ A = \begin{pmatrix} I \\ -I \end{pmatrix},\ N = \begin{pmatrix} B_{max} \\ -B_{min} \end{pmatrix}$. The MPAC control algorithm is finally expressed as

$$B^* = \underset{B}{\operatorname{argmin}} J(k), \quad s.t.\ AB \leq N, \tag{28}$$

and it is solved as a convex quadratic optimizer, benefiting the inherent favorable structure of the problem. In general, in MPAC for nonlinear systems where the problem structure cannot be exploited, other numerical-based search algorithms must be used [60,61]. Based on the receding horizon principle, only the first component of B is extracted and next sent to the plant for actuation, i.e., $\beta'_k = B(1)$, and that implies numerical integration through the artificial integrator augmenting the plant model in the first place.

Notice that in the MPAC, the parameter k_β adapts online with the current linearization point, and hence, it triggers the online update of k_d and of the matrix P. The matrix Ψ is updated online based on the last controlled output. Parameter λ acts as a regularizer that trades off fast response time and robustness against uncertainty and disturbances. The input control constraints also act as regularizers with a similar effect; hence, more hyperparameters lead to more flexibility in the design. The artificial integrator augmenting the base dynamics adds another level of robustness.

4.4. Testing the Controllers Designed for OR2

The test scenario for the competitive controllers designed for the region OR2 is captured by a wind speed variation $V(t) = 21 - 11e^{-0.01t}$, initial conditions at time $t = 0$ are $V_0 = 10$ [m/s] (close to V_{MAX} but rounded to a smaller integer value, without generality loss), $n_0 = 38.269$ [rps], $\beta_0 = 0$ [deg] and $P_{TV0} = 2.4423$ [MW]. For time intervals up to several tens of seconds, the variation of $V(t)$ can be considered ramp-like, as will be apparent from the plots.

For robustness, the poles of the closed loops of the linearized system with the double integrator controller are allocated, resulting in $p_1 = -5,\ p_0 = -20$.

For the sliding mode controller, the main parameter is chosen as $K = 10^6$, and for chattering reduction, the sign function in the controller switching is smoothed as $sgn(g) = \tanh(10g)$.

For MPAC application, we choose $N = 3$; the blade pitch angle derivative was saturated within thresholds $\beta_{min} = -40,\ \beta_{max} = 40$, and the control effort on the pitch angle derivative was set to $\lambda = 1$. An interior-point barrier optimizer was employed. A sample period of $T_s = 0.05$ [s] was used, as with the VRFT discrete-time controller.

The control results measured with all proposed controllers are visible in Figure 5. Fast transient responses are obtained with a slight advantage for the sliding mode controller. In the disturbance rejection, the linear double integrator rejects the disturbance with steady-state tracking error close to zero, similarly to the sliding mode controller. This is surprising, as the double integrator is linear; however, it displays sufficient robustness. The MPAC controller displays decreasing steady-state tracking error at a slower pace.

The control in operating region OR2 is deemed feasible and performant with the proposed controllers. That is, reliable operation follows by regulating $P_{TV}(t)$ to the desired value $P^*_{TV}(t) = 1.5$ [MW]. Chattering with $\beta(t)$ is not seen due to its small value; however, its indirect effect is observed with the sliding mode controller, even though the computed $u(t)$ is integrated once to arrive at $\beta(t)$. The results were tested on the entire wind speed variation domain [10; 21] [m/s] and they hold the same control behavior. Due to the fast-transient responses, only the first 50 s are presented in Figure 5. Due to its simplicity and ability to simultaneously reject disturbance and track the reference, the double integrator may be the best tradeoff. However, testing the robustness in extreme conditions under additional operational constraints may leave a significant space for either the sliding-mode controller or for the MPAC one.

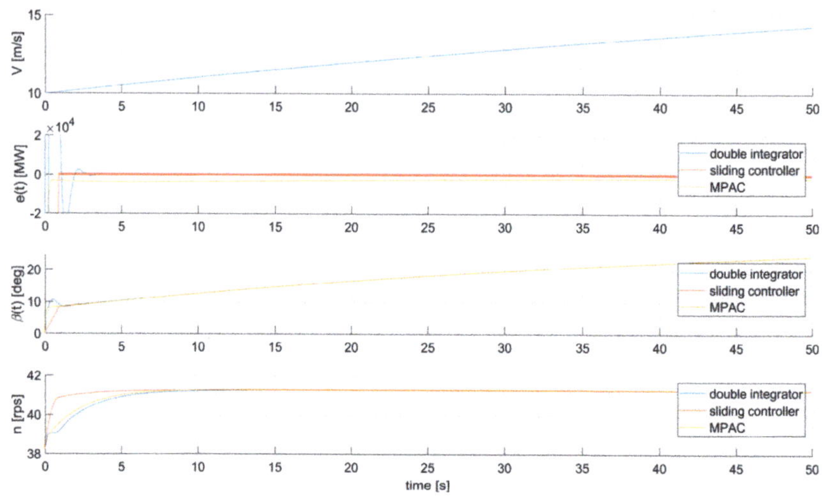

Figure 5. The control of the WT operation in region OR2. The linear double integral controller is tested against the sliding mode controller and against an MPAC controller. Regulation of $e(t)$ to zero indicates that $P_{TV}(t) = P^*_{TV}(t) = 1.5$ [MW] and demonstrates reliable operation in the region of interest.

Regarding the sensitivity of the compared controllers with respect to the parameter's choice, we disclose the following. The linear double integrator provided the baseline performance, with two main criteria, in this order: (1) fast transient response and (2) null steady-state tracking error with respect to the ramp-like wind speed.

For the sliding mode controller, we expected to outperform the linear double integrator; however, we could not make the transient response much faster, since the chattering increased. Notice from the theoretical design that the chattering will be present under any circumstance, since we chose to not compensate explicitly for the uncertainty; thus, we leave it to the switching component to deal with it. This way, the resulting controller has much simpler expression and does not need to evaluate the uncertainty factor σ at each integration time step, so the computational complexity is heavily reduced. With the chattering result, as seen in the plot, the performance was considered good enough, with zero-on-average steady-state tracking error.

For the MPAC controller, although the targeted performance was better than with the linear double integrator, we notice its apparent lower performance when compared with the double integrator. It manifests a significantly longer time needed to bring the tracking error to zero, although the response is similarly fast to the linear controller. There are two advantages, however, to the MPAC controller. The first one is that it only has a single integrator, like the sliding mode controller. The second one is the ability to approach constraints on the controlled variables, which is a unique feature when compared with the other two competitive controllers. Although not visible in the tested scenario, the transient response obtained with MPAC could have been faster, given that the thresholds β_{max}, β_{min} were larger (in absolute value) and the control effort penalty λ was made smaller. However, this would trade faster response for robustness, and this issue must be dealt with carefully, since robustness allows us to use the same hyperparameter settings with a much wider range of scenarios. We choose a more conservative approach to ensure robustness preservation, instead of faster response in this particular scenario.

5. Conclusions

Two important operating regions were analyzed for the 1.5 [MW] WTs found near Oravita, Romania, based on a detailed, realistic mathematical model including an induction generator and two power converters for stator and rotor, which is a unique feature. The first operating region OR1 is intended for small wind speed variations in the range of 3~10 [m/s] and aims for MPP control achieved by MAS control through the stator frequency under a corresponding nominal current in the stator ensured by indirect control through an additional resistance actuated by the voltage of the rotor converter. Linear PI controllers were validated by pole placement and by the VRFT tuning method, and good tracking and disturbance rejection capability were shown in spite of the nonlinear time-varying nature of the analyzed process model. We motivate why a double integrator within the controller is not used, and this requires a performance tradeoff in terms of a small but non-zero steady-state tracking error. In the second operating region OR2, the focus changes to ensuring reliable operation by saturating the MAS and the generator power. In consequence, the WT power has to be regulated using the blade pitch angle. A linear double integrator controller, a sliding-mode controller and an MPAC were validated and compared, again showing acceptable tracking and disturbance rejection capacities, with favorable and fast transients. This operating region requiring reliable operation allows for a double integral controller.

We conclude that the proposed controllers ensure the operation specifications in a wide wind speed range, characteristic of continental wind energy harvesting locations, delivering both maximum power point tracking when possible or reliable operation at higher wind speeds. There are several future work streams related to more accurate model identification of the WT characteristics, inclusion of the converter dynamics into the controlled object model and the development of a global control logic that unifies the control operation dedicated to the two individual regions presented in this work.

Author Contributions: Conceptualization, M.-B.R.; methodology, M.-B.R. and V.-D.M.; software, M.-B.R. and S.C.; validation, M.-B.R., V.-D.M. and S.C.; formal analysis, M.-B.R.; investigation, M.-B.R., V.-D.M. and S.C.; resources, V.-D.M. and S.C.; data curation, V.-D.M. and S.C.; writing—original draft preparation, M.-B.R., V.-D.M. and S.C.; writing—review and editing, M.-B.R., V.-D.M. and S.C.; visualization, M.-B.R., V.-D.M. and S.C.; supervision, M.-B.R. All authors have read and agreed to the published version of the manuscript.

Funding: This research received no external funding.

Data Availability Statement: Data is contained within the article.

Conflicts of Interest: The authors declare no conflicts of interest.

Abbreviations

The following abbreviations are used in this manuscript:

WT	Wind turbine
MPP	Maximum power point
MAS	Mechanical angular speed
VRFT	Virtual Reference Feedback Tuning
PI	Proportional–integral
PD	Proportional–derivative
MM	Mathematical model
OR	Operating region
MPAC	Model predictive adaptive control

References

1. Ye, H.; Ding, Y.; Xiao, L.; Li, Q.; Zheng, C.; Wang, Y. Hydro-Tower Pumped Storage-based Wind Power Generator: Short-t Dynamics and Controls. In Proceedings of the 2023 2nd Asian Conference on Frontiers of Power and Energy (ACFPE), Chen China, 20–22 October 2023; pp. 463–468. [CrossRef]
2. Papakonstantinou, A.G.; Konstanteas, A.I.; Papathanassiou, S.A. Solutions to Enhance Frequency Regulation in an Island Sys with Pumped-Hydro Storage under 100% Renewable Energy Penetration. *IEEE Access* **2023**, *11*, 76675–76690. [CrossRef]
3. Jamii, J.; Mimouni, F. Model of wind turbine-pumped storage hydro plant. In Proceedings of the 2018 9th International Renew Energy Congress, IREC 2018, Hammamet, Tunisia, 20–22 March 2018; pp. 1–6.
4. Sorandaru, C.; Ancuti, M.C.; Musuroi, S.; Svoboda, M.; Muller, V.; Erdodi, M.G.; Edu, E.R. Fundamental Issue for Wind Po Systems Operating at Variable Wind Speeds: The Dependence of the Optimal Angular Speed on the Wind Speed. In Proceed of the 2022 International Conference and Exposition on Electrical And Power Engineering (EPE), Iasi, Romania, 20–22 Oct 2022; pp. 167–171.
5. Rebello, E.; Watson, D.; Rodgers, M. Performance Analysis of a 10 MW Wind Farm in Providing Secondary Frequency Regula Experimental Aspects. *IEEE Trans. Power Syst.* **2019**, *34*, 3090–3097. [CrossRef]
6. Huynh, P.; Tungare, S.; Banerjee, A. Maximum Power Point Tracking for Wind Turbine Using Integrated Generator-Rect Systems. *IEEE Trans. Power Electron.* **2021**, *36*, 504–512. [CrossRef]
7. Ma, Y.; Guo, Z.; Li, Q.; Yan, J.; Ren, H.; Xiao, Y. Processing of Upward leader on the wind turbine blade and critical ler inception criterion. In Proceedings of the 2016 33rd International Conference on Lightning Protection (ICLP), Estoril, Portu 25–30 September 2016.
8. Hussain, J.; Mishra, M.K. An Efficient Wind Speed Computation Method Using Sliding Mode Observers in Wind En Conversion System Control Applications. *IEEE Trans. Ind. Appl.* **2020**, *56*, 730–739. [CrossRef]
9. Edrah, M.; Zhao, X.; Hung, W.; Qi, P.; Marshall, B.; Karcanias, A.; Baloch, S. Effects of POD Control on a DFIG Wind Tur Structural System. *IEEE Trans. Energy Convers.* **2020**, *35*, 765–774. [CrossRef]
10. Sorandaru, C.; Musuroi, S.; Frigura-Iliasa, F.M.; Vatau, D.; Dordescu, M. Analysis of the wind system operation in the opti energetic area at variable wind speed over time. *Sustainability* **2019**, *11*, 1249. [CrossRef]
11. Babescu, M. *Mașina Sincronă—Modelare, Simulare Și Identificare*; Editura Politehnica: Timisoara, Romania, 2003.
12. Deng, X.; Yang, J.; Sun, Y.; Song, D.; Yang, Y.; Joo, Y.H. An Effective Wind Speed Estimation Based Extended Optimal Tor Control for Maximum Wind Energy Capture. *IEEE Access* **2020**, *8*, 65959–65969. [CrossRef]
13. Karthik, R.; Hari, A.S.; Pavan Kumar, Y.V.; Pradeep, D.J. Modelling and Control Design for Variable Speed Wind Turbine En System. In Proceedings of the 2020 International Conference on Artificial Intelligence and Signal Processing (AISP), Amara India, 10–12 January 2020.
14. Sudharsan, G.S.; Vishnupriyan, J.; Anand, K.V. Active flow control in Horizontal Axis Wind Turbine using PI-R contro In Proceedings of the 2020 6th International Conference on Advanced Computing and Communication Systems (ICAC Coimbatore, India, 6–7 March 2020; pp. 1010–1013.
15. Goyal, S.; Maurya, S.K.; Kumar, S.; Agarwal, D. A Consolidation Review of Major Wind Turbine Models in Global Marke Proceedings of the 2020 International Conference on Power Electronics & IoT Applications in Renewable Energy and its Co (PARC), Mathura, India, 28–29 February 2020; pp. 246–251.
16. Baala, Y.; Bri, S. DFIG-Based Wind Turbine Control Using High-Gain Observer. In Proceedings of the 2020 1st International Confer on Innovative Research in Applied Science, Engineering and Technology (IRASET), Meknes, Morocco, 16–19 April 2020.

An, Y.; Li, Y.; Zhang, J.; Wang, T.; Liu, C. Enhanced Frequency Regulation Strategy for Wind Turbines Based on Over-speed De-loading Control. In Proceedings of the 2020 5th Asia Conference on Power and Electrical Engineering (ACPEE), Chengdu, China, 4–7 June 2020; pp. 442–446.

Dobrin, E.; Ancuti, M.C.; Musuroi, S.; Sorandaru, C.; Ancuti, R.; Lazar, M.A. Dynamics of the Wind Power Plants at Small Wind Speeds. In Proceedings of the 2020 IEEE 14th International Symposium on Applied Computational Intelligence and Informatics (SACI), Timisoara, Romania, 21–23 May 2020; pp. 187–192.

Fan, X.; Crisostomi, E.; Zhang, B.; Thomopulos, D. Rotor Speed Fluctuation Analysis for Rapid De-Loading of Variable Speed Wind Turbines. In Proceedings of the 2020 IEEE 20th Mediterranean Electrotechnical Conference (MELECON), Palermo, Italy, 16–18 June 2020; pp. 482–487.

Pali, B.S.; Vadhera, S. An Innovative Continuous Power Generation System Comprising of Wind Energy along with Pumped-Hydro Storage and Open Well. *IEEE Trans. Sustain. Energy* **2020**, *11*, 145–153. [CrossRef]

Yokoyama, S.; Yasuda, Y.; Minowa, M.; Sekioka, S.; Yamamoto, K.; Honjo, N.; Sato, T. Clarification of the mechanism of wind turbine blade damage taking lightning characteristics into consideration and relevant research project. In Proceedings of the 2012 International Conference on Lightning Protection (ICLP), Vienna, Austria, 2–7 September 2012.

Yao, X.; Liu, Y.; Bao, J.; Xing, Z. Research and simulation of direct drive wind turbine VSCF characteristic. In Proceedings of the IEEE International Conference on Automation and Logistics, ICAL 2008, Qingdao, China, 1–3 September 2008; pp. 1683–1687.

Singh, M.; Santoso, S. *Dynamic Models for Wind Turbines and Wind Power Plants*; National Renewable Energy Lab. (NREL): Golden, CO, USA, 2012; ISBN 9781620817872.

en.wind-turbine-models.com. Fuhrlaender FL MD 77. Available online: https://en.wind-turbine-models.com/turbines/357-fuhrlaender-fl-md-77 (accessed on 2 December 2024).

Najih, Y.; Adar, M.; Aboulouard, A.; Khaouch, Z.; Bengourram, M.; Zekraoui, M.; Mabrouki, M. Mechatronic Control Model of a Novel Variable Speed Wind Turbine Concept with Power Splitting Drive Train: A Bond Graph Approach. In Proceedings of the 2020 IEEE 6th International Conference on Optimization and Applications (ICOA), Beni Mellal, Morocco, 20–21 April 2020.

Vadi, S.; Gurbuz, F.B.; Bayindir, R.; Hossain, E. Design and Simulation of a Grid Connected Wind Turbine with Permanent Magnet Synchronous Generator. In Proceedings of the 2020 8th International Conference on Smart Grid (icSmartGrid), Paris, France, 17–19 June 2020; pp. 169–175.

Carstea, C.; Butaru, F.; Ancuti, M.C.; Musuroi, S.; Deacu, A.; Babaita, M.; Stanciu, A.M. Wind Power Plants Operation at Variable Wind Speeds. In Proceedings of the 2020 IEEE 14th International Symposium on Applied Computational Intelligence and Informatics (SACI), Timisoara, Romania, 21–23 May 2020; pp. 205–210.

Stotsky, A.; Egardt, B.Z. Individual pitch control of wind turbines: Model-based approach. *Proc. Inst. Mech. Eng. Part I J. Syst. Control Eng.* **2013**, *227*, 602–609. [CrossRef]

Abd-elwhab, K.T.; Tawfeic, S.R.; Abdel-halim, A. Pitch Control of a Wind Turbine Rotor blade. *Minia J. Eng. Technol.* **2013**, *32*, 27–35.

Civelek, Z.; Çam, E.; Lüy, M.; Mamur, H. Proportional-integral-derivative parameter optimisation of blade pitch controller in wind turbines by a new intelligent genetic algorithm. *IET Renew. Power Gener.* **2016**, *10*, 1220–1228. [CrossRef]

Han, B.; Zhou, L.; Yang, F.; Xiang, Z. Individual pitch controller based on fuzzy logic control for wind turbine load mitigation. *IET Renew. Power Gener.* **2016**, *10*, 687–693. [CrossRef]

Soued, S.; Ebrahim, M.A.; Ramadan, H.S.; Becherif, M. Optimal blade pitch control for enhancing the dynamic performance of wind power plants via metaheuristic optimisers. *IET Electr. Power Appl.* **2017**, *11*, 1432–1440. [CrossRef]

Laina, R.; Lamzouri, F.E.Z.; Boufounas, E.M.; El Amrani, A.; Boumhidi, I. Intelligent control of a DFIG wind turbine using a PSO evolutionary algorithm. *Procedia Comput. Sci.* **2018**, *127*, 471–480. [CrossRef]

Parvaresh, A.; Abrazeh, S.; Mohseni, S.R.; Zeitouni, M.J.; Gheisarnejad, M.; Khooban, M.H. A novel deep learning backstepping controller-based digital twins technology for pitch angle control of variable speed wind turbine. *Designs* **2020**, *4*, 15. [CrossRef]

Kane, M.B. Machine Learning Control for Floating Offshore Wind Turbine Individual Blade Pitch Control. In Proceedings of the 2020 American Control Conference (ACC), Denver, CO, USA, 1–3 July 2020; pp. 237–241.

Badihi, H.; Zhang, Y.; Pillay, P.; Rakheja, S. Fault-Tolerant Individual Pitch Control for Load Mitigation in Wind Turbines with Actuator Faults. *IEEE Trans. Ind. Electron.* **2021**, *68*, 532–543. [CrossRef]

Coquelet, M.; Bricteux, L.; Moens, M.; Chatelain, P. A reinforcement-learning approach for individual pitch control. *Wind Energy* **2022**, *25*, 1343–1362. [CrossRef]

Bouregba, H.; Hachemi, M.; Bey, M.; Hamidat, A. Stability analysis of the pitch angle control of large wind turbines using different controller strategies. *Adv. Mech. Eng.* **2022**, *14*, 16878132221139926. [CrossRef]

Chen, Z.; Shi, T.; Song, P.; Li, C.; Cao, Y.; Yan, Y. Improved pitch control strategy for the robust operation of wind energy conversion system in the high wind speed condition. *Int. J. Electr. Power Energy Syst.* **2023**, *153*, 109381. [CrossRef]

Zhou, Z.; Wang, S.; Jiang, J.; Li, H.; Zhao, J.; Yu, D. Enhancing the Tracking Performance of Wind Turbine Blade Pitch Angle Control via Model-Free Adaptive Control Algorithm Utilizing Input-Output Differential. 2024. Available online: https://www.researchsquare.com/article/rs-4447247/v1 (accessed on 2 December 2024).

41. Owayjan, M.; Houari, A.; Achkar, R.; Ait-Ahmed, M.; Tahliati, M.; Ferahtia, S. Robust Model-Free Control of a Floating Offsh Wind Turbine under High Wind & Wave Conditions. In Proceedings of the 2024 International Conference on Control, Automa and Diagnosis, ICCAD 2024, Paris, France, 15–17 May 2024; pp. 1–6.
42. Edu, E.R.; Radac, M.B. Control of Wind Turbines Operating at Significantly Variable Wind Speeds Over Time. In Proceeding the 2024 International Conference on Electrical, Computer and Energy Technologies (ICECET), Sydney, Australia, 25–27 July 2 [CrossRef]
43. Babescu, M. *Mașina Asincronă—Modelare, Simulare Și Identificare*; Editura Politehnica: Timisoara, Romania, 2002.
44. Formentin, S.; Campi, M.C.; Carè, A.; Savaresi, S.M. Deterministic continuous-time Virtual Reference Feedback Tuning (VR with application to PID design. *Syst. Control Lett.* **2019**, *127*, 25–34. [CrossRef]
45. Yonezawa, A.; Yonezawa, H.; Yahagi, S.; Kajiwara, I. Simple controller design to achieve iso-damping robustness: Non-itera data-driven approach based on fractional-order reference model. *arXiv* **2024**, arXiv:2409.20375.
46. D'Amico, W.; La Bella, A.; Farina, M. An Incremental Input-to-State Stability Condition for a Class of Recurrent Neural Netwo *IEEE Trans. Automat. Contr.* **2023**, *69*, 2221–2236. [CrossRef]
47. Radac, M.-B. Trajectory Tracking within a Hierarchical Primitive-Based Learning Approach. *Entropy* **2022**, *24*, 889. [Cross [PubMed]
48. Lala, T.; Chirla, D.-P.; Radac, M.-B. Model Reference Tracking Control Solutions for a Visual Servo System Based on a Virtual S from Unknown Dynamics. *Energies* **2022**, *15*, 267. [CrossRef]
49. Radac, M.-B.; Borlea, A.-I. Virtual State Feedback Reference Tuning and Value Iteration Reinforcement Learning for Unkno Observable Systems Control. *Energies* **2021**, *14*, 1006. [CrossRef]
50. Li, Y.; Li, H. A Study on the Vehicle Antilock System Based on Adaptive Neural Network Sliding Mode Control. *Math. Probl.* **2024**, *2024*, 3359266. [CrossRef]
51. Naderian, S.; Farrokhi, M. Adaptive Back-Stepping Data-Driven Terminal Sliding-Mode Controller for Nonlinear MIMO Syst With Disturbance Observer. *IEEE Access* **2023**, *11*, 78059–78073. [CrossRef]
52. Chereji, E.; Radac, M.-B.; Szedlak-Stinean, A.-I. Sliding Mode Control Algorithms for Anti-Lock Braking Systems with Performa Comparisons. *Algorithms* **2021**, *14*, 2. [CrossRef]
53. Ismael, O.Y.; Noaman, M.N.; Abdullah, I.K. Fick's Law Algorithm Based-Nonlinear Model Predictive Control of Twin R MIMO System. *J. Robot. Control.* **2024**, *5*, 694–705.
54. Ebirim, K.U.; Lecchini-Visintini, A.; Rubagotti, M.; Prempain, E. Constrained Model Predictive Control With Integral Action Twin Rotor MIMO Systems. *J. Dyn. Syst. Meas. Control.* **2023**, *145*, 081006. [CrossRef]
55. Mokhtari, M.A.; Rostmi, M. Adaptive Data-driven Controller Design for a Control Simulator with a Common Single M Rotor-single Tail Rotor Configuration. *Iran. J. Mech. Eng.* **2023**, *25*, 80–96. [CrossRef]
56. Pan, T.; Hou, J.; Jin, X.; Yu, Z.; Zhou, W.; Wang, Z. Distributed Control of Hydrogen-Based Microgrids for the Demand S A Multiagent Self-Triggered MPC-Based Strategy. *Algorithms* **2024**, *17*, 251. [CrossRef]
57. Nebeluk, R.; Ławryńczuk, M. Tuning of Multivariable Model Predictive Control for Industrial Tasks. *Algorithms* **2021**, *14*, [CrossRef]
58. Ates, C.; Bicat, D.; Yankov, R.; Arweiler, J.; Koch, R.; Bauer, H.-J. Model Predictive Evolutionary Temperature Control Neural-Network-Based Digital Twins. *Algorithms* **2023**, *16*, 387. [CrossRef]
59. Gong, L.; Yu, M.; Kollias, S. Optimizing Crop Yield and Reducing Energy Consumption in Greenhouse Control Using PSO-M Algorithm. *Algorithms* **2023**, *16*, 243. [CrossRef]
60. Radac, M.B.; Nicolae, T. Leveraging simplex gradient variance and bias reduction for black-box optimization of noisy and co functions. *IEEE Access* **2025**, *13*, 14304–14316. [CrossRef]
61. Yonezawa, H.; Yonezawa, A.; Kajiwara, I. Efficient Tuning Scheme of Mode-Switching-Based Powertrain Oscillation Contro Considering Nonlinear Backlash. *IEEE Access* **2023**, *11*, 93935–93947. [CrossRef]

algorithms

MDPI

cle

eep-Learning-Based Optimization of the Signal/Background atio for Λ Particles in the CBM Experiment at FAIR

n Kisel [1,2,3,4,*,†], Robin Lakos [1,2,*,†] and Gianna Zischka [2,*,†]

1 Frankfurt Institute for Advanced Studies, 60438 Frankfurt am Main, Germany
2 Institute of Computer Science, J. W. Goethe University, 60629 Frankfurt am Main, Germany
3 GSI Helmholtz Centre for Heavy Ion Research, 64291 Darmstadt, Germany
4 Helmholtz Research Academy Hesse for FAIR, 60438 Frankfurt am Main, Germany
* Correspondence: i.kisel@compeng.uni-frankfurt.de (I.K.); lakos@fias.uni-frankfurt.de (R.L.); g.zischka@gsi.de (G.Z.)
† These authors contributed equally to this work.

Abstract: Machine learning algorithms have become essential tools in modern physics experiments, enabling the precise and efficient analysis of large-scale experimental data. The Compressed Baryonic Matter (CBM) experiment at the Facility for Antiproton and Ion Research (FAIR) demands innovative methods for processing the vast data volumes generated at high collision rates of up to 10 MHz. This study presents a deep-learning-based approach to enhance the signal/background (S/B) ratio for Λ particles within the Kalman Filter (KF) Particle Finder framework. Using the Artificial Neural Networks for First Level Event Selection (ANN4FLES) package of CBM, a multi-layer perceptron model was designed and trained on simulated data to classify Λ particle candidates as signal or background. The model achieved over 98% classification accuracy, enabling significant reductions in background—in particular, a strong suppression of the combinatorial background that lacks physical meaning—while preserving almost the whole Λ particle signal. This approach improved the S/B ratio by a factor of 10.97, demonstrating the potential of deep learning to complement existing particle reconstruction techniques and contribute to the advancement of data analysis methods in heavy-ion physics.

Keywords: artificial neural network; Compressed Baryonic Matter experiment; deep learning; heavy-ion experiment; Kalman Filter Particle Finder; multi-layer perceptron

1. Introduction

During the last decade, machine learning has become a cornerstone in numerous scientific and industrial domains, providing powerful tools for fast and efficient data processing applications. To name a few examples, these applications include highly accurate skin cancer recognition [1], complex protein folding predictions [2], and advanced financial strategies like deep hedging, which uses machine learning to optimize hedging strategies under realistic market conditions [3].

In recent years, machine learning has also become instrumental in particle physics experiments [4–6]. These experiments, typically conducted at particle accelerators, involve colliding heavy atomic nuclei—such as gold or lead—at nearly the speed of light, creating an extremely hot or dense fireball to study the properties of nuclear matter under extreme conditions [7–9]. To search for rare probes, some of these experiments have trended toward higher collision rates [10,11], driving the need for sophisticated data processing techniques capable of handling massive datasets on high-performance computing resources. Machine learning methods are increasingly used to address challenges such as particle identification and event classification in these data-intensive environments.

The future heavy-ion experiment Compressed Baryonic Matter (CBM) at the Facility for Antiproton and Ion Research (FAIR) [12] in Darmstadt, Germany, is such an experiment, targeting a collision rate of up to 10 MHz [13]. This unprecedented rate of collisions will generate vast volumes of about 1 TByte of data per second [14], demanding real-time event reconstruction and analysis capabilities that go beyond traditional methods, as it is simply not feasible to store all the data produced [15]. To meet these requirements, CBM will rely on high-performance computing infrastructure combined with highly efficient algorithms for tasks such as online event reconstruction [16] and event selection [17,18], identifying events of particular scientific interest to retain for further analysis. Newly developed machine learning applications will complement the existing algorithm packages by increasing reconstruction efficiency and improving the quality of physics measurements [19–21], enabling more precise insights into the conditions created in heavy-ion collisions.

One of the core packages of CBM, the Kalman Filter (KF) Particle Finder [22], was developed for the online reconstruction and selection of short-lived particles. Due to their instability, these particles decay before or in the tracking system and, therefore, cannot be directly detected or reconstructed [23]. To reconstruct them, their decay products, known as daughter particles, are analyzed to infer the original particle, referred to as the mother particle. During the reconstruction process, when a decay is identified, all potential mother particles are created to ensure that no real particle signal is inadvertently discarded due to an incorrect hypothesis. However, this method leads to noise, the so-called background, which contains both incorrectly reconstructed particles (referred to as combinatorial background or ghosts) and particles that have been finally assigned to the wrong particle type (physical background). The KF Particle Finder is part of the First-Level Event Selection (FLES) package [17], which selects the most interesting events for the current research online.

Previous work has investigated machine learning techniques to enhance particle reconstruction quality and background suppression. Boosted Decision Trees have been employed to automatically optimize cut parameters for Λ particle selection [24], while neural networks have been integrated into the KF Particle Finder's particle competition to reduce the mutual background between short-lived particle candidates through particle classification [25], demonstrating promising improvements in reconstruction performance.

In this work, the KF Particle Finder is extended by a deep-learning-based approach to investigate the capabilities of improving the signal/background (S/B) ratio for Λ particles by classifying the Λ particle candidates into signal and background using neural networks. For this task, the neural network package Artificial Neural Networks for First-Level Event Selection (ANN4FLES) [26] (p. 161) is used, which is primarily developed for use within the CBM experiment. Improving the reconstruction quality of short-lived particles, such as the Λ particle, is essential not only for extracting rare physical signals in the high-rate environment of CBM but also for enabling a more accurate interpretation and analysis of the underlying physical processes.

2. Materials and Methods

The investigated particle Λ is a neutral baryon consisting of an up quark, a down quark, and a strange quark. Strange quarks are significant because their presence is expected to indicate deconfined matter, such as Quark Gluon Plasma [27]. Additionally, Λ particles are abundantly produced within the energy range of the CBM experiment. Since Λ is an electrically neutral particle with a short lifetime [28] (p. 81), it must be reconstructed by its decay products. The Λ particle decays predominantly into a proton (p) and a negatively charged pion (π^-), with a branching ratio of approximately 63.9% $\pm$ 0.5 [28] (p. 81). This common decay mode with two detectable daughter particles, along with the Λ particle's abundant production and relevance in heavy-ion physics, makes it a suitable candidate for initial performance tests of neural networks in classification tasks, such as the one in this work.

In CBM, the FLES package is utilized for online full event reconstruction, covering everything from combining detector measurements for track reconstruction to identifying particles, decays, and decay chains. Once the tracks have been reconstructed, they are classified as either primary or secondary in the KF Particle Finder [22] (p. 88). Primary tracks are those that, when extrapolated to the primary vertex (the collision point), are statistically likely to originate from it. In contrast, secondary tracks are those produced at the decay point of another particle, known as the secondary vertex. Tracks are further grouped by the charge of the associated particle (negative or positive) [22] (p. 88). To reconstruct short-lived particles, potential daughter tracks are extrapolated to locate a possible secondary vertex. When combining secondary tracks to form potential mother particle candidates, tracks are combined, such as one positive and one negative track, which are potential candidates for the reconstruction of the $\Lambda \rightarrow p\pi^-$ decay. Once a secondary vertex is identified, all potential mother particle candidates for that decay are reconstructed. However, as only one true mother particle decays at a given secondary vertex, reconstructing all possible candidates introduces noise (referred to as background) which can reduce the quality of subsequent physics analyses. In addition to real particles that are misclassified (physical background), the background also includes non-existent particles that lack physical meaning (combinatorial background). The observation that daughter particles can also act as mother particles after decaying into their own daughter particles implies a hierarchy of decays, where reconstructed particles at one level might serve as components for reconstructing higher-level particles. This layered reconstruction approach increases the complexity of the analysis, as each new hypothesis of a mother particle at one level introduces potential combinations that could add to the background, further challenging the extraction of true physical signals.

To mitigate this issue and reduce background, statistical cuts are applied to discard unlikely mother particles that are incorrectly reconstructed. Additionally, particle competition methods can be employed to further minimize the background introduced during this process. For this work, the competition is not enabled.

2.1. Selection of Input Features for the Deep Learning Approach

In the KF Particle Finder, various cuts are applied to determine whether reconstructed particles align with the assumptions of the underlying particle model. If a particle is statistically unlikely to match the model, it is excluded. However, since particles are typically assigned to multiple model hypotheses initially, this exclusion does not necessarily remove the particle entirely from the analysis.

In this work, ten input features, five of which are χ^2 values used for cuts, are used for the neural-network-based approach. One of them is χ^2_{prim}, which determines whether a particle's track is classified as a primary or secondary track. This distinction is particularly important for daughter tracks, as they should be secondary tracks originating from a particle decay (here of Λ) and not pointing directly to the primary vertex. Pairs of secondary tracks often overlap in time and space, suggesting they may have originated from a common mother particle. To identify such mother particle candidates, χ^2_{geo}, evaluates the quality of the intersection point of the daughters' tracks, indicating a likely point of decay. The third χ^2 value, χ^2_{topo}, defined as the sum of χ^2_{geo} and χ^2_{prim}, captures the overall topology of the particle. In addition to these χ^2 values for the Λ particle, other features are used as input for the classification model. These include the decay length normalized by its error, the particle mass, transverse momentum (momentum perpendicular to the beam axis), and the transverse momentum and χ^2_{prim} values of the mother particle candidate's daughter particles. The complete list of input features is shown in Table 1.

Table 1. Selected input features for the deep learning approach.

Input Features	Description
m	Mass of the reconstructed Λ particle.
p_T	Transverse momentum of the reconstructed Λ particle.
χ^2_{geo}	χ^2 geometry value of the reconstructed Λ, used for constructing mother particle candidates.
χ^2_{prim}	χ^2 primary value of the reconstructed Λ, used to separate primary and secondary particles/track
χ^2_{topo}	χ^2 topology value of the reconstructed Λ that is used for evaluating the reconstructed particle's topology. $(\chi^2_{topo} = \chi^2_{geo} + \chi^2_{prim})$
$l/\Delta l$	Decay length normalized by its error (uncertainty) of the reconstructed Λ.
$p_{T_{daughter1}}$	Transverse momentum of the positively charged daughter particle of the reconstructed Λ.
$p_{T_{daughter2}}$	Transverse momentum of the negatively charged daughter particle of the reconstructed Λ.
$\chi^2_{prim_{daughter1}}$	χ^2_{prim} of the positively charged daughter particle of the reconstructed Λ.
$\chi^2_{prim_{daughter2}}$	χ^2_{prim} of the negatively charged daughter particle of the reconstructed Λ.

To support the subsequent application of the deep learning model, it is crucial to avoid prematurely discarding particles that may be misclassified as background due to not meeting the cut criteria. Therefore, the thresholds for χ^2_{prim}, χ^2_{geo}, and $l/\Delta l$ were relaxed to retain more particles. In the KF Particle Finder, the threshold value of χ^2_{prim} is, unlike the other two threshold values that are directly hard-coded, calculated by a function that converts a given probability of incorrectly identifying a primary track as a secondary track into a corresponding threshold value. Here, the probability was relaxed from 0.0001 to 0.1. All resulting cut thresholds are shown in Table 2. This provides the network with greater room for decision-making, ensuring the cuts do not preemptively reject particles that the model might classify as signal.

Table 2. Default cut thresholds of the KF Particle Finder for the CBM setup and the relaxed cut thresholds used in the presented deep learning approach.

Default Cut	Relaxed Cut	Cut Description
$\chi^2_{prim} > 18.42$	$\chi^2_{prim} > 4.605$	A particle's track is considered a secondary track when χ^2_{prim} is larger than the threshold.
$\chi^2_{geo} < 3$	$\chi^2_{geo} < 6$	The χ^2_{geo} criterion evaluates the quality of a possible intersection of two daughter particle candidates' tracks.
$l/\Delta l > 3$	$l/\Delta l > 2$	Ensures the candidate's decay point is significantly distant from the primary verte normalized by its uncertainty.

2.2. Simulated Data and Deep Learning Model for Λ Particle Classification

Since the CBM experiment is still under construction, applying the algorithms to real data is not yet feasible. However, well-established simulation frameworks for heavy-ion physics are widely accepted and utilized. One such tool is the Ultra-relativistic Quantum Molecular Dynamics (UrQMD) framework [29], which generates raw heavy-ion collision data across a wide range of energies. These simulated datasets offer the advantage of known ground truth, making them ideal for supervised learning approaches . The data used in this work originate from CBM repositories, which provide a collection of validated datasets specifically prepared for algorithm development and testing. The CBM event reconstruction pipeline utilizes the Monte Carlo (MC) information from the simulation by making comparisons between algorithmic results and MC information at each phase. For instance, in the KF Particle Finder package, one attempts to match reconstructed particles with their respective MC particles. A reconstructed particle is called a signal if it is reconstructed and matched with the respective particle of the same type from the MC data. Physical background refers to reconstructed particles that match an MC particle but of a different type. Thus, this background is usually produced by other types of particles that have a similar topology. Combinatorial background (or ghosts) are reconstructed particles that do not match any MC particle and, therefore, lack physical meaning.

The deep learning model, a multi-layer perceptron [30] constructed using ANN4FLES, is composed of an input layer with 10 neurons for the input features, four hidden layers with 64 neurons each, and an output layer with 2 neurons for the classification of signal and background. LeakyReLU with a negative slope of 0.1 serves as the activation function for the hidden layers, while Softmax is applied in the output layer. The model is trained using categorical cross-entropy loss and the Adam [31] weight optimization algorithm, set up with $\alpha = 0.001$, $\beta_1 = 0.9$, and $\beta_2 = 0.999$ and $\epsilon = 10^{-8}$. This model was selected through manual tuning. Initial tests with smaller models showed comparable results, suggesting a trade-off between classification performance and runtime. Automated hyperparameter optimization was not yet applied, as the chosen configuration performed well for our initial tests. The model architecture can be seen in Figure 1.

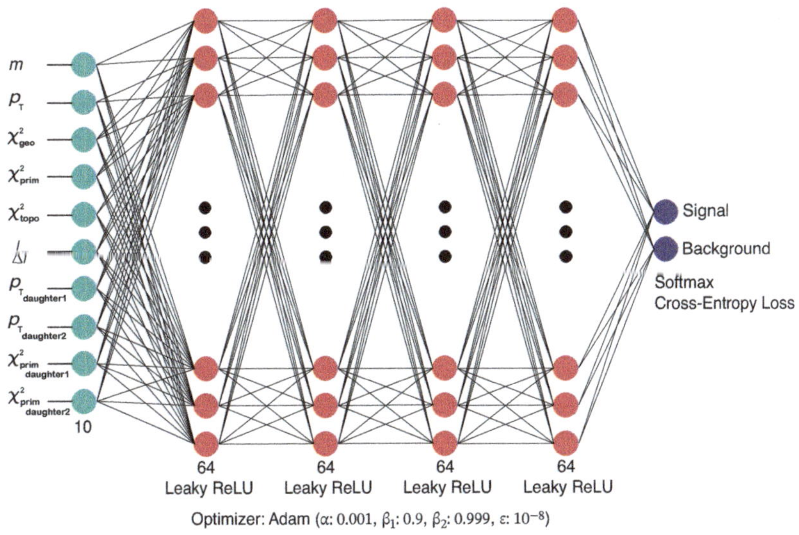

Figure 1. Illustration of the deep learning model used for the presented results.

3. Results

For the results presented in this work, UrQMD-simulated gold–gold central collisions at 10 GeV were utilized. The training and validation datasets were artificially balanced to contain 50% signal and 50% background, ensuring even representation for training. A total of 787,000 Λ particles were used, with an 80:20 split for training and validation, respectively.

The training was performed over 30 epochs with a batch size of 100 samples. The deep learning model achieved a classification accuracy of 98.76% on the validation set, which was used to select a well-performing model. The progression of the training process over 30 epochs is shown in Figure 2.

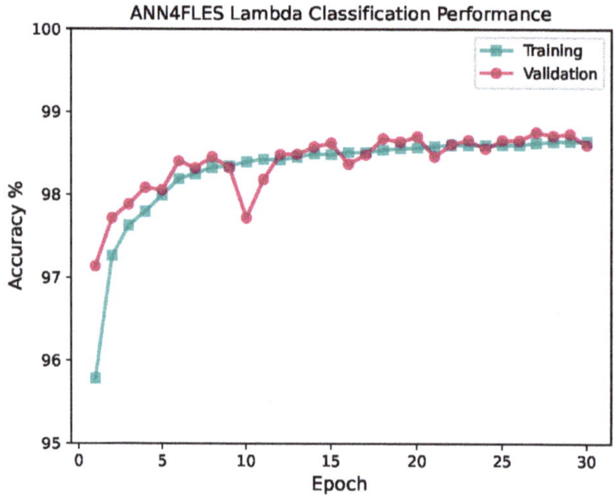

Figure 2. Accuracy over 30 epochs of training and validation with a peak performance of 98.76% on the validation set.

Following the training phase, the pre-trained model was integrated into the KF Particle Finder to classify Λ particles within the CBM reconstruction pipeline. This classification was performed using 46,000 new collisions. The subsequent results presented here are directly derived from the KF Particle Finder package 22.2.99.

In Figure 3, the mass distribution in the range from 1.06 GeV/c^2 to 1.2 GeV/c^2 for all reconstructed Λ particles is shown, consisting of signal, physical background, and ghosts. The actual Λ particles are concentrated around the mass region of 1.115 GeV/c^2, corresponding to the expected Λ mass. While background particles may also appear near the Λ mass region, the majority are located in the surrounding areas. As shown, the overall number of reconstructed Λ particles is reduced by the deep learning approach (red) compared to the default method (blue), with the reduction primarily occurring in regions dominated by background.

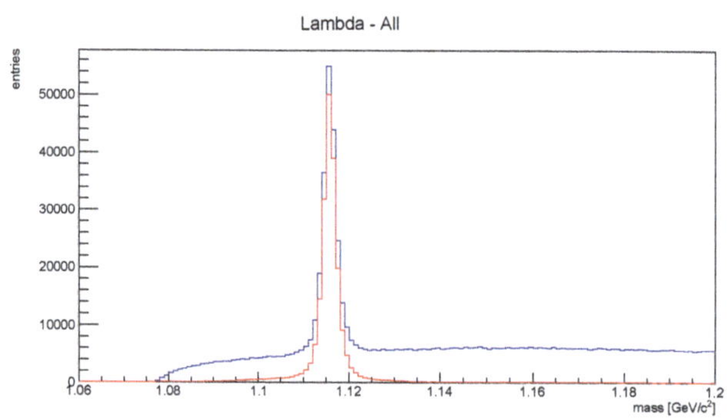

Figure 3. Comparison of all created Λ particles (signal and background) of the default approach (blue) and deep learning approach (red) in the mass range from 1.06 GeV/c^2 to 1.2 GeV/c^2.

True positives are those Λ particles that are correctly reconstructed and identified, also known as signal. The histogram of the true positives of the default approach and the deep learning approach can be seen in Figure 4a. In the mass range of 1.1 GeV/c^2 to 1.135 GeV/c^2, the deep learning approach has reconstructed 179,891 true positives, 1.36% fewer true Λ particles than the default approach, which reconstructs 182,364 true Λ particles. Thus, slightly more Λ particles were incorrectly classified as background in comparison to the default approach based on pre-defined cuts.

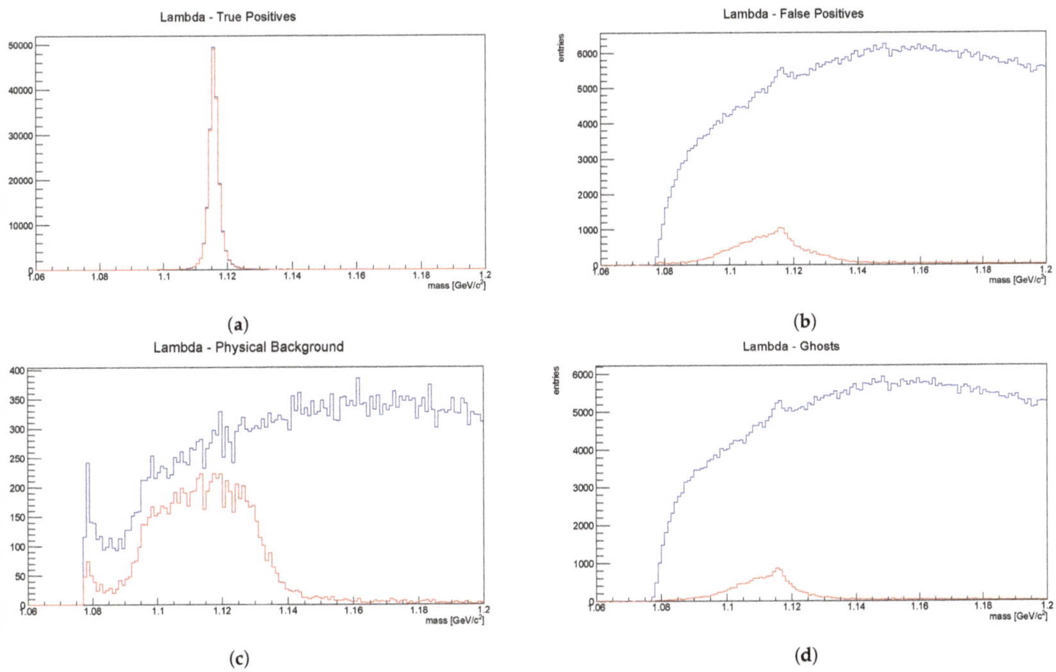

Figure 4. Comparison of the results of the default approach (blue) and the deep learning approach (red) in the mass range from 1.06 GeV/c^2 to 1.2 GeV/c^2. (**a**) True positives (signal) of all reconstructed Λ particles. (**b**) False positive Λ particles (total background). (**c**) Physical background. (**d**) Combinatorial background (ghosts).

The total background, here false positives, can be seen in Figure 4b. With 25,761 incorrectly classified Λ particles, the deep learning approach produces 95.94% less total background than the default approach, which incorrectly classified 633,771 particles as Λ.

Since there are two types of background with different meanings for physics analysis, it is important to analyze both separately. In Figure 4c, the results of the physical background can be seen. Both approaches encountered difficulties in the removal of the background in the anticipated mass region of the Λ particle. Nevertheless, the deep learning approach exhibited superior performance in the reduction of background in comparison to the standard method. In the remaining regions, the reductionof background is more evident. Here, the deep learning approach demonstrated a markedly superior reduction compared to the default approach. Overall, within the range of 1.06 GeV/c^2 to 1.2 GeV/c^2, the standard approach misclassified 34,746 of the observed particles, while the deep learning approach misclassified only 8314.

Since ghosts are particles that do not exist, these incorrectly created particles are of no use for physics analysis. It would be desirable to completely avoid any ghost particles being misclassified as Λ. The proposed approach significantly reduces these reconstructed particles, as shown by the data presented in Figure 4d. While a small peak remains visible within the range of the mass of Λ, this range has been significantly constrained. Overall, the combinatorial background was reduced from 599,025 ghosts to 17,447 ghosts, achieving a reduction factor of 34.33.

In total, within and beyond the shown mass ranges, 2758 Λ particles were incorrectly classified as background, while 2,006,910 particles were correctly identified as such. Therefore, the number of rejected Λ particle signal remains within a manageable range.

Given the absolute numbers from the evaluation, the dataset's imbalance—containing significantly more background than signal—is clearly evident. In such cases, accuracy alone can be misleading. Therefore, to more reliably assess the performance of the deep learning approach, additional classification metrics are presented in Figure 5, including the confusion matrix of the evaluation results. On the test dataset, within the KF Particle Finder, the accuracy dropped slightly in comparison to the validation (from 0.9876 to 0.9859). The results show a precision of 0.9852, indicating that the vast majority of particles identified as Λ were correctly classified, with less than 2% of the background being misclassified as Λ. The recall of 0.8651 reflects the model's ability to recover most true Λ particles. However, this also implies that some Λ particles were misclassified as background, leading to the omission of these true Λ particles in the physics analysis. The F1-score of 0.9212 demonstrates a good balance between precision and recall, and the high specificity of 0.9986 confirms that background particles were effectively rejected, highlighting the method's strength in minimizing false positives, as desired.

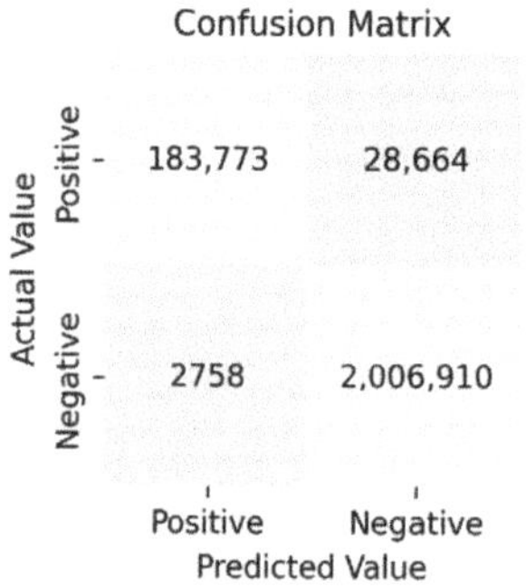

(a)

Metric	Value
Accuracy	0.9859
Precision	0.9852
Recall	0.8651
F1-Score	0.9212
Specificity	0.9986

(b)

Figure 5. Confusion matrix (**a**) and evaluation metrics (**b**) of the deep learning model evaluated on all classified particles during the final test in the KF Particle Finder.

In Table 3, the S/B ratio and significance of both the default approach and the deep learning approach are presented. In each case, the signal (S) and background (B) are determined using the integrals of two function fits—one for the signal and one for the background—performed with the CbmRoot framework [32]. The S/B ratio quantifies the proportion of signal to background, while the significance reflects the confidence in distinguishing the signal of a particle type from the background. A significance of 1 indicates no distinction, while a significance of 5 marks the threshold for identifying a real particle signal, ensuring it is unlikely to be a statistical fluctuation and typically resulting in a clear peak.

The deep learning approach improved the S/B ratio significantly, from 3.49 to 38.28—an increase by a factor of 10.97. While these values depend on the functions used for fitting the signal and background, the improvement in the S/B ratio is evident. Additionally, the significance increased slightly, from 11.38 to 12.95—a factor of 1.14. In both approaches, the significance remains well above the threshold. However, the increased significance demonstrates that the deep learning approach enhances the distinguishability of the Λ particle signal.

Table 3. Comparison of the S/B ratio and significance $(S/\sqrt{S+B})$ of the default approach and the deep-learning-based approach.

	S/B	$S/\sqrt{S+B}$
Default	3.49	11.38
Neural Network	38.28	12.95
Improvement Factor	10.97	1.14

4. Discussion

The results of this work demonstrate a significant reduction in background while keeping most of the particles' signal, as shown in Figure 5. This is specifically true when comparing to the Monte Carlo information of the simulated data. However, the mass is typically used as the final observable in physics analyses. Including it—or variables strongly correlated with it—within the classifier may bias the mass spectrum, artificially sharpening the signal peak and suppressing the sidebands. Although the metrics indicate good performance of the neural network, this can compromise the reliability of background estimation and signal extraction, particularly when applying the model to experimental data and therefore requires thorough examination.

To investigate this effect, we conducted tests using the training and validation datasets, excluding the mass and other kinematically correlated variables (specifically, the transverse momenta of Λ and its daughters). The classifier still achieved strong results. When only the Λ mass was removed, the model reached an accuracy of 0.9745, with a precision and F1-score of 0.9746 and 0.9745, respectively. When both the mass and all transverse momenta were excluded—leaving only cut-based features such as primary vertex and track quality variables—the model still achieved an accuracy of 0.9444, with precision and F1-score exceeding 0.94. These results confirm that a comparable signal–background discrimination is achievable even without relying on mass-correlated features, thus preserving the integrity of the mass as an unbiased observable in subsequent physics analyses using experimental data.

It should be emphasized that the results presented in this work were obtained using simulated central collisions, which represent idealized "perfect" scenarios. Future investigations should evaluate the performance of the proposed approach in simulated minimum bias collisions, where less ideal interactions and a wider variety of collision geometries are present. This will provide a more realistic assessment of the method's robustness and its applicability to a broader range of collision conditions—a crucial step toward its use with experimental data. Furthermore, the presented deep learning approach was only trained, validated, and tested on simulated data. While these simulations are typically well studied and assumed to reflect real data reasonably well, the method must be thoroughly studied before being applied to experimental data.

The strong suppression of combinatorial background highlights the potential of machine learning in this domain. However, physical background arises from real particles mistakenly identified as Λ particles. Completely removing such a background negatively impacts the quality of the physics analysis for other particles. To address this, two extensions of the approach are proposed. Firstly, the analysis should include other particles of interest, especially those that typically interact or overlap with Λ particles, contributing to the mutual physical background. Secondly, the deep learning approach could be expanded to classify not only signal and background for Λ but also for multiple particle species. An extended neural network could potentially distinguish physical background for one particle as a valid signal for another, ensuring a more comprehensive and balanced reconstruction process. With such an approach, the physical background might be reduced without compromising the reconstruction quality of other particles while effectively eliminating combinatorial background with no physical significance.

5. Conclusions

Instead of relying solely on statistical cuts, this work employed a deep learning approach using a deep multi-layer perceptron for signal and background classification. The model achieved a high accuracy of about 0.9876 on the validation set used for selecting the best-fitting neural network.

Integrated into the KF Particle Finder package for a final test, the neural network effectively reduced reconstructed background, particularly eliminating ghosts (combinatorial background) that lack physical meaning. Importantly, the Λ particle signal was minimally affected. The model achieved an accuracy of 0.9859, a precision of 0.9852, a recall of 0.8651, an F1-score of 0.9212, and a specificity of 0.9986, indicating strong overall performance in classifying signal and background. However, reducing the physical background and rejecting these particles has implications for other particles and should be carefully investigated in future works.

Overall, this deep learning method significantly improved the S/B ratio by a factor of 10.97 (from 3.49 to 38.28) and also increased the significance by a factor of 1.14 (from 11.38 to 12.95). These advancements highlight the potential of machine learning to improve particle reconstruction and signal clarity, paving the way for more refined analyses in heavy-ion physics. Future work on extending the model to other particle types, integrating inter-particle interactions, and assessing performance under diverse collision conditions will further enhance its utility and impact.

Author Contributions: Conceptualization, I.K.; methodology, R.L. and G.Z.; software, R.L. and G.Z.; validation, R.L. and G.Z.; formal analysis, G.Z.; investigation, R.L. and G.Z.; resources, R.L. and G.Z.; data curation, R.L. and G.Z.; writing—original draft preparation, R.L. and G.Z.; writing—review and editing, I.K., R.L. and G.Z.; visualization, G.Z.; supervision, I.K.; project administration, I.K.; funding acquisition, I.K. All authors have read and agreed to the published version of the manuscript.

Funding: This research was partly funded by the Federal Ministry of Education and Research [grant numbers 01IS21092, 05P24RF3, 05P24RF7], Germany, and Helmholtz Research Academy Hesse for FAIR (project ID 2.1.4.2.5), Germany.

Institutional Review Board Statement: Not applicable.

Informed Consent Statement: Not applicable.

Data Availability Statement: Restrictions apply to the availability of these data. Data were obtained from the Facility of Antiproton and Ion Research (FAIR), Germany, and are available from the authors with the permission of FAIR.

Conflicts of Interest: The authors declare no conflicts of interest.

Abbreviations

The following abbreviations are used in this manuscript:

ANN4FLES	Artificial Neural Networks for First Level Event Selection
CBM	Compressed Baryonic Matter
FAIR	Facility of Antiproton and Ion Research
FLES	First Level Event Selection
KF	Kalman Filter

MC	Monte Carlo
MLP	Multi-Layer Perceptron
S/B	Signal/Background
UrQMD	Ultra-relativistic Quantum Molecular Dynamics

ferences

Esteva, A.; Kuprel, B.; Novoa, R.; Ko, J.; Swetter, S.M.; Blau, H.M.; Thrun, S. Dermatologist-level classification of skin cancer with deep neural networks. *Nature* **2017**, *542*, 115–118. [CrossRef] [PubMed]

Jumper, J.; Evans, R.; Pritzel, A.; Green, T.; Figurnov, M.; Ronneberger, O.; Tunyasuvunakool, K.; Bates, R.; Zıdek, A.; Potapenko, A.; et al. Highly accurate protein structure prediction with AlphaFold. *Nature* **2021**, *596*, 583–589. [CrossRef] [PubMed]

Buehler, H.; Gonon, L.; Teichmann, J.; Wood, B. Deep hedging. *Quant. Financ.* **2019**, *19*, 1271–1291. [CrossRef]

Radovic, A.; Williams, M.; Rousseau, D.; Kagan, M.; Bonacorsi, D.; Himmel, A.; Aurisano, A.; Terao, K.; Wongjirad, T. Machine learning at the energy and intensity frontiers of particle physics. *Nature* **2018**, *560*, 41–48. [CrossRef]

Bourilkov, D. Machine and deep learning applications in particle physics. *Int. J. Mod. Phys. A* **2019**, *34*, 1930019.

Qu, H.; Gouskos, L. Jet tagging via particle clouds. *Phys. Rev. D* **2020**, *101*, 056019. [CrossRef]

Xu, N. An overview of STAR experimental results. *Nucl. Phys. A* **2014**, *931*, 1–12. . [CrossRef]

Acharya, S.; Adamová, D.; Adler, A.; Rinella, G.A.; Agnello, M.; Agrawal, N.; Ahammed, Z.; Ahmad, S.; Ahn, S.U.; Ahuja, I.; et al. The ALICE experiment: A journey through QCD. *Eur. Phys. J. C* **2024**, *84*, 813. [CrossRef]

Agarwal, K.; for the CBM Collaboration. The Compressed Baryonic Matter (CBM) experiment at FAIR—Physics, status and prospects. *Phys. Scr.* **2023**, *98*, 034006. [CrossRef]

Aberle, O.; Adorisio, C.; Adraktas, A.; Ady, M.; Albertone, J.; Alberty, L.; Alcaide, Leon, M.; Alekou, A.; Alesini, D.; et al. *High-Luminosity Large Hadron Collider (HL-LHC): Technical Design Report*; CERN Yellow Reports: Monographs; 10/2020; CERN: Geneva, Switzerland , 2020. . [CrossRef]

Heuser, J.; Müller, W.; Pugatch, V.; Senger, P.; Schmidt, C.J.; Sturm, C.; Frankenfeld, U. (Eds.) *[GSI Report 2013-4] Technical Design Report for the CBM Silicon Tracking System (STS)*; GSI: Darmstadt, Germany, 2013; p. 167.

Sturm, C.; Stöcker, H. The facility for antiproton and ion research FAIR. *Phys. Part. Nucl. Lett.* **2011**, *8*, 865–868. [CrossRef]

Ablyazimov, T.; Abuhoza, A.; Adak, R.P.; Adamczyk, M.; Agarwal, K.; Aggarwal, M.M.; Ahammed, Z.; Ahmad, F.; Ahmad, N.; Ahmad, S.; et al. Challenges in QCD matter physics—The scientific programme of the Compressed Baryonic Matter experiment at FAIR. *Eur. Phys. J. A* **2017**, *53*, 60. [CrossRef]

Friese, V. Simulation and reconstruction of free-streaming data in CBM. *J. Phys. Conf. Ser.* **2011**, *331*, 032008. [CrossRef]

Friese, V.; for the CBM Collaboration. The high-rate data challenge: Computing for the CBM experiment. *J. Phys. Conf. Ser.* **2017**, *898*, 112003. [CrossRef]

Akishina, V. Four-Dimensional Event Reconstruction in the CBM Experiment. Ph.D. Thesis, J. W. Goethe University Frankfurt, Frankfurt, Germany, 2017.

Kisel, I.; Kulakov, I.; Zyzak, M. Standalone First Level Event Selection Package for the CBM Experiment. *IEEE Trans. Nucl. Sci.* **2013**, *60*, 3703–3708. [CrossRef]

Essel, H. FutureDAQ for CBM: On-line event selection. *IEEE Trans. Nucl. Sci.* **2006**, *53*, 677–681. [CrossRef]

Omana Kuttan, M.; Steinheimer, J.; Zhou, K.; Redelbach, A.; Stoecker, H. A fast centrality-meter for heavy-ion collisions at the CBM experiment. *Phys. Lett. B* **2020**, *811*, 135872. [CrossRef]

Omana Kuttan, M.; Zhou, K.; Steinheimer, J.; Redelbach, A.; Stoecker, H. An equation-of-state-meter for CBM using PointNet. *J. High Energy Phys.* **2021**, *2021*, 184. [CrossRef]

Agarwal, K. Status of the Compressed Baryonic Matter (CBM) Experiment at FAIR. *arXiv* **2022**, arXiv:2207.14585. [CrossRef]

Zyzak, M. Online Selection of Short-Lived Particles on Many-Core Computer Architectures in the CBM Experiment at FAIR. Ph.D. Thesis, J. W. Goethe University Frankfurt, Frankfurt, Germany, 2016.

Larionov, P.; for the CBM Collaboration. Overview of the Silicon Tracking System for the CBM experiment. *J. Phys. Conf. Ser.* **2015**, *599*, 012025. [CrossRef]

Khan, S.; Klochkov, V.; Lavoryk, O.; Lubynets, O.; Khan, A.I.; Dubla, A.; Selyuzhenkov, I. Machine Learning Application for Λ Hyperon Reconstruction in CBM at FAIR. In Proceedings of the 19th International Conference of Strangeness in Quark Matter (SQM 2021), New York, NY, USA, 17–22 May 2021; EPJ Web of Conferences; EDP Sciences: Les Ulis, France, 2022 ; Volume 259, p. 13008. [CrossRef]

Belousov, A.; Kisel, I.; Lakos, R. A Neural-Network-Based Competition between Short-Lived Particle Candidates in the CBM Experiment at FAIR. *Algorithms* **2023**, *16*, 383. [CrossRef]

Senger, P.; Friese, V. *CBM Progress Report 2022*; Technical Report CBM Progress Report 2022; GSI: Darmstadt, Germany, 2022. [CrossRef]

Rafelski, J.; Müller, B. Strangeness Production in the Quark-Gluon Plasma. *Phys. Rev. Lett.* **1982**, *48*, 1066. [CrossRef]

28. Amsler, C.; Doser, M.; Bloch, P.; Ceccucci, A.; Giudice, G.F.; Höcker, A.; Mangano, M.L.; Masoni, A.; Spanier, Törnqvist, N.A.; et al. Particle Data Group. *Phys. Lett. B* **2008**, *667*, 1. [CrossRef]
29. Bleicher, M.; Zabrodin, E.; Spieles, C.; Bass, S.A.; Ernst, C.; Soff, S.; Bravina, L.; Belkacem, M.; Weber, H.; Stöcker, H.; e Relativistic hadron-hadron collisions in the ultra-relativistic quantum molecular dynamics model. *J. Phys. G Nucl. Part. P* **1999**, *25*, 1859. [CrossRef]
30. Murtagh, F. Multilayer perceptrons for classification and regression. *Neurocomputing* **1991**, *2*, 183–197. [CrossRef]
31. Kingma, D.P.; Ba, J. Adam: A Method for Stochastic Optimization. In Proceedings of the 3rd International Conference Learning Representations, San Diego, CA, USA, 7–9 May 2015.
32. Al-Turany, M.; Bertini, D.; Koenig, I. CbmRoot: Simulation and analysis framework for CBM experiment. *Comput. High En Nucl. Phys. (CHEP-2006)* **2006**, *1*, 170–171.

algorithms

MDPI

cle

›ileptic Seizure Prediction Using a Combination of Deep :arning, Time–Frequency Fusion Methods, and Discrete avelet Analysis

‹i Sadeghi Khansari [1], Mostafa Abbaszadeh [2,*], Gholamreza Heidary Joonaghany [1], Hamidreza Mohagerani [3] Fardin Faraji [4]

[1] Department of Mathematics and Computer Science, Arak Branch, Islamic Azad University, Arak 3836119131, Iran; h.sadeghikhansari@iau.ac.ir (H.S.K.); ghheydari@iau.ac.ir (G.H.J.)
[2] Department of Applied Mathematics, Faculty of Mathematics and Computer Sciences, Amirkabir University of Technology (Tehran Polytechnic), No. 424, Hafez Ave., Tehran 15914, Iran
[3] Quantum Technologies Research Center, Science and Research Branch, Islamic Azad University, Tehran 1477893855, Iran; mohajeranihr@gmail.com
[4] Department of Neurology, School of Medicine, Arak University of Medical Sciences, Arak 3813873449, Iran; dr.faraji@arakmu.ac.ir
* Correspondence: m.abbaszadeh@aut.ac.ir

Abstract: Epileptic seizure prediction remains a critical challenge in neuroscience and healthcare, with profound implications for enhancing patient safety and quality of life. In this paper, we introduce a novel seizure prediction method that leverages electroencephalogram (EEG) data, combining discrete wavelet transform (DWT)-based time–frequency analysis, advanced feature extraction, and deep learning using Fourier neural networks (FNNs). The proposed approach extracts essential features from EEG signals—including entropy, power, frequency, and amplitude—to effectively capture the brain's complex and nonstationary dynamics. We measure the method based on the broadly used CHB-MIT EEG dataset, ensuring direct comparability with prior research. Experimental results demonstrate that our DWT-FS-FNN model achieves a prediction accuracy of 98.96 with a zero false positive rate, outperforming several state-of-the-art methods. These findings underscore the potential of integrating advanced signal processing and deep learning methods for reliable, real-time seizure prediction. Future work will focus on optimizing the model for real-world clinical deployment and expanding it to incorporate multimodal physiological data, further enhancing its applicability in clinical practice.

Keywords: epileptic seizure; electroencephalogram (EEG); discrete wavelet transform (DWT); feature selection; Fourier neural networks (FNNs)

1. Introduction

Epilepsy is a common neurological disorder marked by frequent and unpredictable seizures that can profoundly impact a person's quality of life. Early and accurate seizure prediction is essential for improving patient outcomes by enabling timely intervention and enhancing overall safety. Electroencephalogram (EEG) signals, which capture the brain's electrical activity, have become central to the development of automated seizure detection and prediction systems. However, the highly nonstationary and complex nature of EEG data presents significant challenges in designing robust and generalizable predictive models.

Recent advancements in machine learning and signal processing have substantially improved EEG-based epileptic seizure prediction models. Li et al. [1] introduced a patient-specific seizure prediction framework using a multichannel feedback capsule network (FB-CapsNet), which processes EEG signals in an end-to-end manner, eliminating the need for manual feature extraction. By leveraging feedback-enabled capsule structures, the model effectively captures complex spatial-temporal dependencies, offering high predictive accuracy and adaptability to individual EEG profiles. However, the model exhibits high computational complexity and limited generalizability, as it requires separate training for each patient. In contrast, Tamanna et al. [2] proposed a generalized approach utilizing discrete wavelet transform (DWT) for feature extraction and support vector machines (SVM) for classification. Their method achieved an average prediction accuracy of 96.38% and anticipated seizures approximately 26.1 min before onset, without requiring patient-specific training. Nevertheless, reliance on a single dataset and sensitivity to preprocessing steps may impact its generalizability and robustness.

Divya et al. [3] introduced a hybrid deep learning model integrating autoencoders for unsupervised feature extraction with convolutional neural networks (CNNs) for classification. The model achieved 92.5% accuracy and demonstrated good generalization across datasets, though it remains slightly behind the best-performing models and still requires clinical validation. Zhang et al. [4] developed a vision transformer (ViT)-based model that processes EEG data by converting signals into image-like formats. This method benefits from self-attention mechanisms that extract patient-specific spatial features. While it offers strong predictive performance, the approach demands large volumes of patient-specific data and significant computational resources, limiting scalability. Wang et al. [5] proposed a seizure prediction model combining dynamic multi-graph convolution with a channel-weighted transformer. This architecture captures intricate spatial and temporal relationships among EEG channels, resulting in enhanced prediction accuracy. However, it is computationally intensive and dependent on high-quality EEG data, which may not always be feasible in clinical settings.

Kapoor et al. [6] introduced a hybrid Cuckoo–Finch optimization algorithm for automatic EEG electrode selection and CNN hyperparameter tuning. Evaluated on the CHB-MIT and Siena datasets, the model achieved an accuracy of 97.76%. Despite its strong performance, the method's computational complexity and lack of testing in real-world IoT scenarios pose challenges for deployment. Zhao et al. [7] proposed a patient-specific approach combining Adder networks and supervised contrastive learning to improve energy efficiency and feature discrimination. The model demonstrated strong sensitivity and specificity while being computationally suitable for wearable devices. However, it heavily relies on patient-specific data and requires further validation in real-time, noisy environments. Bhattacharya et al. [8] developed a Transformer-based model for seizure prediction that captures long-range temporal dependencies with minimal manual preprocessing. Achieving a sensitivity of 98.5% and a low false-positive rate of 0.12/h, the model is well-suited for clinical use. Nonetheless, its generalizability and high resource requirements remain concerns.

In the context of IoMT applications, Torkey et al. [9] proposed a hybrid model combining CNN, LSTM, and GRU layers, incorporating SMOTE for class imbalance and SHAP for model explainability. Designed for real-time deployment, the model achieved 99.13% accuracy. Despite its strengths in scalability and interpretability, limitations include high computational costs and privacy concerns in IoMT ecosystems. Kalitzin et al. [10] presented TOREADA, an adaptive seizure detection algorithm based on topological reinforcement learning. It dynamically adjusts detection parameters using real-time EEG embeddings. While simulation results highlight its robustness, the lack of clinical validation restricts its practical application. Li et al. [11] analyzed variations in fractal dimensions during seizures using CHB-MIT data, applying both Higuchi's and roughness scaling extraction (RSE) methods. Their study clarified discrepancies in prior findings and emphasized the influence of preprocessing. However, its clinical relevance remains limited due to the absence of predictive modeling. The study by Deng et al. [12] introduced HViT, a hybrid vision Transformer architecture for EEG-based seizure prediction that integrates convolutional neural networks (CNNs) to enhance local feature extraction and mitigate top-level gradient vanishing typically seen in pure transformers. On top of this, they incorporate data uncertainty learning (DUL), modeling each EEG embedding as a Gaussian or Laplacian distribution—where the mean is learned by the HViT and a parallel branch predicts variance or scale—thereby increasing robustness to noisy EEG signal representations. Additionally, a learnable constraint coefficient in the loss function is tailored per patient, and a simple uncertainty quantification method is applied to alarms using a k-of-n continuous prediction strategy. Evaluated on two public epilepsy datasets, their approach demonstrates a superior performance, highlighting the combined benefits of CNN-augmented transformers and uncertainty modeling in improving seizure prediction accuracy

Zhu et al. [13] presented a novel EEG-based seizure prediction model that fuses a multidimensional Transformer encoder with LSTM and GRU recurrent neural networks to simultaneously capture both global and local temporal-frequency features from EEG spectrograms. The approach first applies short-time Fourier transform to extract time–frequency representations, then separately processes spectral and temporal dimensions via dual Transformer encoders. Outputs are further refined through LSTM and GRU branches, whose features are gated and fused for classification. Tested on two public datasets—CHB-MIT and Bonn—the model achieved an outstanding performance: on CHB-MIT, it averaged 98.24 sensitivity and 97.27 specificity; on Bonn, it reached 99 accuracy in binary and 98 in three-class classification. Han Wang et al. [14] proposed a lightweight, compressive sensing-based approach to channel estimation in MIMO-FBMC systems, addressing challenges such as intrinsic imaginary interference and low-resource deployment in industrial IoT settings. By modeling the channel as sparse in the delay/Doppler domain, the authors design a low-complexity estimator that avoids dense pilot structures and heavy computations, achieving a comparable or better MSE than classical methods, especially in noisy environments. This methodology offers strong cross-domain relevance to biomedical applications like seizure prediction, where similar constraints—such as real-time processing, noise robustness, and low-power operation exist. Applying these ideas to EEG analysis suggests potential for wavelet-domain sparsity modeling, adaptive recovery algorithms, and improved interpretability in wearable seizure-monitoring systems. To enhance novelty, related biomedical research can integrate these signal-model-driven, sparsity-aware techniques as alternatives to standard deep fusion models. The main aim of [15] is to address angle estimation in arbitrary-manifold array bistatic MIMO radar and propose a joint two-dimensional direction-of-departure (2D-DOD) and two-dimensional direction-of-arrival (2D-DOA) estimation algorithm assisted by IRS. Finally, Mansouri et al. [16] developed a real-time, non-patient-specific algorithm for seizure detection and localization. Utilizing spectral and coherence-based features, the method achieved a median detection latency of 8 seconds. While computationally efficient and generalizable, its accuracy is reduced for brief seizures and requires robust artifact removal for optimal performance.

Because adder networks use the t-norm distance as the similarity measure between input features and filters, the network's gradient behavior changes. To ensure the proper convergence of AddNet-SCL, we introduce an adaptive learning rate strategy. Building upon these innovations, this paper presents a novel epileptic seizure prediction method that integrates DWT-based time–frequency analysis with advanced feature extraction techniques—including entropy, power, frequency, and amplitude—paired with deep learning using Fourier neural networks (FNNs). Evaluated on the well-established CHB-MIT EEG dataset, the proposed approach achieves high prediction accuracy with a zero false positive rate, marking a significant advancement over existing methods. The rest of this paper is structured as follows:

- Section 2 describes the preprocessing steps, including discrete wavelet transform and feature selection methods.
- Section 3 details the deep learning approach using Fourier neural networks.
- Section 4 details the experimental results and provides a comparative analysis of the proposed method with current approaches.

The originality and primary contributions of this paper can be summarized as follows:

- Sparse signal representation in the wavelet domain: Unlike traditional approaches that rely on dense representations followed by deep fusion techniques (e.g., DWT combined with LSTM), our method explicitly models EEG signals as sparse in the wavelet domain. This formulation draws a parallel to the sparsity observed in the delay/Doppler domain of FBMC channels, allowing for more efficient signal analysis.
- Lightweight adaptive recovery framework: We introduce an adaptive sparse recovery module inspired by pursuit-based algorithms, specifically designed to handle the non-stationary and noise-prone nature of EEG signals. While conceptually similar to sparse channel estimation techniques in communication systems, this module is customized for biomedical signal processing applications.
- Optimized for real-time applications: The proposed model significantly reduces computational overhead, making it suitable for deployment on low-power, real-time platforms such as wearable seizure detection devices. This aligns with similar efficiency goals pursued in MIMO-FBMC systems for industrial IoT environments.
- Improved interpretability and clinical relevance: The sparse wavelet coefficients produced by our model enhance the transparency and physiological interpretability of EEG signals. This feature not only supports clinical decision making but also mirrors the interpretability advantages seen in sparse communication channel estimation.

2. Preprocessing

The dataset used in this article is CHB-MIT, which has been used in most similar articles, and this dataset is a standardized dataset, so it has been used to compare the results with other proposed methods in different articles. The paper method includes steps as follows:

2.1. Discrete Wavelet Transform

The discrete wavelet transform (DWT) is a powerful signal processing technique often used for analyzing non-stationary signals, such as electroencephalogram (EEG) data. EEG signals capture electrical activity in the brain, and due to their complex nature, traditional Fourier analysis may not be sufficient to fully characterize their time–frequency features. DWT provides a multi-resolution analysis, making it particularly suitable for EEG signal processing. Here is a description of how DWT is applied to EEG signals: Overview of the discrete wavelet transform wavelet basics: Unlike the Fourier Transform, which uses sine and cosine functions, DWT uses wavelets—short, oscillatory, localized functions that can represent both frequency and time characteristics of a signal. Wavelets can be designed to possess different shapes and properties, allowing for adaptability to various types of signals. The DWT decomposes a signal $x[p]$ using a pair of filters:

- Low-pass filter $h[p]$: extracts approximations (low-frequency components).

- High-pass filter $g[p]$: extracts details (high-frequency components).

Decomposition Equations

$$a_i[k] = \sum_p x[p] \cdot h[2k - p]$$

$$d_i[k] = \sum_p x[p] \cdot g[2k - p]$$

such that

- $a_i[k]$: approximation coefficients at level i.
- $d_i[k]$: detail coefficients at level i.
- $2k$: represents downsampling by 2.

Multi-resolution analysis: DWT decomposes a signal into different frequency components by breaking it down into approximations (low-frequency) and details (high-frequency). The decomposition is performed recursively, producing multiple levels of resolution corresponding to different frequency bands. Decomposition process: The original EEG signal is passed through a series of filters: a low-pass filter (to extract approximation coefficients) and a high-pass filter (to extract detailed coefficients). This process is repeated on the approximation coefficients to yield additional levels of detail, creating a tree-like structure of coefficients. Each level recursively decomposes the approximation coefficients a_j:

$$x[n] \xrightarrow{\text{DWT}} \{a_J[n], d_J[n], d_{J-1}[n], \ldots, d_1[n]\}$$

Coefficients interpretation: The resulting coefficients provide insight into both the coarse (low-frequency) and fine (high-frequency) aspects of the EEG signal. The approximation coefficients are associated with slower brain wave activities (like delta and theta waves), while detailed coefficients tend to correspond to faster activities (like alpha and beta waves).

In our Python 3.13.5 function `apply_dwt`, we initially employed the Daubechies 4 (`'db4'`) wavelet with a fixed decomposition level of 5. The `db4` wavelet is widely used due to its orthogonality, compact support, and its ability to provide a balanced representation in both time and frequency domains, making it suitable for diverse signal types.

However, we recognize that the choice of wavelet should be guided by the specific characteristics of the signal under analysis. For example, the `Haar` wavelet is more effective for signals with abrupt changes, while smoother signals—such as those often found in biomedical applications—are better handled with `Symlets` or `Coiflets`.

Moreover, we improved the adaptability of our approach by avoiding a fixed number of decomposition levels. Instead, the appropriate level is now determined dynamically based on the signal length and the filter length of the chosen wavelet. This is achieved using the `PyWavelets` function:

$$\text{level} = \texttt{pywt.dwt\_max\_level(len(signal), pywt.Wavelet(wavelet).dec\_len)} \quad (1)$$

This ensures that the decomposition captures relevant time–frequency features without unnecessary over-decomposition.

To clarify the process, we have provided an example: Figure 1 displays the original EEG signal, while Figure 2 shows the reconstructed signal using DWT. The aim of this work is to regularize highly irregular EEG signals.

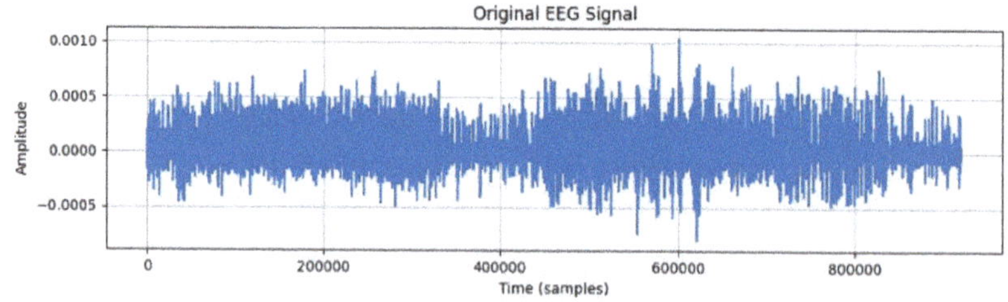

Figure 1. Original EEG signal plotted over time. The signal exhibits high variability and nonstationary characteristics, highlighting the need for advanced preprocessing techniques such as the discrete wavelet transform (DWT) for effective analysis and feature extraction.

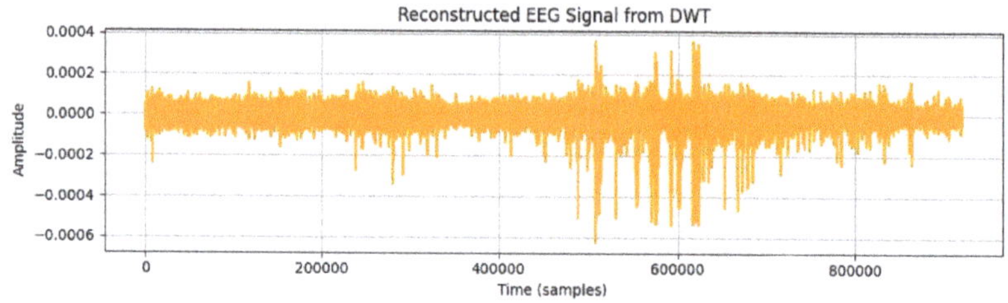

Figure 2. The reconstruction signal from DWT preprocessing and ready to extracted features.

2.2. Features Selection

2.2.1. Calculated Entropy of EEG Signal

Entropy in EEG signals refers to the measurement of irregularity or complexity in the signal. EEG signals originate from the brain's electrical activity and are typically distinguished by characteristic patterns and fluctuations that provide valuable insights into brain activity and function. The entropy analysis of EEG signals involves quantifying the level of disorder and randomness within the signal. Higher entropy values indicate greater complexity and irregularity, while lower entropy values indicate more regular and predictable patterns in the signal. Different entropy measures, such as sample entropy or approximate entropy, can be used to analyze EEG signals and Offer insights into the dynamic processes of brain activity. In our implementation, entropy is calculated using the `scipy.stats.entropy()` function, which computes the Shannon entropy of a discrete probability distribution. To do this, we first create a histogram of the truncated signal using 50 bins:

```
hist = np.histogram(truncated_signal, bins=50)[0]
ent = entropy(hist)
```

This histogram captures the frequency distribution of the signal's amplitude values. The `entropy()` function then normalizes the histogram to produce a probability distribution and applies the Shannon entropy formula:

$$H = -\sum_{i=1}^{n} p_i \log_2(p_i) \tag{2}$$

where p_i denotes the normalized probability associated with the i-th bin.

This approach yields a global measure of the signal's complexity, reflecting the diversity in amplitude values throughout the signal.

The entropy analysis of EEG signals can help in understanding the complexity of neural processes, identifying abnormalities or changes in brain function, and providing valuable information for diagnostic and therapeutic purposes in neurological disorders such as epilepsy and neurodegenerative diseases. Overall, the entropy analysis of EEG signals offers a quantitative and objective way to assess the complexity and dynamics of brain activity, allowing for a deeper understanding of brain function and providing valuable insights for clinical and research applications.

2.2.2. Calculated Power of Signals

The power of a signal is a crucial concept in signal processing that quantifies the average energy contained in the signal over time. It provides insight into the strength and variability of the signal, which can be particularly important for applications in various fields such as telecommunications, audio processing, and biomedical engineering, including EEG analysis. Below is a description of signal power, including its definitions, types, calculations, and implications: Definition of signal power signal power: The power of a signal is defined as the average energy per unit time. It indicates how much energy a signal carries and is often measured in watts (W). Mathematically, for a continuous-time signal $x(t)$, the average power P can be expressed as

$$P = \lim_{T\to\infty} \frac{1}{T} \int_{-T/2}^{T/2} |x(t)|^2 \, dt.$$

Instantaneous power: The instantaneous power of a signal at a given time t is defined as

$$P(t) = |x(t)|^2,$$

where T is the period of the signal. Aperiodic Signals: For aperiodic signals (non-repeating), the average power is calculated over an infinite duration, as shown in the earlier definitions. Power Spectral Density (PSD) The power spectral density (PSD) is a measure that describes how the power of a signal is distributed across different frequency components. It is often used in the context of analyzing signals in the frequency domain. The PSD can be calculated using techniques such as the Fourier transform or the Welch method and provides insight into how signal power varies with frequency.

2.2.3. Calculated Frequency of Signals

Electroencephalography (EEG) measures electrical activity in the brain through electrodes placed on the scalp. The calculated frequency of EEG signals is vital for understanding brain state and mental processes. Here is an overview of EEG frequency bands and their significance: Delta (0.5–4 Hz): Associated with deep sleep and restorative processes. Common in infants and deep anesthetic states. Theta (4–8 Hz): Linked to light sleep, relaxation, and creativity. Often observed during meditation and daydreaming. Alpha (8–12 Hz): Indicates relaxed, yet alert states, often present when the eyes are closed. Attenuates with mental tasks or distraction. Beta (12–30 Hz): Related to active thinking, problem-solving, and focus. Prominent during active concentration and anxiety. Gamma (30 Hz and above): Associated with higher-level cognitive functions, including perception and consciousness. Involves memory recall and sensory processing. Description shown in Figure 3.

2.2.4. Calculating Frequency

To analyze EEG signals, techniques such as fast Fourier Transform (FFT) is used, since this is a mathematical algorithm that transforms time-domain EEG signals into the frequency domain, allowing the identification of predominant frequency components. Wavelet transform: Useful for assessing frequency changes over time, providing a time–frequency representation of EEG data.

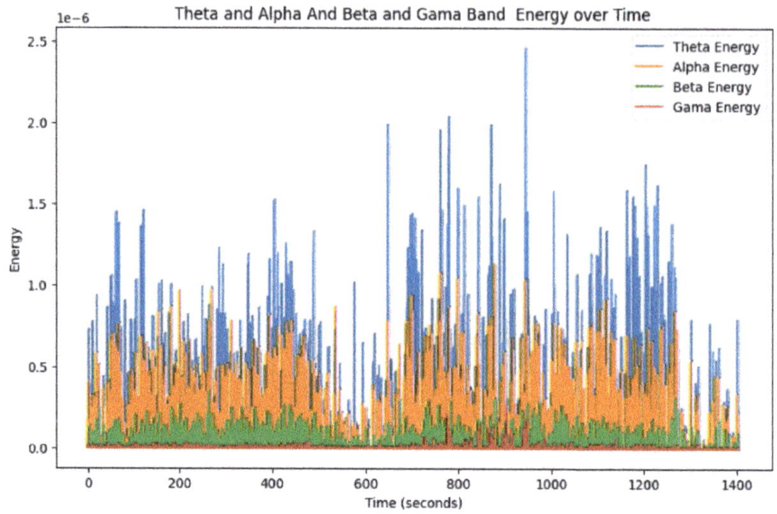

Figure 3. Energy distribution of neural frequency bands (theta, alpha, beta, gamma) over a 1400-s period. Theta (4–8 Hz) and Alpha (8–12 Hz) dominate lower frequencies, while Beta (12–30 Hz) and Gamma (30–100 Hz) show intermittent spikes, suggesting varied cognitive states.

2.2.5. Calculated Amplitude of Signals

Signal amplitude refers to the magnitude or strength of a signal's oscillation or variation over time. It represents the maximum deviation of the signal from its baseline or mean value and is a critical characteristic in analyzing and understanding various types of signals, such as electrical, audio, and biological signals. Key aspects of signal amplitude Measurement: Amplitude can be measured in various units depending on the type of signal: Voltage (V) for electrical signals. Decibels (dB) for sound intensity. Arbitrary units in specific applications. Types of amplitude: Peak amplitude: The maximum positive or negative value of the signal from the center line. Root mean square (RMS) amplitude: A statistical measure that reflects the effective value of a varying signal, often used to compute power in alternating current (AC) circuits. Peak-to-peak amplitude: The total range of the signal, calculated as the difference between the maximum positive and maximum negative peaks. Signal strength: Amplitude indicates the strength of the signal, with higher amplitude correlating to greater intensity or energy. Quality: In communication systems, a higher amplitude generally improves the signal-to-noise ratio (SNR), enhancing clarity and quality. Biological insights: In medical signals (e.g., EEG or ECG), amplitude variations can indicate neural or cardiac activity levels, revealing important health information.

3. Deep Learning

3.1. Fourier Neural Networks

(FNNs) can be particularly effective in analyzing electroencephalography (EEG) signals, which are inherently complex and often contain rhythmic and periodic patterns indicating brain activity. Below is an in-depth description of how FNNs can be applied specifically to EEG signal processing. Given an input vector $x \in \mathbb{R}^d$ and a frequency matrix $B \in \mathbb{R}^{m \times d}$, the Fourier feature mapping is defined as

$$\gamma(x) = [\sin(2\pi Bx), \cos(2\pi Bx)] \in \mathbb{R}^{2m}$$

Here

- B is a matrix with entries often sampled from $\mathcal{N}(0, \sigma^2)$.
- $\gamma(x)$ embeds x into a higher-dimensional space where periodic features are easier to learn.

3.2. FNN Architecture

An FNN uses the Fourier-mapped input as input to a standard neural network:

$$f(x) = \mathcal{N}(\gamma(x); \theta)$$

where

- $\mathcal{N}(\cdot; \theta)$ is a multi-layer perceptron (MLP).
- θ represents the learnable weights and biases.

A basic architecture looks like

$$f(x) = W_2 \cdot \sigma(W_1 \cdot \gamma(x) + b_1) + b_2$$

where

- $W_1 \in \mathbb{R}^{h \times 2m}$, $W_2 \in \mathbb{R}^{1 \times h}$
- b_1, b_2 are biases
- σ is an activation function (e.g., ReLU)

The neural network architecture consists of an input layer followed by two hidden layers with 128 and 64 neurons, respectively. Both hidden layers use ReLU activation functions. The output layer employs a sigmoid activation to perform binary classification, distinguishing between seizure and non-seizure instances.

The model was trained using the Adam optimizer with a binary cross-entropy loss function, a batch size of 32, and over 10 epochs. This configuration was chosen to maintain a balance between computational efficiency and predictive performance.

Although no explicit regularization methods (such as dropout or L2 regularization) were applied, validation metrics were closely monitored throughout training. This helped ensure the model generalized well and did not exhibit signs of overfitting, particularly given the relatively short training duration.

Description for EEG signal processing EEG signal characteristics: EEG signals are composed of electrical activities from the brain, reflecting various states such as sleep, alertness, and cognitive engagement. These signals typically exhibit rhythmic patterns across different frequency bands (e.g., delta, theta, alpha, beta, and gamma). Fourier Transform applications: frequency domain analysis: FNNs can leverage Fourier transforms to convert EEG time-series data into the frequency domain. This transformation allows the network to directly analyze different frequency bands, which are essential for interpreting various mental states and conditions. Feature extraction: Through Fourier transformation, the FNN can automatically extract meaningful features related to brain activity, such as power spectral densities for specific frequency bands, without relying heavily on manual feature engineering. Network Architecture: FNNs designed for EEG may include layers that directly apply Fourier transforms, sinusoidal activations, and other elements suited to model periodic functions relevant to brain activities. Some architectures might blend traditional convolutional or recurrent layers with Fourier layers to capture both temporal and frequency-related information. Learning Temporal Dynamics: By integrating temporal dynamics within the framework of Fourier analysis, FNNs can adaptively learn how specific frequency patterns evolve over time, which is crucial for understanding cognitive processes, detecting seizures, or classifying mental states.

4. Result

We utilized the CHB-MIT Scalp EEG database, which contains recordings from 24 pediatric patients. From this dataset, a total of 827 usable EEG signal segments were extracted following initial preprocessing, which included

- Removing segments with missing or corrupted values.
- Normalizing signal amplitudes using z-score normalization to ensure a standardized range.
- Truncating or zero-padding signals to a fixed length to maintain uniform input dimensions.

To simulate a realistic prediction scenario, the dataset was split chronologically based on recording times. This strategy ensures that the test data reflects unseen future samples, reducing data leakage and offering a more accurate measure of generalization. The data was divided as follows:

- **289 signals** were assigned to the test set.
- **539 signals** were used for training and validation.

This results in a test set comprising approximately 35% of the entire dataset. To enhance the robustness of the evaluation, the model was trained and assessed over 5 independent runs, each with different random seeds and data shuffling.

Table 1 presents a comparison of several deep learning models applied to EEG signal classification, each utilizing distinct preprocessing pipelines.

Table 1. Comparison of EEG classification models with different preprocessing and deep learning techniques.

Preprocessing	Deep Learning	Predict Time	Accuracy	AUC-ROC	FPR
Raw Data	CapsNet	30	95/7	–	0/127
DWT	SVM	25/1	96/38	–	0/19
DWT	Hybrid AE+CNN	–	94/54	0/9215	–
STFT	Transformer based	10	94/6	0/989	–
DWT	FNN	5	98/96	1	0

AUC-ROC (area under the receiver operating characteristic curve) quantifies the model's ability to distinguish between preictal (pre-seizure) and interictal (non-seizure) states across all possible classification thresholds. An AUC of 1.0 indicates perfect discrimination, whereas an AUC of 0.5 suggests a performance equivalent to random guessing. This metric is particularly important in medical diagnosis tasks such as epilepsy prediction, where both false positives and false negatives can have significant consequences. A high AUC signifies that the model is effective at ranking true preictal events above interictal ones, which is vital for providing timely and accurate seizure warnings.

FPR (false positive rate) refers to the proportion of interictal (non-seizure) segments that are incorrectly classified as preictal. In the context of epilepsy prediction, maintaining a low FPR is crucial, as frequent false alarms can cause undue stress, trigger unnecessary interventions, and negatively impact the patient's quality of life. This is especially important in real-time or wearable monitoring systems, where reliability and user trust are paramount.

As shown in Figure 4, the plot illustrates the classification accuracy of various seizure prediction and detection models. The x axis represents different models along with their corresponding preprocessing techniques, while the y axis indicates accuracy values ranging from 93% to 100%. This visualization enables a direct comparison of model performance in terms of classification accuracy.

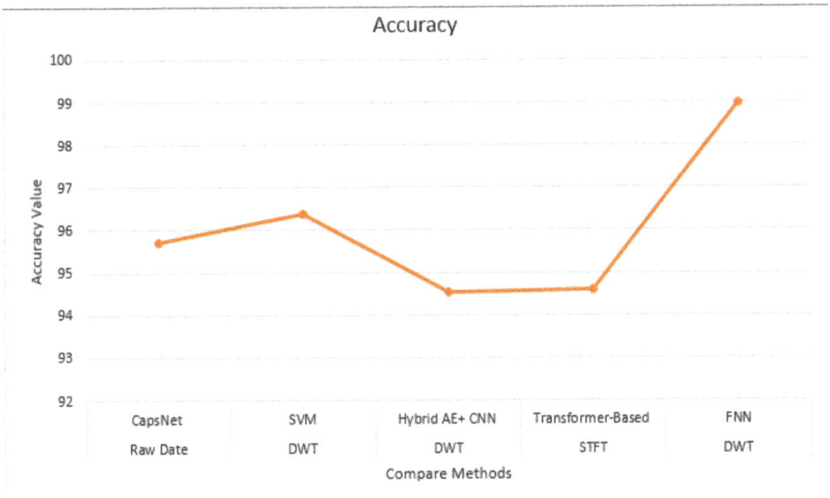

Figure 4. Model accuracy rankings. Higher values denote a better classification performance.

Figure 5 presents a line graph comparing the AUC-ROC scores of several seizure prediction or detection models, providing insight into their discriminative power. Higher AUC values (closer to 1.0) indicate better performance. The y axis ranges from 0.88 to 1.02, focusing on high-performing models, while the x axis lists the models along with their EEG preprocessing methods: CapsNet (Raw Data), SVM (DWT), Hybrid AE + CNN (DWT), Transformer based (STFT), and FNN (DWT). The curve begins at approximately 0.92 for the Hybrid AE + CNN model, rises to about 0.98 for the Transformer-based model, and peaks near 1.0 for the FNN model, indicating the highest classification performance. CapsNet and SVM models are not plotted, possibly due to low or unavailable AUC values. Overall, the figure highlights the superior discriminative capability of the FNN model and the importance of effective EEG preprocessing combined with deep learning architectures.

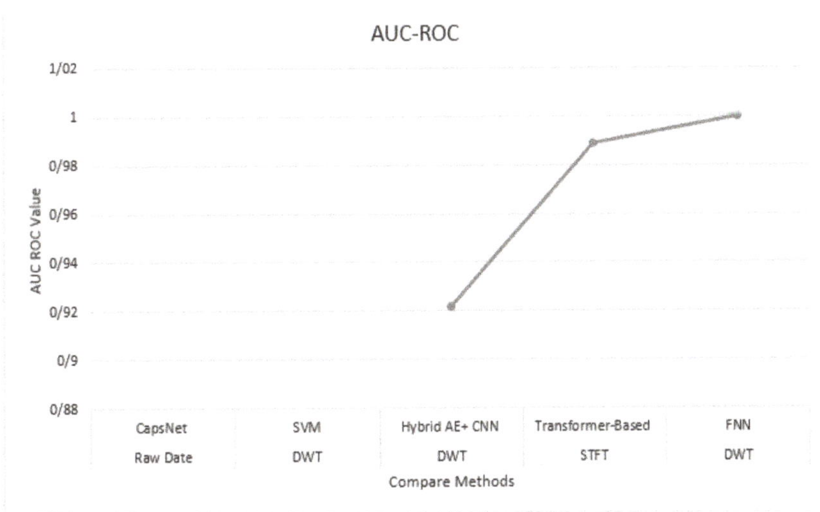

Figure 5. AUC-ROC curves for model comparisons. Scores closer to 1 indicate superior classification ability.

Figure 6 displays a line graph showing the false positive rate (FPR) across various seizure detection models, where lower FPR values indicate better resistance to false alarms. The y axis spans from 0 to 0.20 to capture clinically significant variations, while the x axis shows the models alongside their respective EEG preprocessing techniques: CapsNet (raw data), SVM (DWT), hybrid AE + CNN (DWT), Transformer-based (STFT), and FNN (DWT). Among the visible data points, the SVM model starts at an FPR of approximately 0.13, and the hybrid AE + CNN model rises to around 0.19, indicating weaker performance. In contrast, the FNN model demonstrates the best outcome, with an FPR close to zero. CapsNet and Transformer-based models lack visible data points, possibly due to missing values or values outside the displayed range.

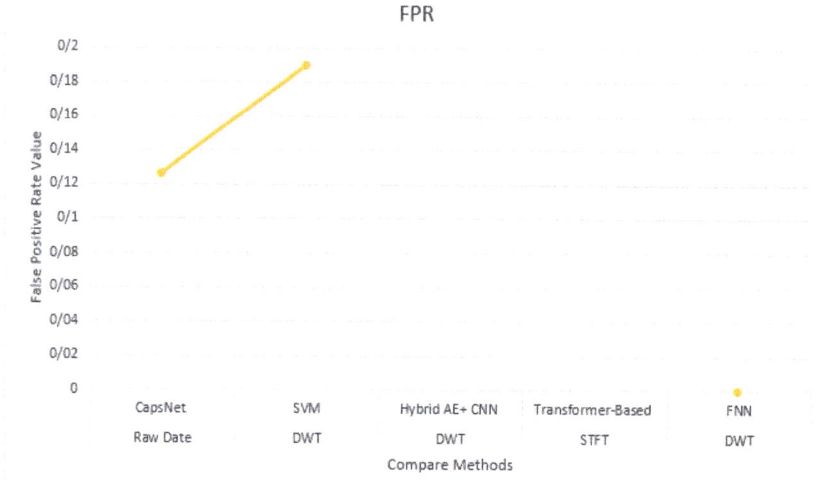

Figure 6. False positive rate (FPR) across models. Lower values indicate better robustness against false alarms.

5. Conclusions

However, several challenges were identified:

- **Data scarcity and imbalance:** Despite access to a relatively large EEG database, only 827 segments were usable after filtering, limiting model generalization. Furthermore, certain models showed skewed performance (e.g., perfect FPR but low AUC), likely due to class imbalance or overfitting.
- **Interpretability of deep models:** While deep models like Transformers and CNNs yielded competitive results, their black-box nature raises concerns in clinical applications where decision transparency is critical.
- **Variability in signal quality:** EEG signals are inherently noisy and patient-specific. Although normalization was applied, inter-patient variability remains a key obstacle, potentially impacting model robustness in broader clinical settings.
- **Computational Trade-offs:** Some models, such as the Transformer-based approach, offer competitive accuracy with reduced prediction time, making them suitable for real-time use. Others, while more accurate, require more extensive computation or more complex preprocessing, which may limit deployment in resource-constrained environments.

The integration of discrete wavelet transform (DWT) with deep learning models led to significant improvements in performance. Notably, the combination of DWT with a

Fourier neural network (FNN) achieved the highest performance across all metrics. This configuration recorded an accuracy of 98/96, an AUC-ROC score of 1.0, and an FPR of 0, with the shortest prediction time of 5 units. These results indicate a highly effective model capable of rapid and precise EEG signal classification.

In contrast, the use of raw EEG data with a CapsNet model, while achieving a reasonable accuracy of 95/7, resulted in the highest false positive rate (0/127) and the longest prediction time (30 units), underscoring the limitations of bypassing signal preprocessing. Other DWT-based approaches, such as DWT + SVM and DWT + hybrid AE+CNN, also demonstrated solid accuracy and low false positive rates, though they did not surpass the FNN model. Meanwhile, the STFT + Transformer-based method showed moderate accuracy (94/6) and AUC-ROC performance but fell short in comparison to the top-performing DWT-based configuration. The experimental results confirm that applying discrete wavelet transform (DWT) as a preprocessing step significantly enhances the effectiveness of deep learning models for EEG signal classification. Among the tested methods, the DWT + FNN configuration stands out for its superior accuracy, perfect AUC-ROC score, zero false positives, and minimal prediction time. These findings highlight the potential of combining multi-resolution signal analysis with lightweight neural architectures to develop robust and efficient EEG-based diagnostic and brain–computer interface systems.

Author Contributions: H.S.K.: Responsible for the implementation of the model and initial manuscript drafting. M.A.: Led the development of the mathematical modeling framework and performed validation and verification of the results. G.H.J.: Conducted result analysis and contributed to the generation and refinement of visual figures. H.M.: Performed detailed dataset analysis and preprocessing. F.F.: Conceived and defined the structure and characteristics of the dataset used in the study. All authors have read and agreed to the published version of the manuscript.

Funding: This research received no external funding.

Data Availability Statement: Data sharing is not applicable.

Acknowledgments: The authors would like to sincerely thank the anonymous referees for their careful reading, insightful comments, and valuable suggestions, which have greatly improved the clarity, quality, and overall presentation of this paper.

Conflicts of Interest: The authors declared that they have no conflict of interest.

ferences

Li, C.; Zhao, Y.; Song, R.; Liu, X.; Qian, R.; Chen, X. Patient-specific seizure prediction from electroencephalogram signal via multichannel feedback capsule network. *IEEE Trans. Cogn. Dev. Syst.* **2022**, *15*, 1360–1370. [CrossRef]

Tamanna, T.; Rahman, M.; Sultana, S.; Haque, M.; Parvez, M. Predicting seizure onset based on time-frequency analysis of eeg signals. *Chaos Solitons Fract.* **2021**, *145*, 110796. [CrossRef]

Divya, P.; Devi, B.; Prabakar, S.; Porkumaran, K.; Kannan, R.; Nor, N.; Elamvazuthi, I. Identification of epileptic seizures using autoencoders and convolutional neural network. In Proceedings of the 2020 8th International Conference on Intelligent and Advanced Systems (ICIAS), Kuching, Malaysia, 13–15 July 2021; pp. 1–6.

Zhang, X.; Li, H. Patient-specific seizure prediction from scalp eeg using vision transformer. In Proceedings of the 2022 IEEE 6th Information Technology and Mechatronics Engineering Conference (ITOEC), Chongqing, China, 4–6 March 2022; pp. 1663–1667.

Wang, Y.; Cui, W.; Yu, T.; Li, X.; Liao, X.; Li, Y. Dynamic multi-graph convolution based channelweighted transformer feature fusion network for epileptic seizure prediction. *IEEE Trans. Neural Syst. Rehabil.* **2023**, *31*, 99. [CrossRef] [PubMed]

Kapoor, B.; Nagpal, B. Hybrid cuckoo finch optimisation based machine learning classifier for seizure prediction using eeg signals in iot network. *Clust. Comput.* **2024**, *27*, 2239–2260. [CrossRef]

Zhao, Y.; Li, C.; Liu, X.; Qian, R.; Song, R.; Chen, X. Patient-specific seizure prediction via adder network and supervised contrastive learning. *IEEE Trans. Neural Syst. Rehabil. Eng.* **2022**, *30*, 1536–1547. [CrossRef] [PubMed]

Bhattacharya, A.; Baweja, T.; Karri, S.P.K. Epileptic seizure prediction using deep transformer model. *Int. J. Neural Syst.* **2022**, *32*, 2150058. [CrossRef] [PubMed]

9. Torkey, H.; Hashish, S.; Souissi, S.; Hemdan, E.E.-D.; Sayed, A. Seizure detection in medical iot: Hybrid cnn-lstm-gru model data balancing and xai integration. *Algorithms* **2025**, *18*, 77. [CrossRef]
10. Kalitzin, S. Topological reinforcement adaptive algorithm (toreada) application to the alerting of convulsive seizures validation with monte carlo numerical simulations. *Algorithms* **2024**, *17*, 516. [CrossRef]
11. Li, Z.; Li, J.; Xia, Y.; Feng, P.; Feng, F. Variation trends of fractal dimension in epileptic eeg signals. *Algorithms* **2021**, *14*, [CrossRef]
12. Deng, Z.; Li, C.; Song, R.; Liu, X.; Qian, R.; Chen, X. EEG-based seizure prediction via hybrid vision transformer and uncertainty learning. *Eng. Appl. Artif. Intell.* **2023**, *123*, 106401. [CrossRef]
13. Pan, W.; Liu, J.; Shang, J. Epileptic seizure prediction via multidimensional transformer and recurrent neural network fusic *Transl. Med.* **2024**, *22*, 895. [CrossRef] [PubMed]
14. Wang, H.; Xu, L.; Yan, Z.; Gulliver, T.A.; Gulliver, T.A. Low-Complexity MIMO-FBMC Sparse Channel Parameter Estimatio Industrial Big Data Communications. *IEEE Trans. Ind. Inform.* **2021**, *17*, 3422–3430. [CrossRef]
15. Xue, X.; Wen, F.; Wang, H. Two-Dimensional Estimation Method for Bistatic MIMO Radar Assisted by Intelligent Reflec Surfaces. In Proceedings of the 2025 IEEE 34th Wireless and Optical Communications Conference (WOCC), Taipa, Macao, 2 May 2025; pp. 260–264. [CrossRef]
16. Mansouri, A.; Singh, S.P.; Sayood, K. Online eeg seizure detection and localization. *Algorithms* **2019**, *12*, 176. [CrossRef]

algorithms

cle

n Solving the Minimum Spanning Tree Problem with onflicting Edge Pairs

erto Montemanni [1,*] and Derek H. Smith [2]

1 Department of Sciences and Methods for Engineering, University of Modena and Reggio Emilia, 42122 Reggio Emilia, Italy
2 Faculty of Computing, Engineering and Science, University of South Wales, Pontypridd CF37 1DL, UK; derek.smith@southwales.ac.uk
* Correspondence: roberto.montemanni@unimore.it; Tel.: +39-0522-522-126

Abstract: The Minimum Spanning Tree with Conflicting Edge Pairs is a generalization that adds conflict constraints to a classical optimization problem on graphs used to model several real-world applications. In recent years, several heuristic and exact approaches have been proposed to tackle this problem. In this paper, we present a mixed-integer linear program not previously applied to this problem, and we solve it with an open-source solver. Computational results for the benchmark instances commonly adopted in the literature of the problem are reported. The results indicate that the approach we propose obtains results aligned with those of the much more sophisticated approaches available, notwithstanding it being much simpler to implement. During the experimental campaign, six instances were closed for the first time, with nine improved best-known lower bounds and sixteen improved best-known upper bounds over a total of two hundred thirty instances considered.

Keywords: minimum spanning tree; conflict constraints; exact solutions; heuristic solutions

1. Introduction

The Minimum Spanning Tree Problem with Conflicting Edge Pairs (MSTC) is a variant of the classical minimum spanning tree (MST) problem recently introduced [1]. Given a connected undirected graph with costs on the edges and a set of edge pairs in conflict with each other, the MSTC consists of finding the spanning tree with the minimum total cost that uses at most one of the edges of each conflicting pair. The MSTC was first introduced by Darmann et al. [2]. It was shown that under general settings, the problem cannot be solved in polynomial time, although some special cases are shown to be polynomially solvable. Several heuristic methods were subsequently proposed in [3], while a branch-and-cut based on a mathematical programming model and some valid inequalities was presented in [4]. More recently, a metaheuristic method was designed and presented in [5], while some new methods based on Lagrangian relaxations, able to produce high-quality lower bounds and heuristic solutions, were introduced in [6]. Finally, a new branch-and-cut approach based on some new valid inequalities was discussed in [7] and shown to represent the current state-of-the-art exact solving methods.

In the literature of graph theory and algorithms, several classic optimization problems have been studied in one or more variants involving conflict constraints, witnessing increasing popularity of the topic due to the number of related real-world applications. For example, for the Assignment Problem with Conflicts, theoretical results on the computational complexity, together with some approximation results, can be found in [2]. Further

 https://doi.org/10.3390/a18080526

results for special polynomially solvable settings were presented in [8], together with some heuristics and lower-bounding schema. More contributions can be found in [9,10], where some Mixed-Integer Linear Programming models, exact Branch-and-Bound methods, and heuristic ideas are introduced. The concepts of the last two papers were later summarized and extended in [11]. For the Knapsack Problem with Conflicts, a local-search heuristic and a branch-and-bound method based on Lagrangian relaxation are discussed in [12]. In [13], the authors proposed some preprocessing techniques and a different branch-and-bound algorithm. Heuristic methods for this problem were discussed in [14,15]. Metaheuristic approaches were finally presented in [16,17]. Finally, a branch-and-bound exact method, based on binary branching, was proposed in [18], while another branch-and-bound schema, based on n-ary branching, was developed and tested in [19]. Different Set-Covering Problems with Conflicts were proposed in [20,21], together with approximation algorithms and computational complexity results. Different families of valid inequalities for a model representing the problem were presented in [22], together with some preprocessing and speed-up routines. A specialization of the same problem in geometric settings was discussed in [23], where some approximation results were presented. The Shortest Path Problem with Conflicts can be found in [24], where critical variants of the shortest path problem arising in the automatic generation of test paths for programs were introduced, and in [25], where the first definition of conflict pairs was presented, although nodes instead of arcs were a part of the conflicts. A procedure to solve the problem was discussed in [26]. A polyhedral study of the problem was presented in [27], while branch-and-bound and dynamic programming approaches were recently proposed in [28,29]. The Maximum Flow Problem with Conflicts was first studied in [30], where the NP-hardness of the problem is shown. Later, some mixed-integer linear programming formulations and exact methods, such as a Benders Decomposition, a Branch-and-Bound, and a Russian Doll Search were presented in [31]. More recently, the authors of [32] proposed a heuristic approach for the problem called Kernousel, obtained by merging two metaheuristic approaches, one based on Carousel Greedy [33] and the other on Kernel Search [34].

The MSTC can be used to represent real applications arising in different domains. For example, the design of an offshore wind farm network, where the wind turbines have to be connected together, and the different possible point-to-point connections are characterized by different costs. Technical reasons prevent the use of overlapped cables in such a context [35], and this generates conflict constraints. Other practical applications are in the design and installation of long-distance pipelines, where conflicts typically represent the impossibility of using infrastructures owned by competitor service providers or, alternatively, the impossibility of crossing countries with reciprocal political issues with the same line [36].

In this paper, a compact mixed-integer linear programming model for the MSTC is introduced in the context of the MSTC. It is based on multi-commodity flow concepts and extends known formulations for the MST problem ([37,38]) to the case with conflicts. Notice that multi-commodity flow models are common for problems related to the MST problem (see, for example, [39] for the Min-degree Constrained MST and [40] for the Diameter-Constrained MST). The model we propose is solved by the open-source solver CP-SAT, which is a part of the Google OR-Tools [41] optimization suite. Normally, models based on multi-commodity flow are not very effective in the context of integer programming, due to the poor linear relaxation, but we believe such a formulation might perform well when solved with CP-SAT. Successful application of this solver on optimization problems with characteristics similar to the problem under investigation, such as the Parallel Drone-Scheduling Traveling Salesman Problem and Vehicle Routing Problems [42,43], the Maximum Flow Problem with Conflict Constraints [44], and the Home Healthcare-Routing and Scheduling Problem [45], motivated this study. A comprehensive experimental campaign is conducted and reported on the benchmark instances previously used in the literature.

The overall organization of the paper can be summarized as follows: Section 2 is dedicated to the formal introduction and definition of the Minimum Spanning Tree Problem with Conflicting Edge Pairs. Section 3 presents a compact mixed-integer linear programming model to represent the problem. In Section 4, the new model is validated through an extensive experimental perspective. After the description of the benchmark instances considered and of the methods used for comparison purposes, the detailed results obtained by solving the new model are reported. Some conclusions about the work presented and the results achieved are drawn in Section 5 to close the paper.

2. Problem Description

The Minimum Spanning Tree Problem with Additional Conflicts can be defined on an undirected graph ($G = (V, E)$), with V denoting the set of nodes and E the set of edges. Each edge ($\{i, j\} \in E$) is associated with a cost ($u_{ij} \in \mathbb{N}^+$). The following feature differentiates the problem from the classic Minimum Spanning Tree Problem and increases the theoretical computational complexity of the problem to $\mathcal{NP}$–hard [2]: Two edges ($\{i, j\}, \{k, l\} \in E$) are said to be *in conflict* if, at most, one of them can be included in a feasible solution. The set of edges in conflict with the edge ($\{i, j\} \in E$) is contained in the set δ_{ij}. The goal of the MSTC is to find the minimum-cost-spanning tree that satisfies all the conflict constraints.

An example of an MFPC instance and the optimal solution for the same instance are provided in Figure 1.

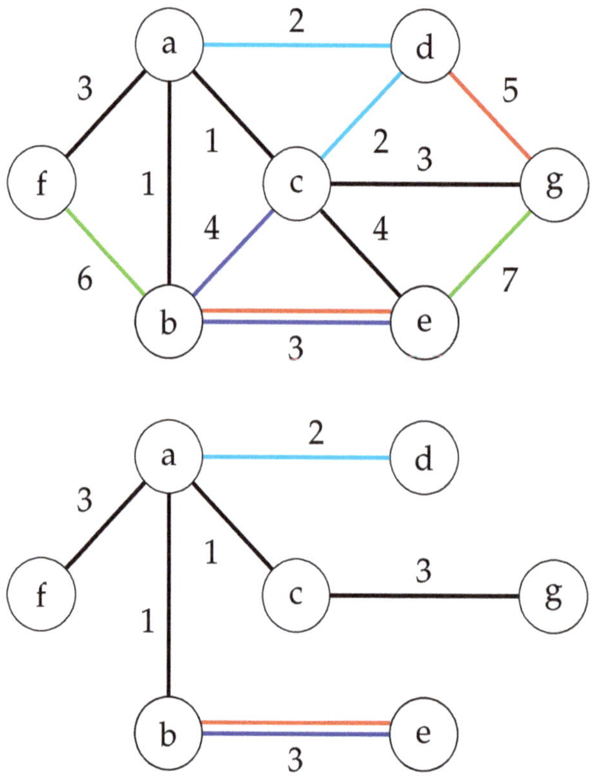

Figure 1. (Top) An example of a small MSTC instance is shown, where the edge costs are placed by the edges. Edges in black are not affected by conflicts, while any two edges sharing the same red, cyan, blue, or green color are in conflict. According to the notation $\delta_{ab} = \delta_{ac} = \delta_{af} = \delta_{ce} == \delta_{cg} = \emptyset$, $\delta_{ad} = \{\{c,d\}\}$, $\delta_{bc} = \{\{b,e\}\}$, $\delta_{be} = \{\{b,c\},\{d,g\}\}$, $\delta_{bf} = \{\{e,g\}\}$, $\delta_{cd} = \{\{a,d\}\}$, $\delta_{dg} = \{\{b,e\}\}$, and $\delta_{eg} = \{\{b,f\}\}$. (Bottom) the optimal solution that does not violate any conflict is reported. Note that no edge of the green conflict is included.

3. A Mixed-Integer Linear Programming Model

In this section, a model for the MSTC—obtained by extending a classical model for the Minimum Spanning Tree Problem [37]—is proposed. The compact model is based on multi-commodity flow, characterized by the number of variables in the order of $O(|V|^2)$ and the number of constraints in the order of $O(|V|^2)$, making it compact and suitable to be attacked directly by a solver. Conversely, the approaches previously considered in the literature rely on models with an exponential number of constraints [4,7], which require a more complex implementation of dynamic and iterative mechanisms to generate violated constraints during the solving process. Our approach is expected to have a weaker linear relaxation than the exponential models, but we believe it has potential when approached with solvers able to do logical inferences, as is done herein. The new model uses a set (A) of (directed) arcs, obtained by including the two arcs ((i,j) and (j,i)) for each edge ($\{i,j\} \in E$). A node (s) is arbitrarily selected as the root (node 0 in our implementation), and the model aims to send one unit of flow from the source to each other node.

The new model can be formally defined as follows: A variable ($x_{ij} \in \mathbb{Z}_0^+$) is introduced for each $(i,j) \in A$ and takes the value of the flow transiting the arc ($(i,j) \in A$). An additional set of variables is introduced to link the multi-commodity flow formulation to the MSTC. Then, a binary variable (y_{ij}) is defined for each edge ($\{i,j\} \in E$). It takes a value of 1 if the edge is a part of the solution and 0 otherwise. The resulting compact model, characterized by a polynomial number of variables and constraints, is as follows:

$$\min \sum_{\{i,j\}\in E} u_{ij}y_{ij} \tag{1}$$

$$\text{s.t.} \sum_{(j,i)\in A} x_{ji} - \sum_{(i,j)\in A} x_{ij} = \begin{cases} -|V|+1 & \text{if } i = s \\ +1 & \text{if } i \neq s \end{cases} \qquad i \in V \tag{2}$$

$$x_{ij} \leq (|V|-1)y_{ij} \qquad \{i,j\} \in E \tag{3}$$

$$x_{ji} \leq (|V|-1)y_{ij} \qquad \{i,j\} \in E \tag{4}$$

$$y_{ij} + y_{kl} \leq 1 \qquad \{i,j\} \in E, (k,l) \in \delta_{ij} \tag{5}$$

$$x_{ij} \geq 0 \qquad (i,j) \in A \tag{6}$$

$$y_{ij} \in \{0,1\} \qquad \{i,j\} \in E \tag{7}$$

The objective function (1) minimizes the cost of the spanning tree. Constraints (2) implement a classical multi-commodity flow model on the directed network and impose that one unit of the commodity has to exit the source (s) for each other node of V (case $i = s$) and that each node different from s has to retain exactly one unit of the commodity (case $i \neq s$). An example of the flow associated with the solution reported in Figure 1 is available in Figure 2.

Inequalities (3) and (4) connect the x and y variables by imposing that y_{ij} has to take a value of 1 as soon as either x_{ij} or x_{ji} takes a positive value. Constraints (5) encode conflict constraints by ensuring that conflicting edges are not selected simultaneously. Finally, the domains of the variables are specified in constraints (6) and (7) for the x and y variables, respectively.

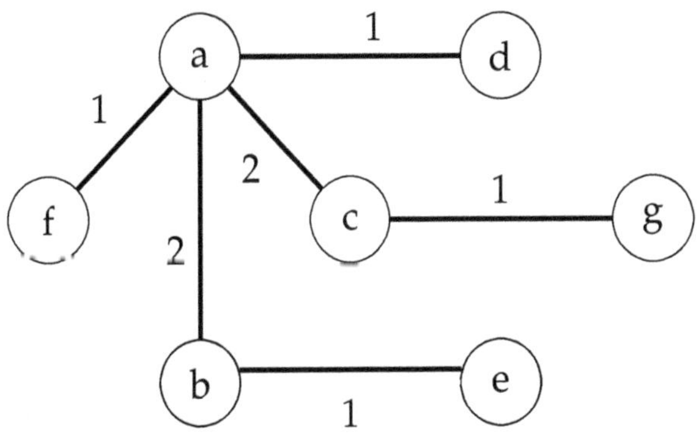

Figure 2. Assignment of flow variables (f) for the solution reported in Figure 1, assuming node a is designed to be the source node (s).

4. Computational Experiments

This section is devoted to the experimental validation of the new compact model introduced in Section 3. The model's results are compared to those of existing methods for the standard benchmark instances from the literature. In detail, Section 4.1 is devoted to the description of the benchmark instances previously introduced in the literature and used in the present study. An extensive comparison between the results achieved in this work and the results previously published is presented in Section 4.2.

4.1. Benchmark Instances

The benchmark sets originally proposed in [3,7], which have been widely used in the previous literature to validate and compare solving methods, are adopted for the experiments reported in the present work.

From the benchmark set proposed in [3], the 50 most challenging instances are considered, since the other ones can easily be solved to optimality by any recent method. The instances are generated at random and have a number of nodes that ranges between 50 and 300 and a number of edges between 200 and 1000. The edge costs are between 0 and 500, and different densities for the conflict graph are considered. We refer the interested reader to [3] for full details on instance generation.

A newer set of benchmark instances was recently introduced in [7] and is formed by random instances with the number of nodes between 25 and 100 and the edge density equal to 0.2, 0.3, or 0.4 (notice that the previous set of benchmarks was characterized by lower densities). Costs are between 1 and 30, and the density of the conflict graph is 0.01, 0.04, or 0.07. All 180 instances of the set are considered for the experiments reported in the present work. We refer the reader interested in the generation process of the instances to [7] for full details.

4.2. Experimental Results

The model discussed in Section 3 has been solved with the Google OR-Tools CP-SAT solver [41] version 9.12. The CP-SAT solver is designed to work in a multi-thread environment (compatible with all new processors) and implements a portfolio strategy with effective data exchange among the different threads. The main process runs a Constraint-Programming Solver based on Lazy Clause Generation (LCG) [46]. The concept behind LCG involves the (incremental) transformation of the problem to an SAT formula, subsequently employing an SAT solver to seek a solution (or prove bounds for infeasibility). The input model is also linearized, the corresponding linear program is (partially) solved with the (dual) simplex algorithm, and other classical MILP techniques are run to enhance bounds and retrieve new solutions, aiming at supporting the satisfiability model. Finally, instances of metaheuristic methods, seeking high-quality feasible solutions, are executed.

We believe a compact model heavily based on binary variables, like those discussed in Section 3, might be very suitable to be attacked with a solver with the characteristics of CP-SAT.

The experiments have been run on a computer equipped with an Intel Core i7 12700F CPU, but the computational times were normalized using the Intel Core i7-3770 CPU used for the experiments reported in [5–7], as a baseline. This ensures fair comparisons across methods. The normalization of the computation times has been carried out according to the conversion ratios inferred from [47]. Notice that ref. [47] is commonly used in the community to compare results obtained on different machines (see, for example, [32,44]). In accordance with the tests previously reported in [7], a maximum computation time of 5010 s is allowed for all the methods for which a computation time is reported in the tables that follow.

The first experiments have been carried out on the instances proposed in [3] and are summarized in Table 1. The first columns identify each instance (n is the number of nodes, m is the number of edges, and p is the number of conflicts, following the parameters used to generate the instances), while the rest of the table summarizes all the relevant results presented in the previous literature. The (not necessarily) optimal results obtained by solving a Mixed-Integer Linear Programming (MILP) model and two lower-bounding procedures (LB-MST and LB-MI) are taken from [3] (with no computation time). The lower and upper bounds (HDA and HDA+, respectively) from [6] are reported together with the upper bounds obtained with the multi-ethnic genetic metaheuristic method that appeared in [5] (Mega) and the lower and upper bounds obtained by the two branch-and-cut approaches discussed in [4] (unfortunately, without computation times) and [7], respectively (BC). Finally, the results obtained by the method presented in this paper are presented in the last five columns (CP-SAT). On top of the lower and upper bounds obtained and the relative computation time, the percentage deviation (Dev%) against the best lower and upper bounds is also reported to better position the new approach. These deviations are calculated as $100 \cdot \frac{BK_{LB}-LB}{BK_{LB}}$ and $100 \cdot \frac{UB-BK_{UB}}{BK_{UB}}$, respectively, where BK_{LB} and BK_{UB} are the best-known lower and upper bounds available from the previous literature, and LB and UB are the values provided by CP-SAT. Negative deviations (corresponding to improved best-known results) are highlighted in bold.

The results in Table 1 suggest that the approach we propose (CP-SAT) is particularly effective in identifying infeasible instances: Five such instances were identified for the first time in this study by the powerful feasibility checker provided by the adopted solver (notice that infeasible instances are marked as Infeas in the table). This corroborates the intuition that the logical inference carried out by CP-SAT can be effective on the compact model we propose. Moreover, another best-known upper bound has been improved. In general, the new approach has a performance comparable with those of the other state-of-the-art methods available, with deviation gaps remaining below 8.5% (and, in general, substantially below) from best-known bounds (taken as the best of the results obtained by several different algorithms). We observe that the average deviations reported are not very significant because they are heavily affected by the figures for the infeasibility proofs. Notably, CP-SAT consistently provides meaningful lower and upper bounds, demonstrating a level of robustness—especially on the upper bounds—that is uncommon among other methods. On the other hand, the lower bounds found by CP-SAT appear sometimes worse than those of BC (from [7]) in some of the most challenging instances. This might indicate scalability issues. When observing computation times, CP-SAT often appears slower than the other methods. This likely depends on the model we propose, which is characterized by a poor linear relaxation, which, in turn, means that no strong lower bound from linear programming is available to the solver. CP-SAT effectively compensates for this lack of information by applying logical inference, although this takes a longer time, showing that the solver is suitable for the new model, and the combination leads to very good results.

The percentage deviations from the best-known (before the present study) lower and upper bounds are plotted for all the methods considered and for each instance of the first benchmark set in Figures 3 and 4. The plots help to position the new approach even more clearly. A plot representing the computation times required to close each instance by the two exact methods for which such information is available (BC [7] and CP-SAT) is provided in Figure 5. A negative value is plotted when no result is available for the solver BC. The plot suggests how CP-SAT is often generally slower in the instances solved by the two methods, but, on the other hand, the number of instances solved by such an approach is higher.

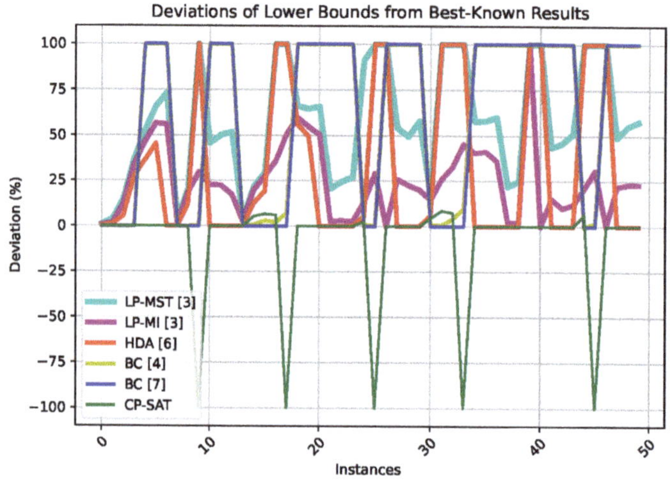

Figure 3. Percentage deviations from the best-known lower bounds in the instances of the first benchmark set.

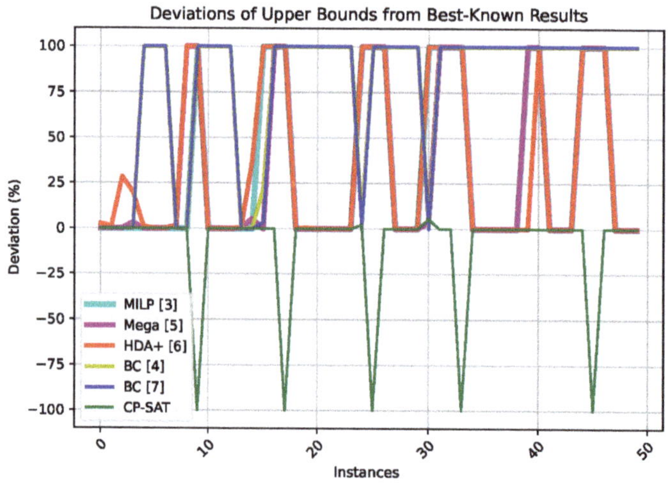

Figure 4. Percentage deviations from the best-known upper bounds in the instances of the first benchmark set.

A second set of experiments has been carried out on the instances proposed in [7], and the results are summarized in Table 2. The meaning of the column matches that of the column in Table 1, with the addition of parameter s, which is the seed used to generate the instances and helps to distinguish among instances with the same characteristics. The results of all the methods for which results are available in this dataset (namely, the most recent approaches) are reported. Computational times are available for all the methods reported.

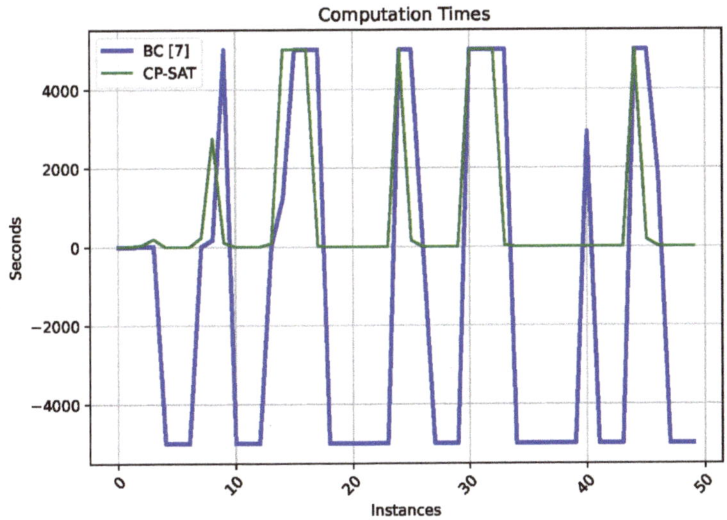

Figure 5. Computation times for two exact methods in the instances of the first benchmark set.

The comparison proposed in Table 2 shows that the approach we propose (CP-SAT) also performs well in this second set of benchmark instances, with average deviations from the previously best-known results of 0.4% concerning the lower bounds and 0.8% concerning the upper bounds. These figures are very good, considering the abundance of methods considered while calculating the (previous) best-known results. The maximum deviation is negligible for most of the instances, with only a few cases above 10% for upper bounds and never above 2.2% for lower bounds. Notice that for some of the instances of this benchmark set, CP-SAT suffers on the heuristic solution side (upper bounds). This indicates that several tailored heuristics presented for the problem were well motivated. A total of four new best-known lower bounds and ten new best-known upper bounds have been produced during the experimental campaign, with one instance (50-245-2093-349) closed for the first time during this experimental campaign. The same conclusion drawn for computation times in Table 1 also applies to these experiments too.

Analogous to what was done for the first benchmark set, the percentage deviations from the best-known (before the present study) lower and upper bounds are plotted for all the methods considered and for each instance of the first benchmark set in Figures 6 and 7. The plots help to position the new approach even more clearly, although the dominance of CP-SAT here is not as clear as in Figures 3 and 4. We plot the computation times required to close each instance by the two exact methods for which such information is available in Figure 8. The plot suggests that for the second benchmark set, BS converges faster (and closes a few more instances) than CP-SAT.

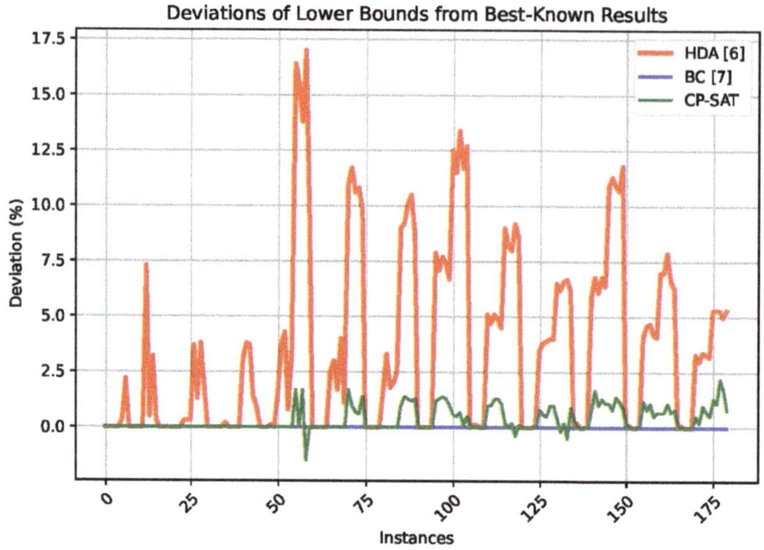

Figure 6. Percentage deviations from the best-known lower bounds in the instances of the second benchmark set.

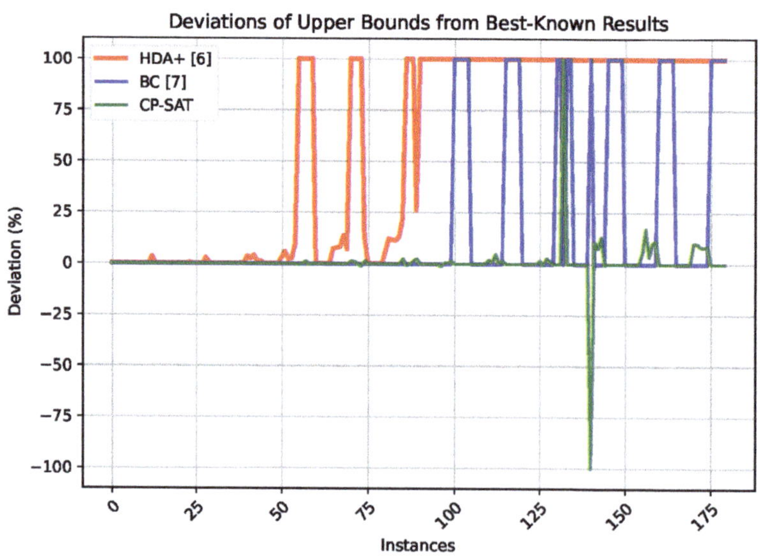

Figure 7. Percentage deviations from the best-known upper bounds in the instances of the second benchmark set.

Instances			MILP [3]	LB-MST [3]	LB-MI [3]	HDA [6]		Mega [5]		HDA+ [6]		BC [4]		BC [7]			CP-SAT			Dev%	
n	**m**	**p**	**UB**	**LB**	**LB**	**LB**	**Sec**	**UB**	**Sec**	**UB**	**Sec**	**LB**	**UB**	**LB**	**UB**	**Sec**	**LB**	**UB**	**Sec**	**LB**	**UB**
50	200	199	708	701.1	702.8	705.5	0.3	708	0.7	726	0.4	708.0	708	708.0	708	0.2	708	708	5.1	0.0	0.0
50	200	398	770	739.8	757.8	761.0	0.3	770	0.7	780	0.5	770.0	770	770.0	770	0.5	770	770	9.2	0.0	0.0
50	200	597	917	782.7	807.8	867.7	0.4	917	0.6	1176	0.6	917.0	917	917.0	917	1.8	917	917	46.0	0.0	0.0
50	200	995	1324	835.7	877.5	961.9	0.4	1365.4	0.6	1587	0.8	1324.0	1324	1324.0	1324	7.4	1324	1324	199.6	0.0	0.0
50	200	3903	1636	775.1	877.5	1042.8	1.2	1636	0.5	1653	2.2	-	-	-	-	-	1636	1636	0.1	0.0	0.0
50	200	4877	2043	698.7	887.5	1116.3	1.6	2043	0.5	2043	2.5	-	-	-	-	-	2043	2043	0.2	0.0	0.0
50	200	5864	2338	626.9	1030.3	2338.0	0.8	2338	0.6	2338	0.8	-	-	-	-	-	2338	2338	0.1	0.0	0.0
100	300	448	4041	3893.5	3991.2	4036.6	0.9	4099.2	0.6	4099	1.2	4041.0	4041	4041.0	4041	4.6	4041	4041	232.0	0.0	0.0
100	300	897	5658	4508.2	4624.2	4982.0	1.4	-	1.9	-	2.1	5658.0	5658	5658.0	5658	178.5	5658	5658	2758.6	0.0	0.0
100	300	1344	-	-	4681.3	-	-	-	2.9	-	-	6621.2	-	6635.4	-	5010.0	Infeas	Infeas	104.6	**−100.0**	**−100.0**
100	300	8609	7434	4043.4	5754.9	7434.0	0.6	7434	1.9	7434	0.6	-	-	-	-	-	7434	7434	0.1	0.0	0.0
100	300	10,686	7968	3970.5	6192.3	7968.0	0.6	7968	1.8	7968	0.5	-	-	-	-	-	7968	7968	0.2	0.0	0.0
100	300	12,761	8166	3936.3	6758.6	8166.0	0.5	8166	1.9	8166	0.5	-	-	-	-	-	8166	8166	0.1	0.0	0.0
100	500	1247	4275	4124.5	4165.7	4268.6	2.3	4291.2	5.3	4301	3.0	4275.0	4275	4275.0	4275	11.5	4275	4275	86.6	0.0	0.0
100	500	2495	5997	4701.9	4805.4	5238.2	2.5	6325	5.0	8214	5.5	5951.4	6006	5997.0	5997	1239.4	5676	6005	5010.0	5.4	0.1
100	500	3741	7665	4743.8	4871.3	5418.8	2.6	7788	3.2	-	6.8	6510.8	9440	6707.8	8049	5010.1	6267	7787	5010.0	6.6	**−0.013**
100	500	6237	-	-	4969.0	-	-	-	5.0	-	-	7568.7	-	7729.3	-	5010.0	7259	-	5010.0	6.1	0.0
100	500	12,474	-	-	5194.7	-	-	-	6.9	-	-	9816.9	-	10,560.2	-	5010.0	Infeas	Infeas	15.1	**−100.0**	**−100.0**
100	500	24,740	12,652	4289.9	5104.9	5565.2	9.0	12,652	3.4	12,681	20.8	-	-	-	-	-	12,652	12,652	0.1	0.0	0.0
100	500	30,886	11,232	3972.7	5078.8	5672.7	15.5	11,232	3.6	11,287	26.4	-	-	-	-	-	11,232	11,232	0.1	0.0	0.0
100	500	36,827	11,481	3918.1	5710.8	11,481.0	22.9	11,481	3.6	11,481	24.4	-	-	-	-	-	11,481	11,481	0.2	0.0	0.0
200	400	13,660	17,728	14,085.8	17,245.9	17,728.0	1.3	17,728	7.7	17,728	1.4	-	-	-	-	-	17,728	17,728	0.1	0.0	0.0
200	400	17,089	18,617	14,067.3	18,048.2	18,617.0	1.5	18,617	7.7	18,617	1.4	-	-	-	-	-	18,617	18,617	0.1	0.0	0.0
200	400	20,470	19,140	13,998.7	18,646.2	19,140.0	1.4	19,140	7.6	19,140	1.4	-	-	-	-	-	19,140	19,140	0.1	0.0	0.0
200	600	1797	15,029	1111.6	11,425.8	12,451.6	4.9	-	12.6	-	8.6	13,072.9	14,707	13,171.2	14,086	5010.0	12,841	14,405	5010.0	2.5	2.3
200	600	3594		-	12,487.0		-	-	24.0	-	-	17,532.7	-	17,595.0	-	5010.0	0	0	158.9	**−100.0**	**−100.0**
200	600	5391		-	12,873.2		-	-	31.6	-	-	Infeas	Infeas	Infeas	Infeas	16.4	Infeas	Infeas	0.0	0.0	0.0
200	600	34,504	20,716	9466.1	15,393.1	20,716.0	3.0	20,716	11.6	20,716	3.0	-	-	-	-	-	20,716	20,716	0.1	0.0	0.0
200	600	42,860	18,025	9100.6	13,971.5	18,025.0	2.1	18,025	12.0	18,025	2.2	-	-	-	-	-	18,025	18,025	0.2	0.0	0.0
200	600	50,984	20,864	8734.5	16,708.1	20,864.0	1.9	20,864	12.5	20,864	2.0	-	-	-	-	-	20,864	20,864	0.1	0.0	0.0
200	800	3196	22,110	17,428.8	17,922.6	19,685.1	8.6	22,350.8	22.2	-	18.9	20,744.2	21,852	20,941.5	21,553	5010.1	20,030	22,722	5010.0	4.4	5.4
200	800	6392	-	-	19,705.7	-		-	28.4	-	-	26,361.3	-	26,526.7	-	5010.1	24,259	-	5010.0	8.5	0.0
200	800	9588	-	-	20,684.8	-		-	38.3	-	-	29,443.6	-	30,634.2	-	5010.0	28,351	-	5010.0	7.5	0.0
200	800	15,980	-	-	20,226.9	-		-	48.0	-	-	33,345.1	-	36,900.2	-	5010.0	0	0	35.4	**−100.0**	**−100.0**
200	800	62,625	39,895	16,806.5	23,792.3	39,895.0	43.3	39,895	16.7	39,895	45.8	-	-	-	-	-	39,895	39,895	0.2	0.0	0.0
200	800	78,387	37,671	15,803.1	22,174.2	37,671.0	7.7	37,671	15.9	37,671	8.2	-	-	-	-	-	37,671	37,671	0.2	0.0	0.0
200	800	93,978	38,798	15,470.1	24,907.0	38,798.0	4.5	38,798	17.3	38,798	4.7	-	-	-	-	-	38,798	38,798	0.1	0.0	0.0

Table 1. *Cont.*

Instances			MILP [3]	LB-MST [3]	LB-MI [3]	HDA [6]		Mega [5]		HDA+ [6]		BC [4]		BC [7]			CP-SAT			Dev%	
n	m	p	UB	LB	LB	LB	Sec	UB	Sec	UB	Sec	LB	UB	LB	UB	Sec	LB	UB	Sec	LB	UB
300	600	31,000	43,721	34,154.2	42,720.6	43,721.0	3.0	43,721	19.2	43,721	3.4	-	-	-	-	-	43,721	43,721	0.1	0.0	0.0
300	600	38,216	44,267	33,320.1	43,486.7	44,267.0	3.1	44,267	22.3	44,267	3.4	-	-	-	-	-	44,267	44,267	0.2	0.0	0.0
300	600	45,310	43,071	32,072.3	42,149.0	43,071.0	3.0	43,071	24.6	43,071	3.1	-	-	-	-	-	43,071	43,071	0.3	0.0	0.0
300	800	3196	-	-	30,190.1	-	-	-	62.8	-	-	Infeas	Infeas	Infeas	Infeas	2911.1	Infeas	Infeas	3.3	0.0	0.0
300	800	59,600	43,125	24,384.3	36,629.6	43,125.0	3.3	43,125	32.7	43,125	3.1	-	-	-	-	-	43,125	43,125	0.1	0.0	0.0
300	800	74,500	42,292	22,913.2	38,069.3	42,292.0	3.2	42,292	35.6	42,292	3.2	-	-	-	-	-	42,292	42,292	0.3	0.0	0.0
300	800	89,300	44,114	21,624.6	38,843.0	44,114.0	3.4	44,114	35.4	44,114	3.2	-	-	-	-	-	44,114	44,114	0.1	0.0	0.0
300	1000	4995	-	-	40,732.7	-	-	-	79.3	-	-	51,451.3	-	51,398.4	-	5010.0	48,180	-	5010.0	6.4	0.0
300	1000	9990	-	-	42,902.5	-	-	-	119.1	-	-	60,907.8	-	61,878.9	-	5010.0	Infeas	Infeas	181.3	**−100.0**	**−100.0**
300	1000	14,985	-	-	44,639.1	-	-	-	141.3	-	-	Infeas	Infeas	Infeas	Infeas	1820.0	Infeas	Infeas	9.7	0.0	0.0
300	1000	96,590	71,562	36,544.7	56,048.3	71,562.0	9.2	71,562	41.5	71,562	9.5	-	-	-	-	-	71,562	71,562	0.1	0.0	0.0
300	1000	120,500	76,345	34,380.8	58,780.1	76,345.0	6.6	76,345	33.4	76,345	6.7	-	-	-	-	-	76,345	76,345	0.2	0.0	0.0
300	1000	144,090	78,880	33,481.2	60,810.8	78,880.0	5.2	78,880	36.9	78,880	5.4	-	-	-	-	-	78,880	78,880	0.1	0.0	0.0
Averages																				−9.1	−9.8

Table 2. Computational results for the instances introduced in [7].

Instances			HDA [6]		HDA+ [6]		BC [7]			CP-SAT				Dev%	
m	*p*	*s*	LB	Sec	UB	Sec	LB	UB	Sec	LB	UB	Sec	LB		UB
60	18	1	347.0	0.04	347	0.05	347.0	347	0.0	347	347	0.23	0.0		0.0
60	18	7	389.0	0.04	389	0.04	389.0	389	0.0	389	389	0.18	0.0		0.0
60	18	13	353.0	0.04	353	0.04	353.0	353	0.0	353	353	0.19	0.0		0.0
60	18	19	346.0	0.04	346	0.05	346.0	346	0.0	346	346	0.19	0.0		0.0
60	18	25	336.0	0.04	336	0.04	336.0	336	0.0	336	336	0.18	0.0		0.0
90	71	31	379.6	0.09	381	0.07	381.0	381	0.0	381	381	0.45	0.0		0.0
60	71	37	381.5	0.05	390	0.07	390.0	390	0.1	390	390	0.32	0.0		0.0
60	71	43	372.0	0.05	372	0.06	372.0	372	0.0	372	372	0.44	0.0		0.0
60	71	49	357.0	0.05	357	0.06	357.0	357	0.0	357	357	0.24	0.0		0.0
60	71	55	406.0	0.05	406	0.06	406.0	406	0.0	406	406	0.38	0.0		0.0
60	124	61	385.0	0.06	385	0.07	385.0	385	0.0	385	385	0.18	0.0		0.0
60	124	67	432.0	0.06	432	0.07	432.0	432	0.0	432	432	0.20	0.0		0.0
60	124	73	424.5	0.07	474	0.1	458.0	458	0.3	458	458	0.48	0.0		0.0
60	124	79	398.0	0.07	400	0.08	400.0	400	0.0	400	400	0.45	0.0		0.0
60	124	85	406.8	0.08	421	0.12	420.0	420	0.0	420	420	0.42	0.0		0.0
90	41	91	310.1	0.05	311	0.05	311.0	311	0.0	311	311	0.54	0.0		0.0
90	41	97	306.0	0.05	306	0.06	306.0	306	0.0	306	306	0.36	0.0		0.0
90	41	103	299.0	0.05	299	0.05	299.0	299	0.0	299	299	0.31	0.0		0.0
90	41	109	297.0	0.05	297	0.05	297.0	297	0.0	297	297	0.30	0.0		0.0
90	41	115	318.0	0.05	318	0.05	318.0	318	0.0	318	318	0.25	0.0		0.0
90	161	121	305.0	0.08	305	0.09	305.0	305	0.0	305	305	0.54	0.0		0.0
90	161	127	339.0	0.12	339	0.11	339.0	339	0.0	339	339	0.29	0.0		0.0
90	161	133	344.0	0.08	344	0.09	344.0	344	0.0	344	344	0.23	0.0		0.0
90	161	139	328.0	0.09	331	0.11	329.0	329	0.0	329	329	0.61	0.0		0.0
90	161	145	325.0	0.08	327	0.11	326.0	326	0.0	326	326	0.89	0.0		0.0
90	281	151	347.9	0.1	349	0.13	349.0	349	0.0	349	349	0.56	0.0		0.0
90	281	157	370.6	0.1	385	0.16	385.0	385	0.5	385	385	2.67	0.0		0.0
90	281	163	330.8	0.11	335	0.14	335.0	335	0.0	335	335	0.66	0.0		0.0
90	281	169	334.7	0.1	358	0.18	348.0	348	0.1	348	348	1.91	0.0		0.0
90	281	175	350.1	0.1	359	0.17	357.0	357	0.0	357	357	0.98	0.0		0.0
120	72	181	282.0	0.07	282	0.06	282.0	282	0.0	282	282	0.24	0.0		0.0
120	72	187	294.0	0.06	294	0.06	294.0	294	0.0	294	294	0.90	0.0		0.0
120	72	193	284.0	0.06	284	0.08	284.0	284	0.0	284	284	0.48	0.0		0.0
120	72	199	281.0	0.06	281	0.07	281.0	281	0.0	281	281	0.53	0.0		0.0
120	72	205	292.0	0.06	292	0.06	292.0	292	0.0	292	292	0.30	0.0		0.0
120	286	211	320.3	0.12	321	0.16	321.0	321	0.0	321	321	1.06	0.0		0.0
120	286	217	317.0	0.12	317	0.17	317.0	317	0.0	317	317	0.64	0.0		0.0
120	286	223	284.0	0.56	284	0.12	284.0	284	0.0	284	284	0.31	0.0		0.0
120	286	229	311.0	0.12	312	0.17	311.0	311	0.0	311	311	0.58	0.0		0.0
120	286	235	290.0	0.13	290	0.13	290.0	290	0.0	290	290	0.36	0.0		0.0
120	500	241	319.2	0.16	341	0.26	329.0	329	0.1	329	329	4.72	0.0		0.0
120	500	247	326.1	0.16	347	0.25	339.0	339	0.5	339	339	1.84	0.0		0.0
120	500	253	354.5	0.16	383	0.3	368.0	368	0.4	368	368	1.55	0.0		0.0
120	500	259	306.5	0.16	314	0.22	311.0	311	0.0	311	311	0.65	0.0		0.0
120	500	265	318.0	0.16	325	0.25	321.0	321	0.0	321	321	0.74	0.0		0.0
245	299	271	619.0	0.34	619	0.37	619.0	619	0.0	619	619	2.75	0.0		0.0
245	299	277	604.0	0.36	604	0.38	604.0	604	0.0	604	604	1.49	0.0		0.0
245	299	283	634.0	0.34	634	0.35	634.0	634	0.0	634	634	0.72	0.0		0.0
245	299	289	615.5	0.34	616	0.4	616.0	616	0.1	616	616	1.49	0.0		0.0
245	299	295	595.0	0.34	595	0.44	595.0	595	0.0	595	595	7.28	0.0		0.0
245	1196	301	668.5	0.57	698	0.96	678.0	678	1.4	678	678	27.19	0.0		0.0
245	1196	307	655.5	0.56	721	0.99	681.0	681	3.2	681	681	51.96	0.0		0.0
245	1196	313	678.2	0.59	725	1	709.0	709	6.3	709	709	612.25	0.0		0.0
245	1196	319	634.0	1.26	656	0.86	639.0	639	1.5	639	639	16.54	0.0		0.0
245	1196	325	658.8	0.56	748	1.01	681.0	681	3.8	681	681	57.54	0.0		0.0
245	2093	331	661.3	0.76	-	-	791.2	820	5010.0	778	816	5010.00	1.7		**−0.5**
245	2093	337	706.0	0.75	-	-	835.0	835	1938.7	835	835	4603.22	0.0		0.0
245	2093	343	666.5	0.74	-	-	773.2	811	5010.1	760	822	5010.00	1.7		1.4
245	2093	349	680.8	0.76	-	-	820.0	836	5010.1	832	832	2874.48	**−1.5**		**−0.5**
245	2093	355	693.9	0.74	-	-	769.0	769	25.7	769	769	266.66	0.0		0.0
367	672	361	570.0	0.82	570	0.88	570.0	570	0.1	570	570	8.05	0.0		0.0
367	672	367	561.0	0.86	561	0.98	561.0	561	1.4	561	561	10.48	0.0		0.0
367	672	373	573.0	0.86	573	1.06	573.0	573	0.0	573	573	2.98	0.0		0.0
367	672	379	560.0	0.86	560	0.87	560.0	560	0.0	560	560	1.61	0.0		0.0
367	672	385	549.0	0.83	551	0.99	549.0	549	0.5	549	549	17.12	0.0		0.0
367	2687	391	596.4	1.26	657	2.37	612.0	612	7.5	612	612	230.76	0.0		0.0
367	2687	397	596.7	1.27	663	2.24	615.0	615	6.6	615	615	154.67	0.0		0.0
367	2687	403	577.1	1.26	635	2.33	587.0	587	3.0	587	587	35.79	0.0		0.0
367	2687	409	608.5	1.26	721	2.4	634.0	634	7.3	634	634	508.17	0.0		0.0
367	2687	415	636.1	3.08	688	2.45	643.0	643	3.2	643	643	72.48	0.0		0.0

Table 2. *Cont.*

Instances				**HDA [6]**		**HDA+ [6]**		**BC [7]**			**CP-SAT**			**Dev%**
n	*m*	*p*	*s*	**LB**	**Sec**	**UB**	**Sec**	**LB**	**UB**	**Sec**	**LB**	**UB**	**Sec**	**LB**
50	367	4702	421	624.4	1.66	-	-	701.3	726	5010.1	689	735	5010.00	1.7
50	367	4702	427	635.4	1.65	-	-	719.5	753	5010.0	712	762	5010.00	1.0
50	367	4702	433	646.9	1.64	-	-	723.9	786	5010.0	719	784	5010.00	0.7
50	367	4702	439	597.5	1.72	-	-	669.8	711	5010.0	666	702	5010.00	0.6
50	367	4702	445	665.1	1.71	868	3.36	737.3	764	5010.0	727	775	5010.00	1.4
50	490	1199	451	548.0	1.68	552	2.03	548.0	548	0.1	548	548	8.41	0.0
50	490	1199	457	530.0	1.66	531	1.88	530.0	530	0.5	530	530	11.77	0.0
50	490	1199	463	549.0	1.65	549	1.76	549.0	549	0.0	549	549	3.08	0.0
50	490	1199	469	540.0	1.67	541	2.01	540.0	540	0.2	540	540	46.21	0.0
50	490	1199	475	540.0	1.65	540	1.71	540.0	540	0.0	540	540	4.77	0.0
50	490	4793	481	584.3	2.38	629	4.63	594.0	594	7.8	594	594	109.31	0.0
50	490	4793	487	559.9	2.4	650	4.9	579.0	579	13.8	579	579	1473.29	0.0
50	490	4793	493	578.3	2.43	657	4.75	589.0	589	3.0	589	589	31.17	0.0
50	490	4793	499	565.4	2.39	643	4.74	577.0	577	7.5	577	577	118.57	0.0
50	490	4793	505	577.4	2.4	670	4.71	592.0	592	6.0	592	592	40.34	0.0
50	490	8387	511	575.0	2.4	812	6.54	632.2	666	5010.0	626	683	5010.00	1.0
50	490	8387	517	569.0	3.07	-	-	626.7	651	5010.0	618	646	5010.00	1.4
50	490	8387	523	592.2	3.08	-	-	658.4	678	5010.0	650	676	5010.00	1.3
50	490	8387	529	592.5	3.07	-	-	662.2	682	5010.1	654	692	5010.00	1.2
50	490	8387	535	587.5	3.09	828	6.95	644.2	657	5010.0	636	674	5010.00	1.3
75	555	1538	541	868.0	2.51	-	-	868.0	868	0.7	868	868	75.24	0.0
75	555	1538	547	870.9	2.49	-	-	871.0	871	3.0	871	871	58.57	0.0
75	555	1538	553	838.0	2.45	-	-	838.0	838	0.3	838	838	33.73	0.0
75	555	1538	559	855.0	2.47	-	-	855.0	855	4.4	855	855	44.64	0.0
75	555	1538	565	857.0	2.47	-	-	857.0	857	4.1	857	857	48.19	0.0
75	555	6150	571	942.3	3.49	-	-	1023.7	1047	5010.0	1011	1048	5010.00	1.2
75	555	6150	577	937.6	3.54	-	-	1008.8	1069	5010.2	996	1054	5010.00	1.3
75	555	6150	583	910.9	3.48	-	-	987.3	1040	5010.1	973	1044	5010.00	1.4
75	555	6150	589	913.0	3.53	-	-	985.6	998	5010.1	973	1004	5010.00	1.3
75	555	6150	595	897.9	3.54	-	-	962.6	994	5010.1	953	1009	5010.00	1.0
75	555	10,762	601	922.5	4.44	-	-	1054.5	-	4647.3	1048	-	5010.00	0.6
75	555	10,762	607	948.0	12.01	-	-	1070.9	-	3483.6	1066	-	5010.00	0.5
75	555	10,762	613	901.9	4.44	-	-	1041.0	-	5010.0	1034	-	5010.00	0.7
75	555	10,762	619	888.4	4.44	-	-	1006.4	-	5010.0	1005	-	5010.00	0.1
75	555	10,762	625	914.7	4.42	-	-	1048.1	-	3208.1	1043	-	5010.00	0.5
75	832	3457	631	797.8	6.86	-	-	798.0	798	4.8	798	798	78.24	0.0
75	832	3457	637	820.0	6.83	-	-	821.0	821	1.1	821	821	637.56	0.0
75	832	3457	643	815.3	6.87	-	-	816.0	816	4.0	816	816	262.59	0.0
75	832	3457	649	820.0	7.16	-	-	820.0	820	23.9	820	820	184.06	0.0
75	832	3457	655	815.0	7.23	-	-	815.0	815	1.4	815	815	84.81	0.0
75	832	13,828	661	830.9	9.08	-	-	875.7	891	5010.0	867	909	5010.00	1.0
75	832	13,828	667	859.5	9.05	-	-	901.8	947	5010.1	893	956	5010.00	1.0
75	832	13,828	673	829.0	9.04	-	-	873.7	892	5010.0	862	934	5010.00	1.3
75	832	13,828	679	842.2	8.98	-	-	885.6	915	4570.8	874	918	5010.00	1.3
75	832	13,828	685	846.7	9.05	-	-	886.9	896	5010.0	877	911	5010.00	1.1
75	832	24,199	691	870.0	12.24	-	-	955.8	-	1305.3	954	-	5010.00	0.2
75	832	24,199	697	837.7	12.33	-	-	913.0	-	1161.2	913	-	5010.00	0.0
75	832	24,199	703	842.0	27.17	-	-	915.0	-	953.0	913	-	5010.00	0.2
75	832	24,199	709	863.0	11.98	-	-	950.4	-	5010.1	954	-	5010.00	**−0.4**
75	832	24,199	715	878.7	12.14	-	-	960.8	-	962.3	960	-	5010.00	0.1
75	1110	6155	721	787.0	14.88	-	-	787.0	787	2.1	787	787	237.82	0.0
75	1110	6155	727	785.0	14.82	-	-	785.0	785	5.4	785	785	214.71	0.0
75	1110	6155	733	783.0	14.78	-	-	783.0	783	0.0	783	783	102.86	0.0
75	1110	6155	739	783.9	14.94	-	-	784.0	784	3.3	784	784	128.21	0.0
75	1110	6155	745	796.5	14.86	-	-	797.0	797	5.7	797	797	479.97	0.0
75	1110	24,620	751	816.9	19.16	-	-	846.5	857	5010.0	840	871	5010.00	0.8
75	1110	24,620	757	798.0	19.28	-	-	829.2	851	4573.5	824	847	5010.00	0.6
75	1110	24,620	763	808.4	19.44	-	-	841.5	892	2189.8	837	917	5010.00	0.5
75	1110	24,620	769	808.0	19.31	-	-	841.6	864	2866.0	833	876	5010.00	1.0
75	1110	24,620	775	804.0	19.32	-	-	837.8	868	5010.1	829	868	5010.00	1.0
75	1110	43,085	781	817.0	27.33	-	-	873.5	-	2357.1	870	-	5010.00	0.4
75	1110	43,085	787	804.0	26.74	-	-	857.0	-	3106.8	859	-	5010.00	**−0.2**
75	1110	43,085	793	827.3	26.9	-	-	885.9	1194	3443.8	884	-	5010.00	0.2
75	1110	43,085	799	799.0		-	-	856.70	-	3448.3	861	-	5010.00	**−0.5**
75	1110	43,085	805	806.0	27.14	-	-	859.1	-	3146.2	851	-	5010.00	0.9
100	990	4896	811	1118.5	11.59	-	-	1119.0	1119	43.7	1116	1121	5010.00	0.3
100	990	4896	817	1134.7	11.43	-	-	1137.0	1137	11.8	1137	1137	1091.57	0.0
100	990	4896	823	1112.5	11.71	-	-	1113.0	1113	71.8	1113	1113	493.89	0.0
100	990	4896	829	1109.6	11.48	-	-	1110.0	1110	48.6	1110	1110	942.31	0.0
100	990	4896	835	1088.7	11.99	-	-	1090.0	1090	35.8	1090	1090	357.10	0.0
100	990	19,583	841	1175.6	15.37	-	-	1249.4	-	5010.0	1239	1570	5010.00	0.8
100	990	19,583	847	1142.0	14.98	-	-	1225.8	1491	5010.0	1205	1650	5010.00	1.7
100	990	19,583	853	1140.7	14.8	-	-	1215.0	1510	5010.0	1203	1623	5010.00	1.0

Table 2. *Cont.*

Instances			HDA [6]		HDA+ [6]		BC [7]			CP-SAT			Dev%	
m	p	s	LB	Sec	UB	Sec	LB	UB	Sec	LB	UB	Sec	LB	UB
990	19,583	859	1178.1	14.82	-	-	1264.2	1441	5010.2	1248	1632	5010.00	1.3	13.3
990	19,583	865	1176.4	15.36	-	-	1257.3	1560	5010.1	1244	1555	5010.00	1.1	**−0.3**
990	34,269	871	1126.4	22.2	-	-	1264.8	-	5010.0	1251	-	5010.00	1.1	0.0
990	34,269	877	1148.9	24.59	-	-	1295.6	-	5010.0	1285	-	5010.00	0.8	0.0
990	34,269	883	1179.9	21.17	-	-	1323.7	-	5010.0	1305	-	5010.00	1.4	0.0
990	34,269	889	1146.7	20.3	-	-	1283.6	-	5010.0	1268	-	5010.00	1.2	0.0
990	34,269	895	1155.0	20.42	-	-	1309.1	-	5010.0	1297	-	5010.00	0.9	0.0
1485	11,019	901	1077.9	34.81	-	-	1079.0	1079	248.6	1077	1081	5010.00	0.2	0.2
1485	11,019	907	1054.9	34.46	-	-	1056.0	1056	113.4	1056	1056	757.17	0.0	0.0
1485	11,019	913	1059.0	34.29	-	-	1059.0	1059	47.9	1059	1059	503.94	0.0	0.0
1485	11,019	919	1046.0	34.09	-	-	1046.0	1046	195.2	1046	1046	1206.51	0.0	0.0
1485	11,019	925	1071.2	34.17	-	-	1072.0	1072	249.6	1071	1072	5010.00	0.1	0.0
1485	44,075	931	1096.9	46.07	-	-	1144.0	1374	3018.3	1130	1444	5010.00	1.2	5.1
1485	44,075	937	1091.0	45.6	-	-	1143.6	1291	2144.6	1134	1511	5010.00	0.8	17.0
1485	44,075	943	1084.4	46.54	-	-	1137.6	1344	3075.6	1125	1390	5010.00	1.1	3.4
1485	44,075	949	1089.4	46.01	-	-	1136.9	1286	3523.3	1131	1417	5010.00	0.5	10.2
1485	44,075	955	1088.4	45.84	-	-	1134.6	1370	2954.2	1127	1524	5010.00	0.7	11.2
1485	77,131	961	1083.5	60.68	-	-	1164.4	-	4773.8	1156	-	5010.00	0.7	0.0
1485	77,131	967	1086.0	60.29	-	-	1168.2	-	5010.0	1160	-	5010.00	0.7	0.0
1485	77,131	973	1094.0	60.69	-	-	1187.8	-	5010.0	1175	-	5010.00	1.1	0.0
1485	77,131	979	1105.9	60.83	-	-	1183.7	-	5010.0	1175	-	5010.00	0.7	0.0
1485	77,131	985	1090.9	60.63	-	-	1164.5	-	5010.0	1155	-	5010.00	0.8	0.0
1980	19,593	991	1030.9	76.15	-	-	1031.0	1031	214.4	1031	1031	919.88	0.0	0.0
1980	19,593	997	1034.9	76.02	-	-	1036.0	1036	42.8	1036	1036	1298.69	0.0	0.0
1980	19,593	1003	1024.0	76.43	-	-	1024.0	1024	21.8	1024	1024	622.64	0.0	0.0
1980	19,593	1009	1025.0	76.67	-	-	1025.0	1025	27.4	1025	1025	546.97	0.0	0.0
1980	19,593	1015	1027.5	77.49	-	-	1028.0	1028	151.0	1028	1028	1964.48	0.0	0.0
1980	78,369	1021	1060.5	106.68	-	-	1097.0	1234	5010.1	1091	1358	5010.00	0.5	10.0
1980	78,369	1027	1034.0	106.82	-	-	1065.6	1187	5010.1	1064	1305	5010.00	0.2	9.9
1980	78,369	1033	1050.5	104.96	-	-	1087.4	1213	5010.1	1076	1314	5010.00	1.0	8.3
1980	78,369	1039	1048.1	103.83	-	-	1083.5	1221	5010.1	1076	1320	5010.00	0.7	8.1
1980	78,369	1045	1048.9	103.99	-	-	1084.1	1245	5010.1	1079	1353	5010.00	0.5	8.7
1980	137,145	1051	1041.8	129.47	-	-	1100.6	-	5010.1	1086	-	5010.00	1.3	0.0
1980	137,145	1057	1066.5	129.26	-	-	1126.3	-	5010.1	1114	-	5010.00	1.1	0.0
1980	137,145	1063	1052.4	130.38	-	-	1111.3	-	5010.1	1087	-	5010.00	2.2	0.0
1980	137,145	1069	1062.9	130.01	-	-	1118.7	-	5010.1	1100	-	5010.00	1.7	0.0
1980	137,145	1075	1055.5	130.01	-	-	1114.1	-	5010.1	1105	-	5010.00	0.8	0.0
rages													0.4	0.8

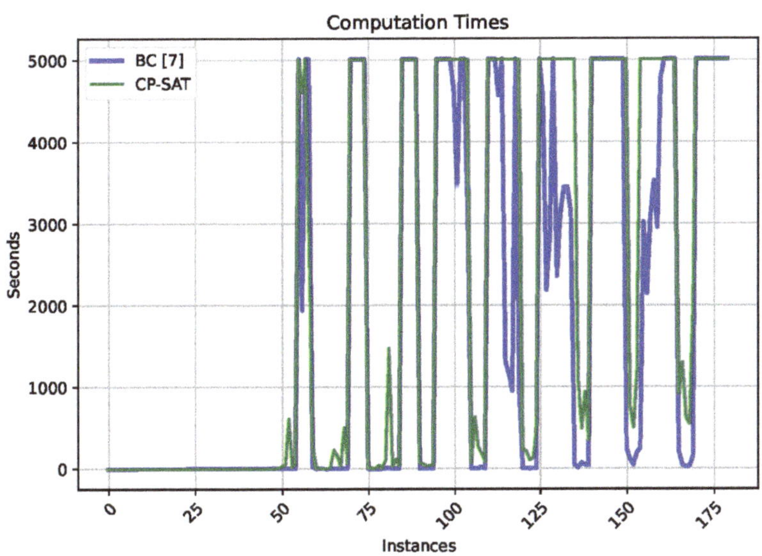

Figure 8. Computation times for two exact methods in the instances of the second benchmark set.

As a general conclusion, the proposed model closely matches or improves upon the best-known results available prior to this work. The proposed method also demonstrates consistent robustness across the entire dataset, although its convergence times appear slower than those of some of the methods previously proposed.

5. Conclusions

A compact mixed-integer linear formulation for the Minimum Spanning Tree Problem with Conflicting Edge Pairs was proposed for the first time in the context of this problem and solved via an open-source solver.

The results of a vast experimental campaign run on the benchmark instances adopted in the previous literature are reported. The results indicate that the proposed approach achieves computational results comparable with the best of those achieved by the substantially more complex methods that appeared in the prior literature, although, sometimes, the computation times are longer due to the mechanics of the solver. A total of six instances were closed for the first time, with nine best-known lower bounds and sixteen best-known upper bounds improved out of the two hundred thirty instances considered. In some of the instances, the new approach still performs slightly worse than some among the other methods it is compared against, but overall, it guarantees robust results, with improvements in instances attacked and solved in the research community for more than a decade.

Future research directions might be twofold. On the one hand, compact models, like the one we propose, might be employed on problems with conflicts similar to the one treated in this paper or employ soft constraints (that can be violated at the price of a penalty), which, by their nature, would pose new challenges. On the other hand, variants of the Minimum Spanning Tree, characterized by soft constraints, with penalties to be paid if violated, might be considered.

Author Contributions: Conceptualization, R.M. and D.H.S.; methodology, R.M.; software, R.M.; validation, R.M. and D.H.S.; formal analysis, R.M. and D.H.S.; investigation, R.M.; resources, R.M.; data curation, R.M.; writing—original draft preparation, R.M.; writing—review and editing, R.M. and D.H.S.; visualization, R.M. and D.H.S. All authors have read and agreed to the published version of the manuscript.

Funding: This work was partially supported by the Google Cloud Research Credits Program.

Data Availability Statement: The instances used for the experiments, originally introduced in [3,7], are available upon request to the corresponding author.

Acknowledgments: The authors have reviewed and edited the output and take full responsibility for the content of this publication.

Conflicts of Interest: The authors declare no conflicts of interest.

References

1. Prim, R.C. Shortest connection networks and some generalizations. *Bell Syst. Tech. J.* **1957**, *6*, 1389–1401. [CrossRef]
2. Darmann, A.; Pferschy, U.; Schauer, J.; Woeginger, G. Paths, trees and matchings under disjunctive constraints. *Discret.* *Math.* **2011**, *16*, 1726–1735. [CrossRef]
3. Zhang, R.; Kabadi, S.; Punnen, A. The minimum spanning tree problem with conflict constraints and its variations. *Di* *Optim.* **2011**, *2*, 191–205. [CrossRef]
4. Samer, P.; Urrutia, S. A branch and cut algorithm for minimum spanning trees under conflict constraints. *Optim. Lett.* *1*, 41–55. [CrossRef]
5. Carrabs, F.; Cerrone, C.; Pentangelo, R. A multi-ethnic genetic approach for the minimum conflict weighted spanning problem. *Networks* **2019**, *2*, 134–147. [CrossRef]
6. Carrabs, F.; Gaudioso, M. A Lagrangian approach for the minimum spanning tree problem with conflicting edge pairs. *Netw* **2021**, *1*, 32–45. [CrossRef]
7. Carrabs, F.; Cerulli, R.; Pentangelo, R.; Raiconi, A. Minimum spanning tree with conflicting edge pairs: A branch-and approach. In *Annals of Operations Research*; Springer: Berlin/Heidelberg, Germany, 2019; pp. 65–78.

Öncan, T.; Zhang, R.; Punnen, A.P. The minimum cost perfect matching problem with conflict pair constraints. *Comput. Oper. Res.* **2013**, *40*, 920–930. [CrossRef]
Öncan, T.; Altınel, I.K. Iterated exact and heuristic algorithms for the minimum cost bipartite perfect matching problem with conflict constraints. In Proceedings of the 2017 IEEE International Conference on Industrial Engineering and Engineering Management (IEEM), Singapore, 10–13 December 2017; pp. 1032–1036.
Öncan, T.; Altınel, I.K. A Branch-and-Bound Algorithm for the Minimum Cost Bipartite Perfect Matching Problem with Conflict Pair Constraints. *Electron. Notes Discret. Math.* **2018**, *64*, 5–14. [CrossRef]
Öncan, T.; Şuvak, Z.; Akyüz, M.H.; Altınel, I.K. Assignment problem with conflicts. *Comput. Oper. Res.* **2019**, *111*, 214–229. [CrossRef]
Yamada, T.; Kataoka, S.; Watanabe, K. Heuristic and exact algorithms for the disjunctively constrained knapsack problem. *Informs J. Comput.* **2002**, *43*, 2864–2870.
Hifi, M.; Michrafy, M. Reduction strategies and exact algorithms for the disjunctively constrained knapsack problem. *Comput. Oper. Res.* **2007**, *34*, 2657–2673. [CrossRef]
Hifi, M.; Michrafy, M. A reactive local search-based algorithm for the disjunctively constrained knapsack problem. *J. Oper. Res. Soc.* **2006**, *57*, 718–726. [CrossRef]
Akeb, H.; Hifi, M.; Ould Ahmed Mounir, M.E. Local branching-based algorithms for the disjunctively constrained knapsack problem. *Comput. Ind. Eng.* **2011**, *60*, 811–820. [CrossRef]
Hifi, M.; Omani, N. An algorithm for the disjunctively constrained knapsack problem. *Int. J. Oper. Res.* **2012**, *13*, 22–43. [CrossRef]
Hifi, M. An iterative rounding search-based algorithm for the disjunctively constrained knapsack problem. *Eng. Optim.* **2014**, *46*, 1109–1122. [CrossRef]
Bettinelli, A.; Cacchiani, V.; Malaguti, E. A Branch-and-Bound Algorithm for the Knapsack Problem with Conflict Graph. *INFORMS J. Comput.* **2017**, *29*, 457–473. [CrossRef]
Coniglio, S.; Furini, F.; San Segundo, P. A new combinatorial branch-and-bound algorithm for the Knapsack Problem with Conflicts. *Eur. J. Oper. Res.* **2021**, *289*, 435–455. [CrossRef]
Carrabs, F.; Cerulli, R.; Mansini, R.; Moreschini, L.; Serra, D. Solving the Set Covering Problem with Conflicts on Sets: A new parallel GRASP. *Comput. Oper. Res.* **2024**, *166*, 106620. [CrossRef]
Jacob, A.; Majumdar, D.; Raman, V. Parameterized complexity of conflict-free set cover. *Lect. Notes Comput. Sci.* **2019**, *11532*, 191–202.
Saffari, S.; Fathi, Y. Set covering problem with conflict constraints. *Comput. Oper. Res.* **2022**, *143*, 105763. [CrossRef]
Banik, A.; Panolan, F.; Raman, V.; Sahlot, V.; Saurabh, S. Parameterized Complexity of Geometric Covering Problems Having Conflicts. *Algorithmica* **2020**, *82*, 1–19. [CrossRef]
Gabow, H.; Maheshwari, S.; Osterweil, L. On Two Problems in the Generation of Program Test Paths. *IEEE Trans. Softw. Eng.* **1976**, *SE-2*, 227–231. [CrossRef]
Krause, K.W.; Goodwin, M.A.; Smith, R.W. *Optimal Software Test Planning Through Automated Network Analysis*; TRW Systems Group: Redondo Beach, CA, USA, 1973; pp. 18–22.
Srimani, P.K.; Sinha, B.P. Impossible pair constrained test path generation in a program. *Inf. Sci.* **1982**, *28*, 87–103. [CrossRef]
Blanco, M.; Borndörfer, R.; Brückner, M.; Hoang, N.D., Schlechte, T. On the Path Avoiding Forbidden Pairs Polytope. *Electron. Notes Discret. Math.* **2015**, *50*, 343–348. [CrossRef]
Ferone, D.; Festa, P.; Salani, M. Branch and Bound and Dynamic Programming Approaches for the Path Avoiding Forbidden Pairs Problem. In *Optimization and Decision Science: ODS, Virtual Conference, November 19, 2020*; Cerulli, R., Dell'Amico, M., Guerriero, F., Pacciarelli, D., Sforza, A., Eds.; Springer International Publishing: Cham, Switzerland, 2021; pp. 227–235.
Cerulli, R.; Guerriero, G.; Scalzo, E.; Sorgente, C. Shortest paths with exclusive-disjunction arc pairs conflicts. *Comput. Oper. Res.* **2023**, *152*, 106158. [CrossRef]
Pferschy, U.; Schauer, J. The maximum flow problem with disjunctive constraints. *J. Comb. Optim.* **2013**, *26*, 109–119. [CrossRef]
Şuvak, Z.; Altınel, I.K.; Aras, N. Exact solution algorithms for the maximum flow problem with additional conflict constraints. *Eur. J. Oper. Res.* **2020**, *287*, 410–437. [CrossRef]
Carrabs, F.; Cerulli, R.; Mansini, R.; Serra, D.; Sorgente, C. Hybridizing Carousel Greedy and Kernel Search: A new approach for the maximum flow problem with conflict constraints. *Eur. J. Oper. Res.* **2025**, *324*, 414–435. [CrossRef]
Cerrone, C.; Cerulli, R.; Golden, B. Carousel greedy: A generalized greedy algorithm with applications in optimization. *Comput. Oper. Res.* **2017**, *85*, 97–112. [CrossRef]
Angelelli, E.; Mansini, R.; Speranza, M.G. Kernel search: A new heuristic framework for portfolio selection. *Comput. Optim. Appl.* **2012**, *51*, 345–361. [CrossRef]
Klein, A.; Haugland, D.; Bauer, J.; Mommer, M. An integer programming model for branching cable layouts in offshore wind farms. In *Advances in Intelligent Systems and Computing*; Springer: Berlin/Heidelberg, Germany, 2015; pp. 27–36.

36. Darmann, A.; Pferschy, U.; Schauer, J. Determining a minimum spanning tree with disjunctive constraints. In *Lecture Note* *Computer Science*; Springer: Berlin/Heidelberg, Germany, 2009; pp. 414–423.
37. Magnanti, T.L.; Wolsey, L. Optimal trees. In *Handbook in Operations Research and Management Science*; Ball, M.O., Magnanti, Monma, C.L., Nemhauser, G.L., Eds.; North Holland Publishing: Amsterdam, The Netherlands, 1995; pp. 503–615.
38. Abdelmaguid, T.F. An Efficient Mixed Integer Linear Programming Model for the Minimum Spanning Tree Problem. *Mathem* **2018**, *6*, 183. [CrossRef]
39. de Almeida, A.M.; Martins, P.; de Souza, M.C. Min-degree constrained minimum spanning tree problem: complexity, proper and formulations. *Int. Trans. Oper. Res.* **2012**, *19*, 323–352. [CrossRef]
40. Gouveia, L.; Magnanti, T.L. Network flow models for designing diameter-constrained minimum-spanning and Steiner t *Networks* **2003**, *41*, 159–173. [CrossRef]
41. Perron, L.; Didier, F. Google OR-Tools-CP-SAT. 2025. Available online: https://developers.google.com/optimization/cp/ solver/ (accessed on 9 July 2025).
42. Montemanni, R.; Dell'Amico, M. Solving the parallel drone scheduling traveling salesman problem via constraint programm *Algorithms* **2023**, *16*, 40. [CrossRef]
43. Montemanni, R.; Dell'Amico, M.; Corsini, A. Parallel drone scheduling vehicle routing problems with collective drones. *Com* *Oper. Res.* **2024**, *163*, 106514. [CrossRef]
44. Montemanni, R.; Smith, D.H. On Solving the Maximum Flow Problem with Conflict Constraints. In Proceedings of the 2 Industrial Electronics and Applications Conference, Sabah, Malaysia, 8–9 September 2025.
45. Montemanni, R. Solving a Home Healthcare Routing and Scheduling Problem with Real-World Features. In *Machine Learning* *Soft Computing, Proceedings of International Conference on Machine Learning and Soft Computing, Tokyo, Japan, 24–26 January 2* Springer: Singapore, 2025; pp. 111–119.
46. Stuckey, P.J. Lazy Clause Generation: Combining the Power of SAT and CP (and MIP?) Solving. In Proceedings of International Conference on Integration of Artificial Intelligence and Operations Research Techniques in Constraint Programm (CPAIOR), Bologna, Italy, 14–18 June 2010; pp. 5–9.
47. GEne Network Expansion. CPU Performance. 2025. Available online: https://gene.disi.unitn.it/test/cpu_list.php (accesse 9 July 2025).

algorithms

MDPI

cle

ɘconstructing a Minimalist Transformer Architecture for ɿivariate Time Series Forecasting

po Garagnani [1] and Vittorio Maniezzo [2,*]

1 "Enzo Ferrari" Department of Engineering, University of Modena and Reggio Emilia, 41121 Modena, Italy; 298707@studenti.unimore.it
2 Department of Computer Science, University of Bologna, 40126 Bologna, Italy
* Correspondence: vittorio.maniezzo@unibo.it

Abstract: This paper provides a detailed breakdown of a minimalist, fundamental Transformer-based architecture for forecasting univariate time series. It describes each processing step in detail, from input embedding and positional encoding to self-attention mechanisms and output projection. All of these steps are specifically tailored to sequential temporal data. By isolating and analyzing the role of each component, this paper demonstrates how Transformers capture long-term dependencies in time series. A simplified, interpretable Transformer model named 'minimalist Transformer' is implemented and showcased using a simple example. It is then validated using the M3 forecasting competition benchmark, which is based on real-world data, and a number of data series generated by IoT sensors. The aim of this work is to serve as a practical guide and foundation for future Transformer-based forecasting innovations, providing a solid baseline that is simple to achieve but exhibits a stable forecasting ability not far behind that of state-of-the-art specialized designs.

Keywords: data series forecasting; Transformer models; machine learning; attention mechanism; interpretable results; pedagogical breakdown

1. Introduction

Time series forecasting is a key topic in data science and has a wide range of applications in areas such as economics, energy, healthcare, logistics and environmental monitoring. Accurate forecasting enables informed decision-making, efficient resource allocation and risk mitigation. Traditional statistical methods such as ARIMA and exponential smoothing have long been used for this purpose and often produce good results when the necessary assumptions are met. However, these methods often struggle to capture complex patterns and long-term dependencies in the data, an area in which deep learning methods, especially sequence models such as recurrent neural networks (RNNs), have often demonstrated superior performance.

Transformer models, which were initially designed for natural language processing tasks, have recently shown remarkable success in understanding and generating sequential data, demonstrating their effectiveness in modeling long-range dependencies. Transformers are attention-based models that eliminate the need for recurrence and convolution, relying instead on a self-attention mechanism to capture global context across sequences. This architecture has had a revolutionary impact on NLP, and its application to time series forecasting is a rapidly growing area of research.

Unlike natural language, time series are composed of continuous values and frequently exhibit seasonality, trends, and influence from exogenous variables. While recent studies have

https://doi.org/10.3390/a18100645

proposed various adaptations of the Transformer to address the unique properties of time series data, many of these models are treated as opaque black boxes. This means that there is limited clear understanding of how each component relates to temporal information and contributes to forecasting performance. Furthermore, the implementation details are frequently insufficiently specified, which makes reproducibility and interpretability challenging.

The aim of this paper is to 'deconstruct' the forecasting process of Transformer-based models when applied to univariate time series. The objective is to provide a transparent, modular and pedagogical account of how univariate time series are transformed and processed within these models to generate future trajectories. Each processing step is described in detail, including data normalization, input windowing, positional encoding, encoder and decoder architecture, training strategies, and prediction generation. Both the theoretical basis and the practical design choices are highlighted, showing how each element contributes to predictive accuracy and attempting to bridge the gap between theoretical advancements and practical implementation.

To validate the methodology, a basic Transformer-based model has been implemented and evaluated on a significant benchmark of univariate time series. These were selected from the well-known M forecasting competition benchmarks and included macro- and micro-economic, industrial, financial, and demographic series with varying statistical properties. This work combines theoretical explanation with empirical validation to serve as a comprehensive guide to deconstructing Transformer-based time series forecasting, providing a tutorial for newcomers and a reference for practitioners.

This paper is structured as follows. Section 2 reviews the related works in time series forecasting, with particular emphasis on recent advancements leveraging Transformer architectures. Section 3 presents the workflow of a minimalist Transformer module to produce a multipoint forecast for a univariate time series. Section 4 analyses some results in applying the described architecture on benchmark data series and comparing it with another standard methodology.

2. Related Work

Transformer modules for processing graph-like structures were originally introduced in [1] for a check-reading task; however, it was only in [2] that the current Transformer architecture for sequence modeling was proposed. Already, the very first line of the introduction of this seminal paper frames the transformer architecture among established time series modeling and forecasting algorithms, citing LSTM [3] and GRU [4], i.e., the two main architectures for recurrent neural networks (RNNs) applied to time series modeling.

Indeed, RNNs can be effective in capturing long-term dependencies within data, but they suffer from slow training, vanishing gradients, and high sensitivity to hyperparameter settings. Furthermore, the most well-established statistical methods, such as autoregressive integrated moving average (ARIMA) [5] and exponential smoothing (ETS) [6,7], are highly effective for stationary data but struggle with complex nonlinear patterns.

Transformer architectures are immune to these drawbacks because they do not rely on the assumption of stationarity. They capture global dependencies in input sequences without relying on recurrence, instead leveraging self-attention mechanisms to enable the direct modeling of long-range dependencies. This supports full parallelization during training and allows the model to focus on relevant time steps, regardless of their position in the sequence.

A key challenge in applying Transformers to univariate time series is the absence of the rich semantic tokens found in language. Unlike words in a sentence, time series values are continuous and lack discrete meaning, making it more difficult to learn meaningful attention patterns. Therefore, Transformers need to be adapted for time series forecasting. Some adaptations of Transformers for use with time series data include: *Informer* [8], which introduces a sparse self-attention mechanism to reduce the quadratic complexity of self-attention, making it more efficient for long sequence time series forecasting; *Autoformer* [9], which integrates a series decomposition block within the Transformer to separate trend and seasonal components, obtaining decomposition-based attention for better seasonal-trend modeling, improving interpretability and long-horizon forecasting accuracy; *FEDformer:* [10], which incorporates Fourier transformations into the attention mechanism to better exploit frequency-domain characteristics; *PatchTST:* [11], which employs a splitting mechanism to time series, converting multiple timesteps (i.e., a patch) into a single token, enabling a vanilla Transformer architecture to capture long-term dependencies with fewer tokens; *Chronos* [12], a family of pretrained time series forecasting models based on language model architectures. Chronos models have been trained on a large corpus of publicly available time series data, with particular interest in their zero-shot performance; *TCANs* (Temporal Convolution Attention Networks) [13], which combine temporal convolutional networks and attention mechanisms.

Recently, an explosion of adaptations has appeared, together with dedicated surveys and tutorials [14–16]. However, these models are often complex, incorporating multiple components such as static covariates, gating mechanisms, and probabilistic outputs. While these additions have shown empirical gains, they frequently obscure the core dynamics of the attention mechanism and make the models less accessible for analysis or adaptation.

In contrast, there is interest in minimal Transformer implementations, which isolate the effectiveness of self-attention in forecasting tasks. Informer has already demonstrated that a simplified Transformer, devoid of specialized components, can outperform classical models and RNNs on certain benchmarks when properly tuned. Similarly, ref. [17] proposed the 'Temporal Attention' module within a lightweight Transformer framework, demonstrating that attention over timesteps alone can achieve comparable performance on univariate series. Other studies, such as iTransformer [18], investigate how the performance of standard Transformers is affected by different initialization, normalization, or positional encoding strategies. This sheds light on the contribution of each component to forecasting accuracy.

This body of work highlights the growing interest in demystifying Transformer-based time series models by removing layers of abstraction. In line with this perspective, a minimalist Transformer specifically designed for univariate forecasting is proposed. A minimal version of the Transformer encoder has been developed by maintaining only the essential self-attention and feedforward components. By simplifying the model, the aim of this study is to understand the fundamental processes that enable Transformers to succeed in this domain and to provide a transparent and reproducible basis for further research.

3. The Transformer Processing Pipeline

This section describes the successive processing phases carried out by a minimalist Transformer module to produce a multipoint forecast of a univariate data series. The relevant Python code can be found in [19]. Successive processing stages are here showcased on a tiny time series obtained by querying Google Trends [20] on the term "restaurant". The series shows a trend (at the time of writing, it is holiday season in Italy and interest in dining out is increasing) as well as seasonality, due to increased interest on weekends.

Only 35 data points are considered, 7 of which are kept for validation and 28 are used for training. The series $s(t)$ is the following:

$$s(t) = (44, 48, 51, 48, 50, 63, 66, 48, 53, 56, 52, 57, 70, 67, 56, 60, 62, 60, 58, 75, 73, 59, 61, 65, 63, 63, 78, 80, 63, 64, 67, 65, 70, 87, 84)$$

The data processing cycle consists of three main phases: encoding, decoding, and learning. A view of the whole model can be seen in Figure 1. The following subsections provide details on each phase; the reader is referred to [2] for a more exhaustive exposition.

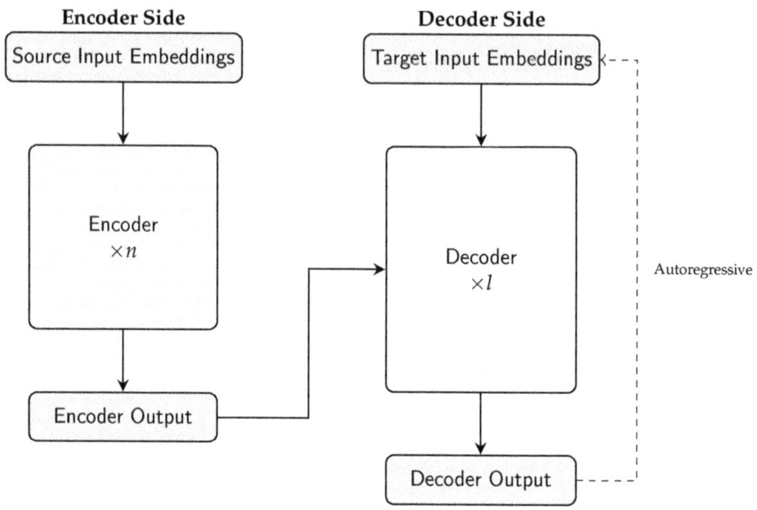

Figure 1. The vanilla Transformer architecture.

3.1. Encoding

The objective of the encoding component (i.e., the *encoder*) in a Transformer architecture is to process an input sequence and convert the raw input into a contextually enriched representation that captures both local and global dependencies. This representation can then be used effectively by the rest of the model.

The general structure of the encoding module is represented by the pseudocode in Algorithm 1 and sketched in Figure 2. All intermediate numerical results obtained for the restaurant series case study are reported in the text or in Appendix A when they are too big to be presented inline. This is to enable the interested reader to immediately grasp the dimensionalities and values involved in this tiny example, and possibly to follow the corresponding evolution of a run of the code provided in [19].

In the case of the running example, the following input parameter values are used: $n = 7$, $m = 4$, $k = 2$, $d_k = d_v = 2$, $p = 16$.

The individual steps are detailed below.

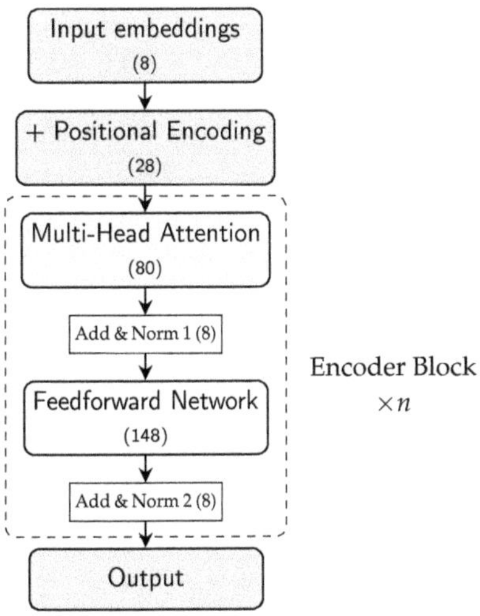

Figure 2. The encoding process. For each block, the total number of learnable parameters for the restaurant series example is shown.

Algorithm 1: The encoding module

Procedure encoding(s,n,m,k,d_k,d_v,p)
Input : A time series $\mathbf{s} = [s_i], i = 0, \ldots, t$
Output: A 2D matrix Z
`// Input Projection`
`// transform the array s into the 2D embedding matrix (tensor) X`
for $i = 0, \ldots, t$ **do**
  Expand value s_i into a row $X_i = (s_i W_i) + b_i$
end
$X' = X + P$; `// Positional encoding`
for *n times* **do**
  `// multihead attention`
  for $h = 1, \ldots, k$ **do**
    `// attention`
    Compute $Q^h = (X' \cdot W_q^h) + b_q^h$;
    Compute $K^h = (X' \cdot W_k^h) + b_k^h$;
    Compute $V^h = (X' \cdot W_v^h) + b_v^h$;
    Let d_k = num columns of W_k^h;
    Let $A^h = \frac{Q \cdot K^T}{\sqrt{d_k}}$; `// init attention function`
    Let $A^h = softmax\left(A^h\right)$; `// softmax over all rows`
    Let $A^h = A^h \cdot V^h$; `// completed attention function`
  end
  Let $A = concatenate(A^h), h = 0, \ldots, k$;
  Let $A = A \cdot W_O$; `// output projection`
  Let $X' = LayerNorm(X' + A)$;
  Let $F = feedforward(X')$; `// feedforward layer`
  Let $X' = LayerNorm(X' + F)$;
end
Let $Z = X'$;

(*Input arguments*)

The input consists of the data series to be forecast—in this case, it is an array $s \in \mathbb{R}^n$ and of six control hyperparameters.

For the restaurant time series, a straightforward preprocessing step has been applied: *min-max* normalization of the raw data. Subsequently, each sequence was constructed using a sliding window of length $n = 7$ over the series.

Lines 2–4: (*Input Projection*)

Single scalar values for each single timestep may not be expressive enough to capture contextual information. Each data point is projected into a higher-dimensional space where nonlinear dependencies between features can be easier to identify.

In the minimalist Transformer model proposed in this study, the projections, also known as *embeddings*, were obtained by multiplying each datapoint by a shared real-valued vector $W_i \in \mathbb{R}^m$ initialized as a random Gaussian vector, and by adding a bias array $b_i \in \mathbb{R}^m$. These values can later be learned. In this way, a matrix $X \in \mathbb{R}^{n \times m}$ is computed, which contains, for each original timestep, its m-dimensional representation.

In the restaurant series, the projections were based on vectors of 4 values, obtaining a set of matrices, each of which with $n = 7$ rows and $m = 4$ columns, leaving 4 parameters to be learned for the projection vector and the other 4 for the bias array. Each matrix $\mathbf{X}$ represents a window over the input time series; the first of these matrices is presented in the Appendix A as Equation (A1). The learned arrays W_i, b_i are also shown in the Appendix A, as Equation (A2).

Line 5: (*Positional Encoding*)

The basic attention mechanism, which will be implemented in lines 12–14, is insensitive to the permutation of the input values [2] and is in itself unusable for modeling data series. Therefore, the model does not inherently deal with the sequential position of the elements: the attention only depends on the set of elements, not on their order. To inject ordering information, each input embedding X^j is added to a positional vector. This is obtained by means of a matrix $P \in \mathbb{R}^{n \times m}$, which yields the transformed input:

$$X' = X + P \tag{1}$$

where n denotes the sequence length and m denotes the embedded dimension.

The matrix P can be either *static*, remaining fixed during the training phase, or *learnable*, changing at each step to better adapt to the task at hand. It can also be either *absolute*, depending solely on the element's position, or *relative*, in which case the element itself influences the values of the matrix's rows.

In the proposed minimalist architecture, matrix $P \in \mathbb{R}^{7 \times 4}$ is an absolute, learnable positional encoding, in the restaurant use case consisting of 7 rows and 4 columns. This equates to a further 28 parameters that need to be learned. The matrix P used in the running example is presented in the Appendix A as Equation (A3).

Lines 6–21: (*Encoding Blocks*)

The main loop of the algorithm repeats a block of code called an *Encoding Block* n times. In it, matrix $\mathbf{X}$ is first passed to a module implementing Multihead Attention (Lines 7–15). The outputs of the heads are then concatenated and projected to keep the size consistent (Lines 16–17). Next, a residual connection with a normalization is applied (Line 18). The output is then passed through a small feedforward network, after which another residual connection and normalization are applied (Lines 19–20). It is important to note that each iteration uses its own set of parameters for the projections, attention weights, and feedforward layers; parameters are not shared between iterations. All these steps are detailed in the following.

Lines 7–15: (*Multihead Attention*)

This loop iterates a basic attention mechanism that dynamically weighs the contribution of each past point in the series when computing the representation of those under scrutiny. It computes a set of attention scores relating the "query" vector of the current point and "key" vectors of all sequence values. In the sample application, a query comes from the embedding of the last known observation, while the keys correspond to those of all past observations. The resulting attention weights determine which points matter most and the forecast is then given by a weighted sum of the corresponding "value" vectors.

Queries (the elements currently focused on), keys (descriptors of the corresponding values), and values (the actual information) are all represented as matrices. Typically, queries and keys share the same inner dimension d_k, while values may have a different dimension d_v. At each iteration, the corresponding set of query, key, and value is referred to as a *head*. The matrices and the bias identified for the two heads used in the running example are reported in the Appendix A in Equations (A4) and (A5).

Line 8: generates the $h-th$ query matrix and projects the input embeddings into vectors that represent what has been looked for in the past. This is achieved by using a dynamic parameter matrix $W_q^h \in \mathbb{R}^{m\times d_k}$ and a bias array $b_q^h \in \mathbb{R}^{d_k}$, which are learnt.

Line 9: generates the $h-th$ key matrix and projects the input embeddings into vectors that represent the information content of each corresponding embedding. This is achieved by using a dynamic parameter matrix $W_k^h \in \mathbb{R}^{m\times d_k}$ and a bias array $b_k^h \in \mathbb{R}^{d_k}$, which are learnt.

Line 10: generates the $h-th$ value matrix and projects the input embeddings into vectors that represent the relevant information of each available embedding. This is achieved by using a dynamic parameter matrix $W_v^h \in \mathbb{R}^{m\times d_v}$ and a bias array $b_v^h \in \mathbb{R}^{d_k}$, which are learnt.

Line 11: initializes the scaling factor.

Line 12: implements the first part of the attention function, in this case using the *Scaled Dot-Product Attention* [2]. The similarity between sequence elements is computed from Q and K through a dot product. The key matrix is transposed so that the operation compares each feature of every query with the corresponding feature of every key. This initial A matrix will contain similarity values $a_{ij} \in \mathbb{R}$ between every query vector and every key vector.

Line 13: transforms the similarity values into 'probability' scores. The *softmax*() operator is applied to all elements a_{ij} over every row: $a_{ij} = e^{a_{ij}} / \sum_k e^{a_{kj}}, \forall i, j = 1, \ldots, n$. In this way, for every query vector, normalized weights of similarity towards key vectors are obtained.

Line 14: completes the computation of the attention function by implementing a weighted sum of the value vectors, $A^h = A^h \cdot V^h$, thereby aggregating information from the relevant timesteps.

Line 16: lines 7–15 are repeated k times, each time obtaining an attention matrix A^h, $h = 1,\ldots,k$. This line concatenates all these matrices into a single bigger one, $A = [A^1\ A^2\ \ldots\ A^h]$. The matrix A obtained for the running example is reported in the Appendix A as Equation (A6).

Line 17: since concatenation may modify the dimensionality, a final output projection $W^O \in \mathbb{R}^{hd_v\times m}$ is applied to ensure that the original size is kept $X' = A \cdot W^O$.

In the running example, we set $h = d_k = d_v = \frac{m}{2} = 2$. This produced 6 matrices, all of size 4×2, totaling 48 more parameters to learn. The output matrix W^O is, instead, of size 4×4. Matrix W^O for the running example is reported in Equation (A7) of the Appendix A.

Lines 18, 20: (*Add and Norm*)

This block tries to stabilize training by normalizing activations while keeping a residual path. It is implemented by a layer function $LayerNorm : \mathbb{R}^{n \times m} \to \mathbb{R}^{n \times m}$, which operates independently for each row i (i.e., for each embedding), computing the mean $\mu_i \in \mathbb{R}$ and the variance $\sigma_i \in \mathbb{R}$, and updating the features of row i as $x_{ij} = \gamma_j \cdot \frac{x_{ij} - \mu_i}{\sigma_i} + \beta_j$, where $\gamma, \beta \in \mathbb{R}^m$ are learnable parameters.

In the running example, having set $m = 4$, and having two different *LayerNorm* blocks, 16 parameters were set to be learned. For the first layer:

$$\gamma = \begin{bmatrix} 0.8659 & 1.1768 & 0.4843 & 1.2575 \end{bmatrix} \quad \beta = \begin{bmatrix} -0.3721 & 0.1294 & -0.0496 & 0.3132 \end{bmatrix}$$

While for the second layer:

$$\gamma = \begin{bmatrix} 0.8747 & 0.7511 & 0.6320 & 0.7074 \end{bmatrix} \quad \beta = \begin{bmatrix} -0.1117 & -0.1993 & 0.0806 & 0.1641 \end{bmatrix}$$

Line 19: (*Feedforward Network*)

The final processing step of the minimalist Transformer architecture implements a two-layer network with a ReLU activation function between them:

$$s' \leftarrow \max(0, s' \cdot W_1 + b_1) \cdot W_2 + b_2 \tag{2}$$

where:

$$W_1 \in \mathbb{R}^{m \times p}, \quad b_1 \in \mathbb{R}^p$$
$$W_2 \in \mathbb{R}^{p \times m}, \quad b_2 \in \mathbb{R}^m$$

The ReLU function is applied element-wise. The intermediate dimension p is typically chosen to be larger than m to improve model capacity and generalization.

In the model, we set $p = 4 \times m = 16$, meaning a total number of $16 \times 4 \times 2 + (16 + 4) = 148$ parameters, as resulting also in Figure 2. The values learned by the sample architecture is reported in the Appendix A in Equations (A8) and (A9).

Line 22: (*Output*)

The full output, stored in matrix X', contains the *encoded* representation of the input timesteps. In order to distinguish it thereafter, it will be denoted as Z.

3.2. Decoding

The objective of the decoding component (i.e., the decoder) in a Transformer architecture is to generate an output sequence step by step. This is achieved by using the encoded representation of the input and the output data generated by the encoding component.

The general structure of the decoding module is represented by the pseudocode in Algorithm 2 and in Figure 3. The individual steps are detailed below.

Lines 1–2: (*Input*)

The decoder takes the encoder output $Z \in \mathbb{R}^{n \times m}$ as its main input (Line 1) and iteratively updates a sequence represented by matrix $\mathbf{Y} \in \mathbb{R}^{no+1 \times m}$, where each row Y_{i+1} represents the i-th output embedding, except for the first row, which has a special row. Initially, the matrix is zero-initialized (Line 2). The first row is set as the `<CLS>` token (Line 3), a learnable embedding used in order to kick-start the learning process. The sequence is then updated autoregressively, i.e., one timestep at a time, with each new element depending on the previously generated ones.

The learned `<CLS>` token for the restaurant series is the following vector:

$$\texttt{<CLS>} = \begin{bmatrix} 0.3162 & -0.1322 & 0.3443 & 0.2043 \end{bmatrix}$$

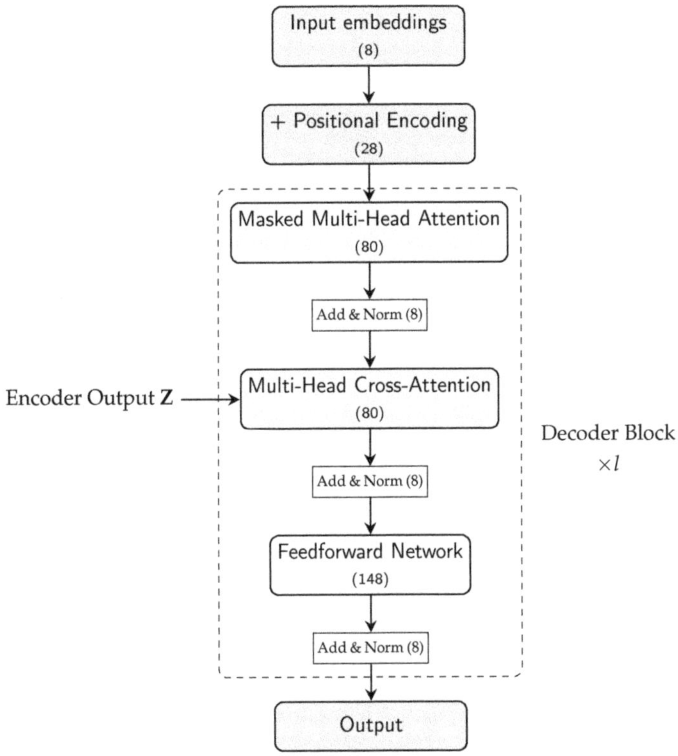

Figure 3. The Decoding Process. For each block, the total number of learnable parameters for the restaurant series example is shown.

Lines 5–24: (*Decoding Blocks*)

Just as in the encoding phase, the main loop of the algorithm updates for l iterations (Lines 5–24) the matrix **Y**. The block of code implementing each iteration is called a *Decoding Block*. In the block, Matrix **Y** is first processed by the *Multihead Masked Self-Attention*, which enables the decoder to process to previous positions in the output sequence while preventing it from attending to future positions, thereby enforcing autoregressive generation. Next, **Y** interacts with the encoder output **Z** through a *Multihead Cross-Attention module*, which enables the model to selectively focus on relevant parts of the input sequence (as encoded by the encoder) when generating each output token. This is the key mechanism that connects the encoder and decoder. Finally, the output is passed through some postprocessing steps to produce the final result of the single iteration.

The general procedure outlined above is explained in more detail below.

Lines 6–20: (*Masked Self-Attention*)

The Masked Self-Attention mechanism works in the same way as a Multihead Attention function, but it ensures that the generation of each successive sequence value can only consider the present or the past, never the future. This is achieved using a look-ahead mask that prevents feedback in time. The following operations are performed inside each loop (i.e., each head).

Line 7: generates the query, key, and value matrices, projecting the already-generated embeddings into semantic vectors. This projection is achieved by using dynamic parameter matrices and a dynamic bias array, both of which must be learnt.

Line 8: computes the first part of the *Scaled-Dot Product Attention* function.

Line 9: masks out any similarity values computed between a query vector from a timestep and a key vector coming from a future timestep. During the subsequent softmax step, the value $-\infty$ becomes 0, thus avoiding dependency on the future.

Line 10: computes the last part of the attention function.

After the loop of Lines 7–10 is completed, the h^1 different output matrices must be aggregated together.

Line 12: the h^1 matrices are concatenated by row, obtaining the complete $\mathbf{A}$ matrix.

Line 13: the matrix $\mathbf{A}$ is multiplied by $W_{o1} \in \mathbb{R}^{h^1 d_v \times m}$. The latter matrix is a learnable parameter.

The operations above are referred to as 'Self-Attention' because the projections of Q, K and V all come from the same input vector, $\mathbf{Y}$. In the example architecture, we set the number of heads for the self-attention layers to $h^1 = 2$.

Lines 14, 21, 23: (*Add and Norm*)

Each operation in the decoding stage is followed by a residual connection and a normalization step. The LayerNorm() function works row-wise on the embeddings, standardizing them with learnable scaling and shifting parameters (γ, β).

Lines 15–20: (*Cross-Attention*)

The second Attention step in the decoding phase links the partially generated output with the encoder's representation of the input. Specifically, the decoder's current output is projected into queries, while the encoder's output provides the keys and values. Similar to Multihead Attention, this process involves a loop (Lines 15–18) and an aggregation step at the end (Lines 19–20).

Line 16: generates the query, key, and value matrices, projecting the decoder's current output into queries and the encoder's output into keys and values. Each projection uses a learnable parameter matrix to transform the embeddings into semantic vectors.

Line 17: computes the attention function, using the already computed matrices.

The above operations are repeated h^2 times, getting h^2 attention outputs.

Line 19: All the head's outputs are concatenated by the rows in a single matrix $\mathbf{A}$.

Line 20: The attention matrix $\mathbf{A}$ is multiplied by $W_{o2} \in \mathbb{R}^{h^2 d_v \times m}$, which is a learnable parameter.

The name Cross-Attention is due to the fact that the output of the encoding phase Z and the decoding current output $\mathbf{Y}$ are combined, *crossing* the two matrices together. In the example, we set the number of heads of the Cross-Attention layer to $h^2 = 2$.

Line 22: (*Feedforward Network*)

The decoder applies a position-wise two-layer feedforward network with ReLU activation, as was done in the encoder (Line 22):

$$\mathbf{Y} \leftarrow \max(0, \mathbf{Y} \cdot W_1 + b_1) \cdot W_2 + b_2$$

Line 25: (*Projecting the Output*)

At the end of the decoding loop, matrix $\mathbf{Y} \in \mathbb{R}^{o \times m}$ is obtained. Before mapping the j-th embedding back into its scalar prediction, Y_j is passed through a final feedforward network and regularized (Line 25):

$$Y_j \leftarrow feedforward(Y_j) * scale(\mathbf{Z}) + bias(\mathbf{Z})$$

For enhanced regularization purposes, a scale value and a bias value are determined through two learnable matrices $W_{\text{scale}}, W_{\text{bias}} \in \mathbb{R}^{m \times m}$, based upon the mean across the timesteps of the encoded input series $\mathbf{Z}$:

$$scale(\mathbf{Z}) = \sigma\left(W_{\text{scale}} \cdot \sum_i \frac{\mathbf{Z}_i}{d}\right), \quad bias(\mathbf{Z}) = W_{\text{bias}} \cdot \sum_i \frac{\mathbf{Z}_i}{d}$$

where σ represents the sigmoid function.

If we are at the i-th iteration of the outer output cycle (Lines 4–27), the output matrix $\mathbf{Y}$ contains in position i the predicted embedding Y_i for timestep i.

Algorithm 2: The decoding module

1 **Procedure** decoding($\mathbf{Z}$,no,l,h^1,h^2)

Input : Matrix $\mathbf{Z}$ from encoding, *no* num data series points in output, l number of decoding blocks, h^1 and h^2 head numbers

Output: A 2D matrix $\mathbf{Y}$

`// subscripts indicate rows, superscripts columns`

2 $\mathbf{Y} = \mathbf{0}_{no+1 \times m}$

3 Let $Y^0 =$ <CLS>

4 **for** $i = 0, \ldots, no$ **do**

5   **for** l *times* **do**

`// Masked self-attention`

6   **for** $j = 0, \ldots, h^1$ **do**

7   Let $Q^j = (\mathbf{Y}W^j_{q1}) + b^j_{q1}, \quad K^j = (\mathbf{Y}W^j_{k1}) + b^j_{k1}, \quad V^j = (\mathbf{Y}W^j_{v1}) + b^j_{v1}$

8   Let $S^j = \frac{Q^j {K^j}^T}{\sqrt{d_k}}$

9   Set $S^j_i = -\infty$ for all $i > j$; `// mask future positions`

10   Let $A^j = softmax(S^j)V^j$

11   **end**

12   Let $\mathbf{A} = concatenate(A^j), j = 0, \ldots, h^1$

13   Let $\mathbf{A} = \mathbf{A} \cdot \mathbf{W_{o1}}$; `// for dimensionality coherence`

14   Let $\mathbf{Y} = LayerNorm(\mathbf{Y} + \mathbf{A})$

`// Cross-attention`

15   **for** $j = 0, \ldots, h^2$ **do**

16   Let $Q^j = (\mathbf{Y} \cdot W^j_{q2}) + b^j_{q2}, \quad K^j = (\mathbf{Z} \cdot W^j_{k2}) + b^j_{k2}, \quad V^j = (\mathbf{Z} \cdot W^j_{v2}) + b^j_{v2}$

17   Let $A^j = softmax\left(\frac{Q^j {K^j}^T}{\sqrt{d_k}}\right)V^j$

18   **end**

19   Let $\mathbf{A} = concatenate(A^j), j = 0, \ldots, h^2$

20   Let $\mathbf{A} = \mathbf{A} \cdot \mathbf{W_{o2}}$

21   Let $\mathbf{Y} = LayerNorm(\mathbf{Y} + \mathbf{A})$

22   Let $F = feedforward(\mathbf{Y})$

23   Let $\mathbf{Y} = LayerNorm(\mathbf{Y} + F)$

24   **end**

25   $Y^{i+1} = feedforward(Y^{i+1}) * scale(\mathbf{Z}) + bias(\mathbf{Z})$

26   $y_i = (Y^{i+1})W_o + b_o$

27 **end**

3.3. Learning

The encoding and decoding processes described in Sections 3.1 and 3.2 are actually included in an overarching loop that implements learning by adjusting all parameters (e.g., weights of projection matrices, attention heads, feed-forward layers, etc.) to minimize a loss function over the training data. This is typically achieved through stochastic gradient descent (SGD)-based optimization, usually backpropagation.

The process is the standard neural learning process, flowing through three main phases:

1. a *forward pass* where input sequences (time series points) are embedded into vectors, flowing through layers of multi-head self-attention and feed-forward networks obtain a forecasted value.
2. *loss computation*, where the loss function measures how far the predictions are from the ground truth. In the case of forecasting data series, the most commonly used loss functions are Mean Squared Error (MSE) or Root Mean Squared Error (RMSE), Mean Absolute Error (MAE), and Huber loss, which combines the robustness of MAE with the smoothness of MSE.
3. a *backward pass*, where gradients of the loss with respect to the parameters are computed via backpropagation and parameters are updated using an optimization algorithm (usually a variant of gradient descent).

The backward pass implements the actual learning process by reversing the computation flow that was used to make the forecast, as presented in Figure 2. A Transformer's computation graph has many layers, including an embedding layer, multiple self-attention blocks (each with projections W_Q, W_K, W_V, W_O), feed-forward networks, layer norms, residual connections, etc. During backpropagation, the chain rule of calculus is applied to each layer, as with standard MLPs, and the gradient flows backwards through each operation. This means that the W_Q, W_K, W_V, W_O, feed-forward weights, embedding matrices, and LayerNorm parameters all receive gradient-based updates depending on the value of the loss function.

Learning is a computationally intensive phase based on standard gradient descent optimizers, and it greatly benefits from GPU-optimized codes. In the minimalist architecture, the backward computations have been delegated to the relevant PyTorch classes [21].

The embedding matrices W_i and W_o are initialized such that $W_i \cdot W_o = 1$ to represent exactly the same projection. Specifically, W_i is initialized by drawing each of its elements from a uniform distribution, and W_o is set to be $\frac{W_i}{||W_i||^2}$ since the bias arrays b_i, b_o are zero-initialized. Then, during training, they are set to change without any constraint.

The training technique is as follows. The input sequence $\mathbf{X}$ of fixed length n is given to the model. The predicted element at the i-th timestep $\hat{y}_i$ is looked at, and the loss function between the ground truth element y_i is computed. The employed loss is the MSE. The backpropagation step, which updates the internal parameters of the mode, follows. Then, with probability p, the $\mathbf{Y}$ matrix is filled not with the predicted element $\hat{y}_i$ but with the actual one, y_i. The probability of that happening is gradually decreased during the training phase in order to let the model be more reliant on its own predictions, as it will be during inference.

In the case of the running example, the total number of parameters to learn in the Transformer model was 737.

3.4. Forecasting

Sections 3.1–3.3 describe the complete process to obtain one forecasted value. If more than one value is to be forecast, each additional forecast is appended to the end of the series, after which the process is repeated using the same fixed parameter matrices.

Figure 4 shows the results for the tiny example data series. The blue line depicts the training set, the green line the validation set, and the dashed line the model's results. Training was implemented using windows consisting of seven inputs and one output; therefore, the first seven values are not modeled. The forecast was made using seven validation values in the recursive forecasting fashion outlined above.

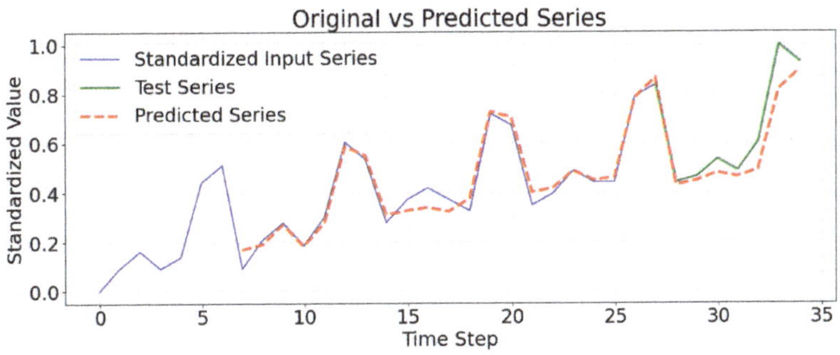

Figure 4. The Google trends restaurants dataseries.

Despite the limited data and restrictive configuration, the Transformer is highly effective in modeling the input series, though its forecasting abilities are, as would be expected, less accurate. More significant tests are reported in Section 4.

4. Computational Results

This section presents results obtained using the minimalist Transformer architecture in forecasting well-known univariate benchmark data series.

First, we showcase the successive processing stages on the archetypal Airline Passenger data series [5]. Then, we present illustrative quantitative results on standard forecasting benchmark instances. Unless otherwise specified, the hyperparameters were optimized using the Optuna package [22], and all experiments were performed on a machine equipped with 32 GB of RAM and a GPU featuring 16 GB of dedicated memory. All models were trained using PyTorch 2.8.0 on CUDA-enabled devices (with CUDA version 12.8) to leverage GPU acceleration.

4.1. The Airline Passengers Test Case

The Airline Passengers time series is one of the most famous and widely used in data analysis and forecasting. It consists of 144 observations of the monthly total number of international airline passengers in thousands between 1949 and 1960. As it is a real-world case that is very easy to model and predict (it is known to be an ARMA(1,1)), it is commonly used as a first validation for new forecasting approaches.

When the model is applied to this series, setting aside the last 12 values for validation and accounting for the obvious 12-month seasonality, the successive encoding steps through the positional embedding–multi-head attention–layer norm pipeline produce the results shown in Figure 5.

The series was preprocessed only via standard min–max normalization, then it was projected into embeddings of size $m = 12$. Employing only $n = 12$ timesteps at a time, 118 matrices $X \in \mathbb{R}^{12\times 12}$ are obtained. Matrix P used for positional embedding has the same dimensionality.

Next comes multi-head attention. We used 2 heads, and for each head, we set $d_k = d_v = \frac{12}{2} = 6$. Therefore, all matrices W_Q^h, W_K^h, and W_V^h had dimensions 12×6. These provide the bases for computing the attention function, where each *h-th* head gives rise to the matrix $A^h = \frac{Q_h K_h'}{d_h} \in \mathbb{R}^{n \times n}$, in this study $A^h \in \mathbb{R}^{12\times12}$. The successive *softmax* function does not change its dimensionality. After multiplying by V_h, we obtain the output of each head, of dimension 12 × 6. All outputs are then concatenated by row, giving rise to a matrix $A \in \mathbb{R}^{12\times12}$. The input dimension is then kept, when the output attention matrix is multiplied by matrix $W_O \in \mathbb{R}^{hd_v \times m}$—in the example, of dimension 12 × 12. In summary, the values used for the parameters were $n = 12$, $m = 12$, $k = 2$, $d_k = d_v = 6$, $p = 48$.

The number of epochs set for learning was 400, and the total number of parameters to learn in the transformer model resulted to be 5413.

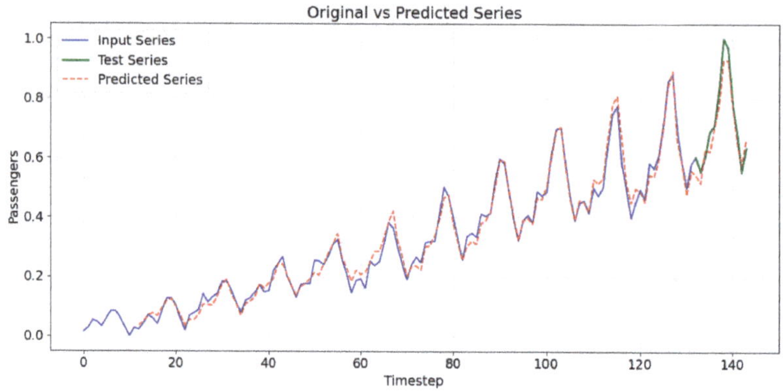

Figure 5. The predictions of the model on the full airline series, comprising 132 training data-points and 12 evaluation points.

4.2. Benchmark Results

This study aims to provide a basic, simple architecture that can be used to fully understand the internal functioning of the Transformer and possibly form the basis for improvements, rather than a best-of-class architecture. However, it is important to validate its effectiveness in order to determine how representative it is of the possibilities offered by the Transformer approach to data series forecasting. To this end, we ran both the described system and a standard random forest forecaster, the RandomForestRegressor from scikit-learn [23], on a standard forecasting benchmark.

The benchmark consisted of the monthly series from the M3 forecasting competition [24]. The M3 dataset comprises a variety of time series from different domains and frequencies, including yearly, quarterly, monthly, and other intervals. It contains the kind of seasonal and noisy data commonly encountered in business forecasting. The monthly data subset includes 1428 real-world time series collected at monthly intervals covering a wide range of domains, classified as:

- *Macroeconomics* (e.g., unemployment rates, inflation, industrial production),
- *Microeconomics* (e.g., sales, orders, inventory levels for individual companies),
- *Industry* (e.g., combined production, sales, or demand in a broader industrial sector, not just a single firm)
- *Finance* (e.g., stock prices, exchange rates, interest rates),
- *Demographics* (e.g., population statistics, birth/death rates),
- *Others*, i.e., diverse, real-world time series that do not belong to traditional economic or financial domains (e.g., energy consumption, transportation data)

The length of the monthly series varies, typically ranging from 48 to 126 observations (i.e., 4 to over 10 years of data), and for each series, participants were asked to forecast the next 18 months. This same forecast horizon has been used in all relevant tests, along with the following argument values: $n = 24$, $m = 36$, $k = 4$, $d_k = d_v = 12$, $p = 144$. The number of epochs set for network learning was 400, and the total number of parameters to learn in the Transformer model was 46,189.

We ran each model on all the benchmark series, computing the RMSE on both the training and test sets. To determine whether the difference in forecast effectiveness was significant, a Mann–Whitney U-test was conducted on the RMSE results for each aggregate separately. Table 1 shows the results of the comparison aggregated over the type feature. The columns show:

- *type*: type of the aggregate,
- *num*: number of series in the aggregate,
- *len*: average length of the series of the aggregate,
- *train*: number of series where the Transformer had a lower RMSE on the training set,
- *test*: number of series where the Transformer had a lower RMSE on the number of series where the Transformer had a lower RMSE on the training set,
- *perc*: percentage of aggregate series where the Transformer had a lower RMSE on the training set
- *pval*: p-value of the Mann–Whitney U test.

Table 1. Minimalist Transformer and random forest, aggregate results.

Type	Num	Len	Train	Test	Perc	Pval
MICRO	474	92.65	6	134	28.27	0.000
INDUSTRY	334	140.02	3	123	36.83	0.042
MACRO	312	130.88	3	101	32.37	0.021
FINANCE	145	124.40	1	68	46.90	0.247
DEMOGRAPHIC	111	123.33	3	33	29.73	0.021
OTHER	52	82.98	0	29	55.77	0.661

The results in Table 1 show that, despite being outperformed as a modeler of the known part of the series, the Transformer solution can already be competitive in forecasting, despite the limiting operational restrictions. The quality of the forecast depends on the structure of the data, resulting from dependency on the application domain. In the MICRO and DEMOGRAPHIC domains, Transformers performed better than random forest in less than one-third of cases, whereas in FINANCE, it was almost one-half, and in the OTHER domain, it was even more than half the time. There is no statistical difference in performance between the two approaches for these last two domains, while random forest has a significantly lower average RMSE for the other four. The results of the tests are highly dependent on sample size. It is not surprising that the greatest indifference is observed for the least numerous sample. However, no aggregate has a sample size that renders the test irrelevant.

As the M3 benchmark has been studied in depth, we can tentatively interpret these observations. Financial data is characterized by high volatility and weak or non-existent trends or seasonality. They therefore have a higher noise component, which appears to be better handled by Transformers. In contrast, industry and macro data have stronger deterministic components, such as trends and seasonality (due to business cycles, yearly production seasonality, etc.), which are better captured by a decision tree-based model. Seasonality is in fact much more pronounced in industry and demographics series, while finance has very weak seasonality and is often dominated by idiosyncratic shocks. A similar situation applies to trends in the series, where demographic and macroeconomic series exhibit clear long-term growth or decline. Finally, and most significantly, financial and 'other' series are subject to frequent regime shifts, whereas industry and macroeconomic series undergo structural breaks less frequently and exhibit more persistent regimes.

Table 2 shows details of the instances in each category for which Transformers achieved the best and worst test results compared to random forest. The columns of the table contain data that refer to scaled series and are:

- *id*: the id of the data series in the M3 collection;
- *type*: the category of the data series;
- *trtrain*: the absolute RMSE of the Transformer model on the training part;
- *trtest*: the absolute RMSE of the Transformer model on the test part, i.e., on the last 18 data points;
- *rftrain*: the absolute RMSE of the random forest model on the training part;
- *rftest*: the absolute RMSE of the random forest model on the test part, i.e., on the last 18 data points;
- Δ*train*: the RMSE difference between Transformers and random forest on the training part;
- Δ*test*: the RMSE difference between Transformers and random forest on the test part;
- *trtime*: the average time in seconds needed to train the Transformer on the respective series for a single epoch;
- *rftime*: the time in seconds needed to fit the random forest model on the training set.

Table 2. Minimalist Transformer and random forest, aggregate results, scaled data.

id	Type	Trtrain	Trtest	Rftrain	Rftest	ΔTrain	ΔTest	Trtime	Rftime
N1652	MICRO	0.061	0.262	0.062	0.335	−0.001	−0.072	0.07	0.15
N1546	MICRO	0.168	0.526	0.068	0.306	0.1	0.219	0.04	0.14
N1894	INDUSTRY	0.133	0.290	0.058	0.433	0.074	−0.142	0.11	0.22
N2047	INDUSTRY	0.144	0.667	0.056	0.428	0.088	0.238	0.12	0.21
N2255	MACRO	0.068	0.088	0.021	0.494	0.046	−0.406	0.13	0.20
N2492	MACRO	0.130	0.626	0.054	0.249	0.076	0.377	0.18	0.21
N2594	FINANCE	0.074	0.597	0.015	0.737	0.059	−0.140	0.13	0.19
N2658	FINANCE	0.126	0.656	0.046	0.435	0.080	0.220	0.03	0.13
N2737	DEMOGRAPHIC	0.074	0.129	0.046	0.209	0.028	−0.079	0.32	0.21
N2758	DEMOGRAPHIC	0.214	1.007	0.034	0.310	0.180	0.696	0.05	0.13
N2817	OTHER	0.079	0.125	0.036	0.441	0.043	−0.315	0.06	0.13
N2823	OTHER	0.116	0.166	0.066	0.081	0.050	0.085	0.11	0.13

The results in the table confirm that the RMSE values are comparable in all cases and that there are never differences in the order of magnitude, with values remaining relatively low, even when considering that they were computed on max–min scaled series. In all categories, the Transformers achieved a lower RMSE in at least one series. Figures 6 and 7 show plots of the actual series and the forecasts of the Transformers and the random forest in cases where the Transformers performed better and worse than the random forest, respectively.

To evaluate the scalability of the attention mechanism in capturing patterns, we conducted experiments on four longer time series. The series were produced in the context of the SMARTLAGOON project [25], an EU H2020 project with the objective of real-time monitoring, analysis, and prediction of the socio-environmental evolution of the vulnerable area Mar Menor area, the largest saltwater coastal lagoon in Europe. As part of the project, smart buoys were deployed in the lagoon, and their sensors generated IoT series on different physical variables at different sampling frequencies from August 2022 to April 2023. Table 3 below reports the results of forecasting the series in relation to water temperature at a depth of 1 m (*SDI_Temp_1m*), steam pressure (*Vapor_Pressure*), wind speed (*WS_ms*), and water temperature at a depth of 1 m (*WTemp_C1*). Each run had 24 timesteps as input and had to predict 18 points in time. Each dataset, instead, had 870 samples in the training set and 187 in the test set. Two plot examples of long series can be seen in Figure 8. The results presented in Table 3 show much lower variance than those in Table 2, as they refer to a single application domain. Interestingly, in this particular domain, the minimalist Transformer performs particularly well in comparison to the random forest regressor. Despite achieving a higher RMSE error in the training phase, it was able to deliver better forecasting performance across all series.

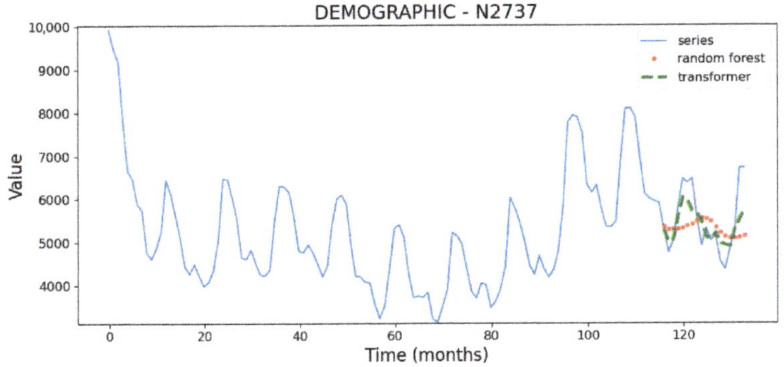

Figure 6. Actual data, Transformers and random forest forecast on series N2737.

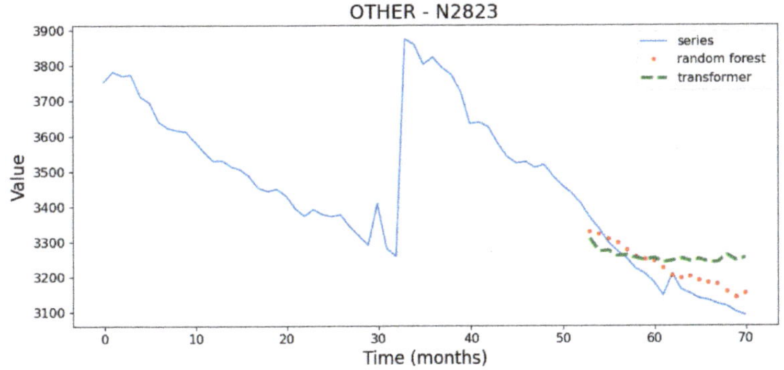

Figure 7. Actual data, Transformers and random forest forecast on series N2833.

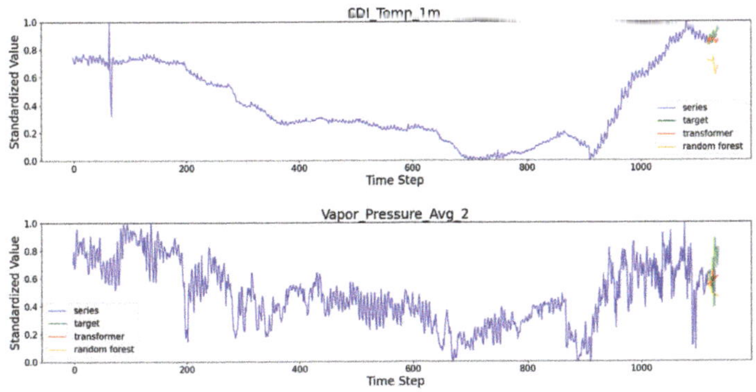

Figure 8. The series and the respective predictions of the Minimalistic Transformer model along with the Random Forest regressor.

To provide a more comprehensive view of the forecasting models, further comparisons have been made against different forecasting models, including recent Transformer-based approaches, in addition to the random forest baseline. These include the Chronos model [12], TCAN (Temporal Convolution Attention Network) [13], the ARIMA (AutoRegressive Integrated Moving Average) (ARIMA), and an ETS model (Exponential Smoothing), specifically a Holt and Winters forecaster. The autoregressive models relied on their statsmodels implementation [26] using the stepwise approach of pmdarima for hyperparameter tuning [27]. The RMSE test results are shown for the series listed in Table 4.

Table 3. Minimalist Transformer results over longer time series.

Name	Trtrain	Trtest	Rftrain	Rftest	ΔTrain	ΔTest	Trtime	Rftime
SDI_Temp_1m	0.047	0.143	0.012	0.170	0.035	−0.027	5.06	2.52
Vapor_Pressure	0.114	0.167	0.038	0.170	0.076	−0.003	4.93	10.99
WS_ms	0.175	0.190	0.061	0.191	0.114	−0.001	4.96	19.28
WTemp_C1	0.047	0.157	0.011	0.195	0.036	−0.038	4.93	12.73

Table 4. Minimalist Transformer compared to other baseline models.

id	Trtest	Chronos	Tcan	Arima	Ets
N1652	0.262	0.523	0.074	0.119	0.120
N1546	0.526	0.410	0.170	0.238	0.234
N1894	0.290	0.380	0.250	0.408	0.364
N2047	0.667	0.463	0.254	0.133	0.150
N2255	0.088	0.409	0.106	0.201	0.033
N2492	0.626	0.317	0.220	0.284	0.223
N2594	0.597	0.364	0.115	0.013	0.047
N2658	0.656	0.362	0.191	0.248	0.369
N2737	0.129	0.211	0.117	0.238	0.306
N2758	1.007	0.410	0.358	0.212	0.193
N2817	0.125	0.538	0.158	0.143	0.126
N2823	0.166	0.449	0.304	0.302	0.325
avg.	0.428	0.403	0.193	0.211	0.207

As shown in Table 4, there is no clear dominance among the different methods. Even though the specialized convolutional Transformer architecture achieves the lowest average error, the two autoregressive approaches follow closely behind. Fine-tuned models are clearly more effective than the zero-shot approach used with Chronos; even the minimalist architecture achieves comparable performance to their specialized one.

4.3. Ablation Studies

In Table 5 it is possible to see the effects of removing or editing computational blocks of the encoder, as shown in Figure 2, on the performance of the entire model. Each cell reports the training and the testing loss of the configuration in the respective row and column, and the corresponding loss, while the columns show:

- *id*: the id of the data series in the M3 collection;
- *1-sized embeddings*: results using embeddings of a single value (i.e., no embedding), lines 2–4 of Algorithm 1;
- *No PE*: results without positional encoding, line 5 of Algorithm 1;
- *Single Head*: results with single head instead than mutihead attention, lines 7–15 of Algorithm 1;
- *No Add&Norm 1*: results removing the first Add and Norm block, line 18 of Algorithm 1;
- *No FF*: results removing the feedforward network, line 19 of Algorithm 1;
- *No Add&Norm 2*: results removing the second Add and Norm block, line 20 of Algorithm 1;
- *Baseline*: results of the complete model.

id	Single Head	No FF	No Add&Norm 1	No Add&Norm 2	1-Sized Embeddings	No PE	No Output	Baseline
N1652	0.175/0.327	0.188/0.329	0.183/0.332	0.180/0.327	0.410/0.568	0.183/0.301	0.183/0.323	0.179/0.337
N1546	0.194/0.353	0.185/0.290	0.211/0.480	0.190/0.330	0.605/0.319	0.190/0.301	0.195/0.407	0.197/0.354
N1894	0.142/0.496	0.188/0.385	0.132/0.325	0.156/0.524	0.243/0.370	0.108/0.512	0.149/0.260	0.152/0.211
N2047	0.161/0.252	0.157/0.448	0.168/0.255	0.134/0.432	0.181/0.253	0.099/0.488	0.141/0.324	0.173/0.344
N2255	0.117/0.619	0.126/0.587	0.124/0.603	0.121/0.608	0.775/0.208	0.068/0.596	0.097/0.566	0.119/0.577
N2492	0.157/0.438	0.113/0.272	0.154/0.571	0.143/0.598	0.267/0.340	0.097/0.559	0.133/0.380	0.114/0.167
N2594	0.133/0.728	0.125/0.800	0.115/0.640	0.154/0.656	0.542/0.121	0.082/0.615	0.118/0.523	0.137/0.653
N2658	0.143/0.547	0.210/0.268	0.182/0.313	0.184/0.418	0.215/0.246	0.166/0.428	0.190/0.234	0.186/0.380
N2737	0.164/0.226	0.137/0.245	0.131/0.316	0.116/0.255	0.168/0.198	0.099/0.199	0.160/0.215	0.154/0.193
N2758	0.238/0.392	0.273/0.335	0.276/0.401	0.253/0.479	0.371/0.221	0.091/0.711	0.272/0.366	0.229/0.357
N2817	0.267/0.422	0.254/0.414	0.262/0.428	0.240/0.294	0.588/0.200	0.167/0.466	0.226/0.386	0.268/0.341
N2823	0.300/0.200	0.307/0.221	0.308/0.347	0.293/0.178	3.025/2.723	0.233/0.177	0.286/0.218	0.308/0.220
avg.	0.183/0.417	0.189/0.383	0.187/0.418	0.180/0.425	0.616/0.481	0.132/0.446	0.179/0.350	0.185/0.345

As the model is quite small, comprising just a single encoder block and a single decoder block, the overall effect is visible but not particularly impactful. As expected, the baseline model achieves the best loss value over the validation data, while the model without the feedforward network is still almost equivalent to it, and removing any other component has a comparable highly disruptive effect. Furthermore, the full model has the fourth highest training loss value. This, alongside the validation result, indicates the model's ability to generalize over the training data.

4.4. Interpretability

Figure 9 provides an additional view of the effects of learning. It illustrates the contribution of each timestep provided by the decoder to each generated output value. These contributions are made by both the encoded input time series and by the autoregressively generated output timestep, and are demonstrated using the Google Trends restaurant series. The larger the circle around a certain timestep, the greater the attention weight given by the trained model for inference.

More specifically, the attention contribution of the input series-in blue-is extracted from the weights of the Cross-Attention layer, while the attention contribution of the generated series—in green—is extracted from the Self-Attention layer.

The results align with what one might expect the model to learn about a seasonal trajectory. For example, it can be seen that, when generating the first timestep (labeled "Step 1" in Figure 9), the model relies on the timestep seven days prior, when a slight seasonal increase occurs. A similar argument could be made by observing that, from the generation of the fifth timestep onwards, the model relies heavily on the peak value of the input series, probably in order to extract information about the correct value of the new seasonal peak.

Another interesting observation that emerges from the above example is that the model focuses on specific timesteps while ignoring others entirely. Since the difference between these timesteps is small, the model attempts to gather as much information as possible from a few significant timesteps rather than relying on too many similar ones.

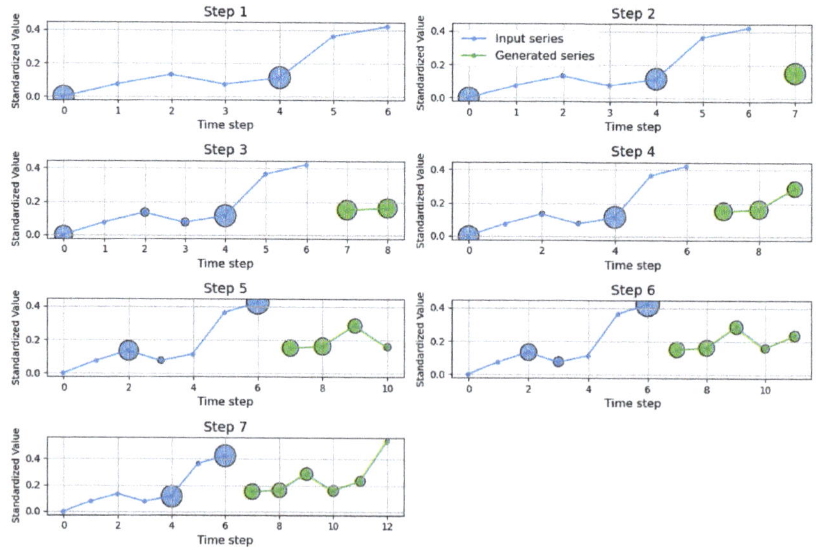

Figure 9. The contribution of each timestep to each generated output value.

4.5. Scalability

The model has also been evaluated in terms of the scalability of its components, i.e., how the number of parameters relates to training and inference time and performance. These tests were performed on the M3 dataseries with ID *N2047*, against which the minimalist model produced unfavorable testing results. The outcomes of these tests are reported in Tables 6 and 7. In Table 6, the embedding size was 8 and the number of training epochs was 20. The columns show:

- *Encoder*: number of encoder layers;
- *Decoder*: number of decoder layers;
- *trtrain*: absolute RMSE of the Transformer model on the training part;
- *trtest*: absolute RMSE of the Transformer model on the test part, i.e., on the last 18 data points;
- *nparams*: number of model parameters to train;
- *trtime*: training time, in seconds per epoch;
- *inftime*: inference time, in seconds.

Table 6. Scalability results.

Encoder	Decoder	Trtrain	Trtest	Nparams	Trtime	Inftime
1	1	0.181	0.397	2697	0.32	0.028
2	2	0.200	0.365	4745	0.37	0.049
3	3	0.191	0.251	6793	0.53	0.051
4	4	0.188	0.162	8841	0.69	0.078

A brief examination of the above results shows that as the number of encoder and decoder blocks increases, so does the number of parameters (*nparams*), which directly influences the training time (*trtime*) and inference time (*inftime*). While the training loss remains largely stable, the model's ability to generalize is reflected in the decreasing test loss values. As will also be apparent from the following Table 7, there is no direct correlation between training and testing loss.

Table 7, which includes a new *embed* column to report the size of the embeddings, shows the results of a model in which both the model size and the size of the internal embeddings change. In this case, the number of epochs is set to 100: this leads to better convergence on the training set, but worse results (with respect to Table 6). It should also be noted that the series in question is relatively short; therefore, increasing the network size — and thus the number of parameters — beyond a certain threshold does not affect performance.

Table 7. Scalability results.

Encoder	Decoder	Embed	Trtrain	Trtest	Nparams	Trtime	Inftime
1	1	4	0.175	0.592	805	0.21	0.023
1	1	40	0.135	0.417	57001	0.21	0.033
2	2	4	0.164	0.508	1381	0.34	0.037
2	2	40	0.176	0.422	103081	0.37	0.043
4	4	4	0.132	0.433	2533	0.68	0.083
4	4	40	0.180	0.294	195241	0.70	0.093

5. Conclusions

This work presents a minimalist Transformer architecture that is specifically designed for univariate time series forecasting. Rather than trying to propose yet another cutting-edge variant, the contribution of this study lies in systematically reducing the architecture to its essential components and documenting all relevant steps of the encoder, decoder and learning procedures in pseudocode. This study aimed to provide a transparent and replicable baseline for researchers, and practitioners interested in understanding the core mechanisms of transformers when applied to forecasting tasks.

The model is evaluated using a set of standard forecasting benchmarks and its performance is compared with that of a random forest forecaster. Although the minimalist Transformer does not outperform the most sophisticated state-of-the-art models, it consistently achieves comparable accuracy, particularly for time series with long-term dependencies, where attention mechanisms can exploit global context more effectively than purely tree-based methods.

Beyond raw predictive performance, the computational findings highlight two key outcomes: clarity and accessibility. By explicitly exposing each functional step, the proposed framework lowers the barrier for newcomers to the Transformer literature and the field of time series forecasting.

The robustness of the Transformer paradigm is also evident, as even a stripped-down version of the model demonstrates stable forecasting ability. This suggests that many performance gains in advanced variants stem from relatively minor architectural refinements.

Although the proposed architecture is designed for univariate forecasting, it can be readily extended to include external predictors and the multivariate case. This can be achieved by adapting the input encoding to represent both the target variable and the external predictors, or multiple variables. This enables the model to explicitly learn and exploit correlations between them.

In a research landscape often dominated by increasingly complex architectures, this study highlights the importance of transparent baselines. Future work may explore the impact of specific enhancements, such as seasonal embeddings, multi-head configurations or hybridization with statistical components, on forecasting performance when added to this minimalist core.

Author Contributions: All authors (F.G. and V.M.) contributed equally to all activities related to this work. All authors have read and agreed to the published version of the manuscript.

Funding: This research received no external funding.

Data Availability Statement: All codes and data are available in publicly accessible repositories, as referenced in the text.

Acknowledgments: No generative AI has been used for purposes such as generating text, data, or graphics, or for study design, data collection, analysis, or interpretation of data. AI-assisted tools were only used to check the spelling, syntax and style of the writing.

Conflicts of Interest: The authors declare no conflicts of interest.

Appendix A

This appendix contains all values of the trained matrices obtained for the encoding of the running example described in Section 3.

Equation (A1) shows the first embedded matrix, X, which encodes the input series. The matrix has been transposed for the sake of compact presentation.

The first 7×4 embedded matrix X used in the encoding process.

$$X^T = \begin{bmatrix} -0.4499 & -0.3722 & -0.3139 & -0.3722 & -0.3333 & -0.0808 & -0.0225 \\ 0.3955 & 0.1987 & 0.0512 & 0.1987 & 0.1004 & -0.5389 & -0.6865 \\ 0.0499 & 0.2140 & 0.3371 & 0.2140 & 0.2961 & 0.8295 & 0.9526 \\ -0.0958 & -0.0135 & 0.0483 & -0.0135 & 0.0277 & 0.2953 & 0.3570 \end{bmatrix} \quad (A1)$$

The projection vectors used to convert each scalar timestep in an embedding, and viceversa.

$$W_i = \begin{bmatrix} 0.8354 \\ -2.1147 \\ 1.7644 \\ 0.8851 \end{bmatrix} \quad b_i = \begin{bmatrix} -0.4499 \\ 0.3955 \\ 0.0499 \\ -0.0958 \end{bmatrix} \qquad W_o = \begin{bmatrix} 0.3003 \\ -0.1796 \\ 0.3854 \\ 0.0305 \end{bmatrix} \quad b_o = \begin{bmatrix} 0.0597 \end{bmatrix} \tag{A2}$$

Equation (A3) shows the positional encoding matrix, P. The matrix has been transposed for the sake of compact presentation.

The 7×4 positional encoding matrix P.

$$P^T = \begin{bmatrix} 0.2843 & -0.8508 & -0.7088 & -1.1406 & 1.0270 & 0.9304 & 0.4463 \\ 1.0329 & -0.4291 & 0.0881 & -0.1644 & -0.6551 & 0.6012 & -0.3370 \\ 0.8908 & -0.2810 & 0.8743 & 0.5641 & -1.0543 & -0.4678 & 1.4571 \\ 0.4260 & 0.2978 & -0.8110 & -0.1593 & -0.5840 & -1.0103 & -0.7960 \end{bmatrix} \tag{A3}$$

Equation (A4) presents the query matrices W_q^1 and W_q^2, the key matrices W_k^1 and W_k^2 and the value matrices W_v^1 and W_v^2 for the two heads used in the restaurant running example.

Query, key, and value matrices.

$$\begin{aligned} W_q^1 &= \begin{bmatrix} 0.1310 & 0.5068 & 0.2681 & 0.2951 \\ 0.3385 & 1.0323 & -0.0560 & 0.2226 \end{bmatrix} & W_q^2 &= \begin{bmatrix} -0.8557 & 0.4819 & -0.5107 & 0.1844 \\ 0.4872 & -0.1906 & 0.6404 & -0.7132 \end{bmatrix} \\ W_k^1 &= \begin{bmatrix} -0.7092 & -0.1109 & -0.6519 & -0.1403 \\ -0.4628 & -0.4405 & 0.3128 & 0.2569 \end{bmatrix} & W_k^2 &= \begin{bmatrix} 0.3696 & -0.8603 & -0.1482 & 1.2098 \\ -0.2819 & 0.7551 & -0.4609 & -1.2695 \end{bmatrix} \\ W_v^1 &= \begin{bmatrix} 0.2794 & -0.8501 & 0.0569 & -0.0530 \\ -0.5428 & 0.9581 & -0.0329 & -0.2587 \end{bmatrix} & W_v^2 &= \begin{bmatrix} 0.0266 & -0.8855 & 0.0607 & -0.1688 \\ -0.9599 & -0.0645 & -0.2187 & -0.3482 \end{bmatrix} \end{aligned} \tag{A4}$$

The additive bias arrays learned for projection.

$$\begin{aligned} b_1^Q &= \begin{bmatrix} 0.6879 \\ 0.3649 \end{bmatrix} b_1^K = \begin{bmatrix} 0.1048 \\ -0.0416 \end{bmatrix} b_2^Q = \begin{bmatrix} -0.4185 \\ 0.8086 \end{bmatrix} b_2^K = \begin{bmatrix} -0.2673 \\ 0.0098 \end{bmatrix} \\ b_1^V &= \begin{bmatrix} -0.1740 \\ 0.0893 \end{bmatrix} b_1^O = \begin{bmatrix} -0.3292 \\ 0.4357 \end{bmatrix} b_2^V = \begin{bmatrix} 0.0213 \\ -0.0516 \end{bmatrix} b_2^O = \begin{bmatrix} -0.2850 \\ -0.2149 \end{bmatrix} \end{aligned} \tag{A5}$$

Equation (A6) presents the attention matrix as resulting after the multihead attention phase for the restaurant time series.

The matrix A obtained.

$$A = \begin{bmatrix} 0.0531 & -0.1152 & -0.0142 & -0.0760 & -0.0043 & 0.1103 & 0.1638 \\ 0.1000 & 0.2736 & 0.1393 & 0.2191 & 0.1116 & 0.0060 & -0.0616 \\ -0.4575 & -0.3464 & -0.4285 & -0.3830 & -0.4366 & -0.4860 & -0.4923 \\ 0.4941 & 0.1239 & 0.2288 & 0.1804 & 0.1319 & 0.2962 & 0.1124 \end{bmatrix} \tag{A6}$$

Equation (A7) shows the matrix used to restore the needed dimensionality after the multihead attention computation.

The matrix W^O used for reprojection of the running example.

$$W^O = \begin{bmatrix} -0.1143 & 0.3255 & 0.1047 & 0.5301 \\ 0.1422 & -0.2276 & 0.0155 & -0.5644 \\ 0.1575 & -0.1060 & 0.1315 & -0.1953 \\ 0.3641 & 0.9191 & -0.2459 & -0.0482 \end{bmatrix} \tag{A7}$$

Equations (A8) and (A9) show the weights learnt by the feed-forward neural network used at the end of the encoding phase. They show the weights of the hidden and output layers, respectively.

Feedforward network, weights of the internal layer.

$$W_1^T = \begin{bmatrix} 0.3067 & 0.1809 & 0.0673 & 0.5560 \\ -0.1806 & -0.0553 & -0.2755 & 0.2545 \\ -0.1128 & -0.1211 & -0.4158 & 0.5880 \\ -0.1154 & 0.1402 & 0.0267 & 0.5364 \\ 0.0962 & -0.6581 & -0.2307 & 1.0214 \\ 0.0897 & -0.2100 & 0.1455 & 0.3424 \\ -0.4518 & 0.2141 & -0.9220 & 1.0428 \\ -0.3704 & 0.0218 & -0.4648 & 0.0920 \\ -0.1018 & -0.1424 & -0.3883 & 0.4627 \\ -0.0223 & 0.2030 & -0.2052 & 0.6145 \\ 0.1926 & -0.8201 & -0.0567 & 0.3366 \\ 0.0048 & -0.0324 & -0.0757 & 0.3328 \\ -0.2997 & 0.3305 & -0.5676 & 0.5782 \\ 0.0013 & -0.1013 & -0.1348 & -0.1666 \\ 0.0737 & 0.0930 & 0.0206 & 0.0936 \\ -0.2211 & -0.2244 & -0.3285 & -0.1195 \end{bmatrix} \quad b_1 = \begin{bmatrix} -0.3033 \\ -0.4938 \\ -0.3991 \\ -0.7121 \\ -0.7605 \\ -0.4844 \\ -0.7139 \\ -0.4224 \\ -0.4635 \\ -0.7017 \\ -0.4705 \\ -0.2822 \\ -0.3001 \\ -0.3100 \\ -0.2118 \\ -0.3648 \end{bmatrix} \tag{A8}$$

Feedforward network, weights of the output layer.

$$W_2 = \begin{bmatrix} -0.0902 & 0.0623 & -0.0051 & -0.0214 \\ 0.2824 & -0.1389 & 0.1038 & 0.0440 \\ -0.1227 & 0.1329 & -0.0587 & -0.3040 \\ 0.2578 & -0.4245 & 0.7379 & 0.2276 \\ -0.1491 & 0.4089 & -0.2755 & -0.6134 \\ 0.0673 & 0.0081 & -0.1963 & -0.0560 \\ 0.3649 & -0.1506 & -0.5302 & 0.6227 \\ 0.0849 & -0.1017 & -0.0649 & 0.2134 \\ 0.2211 & 0.0406 & 0.0487 & 0.1118 \\ 0.0785 & 0.1100 & -0.1416 & 0.1657 \\ -0.0010 & -0.3243 & -0.2919 & 0.5994 \\ -0.1367 & -0.1310 & 0.1522 & 0.0323 \\ -0.2234 & -0.0427 & -0.1288 & 0.0573 \\ -0.0032 & -0.0585 & -0.0134 & -0.1194 \\ -0.1594 & -0.1936 & -0.1171 & 0.0181 \\ 0.0751 & 0.1026 & 0.1138 & 0.1537 \end{bmatrix} \quad b_2 = \begin{bmatrix} 0.0467 \\ 0.0970 \\ -0.1583 \\ -0.2808 \end{bmatrix} \tag{A9}$$

References

1. Cun, Y.L.; Bottou, L.; Bengio, Y. Reading checks with multilayer graph transformer networks. In Proceedings of the 1 IEEE International Conference on Acoustics, Speech, and Signal Processing, Munich, Germany, 21–24 April 1997; Volum pp. 151–154.
2. Vaswani, A.; Shazeer, N.; Parmar, N.; Uszkoreit, J.; Jones, L.; Gomez, A.N.; Kaiser, L.U.; Polosukhin, I. Attention is All you N In *Advances in Neural Information Processing Systems*; Guyon, I., Luxburg, U.V., Bengio, S., Wallach, H., Fergus, R., Vishwanat S., Garnett, R., Eds.; Curran Associates, Inc.: Red Hook, NY, USA, 2017; Volume 30.
3. Hochreiter, S.; Schmidhuber, J. Long Short-Term Memory. *Neural Comput.* **1997**, *9*, 1735–1780. [CrossRef] [PubMed]
4. Chung, J.; Gulcehre, C.; Cho, K.; Bengio, Y. Empirical Evaluation of Gated Recurrent Neural Networks on Sequence Model *arXiv* **2014**, arXiv:1412.3555. [CrossRef]

Box, G.; Jenkins, G. *Time Series Analysis: Forecasting and Control*; Holden-Day series in time series analysis and digital processing; Holden-Day: San Francisco, CA, USA, 1970.

Holt, C.C. Forecasting trends and seasonals by exponentially weighted moving averages. *ONR Memo.* **1957**, *52*, 5–10.

Winters, P.R. Forecasting Sales by Exponentially Weighted Moving Averages. *Manag. Sci.* **1960**, *6*, 324–342. [CrossRef]

Zhou, H.; Zhang, S.; Peng, J.; Zhang, S.; Li, J.; Xiong, H.; Zhang, W. Informer: Beyond Efficient Transformer for Long Sequence Time-Series Forecasting. *arXiv* **2021**, arXiv:2012.07436. [CrossRef]

Wu, H.; Xu, J.; Wang, J.; Long, M. Autoformer: Decomposition Transformers with Auto-Correlation for Long-Term Series Forecasting. *arXiv* **2022**, arXiv:2106.13008.

Zhou, T.; Ma, Z.; Wen, Q.; Wang, X.; Sun, L.; Jin, R. FEDformer: Frequency Enhanced Decomposed Transformer for Long-term Series Forecasting. In *International Conference on Machine Learning*; Chaudhuri, K., Jegelka, S., Song, L., Szepesvari, C., Niu, G., Sabato, S., Eds.; PMLR: New York, NY, USA, 2022; Volume 162, pp. 27268–27286.

Nie, Y.; Nguyen, N.H.; Sinthong, P.; Kalagnanam, J. A Time Series is Worth 64 Words: Long-term Forecasting with Transformers. *arXiv* **2023**, arXiv:2211.14730. [CrossRef]

Ansari, A.F.; Stella, L.; Turkmen, C.; Zhang, X.; Mercado, P.; Shen, H.; Shchur, O.; Rangapuram, S.S.; Pineda Arango, S.; Kapoor, S.; et al. Chronos: Learning the Language of Time Series. *arXiv* **2024**, arXiv:2403.07815. [CrossRef]

Lin, Y.; Koprinska, I.; Rana, M. Temporal Convolutional Attention Neural Networks for Time Series Forecasting. In Proceedings of the IEEE International Joint Conference on Neural Networks (IJCNN), Shenzhen, China, 18–22 July 2021.

Wen, Q.; Zhou, T.; Zhang, C.; Chen, W.; Ma, Z.; Yan, J.; Sun, L. Transformers in time series: A survey. In Proceedings of the Thirty-Second International Joint Conference on Artificial Intelligence, 2023, IJCAI '23, Macao, China, 19–25 August 2023.

Ahmed, S.; Nielsen, I.E.; Tripathi, A.; Siddiqui, S.; Ramach, R.P.; Rasool, G. Transformers in Time-Series Analysis: A Tutorial. *Circuits Syst. Signal Process.* **2023**, *42*, 7433–7466. [CrossRef]

Su, L.; Zuo, X.; Li, R.; Wang, X.; Zhao, H.; Huang, B. A systematic review for transformer-based long-term series forecasting. *Artif. Intell. Rev.* **2025**, *58*, 1573–7462. [CrossRef]

Lim, B.; Sercan, O.; Loeff, N.; Pfister, T. Temporal Fusion Transformers for interpretable multi-horizon time series forecasting. *Int. J. Forecast.* **2021**, *37*, 1748–1764. [CrossRef]

Liu, Y.; Hu, T.; Zhang, H.; Wu, H.; Wang, S.; Ma, L.; Long, M. iTransformer: Inverted Transformers Are Effective for Time Series Forecasting. In Proceedings of the Twelfth International Conference on Learning Representations, Vienna, Austria, 7–11 May 2024.

Garagnani, F. Deconstructing-Transformers. 2025. Available online: https://github.com/FGaragnani/deconstructing-transformers (accessed on 8 August 2025).

Google. Google Trends. 2025. Available online: https://trends.google.com (accessed on 27 August 2025).

PyTorch Transformer. 2025. Available online: https://docs.pytorch.org/docs/stable/generated/torch.nn.Transformer.html (accessed on 8 August 2025).

Akiba, T.; Sano, S.; Yanase, T.; Ohta, T.; Koyama, M. Optuna: A Next-generation Hyperparameter Optimization Framework. *arXiv* **2019**, arXiv:1907.10902. [CrossRef]

Geurts, P.; Ernst, D.; Wehenkel, L. Extremely randomized trees. *Mach. Learn.* **2006**, *63*, 3–42. [CrossRef]

Makridakis, S.; Hibon, M. The M3-Competition: Results, conclusions and implications. *Int. J. Forecast.* **2000**, *16*, 451–476. [CrossRef]

Cecilia, J.M.; Manzoni, P.; Trolle, D.; Nielsen, A.; Blanco, P.; Prandi, C.; Peña Haro, S.; Barkved, L.; Pierson, D.; Senent, J. SMARTLAGOON: Innovative modelling approaches for predicting socio-environmental evolution in highly anthropized coastal lagoons. In Proceedings of the Conference on Information Technology for Social Good, GoodIT '21, New York, NY, USA, 9–11 September 2021; pp. 204–209.

Seabold, S.; Perktold, J. statsmodels: Econometric and statistical modeling with python. In Proceedings of the 9th Python in Science Conference, Austin, TX, USA, 28 June–3 July 2010.

Smith, T.G. pmdarima: ARIMA Estimators for Python. 2017. Available online: https://alkaline-ml.com/pmdarima/index.html (accessed on 29 September 2025).

algorithms

Article

Single Machine Scheduling Problems: Standard Settings and Properties, Polynomially Solvable Cases, Complexity and Approximability

Nodari Vakhania [1,*], Frank Werner [2,*] and Kevin Johedan Ramírez-Fuentes [1]

[1] Centro de Investigación en Ciencias, Universidad Autónoma del Estado de Morelos, Cuernavaca 62209, Mexico; johedan20012@gmail.com
[2] Faculty of Mathematics, Otto-von-Guericke University, 39106 Magdeburg, Germany
* Correspondence: nodari@uaem.mx (N.V.); frank.werner@ovgu.de (F.W.)

Abstract

Since the publication of the first scheduling paper in 1954, a huge number of works dealing with different types of single machine problems have appeared. They addressed many heuristics and enumerative procedures, complexity results or structural properties of certain problems. Regarding surveys, often particular subjects like special objective functions were discussed or more general scheduling problems were surveyed, in which a substantial part was devoted to single machine problems. In this paper, we focus on standard settings, basic structural properties of these settings, polynomial algorithms and complexity and approximation issues, which have not been reviewed so far, and suggest some future work in this area.

Keywords: single machine scheduling; polynomial algorithms; complexity; approximation algorithms

1. Introduction

Scheduling problems arise in many real-life applications, including in our everyday life. We commonly desire to optimize our time by arranging different activities, where the time is limited and the resources that we use are also scarce. We wish to optimize some of our personal criteria, but we also depend on the availability of the above-mentioned resources. As a simple but very common daily example, consider an apartment with a single bathroom, where a small family lives. The family members get up at some fixed time, and all of them need to spend some time in the bathroom, which is a scarce *resource* (or machine). Typically such a (renewable) resource may serve a single object or *job*, a family member in our example. Every member of the family needs to leave the apartment at some fixed time to reach their job or school without delay. This time can be different for different members of the family. Here arises a small optimization problem that requires us to schedule the time interval for each member of the family in order to meet the deadline of each member of the family.

Generally, in a scheduling problem we are given *jobs* or *tasks*, which are requests that need to be performed by some resource, such as a *machine* or a *processor*. In our small example, the bathroom requirements for each member of the family are jobs and the bathroom is a machine. We can give a vast number of examples of jobs and machines in our practical life, e.g., a job in a factory or a software application on a computer or smart phone or a lesson at school. Here machines, computers, smart phones, classrooms and teachers are resource examples. Every job requires some time units on a resource, whereas a resource is able to process at most one job at a time. Indeed, one classroom cannot be used for two different classes simultaneously, or a teacher cannot give two or more classes at the same time. There is a restriction on the whole time window during which a factory or a teacher can work. It is a scheduling task to arrange the order for processing the jobs. Often, there is some minimization or maximization criterion called an *objective function*. For example, a very common criterion is to minimize the maximum job or machine completion time, called the *makespan* $C_{\max}$.

In this paper, we consider single machine scheduling problems. These problems are important for some practical multi-machine scheduling applications. Often there exists a bottleneck machine in a manufacturing environment. If one can solve the scheduling problem on the bottleneck machine optimally, this is at least a very good base for the overall schedule. An intelligent solution method for a single machine scheduling problem may also lead to important insights for the solution of more general shop and multiprocessor scheduling problems. We concentrate our attention on standard settings, basic properties for these settings, polynomial-time algorithms and complexity and approximability issues. Regarding standard settings, most single machine scheduling problems are relatively easy for simultaneously released jobs given that no weight function is associated with the jobs. With non-simultaneously released jobs, single machine scheduling problems become more challenging and essentially more complicated. Here, we deal with such settings, where the jobs, besides release times, are characterized by due dates and consider due-date-oriented objective functions. We review the most important ideas, properties and approaches related to classical standard settings at the borderline between polynomial solvability/approximability on one side and complexity issues on the other side, where a review of the extensive literature on single machine scheduling that considers mostly offline settings is still missing.

Most of the results we review were obtained after the early seminal works by Lenstra et al. [1] and Chen et al. [2], which covered a wide range of scheduling problems, including those on one machine. In general, there is a huge number of papers dealing with single machine problems. Since the publication of [1,2], surveys are mostly restricted to special subjects and/or consider more general problem settings. As an example, there exist three very detailed surveys on scheduling problems with setup times or costs, see [3–5]. For problems with so-called p-batching (i.e., several jobs can be processed in parallel in a batch), a survey was given by Fowler and Mönch [6]. The case of equal processing times was surveyed by Kravchenko and Werner [7]. Recently, several works have dealt with single machine problems with learning effects. The first paper on this subject was given by Briskorn [8]; for a survey on learning effects and periodic maintenance, see [9]. The paper by Koulamas and Kyparisis [10] reviews different kinds of dynamic programming algorithms for single machine scheduling problems. Other surveys on single machine problems deal with particular objective functions. As a few examples, we can mention, e.g., a survey on the total weighted tardiness problem [11] and on the weighted number of tardy jobs problem [12]; for more general problems, we mention a survey on scheduling with late work criteria [13] or more recently on early and late work scheduling [14], where a substantial part is dedicated to single machine scheduling. While mostly a minimization problem is considered, Gafarov et al. [15] reviewed algorithms and complexity issues for single machine maximization problems.

In Section 2, we study general structural properties of feasible schedules. These properties have been used for the construction of polynomial-time algorithms, and they may further be useful to build new efficient algorithms for both polynomially solvable and open versions of scheduling problems with job release and due times in general.

 https://doi.org/10.3390/a19010038

Then in Section 3, we discuss polynomial algorithms, complexity and approximability issues, implicit enumeration algorithms and lower bounds for due-date-oriented objective functions with an emphasis on the classical maximum job lateness objective function. We also outline some subjects for future research, which includes in part more general multi-machine scheduling problems. This paper ends with concluding remarks in Section 4.

In Tables 1 and 2, we summarize most of the reviewed works concerning exact and approximation algorithms for single machine scheduling problems. We refer to the particular sections where the corresponding algorithms are discussed. In the time complexity expressions, the variable n stands for the total number of jobs, while additional parameters are defined in the corresponding subsections. The criterion $D_{\max}$ is defined in the following subsection.

Table 1. Overview of exact algorithms.

Problem	Time Complexity	Reference
Section 3.1		
$1\|r_j\|L_{\max}$	Exponential in n	McMahon and Florian [16]
$1\|r_j\|D_{\max}$	Exponential in n	Carlier [17]
$1\|r_j\|D_{\max}$	Exponential in n	Pan and Shi [18]
$1\|r_j\|D_{\max}$	$O(\nu!n\log n)$ (Exponential in ν)	Vakhania [19]
$1\|r_j=r\|L_{\max}$	$O(n\log n)$	Jackson [20]
$1\|d_j=d\|L_{\max}$	$O(n\log n)$	Jackson [20]
$1\|r_j,p_j=1\|L_{\max}$	$O(n\log n)$	Horn [21]
$1\|r_j,pmtn\|L_{\max}$	$O(n\log n)$	Horn [21]
$1\|r_j,p_j=p\|L_{\max}$	$O(n\log n)$	Garey et al. [22]
$1\|p_j\in\{p,2p\},r_j\|D_{\max}$	$O(n^2\log n\log p)$	Vakhania [23]
$1\|r_j,div\|D_{\max}$	$O(n^2\log n\log p_{\max})$	Vakhania [24]
$1\|p_{\max}\le P(n),\|r_j-r_i\|<R\|L_{\max}$	$O(n^{k+1}\log n\log p_{\max})$	Vakhania and Werner [25]
$1\|r_j,p_j=p\|C_{\max},L_{\max}$	$O(n^3\log n)$	Lazarev et al. [26]
$1\|r_j,embedded\|L_{\max}$	$O(n\log n)$	Vakhania [27]
$1\|r_j\in\{r_1,r_2\},d_j\in\{d_1,d_2\}\|L_{\max}$	$O(n\log n)+SUBSETSUM$	Reynoso and Vakhania [28]
$1\|r_j,prec,pmtn\|f_{\max}$	$O(n\log n)$	Azharonok et al. [29]
Section 3.2.1		
$1\|r_j\|\sum U_j$	$O(n^3\log n)$	Vakhania [30]
$1\|r_j;p_j=p\|\sum U_j$	$O(n^3\log n)$	Vakhania [30]
Section 3.2.2		
$1\|r_j;pmtn\|\sum U_j$	$O(n^5)$	Lawler [31]
$1\|r_j;pmtn\|\sum U_j$	$O(n^4)$	Baptiste [32]
$1\|r_j;pmtn\|\sum U_j$	$O(n^3)$	Vakhania [33]
Section 3.3		
$1\|r_j;p_j;pmtn\|\sum w_jU_j$	$O(n^{10})$	Baptiste [34]
$1\|r_j;p_j;pmtn\|\sum w_jU_j$	$O(n^4)$	Baptiste et al. [35]
Section 3.5		
$1\|r_j,p_j=p\|\sum w_jT_j$ Ordered weights	$O(n^9)$	Gafarov et al. [36]
$1\|(nd)\|\sum T_j$	$O(n^2)$	Gafarov et al. [15]
Section 3.7		
$1\|r_j,p_j=1,e_j\|L_{\max}$	$O(n\log n)$	Ramirez et al. [37]
$1\|rm=1,p_j=1\|L_{\max}$	$O(n^2\log n)$	Grigoriev et al. [38]

Since for the borderline problems between polynomial solvability/approximability we outline here heuristic and meta-heuristic algorithms are usually not applied, we do not discuss the big variability of such algorithms for single machine problems. For the interested reader, we mention that for more general NP-hard single machine problems, the standard meta-heuristic techniques are applied. In the recent literature, one can find

https://doi.org/10.3390/a1901(

papers dealing with a genetic algorithm (see, e.g., [39]), both simulated annealing and tabu search (see [40]), ant colony optimization (see, e.g., [41]), variable neighborhood search (see, e.g., [42] or [43]), iterated local search (see [44]), differential evolution (see, e.g., [45]), the meerkat clan algorithm and bald eagle search (see [46]) or gray wolf optimization (see [47]). In addition, particular meta-heuristics have been developed, e.g., for stable scheduling on a single machine [48], a self-adaptive meta-heuristic for the problem with flexible and variable maintenance [49] or a data-driven heuristic combining machine learning with problem-specific characteristics [50], to name a few.

Table 2. Overview of approximation algorithms.

Problem	Time Complexity	Reference	Approximation Factor
tion 3.1			
$1\|r_j\|D_{\max}$	$O(n \log n)$	Schrage [51]	2
$1\|r_j\|D_{\max}$	$O(n^2 \log n)$	Potts [52]	$3/2$
$1\|r_j\|D_{\max}$	$O(n \log n)$	Nowicki and Smutnicki [53]	$3/2$
$1\|r_j\|D_{\max}$	$O(n^2 \log n)$	Hall and Shmoys [54]	$4/3$
$1\|r_j\|D_{\max}$	$O(16^k (nk)^{3+4k})$	Hall and Shmoys [54]	$(1+1/k)$ (PTAS)
$1\|r_j\|D_{\max}$	$O(n \log n + n(4k)^{8k^2+8k+2})$	Hall and Shmoys [54]	$(1+1/k)$ (PTAS)
$P\|r_j\|D_{\max}$	$O(n + k^{O(k)})$	Mastrolilli [55]	$(1+1/k)$ (PTAS)
$1\|r_j\|D_{\max}$	$O(\kappa! \kappa_{1.1} n^2 \log n)$	Vakhania [19]	$(1+1/k)$ (PTAS)
tion 3.6			
$\|r_j\|D_{\max}$ *Online version*	$O(n \log n)$	Hoogeveen and Vestjens [56]	$(\sqrt{5}+1)/2 \approx 1.61803$

Basic Notation and Terminology

We shall denote the given set of n jobs by $\{1, 2, \ldots, n\}$. A *schedule* S prescribes to each job j the *starting time* s_j^S on the machine (creating in this way a total order on the set of jobs by sequencing the jobs on the machine). Problem restrictions on the way in which the jobs are to be performed by the machine define the set of *feasible schedules*. For example, a machine can process at most one job simultaneously; the *precedence relations* defined on the set of jobs restrict the relative order in which the jobs can be scheduled. Scheduling problems are sometimes referred to as *sequencing problems* since the jobs need to be scheduled in a sequential manner (as no job overlapping is permitted). The precedence relations between the jobs can be represented by directed graphs, which are often referred to as *precedence (task) graphs*. In such graphs, nodes represent jobs, and there is an arc (i, j) if and only if job i immediately precedes job j.

Job *preemptions* might be allowed or not. In a preemptive scheduling problem, a job can be interrupted and later resumed on the machine. In a non-preemptive scheduling problem, job j, once scheduled on the machine, should be processed without any interruption until its full completion on that machine. The machine is called *idle* at some moment t if no job is processed by the machine at that moment, otherwise it is said to be *busy*.

Job j, once scheduled on the machine, needs the *processing time* p_j on that machine. Thus, if this job is processed without any interruption, its *completion time on the machine* in the schedule S is $c_j^S = s_j^S + p_j$. Since basically all scheduling problems imply resource restrictions, in any feasible schedule S, if job j is scheduled on the machine, then $s_j^S \geq s_i^S + p_i$ for any job i scheduled earlier on the machine in the schedule S.

Besides the processing time, job j may possess additional parameters (job parameters can normally be assumed to be non-negative integral numbers). For example, the time moment when it becomes available to be processed by the machine is called its *release or readiness time* and is commonly denoted by r_j. Thus, $s_j^S \geq r_j$, for any feasible schedule S and any job j. The *due date* d_j of job j is the "desirable" completion time of job j on the machine.

https://doi.org/10.3390/a19010038

It is a common situation in real-life applications that it is desirable for a job to be completed by some date, as otherwise it becomes less important.

With job due dates, the quality of a solution is measured by a due-date-oriented objective function. We can judge the urgency of a job j based on its *slack* $d_j - r_j - p_j$: the earliest job j can be started is at time r_j, and hence, the earliest it can be completed is at time $r_j + p_j$. If $r_j + p_j > d_j$, then there is no feasible schedule in which job j completes by its due date. Otherwise, the tighter d_j is, equivalently, the less slack of job j is and the more urgent it is.

In some cases, we impose the condition that job j cannot be completed after its due date. Then the term *deadline* instead of "due date" is commonly used; in a feasible schedule, every job is to be completed by its deadline (in some applications, job deadlines are important since if a job is not completed by its deadline, then its benefit or functionality becomes negligible). Thus, if job deadlines are given, our objective is to find a feasible schedule, one in which all jobs are completed before or at their deadlines on the machine.

In a number of applications, a job, once completed by the machine, needs to be delivered to the customer. The delivery is carried out by an independent transportation unit, which is not a scarce resource in a given scenario. The *delivery time* of job j is commonly denoted by q_j. On the one hand, job delivery takes no machine time. On the other hand, q_j contributes to the *full* completion time of job j: In a given schedule S, the *full completion time* of job j is $C_j^S = c_j^S + q_j$ (whereas c_j^S is the completion time of job j *on the machine* in that schedule). Thus, the full completion time of a job depends on both, its completion time on the machine and its delivery time. Job due-dates and delivery times are alternative job parameters in the sense that they typically are not present together. With job delivery times, one wishes to minimize maximum job full completion time, whereas with job due-dates one wishes to minimize some due-date-oriented objective function (see below).

Concerning the objectives, an *optimal schedule* is a feasible schedule which minimizes or maximizes a given objective (goal) function. With job due dates, for example, our objective can be to minimize or maximize some due-date-oriented objective function. For example, let the *lateness* of a job in schedule S be $L_j(S) = c_j^S - d_j$, i.e., it is the difference between the completion time of job j on the machine and its due date. One of the common due-date-oriented objective functions is the maximal job lateness $L_{\max}$ (which is to be minimized). Another such common objective function that is to be minimized is $\sum U_j$, the number of *late* jobs, ones completed on the machine after their due dates (U_j is a 0–1 variable indicating whether job j is completed on time or not completed on time on the machine in a given schedule). We may allow the omission of some jobs in the case when the total workload is more than the machine capacity, maximizing the *throughput*, which is the number of jobs completed *on time*, i.e., before or at their due dates. We may also consider more general criteria to maximize some profits. The profit of job j can be expressed by its *weight*, commonly denoted by w_j.

If jobs have no due dates and no delivery times, then one typically wishes to minimize the maximum job completion time on the machine, the makespan $C_{\max} = \max_j c_j$. If jobs have delivery times (then the full completion time of every job with a positive delivery time is more than its completion time on the machine), the makespan is defined as the maximum job *full* completion time $C_{\max} = \max_j C_j$. With job delivery times, to avoid a possible confusion between two job completion times c_j and C_j, recently Jan Karel Lenstra [57] suggested to use $D_j = c_j + q_j$ (instead of C_j) for the full completion time of job j. With this notation, one wishes to minimize $D_{\max} = \max_j D_j$. This extends the three-field notation introduced much earlier by Graham, Lawler, Lenstra and Rinnooy Kan [58], a commonly used way to abbreviate scheduling problems. In this notation, the first, the second and the third fields define the machine environment, the job characteristics and the

https://doi.org/10.3390/a1901

objective function, respectively. For example, for the single machine scheduling problems considered here, a "1" is used in the first field; the problem with job release times and due dates to minimize the maximum job lateness is abbreviated by $1|r_j|L_{\max}$; and the problem with job release and delivery times to minimize the maximum job full completion time can be expressed either by $1|r_j, q_j|C_{\max}$ or by using the new notation [57] it can alternatively be expressed by $1|r_j|D_{\max}$. Notice that we omit the parameters d_j and q_j in the $1|r_j|L_{\max}$ and $1|r_j|D_{\max}$ notations, respectively, which are implicitly assumed to be present; the use of $L_{\max}$ implies that due dates d_j have been specified, and the use of $D_{\max}$ implies that delivery times q_j have been specified. Note that both job delivery times and due dates specify the urgency of job j: the larger q_j is, the more urgent job j is (as its delivery will take a "considerable time"); in contrast, the less d_j is, the more urgent job j is (as it has a "small" slack).

The mathematical equivalence of the two above settings $1|r_j|L_{\max}$ and $1|r_j|D_{\max}$ ($1|r_j, q_j|C_{\max}$) is established by letting $q_j = -d_j$ for all j. We can avoid a slightly unnatural due-date negativity constraint considering an alternative setting, which is practically intuitive. We can still conserve non-negative job due dates by the following transformation from an instance of the problem $1|r_j, q_j|C_{\max}$ ($1|r_j|D_{\max}$) to an equivalent instance of the problem $1|r_j|L_{\max}$. Let K be a large constant, say, no less than the maximum job delivery time, and let the due date of each job j be $d_j = K - q_j$. Vice versa, given an instance of problem $1|r_j|L_{\max}$, an equivalent instance of the problem $1|r_j, q_j|C_{\max}$ ($1|r_j|D_{\max}$) is obtained by letting $q_j = D - d_j$ for a large constant D no less than the maximum job due date. It is easy to see that whenever the makespan for the version $1|r_j, q_j|C_{\max}$ is minimized, the maximum job lateness in the problem $1|r_j|L_{\max}$ is minimized, and vice versa, see an early paper by Bratley et al. [59] for the details. It should be noted that, for the approximation purposes, the setting $1|r_j|L_{\max}$ is inappropriate as the maximum job lateness in a schedule can be positive, negative or even 0. However, the problem $1|r_j|L_{\max}$ can be approximated via its alternative formulation $1|r_j|D_{\max}$ (see Section 3.1).

2. Some Basic Concepts and Properties

In this section, we give some basic concepts and schedule properties that have been used in the study of single machine scheduling problems. Single machine scheduling problems are trivial if every job has a single parameter, its processing time. For minimizing the makespan, it suffices to schedule the jobs in any order without leaving a machine with idle time or a *gap*: a *gap* on a machine is the longest time interval during which this machine is idle, i.e., it processes no job. A *block* is a consecutive part in a schedule which is preceded and succeeded by a gap.

Thus, from *any* permutation of n jobs, an optimal makespan schedule can be constructed in linear time by assigning the jobs from that permutation without leaving any idle time interval on the machine. In particular, if all jobs are simultaneously released, any non-idle time schedule minimizes the makespan $C_{\max}$. Single machine scheduling problems get less trivial if jobs are not simultaneously released, i.e., they have individual release times. Then, to minimize the makespan, we just need to keep the machine busy whenever this is possible. This goal will be achieved if we just order the jobs according to non-decreasing release times and include them in this order without leaving any avoidable gap. This procedure will take $O(n \log n)$ time due to the preprocessing step.

Minimizing maximum job lateness $L_{\max}$ is a bit more complex. If only the job due dates are given (all the jobs being released at time 0), the venerable ED-heuristic (earliest due date) obtains an optimal schedule, minimizing maximum job lateness by scheduling the jobs in non-decreasing order of their due dates without any idle time intervals (we describe this optimization algorithm later in more detail). Vice versa, if only job release

https://doi.org/10.3390/a19010038

times are given, the earliest release time (ER) heuristic generates an optimal makespan schedule. In that algorithm, initially, the minimum job release time is assigned to the current scheduling time, and any job released at that time is assigned to the machine. Iteratively, the next scheduling time is defined as the maximum between the completion time of the latest-so-far-assigned job and the minimum release time taken among the yet unscheduled jobs. Again, any (unscheduled) job released at the current scheduling time is assigned to the machine.

Because of the job release times, a schedule created by the ER-heuristic may contain a gap. However, it may contain no gap that might be avoided. In particular, the total gap length in such a schedule is the minimal possible one. We can also use this heuristic if all the jobs have a common due date d. In other words, all jobs are equally urgent. Then, as is easy to see, an optimal schedule minimizing the maximum job lateness contains no gap that might be avoided, and it has the minimum possible total gap length. Therefore, the ER-heuristic also minimizes the maximum job lateness.

It is easy to see that the ER-heuristic will not further minimize the maximum job lateness even if only two possible job due dates are allowed. For example, consider an instance with two jobs, job 1 released at time 0 and having the due date 11 and job 2 released at time 1 with the due date 6. The ER-heuristic will assign job 1 to the time interval $[0,5)$ and job 2 to the time interval $[5,10)$, resulting in a maximum job lateness of 4 (that of job 2). Observe that this schedule contains no gap. At the same time, an optimal schedule does contain a gap $[0,1)$: it assigns job 2 to the time interval $[1,6)$ and then job 1 to the time interval $[6,11)$, completing both jobs on time with the maximum job lateness equal to 0.

If with job release times and due dates job preemptions are allowed, then we have a simple method to solve the problem optimally and even online. We usually start at the earliest job release time and initially set the current time t to that magnitude. Iteratively, among the available jobs, we schedule the next most urgent job, one with the smallest due date (or the maximum delivery time for the problem $1|r_j|D_{\max}$). However, if during the execution of that job another more urgent job gets released, the former job is interrupted at the release time of the latter job. The latter job is then included at its release time. In this way, there will occur no forced delay for any urgent job by a less urgent one; the *delay* of job j in the schedule S is $c_j^S - r_j$ (recall that a job is more *urgent* than another job if the former one has a larger delivery time or a smaller due date). Note that the so-constructed schedule also minimizes the makespan, since it has no avoidable machine idle time.

Suppose now a job preemption is not allowed and that job i is processed by the machine at time r_j in schedule S, where a yet unscheduled job j is such that $d_j < d_i$; more precisely, job j gets released within the execution interval of job i so that job i delays the starting of job j. Note that this delay will be less than p_i if upon the completion of job i, job j is immediately scheduled. The delay of job j may, however, result in a non-optimal schedule. Indeed, this will be the case when job j is urgent "enough" that in an optimal schedule it should be included with no or with a smaller delay.

Now we give a description of the non-preemptive version of the heuristic. This popular greedy algorithm, commonly referred to as *earliest due date* ED-heuristic, has been widely used in the process of the solution of variants of single machine, multiprocessor and also shop scheduling problems. As in the above described preemptive version, it is online. It was initially proposed by Jackson [20] and proved to be optimal for problem $1||L_{\max}$. Later, it was extended for the setting with job release times $1|r_j|L_{\max}$ by Schrage [51]. The extended algorithm is as follows. We let the current scheduling time t be the minimal release time of an unscheduled job or the time when the machine completes the last job, whichever magnitude is larger. If no job is yet scheduled, we let $t := 0$. Iteratively, among the jobs already released by time t, the heuristic schedules the most urgent job (it breaks

https://doi.org/10.3390/a1901(

ties by selecting the longest job). So for problem $1|r_j|L_{\max}$, the most urgent job is an already released one with the smallest due date, whereas for the alternative setting $1|r_j|D_{\max}$, it is an already released one with the largest delivery time. We shall refer to the extended versions of the above greedy algorithm applied to the problems $1|r_j|L_{\max}$ and $1|r_j|D_{\max}$ as the ED-heuristic and LDT-heuristic, respectively. Given the obvious similarity between the two versions of the heuristic and the equivalence of the two settings $1|r_j|L_{\max}$ and $1|r_j|D_{\max}$, we make no distinction between the heuristics, these settings and $L_{\max}$ and $D_{\max}$, which may be used interchangeably.

We now introduce some additional concepts. Among all jobs in the schedule S, it is useful to distinguish the ones whose lateness attains the maximum job lateness $L_{\max}(S)$ in that schedule. In a given block $B \in S$, among all such jobs, the last scheduled one is said to be an *overflow job* o in schedule S. In general, more than one overflow job in the schedule S may exist, each one in a different block of that schedule.

Let e be a job from block B such that $d_e > d_o$ (i.e., job e is less urgent than the overflow job o). Then job e is referred to as an *emerging job* in the schedule S associated with job o. There may exist one or more emerging jobs for the overflow job o. The one scheduled last before job o is referred to as the *delaying* emerging job l associated with job o.

During the scheduling process, it is important to determine an "appropriate" position of each emerging job. Then we might be able to "adjust" the full completion time of the overflow jobs and reduce in this way the makespan. This property makes the "non-urgent" emerging jobs most important during the scheduling process.

Given an ED-schedule S (one constructed by the ED-heuristic) and a block $B \in S$ with the overflow job o, the corresponding *kernel* $K \in B$ consists of the set of jobs included in that block between the delaying emerging job l associated with the overflow job o and job o including the latter job. It immediately follows that the due date of any job of the kernel $K(S)$ is no less than that of job o. Note that any schedule contains the same number of kernels, the overflow jobs and the corresponding delaying emerging jobs. This number cannot be more than the total number of blocks in the schedule.

We illustrate the above concepts using the problem instance with eight jobs from Table 3. The LDT-schedule for that instance is depicted in Figure 1. There are two blocks and one kernel in that schedule. The numbers in the circles indicate the objective value $C_{\max}$ (full completion time) of the corresponding jobs. The kernel jobs are marked in blue, whereas the last overflow job of the kernel is marked in red. The two emerging jobs are marked in green.

Table 3. Data of the example instance for problem $1|r_j|D_{\max}$.

$r_1 = 0$	$p_1 = 6$	$q_1 = 17$
$r_2 = 2$	$p_2 = 7$	$q_2 = 21$
$r_3 = 6$	$p_3 = 10$	$q_3 = 16$
$r_4 = 21$	$p_1 = 5$	$q_1 = 33$
$r_5 = 19$	$p_2 = 7$	$q_2 = 28$
$r_6 = 30$	$p_3 = 7$	$q_3 = 23$
$r_7 = 42$	$p_1 = 9$	$q_1 = 1$
$r_8 = 45$	$p_2 = 7$	$q_2 = 2$

We have the following known optimality condition (see [60] for a proof):

Lemma 1. *The ED-schedule S is optimal if it contains an overflow job with no associated delaying emerging job.*

https://doi.org/10.3390/a19010038

The ED-heuristic is quite a powerful scheduling tool and can be used to "capture" other important structural properties of the problem. For example, another sufficient optimality condition can relatively easily be derived. Suppose we apply the heuristic online. Denote by j_t the job scheduled at time t and denote by S^t the partial ED-schedule constructed by the scheduling time t. Suppose further that once job j_t is scheduled, another job j with $d_j < d_{j_t}$ gets released within the execution interval of the former job (job j_t is "pushing" a more urgent job j). Then we shall refer to the scheduling time t as a *conflict* scheduling time. Let σ be the schedule generated by the ED-heuristic for the originally given problem instance.

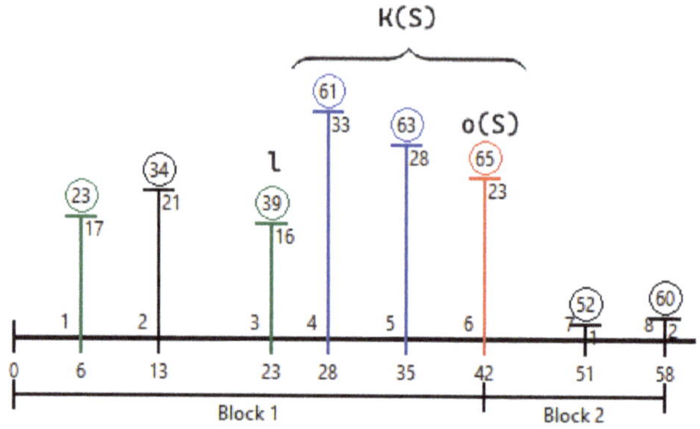

Figure 1. LDT-schedule for the example instance.

Lemma 2. *The ED-schedule σ is optimal if no conflict scheduling time occurs while it is built. If this condition is satisfied for all t, no job released within the execution interval of job j_t can start a kernel at any scheduling time t during the construction of the schedule σ.*

Proof. The lemma follows, since by the hypothesis we can have no overflow job with an associated delaying emerging job in the schedule σ (see Lemma 1). □

Next, we define a lower bound LB on the optimum objective function value OPT. Given an LDT-schedule S (one constructed by the LDT-heuristic) with the kernel K and the corresponding delaying emerging job $l(K)$, we have a lower bound

$$LB \geq D_{\max}(S) - p_{l(K)} \tag{1}$$

(see, e.g., [60] for a proof). Combining this lower bound with other easily seen lower bounds, an overall lower bound on OPT is

$$LB = \max\{\max_{K \in S}(D_{\max}(S) - p_{l(K)}), P, \max_j\{r_j + p_j + q_j\}\},$$

where P is the total processing time of all jobs.

Inequality (1) has useful implications for approximation purposes, where we consider the setting with job delivery times $1|r_j|D_{\max}$. Indeed, it is obvious how the approximation can be measured for this setting, unlike the setting $1|r_j|L_{\max}$, where, for example, we may have a negative lateness. By the mere observation that $LB \leq$OPT and $p_{l(K)} \leq$OPT, we obtain that

$$D_{\max}(S) \leq 2\text{OPT}, \tag{2}$$

i.e., the LDT-heuristic already delivers a two-approximation schedule. Furthermore, suppose we are interested in a $(1 + 1/k)$-approximation solution for the problem $1|r_j|D_{\max}$ for

 https://doi.org/10.3390/a1901

a given constant k. By the next lemma, there exist certain values for k that guarantee such an approximation:

Lemma 3. *The inequality* $|S|/\mathrm{OPT} < (1 + 1/k)$ *holds if* $k \leq LB/p_{l(K)}$.

Proof. From $LB \geq L_{\max}(S) - p_{l(K)}$, we obtain that $|S|/\mathrm{OPT} < (\mathrm{OPT}+p_{l(K)})/\mathrm{OPT} = 1 + p_{l(K)}/\mathrm{OPT} \leq 1 + p_{l(K)}/LB \leq 1 + 1/k$. □

If an ED-schedule S is not optimal, then an overflow job o in it is to be restarted earlier. By increasing artificially the release time of a corresponding emerging job and applying the ED-heuristic to such a modified instance, different ED-schedules can be constructed. We intend to reduce $L_{\max}(S)$ in this way by *activating* an emerging job e for the kernel K, i.e., rescheduling it after that kernel. The activation is carried out in two steps. In step 1, the release time of job e is increased to a magnitude no less than the largest job release time in kernel K. In step 2, the ED-heuristic is applied to the modified job in this way for this problem instance. Since now the release time of job e is no less than that of any job of kernel $K(S)$ and d_e is larger than the due date of any job from kernel K, the ED-heuristic will give the priority to the jobs of kernel K and will reschedule job e after all former jobs. The ED-schedule $\{S\}_e$, obtained in this way, is referred to as *(weakly) complementary* to the S schedule.

Note that in the schedule S, some emerging jobs might have been originally included after kernel K. Then such an emerging job can be included before the jobs of kernel K in the schedule $\{S\}_e$ by the ED-heuristic (since no job of kernel K is released at time $s_e(S)$). As a result, kernel K may not be restarted at the earliest possible time. However, this will happen if the above emerging jobs are forced to remain after kernel K: we increase the release times of these jobs similar to how we did this for job l. The ED-schedule S_e, obtained by the ED-heuristic for the modified job in this way for this problem instance, is referred to as *(strongly) complementary* to the S schedule and is denoted by . The complementary schedule is referred to as a *C-schedule*.

Note that there is exactly one job less included before kernel K in a strong C-schedule S_e compared to schedule S. The same condition does not hold for a weak C-schedule $\{S\}_e$. In fact, we may have more jobs scheduled before kernel K in schedule $\{S\}_e$ than in the schedule S. Then, as is easy to see, the overflow job o will be completed earlier in the schedule S_e than it was completed in the schedule S.

There are polynomial time algorithms and implicit enumeration procedures that repeatedly generate (weak or strong) C-schedules (see, e.g., [19,23–25,30,33]). Depending on a particular solution approach, either weak or strong C-schedules can be enumerated. The enumeration of strong C-schedules is less costly but may not guarantee optimality.

3. The Overview

In the previous section, we gave some basic properties related to single machine scheduling problems. In this section, we survey some state-of-the-art results, concentrating our attention on $L_{\max}$ and $D_{\max}$ criteria, complexity, polynomial solvability and approximability issues for standard settings. (As earlier noted, we do not pretend to cover all the existing literature on single machine scheduling problems, including extended settings with setup times and batch processing.)

3.1. Scheduling Jobs with Release Times with $L_{\max}$ and $D_{\max}$ Criteria

Exact algorithms. The general settings $1|r_j|L_{\max}$ and $1|r_j|D_{\max}$ are strongly NP-hard [61]. The problem is fixed-parameter tractable for the parameters $p_{\max}$ and $\delta_{\max}$, where $\delta_{\max}$ is the maximum difference between the job due dates, see Vakhania and Werner [25]. The

https://doi.org/10.3390/a19010038

problem is weakly NP-hard with only two job release times and due dates being allowed: $1|r_j \in \{r_1, r_2\}, d_j \in \{d_1, d_2\}|L_{\max}$ (see Lenstra et al. [1] and Chinos and Vakhania [60]). Apparently, it is a minimal NP-hard special case of the problem $1|r_j|L_{\max}$.

Among early branch-and-bound algorithms, we mention those by McMahon and Florian [16] and Carlier [17]. As to the more recent works on implicit enumeration methods, Pan and Shi [18] proposed branch-and-bound algorithms using the basic framework from that of Carlier [17]. In particular, to each node of the search tree, a complete LDT-schedule is associated, and for each already created LDT-schedule, two possibilities are considered: in the first generated branch of the node, the delaying emerging job is activated for the corresponding kernel, and in the second branch it is forced to be scheduled before that kernel in any further created schedule in this branch (technically, the delivery time of that job is increased so that the LDT-heuristic will always include it before all jobs of the kernel). A lower bound at each node is determined if the kernel of the corresponding LDT-schedule contains at most two jobs. The at most 3! possible feasible solutions for the jobs of the kernel and the delaying emerging job are formed, and the makespan of the best solution is set as a lower bound.

Besides this lower bound, the authors in [18] give a procedure that permits us to discard some sets of jobs in the following enumeration process. In a created LDT-schedule, let i be the last scheduled job of a block such that no job preceding job i in that schedule has a full completion time more than the current lower bound. Then note that the corresponding part of the schedule including job i can be "frozen" (left as is) in any further created LDT-schedule, and the original instance can be *trimmed* in this way.

Della Croce and T'kindt [62] consider the version of the problem $1|r_j|L_{\max}$ with job due dates and propose a lower bound, an alternative to the standard preemptive ED-schedule. Let $1, \ldots, j, \ldots, n$ be the jobs in the preemptive ED-schedule (PED), where j is the first overflow job in that schedule. Four different cases where job j can appear in a non-preemptive optimal schedule S_{OPT} are distinguished:

1. Job j is in the position j in S_{OPT} as in the PED schedule, being preceded by the jobs $1, \ldots, j-1$ and followed by the jobs $j+1, \ldots, n$. Then in schedule S_{OPT}, job j cannot be started before the completion time $c_{ED(1,\ldots,j-1)}$ of the last scheduled job in the non-preemptive ED-schedule $ED(1, \ldots, j-1)$ constructed for the jobs $1, \ldots, j-1$. Hence, $L_{1a} = \max\{r_j, c_{ED(1,\ldots,j-1)}\} + p_j - d_j$ is a lower bound for the lateness of job j in this case. Likewise, since the jobs $j+1, \ldots, n$ come after job j, the release times of these jobs can correspondingly be increased. Let $PED(j+1, \ldots, n)$ be the PED-schedule constructed for an updated sub-instance. Then $L_{1b} = L_{\max}(PED\{j+1, \ldots, n\})$ is another lower bound, and $L_1 = \max\{L_{1a}, L_{1b}\}$ is a lower bound.
2. Job j is in one of the positions $1, \ldots, j-1$ in the schedule S_{OPT}, and the jobs $1, \ldots, j-1$ precede the jobs $j+1, \ldots, n$. Now, let $ED(1, \ldots, j-1, j)$ be the ED-schedule constructed for the first j jobs, i.e., the jobs $1, \ldots, j-1, j$, and let $c_{ED(1,\ldots,j-1,j)}$ be the completion time of the last scheduled job in $ED(1, \ldots, j-1, j)$. Then note that $c_{ED(1,\ldots,j-1,j)} - \max_{i=1,\ldots,j} d_i$ is a lower bound. Again, the release times of the remaining jobs $j+1, \ldots, n$ are updated and then scheduled by the PED-heuristic. In the resultant schedule, the maximum job lateness is a lower bound, and the maximum between this and the former lower bound is another lower bound L_2.
3. Job j has one of the positions $j+1, \ldots, n$ in the schedule S_{OPT}. So j is preceded by the jobs $1, \ldots, j-1$ and at least one more job k from the set $\{j+1, \ldots, n\}$. Similarly, we define the ED-schedule $ED(1, \ldots, j-1, k)$, where k is a job that minimizes the maximum job completion time $c_{ED(1,\ldots,j-1,k)}$ in such an ED-schedule. Then $L_3 = c_{ED(1,\ldots,j-1,k)} + p_j - d_j$ is another lower bound.

https://doi.org/10.3390/a1901

4. There exists a job $h \leq j-1$ that occupies one of the positions $j+1,\ldots,n$ in the schedule S_{OPT}. Now we have at least one job k scheduled before job h. Similarly to case 3, we compute the ED-schedule $ED(1,\ldots,h-1,h+1,\ldots,j,k)$ for the jobs in $\{1,\ldots,h-1,h+1,\ldots,j,k\}$, where k is defined similarly as in case 3. Then $L_4 = c_{ED(1,\ldots,h-1,h+1,\ldots,j,k)} - \max_{i=1,\ldots,h-1,h+1,\ldots,j,k} d_i$ is a lower bound.

The authors in [62] build their last two lower bounds L_5 and L_6 as follows. Given a pair of jobs u,v, they use the fact that

$$L_{u,v} = \min\{\max\{r_u + p_u, r_v\} + p_v - d_v, \max\{r_v + p_v, r_u\} + p_u - d_u\}$$

is a lower bound on $L_{\max}$. Indeed, either u comes before v or vice versa. In the first case, we have the first term and in the second case, we have the second one in the above min expression. Then $L_5 = \max_{i \neq j} L_{i,j}$ and $L_6 = \max_{i \neq o} L_{i,o}$, where j is the first overflow job in the complete preemptive ED-schedule and o is the first overflow job in the non-preemptive ED-schedule. Thus, $LB = \max\{L_5, L_6, \min\{L_1, L_2, L_3, L_4\}\}$ is a lower bound.

Gharbi and Labidi [63] proposed yet another lower bound by applying the common idea that the lower the number of preemptions in a PED-schedule is, the stronger the corresponding lower bound can be. Intuitively, an optimal makespan of a schedule with a "restricted" number of preemptions would approximate better an optimal non-preemptive makespan than a preemptive schedule. Hence, they define a *semi-preemptive* LDT-schedule in which the preemption of some job parts is not allowed. In particular, every job is divided into two smaller jobs, the *fixed* and the *free* parts. The fixed part is considered a job that cannot be preempted, unlike the free part. After that, the decision version of the problem $1|r_j,q_j|C_{\max}$ ($1|r_j|D_{\max}$) with a threshold C is considered: Is there a feasible non-preemptive schedule S with $C_{\max}(S) = C$? Note that in using binary search on the possible values of $C_{\max}$ within an appropriate interval $[L,U]$, the optimization version can be solved using at most $\log(U-L)$ solutions of the decision problem. In the binary search, semi-preemptive LDT-schedules are treated. Observe that if a preemptive schedule S_p has a makespan of more than C, then there will exist no non-preemptive schedule S with a makespan of at most C, since

$$C_{\max}(S) \geq C_{opt} \geq LB = C_{\max}(S_p) > C.$$

For a threshold C in the decision problem, to each job j, a *deadline* $d_j^{\sim} = C - q_j$ is assigned so that in a feasible semi-preemptive schedule, all jobs are to be completed by their deadlines. The fixed part of job j cannot be preempted whenever this job is to be completed by time $\tilde{d}_j$.

The fixed and free parts of job j are defined as follows. Two cases are distinguished. In case 1, $r_j + p_j > \tilde{d}_j - p_j$, and in case 2, $r_j + p_j \leq \tilde{d}_j - p_j$.

Case 1:

- Fixed part j': $r_{j'} := \tilde{d}_j - p_j; p_{j'} := 2p_j - \tilde{d}_j + r_j; \tilde{d}_{j'} := r_j + p_j$.
- Free part j'': $r_{j''} := r_j; p_{j''} := \tilde{d}_j - r_j - p_j; \tilde{d}_{j''} := \tilde{d}_j$.

Case 2:

- Fixed part j': $r_{j'} := r_j + p_j - x_j; p_{j'} := x_j; \tilde{d}_{j'} := \tilde{d}_j - p_j + x_j$.
- Free part j'': $r_{j''} := r_j; p_{j''} := p_j - x_j; \tilde{d}_{j''} := \tilde{d}_j$.

where the parameter $x_j \in [1, p_j - 1]$. We illustrate the concept of fixed and free parts for cases 1 and 2 in Figures 2 and 3.

https://doi.org/10.3390/a19010038

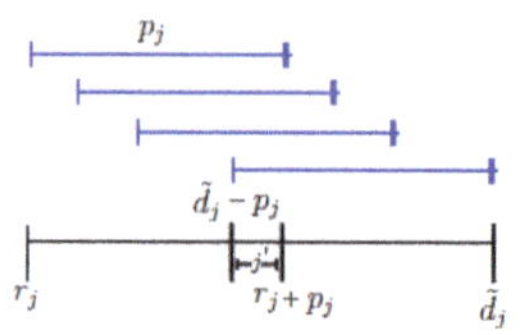

Figure 2. Illustration of the fixed and free parts: case 1.

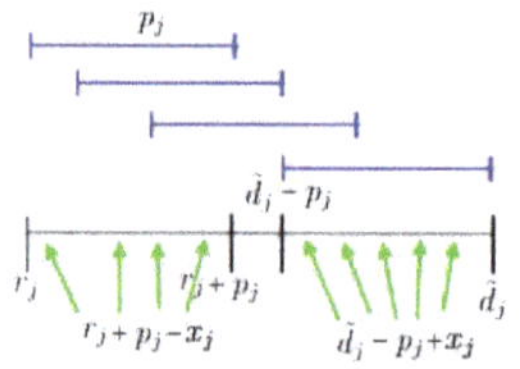

Figure 3. Illustration of the fixed and free parts: case 2.

The binary search procedure can be described as follows: Let J be the set of all jobs.

1. LB := makespan of the LDT-preemptive schedule for set J.
2. UB := makespan of the non-preemptive LDT-schedule for set J.
3. Carry out binary search in the interval $[LB, UB]$. For each derived C, perform the following:
4. Calculate $\tilde{d}_j$ for all $j \in J$.
5. Create a new instance $J' = \{j', j'' | j \in J\}$.
6. Create an LDT-preemptive schedule S' for set J'.
7. IF schedule S' is feasible, i.e., all jobs are completed by their deadlines THEN **increase C**.
8. ELSE **decrease C**.
9. RETURN C and the corresponding feasible semi-preemptive schedule.

Once the above procedure completes, the job release and delivery times are adjusted as follows. Let S_{sp} be the semi-preemptive schedule returned by the above procedure for the obtained threshold C'. Then for each job h:

- $\bar{\bar{r}}_h := c_h(S_{sp}) - p_h$.
- $\bar{\bar{d}}_h = t_h(S_{sp}) + p_h$.

The authors in [63] rely on the following observation (without giving a formal proof): In an optimal non-preemptive schedule, job h cannot start before time $\bar{\bar{r}}_h$ and cannot complete before time $\bar{\bar{d}}_h$. Then the original instance can be modified by $r_h := \bar{\bar{r}}_h$ y $\tilde{d}_h := \bar{\bar{d}}_h$.

A recent implicit enumeration algorithm (IEA) by Vakhania [19] is based on a special kind of parameterized analysis, called the *Variable Parameter* Analysis (VPA). Applying VPA, one can express an exponential dependence in the time complexity expression of an NP-hard optimization problem only in terms of *variable parameters*, the numbers of some specific types of objects and the jobs for the scheduling problem. For scheduling problems with delivery times or due dates, the variable parameter ν can be defined as the number of emerging jobs.

In the IEA from [19], different types of jobs are distinguished. The set of emerging jobs is partitioned into two basic types, the type 1.1 and type 1.2 emerging jobs. Intuitively, a type 1.2 emerging job initially belongs to some kernel, whereas a type 1.1 emerging job comes either before or after some kernel(s). The set of the type 1.1 emerging jobs is formed in a specially constructed iterative procedure, and the set of type 1.2 emerging jobs associated with a given kernel is detected in another iterative procedure that decomposes that kernel. The set of non-emerging jobs is partitioned into two types. The non-type (1.2)

 https://doi.org/10.3390/a1901

kernel jobs are partitioned into type (2) and all the remaining (non-type (1–2)) jobs are of type (4).

The IEA first generates a partial schedule without type (1) emerging jobs in $O(n^2 \log n)$ time using an extension of the LDT-heuristic. To complete this partial schedule, the type (1) jobs are incorporated into that schedule. This can be performed in polynomial time if certain assumptions on the dynamic behavior of the emerging jobs hold. In the worst-case scenario, all possible $\nu^!$ permutations of emerging jobs are enumerated, resulting in an

$$O(n \log n(n - \nu_{1.1})^2 \log(n - \nu_{1.1})\nu^!)$$

running time, where ν ($\nu_{1.1}$) is the variable parameter equal to the total number of the type (1) (type (1.1), respectively) jobs. The author in [19] reports a preliminary computational study according to which the ratio ν/n asymptotically converged to 0.

Polynomial-time approximation algorithms. As to the polynomial-time approximation, recall that the LDT-heuristic gives a two-approximation solution by Inequality (2). Potts [52] showed that by a repeated application of the LDT-heuristic $O(n)$ times, the performance ratio can be improved to 3/2, resulting in an $O(n^2 \log n)$ time performance. Nowicki and Smutnicki [53] proposed another 3/2-approximation algorithm with time complexity $O(n \log n)$. Hall and Shmoys [54] illustrated that the application of the LDT-heuristic to the original problem and a specially defined reversed problem leads to a further improved approximation of 4/3 in $O(n^2 \log n)$ time. Lazarev et al. [64] considered an interesting "metric reduction" approach. Given an arbitrary instance A of the problem, problem instance B, which is the "closest" by a given metric, is built, which is known to belong to a polynomially solvable subclass of the problem. An optimal solution to problem B provides an absolute approximation solution to problem A.

There are polynomial-time approximation schemes (PTASs) for the problem $1|r_j|D_{\max}$. These schemes provide a $(1 + 1/k)$-approximation for an arbitrary constant k, where the exponential-time dependence is only on the parameter k. The first two such PTASs were described by Hall and Shmoys [54]. The two schemes have different time complexities, namely,

$$O(16^k(nk)^{3+4k})$$

and

$$O(n \log n + n(4k)^{8k^2+8k+2}),$$

respectively. Mastrolilli [55] described another approximation scheme for a more general setting with identical processors. It has an aggregated time complexity

$$O(nk^{O(1)} + k^{O(k)}) = O(n + k^{O(k)}).$$

These approximation schemes carry out a complete enumeration of all possible combinations for scheduling specially determined k jobs, yielding a tight exponential-time dependence $O(k^k)$. In these schemes, the set of job release times is artificially reduced to a subset with no more than k elements. As was proved in [54], such a reduction maintains the desired approximation ratio. Below, we give more details on the above three PTASs.

In the first approximation scheme presented in [54], the processing times of jobs are rounded to the nearest multiples of the total processing time P of all jobs, divided by nk. By scaling the remaining job parameters, respectively, the original problem instance is transformed to one in which the total number of job processing times becomes restricted by nk. The obtained simplified instance can then be solved by the proposed dynamic programming algorithm. This algorithm works with the sub-intervals obtained by partitioning the scheduling horizon. The algorithm considers the possible distributions of the total

https://doi.org/10.3390/a19010038

processing time of the jobs assigned to each sub-interval. The way the sub-intervals are constructed permits the LDT-heuristic to schedule optimally the jobs from each sub-interval. Through the construction of the sub-intervals, the dynamic programming algorithm needs to deal with no more than $P^{O(k)}$ distributions. Due to the accomplished rounding of the job processing times, the total number of possible distributions becomes

$$(nk)^{O(k)}.$$

The other two approximation schemes (the second one from [54] and the scheme from [55]) partition the set of jobs into short and long jobs so that there are no more than $O(k)$ long jobs. In the second scheme from [54], as in the first one, $O(k)$ sub-intervals are derived and the possible ways in which long jobs can be distributed into the derived sub-intervals are considered. The short jobs with an appropriate total length together with the corresponding long ones are scheduled by the LDT-heuristic. All the jobs scheduled in a given sub-interval are released at the beginning of this sub-interval, and hence, the LDT-heuristic schedules them optimally.

In the approximation scheme from [55], there is also a constant number of small jobs and no more than $O(k)$ job release times, job processing times and job delivery times. The set of jobs is partitioned into no more than $O(k^2)$ subsets so that each subset contains the jobs with the same release times and delivery times. The jobs of each subset are compiled into longer jobs, with each of these compiled jobs having the same release time and delivery time so that each subset is left with no more than one small job. After these transformations, the cost of a complete enumeration does not depend exponentially on n. Similarly to the second scheme in [54], a constant number of starting times of the long jobs is considered. The jobs are again scheduled by the fast LDT-heuristic.

A recent approximation scheme from Vakhania [19] is based on the earlier mentioned VPA. Like the earlier approximation schemes, it partitions the set of jobs into short and long jobs. The exponential-time dependence in the time complexity expression of this PTAS is only on the number κ of *long emerging* jobs. The total number of long jobs is no more than k, where k is an integer such that the PTAS guarantees the generation of a feasible solution, at most $(1+1/k)$ times an optimal one. A worst-case running time of the PTAS can be expressed as

$$O(\kappa!\kappa_{1.1}n^2\log n),$$

where $\kappa_{1.1}$ is the number of *long* type 1.1 jobs. Note that for any fixed k, the parameter κ is a constant smaller than k.

Polynomially solvable special cases. As we have already seen from Section 2, if all r_j values are equal, then scheduling the jobs in order of non-decreasing due dates gives an optimal schedule in $O(n\log n)$ time, see Jackson [20]. Similarly, if all d_j values are equal, then scheduling the jobs in order of non-decreasing release times is optimal. If all jobs are of unit length, the problem with both job release times and due dates is again solvable. As Horn [21] observed, in this case, the ED-heuristic delivers an optimal solution given that the job release times are integers. Indeed, while applying the ED-heuristic, no job can be released within the execution interval of a currently running job. As a result, no job may potentially cause a forced delay of any more urgent job. With real job release times and unit job processing times, the problem can be scaled to an equivalent one in which all three job parameters are integers and the job processing times are equal (but not unit-length ones). Then, while applying the ED-heuristic (the non-preemptive case), during the execution of a job another more urgent job may be released, which basically makes the heuristic non-optimal for the general setting $1|r_j|L_{\max}$. However, if we allow it to preempt the former job and schedule the latter one at its release time, the preemptive problem

https://doi.org/10.3390/a1901

$1|r_j, pmtn|L_{\max}$ can be solved optimally, as was mentioned in Section 2. The problem with equal (non-unit)-length jobs $1|p_j = p, r_j|L_{\max}$ can still be solved in polynomial $O(n^2 \log n)$ time. Garey et al. [22] used a very sophisticated data structure with a union and find tree with path compression and achieved an improvement of the time complexity to $O(n \log n)$.

The problem with two allowable job processing times p and $2p$ for an arbitrary integer p, denoted as $1|p_j \in \{p, 2p\}, r_j|L_{\max}$, remains polynomially solvable, see Vakhania [23]. The algorithm from the latter reference is optimal when the processing times of only some emerging jobs (which become known during the execution of the algorithm) are restricted to p or $2p$. The algorithm is obtained as a consequence of two implicit enumeration algorithms for the problem $1|r_j|D_{\max}$. The first algorithm is exponential. The second algorithm is a restriction of the first one and runs in $O(n^2 \log n)$ time under certain conditions, which are to be held during its execution. Otherwise, another auxiliary procedure has to be applied to guarantee the optimality. An $O(n^2 \log n \log p)$ implementation of that procedure for the two allowed job processing times yields an algorithm with the same time complexity for this setting.

Relatively recently, it was shown that an essentially more general setting, where every job processing time divides every larger job processing time (for example, the job processing times are powers of 2), $1|div, r_j|D_{\max}$, can be solved optimally in $O(n^2 \log n \log p_{\max})$ time, see Vakhania [24] (here $p_{\max}$ is the maximum job processing time). Note that this is a maximal polynomially solvable special case of the problem with restricted job processing times (as we mentioned earlier, the problem remains strongly NP-hard if the job processing times are from the set $\{p, 2p, 3p, \dots\}$ for any integer p). If the maximum job processing time $p_{\max}$ is bounded by a polynomial function in n, $P(n) = O(n^k)$, and the maximum difference between the job release times is bounded by a constant R, then the corresponding parameterized problem $1|p_{\max} \leq P(n), |r_j - r_i| < R\,|L_{\max}$ can still be solved in polynomial time $O(n^{k+1} \log n \log p_{\max})$, see Vakhania & Werner [25]. Note that in this setting, the general problem is parameterized by $p_{\max}$ and the maximum difference between two job release times.

For the problem $1|p_j = p, r_j|L_{\max}$, Lazarev et al. [26] presented two polynomial algorithms. The first procedure is based on a trisection search and determines an optimal solution in $O(Qn \log n)$ time, where 10^{-Q} represents the accuracy of the parameters of the problem. The second approach uses an auxiliary problem, where the maximum completion time is minimized under the constraint that $L_{\max}$ is bounded by a particular value. Using this approach, the authors determine a solution for the bi-criteria problem with the two criteria $C_{\max}$ and $L_{\max}$ and the Pareto set of optimal solutions in $O(n^3 \log n)$ time.

There are other known conditions that allow a polynomial-time solution of the problem. For example, if the job release times, processing times and due dates are restricted in a specific manner so that each r_j lies within a certain time interval defined by p_j and d_j, then the problem can be solved in $O(n \log n)$ time, see Hoogoveen [65]. If the job parameters are embedded in another special manner, such that for any pair of jobs j, i with $r_i > r_j$ and $d_i < d_j$,

$$d_j - r_j - p_j \leq d_i - r_i - p_i$$

holds, and with

$$r_i + p_i \geq r_j + p_j,$$

$d_i \geq d_j$ holds, then the resultant problem $1|r_j, embedded|L_{\max}$ is solvable in $O(n \log n)$ time, see Vakhania [27]. As was recently observed in Vakhania and Werner [66], allowing the compression of job processing times may lead to an efficient solution of the general problem under some reasonable restrictions (in practice, job compression is accomplished at the cost of using some extra resources). There is an upper limit on the total allowable

https://doi.org/10.3390/a19010038

compression cost, and one looks for a schedule that minimizes the maximum job lateness. The authors propose an $O(n^2 \log n)$ algorithm that determines an amount of additional resources required to solve the problem optimally. If this yields a violation of the restriction on the allowable maximum cost, i.e., the solution is infeasible, it is transformed into a "tight minimal" feasible one in the sense that by increasing the processing time of any compressed job by some amount of time, the maximum job lateness in the resultant solution will increase by the same amount. As is shown, it suffices to compress only some emerging jobs.

As already mentioned, the problem with only two allowable job release times and due dates $1|r_j \in \{r_1, r_2\}, d_j \in \{d_1, d_2\}|L_{\max}$ is weakly *NP*-hard. Reynoso and Vakhania [28] considered this setting. They established structural properties of feasible schedules that have led to a number of optimality conditions, under which the problem was solved in $O(n \log n)$ time. For bottleneck instances, where none of these conditions apply, the problem is reduced to the SUBSET SUM problem. The authors presented the results of computational experiments accomplished for 50 million randomly generated problem instances, reporting that almost all these instances were solved optimally by one of the established optimality conditions. Remarkably, the heuristic algorithms that incorporate the above optimality conditions also succeeded in solving the SUBSET SUM problem optimally for almost all 50 million instances. A more recent work considered a natural generalization of the latter problem with any fixed number of release times (see Escalona [67]). For this setting, the optimality conditions were derived, and again it was shown how the problem can be reduced to the SUBSET SUM problem. It is a challenging question regarding to what extent the above obtained results can be generalized for any fixed number of release and delivery times, a setting with still wider practical applications.

In Azharonok et al. [29], a general objective function $f_{\max}$ defined as the maximum of non-decreasing cost functions f_j was considered for the preemptive problem $1|r_j, prec, pmtn|f_{\max}$. It is assumed that for any pair i, j of jobs, the cost functions fulfill either the order relation $f_i(t) \leq f_j(t)$ for any time t or $f_j(t) \leq f_i(t)$ for any time t of the scheduling interval. In the case of tree-like precedence constraints, the derived algorithm has a time complexity of $O(n \log n)$, which improves the complexity of $O(n^2)$ of a known algorithm for the general case [68]. In addition, a parallel algorithm is given with a time complexity of $O(\log^2 n)$ when using $O(n^2 \log n)$ processors.

Some applications. The problem $1|r_j|L_{\max}$ is important on its own and also because of its possible applications for the solution of other more complex scheduling problems and other optimization problems. For example, Carlier and Pinson [69] used the problem as an auxiliary one to obtain a lower bound for the version of the problem with identical processors. Adams, Balas and Zawack [70] used the problem for the solution of the job shop scheduling problem.

The problem can also be used for the solution of Vehicle Routing Problems (VRPs) with k vehicles (salespeople), each starting and ending at a special point 0 called the depot. Each salesperson has to visit a number of clients and return to the depot. The objective is to minimize the total cost of all k tours (see, for example, [71]). In the setting with *time windows*, each client has to be visited within a specified time window (interval). In this setting, there may exist no feasible solution. Hence, it is crucial to determine whether there exists a feasible solution for a given k. More generally, one may be interested in calculating the minimum k for which there exists a feasible solution. Let us consider a simplified version of the problem with $k = 1$, i.e., the Traveling Salesman Problem (TSP) with time windows, TSP-TW. For a given instance of TSP-TW with $n + 1$ clients, we create an instance of the problem $1|p_j = 0, r_j|L_{\max}$ with n jobs, associating job j with client j for each $i = 1, \ldots, n$ and letting the processing time of each job be 0. Note that this is a simplified version of the generic problem $1|r_j|L_{\max}$. In this version, the release and due times of each job are

https://doi.org/10.3390/a1901

determined according to the time window of the corresponding client. In the feasibility version of the problem, one looks for a schedule in which no job has a positive lateness. One can immediately see that if there is no feasible solution to the scheduling problem, there is also no feasible solution for the corresponding instance of TSP-TW. If we let u be an upper bound on the total number of salesmen, we can carry out binary search within the interval $[1, u]$, solving at each iteration an instance of the corresponding scheduling problem $Pk|p_j = 0, r_j|L_{\max}$ with k parallel identical machines and with trial $k \in [1, u]$. In this way, we can find the minimum k for which there exists a feasible solution to the problem (if it exists).

In the capacitated VRP, each vehicle has some capacity and each client has some request. In a feasible vehicle tour, the total demand of all clients in that tour cannot exceed the capacity of that vehicle. A feasible solution consists of k feasible tours. With equal capacity C of all vehicles, one can verify the feasibility by solving the feasibility version of the multiprocessor version of our genetic problem without job release and due times with k identical processors, where the objective is to minimize the makespan (the maximum job or machine completion time), $Pk||C_{\max}$. Here we associate jobs with clients, where the processing time of each job is the demand of the corresponding client, and we wish to know if there exists a feasible solution to the scheduling problem with a makespan at most C. This is an essentially simpler problem than a VRP. Alternatively, strong lower bounds calculated in polynomial time are known for scheduling problems, which, in particular, can be useful to establish that there exists no feasible solution to an instance of a VRP (whenever this is the case).

3.2. *Minimizing the Number of Late Jobs*

Another common objective function with given due dates is the *number of late jobs*: a job in a schedule is called *late* if it is completed after its due date in that schedule, otherwise it is called *on time*. In the problem of this subsection, we deal with n jobs with release times and due dates which have to be scheduled on the machine to maximize the number of on-time jobs, or equivalently, to minimize the number of late jobs. We consider both preemptive and non-preemptive cases and also cases when the jobs have an additional parameter called *weight*.

3.2.1. Non-Preemptive Scheduling to Minimize the Number of Late Jobs: $1|r_j; p_j = p|\sum U_j$

In this subsection, we deal with the non-preemptive version of the problem $1|r_j|\sum U_j$. This problem was studied in Vakhania [30], where two polynomial-time algorithms were proposed. The first one with the time complexity $O(n^3 \log n)$ optimally solves the problem if during its execution no job with some specially defined property occurs. The second algorithm is an adaptation of the first one for the special case of the problem when all jobs have the same length $1|r_j; p_j = p|\sum U_j$. The time complexity of this algorithm is $O(n^3 \log n)$ (it improved an earlier known fastest algorithm with the time complexity of $O(n^5)$ by Chrobak et al. [72]).

3.2.2. Preemptive Scheduling to Maximize the Number of On-Time Jobs: $1|r_j; pmtn|\sum U_j$

In the problem of this subsection, n jobs with release times and due dates have to be scheduled preemptively on a single machine to minimize the number of late jobs, i.e., problem $1|r_j; pmtn|\sum U_j$. We call a job *late* (*on time*, respectively) if it is completed after (at or before, respectively) its due date. We will say that job j is *feasibly* scheduled if it starts no earlier than at time r_j and overlaps with no other job on the machine. A feasible schedule is one which feasibly schedules all jobs. The objective is to find a feasible schedule with a minimal number of late jobs or, equivalently, with the maximal number of on-time jobs.

https://doi.org/10.3390/a19010038

This problem is known to be polynomially solvable. The first polynomial dynamic programming algorithm with a time complexity of $O(n^5)$ and a space complexity of $O(n^3)$ was developed by Lawler [31]. The result was improved by Baptiste [32], who suggested another dynamic programming algorithm with a time complexity of $O(n^4)$ and a space complexity of $O(n^2)$. The latter result was further improved by Vakhania [33], where an algorithm with the time and space complexities of $O(n^3)$ and $O(n)$, respectively, was proposed. Unlike the earlier algorithms, the latter algorithm is not based on dynamic programming. It uses the ED-heuristic for scheduling the jobs. The main task is to construct a schedule in which all jobs are scheduled on time, with the number of such jobs being maximal. As any late job can be scheduled arbitrarily late without affecting the objective function, jobs not included in the former schedule can be later added at the end of it in an arbitrary order. During the construction of the schedule, some jobs are disregarded, whereas other jobs are omitted with the possibility to be included in a later created schedule.

3.3. Preemptive Scheduling to Minimize the Weighted Number of Late Jobs with Equal Length: $1|r_j; p_j = p; pmtn|\sum w_jU_j$

In this section, we consider the weighted version of the problem of the previous section in which preemptions are allowed and all jobs have an equal length. Moreover, w_j is the non-negative integer weight of job j. We minimize the *weighted throughput*, which is the total weight of the completed jobs. Equivalently, we minimize the weighted number of late jobs. The problem can be abbreviated as $1|r_j; p_j = p; pmtn|\sum w_jU_j$.

The first polynomial dynamic programming algorithm of complexity $O(n^{10})$ for the problem was suggested by Baptiste [34]. Baptiste et al. [35] improved the above time complexity and proposed another dynamic programming algorithm, which runs in $O(n^4)$ time.

Next, we briefly discuss some directions for further research. First, we note that for the multiprocessor case, the weighted version is NP-complete [73]. At the same time, the non-weighted version still remains open. In particular, it is not known whether the problem $P|r_j; p_j = p; pmtn|\sum U_j$ can be solved in polynomial time. (Even for two processors, one cannot restrict the search to solely earliest deadline schedules. As an example, consider an instance with three jobs with feasible intervals $(0,3)$, $(0,4)$, and $(0,5)$ and the processing time $p = 3$. There exists a feasible schedule that completes all three jobs, whereas the earliest-deadline schedule completes only jobs 1 and 2.) For the multiprocessor case, it is also interesting to study the preemptive version, where jobs are not allowed to migrate between processors.

3.4. Scheduling to Minimize the Weighted Number of Late Jobs with Deadlines and Release/Due-Date Intervals

In [74], Gordon et al. dealt with the problem where in addition to release and due dates, deadlines are also given. This means that certain jobs have to be completed on time. The authors considered the two cases of similarly ordered release and dues dates (i.e., $r_1 \leq r_2 \leq \ldots \leq r_n$ and $d_1 \leq d_2 \leq \ldots \leq d_n$) as well as nested release and due-date intervals (i.e., none of two such intervals overlap; thus they have at most a joint point or one covers the other one). For these problems, a reduced problem is constructed where the deadlines are eliminated, and it is shown that the optimal solution of the reduced problem can be used to find an optimal solution of the initial problem.

In a later paper, Gordon et al. [75] considered the preemptive version of the above problem with nested release and due-date intervals. They derived necessary and sufficient conditions for the existence of a schedule in which all jobs are completed by their due dates. For the case of oppositely ordered processing times and job weights, a polynomial algorithm of the complexity $O(n \log n)$ was presented.

https://doi.org/10.3390/a1901(

3.5. Scheduling with Tardiness-Based Objectives

The single machine problem $1||\sum T_i$ is known to be NP-hard in the ordinary sense (see [76]). In [77], Swarcz and Mukhopadhyay developed a decomposition rule which is used in a very powerful branch-and-bound algorithm. It turned out that the algorithm can solve problems with 100 jobs even without using any lower bounds, and the authors were able to solve problems until $n = 150$ jobs. This was possible by eliminating dynamic programming and replacing it with the newly developed decomposition rule, which significantly outperformed the earlier rules by Emmons [78].

The single machine problem of minimizing total tardiness has received a lot of attention. An early review on exact and approximation algorithms was given by Koulamas [79] in 1994. Sixteen years later, Koulamas [80] discussed the most important developments for the total tardiness problem up to 2010. The latter survey discusses some theoretical developments, exact algorithms, fully polynomial-time approximation schemes, approximation algorithms, some special cases and also a generalization of the problem as well as the total tardiness problem with assignable due dates. Recall that for the total weighted tardiness scheduling problem, an early review of algorithms was given by Abdul-Razaq et al. [11] in 1990.

Our main focus in this sub-section is on new results in the last 15 years which have not been included in reviews so far. While the problem $1||\sum T_j$ is known to be NP-hard, Gafarov et al. [36] considered the special case of equal processing times, i.e., problem $1|r_j, p_j = p|\sum w_j T_j$. After deriving some properties, they gave polynomial algorithms for two special cases of the problem. If the difference between the maximum due date and the minimum due date is not greater than the processing time p, the problem can be solved by a modification of the algorithm by Baptiste [81] in $O(n^{10})$ time. The special case with ordered weights and processing times according to $w_1 \leq w_2 \leq \ldots \leq w_n$ and $d_1 \leq d_2 \leq \ldots \leq d_n$ can be solved in $O(n^9)$ time by a similar modification from [81].

In [82], Lazarev and Werner presented a new general graphical algorithm which often improves the complexity or at least the running time of dynamic programming algorithms, and it can be used for efficient approximation algorithms. Compared to standard dynamic programming algorithms, the number of states can often substantially be reduced.

In a standard dynamic programming algorithm for permutation problems, the functions $F_l(t)$ and the corresponding partial sequences have to be stored for any stage $l = 1, 2, \ldots, n$ and any time $t = 0, 1, \ldots, UB$. Here, UB is an upper bound for the scheduling interval, e.g., the sum of all processing times (or the maximal due date). The values $F_1(t)$ typically represent the best function value when considering the first l jobs and allowing at most t time units for the processing of the scheduled (e.g., early) jobs. This results in a pseudo-polynomial algorithm of the complexity $O(n \sum p_j)$.

The graphical algorithm combines different states, where the best partial solution does not change and the corresponding objective function $F_l(t)$ can be described by the same linear function. As a result, at each stage l, there are certain intervals separated by the so-called breakpoints $t_1^l < t_2^l < \ldots t_{h_l}^l$, where the structure of the linear function belonging to the best partial solution changes. In addition, for the graphical algorithm, the times t do not need to be integers.

In [83], Gafarov et al. described the application of this graphical algorithm to the approximate solution of various single machine problems. In particular, the graphical algorithm is applied to five total tardiness problems, where a pseudo-polynomial algorithm exists, and the graphical algorithm yields fully polynomial-time approximation schemes, yielding the best known running time.

In [15], Gafarov et al. considered the maximization of total tardiness, and by applying the graphical algorithm, they transformed a pseudo-polynomial algorithm into a poly-

https://doi.org/10.3390/a19010038

nomial one. More precisely, the complexity of $O(n \sum p_j)$ can be reduced to $O(n^2)$, which settled the open complexity status of the problem max $1|(nd)|\sum T_j)$, where *nd* means that no inserted idle times occur. The authors present a detailed numerical example and also give a practical application of such maximization problems, where wind turbines have to be mounted in several regions of a country.

While for more general settings such a graphical algorithm often improves the running time in comparison with existing algorithms, the complexity remains pseudo-polynomial. For instance, in [84], Lazarev et al. presented graphical algorithms with a complexity of $O(n \sum p_j)$ for a special case of a generalized tardiness problem corresponding to the minimization of late work as well as for the minimization of the weighted number of late jobs.

In [85], Lazarev and Werner considered various special cases of the (unweighted) total tardiness problem $1||\sum T_j$. After proving that the special case of oppositely ordered processing times and due dates, i.e., $p_1 \geq p_2 \geq \ldots \geq p_n$ and $d_1 \leq d_2 \leq \ldots \leq d_n$, is already NP-hard in the ordinary sense, they gave several pseudo-polynomial and polynomial algorithms for special cases of this problem. In particular, $O(n^2)$ algorithms were given for the cases $d_j - d_{j-1} > p_j, j = 2, 3, \ldots, n$, as well as for the case when the difference between the maximal and the minimal due date is not greater than 1. In both cases, the processing times do not need to be integers.

In further research, the graphical algorithm can be applied to more general problems, where a pseudo-polynomial algorithm exists and Boolean variables are used for making yes/no decisions.

3.6. Some Online Settings

First, we consider preemptive scheduling models to maximize overall profit. Jobs with release and processing times, deadlines and weights are to be scheduled on a single machine. Job weight reflects its profit. Any job can be preempted during the execution, and the objective is to maximize the overall profit, respecting job deadlines. Notice that in a feasible schedule, all jobs must complete by their deadlines. In particular, there may exist no feasible schedule in which all jobs are included. Hence, we wish to create a feasible schedule in which the overall profit is maximized. Two possible models and the definition of the profit gained by the execution of task j have been studied. In the *standard model*, a completed task j gives the profit $w_j p_j$, whereas a non-completed task gives no profit. In a more flexible *metered model*, a task j executed for $t \leq p_j$ time units gives the profit w_{jt} (this task may not be completed). We just mention here the work by Chrobak et al. [86], who considered both the offline and online metered profit models. For the offline setting, they used a reduction to bipartite matchings and maximal flows to develop a polynomial-time algorithm with a better running time than the solution of a direct linear programming model would yield. For the online metered case, they presented an algorithm with competitive ratio $e/(e-1) \approx 1.5820$ and proved a lower bound of $\sqrt{5} - 1 \approx 1.236$ on the competitive ratio of the algorithms for this problem.

In an online setting with job release times, the jobs arrive over time. The delivery time of a job becomes known at its arrival (release) time. The objective is to minimize the maximum full job completion time, the makespan. In Section 3.1, we considered the corresponding offline problem, which is strongly NP-hard. We also mentioned that the preemptive version can be solved in polynomial time by the preemptive LDT-heuristic, whereas for the non-preemptive case, the LDT-heuristic has a performance guarantee of two. This is the best possible performance ratio unless we allow the machine to be idle

https://doi.org/10.3390/a1901

when there is an unprocessed job available. Hoogeveen and Vestjens [56] developed an online algorithm with the best possible worst-case ratio

$$(\sqrt{5}+1)/2 \approx 1.61803$$

in which a waiting strategy is incorporated. Van den Akker et al. [87] considered an extension of the standard model by allowing job *restarts*: If an urgent job comes while the machine is busy, then the currently running job can be interrupted in favor of the urgent job. In this model, unlike traditional preemptive models, the already processed part of the interrupted job is wasted and this job is to be started all over again. The algorithm proposed in [87] has the best possible worst-case ratio of 1.5 (which is better than the above-mentioned bound for the case without restarts).

As is easy to see, in the offline setting, a mere modification of the LDT-heuristic that removes and postpones each currently running job in favor of a just released more urgent job can deliver a worst-possible non-preemptive schedule. In this sense, restarts do not make much sense in the offline case.

In the online setting, in cases where a job cannot be split, allowing job restarts can be a reasonable compromise. However, note that an almost completed job will be "lost" if a more urgent job arrives just before its completion on the machine. This scenario can be softened if an already completed part of an abandoned job can give some benefit and this job can be restarted from the moment when it was interrupted. Note that a direct compromise would lead us to the standard preemptive case. But other alternative reasonable compromises are possible. For example, the preemptive part may yield some penalty and the total penalty can be minimized. Furthermore, as in the above-mentioned metered model, a partially completed job may still give some benefit. Hence, one may well consider models where an already processed part of an interrupted job counts in one way or another. It is interesting to consider whether there exist better worst-case performance bounds for such models.

3.7. Scheduling with Non-Renewable Resources

Unlike a traditional *renewable resource* which is constantly available and not consumed by a job, a *non-renewable resource* is consumed by a job so that its availability is not permanent and constant. A machine or a processor is a renewable resource, whereas energy, money and fuel, for example, are non-renewable resources that can be created in different ways. Nowadays, different kinds of sustainable energy sources including solar and wind energies are widely available.

Gafarov et al. [88] considered single machine problems with a non-renewable resource (abbreviated NR). This means that at any time $t_i, i = 0, 1, \ldots, UB$, with $t_0 = 0$ and UB as an upper bound on the scheduling interval, one gets an amount $G(t_i) \geq 0$ of the resource, while any job j has a consumption of g_j at the starting time s_j of the job. Hence, the equality

$$\sum_{j=1}^{n} g_j = \sum_{i=0}^{UB} G(t_i)$$

holds. One looks for an optimal permutation $(j_1, j_2, \ldots, j_n)$ for a particular objective function with the starting times $s_{j_1}, s_{j_2}, \ldots, s_{j_n}$ of the jobs such that the resource constraints are satisfied, i.e., the inequality

$$\sum_{l=1}^{i} g_{j_l} \leq \sum \{G(t_v) \mid t_v \leq s_{j_i} \text{ for all } vs. \leq s_{j_i}\}$$

https://doi.org/10.3390/a19010038

holds for any $i = 1, 2, \ldots, n$. Such problems play a role, e.g., for government-financed organizations when a project can only be started after receiving the required funds.

The authors focused on complexity results and proved that the problems $1|NR|f$ with $f \in \{C_{\max}, \sum C_j, \sum U_j\}$ are strongly NP-hard. When minimizing total tardiness $\sum T_j$, the case of equal due dates ($d_j = d$) is already strongly NP-hard. The following special cases with minimizing total tardiness were proven to be weakly NP-hard:

(1) Equal processing times ($p_j = p$);
(2) Equal due dates ($d_j = d$) and equal consumptions ($g_j = g$).

On the other hand, the special case of equal processing times ($p_j = p$) and ordered consumptions and due dates according to $g_1 \leq g_2 \leq \ldots \leq g_n$ and $d_1 \leq d_2 \leq \ldots \leq d_n$ is polynomially solvable.

This paper considered also the budget scheduling problem with the objective to minimize the makespan. Instead of a resource consumption g_j for each job, two values g_j^- and g_j^+ are given, where g_j^- has the same meaning as g_j before. The value g_j^+ describes the additional earnings at the completion time of job j. The authors showed that the problem $1|NR, g_j^-, g_j^+|C_{\max}$ belongs to the class APX of problems, allowing a constant-factor approximation algorithm.

Recently, Ramirez et al. [37] considered a different non-renewable setting on a single machine. In that setting, every job has a release time, processing time and due date, where the execution of job j, besides the machine time, requires e_j amount of the non-renewable resource (it consumes energy e_j). Here, a schedule is a mapping that assigns to each job a starting time on the machine and the required amount of the non-renewable resource. The objective is to minimize the maximum job lateness. The problem is abbreviated as $1|r_j, e_j|L_{\max}$. The authors proposed an $O(n \log n)$-time algorithm for the case, where all jobs have a unit processing time. Earlier, an $O(n^2 \log n)$ time algorithm was suggested for a similar scenario but without job release times by Grigoriev et al. [38]. Note that job release times essentially complicate the problem, even without energy requirements, since the setting without them is polynomially solvable. The algorithm in [37] iteratively takes the next unscheduled job with the minimum due date and schedules it at the earliest time moment where enough energy for that job becomes available. This is an offline algorithm, as the jobs are not scheduled according to their arrival (release) times.

For future work, due to the NP-hardness of the majority of problems, it would be interesting to derive elimination rules and structural properties of optimal solutions which can be used in enumerative algorithms.

4. Concluding Remarks

In this paper, we reviewed some theoretical results on classical single machine scheduling problems. Since there exists a huge number of heuristic/meta-heuristic and enumerative algorithms, our focus was on polynomial algorithms as well as complexity and approximability issues. The summarized polynomial special cases are also of interest when the conditions are not exactly satisfied and the resulting solution can be taken as a good heuristic one. We hope that the reviewed results will stimulate further investigation in related research fields.

For single machine scheduling problems, efficient solution methods can often be found more easily than for the corresponding multiprocessor or shop scheduling problems. However, such methods may give a better insight into the latter, more complex problems and may well serve as a basis for the development of solution methods for these problems. At the same time, optimal solutions to single machine scheduling problems can directly be used to solve the corresponding multiprocessor or shop scheduling problems. For example, for such NP-hard problems, strong lower bounds can be obtained based on the solutions

https://doi.org/10.3390/a1901

of the corresponding single machine problems. Non-strict lower bounds, which are easier and faster to obtain, can be used in any search-tree-based approximation algorithm, such as beam search, for example. Similarly, using strict lower bounds, we obtain exact branch-and-bound algorithms. Once implemented and tested, the above algorithms can be used as an algorithmic engine for the construction of decision support systems. Finally, we note that a number of algorithms for basic single machine problems can relatively easily be adopted using additional graph-completion mechanisms to solve the corresponding extended versions with precedence relations, transportation and setup times and other real-life job scheduling problems.

Author Contributions: Conceptualization, N.V. and F.W.; methodology, N.V. and F.W.; validation, N.V. and F.W.; formal analysis, N.V., F.W. and K.J.R.-F.; investigation, N.V. and F.W.; writing—original draft preparation, N.V. and F.W.; writing—review and editing, N.V. and F.W.; visualization, K.J.R.-F.; funding acquisition, F.W. All authors have read and agreed to the published version of the manuscript.

Funding: The research of the first author was partially supported by the DAAD grant 57507438 for research stays for university academics and scientists.

Data Availability Statement: The original contributions presented in this study are included in the article. Further inquiries can be directed to the corresponding authors.

Acknowledgments: The authors are very grateful to Jan Karel Lenstra and Sergey Sevastyanov for their insightful and careful comments.

Conflicts of Interest: The authors declare no conflict of interest.

erences

Lenstra, J.K.; Rinnooy Kan, A.H.G.; Brucker, P. Complexity of machine scheduling problems. *Ann. Oper. Res.* **1975**, *1*, 343–362.

Chen, B.; Potts, C.N.; Woeginger, G.J. A Review of Machine Scheduling: Complexity, Algorithms and Approximability. In *Handbook of Combinatorial Optimization*; Du, D.-Z., Pardalos, P.M., Eds.; Kluwer: Boston, MA, USA, 1998; Volume 3, pp. 1493–1641.

Allahverdi, A.; Gupta, J.N.D.; Aldowaisan, T. A Review of Scheduling Research Involving Setup Considerations. *Omega Int. J. Manag. Sci.* **1999**, *27*, 219–239. [CrossRef]

Allahverdi, A.; Ng, C.T.; Cheng, T.C.E.; Kovalyov, M.Y. A Survey of Scheduling Problems with Setup Times or Costs. *Eur. J. Oper. Res.* **2008**, *187*, 985–1032. [CrossRef]

Allahverdi, A. The Third Comprehensive Survey on Scheduling Problems with Setup Times/Costs. *Eur. J. Oper. Res.* **2015**, *246*, 345–378. [CrossRef]

Fowler, J.W.; Mönch, L. A Survey of Scheduling with Parallel Batch (p-Batch) Processing. *Eur. J. Oper. Res.* **2022**, *298*, 1–24. [CrossRef]

Kravchenko, S.; Werner, F. Parallel Machine Problems with Equal Processing Times: A Survey. *J. Sched.* **2011**, *14*, 435–444. [CrossRef]

Briskorn, D. Single-Machine Schduling with Learning Considerations. *Eur. J. Oper. Res.* **1999**, *115*, 173–178.

Wu, H.; Zhang, H. Single-Machine Scheduling with Periodic Maintenance and Learning Effect. *Sci. Rep.* **2023**, *13*, 9309. [CrossRef] [PubMed]

Koulamas, C.; Kyparisis, G.J. A Classification of Dynamic Programming Formulations for Offline Deterministic Single-Machine Scheduling Problems. *Eur. J. Oper. Res.* **2023**, *305*, 999–1017. [CrossRef]

Abdul-Razaq, T.S.; Potts, C.; van Wassenhove, L. A Survey of Algorithms for the Single Machine Total Weighted Tardiness Scheduling Problem. *Discret. Appl. Math.* **1990**, *26*, 235–253. [CrossRef]

Adumu, M.O.; Adewumi, A. A Survey of Single Machine Scheduling to Minimize Weighted Number of Tardy Jobs. *J. Ind. Manag. Optim.* **2014**, *10*, 219–241. [CrossRef]

Sterna, M. A Survey of Scheduling Problems with Late Work Criteria. *Omega Int. J. Manag. Sci.* **2011**, *39*, 120–129. [CrossRef]

Sterna, M. Late and Early Work Scheduling: A Survey. *Omega Int. J. Manag. Sci.* **2021**, *104*, 102453. [CrossRef]

Gafarov, E.; Lazarev, A.; Werner, F. Single Machine Total Tardiness Maximization Problems: Complexity and Algorithms. *Ann. Oper. Res.* **2013**, *207*, 121–136. [CrossRef]

McMahon, G.; Florian, M. On Scheduling with Ready Times and due-dates to Minimize Maximum Lateness. *Oper. Res.* **1975**, *23*, 475–482. [CrossRef]

Carlier, J. The One-Machine Sequencing Problem. *Eur. J. Oper. Res.* **1982**, *11*, 42–47. [CrossRef]

 https://doi.org/10.3390/a19010038

18. Pan, Y.; Shi, L. Branch-and-bound Algorithms for Solving Hard Instances of the One-Machine Sequencing Problem. *Eur. J.* *Res.* **2006**, *168*, 1030–1069. [CrossRef]
19. Vakhania, N. Variable Parameter Analysis for Scheduling One Machine. *arXiv* **2022**, arXiv:2211.02107. [CrossRef]
20. Jackson, J.R. Scheduling a Production Line to Minimize the Maximum Tardiness. Ph.D. Thesis, University of Califo Los Angeles, CA, USA, 1955.
21. Horn, W.A. Some Simple Scheduling Algorithms. *Nav. Res. Logist. Q.* **1974**, *21*, 177–185. [CrossRef]
22. Garey, M.R.; Johnson, D.S.; Simons, B.B.; Tarjan, R.E. Scheduling Unit-Time Tasks with Arbitrary Release Times and Deadl *SIAM J. Comput.* **1981**, *10*, 256–269. [CrossRef]
23. Vakhania, N. Single-Machine Scheduling with Release Times and Tails. *Ann. Oper. Res.* **2004**, *129*, 253–271. [CrossRef]
24. Vakhania, N. Dynamic Restructuring Framework for Scheduling with Release Times and Due-Dates. *Mathematics* **2019**, *7*, [CrossRef]
25. Vakhania, N.; Werner, F. Minimizing Maximum Lateness of Jobs with Naturally Bounded Job Data on a Single Machir Polynomial Time. *Theor. Comput. Sci.* **2013**, *501*, 72–81. [CrossRef]
26. Lazarev, A.A.; Arkhipov, D.I.; Werner, F. Scheduling Jobs with Equal Processing Times on a Single Machine: Minimi Maximum Lateness and Makespan. *Optim. Lett.* **2017**, *11*, 165–177. [CrossRef]
27. Vakhania, N. Fast Solution of Single-Machine Scheduling Problem with Embedded Jobs. *Theor. Comput. Sci.* **2019**, *782*, 91- [CrossRef]
28. Reynoso, A.; Vakhania, N. Theoretical and Practical Issues in Single-Machine Scheduling with two Job Release and Deli Times. *J. Sched.* **2021**, *24*, 615–647. [CrossRef]
29. Azhanarok, E.; Gordon, V.; Werner, F. Single Machine Preemptive Scheduling with Special Cost Functions. *Optimization* **199** 271–286. [CrossRef]
30. Vakhania, N. A Study of Single-Machine Scheduling Problem to Maximize Throughput. *J. Sched.* **2013**, *16*, 395–403. [CrossR
31. Lawler, E.L. A Dynamic Programming Algorithm for Preemptive Scheduling of a Single Machine to Minimize the Numb Late Jobs. *Ann. Oper. Res.* **1990**, *26*, 125–133. [CrossRef]
32. Baptiste, P. An $O(n^4)$ Algorithm for Preemptive Scheduling of a Single Machine to Minimize the Number of Late Jobs. *Oper.* *Lett.* **1999**, *24*, 175–180. [CrossRef]
33. Vakhania, N. Scheduling Jobs with Release Times Preemptively on a Single Machine to Minimize the Number of Late Jobs. *Res. Lett.* **2009**, *37*, 405–410. [CrossRef]
34. Baptiste, P. Polynomial Time Algorithms for Minimizing the Weighted Number of Late Jobs on a Single Machine with E Processing Times. *J. Sched.* **1999**, *2*, 245–252. [CrossRef]
35. Baptiste, P.; Chrobak, M.; Dürr, C.; Jawor, W.; Vakhania, N. Preemptive Scheduling of Equal-Length Jobs to Maximize Weig Throughput. *Oper. Res. Lett.* **2004**, *32*, 258–264. [CrossRef]
36. Gafarov, E.; Lazarev, A.; Werner, F. Minimizing Total Weighted Tardiness for Scheduling Equal-Length Jobs on a Single Mac *Autom. Remote Control* **2020**, *81*, 853–868. [CrossRef]
37. Ramirez, K.; Vakhania, N.; Hernandez A. Fast Algorithm for Single Machine Scheduling of Unit-Length Jobs with Non-renew Resource Requirements to Minimize Maximum Job Lateness. In Proceedings of the 12th Annual Conference on Computati Science & Computational Intelligence, Las Vegas, NV, USA, 3–5 December 2025.
38. Grigoriev, A.; Holthuijsen, M.; van de Klundert, J. Basic Scheduling Problems with Raw Material Constraints. *Nav. Res. L* **2005**, *52*, 527–535. [CrossRef]
39. Chaubey, P.K.; Sundar, S. A Steady-State Genetic Algorithms for the Single Machine Scheduling Problem with Periodic Ma nance Availability. *SN Comput. Sci.* **2023**, *4*, 651. [CrossRef]
40. Mexicano, A.; Carmona-Frausto, J.C.; Montes-Dorantes, P.N.; Cervantes, S.; Cervantes, J.-A.; Rodriguez, R. Simulated Annea and Tabu Search for Solving the Single-Machine Problem. In *Advances on P2P, Parallel, Grid, Cloud and Internet Computing*; Spri Cham, Switzerland, 2023; Volume 571, pp. 86–95.
41. Mellouli, A.; Wafi, C.; Mellouli, R. An Efficent Ant Colony Optimization-Based Heuristic for the Single Machine Scheduling Sequence-Dependent Setup Times. In *Advsnces in Mechanical Engineering, Materials and Mechanics II (ICAMEM2024)*; Sprir Berlin/Heidelberg, Germany, 2025; pp. 179–188.
42. Rosa, B.F.; Souza, M.J.F.; de Souza, S.R. Algorithms based on VNS for Solving the Single Machine Scheduling Problem Earliness and Tardiness Penalties. *Electron. Notes Discret. Math.* **2018**, *66*, 47–54. [CrossRef]
43. Benmansour, R.; Todosijevic, R.; Hanafi, S. Variable Neighborhood Search for the Single Machine Scheduling Problem to Mini the Total Early Work. *Optim. Lett.* **2023**, *17*, 2169–2184. [CrossRef]
44. Israni, M.; Sundar, S. An Iterative Local Search for the Single Machine Scheduling Problem with Periodic Machine Availab *SN Comput. Sci.* **2025**, *6*, 108. [CrossRef]
45. Zhao, Y.; Wang, G. A Dynamic Differential Evolution Algorithm for the Dynamic Single-Machine Scheduling Problem Sequence-Dependent Setup Times. *J. Oper. Res. Soc.* **2020**, *71*, 225–236. [CrossRef]

 https://doi.org/10.3390/a1901

Khraibet, T.J.; Kalaf, B.A.; Mansoor, W. A New Metaheuristic Algorithm for Solving Multi-Objective Single-Machine Scheduling Problems. *J. Intell. Syst.* **2025**, *34*, 20240373. [CrossRef]

Moharam, R.; Morsy, E.; Ali, A.F.; Ahmed, M.A.; Mostafa, M.-S.M. A Discrete Grey Wolf Optimization Algorithm for Minimizing Penalties on a Single Machine Scheduling Problem. In Proceedings of the 8th International Conference on Advanced Machine Learning and Technologies and Applications (AMLTA2022), Cairo, Egypt, 5–7 May 2022; Volume 113, pp. 678–687.

Ballestin, F.; Leus, R. Meta-heuristics for Stable Scheduling on a Single Machine. *Comput. Oper. Res.* **2008**, *35*, 2165–2192. [CrossRef]

Corsini, R.R.; Fichera, V.; Longo, L.; Oriti, G. A Self-Adaptive Metaheuristic to Minimize the Total Weighted Tardiness for a Single-Machine Scheduling Problem with Flexible and Variable Maintenance. *J. Ind. Prod. Eng.* **2025**, *42*, 422–439. [CrossRef]

Antonov, N.; Sucha, P.; Janota, M.; Hula, J. Minimizing the Weighted Number of Tardy Jobs: Data-Driven Heuristic for Single-Machine Scheduling. *Comput. Oper. Res.* **2026**, *185*, 107281. [CrossRef]

Schrage, L. (University of Chicago, Chicago, IL, USA). Obtaining Optimal Solutions to Resource Constrained Network Scheduling Problems. Unpublished work, 1971.

Potts, C.N. Analysis of a Heuristic for One Machine Sequencing with Release Dates and Delivery Times. *Oper. Res.* **1980**, *28*, 1436–1441. [CrossRef]

Nowicki, E.; Smutnicki, C. An Approximation Algorithm for Single-Machine Scheduling with Release Times and Delivery Times. *Discret. Appl. Math.* **1994**, *48*, 69–79. [CrossRef]

Hall, L.A.; Shmoys, D.B. Jackson's Rule for Single-Machine Scheduling: Making a Good Heuristic Better. *Math. Oper. Res.* **1992**, *17*, 22–35. [CrossRef]

Mastrolilli, M. Efficient Approximation Schemes for Scheduling Problems with Release Dates and Delivery Times. *J. Sched.* **2003**, *6*, 521–531. [CrossRef]

Hoogeveen, J.A.; Vestjens, A.P.A. A Best Possible Deterministic On-line Algorithm for Minimizing Maximum Delivery Time on a Single Machine. *SIAM J. Discret. Math.* **2000**, *13*, 56–63. [CrossRef]

Lenstra, J.K. (Centrum Wiskunde & Informatica, Science Park 123, 1098 XG Amsterdam, The Netherlands). Private communication, 2024.

Graham, R.L.; Lawler, E.L.; Lenstra, J.K.; Rinnooy Kan, A.H.G. Optimization and Approximation in Deterministic Sequencing and Scheduling: A Servey. *Ann. Discret. Math.* **1979**, *5*, 287–326.

Bratley, P.; Florian, M.; Robillard, P. On Sequencing with Earliest Start Times and Due–Dates with Application to Computing Bounds for *($n/m/G/F_{max}$)* Problem. *Nav. Res. Logist. Q.* **1973**, *20*, 57–67. [CrossRef]

Chinos, E.; Vakhania, N. Adjusting Scheduling Model with Release and due-dates in Production Planning. *Cogent Eng.* **2017**, *4*, 1321175. [CrossRef]

Garey, M.R.; Johnson. D.S. *Computers and Intractability: A Guide to the Theory of NP-Completeness*; Freeman: San Francisco, CA, USA, 1979.

Della Croce, F.; T'kindt, T. Improving the Preemptive Bound for the Single Machine Dynamic Maximum Lateness Problem. *Oper. Res. Lett.* **2010**, *38*, 589–591. [CrossRef]

Gharbi, A.; Labidi, M. Jackson's Semi-preemptive Scheduling on a single Machine. *Comput. Oper. Res.* **2010**, *37*, 2082–2088. [CrossRef]

Lazarev, A.A.; Sadykov, R.R.; Sevastyanov, S.V. A scheme of an approximate solution of the $1|r_j|L_{\max}$ problem. *Diskretn. Anal. Issled. Oper.* **2006**, *13*, 57–76. (In Russian)

Hoogeveen, J.A. Minimizing Maximum Promptness and Maximum Lateness on a Single Machine. *Math. Oper. Res.* **1995**, *21*, 100–114. [CrossRef]

Vakhania, N.; Werner, F. Scheduling a single machine with compressible jobs to minimize maximum lateness: N. Vakhania, F. Werner. *4OR-Q J. Oper. Res.* 2025, *published online*. [CrossRef]

Escalona, D.; Vakhania, N. A Study of Single-Machine Scheduling Problem with a Fixed Number of Release Times and Two Delivery Times. Working Manuscript. Bachelor's Thesis, Universidad Autónoma del Estado de Morelos, Cuernavaca, Mexico, 2024; pp. 1–49. Available online: https://riaa.uaem.mx/xmlui/bitstream/handle/20.500.12055/4772/EACDNN07.pdf?sequence=1&isAllowed=y (accessed on 29 December 2025).

Baker, K.R.; Lawler, E.L.; Lenstra, J.K.; Rinnooy Kan, A.H.G. Preemptive Scheduling of a Single Machine to Minimize Maximum Cost Subject to Release Dates and Precedence Constraints. *Oper. Res.* **1983**, *31*, 381–386. [CrossRef]

Carlier J.; Pinson, E. Jackson's Pseudo Preemptive Schedule for $Pm/r_i, q_i/C_{max}$ problem. *Ann. Oper. Res.* **1998**, *83*, 41–58. [CrossRef]

Adams J., Balas, E.; Zawack, D. The Shifting Bottleneck Procedure for Job Shop Scheduling. *Manag. Sci.* **1988**, *34*, 391–401. [CrossRef]

Pacheco-Valencia, V.H.; Vakhania, N.; Hernández-Mira, F.Á.; Hernández-Aguilar, J.A. A Multi-Phase Method for Euclidean Traveling Salesman Problems. *Axioms* **2022**, *11*, 439. [CrossRef]

https://doi.org/10.3390/a19010038

72. Chrobak, M.; Dürr, C.; Jawor, W.; Kowalik, L.; Kurowski, M. A Note on Scheduling Equal-Length Jobs to Maximize Throughp *J. Sched.* **2006**, *9*, 71–73. [CrossRef]
73. Brucker P.; Kravchenko, S. Preemption can Make Parallel Machine Scheduling Problems Hard. *Osnabrücker Schriften M Fachbereich Mathematik/Informatik, Reihe P* **1999**, *211*.
74. Gordon, V.; Potapneva, E.; Werner, F. Single Machine Scheduling with Deadlines, Release and due-dates. *Optimization* **1997** 219–244. [CrossRef]
75. Gordon, V.; Werner, F.; Yanushkevich, O.A. Single Machine Preepmptive Scheduling to Minimize the Weighted Number of Jobs with Deadlines and Nested Release/due-date Intervals. *RAIRO Oper. Res.* **2001**, *35*, 71–83. [CrossRef]
76. Du, J.; Leung, J.Y.T. Minimizing Total Tardiness on One Processor is NP-hard. *Math. Oper. Res.* **1990**, *25*, 483–495. [CrossRef]
77. Swarcz, W.; Mukhopadhyay, S. Decomposition of the Single Machine Total Tardiness Problem. *Oper. Res. Lett.* **1996**, *19*, 245– [CrossRef]
78. Emmons, H. One-Machine Sequencing to Minimize Certain Functions of Job Tardiness. *Oper. Res.* **1969**, *17*, 701–715. [Cross
79. Koulamas, C. The Total Tardiness Problem: Review and Extensions. *Oper. Res.* **1994**, *42*, 1025–1041. [CrossRef]
80. Koulamas, C. The Single-Machine Total Tardiness Scheduling Problem: Review and Extensions. *Eur. J. Oper. Res.* **2010**, *202*, [CrossRef]
81. Baptiste, P. Scheduling Equal-Length Jobs on Identical Parallel Machines. *Discret. Appl. Math.* **2000**, *103*, 21–32. [CrossRef]
82. Lazarev, A.; Werner, F. A Graphical Realization of the Dynamic Programming Method for Solving NP-Hard Combinato Problems. *Comput. Math. Appl.* **2009**, *58*, 619–631. [CrossRef]
83. Gafarov, E.; Dolgui, A.; Werner, F. A New Graphical Approach for Solving Single Machine Problems Approximately. *Int. J. P Res.* **2014**, *52*, 597–614. [CrossRef]
84. Gafarov, E.; Lazarev, A.; Werner, F. A Note on a Single Machine Scheduling with Generalized Total Tardiness Objective Funct *Inf. Process. Lett.* **2012**, *112*, 72–76. [CrossRef]
85. Lazarev, A.; Werner, F. Algorithms for Special Cases of the Single Machine Total Tardiness Problem and an Application to Even-Odd Partition Problem. *Math. Comput. Model.* **2009**, *49*, 2061–2072. [CrossRef]
86. Chrobak, M.; Epstein, L.; Noga, J.; Sgall, J.; van Stee, R.; Tichý, T.; Vakhania, N. Preemptive Scheduling in Overloaded System *Comput. Syst. Sci.* **2003**, *67*, 183–197. [CrossRef]
87. van den Akker, M.; Hoogeveen, J.; Vakhania, N. Restarts can Help in On-line Minimization of the Maximum Delivery Time Single Machine. *J. Sched.* **2000**, *3*, 333–341. [CrossRef]
88. Gafarov, E.; Lazarev, A.; Werner, F. Single Machine Scheduling Problems with Financial Resource Constraints: Some Comple ResultResults and Properties. *Math. Soc. Sci.* **2011**, *62*, 7–13. [CrossRef]

https://doi.org/10.3390/a1901(

algorithms

MDPI

:le

›efulness of Wearable Devices for Monitoring Motor Activity Patients with Early Myocardial Infarction

ola Boccuto [1], Ugo Lomoio [1], Salvatore De Rosa [1], Daniele Torella [2], Pierangelo Veltri [3] Pietro Hiram Guzzi [1,*]

1 Department of Surgical and Medical Sciences, University of Catanzaro, 88100 Catanzaro, Italy
2 Department of Experimental and Clinical Medicine, University of Catanzaro, 88100 Catanzaro, Italy
3 Departiment of Informatics Modelling and Systems, University of Calabria, 87036 Rende, Italy
* Correspondence: hguzzi@unicz.it

Abstract

The rising incidence of myocardial infarction (MI) in individuals under 50 years of age underscores an urgent need for innovative rehabilitation strategies that extend beyond hospital care, empowering young patients to reclaim active lives through sustained physical activity and remote monitoring. Wearable health technologies hold transformative potential here, as studies demonstrate their ability to boost exercise capacity daily steps while reducing rehospitalizations in post-MI recovery. This study thus assesses the clinical value of wearable devices in remotely tracking motor activity among young adults during early MI rehabilitation. Using the SiDLY Care Pro wristband, continuous non-invasive measurements of heart rate, oxygen saturation, and physical activity were collected from 62 of 80 post-MI patients (<50 years) over seven days, alongside validated questionnaires (IPAQ, SF-36, DASS-21). Time-series clustering and principal component analysis characterized heart rate dynamics and activity patterns. Most participants showed sedentary behavior (2000–4000 steps/day), though self-reported health and psychological well-being were satisfactory. The device provided reliable, clinically meaningful data, particularly when linked to clinician feedback. Participants expressed an interest in using such technologies, especially if supported through reimbursement and professional guidance. Despite limitations—short monitoring timelines, small heterogeneous samples, and accuracy constraints—the findings suggest that wearable systems can enhance remote monitoring, patient engagement, and early intervention in post-MI care. Broader studies and supportive policies are recommended. Overall, integrating wearable technologies with professional oversight and patient participation may substantially improve recovery and outcomes for young MI survivors

Keywords: wearable devices; AMI; questionnaires

1. Introduction

Acute myocardial infarction (AMI) in adults younger than 45 years is an increasingly recognized entity with distinct epidemiological and clinical features, driven by a complex interplay of traditional factors (smoking, dyslipidemia, obesity, insulin resistance) and non-traditional determinants such as chronic inflammation, psychosocial stress, sleep disorders, recreational drug use, and genetic susceptibility. This trend affects individuals in their most productive decades and is associated with substantial long-term risks of recurrent ischemia, arrhythmias, adverse remodeling, and impaired quality of life, which are only partially captured via traditional, episodic clinic-based follow-up [1–3].

Digital health technologies offer new opportunities to address these gaps through the continuous remote monitoring of physiological and behavioral parameters. Contemporary wearable systems integrate photoplethysmography, accelerometry, and oximetry to derive heart rate, activity, sleep, and surrogate measures of autonomic function, enabling a high–temporal resolution assessment of post-AMI recovery in real-world settings. In parallel, advances in bio-integrated flexible electronics—such as conformal hemodynamic patches, electrospun polymeric fibers, and flexible graphene-based transducers—are pushing the frontier toward skin-like, mechanically compliant devices capable of the real-time monitoring of blood pressure, flow, and bioelectrical or biochemical signals for cardiovascular healthcare. Together with artificial intelligence algorithms, these technologies support precision cardiology paradigms that couple multi-parametric sensing with personalized risk stratification and dynamic therapy adjustment [4,5].

Within this evolving landscape, medical-grade wearable devices like the SiDLY Care Pro occupy a pragmatic position between research-grade flexible bioelectronics and routine clinical practice. The SiDLY system provides the validated, non-invasive monitoring of heart rate, oxygen saturation, and physical activity through a wrist-worn multisensor platform, complemented with fall detection, SOS alerting, geolocation, and encrypted cloud-based telemonitoring. Unlike emerging bio-integrated flexible electronics, which prioritize intimate skin conformity and advanced hemodynamic or biochemical sensing, SiDLY emphasizes usability, regulatory compliance, and integration into telemedicine workflows, making it suitable for heterogeneous young AMI populations with variable digital literacy and lifestyles [5–7].

The present study, as summarised in Table 1, enhances existing knowledge by (i) implementing SiDLY-enabled continuous monitoring among young AMI survivors within real-world clinical pathways, (ii) combining objective biosignals with validated patient-reported outcome measures (IPAQ, DASS-21, SF-36) to obtain a multidimensional view of physical, psychological, and behavioral recovery, and (iii) positioning this clinically deployable wearable within the broader context of bio-integrated flexible electronics, highlighting how scalable telemonitoring today can complement and prepare the ground for the future integration of more sophisticated flexible platforms in cardiovascular secondary prevention. While prior studies and meta-analyses show that wearable-supported cardiac rehabilitation increases daily steps, improves exercise capacity, and reduces rehospitalizations in broad coronary artery disease populations [8–10], evidence remains scarce for young AMI survivors under 50 years of age, who display distinct recovery trajectories and a non-negligible burden of recurrent events despite milder angiographic disease and lower short-term mortality compared with older patients [11–13].

Table 1. Statement of significance.

Section	Summary
Problem or Issue	Early myocardial infarction (MI) in adults under 50 is rising, yet post-discharge monitoring remains limited. Traditional follow-up often fails to capture day-to-day physiological fluctuations and physical inactivity, both of which are critical predictors of recovery and recurrent events.
What is Already Known	Wearable devices can monitor heart rate, oxygen saturation, and activity levels, and telemedicine improves follow-up and adherence. However, evidence specific to young MI survivors—regarding real-world usability, clinical relevance, and patient acceptance—is scarce, and existing studies rarely integrate objective biosignals with patient-reported outcomes.

https://doi.org/10.3390/a1902

Table 1. *Cont.*

Section	Summary
What this Paper Adds	This study provides a multidimensional, real-world evaluation of a certified medical wearable for early MI survivors. It combines time-series analytics, clinical metrics, and usability data, showing that continuous monitoring is feasible, clinically meaningful, and strongly accepted by patients when clinician feedback is integrated.
Who Would Benefit	Clinicians, digital-health researchers, policymakers, and rehabilitation specialists seeking evidence for implementing remote monitoring in young post-MI populations.

2. Materials and Methods

The remote monitoring of patients with early myocardial infarction using wearable devices represents a progressive trend in healthcare, reflecting the increased integration of wearable technologies for continuous, real-time health assessment. This approach is particularly relevant in an era where telemedicine and remote patient management are pivotal for chronic disease care and the risk mitigation of acute cardiac events. Wearable devices enable continuous data collection, optimizing patient management and reducing the risk of post-infarction complications. The present work aligns with the evolving landscape of personalized medicine, where technology-driven solutions enhance both treatment effectiveness and patient engagement.

This study specifically targets a younger cohort with early myocardial infarction—an important choice, given their extended post-event life expectancy and heightened risk for developing long-term complications. Personalized monitoring in this group, addressing both physiological and psychological aspects, is critical for proactive management and improved long-term outcomes. The primary aim of this study was to evaluate the utility of wearable devices for the remote monitoring of motor activity in patients following early myocardial infarction.

2.1. Inclusion Criteria

Patients were randomly selected from a large institutional database comprising approximately 800 individuals who had experienced an acute myocardial infarction (AMI) before the age of 50. This registry includes patients with confirmed ST-elevation myocardial infarction (STEMI) and non–ST-elevation myocardial infarction (NSTEMI), documented according to current ESC and ACC/AHA diagnostic criteria, integrating biochemical, electrocardiographic, and imaging-based evidence. For the purposes of this study, stringent inclusion criteria were applied to ensure the homogeneity of the analytical cohort and relevance to the research objectives. Eligible participants met the following conditions:

- Age at the time of the AMI index of less than 50 years, ensuring that the sample reflects the population with premature myocardial infarction.
- A minimum of 12 months elapsed since the index event, permitting the stabilization of acute-phase physiological alterations and enabling a reliable assessment of long-term recovery patterns.
- Evidence of myocardial infarction documented through troponin elevation, ischemic symptoms, and compatible ECG or imaging findings.
- Clinical stability at the time of enrollment, defined as the absence of acute coronary syndromes, decompensated heart failure, or significant arrhythmias in the preceding 3 months.
- An ability to provide informed consent and a willingness to participate in remote monitoring through wearable technology.

https://doi.org/10.3390/a19020137

From the total eligible pool, 80 participants were randomly selected, following a stratified approach to balance sex distribution, index MI type, and treatment modality (PCI vs. conservative). Among these, 62 individuals were equipped with a Sidly Care Pro, Sidly, Poland wearable device, which enabled the continuous monitoring of physiological and behavioral parameters relevant to post-AMI recovery. A schematic representation of the recruitment process and allocation strategy is provided in Figure 1.

Figure 1 ensured a representative, clinically stable, and methodologically coherent sample suitable for downstream analyses involving biosignal acquisition, behavioral profiling, and patient-reported outcomes.

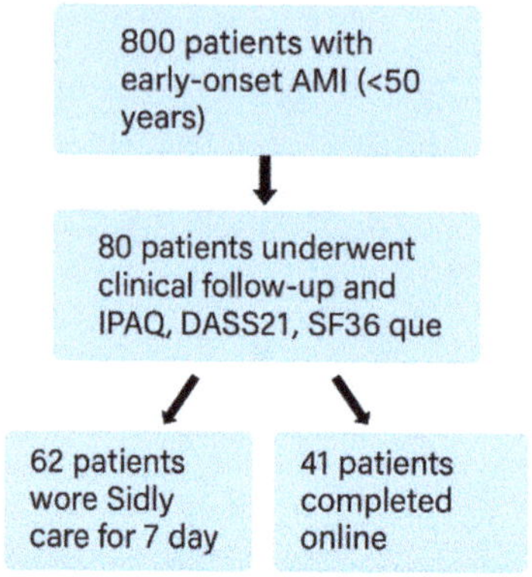

Figure 1. Study cohort and data collection workflow. Flow diagram illustrating patient selection and data acquisition. From an initial cohort of 800 individuals with early-onset acute myocardial infarction (AMI; age < 50 years), 80 participants underwent clinical follow-up and completed standardized questionnaires (IPAQ, DASS21, and SF-36). Among these, 62 patients wore the Sidly Care device for 7 consecutive days, while 41 participants completed the online questionnaire only.

The cohort's male predominance reflects the study's deliberate focus on early-onset AMI in young males, for whom preliminary data from regional registries and prior AI-ECG analyses demonstrate a markedly higher incidence compared to females, often linked to aggressive atherosclerosis and autonomic imbalances.

2.2. Clinical and Instrumental Evaluation

After written informed consent was obtained in accordance with the Declaration of Helsinki and institutional ethical board approval, all enrolled patients underwent a comprehensive and standardized clinical assessment. This multidimensional evaluation was designed to capture cardiovascular status, the comorbidity burden, pharmacological regimens, and potential opportunities for therapeutic optimization. A detailed medical history was collected, including the following: 1. Demographic information and cardiovascular risk profile; 2. Characteristics of the index AMI (STEMI/NSTEMI, culprit vessel, revascularization strategy, complications); 3. Comorbidities such as hypertension, diabetes mellitus, dyslipidemia, chronic kidney disease, and obstructive sleep apnea; 4. Family history of premature coronary artery disease; 5. Lifestyle factors (smoking, alcohol intake, physical activity habits); 6. Pharmacological therapies, with an assessment of adherence and potential drug–drug interactions. A comprehensive physical examination was performed, evaluating vital signs, cardiovascular auscultation, evidence of heart failure (NYHA class, peripheral edema, jugular venous pressure), and anthropometric parameters (weight, BMI, waist circumference). Each participant underwent a standard 12-lead electrocardiogram,

 https://doi.org/10.3390/a1902(

analyzed for residual ischemic changes, Q-waves, conduction abnormalities, ventricular hypertrophy, and arrhythmic patterns. An additional non-invasive hemodynamic evaluation included heart rate, blood pressure measurement following ESC guidelines, and an assessment of autonomic tone through resting heart rate variability when feasible. Venous blood samples were collected in the fasting state to obtain the following: 1. Lipid profile (total cholesterol, LDL-C, HDL-C, triglycerides); 2. Glycemic parameters (fasting glucose, HbA1c); 3. Renal and hepatic function tests; 4. Inflammatory markers when indicated (hs-CRP); 5. Cardiac biomarkers if clinically appropriate. Laboratory results were used to guide therapeutic optimization, with tailored adjustments in lipid-lowering agents, antihypertensives, glucose-lowering medications, or antiplatelet therapy where necessary.

2.3. Tele-Monitoring System Application

At the conclusion of the clinical visit, patients were provided with instructions and fitted with the Sidly wearable device for a seven-day monitoring period. The device records electrical signals from cardiac contractions, converting them into digital heart rate (bpm) readouts. The selection criteria ensured the exclusion of confounding factors such as pre-existing cardiac disease, pharmacological interventions, or lifestyle modifiers (e.g., smoking, caffeine, recent vigorous exercise). Participants received comprehensive instructions to avoid strenuous activity, caffeine, or food intake at least two hours prior to measurement.

The Sidly device was worn on the non-dominant wrist, ensuring good electrode–skin contact and minimal motion artifacts. Device placement and baseline signal stability were verified by trained personnel before the measurement period was started.

This device facilitates remote health monitoring via an online platform directly connected to a Telecenter, enabling real-time health status surveillance and individualized safety thresholds for vital sign alerts. The parameters monitored included heart rate, oxygen saturation, step count, positional changes (syncope risk), and medication timing. All sensors were calibrated prior to the experimental phase to ensure cross-device fidelity.

2.4. Online Questionnaire

After completing seven days of telemonitoring, patients completed an online questionnaire with three sections. The first collected demographic data (age range, gender, educational attainment). The second section assessed computer literacy, including skills in email use, online transactions, information retrieval, social media, and video conferencing. The third section evaluated attitudes toward telemonitoring (e.g., preference for integration with a smartwatch/phone, desire for manual vs. automated updates, the importance of data access, and preferences for direct or clinician-mediated feedback).

2.5. IPAQ

Participants completed the International Physical Activity Questionnaire (IPAQ) to assess physical activity over the preceding week. The IPAQ quantifies time spent in vigorous, moderate, and walking activities, as well as sedentary behavior, considering only activities of at least a 10 min duration.

2.6. SF36

The Short Form Health Survey 36 (SF-36) questionnaire was administered to quantify patient health status and quality of life. The SF-36 measures eight health domains using 36 items, with responses scored on Likert scales. The final item assesses perceived health changes over the past year.

https://doi.org/10.3390/a19020137

2.7. DASS21

To evaluate psychological status, the 21-item Depression, Anxiety, and Stress Scale (DASS-21) was used, assessing symptoms with seven items for each domain.

2.8. Heart Rate Data Analysis

Heart rate data were acquired automatically every 15 min via the Sidly device and stored securely. Data were collected in three time windows: long (24 readings/6 h), medium (12 readings/3 h), and short (6 readings/1.5 h), capturing both acute and circadian variations. After transfer to the secure server, data underwent the following:

- Artifact removal for sensor loss, motion, and extreme values (<40 or >180 bpm);
- Normalization by z-score for interindividual comparison;
- Segmentation into time windows;
- Imputation of isolated missing data via linear interpolation (up to 2 consecutive samples).

Manual and automated annotations defined periods of rest, tachycardia, or bradycardia.

2.9. Dynamic Time Warping Barycenter Averaging (DBA)

The Dynamic Time Warping Barycenter Averaging (DBA) algorithm was applied to compute average heart rate patterns from time series of variable length/alignment. Series within each group were aligned and averaged using DTW, iteratively updated until convergence, to obtain a barycentric profile representative of the group.

2.10. Computational Workflow

The analysis comprised three main stages:

1. Clustering based on DTW distance to group time series by similarity.
2. DBA computation within each cluster to create barycentric patterns.
3. Cluster and barycenter validation by silhouette score, variance, and visual assessment (including PCA-based projection for pattern visualization).

PCA projections facilitated a visualization of cluster separability and pattern structure. These analyses identified diverse dynamic profiles such as rest–tachycardia–rest and sustained tachycardia.

2.11. Statistical Analysis

Group differences were assessed with Chi-squared, ANOVA, or *t*-tests, using Bonferroni correction for multiple comparisons. The variance in barycenter patterns and group membership was related to physiological and subjective variables, providing context for the time-series findings.

3. Results

3.1. Results of the Online Questionnaire

Given the paramount importance of patient confidence in the use of Sidly remote monitoring devices, we developed an online questionnaire to evaluate satisfaction and perceived security associated with device wear. Robust engagement with device features is essential not only for facilitating the timely detection of health deterioration in home settings but also for ensuring effective communication with remote clinical teams.

The cohort predominantly comprised individuals aged 41–50 years (56.1%), males (85.4%), and those with a middle school education (39%). Digital literacy varied: 36.6% demonstrated excellent competency in email communications, with substantial proficiency in online news reading (43.9%) and moderate abilities in banking apps (31.7%), recreational

https://doi.org/10.3390/a1902

gaming (26.8%), television applications (36.6%), video calling/conferencing (31.7%), social media (36.6%), and messaging systems (36.6%).

Nearly half the respondents (48.8%) regarded remote monitoring as essential for both personal health and broader healthcare-system efficacy. Preferences were pronounced for smartwatch-connected systems (73.2%) and those featuring automatic updates (87.8%). A majority favored direct connectivity with specialist telehealth teams (68.3%) and full reimbursement via the national health system (90.2%). The value of the continuous home monitoring of vital parameters was underscored by 61%, with over half desiring health feedback directly from the device (53.7%; Figures 2 and 3) and a clear preference for clinician-generated feedback over AI-based analysis (90.2%).

The distribution of responses to the questionnaire was highly skewed toward the maximum score (Figure 2), with 61% of participants selecting 10 and very few responses below 8. A chi-square goodness-of-fit test was performed to evaluate whether the observed frequencies across the 10 response categories (1–10) were compatible with a uniform distribution under the null hypothesis of no preference. Using the observed counts (0, 0, 0, 0, 1, 2, 1, 5, 7, 25) and an expected count of 4.1 for each category (total $n = 41$), the test yielded $\chi^2 \approx 163.5$ with 9 degrees of freedom (df = 10−1), corresponding to a p-value $p \ll 0.001$, which indicates a statistically significant departure from uniformity and confirms that the responses were overwhelmingly concentrated at the upper end of the scale.

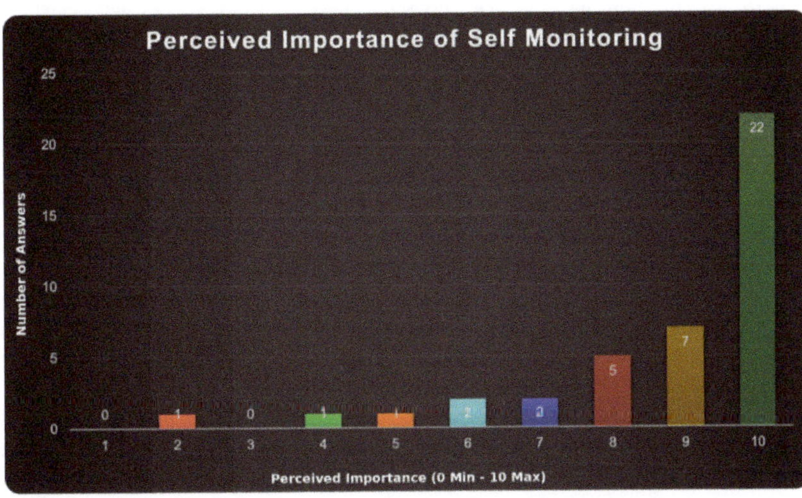

Figure 2. Results concerning self-monitoring importance. The perceived importance of self-monitoring among study participants. The histogram shows that responses are heavily skewed toward the upper end of the 1–10 scale, with the majority of patients assigning ratings of 8–10 and more than half selecting the maximum score, indicating that a high fraction of participants perceive self-monitoring as very important for their care.

For Figure 3, the distribution of responses to this questionnaire item was again markedly skewed toward the highest score, with 53.7% of participants selecting 10 and only a few responses in the lower range. Using the observed counts across the 10 response categories (1–10), namely (0, 1, 0, 1, 1, 2, 2, 5, 7, 22) for a total of $n = 41$ respondents, we tested the null hypothesis of a uniform distribution of answers by applying a chi-square goodness-of-fit test, with an expected frequency of 4.1 per category. The resulting statistic was $\chi^2 \approx 94.9$ with 9 degrees of freedom, corresponding to a p-value $p \ll 0.001$, indicating

https://doi.org/10.3390/a19020137

a highly significant deviation from uniformity and confirming that responses were strongly concentrated at the upper end of the scale.

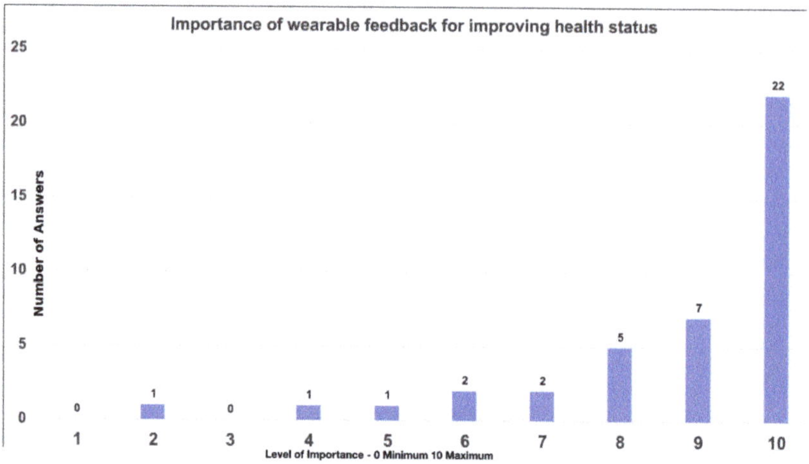

Figure 3. Importance of wearable feedback for improving health status. Perceived importance of device feedback for improving health status. Most respondents rated feedback as highly important (scores 8–10), with a clear peak at 10, while low ratings (1–5) were almost absent, indicating a strong endorsement of feedback functionalities.

3.2. Results of the IPAQ Questionnaire

Patient responses were analyzed to determine the time spent on physical activities during the past seven days. The initial section of the survey addressed occupational activity, revealing that, while most participants were employed outside the home, the predominant group engaged neither in vigorous nor moderate work-related physical activity, with walking during work hours typically lasting less than ten minutes.

An assessment of commuting patterns showed that, over the preceding week, the majority relied on cars for daily travel, averaging approximately two hours per day in the vehicle. Active modalities such as cycling and walking were uncommon; most participants reported no use of bicycles and limited walking for their journeys.

Regarding domestic activity, patients performed minimal physical tasks in or around the home, including chores, gardening, repairs, and family care. The largest subgroup did not undertake vigorous activities (such as heavy lifting, chopping wood, or shoveling snow) or moderate activities (such as light lifting, cleaning windows, or polishing) in the prior week.

Recreational and leisure activity levels were similarly low: most patients did not walk for at least ten minutes or participate in vigorous or moderate exercise or sport during their free time within the last seven days.

The final section of the questionnaire focused on sedentary behavior, capturing time spent seated at work, home, during training courses, or during leisure activities (such as desk work, reading, socializing, or watching television). On both weekdays and weekends, most participants spent approximately two hours each day in sedentary positions.

Demographic profiling identified the largest groups as unemployed, predominantly male, and chiefly holding a middle school diploma.

https://doi.org/10.3390/a1902(

3.3. Results of the SF36 Questionnaire

The majority of patients considered their health to be good and described their health as about the same as the previous year. The largest portion considered themselves partially limited in performing demanding activities like running, lifting heavy objects, or engaging in strenuous sports. In contrast, they did not consider themselves limited in activities requiring moderate physical effort (like carrying grocery bags, climbing one floor of stairs), bending or kneeling, walking one kilometer, 100 m, or a few hundred meters, taking a bath, or dressing themselves. However, a perception of partial limitation in climbing a few flights of stairs emerged. In the last 4 weeks, due to physical health, the majority of patients did not reduce the time spent at work, did not perform less than they would have liked, and did not perceive greater difficulty in doing their work or other activities but had to limit some types of work. The predominant group did not reduce their time at work due to emotional health but did perform less due to it, feeling a drop in concentration. In contrast, their physical and emotional health did not interfere with normal social activities with family and friends. The perception of physical pain was mild and did not interfere with their usual work. Over part of the time in the last 4 weeks, the largest number of patients felt "lively and bright," "very agitated," "calm and serene," "full of energy," "discouraged and sad", almost never down or without energy, tired for a long time, and equally divided between "almost always" happy and happy "some of the time".

The majority believed their health and emotional state hardly interfered with social activities and also stated that they enjoyed excellent health. The patients examined did not have a clear perception of being more likely to get sick than others, nor could they say whether their health was the same as others' or whether there was a possibility of worsening.

3.4. Results of the DASS21 Questionnaire

The DASS21 questionnaire required patients to self-assess symptom frequency over the preceding week, rating each item from zero (never) to three (very often). Most respondents reported rarely experiencing difficulty relaxing and equally infrequent complaints of dry mouth. The largest proportion indicated never feeling unable to experience positive emotions, nor did they report difficulties with breathing (such as an increased respiratory rate or dyspnea at rest) or initiating activities.

Excessive reactions to specific situations were uncommon, with responses divided between "never" and "sometimes." Tremors, significant nervousness, panic episodes, or overwhelming feelings of inadequacy were also notably absent among most patients.

Virtually no participants endorsed hopelessness about the future, while symptoms of stress and difficulty relaxing were rare. The prevailing majority did not report depression, persistent discouragement, intolerance of obstacles, feelings related to imminent panic, a widespread lack of enthusiasm, or worthlessness.

Feelings of irritability were infrequent, and very few patients noted palpitations or tachycardic sensations in the absence of physical exertion. Nearly all respondents ruled out unprovoked fear or a sense that life was meaningless.

3.5. Results Regarding the Application of the Sidly Telemonitoring System

One of the major applications of artificial intelligence is certainly in the field of telemedicine and "smart-home technologies." Thanks to remote patient monitoring and management platforms, it is possible to personalize treatment planning, define the correct medication dosage, and identify patients at risk of adverse events, anticipating potential readmissions. The concept of the "Internet of Things" (IoT) is also increasingly developed: it is based on the use of various electronic devices with embedded sensors in everyday

https://doi.org/10.3390/a19020137

objects, which are then associated with online platforms. The sensor records specific data related to the patient's health status and transmits them to the remote device via specific connectors. By leveraging IoT, medical staff can monitor numerous vital parameters, recognizing early signs of potential health deterioration. The device chosen for our study was the Sidly watch, with the goal of assessing the usefulness of wearable devices in monitoring motor activity among patients with early myocardial infarction. We examined a total of 80 patients, randomly selected from a database of patients with early myocardial infarction. All patients underwent a follow-up visit, but only 66 agreed to use the device for 7 days. The device enables the remote monitoring of heart rate, oxygen saturation, and the number of steps taken each day; it also signals sudden position changes that may indicate syncopal episodes, as well as the exact time to take medication. The maximum and minimum frequency is depicted in Figure 4. The measured heart rate is depicted in Figure 5. The average total number of steps over 24 h was between 2000 and 4000 steps, the daytime steps were between 1200 and 2500, and the total steps in a week were between 10,000 and 20,000 (Figure 6). The average oxygen saturation was consistently around 99%, with minimum values between 70 percent and 78.

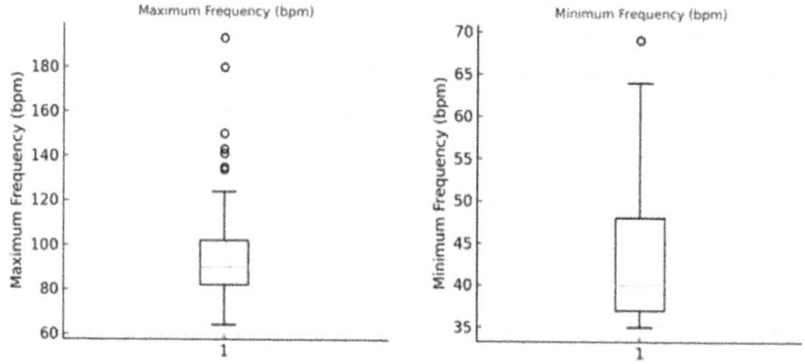

Figure 4. The left panel illustrates the distribution of maximum frequencies, featuring a median of around 110 bpm, an interquartile range from approximately 100 to 120 bpm, and an outlier near 180 bpm. The right panel shows minimum frequencies with a median near 50 bpm, an interquartile range from 45 to 55 bpm, and an outlier approaching 65 bpm; **62 patients wore the Sidly Care device for 7 consecutive days, all the subjects were included in the analysis, and the box plot represents all the subjects.**

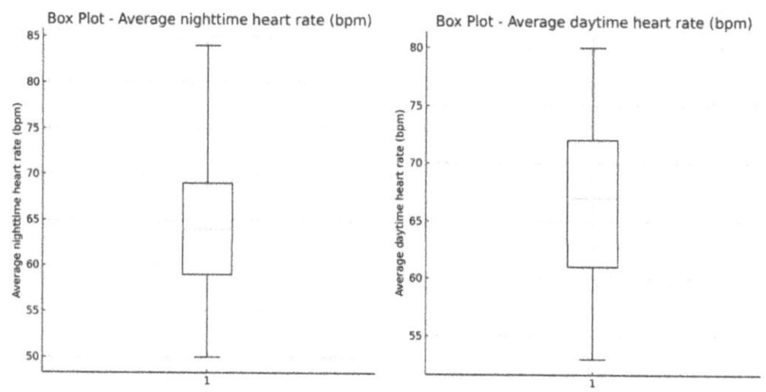

Figure 5. Box plots of average nighttime (left) and daytime (right) heart rates (bpm): the nighttime median is around 66 bpm with a range of 50–85 bpm; the daytime median is around 68 bpm with a range of 55–80 bpm; and 62 patients wore the Sidly Care device for 7 consecutive days, all the subjects were included in the analysis, and the box plot represents all the subjects.

https://doi.org/10.3390/a1902

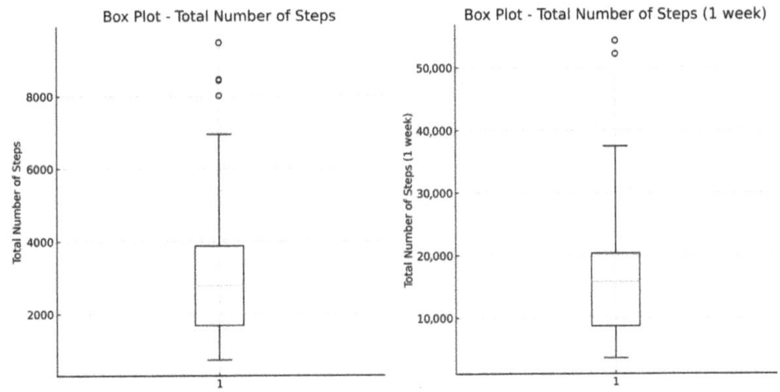

Figure 6. Box plots of total number of steps (left) and total steps over 1 week (right): the daily steps show a median of around 4500 with an IQR of 3500–5500 and outliers of up to 8000; weekly totals showed a median of near 28,000 with an of IQR 22,000–35,000 and outliers of up to 50,000; 62 patients wore the Sidly Care device for 7 consecutive days, all the subjects were included in the analysis, and the box plot represents all the subjects.

3.6. Results on Time-Series Clustering

This section reports the results of the heart rate analysis performed using a multi-scale window extraction strategy. By partitioning the raw heart rate time series into short-, medium-, and long-range windows, we capture variability and structural patterns across distinct temporal resolutions. This approach enables a robust characterization of heart rate dynamics, simultaneously accounting for rapid fluctuations and longer-term trends while mitigating the impact of missing values through interpolation.

Figure 7 presents representative heart rate patterns identified at each temporal scale.

Short-range windows emphasize rapid variability and transient dynamics across clusters, reflecting the system's sensitivity to brief physiological events or artifacts. Each window comprises up to six measurements, with no missing values permitted, and clustering yields 13 DBA *k*-means prototypes. Several clusters are strongly associated with tachycardic activity. In particular, Cluster 10 captures transitions from resting states to tachycardia, characterized by a pronounced rise in heart rate marking the onset of activity. Cluster 7 uniquely represents recovery dynamics, with heart rate declining from tachycardic levels back to rest. Cluster 5 corresponds to prolonged and severe tachycardia, with sustained heart rates exceeding 120 bpm for extended periods, in some cases lasting up to two hours. Conversely, Clusters 11 and 6 are predominantly linked to bradycardic or sleep-related patterns, exhibiting lower and more stable heart rate values indicative of reduced physiological demand. Together, these results demonstrate the ability of short-range clustering to disentangle physiologically meaningful states within long-term heart rate recordings.

Medium-range windows capture intermediate temporal structures, providing insight into ongoing physiological fluctuations and moderate trends that are not discernible at shorter scales. Each window includes up to 12 measurements, allowing for up to one missing value imputed via interpolation. Clustering at this scale yields six representative patterns, reflecting sustained yet dynamic heart rate behavior over intermediate durations.

https://doi.org/10.3390/a19020137

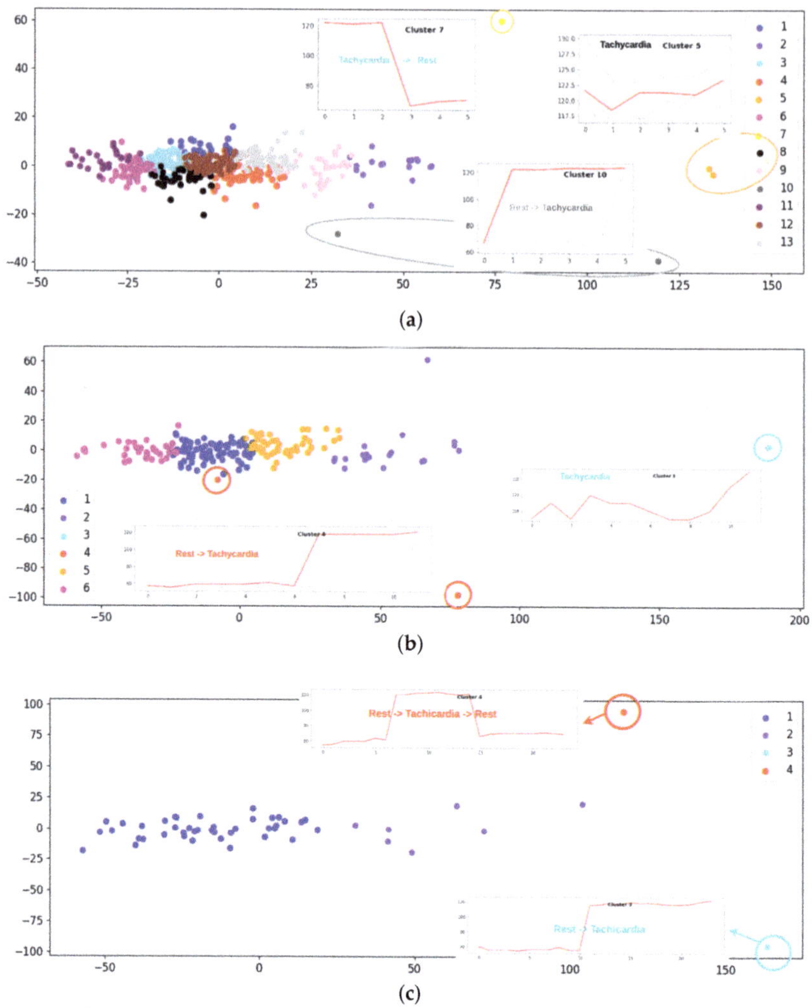

Figure 7. Scatter plots illustrating clusters of heart rate patterns obtained after dimensionality reduction with PCA and unsupervised clustering using DBA *k*-means. The optimal number of clusters in each analysis was selected using the Elbow method. Each point represents a heart rate segment derived from raw ECG recordings and is color-coded according to the cluster assignment. Clusters with a low number of observations correspond to distinctive or atypical physiological patterns, such as episodes of marked tachycardia or abrupt changes in heart rate (e.g., transitions from resting conditions to tachycardia); for these low-populated clusters, the corresponding raw ECG traces are shown alongside the scatter plots to support clinical interpretation. Subfigure (**a**) depicts short-term heart rate patterns derived from short-duration windows, capturing rapid beat-to-beat variability and transient dynamics, resulting in 13 clusters; subfigure (**b**) shows intermediate-term heart rate patterns obtained from medium-duration windows, highlighting short-to-intermediate trends and fluctuations, with 6 clusters identified; subfigure (**c**) presents long-term heart rate patterns derived from long-duration windows, emphasizing broader and more stable heart rate behaviors that may correspond to sustained physiological or clinical states, resulting in 4 clusters. Heart rate segments are extracted from windows containing up to 6, 12, and 24 consecutive measurements for short-, intermediate-, and long-term analyses, respectively, allowing a maximum of 0, 1, and 2 missing measurements per segment, which are imputed through interpolation when present.

https://doi.org/10.3390/a1902(

Long-range windows reveal broad temporal dynamics and support the identification of persistent shifts or gradual modulations in heart rate. These windows comprise up to 24 measurements, with up to two missing values interpolated, and produce four distinct clusters. Clusters 3 and 4 represent outlier patterns: one describes a complete cycle from rest to tachycardia and back to rest, while the other captures a unidirectional transition from rest to tachycardia. In contrast, Clusters 1 and 2 differ primarily in their mean heart rate levels, with Cluster 1 centered around approximately 60 bpm and Cluster 2 around 75 bpm.

Overall, clustering across multiple temporal scales enables a nuanced analysis of heart rate dynamics, facilitating the discrimination between brief, intermediate, and persistent physiological changes. This multi-scale perspective provides a powerful framework for the physiological interpretation and clinically meaningful segmentation of long-term heart rate data.

To further assess the robustness of the proposed clustering framework across heterogeneous physiological signals, we extended the analysis to multiple data modalities, including pedometer-derived activity counts, oxygen saturation (SpO_2) levels, and heart rate measurements. This multi-sensor perspective enables the identification of complementary behavioral and physiological patterns, providing integrated insight into daily activity profiles, cardiorespiratory status, and transitions between functional states.

Figure 8 summarizes the clustering outcomes for each modality, highlighting characteristic groupings and temporal transitions reflected in step activity, oxygen saturation dynamics, and heart rate variability. For consistency across signals, medium-range windows were adopted, and the number of clusters was fixed at six. Within this setting, we systematically compared three variants of time-series k-means—Euclidean k-means, soft-DTW k-means, and DBA k-means—by varying the underlying distance metric while holding all other parameters constant. This design allowed us to evaluate the impact of shape-based versus alignment-aware similarity measures on clustering performance in physiological time series.

Following this comparative analysis, DBA k-means was selected as the primary clustering strategy for subsequent experiments. This choice reflects DBA's ability to capture temporal dynamics through the computation of barycenters under the dynamic time warping (DTW) metric, thereby accommodating temporal shifts and non-linear distortions commonly observed in physiological signals. In contrast to Euclidean-based k-means, DBA k-means yields clusters that are more temporally coherent and physiologically interpretable, making it particularly well suited for multi-modal time-series analysis.

Finally, Figure 9 presents an in-depth analysis of long-range heart rate patterns, revealing sustained temporal dynamics that extend across extended time intervals. By examining these patterns, we capture slow physiological modulations and trends that are often overlooked in short or medium-term analyses. This comprehensive long-range perspective enables the identification of persistent states such as prolonged tachycardia, bradycardia, or recovery phases, which have critical implications for understanding autonomic regulation and cardiovascular health. Through the clustering of these extended windows, distinct phenotypic behaviors emerge, highlighting the significance of the temporal scale in heart rate variability analysis and its potential clinical applications. This approach facilitates an improved characterization of chronic conditions and dynamic physiological responses over hours or longer periods.

https://doi.org/10.3390/a19020137

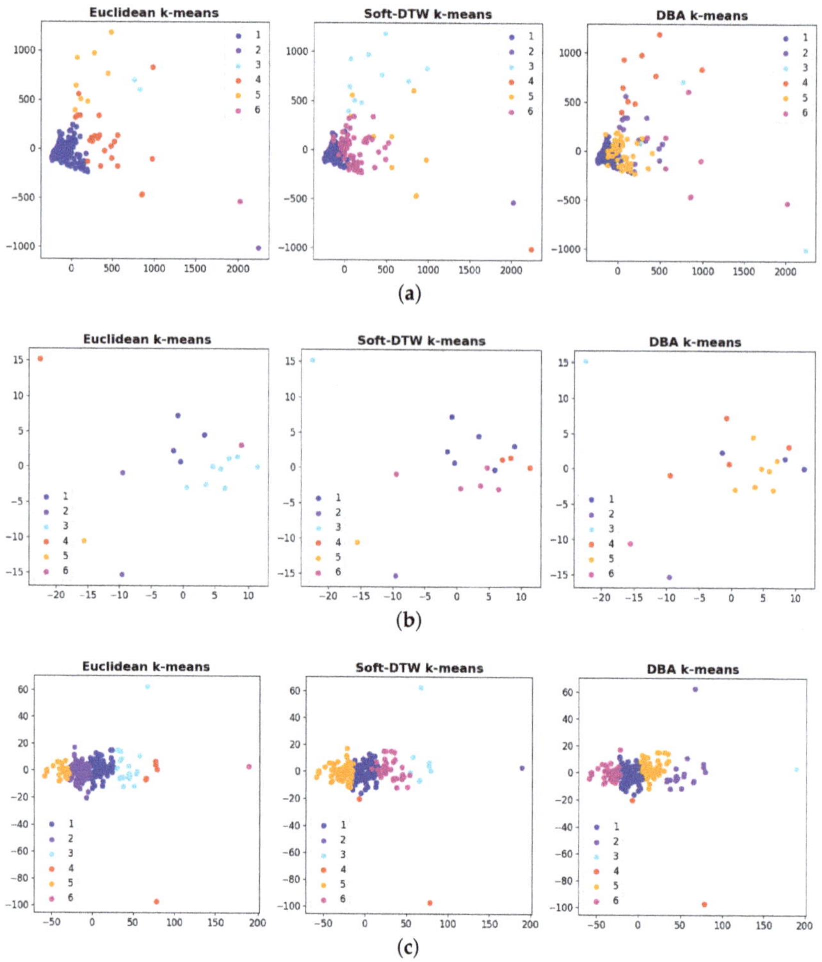

Figure 8. Comparison of clustering outcomes across three types of physiological measurements, employing medium-range segmentation (12-sample windows). **Axes represent the first two principal components obtained from PCA, capturing the dominant modes of variability in the extracted heart rate features. The X-axis is Principal Component 1 (dominant heart rate pattern), while Y is Principal Component 2** . The analysis was conducted using three distinct clustering algorithms, each applied with an identical number of clusters of 6: (**a**) Pedometer data clustered with Euclidean k-means, soft-DTW k-means, and DBA k-means, showing distinct activity distribution patterns. (**b**) Oxygen saturation measurements clustered with the same three methods. (**c**) Heart rate data clustered using Euclidean k-means, soft-DTW k-means, and DBA k-means, emphasizing the increased compactness and separation of temporal patterns achieved via DBA k-means compared with the Euclidean and soft-DTW variants.

Beyond descriptive visualization, the clustering results provide quantitative and qualitative evidence that wearable-derived heart rate data contain structured and clinically interpretable temporal patterns. Across all temporal scales, clusters were not arbitrarily distributed but consistently organized around physiologically meaningful regimes, including resting states, activity-induced tachycardia, recovery phases, and sustained autonomic activation. The recurrence of these patterns across individuals and window lengths supports the internal consistency of the analytical framework and indicates that

 https://doi.org/10.3390/a1902

the extracted clusters reflect underlying cardiac dynamics, rather than noise or random variability. Notably, the identification of low-populated clusters capturing extreme or transitional heart rate behaviors demonstrates the sensitivity of the approach to atypical yet clinically relevant events that would likely be missed through conventional averaging or threshold-based monitoring. Importantly, the clustering framework aims not to diagnose pathological conditions but to characterize recovery-related physiological variability in a post-myocardial infarction population. The results show that continuous wearable monitoring, when combined with time-series analysis, can stratify patients according to dynamic heart rate behaviors over daily life. This stratification provides a richer representation of post-infarction physiology than isolated summary metrics such as the mean heart rate or the total step count, thereby supporting the conclusion that wearable devices can yield clinically meaningful information when interpreted through appropriate analytical models.

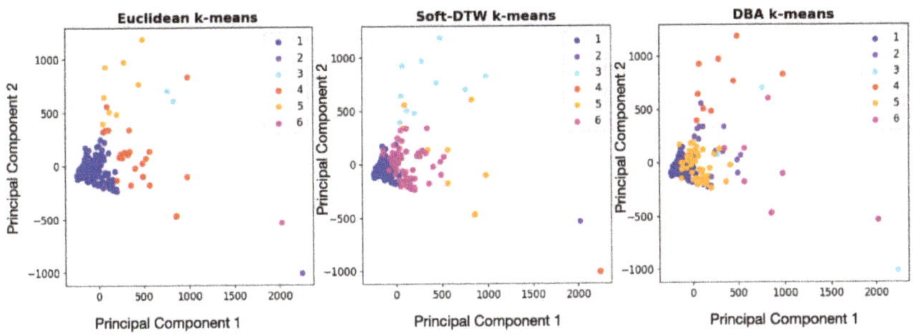

Figure 9. Heart rate pattern analysis using long-range windows extracted from raw ECG data (24 measurements per window). Scatter plots show clusters of heart rate segments projected onto the first two principal components (PC1 and PC2), which represent the dominant and secondary modes of variability in the heart rate data, respectively. Clustering is performed using DBA *k*-means, with each window allowing a maximum of two missing values; when present, missing samples are imputed via interpolation. Each point corresponds to a heart rate window and is color-coded according to its cluster assignment, highlighting both common and less frequent heart rate patterns.

4. Discussion

This study introduces a multi-scale, unsupervised analytical framework for characterizing post-myocardial infarction (MI) physiology using longitudinal data acquired from wearable sensors. By decomposing heart rate dynamics across short-, medium-, and long range temporal windows, the proposed clustering strategy reveals latent autonomic patterns that are not accessible through conventional summary statistics or threshold-based monitoring. This approach enables a form of digital phenotyping, in which physiologically meaningful states emerge directly from a data-driven temporal structure.

At short temporal scales, clustering isolated rapid fluctuations and transient autonomic responses. Distinct clusters captured transitions from rest to tachycardia, recovery trajectories indicative of parasympathetic reactivation, prolonged episodes of sustained tachycardia, and bradycardic or sleep-associated states characterized by autonomic quiescence. The ability to discriminate between activation, recovery, and sustained stress-related patterns highlights the sensitivity of short-range clustering to rapid autonomic regulation and transient perturbations.

Medium-range windows provided an intermediate temporal resolution, capturing autonomic modulations that extend beyond brief fluctuations but do not yet reflect fully sustained physiological states. These clusters revealed diurnal oscillations, stabilization phases during recovery, and activity-associated variability, offering insight into the consis-

https://doi.org/10.3390/a19020137

tency and adaptability of autonomic control during daily life. Importantly, such patterns are often obscured in short-term analyses and diluted in long-term averages.

At longer temporal scales, clustering identified stable physiological phenotypes persisting over several hours. These included complete cycles from rest to tachycardia and back, unidirectional transitions toward sustained tachycardia, and clusters differentiated primarily by baseline heart rate levels. This long-range phenotyping exposes heterogeneity in resting autonomic tone and recovery profiles among young post-MI patients, potentially reflecting differences in autonomic balance, circadian regulation, or cardiovascular conditioning.

From a clinical standpoint, the results demonstrate that wearable-derived data are not merely descriptive but actionable when contextualized temporally. For example, long-range clusters characterized by a persistently elevated baseline heart rate or sustained tachycardia may indicate delayed autonomic recovery or suboptimal rehabilitation engagement, whereas clusters dominated by stable low heart rate patterns are consistent with adequate recovery and parasympathetic reactivation. The ability to distinguish these phenotypes using unsupervised analysis supports the conclusion that wearable monitoring can complement traditional follow-up by revealing latent recovery trajectories that are otherwise inaccessible during intermittent clinical visits.

Extending the clustering framework to pedometer-derived activity counts and oxygen saturation further demonstrated its multimodal applicability. Recurrent patterns linked activity intensity to predictable heart rate responses, while sporadic desaturation clusters emerged as distinct outliers requiring clinical interpretation. Comparative evaluation of Euclidean, soft-DTW, and DBA k-means confirmed that alignment-aware clustering—specifically DBA k-means—more effectively captures the intrinsic temporal variability of physiological signals, reinforcing the importance of time-warp–tolerant methods for wearable-derived data.

From a clinical perspective, early MI—particularly in younger individuals—poses a paradox: patients often regain functional independence yet remain exposed to long-term cardiovascular risk. Traditional follow-up strategies, based on intermittent assessments, are poorly suited to detect subtle physiological deviations or maladaptive recovery trajectories. The findings of this study support wearable-based remote monitoring as a feasible and clinically meaningful complement to standard post-MI care.

Patient acceptance of digital monitoring was high, with a strong preference for smartwatch-based systems and a clear recognition of the importance of reimbursement by national health systems to ensure equitable adoption. Notably, participants overwhelmingly favored personalized feedback delivered by healthcare professionals, underscoring that effective digital health solutions must augment—not replace—clinical relationships. This hybrid model aligns closely with current paradigms in digital medicine, which emphasize human-in-the-loop systems for trust, adherence, and safety.

Objective monitoring revealed low overall physical activity levels, stable oxygen saturation, and predominantly normal heart rate profiles punctuated by rare bradycardic episodes. These findings are consistent with known post-MI recovery patterns, in which reduced activity and subtle autonomic dysregulation may persist despite subjective well-being. Continuous monitoring enables the detection of asymptomatic but potentially relevant events, such as episodic bradycardia or prolonged tachycardia, which may otherwise go unnoticed yet warrant clinical attention.

Importantly, the clustering-based framework moves beyond simple alerting systems by contextualizing physiological signals within temporal patterns. For example, sustained tachycardia clusters may identify individuals requiring intensified rehabilitation, medication adjustment, or closer follow-up, while long-range phenotypes characterized by an elevated baseline heart rate may signal chronic sympathetic predominance and increased

https://doi.org/10.3390/a1902(

long-term risk. Similarly, multimodal patterns linking activity and cardiorespiratory responses can inform personalized rehabilitation intensity and pacing.

More broadly, this approach supports the development of scalable, data-driven secondary prevention strategies. By enabling an automated yet interpretable characterization of physiological states, multi-scale clustering can underpin early warning systems, adaptive rehabilitation programs, and machine-learning–assisted clinical decision support. Such tools are particularly relevant for younger post-MI populations, who are often underrepresented in cardiovascular research despite their extended lifetime risk horizon.

In summary, this work demonstrates how wearable sensing, combined with advanced time-series analytics, can bridge the gap between continuous data acquisition and clinically actionable insight. By aligning methodological innovation with patient-centered design and healthcare system integration, this framework contributes to the evolving landscape of digital cardiovascular medicine and highlights the potential of multi-scale digital phenotyping to support personalized, long-term post-MI care.

To make the clinical translation explicit, clusters can be mapped to predefined actions within a telemonitoring-supported rehabilitation pathway. Short-range clusters capturing minute-to-hour dynamics support real-time safety and workload control: sustained tachycardia patterns (e.g., heart rate above 120 beats per minute for 90–120 min or repeated rest-to-tachycardia transitions within 24 h) would automatically trigger a nurse triage alert on the monitoring dashboard, followed by telephone contact within 24 h to assess symptoms, adherence to exercise prescription, hydration, and medication intake, with escalation to a cardiologist for pharmacological review (for example, beta-blocker titration) or a temporary reduction in training intensity if the pattern persisted for at least three days. Abrupt heart rate variability or frequent transitions not aligned with scheduled exercise sessions would instead prompt targeted lifestyle counseling delivered remotely, focusing on pacing, warm-up and cool-down routines, and stress management, whereas stable low–heart rate clusters compatible with sleep or deep rest predominantly occurring during night-time windows would be documented as physiological recovery without triggering active intervention, providing reassurance to both clinicians and patients.

Medium-range clusters summarizing day-level behavior over several days inform adherence and behavioral monitoring, while long-range clusters extending over weeks enable risk stratification and pathway modulation. Clusters characterized by low step counts and a blunted heart rate response during daytime hours for at least five consecutive days would lead to a nurse-led motivational interview to reinforce rehabilitation goals and explore barriers to activity such as fatigue, anxiety, or musculoskeletal limitations, whereas clusters showing excessive activity combined with an elevated mean heart rate would prompt an adjustment of the exercise prescription and education on safe exertion thresholds. Persistent assignment to sedentary or high resting heart rate clusters over two to three weeks would trigger reclassification to a "sub-optimal recovery" pathway with prioritized in-person assessment and, where appropriate, additional imaging or functional testing, while progressive migration from sedentary to more active clusters with a stable heart rate would support the continuation of the standard rehabilitation pathway with routine follow-up only.

In sum, our findings affirm remote monitoring's utility as an adjunct to conventional post-MI management. When supported through appropriate clinical oversight and human interaction, wearable technologies can facilitate improved recovery trajectories, reduced hospitalizations, and the emergence of a more proactive, responsive, and sustainable model of cardiovascular care.

While the study is exploratory in nature, the convergence of multiple data sources—objective wearable measurements, validated questionnaires, and consistent

https://doi.org/10.3390/a19020137

clustering behavior across temporal scales—provides convergent evidence supporting the study's conclusions. The consistency of observed patterns across heart rate, activity, and oxygen saturation further reinforces the robustness of the findings. Although larger cohorts and longer monitoring periods are required for predictive validation, the present results are sufficient to demonstrate feasibility, interpretability, and clinical relevance of wearable-based multi-scale monitoring among young post-myocardial infarction patients.

5. Limitations

Although wearable devices such as Sidly have provided good accuracy for basic monitoring (heart rate, oxygen saturation, and motor activity), some parameters, such as detecting postural changes in cases of syncope episodes, may be influenced by errors or false positives. It is important to improve the sensitivity of the sensors to minimize such limitations, perform a rigorous validation of wearable devices in real clinical scenarios, and, if necessary, integrate data from the devices with other forms of monitoring or medical consultations. Moreover, the economic sustainability and reimbursement of the device via the national healthcare system were seen as essential for wider technology dissemination. Cost and accessibility are determining factors for the continuation of long-term monitoring and for expanding its use. An additional limitation of the study is the small sample size of patients monitored. The small sample size may compromise the generalizability of the results and increase the risk of biases, as limited samples may not adequately represent the general population. This could lead to unreliable conclusions or an overestimation or underestimation of the effectiveness of the monitored devices. Expanding the sample in future studies will provide more robust and meaningful results, improving the validity and reliability of the conclusions.

A critical aspect that requires attention is the limited duration of monitoring (only 7 days), which, while allowing for immediate and useful data collection to assess the initial treatment response, limits the ability to analyze the long-term effects of wearable devices on post-myocardial infarction recovery and recurrence prevention. Monitoring patients over a more extended period would allow the observation of how the consistency of device use may affect vital parameters over time and whether adopting wearable technologies can indeed reduce the risk of future cardiovascular events.

The heterogeneity of the sample represents another limitation, as the lack of detailed stratification based on relevant factors such as the severity of the cardiac event, comorbidities (e.g., diabetes, hypertension), and the level of physical activity before the infarction can introduce significant biases into the results. Patients with different severities of infarction or pre-existing health conditions may respond very differently to wearable device use, making it more challenging to draw universal conclusions about the effectiveness of remote monitoring. In the future, it would be useful to stratify data for these factors in order to better understand how remote monitoring adapts to the specific needs of different patient types.

These limitations must be considered when planning the future large-scale implementation of remote monitoring through wearable devices. Overcoming the limited study duration, addressing sample heterogeneity, and improving measurement precision are crucial steps to ensure that wearable devices can be truly useful in clinical practice to monitor early myocardial infarction patients effectively and safely over the long term.

6. Future Developments

Future developments of this study will aim to expand the sample and extend the follow-up period to collect long-term data that can provide a more comprehensive view of

https://doi.org/10.3390/a1902

the effectiveness of remote monitoring and recurrence prevention among young patients with early myocardial infarction. Additionally, we plan to include an economic analysis to assess the sustainability of the proposed model, aiming to analyze not only clinical benefits but also the costs associated with large-scale implementation. The economic component is crucial to evaluate the practical feasibility and potential impact of remote monitoring in the healthcare context. Finally, another step may include a direct comparison between different wearable devices to strengthen technological recommendations and select the most effective and cost-efficient solutions to integrate and expand the results obtained so far.

7. Conclusions

The results of this study confirm that wearable devices like Sidly offer significant benefits in monitoring motor activity and vital parameters in patients with early myocardial infarction. Remote monitoring, combined with continuous and personalized feedback, can facilitate recovery and reduce the risk of complications. However, it is necessary to improve the precision of the data (especially regarding acute event detection) and ensure that the healthcare system adequately supports the adoption of these technologies.

Additionally, the active participation of patients, which proved to be crucial in our study, suggests that technology should be integrated into a context that includes both self-management by the patient and continuous support from healthcare professionals. Only through an integrated approach, combining technological innovation and effective communication between the patient and the medical team, will it be possible to maximize the effectiveness of remote monitoring for patients with early myocardial infarction.

Future developments may include the improvement of wearable devices, integration with other healthcare technologies, and a deeper evaluation of the long-term impact of these devices on physical recovery and quality of life for patients.

What emerged from our study could have a significant impact on the applicability of such devices in clinical practice. We consider it essential to promote the implementation of a remote monitoring protocol by integrating wearable devices such as Sidly into the post-infarction follow-up routine. Healthcare professionals could define personalized protocols for each patient, using real-time data to intervene promptly in the case of vital parameter anomalies or during physical activity. The creation of automatic alerts for critical events, such as reduced oxygen saturation or bradycardia episodes, could enhance treatment effectiveness

At the same time, we believe that patient education and awareness are critical. active patient participation was a crucial component of our study. To maximize the benefits of remote monitoring, it is essential that patients receive proper training on the correct use of devices and the interpretation of the data collected. Targeted education sessions could improve self-management and patient awareness of their health status. This would enable the definition of individualized therapeutic paths: data collected via wearable devices could be used to further personalize post-infarction treatment. For example, a patient showing signs of low physical activity or an irregular heart rate could benefit from a more targeted cardiovascular rehabilitation program. In this context, remote monitoring would allow a dynamic adaptation of therapies.

However, economic sustainability and the reformulation of healthcare policies represent the biggest challenges. An important next step for the widespread adoption of technologies like Sidly is the support of the healthcare system. Policies should include incentives for healthcare professionals to adopt remote monitoring devices and ensure financial coverage for patients. Economic sustainability is crucial to make it an available and accessible tool on a large scale. Finally, we recommend that wearable device manufacturers

https://doi.org/10.3390/a19020137

invest in technological improvements, focusing on sensor accuracy and refining the ability to detect acute events. Additionally, further clinical studies should explore the long-term impact of remote monitoring, assessing not only the clinical benefits but also its effect on quality of life, reduction in relapses, and adherence to therapy.

In conclusion, the introduction of remote monitoring devices in the management of myocardial infarction could represent a breakthrough in treatment personalization and complication prevention. However, the real success of this approach will depend on the synergistic integration of technology, healthcare professionals, and patients.

Author Contributions: Conceptualization, P.V. and P.H.G.; methodology, P.V., P.H.G., D.T., and S.D.R.; software, U.L.; formal analysis, F.B.; investigation, F.B. and S.D.R.; resources, D.T. and P.V.; data curation, P.H.G. and U.L.; writing—original draft preparation, P.H.G. and F.B.; writing—review and editing, P.V., P.H.G., and S.D.R.; supervision, P.H.G.; funding acquisition, P.V. and D.T. All authors have read and agreed to the published version of the manuscript.

Funding: This research received no external funding.

Institutional Review Board Statement: The study was conducted in accordance with the Declaration of Helsinki and approved by the local Ethics Review Board (CAL.HUB.RIA protocol, approval no. 137/2023; PACE protocol, approval no. 73/2917). Written informed consent was obtained from all participants prior to enrollment.

Informed Consent Statement: Written informed consent to participate was obtained from the patient(s).

Data Availability Statement: The data that support the findings of this study are available from the corresponding author upon reasonable request. Data are available upon reasonable request.

Conflicts of Interest: The authors declare no conflicts of interest.

References

1. Zhang, T.; Wang, Y.; Feng, X.; Zuo, Y.; Yu, H.; Bao, H.; Jiang, F.; Jiang, S. Flexible electronics for cardiovascular monitorin complex physiological skins. *iScience* **2024**, *27*, 110707. [CrossRef] [PubMed]
2. Wan, X.; Zhao, Y.; Li, Z.; Li, L. Emerging polymeric electrospun fibers: From structural diversity to application in fle bioelectronics and tissue engineering. In *Exploration*; Wiley Online Library: Hoboken, NJ, USA, 2022; Volume 2, p. 2021002
3. Boccuto, F.; De Rosa, S.; Torella, D.; Veltri, P.; Guzzi, P.H. Will artificial intelligence provide answers to current gaps and nee chronic heart failure? *Appl. Sci.* **2023**, *13*, 7663. [CrossRef]
4. Sun, M.; Wang, S.; Liang, Y.; Wang, C.; Zhang, Y.; Liu, H.; Zhang, Y.; Han, L. Flexible graphene field-effect transistors and application in flexible biomedical sensing. *Nano-Micro Lett.* **2025**, *17*, 34. [CrossRef] [PubMed]
5. Gallo, A.; Fregola, S.; Menon, M.; Talarico, F.; Fragkiadaki, S.; Kontaxopolou, D.; Vukojevic, K.; Matijaca, D.; Miljkovic Kožetinac, S.; et al. Using smart devices for monitoring elderly patients in rural areas of calabria after COVID-19 vaccina Experiences within the si4care project. *COVID* **2023**, *3*, 124–130. [CrossRef]
6. Daskalos, A.C.; Theodoropoulos, P.; Spandonidis, C.; Vordos, N. Wearable Device for Observation of Physical Activity with Purpose of Patient Monitoring Due to COVID-19. *Signals* **2022**, *3*, 11–28. [CrossRef]
7. Jena, N.; Singh, P.; Chandramohan, D.; Garapati, H.N.; Gummadi, J.; Mylavarapu, M.; Shaik, B.F.; Nanjundappa, A.; Apala, Toquica, C.; et al. Wearable Technology in Cardiology: Advancements, Applications, and Future Prospects. *Rev. Cardiovasc.* **2025**, *26*, 39025. [CrossRef] [PubMed]
8. Heizmann, A.N.; Chapelle, C.; Laporte, S.; Roche, F.; Hupin, D.; Le Hello, C. Impact of wearable device-based interventi with feedback for increasing daily walking activity and physical capacities in cardiovascular patients: A systematic review meta-analysis of randomised controlled trials. *BMJ Open* **2023**, *13*, e069966. [CrossRef] [PubMed] [PubMed Central]
9. Maximidou, E.; Mons, U. Benefits of wearable-based cardiac rehabilitation interventions in secondary prevention of coror artery disease: A systematic review and meta-analysis. *Am. J. Prev. Cardiol.* **2025**, *23*, 101015. [CrossRef] [PubMed]
10. Yagi, S.; Matsumura, K.; Uchigashima, Y.; Shiroyama, J.; Hase, M.; Nanba, T.; Yamada, N.; Funauchi, Y.; Ueno, M.; Togi, K.; Integration of wearables into a cardiac rehabilitation program and Its Impact on physical activity and exercise capacity in o patients with cardiovascular disease. *Adv. Rehabil. Sci. Pract.* **2025**, *14*, 27536351251343538. [CrossRef] [PubMed]

https://doi.org/10.3390/a1902

ao, H.; Wang, Y.; Shen, A.; Chen, H.; Li, H. Acute myocardial infarction in young men under 50 years of age: Clinical haracteristics, Treatment, and long-term prognosis. *Int. J. Gen. Med.* **2021**, *14*, 9321–9331. CrossRef] [PubMed] [PubMed Central]

amil, G.; Jamil, G.; Mesameh, H.; Qureshi, A.; AlKaabi, J.; Sharma, C.; Aziz, F.; Al-Shamsi, A.R.; Yasin, J. Risk factor comparison 1 young patients presenting with acute coronary syndrome with atherosclerotic coronary artery disease vs. angiographically ormal coronaries. *Int. J. Med. Sci.* **2021**, *18*, 3526–3535. [CrossRef] [PubMed]

Veizman, O.; Simon, T.; Tea, V.; Marijon, E.; Eltchaninoff, H.; Manzo-Silberman, S.; Leclercq, F.; Albert, F.; Bataille, V.; Drouet, E.; t al. Very long-term outcomes after acute myocardial infarction in young men and women: Insights from the FAST-MI program. *rch. Cardiovasc. Dis.* **2023**, *116*, 324–334. [CrossRef] [PubMed]

https://doi.org/10.3390/a19020137

MDPI AG
Grosspeteranlage 5
4052 Basel
Switzerland
Tel.: +41 61 683 77 34

Algorithms Editorial Office
E-mail: algorithms@mdpi.com
www.mdpi.com/journal/algorithms

www.ingramcontent.com/pod-product-compliance
Lightning Source LLC
Chambersburg PA
CBHW061804210926
51850CB00006B/612
9783725872602